Women in the American Civil War

VOLUME II

Lisa Tendrich Frank

Editor

A B C · C L I O

Santa Barbara, California   Denver, Colorado   Oxford, England

Library of Congress Cataloging-in-Publication Data
Women in the American Civil War / Lisa Tendrich Frank, editor.
    v.   cm.
   Includes bibliographical references and index.
   ISBN 978-1-85109-600-8 (hard copy : alk. paper) — ISBN 978-1-85109-605-3 (ebook)   1. United States—History—Civil War, 1861–1865—Women—Encyclopedias.   2. United States—History—Civil War, 1861–1865—Participation, Female—Encyclopedias. 3. United States—History—Civil War, 1861–1865—Biography—Encyclopedias.   4. United States—History—Civil War, 1861–1865—Social aspects—Encyclopedias.   5. Women—United States—History—19th century—Encyclopedias.   6. Women—United States—Biography—Encyclopedias.   I. Frank, Lisa Tendrich.
   E628.W655   2008
   973.7082'03—dc22

                                              2007025822

12 11 10 9 8   1 2 3 4 5 6 7 8 9 10

Production Editor: Alisha Martinez
Production Manager: Don Schmidt
Media Editor: Julie Dunbar
Media Production Coordinator: Ellen Brenna Dougherty
Media Resources Manager: Caroline Price
File Manager: Paula Gerard

This book is also available on the World Wide Web as an eBook.
Visit www.abc-clio.com for details.

ABC-CLIO, Inc.
130 Cremona Drive, P.O. Box 1911
Santa Barbara, California 93116–1911

This book is printed on acid-free paper ∞

Manufactured in the United States of America

For Daniel

Contributors

Adgent, Nancy L.
Rockefeller Archive Center

Allred, Randal
Brigham Young University,
 Hawaii

Anderson, Joe L.
University of West Georgia

Antolini, Katharine Lane
West Virginia University

Bair, Barbara
Library of Congress

Barber, E. Susan
College of Notre Dame of
 Maryland

Beilke, Jayne R.
Ball State University

Blake, Debra A.
North Carolina State Archives

Blalock, Kay J.
St. Louis Community College-
 Meramec

Boccardi, Megan
University of Missouri, Columbia

Bohanan, Robert D.
Jimmy Carter Library

Boswell, Angela
Henderson State University

Broussard, Joyce L.
California State University,
 Northridge

Brown, William H.
North Carolina Office of
 Archives and History

Bruns, Gabrielle
Independent Scholar

Burin, Nikki Berg
University of Minnesota

Campbell, Jacqueline Glass
University of Connecticut

Carter, María Agui
Iguana Films

Castagna, JoAnn E.
University of Iowa

Cole, N. Scott
Longwood University

Coles, David
Longwood University

Confer, W. Clarissa
California University of
 Pennsylvania

Coryell, Janet L.
Western Michigan University

Cox, Karen L.
University of North Carolina at
 Charlotte

Crist, Lynda L.
Rice University

Dunn, Kristina K.
South Carolina Confederate
 Relic Room and Military
 Museum

Eliassen, Meredith
San Francisco State University

Engle, Nancy Driscol
Independent Scholar

Eye, Sara Marie
University South Carolina

Eylon, Dina Ripsman
University of Toronto

Foroughi, Andrea R.
Union College

Frank, Andrew K.
Florida State University

Frank, Ed
University of Memphis

Gallman, J. Matthew
University of Florida

Gerard, Gene C.
Tarrant County College

Gigantino, James
University of Georgia

Graves, Donna Cooper
University of Tennessee at
Martin

Gross, Jennifer Lynn
Jacksonville State University

Halloran, Fiona Deans
Eastern Kentucky University

Hartsock, Ralph
University of North Texas
Libraries

Haynes, Robert W.
Texas A&M International
University

Hinton, Paula Katherine
Tennessee Technological
University

Holcomb, Julie
Navarro College

Hudson, Linda S.
East Texas Baptist University

Jepsen, Thomas C.
Independent Scholar

Kehoe, Karen A.
Saint Vincent College

Kelsey, Sigrid
Louisiana State University
Libaries

Kinzey, Karen
Arlington House

Kuipers, Juliana
Harvard University Archives

Lancaster, Jane
Brown University

Lane, Yvette Florio
Monmouth University

Larson, Kate Clifford
Independent Scholar

Lause, Mark A.
University of Cincinnati

Lewis, Elizabeth Wittenmyer
Independent Scholar

Long, Alecia P.
Louisiana State University

Marszalek, John F.
Mississippi State University

Martinez, Jaime Amanda
University of Virginia

Mays, Gwen Thomas
North Carolina State Archives

McDevitt, Theresa R.
Indiana University of
Pennsylvania Libraries

Minton, Amy
Marymount University

Moody, Wesley
Gordon College

Myers, Barton A.
University of Georgia

Nester, Thomas
Texas A&M University

Neumann, Caryn E.
Ohio Wesleyan University

Nguyen, Julia Huston
Independent Scholar

Nichols, Jennifer Jane
Michigan State University

Nickeson, Dawn Ottevaere
Michigan State University

Nussel, Jill M.
Indiana/Purdue University
Fort Wayne

Nytroe, Sarah K.
Boston College

Oglesby, Catherine
Valdosta State University

Olsen, Christopher J.
Indiana State University

Ott, Victoria E.
Birmingham-Southern College

Prushankin, Jeffrey S.
Pennsylvania State University
Abingdon

Quigley, Paul D. H.
University of Edinburgh

Richard, Patricia
Metropolitan State College
of Denver

Ritter, Charles R.
College of Notre Dame
of Maryland

Roberts, Giselle
La Trobe University

Ross-Nazzal, Jennifer
NASA Johnson Space Center

Rouse, Kristen L.
Independent Scholar

Rubin, Anne Sarah
University of Maryland,
Baltimore County

Sacher, John M.
University of Central Florida

Schoonmaker, Nancy Gray
University of North Carolina
at Chapel Hill

Schroeder, Adriana
University of Central Oklahoma

Schurr, Nancy
University of Tennessee,
Knoxville

Scroggins, Eloise E.
Indiana Historical Society

Selby, Kelly D.
Kent State University

Shaffer, Donald R.
University of Northern Colorado

Sheehan-Dean, Aaron
University of North Florida

Sherman, Dawn M.
Independent Scholar

Smith, Lisa M.
University of Akron

Stabler, Scott L.
Grand Valley State University

Streater, Kristen L.
Collin County Community
College

Sullivan, Regina D.
Independent Scholar

Taylor, Robert A.
Florida Institute of
Technology

Todras, Ellen H.
Independent Scholar

Tolley-Stokes, Rebecca
East Tennessee State University

van Zelm, Antoinette G.
Tennessee Civil War National
Heritage Area Center for
Historic Preservation
Middle Tennessee State
University

Vincent, Thomas
North Carolina Department of
Archives and History

Wamsley, E. Sue
Kent State University-Salem

Warner, Jay
Independent Scholar

Wayne, Tiffany K.
Cabrillo College

Wells, Cheryl A.
University of Wyoming

White, Jonathan W.
University of Maryland, College
Park

Wilkerson, Jessie
Pellissippi State Technical
Community College

Williams, David
Valdosta State University

Wongsrichanalai, Kanisorn
University of Virginia

Wooton, Sarah
South Carolina Confederate
Relic Room & Museum

Wyatt-Brown, Bertram
Richard J. Milbauer Professor
Emeritus, University of
Florida and Visiting Scholar,
Johns Hopkins University

Younger, Karen Fisher
Pennsylvania State University

Contents

List of Entries

Introduction

Until the past few decades, most scholars would have agreed with Margaret Mitchell's narrator, who asserted in *Gone with the Wind,* that war "is men's business, not ladies" (Mitchell, *Gone with the Wind,* 8). Indeed, until recently, only a few scholars dared to treat women as central players in the American Civil War. Instead, the bulk of the scholarship on the war pushed women to the margins, discussing them only as a sidebar to the "important" work done by men on the battlefields and in the political arena. In most accounts, the women stayed at home as unnamed civilians, while the men in their worlds fought the battles that defined the outcome of the war. A few nurses were recognized for their valor, but their wartime efforts remained overshadowed by those of military men, such as William Tecumseh Sherman, Ulysses S. Grant, Thomas "Stonewall" Jackson, and Robert E. Lee, as well by those of politicians like Abraham Lincoln and Jefferson Davis. This book reflects the growing and increasingly sophisticated literature on women during the American Civil War that demonstrates the need to acknowledge women's central roles in pursuing the war and in determining its outcome. Rather than auxiliaries, women across all racial, class, ethnic, religious, and geographic lines were an essential component of the action. Slave women and their white female owners shaped and were shaped by the war, as were female abolitionists, yeoman farmers, recent immigrants, widows, and domestic laborers. Whether living in the North, South, or West or in the countryside or city, women

of all classes and backgrounds found ways to involve themselves in the events shaping their lives.

Although this volume focuses on women in the Civil War period, it does not glorify them for the sake of noticing them. Instead, the entries in this encyclopedia offer a nuanced view of how women survived, contributed to, undermined, and lived through the Civil War. This approach contrasts sharply with that of the literature about Civil War women appearing throughout the nation immediately after the war. These accounts typically elevated women, particularly elite white women, to a mythical status as self-sacrificing feminine patriots. To create this mythology, the accounts, written by both men and women, emphasized women's nurturing roles on the homefront, especially as nurses, seamstresses, and fundraisers for their men on the battlefield. The women of these extensive volumes provided the necessary support for politicians and soldiers, but they rarely played any independent role in the conflict. Instead, they willingly gave up their food, fancy clothes, comfort, homes, and loved ones in support of a cause that they believed in. They never stepped outside the boundaries of what was then considered proper womanhood, but rather performed their wartime tasks with the knowledge that they did them for the men. Those who took on the extraordinary roles as soldiers and spies were often portrayed as doing so in the name of the men they loved.

The reality of women's wartime experiences, however, was much more complicated than this self-sacrificing feminine image suggests. As women stepped outside their traditional roles as sweethearts, wives, mothers, sisters, and daughters, many willingly took on roles that, at the time, some classified as unfeminine. Some white Southern women, for example, vehemently supported or opposed disunion, engaged in political debates, attended secession conventions, and otherwise eagerly participated in the political sphere. Some Northern women similarly joined and helped form abolitionist organizations, petitioned Congress to limit the expansion of slavery, and otherwise became political actors. Once the war began, Northern and Southern women took government jobs, served as spies and soldiers, wrote political and fictional accounts of events, took themselves to the battlefield as frontline nurses, ran farms and plantations to varying degrees of success, worked as doctors, hid deserters and shirkers, protested conscription and wartime shortages, provided information and supplies to enemy soldiers in their midst, offered advice to husbands in military command, and otherwise demonstrated that they made their own choices throughout the war. Enslaved African American women helped turn the war into a fight for emancipation, claiming safety behind Union lines, reuniting with family members, and otherwise pursuing freedom. Free black women helped raise Union regiments, nursed injured and sick soldiers as necessary, and formed aid societies to help the soldiers and widows of their communities. Others remained leery of stepping outside the boundaries of femininity and instead remained on the sidelines as support staff to the men of their families. Many women, regardless of their stances, kept diaries of their experiences and observations of the war and of the people involved. Women of all backgrounds sent letters—filled with words of support, complaint, or requests—to their men at the front. In all cases, however, women could not escape a war that had such wide reaching effects.

To best explore how women experienced and affected the course of the Civil War, this title contains a mixture of types and lengths of entries. The fourteen contextual essays at the beginning outline the general contours of the war, the different types of women, the wartime issues, as well as the experiences of women in particular. These extended entries, appearing at the start of the volume and separated from the traditional alphabetical entries, provide an overview of how various groups of women experienced the era and how women in general shared similar experiences. Specifically, the essays explore abolitionism and Northern reformers, African American women, the Confederate homefront, female spies, female combatants, military invasion and occupation, Northern women, nurses, politics, religion, Southern women, the Union homefront, wartime employment, and wartime literature. Collectively, these essays provide an overview of the female experience during the war. They offer a broad outline of the war experience that is augmented by the individual shorter entries throughout the rest of the volume.

The bulk of the volume consists of more than three hundred entries that detail the experiences of women during the American Civil War without necessarily glorifying them, as was done in the postwar literature. They explore topics that traditionally fall under the headings of military affairs, social life, labor issues, politics, and culture. Some of the entries are explicitly about women, often biographical sketches of well-known and not so well-known participants and observers. Other entries explore famous military and political events, like the Battle of Gettysburg or the wartime elections, introducing and emphasizing the traditionally neglected participation of women. Women's roles in the recruitment of soldiers, the protest of wartime policies, the care of wounded men, and the creation of supplies for the men of both armies are highlighted. In addition, the volume details the cross-dressing women who served as soldiers in the Confederate and Union armies, as well as the employment of women in government and private-sector jobs. It also contains details about emancipation, slave life, and the enlistment of African American soldiers. Even women's homefront lives and roles are explored from various viewpoints. In short, this volume details the contributions and experiences of women across the social, ethnic, and racial spectra.

Each of the alphabetical entries contains the basic components of an encyclopedia—details, dates, names, and the other essential facts for the term—with special attention paid to how the topic relates to the experiences of women during the war. Biographical entries detail the milestones of the person's entire life, but the bulk of their information relates to the individual's wartime experiences. Similarly, entries on battles and other traditional military topics contain the outline of maneuvers and tactics, with special attention paid to the contributions of female spies, civilians, nurses, and soldiers as well as to how women experienced or reacted to the event. Each entry also contains cross references to allow users to flesh out the contours of the wartime experience through a reading of related entries. Finally, all the entries contain a list of specialized books and articles that will allow readers to further explore the topics covered.

The twenty-four primary sources included in the volume offer a first-hand look at women's wartime experiences. They cover a wide array of viewpoints and events, including the Richmond bread riots, the capture of Union spy Pauline Cushman, the formation of United States Sanitary Commission–sanctioned aid societies, the life of a slave woman, the education of freed people by Northern women, and the evacuation of Atlanta. In addition, they offer a brief glance at some of the contemporary popular literature, North and South. The disparate experiences outlined in these sources lend credence to the need for an encyclopedia that examines women's individual wartime experiences. Although these sources are all by or about women, they each offer a specific viewpoint on the war, on its effects, and on women's involvement, demonstrating the impossibility of casting women's wartime experiences in monolithic terms.

Exploring this volume, readers discover the centrality of the Civil War to the lives of American women and American society. Indeed, many scholars paint the Civil War as a defining moment in the history of the United States. Military historians stress its importance as the first modern war—a statement about the tactics, technology, and interaction of civilians. Social historians have uncovered the transformative nature of the war in a host of areas. Many women's historians argue that the wartime participation of Northern women in abolitionism, nursing, and aid societies led to the coales-

cence of a woman's movement in the Northern states. Even scholars of tourism demonstrate how the unprecedented movement around the nation by military troops helped to develop more of a nationwide tourism industry than had existed in antebellum America; soldiers wanted to revisit and bring their loved ones to the places they had fought, and widows and other family members wanted to visit the places where their loved ones had lost their lives. The Civil War did, in fact, alter the lives of all who lived through it. However, individual backgrounds, as well as locations, wartime experiences, and expectations, resulted in lingering effects that each person felt differently.

Readers may also be surprised by the connections between the homefront and the warfront, between civilians and soldiers, and between women and men that this encyclopedia illuminates. Although scholars have often ignored women in their military treatments of the Civil War because they were not on the battlefield, women's omnipresence on the homefront shaped how officers directed their military campaigns and determined what soldiers would eat and wear. Northern and Southern women's often unpaid work as nurses, recruiters, fundraisers, seamstresses, cooks, and laundresses provided essential functions for the waging of war. By performing these tasks, women fulfilled a need for labor and goods that would have otherwise drawn men from their positions on the battlefront. Consequently, women—whether they were rich or poor, black or white, Native American or immigrant, Southern or Northern, rural or urban—helped determine the outcome of the war and in turn were shaped by the events around them.

In addition, for many women, the homefront became the battlefront. Communities in the Shenandoah Valley, for example, constantly shifted between Union and Confederate control, and the residents there found themselves dealing with soldiers on a daily basis. They had to find a way to survive, retain their loyalties, and support their own troops. Similarly, in occupied Southern cities such as Vicksburg, Mississippi, women had to choose between loyalty oaths and possible starvation when occupying Union troops vowed not to do business with Confederates. Some women chose to take loyalty oaths while harboring Confederate allegiance, and others found their fervor for the Southern nation dampened by the realities of war and occupation. In New Orleans, Union officials dealt directly with what they saw as Southern women's insolence. Fed up with the behavior of the city's women, General Benjamin Butler issued the Woman Order to bring Confederate women under control and to force them to behave like ladies with the occupying troops. African American women, who expected the Union army to bring freedom from slavery and its horrors, often found themselves confronted with Northern racism. Much to their surprise, these women faced rape as well as the loss or destruction of their property by those they thought would be their liberators. Northern women, for their part, assumed themselves safe from invasion. However, some faced Confederate soldiers when the troops pushed northward, most notably into Gettysburg, Pennsylvania. Like their Southern counterparts, these women were forced to find ways to protect themselves and their families from enemy soldiers.

Even when they did not face enemy troops, women's roles on the homefront remained essential to the course of the Civil War. As many scholars and participants have noted, women's moral and material support allowed men to leave home for military duty. Women's objections to the course of the war or to the cause that their men supported often proved equally powerful. Some women, unable to handle the business at home on their own, urged their husbands to desert. Other women created underground groups of protest in their communities, such as the secret Unionist circle in Atlanta frequented by Cyrena Stone. In more drastic instances, women took to the streets to make their voices heard. In cities across the South, for example, hundreds of women participated in food riots in 1863, drawing attention to their needs in a time of shortage. That same year, many Northern women participated in draft riots throughout Northern cities.

In addition to the contextual essays and alphabetic entries, this volume also contains two additional resources to help readers understand the experience of women and the Civil War. At the start of the volume, there is a chronology that integrates women's participation in the Civil War with the traditional military and political events. At the end of the volume, an extensive bibliography offers researchers a way to begin their search for information on the topics covered and on the Civil War in general.

Margaret Mitchell may have penned her famous and misleading words about the Civil War a couple of generations ago, but her message resonates to this day. Hopefully, this encyclopedia helps illuminate the falsehood of treating war as men's work and of ignoring women in our interpretations and understandings of the Civil War. This volume, as well as the growing literature on women and the war, should make it clear that war is also women's work.

Chronology

January 1831
Abolitionist William Lloyd Garrison publishes the first issue of *The Liberator*.

December 1833
The American Anti-Slavery Society forms in Philadelphia.

July 1840
Abby Kelly is elected to the board of the American Anti-Slavery Society. Subsequent debate over the role of women in the abolitionist movement results in some members forming the separate American and Foreign Anti-Slavery Society. William Lloyd Garrison remains with the American Anti-Slavery Society.

July 1848
Lucretia Mott, Elizabeth Cady Stanton, and other supporters of women's rights hold a convention at Seneca Falls, New York, and issue a Declaration of Sentiments.

September 1850
President Millard Fillmore signs a series of bills that deals with states' rights and the extension of slavery into the new territories of the United States that becomes known as the Compromise of 1850.

May 1851
Sojourner Truth delivers her "Ain't I a Woman?" speech at a women's rights convention in Akron, Ohio.

June 1851
Washington-based abolitionist newspaper, *The National Era*, begins publishing in serial form Harriet Beecher Stowe's *Uncle Tom's Cabin; Or, Life among the Lowly*.

March 1852
Uncle Tom's Cabin; Or, Life among the Lowly is published in book form.

April 1853
Harriet Tubman begins working on the Underground Railroad.

May 1854
Congress passes the Kansas-Nebraska Act.

March 1857
The Supreme Court makes its *Dred Scott v. Sanford* ruling.

October 1859
Abolitionist John Brown leads a raid on the federal arsenal at Harper's Ferry, Virginia, hoping to initiate a slave rebellion.

April 1860
Anna Dickinson delivers "The Rights and Wrongs of Women" at a Quaker meeting.

November 1860
Abraham Lincoln is elected president of the United States.

December 1860
South Carolina secedes from the Union.

January 1861
Mississippi, Florida, Alabama, Georgia, and
    Louisiana secede.
Harriet Jacobs [Linda Brent] publishes *Incidents
    in the Life of a Slave Girl*.

February 1861
Texas secedes.
Seceded states hold convention in Montgomery,
    Alabama, where they adopt a Confederate Con-
    stitution and elect Jefferson Davis president of
    the Confederate States of America.

March 1861
Abraham Lincoln is inaugurated as president of
    the United States.

April 1861
Rebecca Harding Davis publishes "Life in the Iron
    Mills" in *The Atlantic Monthly*.
Confederates fire on and capture Fort Sumter in
    South Carolina.
Lincoln calls for troops to put down the insurrec-
    tion, and he orders a naval blockade of Confed-
    erate seaports. Virginia secedes. Lincoln also
    orders all civilian employees within the execu-
    tive branch to take a loyalty oath.
Riots erupt in Baltimore, Maryland.
New York City women form the Women's Central
    Association of Relief.
Dorothea Dix is appointed Superintendent of the
    United States Army Nurses.

May 1861
Arkansas and North Carolina secede.
Dorothea Dix organizes the first military hospitals
    in the United States.

June 1861
The Women's Central Association of Relief is sanc-
    tioned by Lincoln, and it becomes the United
    States Sanitary Commission.

After speaking at a pro-Union rally, Sojourner
    Truth is arrested for breaking a state law that
    prohibited African Americans from entering
    Indiana.
Mary Ann Bickerdyke begins her work at Union
    hospitals.
Western counties in Virginia secede from the state
    and form West Virginia.

July 1861
Congress authorizes the enlistment of half a mil-
    lion soldiers and passes the Crittenden Resolu-
    tion, which declares that the United States was
    waging war to reunify the nation rather than to
    eliminate or restrict slavery.
The Confederate and Union armies face each
    other for the first time at the Battle of Bull Run
    (Manassas). During that battle, Anne Blair
    Etheridge and other women witness their first
    combat as frontline nurses.

August 1861
Lincoln declares the Confederate states to be in a
    state of insurrection.
Congress passes the first Confiscation Act.
The United States Secret Service arrests and
    imprisons Rose O'Neal Greenhow for spying on
    behalf of the Confederacy.
Anne Ella Carroll publishes *Reply to the Speech of
    Honorable John C. Breckinridge*.

September 1861
Sally Louisa Tompkins becomes a commissioned
    Confederate officer in order to keep Robertson
    Hospital open in Richmond, Virginia.

October 1861
Charlotte Forten goes to Port Royal, South Car-
    olina, to work as a teacher for recently freed
    African Americans.

November 1861
General Winfield Scott resigns his post as head of
    the United States Army. Lincoln appoints
    George B. McClellan to replace him.

The Young Men's Christian Association establishes the United States Christian Commission.

January 1862
The Port Royal Experiment begins on the Union-occupied Sea Islands in South Carolina.

February 1862
Julia Ward Howe publishes "The Battle Hymn of the Republic" in *The Atlantic Monthly.*

March 1862
The Confederate ironclad *Merrimac* and Union ironclad *Monitor* fight to a draw.
The Peninsular Campaign begins.
The United States Congress passes the Impressment Act.

April 1862
The Battle of Shiloh takes place.
Congress abolishes slavery in the District of Columbia.
The Confederacy passes its first Conscription Act.

May 1862
Union General Benjamin Butler takes command of occupied New Orleans, Louisiana. He issues his General Order Number 28, the Woman Order.

June 1862
Virginian Robert E. Lee assumes command of the Confederate army.

July 1862
Lee and McClellan face each other at the Seven Days Battle.
General Henry Halleck takes control of the Union army.
Confederate spy Belle Boyd is imprisoned at the Old Capital Prison.

August 1862
Confederate soldiers defeat the Union army at the Second Battle of Bull Run.

September 1862
Lee's Army of Northern Virginia invades the North. The deadliest day of fighting occurs when twenty-six thousand soldiers die at the Battle at Antietam in Maryland.
Lincoln issues a preliminary Emancipation Proclamation.
Laura M. Towne establishes a school for freedmen and freedwomen on St. Helena Island, South Carolina.
An explosion at the Allegheny Arsenal kills seventy-eight workers, mostly young women.

November 1862
General Ambrose E. Burnside replaces McClellan as commander of the Union's Army of the Potomac.

December 1862
Confederates defeat Union forces at the Battle of Fredericksburg.
Louisa May Alcott begins work at Union Hospital in Washington, D.C.

January 1863
Lincoln's Emancipation Proclamation goes into effect.
General Joseph Hooker replaces Ambrose Burnside, and Union General Ulysses S. Grant takes control of the Army of the West.
Recruitment begins for the Fifty-fourth Massachusetts Infantry Regiment, the nation's first African American unit.

March 1863
An explosion at an ordnance lab in Richmond, Virginia, kills thirty-four women.
Women in Salisbury, North Carolina, riot in response to their shortage of salt and flour.
Mary Abigail Dodge [Gail Hamilton] publishes "A Call to My Country-Women" in *The Atlantic Monthly.*

April 1863
Women in Richmond, Virginia, engage in bread riots to protest the wartime shortages.

The Battle of Chancellorsville begins.

Confederate Mary Frances "Fanny" Battle is arrested for spying.

The Union's policy of conscription goes into effect.

May 1863

Lee defeats Hooker at Chancellorsville.

The National Women's Loyal League meets for the first time.

Louisa May Alcott begins to publish in serial form her *Hospital Sketches*.

Fanny Kemble publishes her *Journal of a Residence on a Georgian Plantation* while in England; it is published in the United States that July.

Union spy Pauline Cushman is captured.

June 1863

Lee again invades the North, and General George G. Meade becomes the Union commander of the Army of the Potomac.

Residents of Vicksburg, Mississippi, evacuate to nearby caves to avoid Union shelling.

Western Virginia separates from Virginia and re-enters the Union.

July 1863

The Union army defeats Lee at the Battle of Gettysburg.

Union forces under Grant capture Vicksburg and takes control of the Mississippi River.

The Battle of Honey Springs takes place in Indian Territory.

Draft riots in New York expose homefront frustrations. Similar riots occur in Boston, Massachusetts, Holmes County, Ohio, and elsewhere across the Union.

August 1863

Confederate William C. Quantrill and four hundred and fifty supporters raid Lawrence, Kansas.

September 1863

Confederates win the Battle of Chickamauga.

October 1863

Lincoln calls for a national day of thanksgiving to be held in November.

Grant takes control of all operations in the Western theater.

The United States Sanitary Commission holds one of its most successful sanitary fairs in Chicago.

November 1863

Lincoln delivers the Gettysburg Address at the dedication of a national cemetery.

Grant repels the Confederate siege at Chattanooga, Tennessee.

February 1864

Confederates win the Battle of Olustee in Florida.

The National Women's Loyal League presents Congress with a petition demanding the abolition of slavery.

Rebecca Lee becomes the first African American woman to earn an M.D. degree.

March 1864

Grant takes control of all the armies of the United States, and General William T. Sherman assumes control of Union forces in the West.

Women protest for peace in High Point, North Carolina.

April 1864

The United States Sanitary Commission holds a three-week fundraising fair in New York that raises $1 million.

A bread riot erupts in Savannah, Georgia.

May 1864

Union troops under Grant's command fight Confederate forces led by Lee at the Battles of the Wilderness and Spotsylvania.

Sherman advances toward Atlanta and the Army of the Tennessee.

June 1864

Confederates win the Battle of Cold Harbor.

Grant begins a nine-month siege of Petersburg, Virginia.

July 1864
Sherman forcefully evacuates female workers and
their families from the textile mill town of
Roswell, Georgia.

September 1864
Sherman captures Atlanta and issues Special Field
Orders, Number 67, evacuating the city of all
civilians. The order primarily affects the city's
women and children.
Frustrations lead to bread riots in Mobile,
Alabama.

October 1864
Union General Philip H. Sheridan defeats General
Jubal Early's Confederate troops in the Shenan-
doah Valley.

November 1864
Lincoln defeats McClellan in the presidential race.
Sherman burns Atlanta and begins his March to
the Sea.

December 1864
General George H. Thomas defeats the Army of
the Tennessee.
Sherman captures Savannah, Georgia.

January 1865
Freed slaves obtain control of the Sea Islands
between Jacksonville, Florida, and Charleston,
South Carolina, when Sherman issues Special
Field Order, Number 15. Sherman marches
through South Carolina, destroying much
of Charleston, Columbia, and the
surrounding areas.
Before Sherman arrives, the women of Columbia
hold the Confederacy's largest fundraising
bazaar.
Freed slave and Union spy Mary Elizabeth Bowser
flees from Confederate President Jefferson
Davis's Richmond home.

February 1865
African American Julia C. Collins begins publishing "The Curse of Caste; or, The Slave Bride" as

a serial in the *Christian Recorder,* a weekly
newspaper run by the African Methodist Episcopal Church.

March 1865
Grant defeats Lee at the Battle of Petersburg.
Congress creates the Freedmen's Bureau to help
former slaves in their transition to freedom.
Clara Barton establishes the Office of Correspon-
dence with Friends of the Missing Men of the
United States Army.

April 1865
Confederate forces evacuate Richmond, Virginia.
Lee surrenders to Grant at Appomattox Court-
house, Virginia.
John Wilkes Booth assassinates President Lincoln
at Ford's Theater in Washington, D.C.
Andrew Johnson becomes president.

May 1865
General Oliver Otis Howard becomes head of the
Freedmen's Bureau.
Northerners celebrate the Union victory with
a parade down Pennsylvania Avenue in
Washington, D.C.

July 1865
Mary Surratt is hanged for her involvement in the
conspiracy to assassinate Lincoln.

November 1865
Mississippi passes the first black code.

December 1865
Congress ratifies the Thirteenth Amendment,
abolishing slavery.
The Ku Klux Klan forms in Pulaski, Tennessee.

March 1866
Congress enacts the Civil Rights Act of 1866.

May 1866
Susan B. Anthony and Elizabeth Cady Stanton
organize the Eleventh National Women's Rights
Convention in New York City.

July 1866
A race riot erupts in New Orleans.

July 1867
The Ladies' Memorial Association unveils the first monument to the Confederate dead in Cheraw, South Carolina.

July 1868
The Fourteenth Amendment is ratified. It grants citizenship to all men born or naturalized in the United States. The amendment introduces the term "male" to the Constitution.

November 1868
Ulysses S. Grant is elected president.

February 1869
Congress passes the Fifteenth Amendment that prevents states from denying voters the right to voice on the basis of race, color, or previous condition.

May 1869
Susan B. Anthony and Elizabeth Cady Stanton establish the National Woman Suffrage Association.

December 1869
Wyoming passes the first women's suffrage law in the United States.

April 1871
Congress passes the Civil Rights Act of 1871, also known as the Ku Klux Klan Act.

June 1872
Congress abolishes the Freedmen's Bureau.

March 1875
The United States Supreme Court, in *Miner v. Happersett,* concludes that citizenship does not guarantee suffrage.
The Civil Rights Act of 1875 guarantees that African Americans receive equal treatment in public facilities.

November 1876
Rutherford B. Hayes is elected president.

April 1877
Hayes orders the last federal troops to leave South Carolina, and Reconstruction comes to a formal end.

May 1881
Former Civil War nurse Clara Barton forms the American Association of the Red Cross.

September 1894
The United Daughters of the Confederacy is formed.

H

Habersham, Josephine Clay (1821–1893)

The descendant of a prominent Georgia family, Josephine Clay Habersham kept a diary for several months in 1863 at the height of the Civil War. A staunch supporter of the Confederacy, Habersham cataloged unfolding news of the warfront and described in some detail her experiences caring for sick soldiers in two nearby hospitals. In her journal, she also discussed the war's economic and emotional toll on her family and community.

Born on January 14, 1821, one of seven children born to Dr. Joseph Clay Habersham and Anna Wylly Adams, Josephine Habersham inherited a genteel name and high social standing. Her great-grandfather, James Habersham, immigrated to Georgia from England in 1738, where he built a wealthy estate through commercial trade and rice plantations. Both the maternal and paternal sides of her family fought in the American Revolution and held high-level political posts in Georgia throughout the eighteenth and nineteenth centuries. Furthermore, George Washington appointed Josephine's great-uncle, Joseph Habersham, as postmaster general of the United States. A county in Georgia named after the family signifies the Habershams' legacy in that state.

Josephine married William Neyle Habersham, her distant cousin, in 1840. A rice merchant at the time of their marriage, William inherited his father's commercial shipping firm upon the elder Habersham's death. The couple settled in Savannah but maintained a summer home, called Avon Hall, 10 miles away in White Bluff, Georgia, on the bank of the Vernon River. Josephine gave birth to twelve children over the course of twenty years. Three died in infancy, and two more died as young children. Her two eldest sons, Joseph Clay, twenty-three, and William Neyle, twenty, fought at and died in the Battle of Atlanta on July 22, 1864.

Habersham's original diary documents her life from June 17 through November 1, 1863, the time her family spent at Avon Hall that year. The diary ends abruptly upon her return to Savannah. The second-to-last entry describes meeting Jefferson Davis at a Masonic Hall in Thunderbolt, Georgia.

In her journal, Habersham's anxieties over the fate of her enlisted sons and concerns about the Confederate army's progress shared space with descriptions of daily family activities, including dinners, dances, visitors, and the cheerful presence of her infant son. The overall content suggests that the Habershams were spared the worst troubles of the war during the time the diary was kept. A devoted Christian, avid reader, and accomplished pianist, Habersham frequently referenced scripture, British literature, and classical composers.

Habersham also wrote poems under the pen name Tallulah. At least one of these poems was included in a booklet of verse that was published and sold to benefit the Episcopal Orphans' Home in Savannah, Georgia, but no records exist that suggest she published elsewhere.

Josephine Clay Habersham died on November 6, 1893.

Jennifer Jane Nichols

See also Confederate Homefront; Davis, Jefferson (1808–1889); Diaries and Journals; Family Life, Confederate; Hospitals; Nationalism, Confederate; Nurses; Religion; Southern Women.

References and Further Reading

Bulloch, Joseph Gaston Baillie. 1901. *A history and genealogy of the Habersham family: in connection with the history, genealogy, and mention of the families of Clay, Stiles, Cumming, King, Elliott, Milledge, Maxwell, Adams, Houstoun, Screvens, Owens, Demere, Footman, Ellis, Washington, Newell, deTreville, Davis, Barrington, Lewis, Warner, Cobb, Flournoy, Pratt, Nephew, Bolton, Bowers, Cuthbert, and many many other names.* Columbia, SC: R.L. Bryan Company.

King, Spencer Bidwell, Jr., ed. 1958. *Ebb Tide: As Seen through the Diary of Josephine Clay Habersham, 1863.* Athens: University of Georgia Press.

Smith, Anna Habersham Wright, ed. 1999. *A Savannah Family, 1830–1901: Papers from the Clermont Huger Lee Collection.* Milledgeville, GA: Boyd Publishing Company.

Hague, Parthenia Antoinette Vardaman (1838–n.d.)

The daughter of a prominent slaveholding family, Parthenia Hague was employed as a teacher in rural Alabama when the Civil War began. She lived on the plantation of a wealthy slaveholder near Eufaula, and there she experienced the hardships of the Union naval blockade that she recorded in her memoir, *A Blockaded Family.*

Parthenia Antoinette Vardaman was born in Hamilton County, Georgia, on November 19, 1838. She was the second child and oldest daughter of Thomas Butts and Emily Adeline Evans Vardaman's eleven children. She attended Hamilton Academy and, after finishing her education, moved to Alabama to become a teacher.

In 1888, Hague published a memoir of her Civil War experiences. Steeped in Lost Cause ideology and romanticism about the Old South and slavery, Hague's work offers a rare glimpse into the details of daily life in wartime Alabama. In particular, she presented a meticulous accounting of homefront measures taken to ensure that Southerners, who had depended heavily on Northern imports, were fed and clothed during the years of the blockade.

Hague's descriptions of homefront life reveal how Southerners dealt with wartime shortages. Civilians found ways to find necessities such as oil, sugar, shoes, and leather, and they found substitutes for things they could not procure. Hague's detailed descriptions of tasks from her daily life, which included activities such as constructing a rice mill or fashioning buttons, offer a glimpse into the productive aspects of wartime life on a plantation. Textile manufacture was important for military and civilian clothing and linens, and Hague devoted lengthy passages to the female labors of weaving, dyeing, spinning, and sewing. In many cases, Hague played the part of observer to the female slaves who performed the work.

Hague, a religious Baptist, stressed that civilians depended on self-reliance and faith in God and the Cause to endure their material privations. She also emphasized that, despite the trials of wartime life, the spirits of Southerners not only survived, but they also thrived. Her book advanced her belief that Southern women had forged a new identity. United in their struggle, women played a special role in preserving body and soul and had emerged not conquered but victorious.

Hague claimed that her book was simply an account of life during wartime and a plea for reconciliation. Interwoven with her everyday observations, however, are homilies and anecdotes meant to validate the Confederacy and lament what she saw as a lost way of life. Like other postwar authors, Hague's idealized reminiscence served to romanticize slavery and encourage racism and Jim Crow.

The details of Hague's life after the publication of her memoir are shrouded in obscurity. The date of her death is unknown.

Yvette Florio Lane

See also African American Women; Baptist Women; Civilian Life; Confederate Homefront; Homespun; Religion; Shortages; Southern Women; Wartime Literature.

References and Further Reading

Fahs, Alice. 1999. "The Feminized Civil War: Gender, Northern Popular Literature and the Memory of the Civil War, 1861–1900." *Journal of American History* 85: 1461–1494.

erst.

Faust, Drew Gilpin. 1996. *Mothers of Invention: Women of the Slaveholding South in the American Civil War.* Chapel Hill: University of North Carolina Press.

Fox-Genovese, Elizabeth. 1988. *Within the Plantation Household: Black and White Women of the Old South.* Chapel Hill: University of North Carolina Press.

Gardner, Sarah E. 2004. *Blood and Irony: Southern White Women's Narratives of the Civil War, 1861–1937.* Chapel Hill: University of North Carolina Press.

Hague, Parthenia Antoinette. [1888] 1991. *A Blockaded Family: Life in Southern Alabama During the Civil War.* Lincoln: University of Nebraska Press.

Hale, Sarah Josepha (1788–1879)

Sarah Josepha (Buell) Hale was one of the most influential magazine editors of the nineteenth century. Her power was somewhat diminished during the Civil War by her publisher's insistence that she minimize attention to the war in *Godey's Lady's Book* to avoid offending any readers. Nevertheless, Hale had a lasting impact on the country through her efforts to establish a national Thanksgiving Day holiday and through the role taken by *Godey's* before and after the war. Under Hale's leadership, the magazine consistently supported national reconciliation.

Born October 24, 1788, in Newport, New Hampshire, she was a lifelong patriot, who, although she did not support suffrage for women, believed women should be deeply engaged in political issues. She was also a lifelong writer, who began her literary career even before the death of her husband in 1822. Throughout her life, she was committed to encouraging a sense of community and union for the country and increasing women's opportunities for education and employment. While upholding the ideology of separate spheres, she saw women as having a central responsibility to encourage a moral and progressive civil life.

Her first novel, *Northwood* (1827), included a discussion of the problem of slavery for the country, as well as a description of a Thanksgiving dinner in a country home, bringing together two themes that remained important to her throughout her career.

Sarah Josepha Hale, novelist, editor of the influential *Godey's Lady's Book*, and promoter of a national Thanksgiving Day holiday (1788–1879). (Library of Congress)

Northwood expresses some sympathy for Southern slaveholders, while recognizing the evil of slavery. Hale hoped for, and used her personal connections to work toward, a peaceful compromise that would end slavery without significant injury to the South. As tensions mounted in the country, Hale revised *Northwood* in 1852 to add the idea of purchasing the emancipation of slaves, and, in columns and a new novel *Liberia* (1853), she supported the ideas of the American Colonization Society, whose solution to the problem of slavery was the education of slaves and their removal to the new African country of Liberia.

Hale also spent years promoting a national Thanksgiving Day as a time when the nation would come together as families. She saw the private home celebration as a model for the loving unity she wanted to see in the country. Hale imagined Thanksgiving as a time when families would gather together, reinforce their ties, and thus be strengthened to form a more united country. She began her campaign for a nationally recognized Thanksgiving Day as early as 1827, with articles and letters to politicians at every level. She intensified her efforts in 1846, as it became clear that the threat to the country's union was increasing. She argued, in *Godey's* and in letters to the president and to the governors of states and territories that a national day of thanksgiving, celebrated throughout the nation, would help to preserve the union. Finally, in 1863, in the midst of war, President Abraham Lincoln proclaimed a national day of Thanksgiving.

Hale died April 30, 1879.

JoAnn Castagna

See also Fiction Writers, Northern; Northern Women; Poets, Northern; Separate Spheres; Union Homefront; Wartime Literature

References and Further Reading

Hoffman, Nicole Tonkovich. 1990. "Legacy Profile: Sarah Josepha Hale." *Legacy* 7 (2): 47–55.

Okker, Patricia. 1995. *Our Sister Editors: Sarah J. Hale and the Tradition of Nineteenth-Century American Women Editors.* Athens: University of Georgia Press.

Pleck, Elizabeth. 1999. "The Making of the Domestic Occasion: The History of Thanksgiving in the United States." *Journal of Social History* 32 (4): 773–790.

Rogers, Sherbrooke. 1985. *Sarah Josepha Hale: A New England Pioneer 1788–1879.* Grantham, NH: Thompson and Rutter.

Hancock, Cornelia (1840–1926)

Abolitionist and reformer Cornelia Hancock did not allow anyone or anything to deter her from her objectives. Even the strong-willed Dorothea Dix, Superintendent of the United States Army Nurses, could not prevent Hancock from participating in the war effort as an independent nurse for the Union troops.

Hancock was born to Thomas Yorke and Rachel Nicholson Hancock, February 8, 1840, in Salem County, New Jersey. The Hancocks were Quakers, and Cornelia received an early education in abolitionist beliefs.

Hancock's desire to do her duty for the Union was initially sidetracked by Dorothea Dix. In July 1863, Dix refused to allow Hancock to sign on as a nurse for the Union army, telling her that she was too young and too pretty. Dix wanted only plain, married, or widowed women, over the age of thirty. The twenty-three-year-old Hancock was undeterred. She sneaked onto a train bound for Gettysburg, where she met up with her brother-in-law, Dr. Henry T. Child, a doctor with the Second Pennsylvania Regiment. Hancock traveled extensively during the war, serving in several hospitals in Pennsylvania and Virginia. Much of her work concerned obtaining supplies and helping in the hospital kitchens. Toward the end of the war, she helped black refugees in Washington, serving as a nurse and helping them obtain shelter and food.

Hancock's war work did not end with the fall of Richmond. In 1866, during Reconstruction, she founded a school for former slaves in South Carolina. Hancock and Laura Towne, with the support of the Philadelphia Friends Association for the Aid and Elevation of the Freedmen, opened the Laing School in Mount Pleasant, South Carolina. She taught there for ten years, and also served as principal until 1875. In 1878 she helped establish a children's aid society in Pennsylvania and the Society for Organizing Charity. Six years later Hancock began settlement work in Philadelphia in a run-down neighborhood called Wrightsville.

In her later years, Hancock moved to Atlantic City, New Jersey. She died of nephritis December 31, 1926.

Paula Katherine Hinton

See also Abolitionism and Northern Reformers; Hospitals; Northern Women; Nurses; Quaker Women; Reconstruction (1865–1877); Teachers, Northern; Towne, Laura Matilda (1825–1901); Wartime Employment.

References and Further Reading

Hancock, Cornelia. 1998. *Letters of a Civil War Nurse: Cornelia Hancock, 1863–1865,* edited by Henrietta Stratton Jaquette. Lincoln: University of Nebraska Press.

Jaquette, Henrietta Stratton, ed. 1937. *South after Gettysburg: Letters of Cornelia Hancock, 1863–1865.* New York: Thomas Y. Crowell & Company.

Schultz, Jane E. 2004. *Women at the Front: Hospital Workers in Civil War America.* Chapel Hill: University of North Carolina Press.

Harper, Frances Ellen Watkins (1825–1911)

Abolitionist, Underground Railroad agent, journalist, poet, novelist, civil rights activist, and suffragist, Frances Ellen Watkins Harper was one of the nineteenth century's most prolific and influential African American writers and social reformists.

Born free in the slave state of Maryland on September 24, 1825, Harper was orphaned by the time she was three years old. Raised by an aunt and uncle, Henrietta and Reverend William Watkins, in Baltimore, she was fortunate to attend her uncle's renowned William Watkins Academy for Negro Youth. She exhibited an early brilliance, fostered by the extensive range of classical studies offered at the Academy. Employment opportunities for bright young African American women were limited, however, forcing her to take a job as a domestic helper. Fortunately, her employers recognized her great intellect and encouraged her interest in reading and writing. By 1850, virulent racism in Baltimore finally forced the closing of the Academy, and Harper's uncle and his family moved to Canada. Harper moved to Ohio to teach at Union Seminary (later known as Wilberforce University) and then at a school in Pennsylvania. In 1853, she moved in with the family of famed Underground Railroad agent William Still, in Philadelphia, to devote her talents to the antislavery cause. Within a year, she was on the antislavery lecture circuit, traveling throughout New England, Canada, and the West, as well as to Detroit and Cincinnati. She soon began publishing essays, poetry, and political commentaries in abolitionist publications and antislavery newspapers. Renowned for her passionate lectures, her writings reached an even larger audience. Her first book of poetry, *Poems on Miscellaneous Subjects,* sold over ten thousand copies. Although some of her poetry addressed the plight of the enslaved, her work also focused on temperance, religion, women's rights, racism, politics, and African American life and culture.

Harper was a devout Methodist whose faith guided her unyielding determination to advocate the end of slavery and the provision of better educational opportunities for African Americans, as well as to serve those less fortunate. She did not shy away from controversial subjects, and her calls for action included boycotts, mass protest, and civil disobedience. She also demanded public action on the part of those who professed sympathy with the antislavery cause. Personal moral responsibility, she believed, was the foundation of any social movement. Though she traveled and spoke frequently for the "cause of freedom," she also acted on her principles: Her home in Philadelphia became a refuge on the Underground Railroad, and she became intimately involved with some of the most powerful activists of her day, including Frederick Douglass, Sojourner Truth, Henry Highland Garnett, and Susan B. Anthony.

In 1860, she married Fenton Harper, a widower in Cincinnati, and, with the help of her earnings, they purchased a small farm on the outskirts of Columbus, Ohio. She gave birth to a daughter, Mary; motherhood forced her to cut back on her lecturing, though she continued to write for major newspapers and magazines. With the onset of the Civil War, Harper became a tough campaigner for the emancipation of the slaves. She was thrilled when President Abraham Lincoln announced the Emancipation Proclamation in the fall of 1862.

When her husband died in 1864, Harper resumed lecturing and writing on more of a full-time basis. After the Civil War, she devoted herself to working with the freedmen in the South, and, critical of the injustices she saw perpetrated against the newly freed slaves, she campaigned for more schools, better wages, and equal rights.

Even though she had been a supporter of the American Equal Rights Association, the national woman's suffrage organization of the day, she threw her support behind the passage of the Fifteenth Amendment. This Reconstruction era amendment gave black men, but not women of any color, the right to vote. Harper believed that universal suffrage was unattainable at that time and decided that suffrage for African American men was more important than no vote at all. Her support of the amendment, however, alienated her from longtime suffrage friends Susan B. Anthony and Elizabeth Cady Stanton. She went on to help found the

American Woman Suffrage Association, was a member of the national board of the Women's Christian Temperance Union, and was a founding member of the National Association of Colored Women. She continued to write and spent much of her time devoted to African American causes and institution building. At the age of sixty-seven, she published her most famous work, a novel, *Iola Leroy*.

Harper struggled with ill health throughout her later years, and she died in Philadelphia on February 22, 1911.

Kate Clifford Larson

See also Abolitionism and Northern Reformers; African American Women; Anthony, Susan B. (1820–1906); Antislavery Societies; Douglass, Frederick (ca. 1818–1895); Emancipation Proclamation (January 1, 1863); Fifteenth Amendment; Methodist Women; Stanton, Elizabeth Cady (1815–1902); Truth, Sojourner [Isabella Baumfree] (1797–1883).

References and Further Reading

Boyd, Melba Joyce. 1994. *Discarded Legacy: Politics and Poetics in the Life of Frances E.W. Harper, 1825–1911*. Detroit, MI: Wayne State University Press.

Foster, Frances Smith. 2005. "Frances Ellen Watkins Harper." In *Black Women in America*, edited by Darlene Clark Hine, 2, 532–537. New York: Oxford University Press.

Still, William. 1970. *The Underground Railroad: a record of facts, authentic narratives, letters, &c., narrating the hardships, hair-breadth escapes, and death struggles of the slaves in their efforts for freedom, as related by themselves and others or witnessed by the author: together with sketches of some of the largest stockholders and most liberal aiders and advisers of the road*. Chicago, IL: Johnson Publishing. (Orig. pub. 1872.)

Hart, Nancy (ca. 1843–1902)

Nancy Hart, a young and beautiful Confederate spy, served as a scout, guide, and cavalry trooper for the Southern cause before experiencing a dramatic capture and escape from Northern soldiers.

Not to be confused with the Nancy Hart of Revolutionary War fame, Hart was born in the early 1840s. As an infant, she moved from Raleigh, North Carolina, to Tazewell, Virginia (later West Virginia).

Hart became an expert horsewoman and cultivated a familiarity with the Virginia outdoors. Although she never learned to read or write, she explored the wilderness and became a deadeye riflewoman. In 1861 Hart visited the home of her sister and brother-in-law, William Price, just as Union soldiers arrived to escort Price to the nearby town of Spencer to speak in favor of the Union. Price never arrived in Spencer; he was found on the road shot in the back, sparking in Hart a hatred for Union soldiers. Soon after, at a party celebrating the departure of her neighbor's sons for the Confederate army, Union soldiers rode by during the affair and fired a rifle several times at the home. Three days later Hart rode off to join the Confederate cause.

Hart joined the Moccasin Rangers, a pro-Southern guerrilla unit. She served as a scout, guide, and spy, carrying messages while traveling alone between Southern armies by night. Hart peddled eggs and vegetables to Northern troops to gain access to information. She also visited Northern outposts in the mountains to learn and report of their strength, population, and vulnerability.

In July 1862, Union forces offered a large reward for Hart's capture. Union soldiers under the command of Lieutenant Colonel William C. Starr of the Ninth West Virginia arrested Hart at a log cabin where she was crushing corn with a young female friend. Hart was jailed in the upper portion of a dilapidated house turned makeshift jail in the nearby town of Sommersville, in western Virginia, guarded by a sentry at the door, quartered soldiers downstairs, and troops on patrol around the building. A young woman of striking beauty, Hart beguiled a young soldier who allowed her to examine his weapon, upon which she promptly shot him in the head. Hart jumped out a second story window, stole Starr's horse, and rode off for Confederate territory. On July 25, 1862, she returned, still riding Starr's horse, along with approximately two hundred of General Stonewall Jackson's cavalrymen. During the raid of Sommersville, Southern soldiers took mules, horses, and several prisoners (including Starr), and they burned much of the town to the ground.

During the war, Hart met Joshua Douglas, also a former Ranger, and nursed him back to health following his near fatal wounds. He left and joined the Confederate army, but after the war he returned to the area, found Hart, and married her. They settled in Greenbriar County, where they lived until her death in 1902. Nancy Hart is buried in Mannings Knob, Greenbriar Country, West Virginia.

Eloise E. Scroggins

See also Confederate Homefront; Domesticity; Female Combatants; Female Spies; Guerrilla Warfare; Imprisonment of Women; Separate Spheres; Southern Women.

References and Further Reading
Broadwater, Robert P. 1993. *Daughters of the Cause: Women in the "Civil War."* Santa Clarita, CA: Daisy Publishing Company.
Colman, Penny. 1992. *Spies! Women in the Civil War.* White Hall, FL: Shoe Tree Press.
Larson, Rebecca D. 1996. *Blue and Grey Roses of Intrigue.* Gettysburg, PA: Thomas Publications.
Leonard, Elizabeth D. 1999. *All the Daring of the Soldier: Women of the Civil War Armies.* New York: W. W. Norton & Company.

Haviland, Laura Smith (1808–1898)

A birthright member of the Religious Society of Friends (Quakers), Laura Smith Haviland was an abolitionist whose work for the Underground Railroad was so effective that Southern slave owners once offered a $3,000 reward for her capture.

Born in Canada in 1808, Laura's family moved to western New York State when she was seven. In 1829, she, her husband Charles, and their children relocated to southeastern Michigan. In 1834, she and Elizabeth Chandler founded the Logan Female Anti-Slavery Society, the first antislavery society in Michigan. She and Charles established the first station on the Underground Railroad in Michigan, assisting fugitives to Canada. In 1836, they founded the Raisin Institute, in Adrian, Michigan, primarily for orphans. Coeducational and interracial, the Institute also trained students for careers in education.

In 1845, Laura's husband, parents, sister, and baby died from erysipelas, an acute bacterial skin infection. Although she was a widowed mother of seven children with few resources, she intensified her involvement in the Underground Railroad, making daring trips to Cincinnati and the South to help escaping slaves. In 1847, Laura tried to rescue the family of John White, a fugitive who was a farmhand in the neighborhood of Raisin Institute. When Haviland's scheme failed, White was arrested and jailed after making a similar attempt. He was released when Haviland purchased him for $350. In 1852, she opened a day school and Sunday school at the Refugees' Home, one of three black settlements established in Canada for fugitive slaves.

Like many of her male counterparts, Laura took an uncompromising stand against slavery. She displayed a zealous belief in her convictions, both religious and humanitarian. When the Civil War commenced, her attention turned to relief work for recently emancipated slaves and wounded and ill soldiers. She delivered clothing to the freedpersons and medical and food supplies to army hospitals. She made several fundraising trips to Michigan to continue her work. In New Orleans, Louisiana, she badgered government officials for the release of three thousand Union prisoners being held for trivial offenses in prison camps that had deplorable conditions. Beginning in 1864, she worked among destitute African Americans and white Southerners who had migrated to Kansas, providing aid and helping to found an educational institution. After the war, she continued to bring emancipated slaves to Michigan as settlers, and she worked in a mission near Kansas City. In recognition, Haviland, Kansas, was named in her honor.

Drawn to Methodism as a child, Laura and her husband withdrew from the Society of Friends and joined the Wesleyan Methodist Church, which was more amenable to both abolitionism and evangelism. Toward the end of her life, however, Laura rejoined the Quakers. In 1909, a life-size statue of her was erected in front of the city hall at Adrian, Michigan.

Jayne R. Beilke

See also Abolitionism and Northern Reformers; Aid Societies; Methodist Women; Quaker Women.

References and Further Reading
Haviland, Laura Smith. 1881. *A Woman's Life Work: Labors and Experiences of Laura S. Haviland.* Cincinnati, OH: Walden and Stowe.

Hawks, Esther Hill (1833–1906)

Dr. Esther Hill Hawks taught school and provided medical assistance during the Civil War to the United States Colored Troops (USCT) and to freedmen in the South Carolina Sea Islands.

Esther was born in Hooksett, New Hampshire, on August 4, 1833. She was the fifth of eight children born to Parmenas and Jane Kimball Hill. Esther attended public school in Rhode Island and an academy at Kingston, and then she went on to teach public school. In October 1854, Esther married Dr. John Milton Hawks. Through his support, she attended New England Female Medical College and graduated with her medical degree in 1857.

At the outbreak of the Civil War, Esther volunteered her medical services to the Union army. Immediately rebuffed as a doctor because of her sex, Esther attempted to become a nurse. Her youth and beauty, however, caused Dorothea Dix to reject Esther's services. Undeterred, Esther returned to Manchester to assist with the war effort in her local community and became the secretary of the Manchester Soldier's Aid Society. During this time, she was also elected as an officer of the Ladies Medical Academy.

In April 1862, Dr. John Hawks arrived in the Sea Islands of South Carolina under the authority of the National Freedmen's Aid Association. He worked to secure a position for his wife to join him and was finally successful that fall. Esther had independently managed to obtain a position as a teacher in the South Carolina Sea Islands with the National Freedmen's Relief Association. In October 1862, the Hawks settled in Beaufort, South Carolina.

Initially, established gender roles limited Esther to teaching the freedmen and African American soldiers in the Sea Islands instead of serving as a doctor. In April 1862, the Hawks helped to open General Hospital Number 10 for Colored Troops, which established the medical segregation of white and black Union troops. Esther assisted her husband as much as the Union army would allow. Nevertheless, her role remained primarily that of a teacher. The massive arrival of USCT wounded after the assault on Fort Wagner, however, permitted Esther the opportunity to demonstrate her medical expertise without interference. Her skill tending to the wounded soldiers in the Fifty-fourth Massachusetts Infantry allowed Esther to gain the respect of the local Union officials, who allowed her to continue practicing medicine. During the remainder of the war, Esther traveled to parts of Florida, to Charleston, and throughout the Sea Islands, teaching school as well as providing medical assistance to the USCT and local freedmen.

After the Civil War, Esther returned to Massachusetts to join a medical partnership and remained active in charitable and reform organizations, especially woman suffrage. Esther Hill Hawks died at her home in Lynn, Massachusetts, on May 6, 1906.

Kristina K. Dunn

See also Nurses; Teachers, Northern.

References and Further Reading
Schwartz, Gerald, ed. 1984. *A Woman Doctor's Civil War: Esther Hill Hawks' Diary.* Columbia: University of South Carolina Press.

Hayes, Lucy Ware Webb (1831–1889)

The wife of post-Reconstruction President Rutherford B. Hayes, Lucy Ware Webb Hayes was the first president's wife to be referred to as the First Lady.

Born on August 28, 1831, in Chillicothe, Ohio, to Dr. James Webb and Maria Cook Webb, Lucy grew up in Delaware, Ohio. She graduated from Cincinnati Wesleyan Female College in 1850 and married lawyer Rutherford B. Hayes in December 1852. The couple had eight children, five of whom survived to adulthood.

When the Civil War began, thirty-nine-year-old Rutherford was representing runaway slaves trying to stay in Ohio. Lucy, a strong opponent of slavery, had urged him to take an active role in the abolition movement. The fall of Fort Sumter changed the Hayes' focus. Although they had imagined a peaceful resolution to the nation's problems, they understood the need for military action to reunite the Union and end slavery. Rutherford was awarded the rank of major and assigned to help command the newly formed Twenty-third Ohio Volunteer Infantry Regiment. Despite criticism from family and friends for Rutherford's eagerness in joining the military, Lucy proudly supported her husband, despite the hardships his military service would cause her and their three young children. Over the course of the war, Rutherford, who remained in the service until the end of the war, would rise to the rank of brigadier general in the army, and his wartime military service led to a successful postwar political career. Lucy's support proved crucial to his success in both endeavors.

Like so many men at war, Rutherford treasured the numerous letters Lucy sent him and saw them as a constant source of strength. Her letters offered not only moral support, but also insights about the political and cultural situation on the homefront.

Lucy constantly worried about her husband. When Rutherford's unit was sent to what is now West Virginia, Lucy's pregnancy, combined with a fear of Confederate invasion and the constant danger faced by her husband, led to depression. To help ease Lucy's mind, Rutherford or her brother, a surgeon attached to his regiment, would telegraph her after each battle to let her know that they had survived. These messages kept her from having to depend on the incomplete and inaccurate reports in the newspapers. Understanding the value of accurate information, Lucy convinced Rutherford to write to the families of the men under his command who were killed.

Wartime was lonely, but Lucy had many visitors. Soldiers on leave often came by the family's home in Cincinnati to deliver messages to Lucy or to praise her husband and pay their respects. Rutherford returned home for a visit early in the war to see his new daughter. In addition, Lucy visited her husband twice in western Virginia, where she and their two oldest sons spent several months with Rutherford.

Lucy also hurried to her husband's side when he was wounded in the fall of 1862. She received a telegram from Rutherford telling her he was

Lucy Webb Hayes, wife of President Rutherford B. Hayes (1831–1889). (Library of Congress)

wounded and he wanted her there. Lucy left the children with relatives and, along with a family friend, took the train to Washington. She arrived a week after her husband was wounded but could not find him. At the military hospitals and the Surgeon General's headquarters, clerks—too busy to give her any information—treated Lucy rudely. At the U.S. Patent Office, which had been turned into a hospital, Lucy noticed several soldiers with "23" pins on their hats. After she called out "Twenty-third Ohio," several soldiers recognized her and told her where she could find Rutherford. Lucy spent two weeks in Middletown, Maryland, caring for her husband as well as visiting other wounded soldiers. Two weeks later, Lucy shepherded her husband and six other wounded soldiers back to Ohio. Seven weeks later, Rutherford left again for active duty.

When the war ended, Rutherford resigned from the army. Already elected to Congress, Rutherford traveled to Washington with Lucy, where they watched the Grand Review of the Army of the Republic. Rutherford served in Congress for two terms, as governor of Ohio for three terms, and as president for one term. Throughout these years, Lucy worked for the welfare of veterans and their families, using her influence to aid others.

Lucy Hayes died on June 25, 1889, after suffering a stroke.

Wesley Moody

See also Letter Writing; Northern Women; Union Homefront; Wounded, Visits to.
References and Further Reading
Geer, Emily Apt. 1984. *The First Lady, The Life of Lucy Webb Hayes.* Kent, OH: Kent State University Press.
Hoogenboom, Ari. 1995. *Rutherford B. Hayes.* Lawrence: University Press of Kansas.

Heyward, Pauline DeCaradeuc (1843–1914)

A young female diarist on the Confederate home front, Pauline DeCaradeuc Heyward chronicled her life in South Carolina and her experiences during General William T. Sherman's campaign in the Carolinas.

Born into an elite, slaveholding family near Aiken, South Carolina, Pauline, age seventeen, was enjoying the freedom of attending social functions and engaging in courtships when the war commenced. Her homefront experiences transformed Pauline from a protected belle into a self-reliant and outspoken young woman. As an ardent supporter of the Confederate cause, she followed news of military engagements and made clothing for soldiers. She also confronted the hardships of war resulting from the death of family and friends serving on the military front, from financial downturns, and from the demise of the slave system.

Pauline sought normalcy as the war disrupted her life. She attended dances and parties and made extended visits to kin in South Carolina and Georgia. In 1863, she invited a friend to stay with her for the remainder of the war to ease her anxiety and loneliness. She carried on flirtations with soldiers with whom she came into contact. Yet the death of two brothers from typhoid fever while serving in the Confederate army was a constant source of emotional pain for Pauline. The war also took a financial toll on the DeCaradeuc household because the

deflation of Confederate currency and shortages of supplies caused prices to soar. In spite of these hardships, the family welcomed Confederate soldiers and war refugees into their home.

Sherman's march through the Carolinas, beginning in February 1865, brought the war to Pauline's community. As news spread of an impending invasion, she began carrying a pistol for protection. Troops under the command of General Hugh Judson Kilpatrick arrived in Aiken, and Pauline's father fled the home to avoid arrest. The wealth and Confederate sympathies of the DeCaradeucs made their estate a target of Union troops foraging the countryside for supplies. Pauline watched as soldiers looted and threatened to burn the home until her mother and grandmother intervened. Federal soldiers continued to visit the home when the war ended and on one occasion physically assaulted Pauline's father. In response, the young woman traveled with a male escort to nearby Augusta, Georgia, to meet with the Federal commander and request a protective guard.

Pauline continued to demonstrate loyalty to the Confederate cause even at the war's end. She lauded Jefferson Davis's attempts to regroup troops in the West and refused to attend a picnic marking the end of the war. Eventually, Pauline accepted defeat and tried to return to the life of comfort she once knew. In August 1865, she began a courtship with Guerard Heyward, a former Confederate soldier and a member of an elite family, and the two married in 1866.

Pauline DeCaradeuc Heyward died in 1914.

Victoria E. Ott

See also Confederate Homefront; Courtship and Marriage; Destruction of Personal Property; Sherman's Campaign (1864–1865); Southern Women.
References and Further Reading
Campbell, Jacqueline Glass. 2003. *When Sherman Marched North from the Sea: Resistance on the Confederate Homefront.* Chapel Hill: University of North Carolina Press.
Robertson, Mary D., ed., 1992. *A Confederate Lady Comes of Age: The Journal of Pauline DeCaradeuc Heyward.* Columbia: University of South Carolina Press.

Hispanic Women

During the Civil War era, Hispanic women in America lived primarily in former Spanish colonies: California; the territories of Texas, Arizona, and New Mexico; and in the Gulf areas of southern Florida, Louisiana, and Alabama. For most of these women, the war existed in relation to larger geopolitical forces intimately tied to Spain and her colonies in the Americas. In 1860 approximately thirty thousand foreign-born Mexican Hispanics lived in the Southwest regions. By 1861 Mexican women whose homelands had been transferred over to the United States in the wake of the Mexican War had been American citizens for only thirteen years. Even so, ten thousand of their husbands and sons joined the Civil War armies.

The majority of Hispanic women were Mestizas—a combination of European Spanish with varying degrees of Indian blood. Others were Mulattas, such as the Louisiana Creoles of color whose men joined the Louisiana Native Guard, as well as a variety of other Hispanics including Ladinas, Sephardic Jews whose men joined Georgia and South Carolina units, and a handful of Spanish-Philippinas, whose men are found on Confederate rosters.

More Hispanic families would side with the Union, but approximately thirty-six hundred soldiers with Hispanic surnames appear on the Confederate rosters. These men enlisted to prove their citizenship or to gain access to the body politic, as well as for social, class-related, and economic reasons. Hispanic soldiers were less motivated by issues of slavery and states' rights than other soldiers. The majority of Confederate Hispanics were not slave owners; by the 1860s, slavery had been abolished in Spain and in most of the Americas, surviving only in Cuba and Puerto Rico, which were then still Spanish colonies. However, the Confederacy appealed to Southwestern families by promising to honor Latinos' pre-existing land grants, for example, or by offering income and bounty for soldiers to send home.

Even though they were recruited, Hispanics were not always welcomed by the armies of the North or the South. Juanita Chacon waited in vain for her husband's pay to reach her. After years of service and numerous promotions, the Union did not pay Major Manuel Chacon or his men, provide proper equipment, or feed their horses. He resigned in 1864, citing his wife's problems on the homefront. Another group of Mexican soldiers' wives welcomed their husbands home unexpectedly when an entire battalion of Mexican Confederate soldiers deserted upon learning they were about to be lynched by their fellow Confederate soldiers for being "greasers."

Some Hispanic women took a more direct role in the war. Cuban-born and New Orleans–raised, Loreta Janeta Velazquez disguised herself as a man to raise and outfit Confederate recruits with her own money, fought in the Battle of First Bull Run, was wounded at Shiloh, and spied for the Confederacy. A wealthy, educated member of the upper class, Velazquez supported the Southern war effort and condoned slavery, but she chafed at the gender restrictions of her time. Despite reports that she exaggerated her exploits in her 1876 memoir, *A Woman in Battle*, Velazquez played an important role in the war. Her independent wealth allowed her to fund her exploits. As a Hispanic woman under Spanish law and customs, she retained her dowry and property during marriage and as a widow.

Many Hispanic women enjoyed other freedoms unknown to most Anglo women in America. For example, they could run farms, ranches, and other businesses on their own behalf. Furthermore, Hispanic women could testify in court and act as executors of estates. Union widow and novelist Maria Amparo Ruiz de Burton began a series of land court petitions over property after her husband's death. Ruiz married Union Colonel Henry S. Burton, and spent a decade in the Northeast, becoming a close friend of Mary Todd Lincoln and moving in the highest social circles. She published several works after the war, providing a biting critique of Northeastern racism against Hispanics and the corruption of the military, the clergy, and the political system during the nineteenth century. Her satirical novel, *Who Would Have Thought It?* (1872), tells the story of an orphaned Spanish girl raised by a hypocritical abolitionist New England adoptive mother who could not accept a brown child. The novel attempted to counter the prevailing American contempt for things Spanish and Mexican in the wake of the U.S.-Mexican War.

Other Hispanic women took actions against hostile troops. Lola Sanchez, whose family hacienda was repeatedly raided by Union soldiers, longed for revenge. Her elderly father, Cuban immigrant Mauritia Sanchez, was imprisoned near their home outside St. Augustine, Florida, on charges of being a Confederate spy. Her brother had joined the Confederacy, and Lola served briefly as a spy. One night, while Federal soldiers dined at her home and flirted with her sisters, Eugenia and Panchita, Lola stole away to alert the nearest Confederate camp about planned Federal troop movements. As a result of her efforts, the Union lost a unit, a gunboat, and a general.

María Agui Carter

See also Bull Run/Manassas, First Battle of (July 21, 1861); Confederate Homefront; Female Combatants; Female Spies; Northern Women; Shiloh, Battle of (April 6–7, 1862); Southern Women; Union Homefront; Velazquez, Loreta Janeta [Harry T. Buford] (1842–1897); Wartime Literature.

References and Further Reading
Lonn, Ella. 2002. *Foreigners in the Confederacy.* Chapel Hill: University of North Carolina Press.
O'Donnell-Rosales, John. 1997. *Hispanic Confederates.* Baltimore, MD: Clearfield Co.
Padilla, Genaro M. 1993. *My History, Not Yours: The Formation of Mexican American Autobiography.* Madison: University of Wisconsin Press.
Ruiz de Burton, Maria Amparo. 1995. *Who Would Have Thought It?* Houston, TX: Arte Público Press.
Thompson, Jerry D. 2000. *Vaqueros in Blue and Gray.* Austin, TX: State House Press.
Velazquez, Loreta Janeta. 2003. *A Woman in Battle: The Civil War Narrative of Loreta Janeta Velazquez, Cuban Woman and Confederate Soldier.* Madison: University of Wisconsin Press.

Hodgers, Jennie [Albert D. J. Cashier] (ca. 1843–1915)

Disguised as a man, Jennie Hodgers served as a Union soldier throughout the Civil War. With her regiment, Company G, Ninety-fifth Illinois Volunteer Infantry, Hodgers fought in Tennessee, Mississippi, Missouri, and Alabama. Retaining a male identity after mustering out, Hodgers returned to Illinois where she worked as a farm laborer and handyman. Her true gender was kept secret until after the sixty-eight-year-old veteran became a resident of the Illinois State Soldiers' and Sailors' Home.

Although her military service is unequivocal, details of Hodgers's early life are sparse and nebulous, in part because her mental condition had deteriorated by the time her real identity was discovered and questions arose. Her admission application to the Soldiers' and Sailors' Home indicates that she was born in Ireland on December 25 "about 1844," rather than in New York as she occasionally said. In subsequent conversations with hospital personnel, Hodgers gave Cloger Head as her birth town. Hodgers and people claiming to be her relatives gave various explanations for her initial breach of gender roles. In one account, Hodgers said that she wore boy's clothing as either a stowaway or a cabin boy during the journey to America. Alleged relatives opined that her coachman and horse trader father dressed her as a boy for safety while she traveled with him across Ireland. In other conversations, Hodgers maintained that her stepfather instructed her to impersonate a boy in order to work in a New York shoe factory.

Hodgers's residence and visage between immigration and military enlistment as nineteen-year-old farmer Albert D. J. Cashier in Belvidere, Illinois, are unclear, as are her reasons for joining the army. August 1862 induction documents describe her as five feet three inches tall with blue eyes, light brown hair, and fair complexion. Complete physical examinations were rarely performed on recruits, and female soldiers who escaped illness, wounding, or capture could avoid detection throughout their service. Initially dispatched to Kentucky, her regiment continued to Jackson, Tennessee, joining the command of General Stephen A. Hurlbut, then merged with the Army of Tennessee under General Ulysses S. Grant. Hodgers's unit fought at the Battle of Vicksburg before being ordered to West Tennessee and northern Mississippi, ultimately engaging Confederate troops at Brice's Crossroads,

Tennessee, where many of her comrades succumbed to heat prostration and bullet wounds. After regrouping in Memphis, the Ninety-fifth Illinois fought the Rebels in Missouri at the Battles of Spring Hill, Franklin, and Nashville, and along the Gulf Coast.

Having fulfilled its three-year obligation, Private Cashier's unit was mustered out. Hodgers eventually settled in Saunemin, Illinois, where the illiterate veteran earned a living performing jobs including lamplighter and church janitor. At least three times after her military service ended, Hodgers's real gender was revealed; however, all who knew the truth honored her request for secrecy. In early 1911, while working on Senator Ira M. Lish's property, Hodgers suffered injuries when the senator accidentally backed his car into her. Both the senator and the attending physician agreed to keep her gender confidential, as did the superintendent and examining physician at the Soldiers' and Sailors' Home in Quincy, Illinois, when she applied for admission there on April 29, 1911. Soon thereafter, attendants attempting to bathe the veteran discovered she was not a man and the subterfuge crumbled. Perhaps to verify that Hodgers and Cashier were the same person, her former army captain visited her. To support her pension increase request, other Ninety-fifth Illinois veterans attested to her identity and combat record, recalling her reclusive nature, dependability, and bravery.

Exhibiting symptoms of dementia, Hodgers was transferred to the state mental institution in 1913. Two years later, she died there on October 11. She was buried in uniform with full military honors at Saunemin's Sunnyslope Cemetery. After a nine-year investigation, her conservator was unable to authenticate any surviving relatives.

Nancy L. Adgent

See also Domesticity; Female Combatants; Immigrant Women; Northern Women; Wartime Employment.

References and Further Reading

Blanton, DeAnne, and Lauren McCook. 2002. *They Fought Like Demons: Women Soldiers in the American Civil War.* Baton Rouge: Louisiana University Press.

Leonard, Elizabeth. 1999. *All the Daring of a Soldier: Women of the Civil War Armies.* New York: W. W. Norton & Company.

Hoge, Jane Currie Blaikie (1811–1890)

Born in Philadelphia in 1811, Jane Hoge (pronounced Hodge) worked throughout the Civil War to aid United States soldiers and citizens. At the outset of the war she provided relief supplies. She later became an associate manager of the northwestern branch of the United States Sanitary Commission in Chicago. In this position she came to see herself as a mother figure to the many men who fought for the Union. After the war ended, she published a book focusing on the experiences of the army's rank and file. Hoge's *The Boys in Blue* remains one of the few volumes that offers a glimpse into the lives of everyday soldiers in the Civil War.

Hoge shared her position at the Sanitary Commission with Mary A. Livermore. The two women worked smoothly together, imposing strict business standards on the Chicago branch and overseeing a massive supply effort. While the two women shared the office with two men, an accountant and a handyman, Hoge and Livermore represented the

Jane Currie Blaikie Hoge was a manager of the United States Sanitary Commission in Chicago and worked tirelessly to help U.S. soldiers (1811–1890). (Library of Congress)

Commission to the hundreds of donors, family members, women, and soldiers who visited. They wrote thousands of letters, telling folks at home about the needs at the front and facilitating correspondence between the soldiers and their loved ones. In addition, they traveled extensively. For example, early in 1863 Hoge spent weeks on a boat floating in the Mississippi River operating a supply depot and hospital to aid the Union troops fighting to take control of Vicksburg. Finally, in an era when women believed that speaking to mixed audiences was promiscuous, she learned to give moving and dynamic public speeches, telling stories about the soldiers.

Hoge's job with the Sanitary Commission proved highly demanding, but she also enjoyed its benefits. The skills she learned—nursing, public speaking, and the ability to gather bandages, basic clothing, and specific foods, on a scale large enough to provide for the needs of entire armies—took her beyond traditional women's roles. Yet Hoge, the mother of eight surviving children, found her ultimate wartime inspiration in the soldiers. After the war she returned to private life, but she remained a preeminent woman in the eyes of many until she died in Evanston, Illinois, in 1890. To the thousands of men she had visited in the hospital and their families, she would long be remembered as a mother figure who had given her exceptional talents to aid the Union's cause.

Nancy Driscol Engle

See also Livermore, Mary Ashton Rice (1820–1905); Nurses; United States Sanitary Commission.

References and Further Reading
Brockett, Linus P., and Marcy C. Vaughan. 1867. *Woman's Work in the Civil War.* Philadelphia, PA: Zeigler, McCurdy & Co.
Hoge, Jane (Mrs. A. H.). 1867. *The Boys in Blue, or Heroes of the "Rank and File."* New York: E. B. Treat and Company.
Livermore, Mary A. 1889. *My Story of the War.* Hartford, CT: A. D. Worthington and Company.

Holmes, Emma Edwards (1838–1910)

South Carolina diarist Emma Edwards Holmes chronicled life in the Palmetto State from secession through early Reconstruction.

Born in Charleston, the daughter of Dr. Henry McCall Holmes and Eliza Ford Gibbes Holmes, Emma Holmes came from a distinguished Southern lineage. When the Civil War began, her mother was already a widow and the head of a family of ten children, ranging in age from thirteen to thirty-one. Emma was twenty-three and unmarried. Her single state was a matter of concern to both her and her mother. Although she had numerous beaux during her life, Emma never married, no doubt because of what she once called her "high standards" and what her mother described as her "dictatorial character & prejudiced views."

Emma Holmes's contribution to the history of the period is the detailed diary she left behind, which she faithfully kept throughout the Civil War and early Reconstruction years. She lived in Charleston for the early part of the war, then in 1862, after the accidentally set Charleston Fire of 1861 destroyed her family home on the Battery, she worked as a teacher and tutor in Camden and its environs. She did not return to Charleston, except for visits, until sometime after the war when she continued her teaching career in the city she so loved.

Emma Holmes's diary is valuable for several reasons: her presence during many key events in the war; her intellectual curiosity, which caused her to view the events carefully and detail them passionately in her writings; her opportunities to travel around the state; her willingness to comment on people and events around her; and her active participation in the social and interracial life of the times. She was an intelligent Southern white woman who chronicled what she was experiencing, what she read about in newspapers and books, and what she learned from others, all from a completely pro-Confederate viewpoint. Thus her diary describes Fort Sumter from a site on Charleston's Battery and the 1861 fire from the point of view of one of its victims. She visited Confederate army camps; she lived in both city and rural areas; she was a refugee after the fire; and she experienced invasion by General William T. Sherman's army and black troops. She attended contemporary social events, and she interacted directly with slaves throughout the state. She discussed women's roles in the war, talked about books and articles she was reading, expressed Confederate optimism, then displayed pessimism about the war's progress, and, perhaps most important, detailed the impact of the war's end on white society, particularly on its race relations. Her diary provides one of the best contemporary insights into the impact of the Civil War on a single white woman and on Southern society as a whole.

John F. Marszalek

See also Confederate Homefront; Diaries and Journals; Fort Sumter (April 12–14, 1861); Sherman's Campaign (1864–1865); Southern Women.
References and Further Reading
Marszalek, John F., ed. 1994 [1979]. *The Diary of Miss Emma Holmes, 1861–1866.* Baton Rouge: Louisiana State University Press.

Homespun

Homespun, a homemade fabric made of cotton, linen, or wool, became a symbol of Confederate nationalism during the Civil War.

In the early nineteenth century, homespun was produced and worn mostly by poor whites and slaves. During the war, the Union blockade of Southern seaports prevented the importation of manufactured goods into the South, a region whose industrial capabilities remained underdeveloped in 1861. The exorbitant cost and scarcity of an array of household items, including fabrics, lace, ribbons, and stockings, forced women of all classes to revert to home manufacturing. Southern politicians, newspaper editors, and civic leaders urged women to replace ornamental pursuits with the patriotic tasks of spinning and weaving cloth. Textile production was most popular in rural communities, where there was limited access to blockade-run goods and the equipment required for spinning and weaving was readily available. Women produced homespun for both themselves and the Confederate army. Soldiers who wore uniforms made of homespun were often referred to as butternuts due to the golden brown appearance of the cloth, which was often dyed using the husks of the walnut tree. Women of all classes also used homespun to make clothing for themselves and their families. The significance of the

fabric as a symbol of Southern nationalism was reflected in a popular song entitled "The Homespun Dress," which urged women to sacrifice their finery in support of the cause. Elite women found this sacrifice particularly difficult because they had always used clothing as a way to define their status and gentility. The inclusive nature of homespun as a symbol of patriotism thus challenged antebellum expressions of class.

Giselle Roberts

See also Confederate Homefront; Nationalism, Confederate; Shortages; Southern Women.
References and Further Reading
Faust, Drew Gilpin. 1996. *Mothers of Invention: Women of the Slaveholding South in the American Civil War.* Chapel Hill: University of North Carolina Press.
Roberts, Giselle. 2004. *The Confederate Belle.* Columbia, OH: University of Missouri Press.

Honor

The concepts of honor and its opposite, the apprehension of shame, appeal especially to the conservative frame of mind. Honor's exclusivity and reliance on public notice set it apart from the more introspective and self-abnegating ethic of conscience and guilt. Before, during, and after the Civil War, Southern whites—both male and female, slaveholders and nonslaveholders—found the South's rules governing behavior as important as a steady faith in God. Under the code, the female role was traditionally subordinated to the male. Feminine honor consisted largely of do-nots. Women were never to challenge outright men's deeds or opinions. Males were their "lords and masters," a phrase women sometimes muttered in quiet protest among themselves. Nor could they, whether married or virginal, ever relish the sexual license that unmarried and in some respects discreet married men enjoyed. Honor was conferred on women who married appropriately and bore children, preferably male. To be unwed and childless was a doubling of pity and even of shame.

Addressing the physical differences of men and women, a Virginia theologian declared that God had made them so in order to signify that the women, being the morally weaker sex, possessed a lesser claim to the "points of honor." For instance, he noted, men might regain a ruined reputation simply by repudiating their formerly lusty ways. On the other hand, women could be touched by not even the slightest doubt. Once lost, a woman's good name was unrecoverable. The dread of social ostracism and the prospect of church expulsion were usually enough to secure womanly virtue. At the same time, it was a mother's duty to raise sons to fulfill the virile obligations of their sex and to train daughters to show modesty, practice efficient domesticity, retain their chastity, and forbear unseemly adventures. That assignment gave women a degree of steely power by demanding that men live up to their own manly ideals—or suffer under the hammer of hard, shaming words. Extolling the virtue of violence for the sake of honor insulted, a Virginia female propagandist for secession believed that assault and battery and the duel were the sole means to protect one's sense of honor against the calumnies of one's enemies. No less than the male secessionists, she despised the Southern Unionists—cowards or submissionists, as they were called. Southern women were very strong-minded. Yet women of her persuasion above all else treasured their domestic position as keepers of the hearth, the kitchen, and the children's quarters.

In contrast to the constrictions that Southern women endured—and ordinarily enjoyed—their middle-class Northern compatriots were gradually forsaking the restrictive conventions that had previously governed them. Rather, they came to believe that women were morally and possibly intellectually superior to men. Self-control, not public scrutiny, should propel them toward the moral high ground. Conscience, not dread of public shame, should guide the way. A solid sense of guilt and remorse was considered far more preferable to reliance on fear of being publicly shamed.

One of the acute sectional divisions concerned the relative freedom of Northern women to breach conventional ethics. In the 1830s, South Carolinians Sarah and Angelina Grimké were the first of either region to address what were called promiscu-ous assemblies, that is, audiences of both sexes. Their antislavery convictions led them to such a seeming extremity. These courageous abolitionist performances initially aroused fury in all sectors of the nation, but ultimately their tours proved to be the first steps toward the cause of women's rights, a cause supported by some Northerners and disdained throughout the South.

That spirit of gender reform won only scorn and contempt in the slave states. It fed into the crisis over secession in 1860 and 1861. Insulted by years of Northern criticism of slavery, Southerners, both male and female, were likely to charge that New England had become a refuge for men of lascivious minds and women of loose morals. Such alien ideas as socialism, free love, and the abolition of slavery were loose in the land. One Charleston matron objected to the proliferation of Yankee rabble who made a mockery of true democracy, to the godless, to the women in Bloomer costumes, to the fleeing slaves whom abolitionists helped to escape, and to those advocating the intermixing of the races. Yankee manhood also came under attack. Rebel enthusiasts claimed that Northern men had grown too effeminate to win battles, whereas their women were turning themselves into brazen amazons.

While slavery was the root cause of the war, the issue of honor and its sexual differentiations were instrumental in setting the slave and free states on their antagonistic courses. Both sections considered the honor and intellect of whites far superior to those of people of color. Nonetheless, the degrees of racism contrasted enormously between the sections. The centrality of women's honor was most evident in white Southern attitudes. Interracial sex, or amalgamation as it was called, was the most horrifying of all the possibilities that might befall a Southern family. Under the honor code, the preservation of racially pure bloodlines was a matter of almost sacred obligation. In early 1861, a politician arrived in Richmond to present the secessionist principles of South Carolina to the Virginia convention, and the delegates were hotly debating the merits of disunion. Some argued that the abolitionists were bent on humiliating the South by compelling its white women to cohabit with blacks. The politician pompously claimed that no civilization could possibly tolerate or survive rampant sexual unions between races so different in status, color, and intelligence. The honor of the white woman was such a visceral issue that in the post–Civil War years, their protection from the alleged lust of freedmen justified, as Southern whites saw it, the employment of lynch law.

Although often the objects of jealous male guardianship, Southern women could take a more active role in their lives. During the early stages of the war, in the name of honor, Confederate women appointed themselves as public scolds of male slackers. Men were expected to uphold the honor of their sex by undertaking a mandatory rush to arms. Otherwise, the ladies might place a petticoat over the young bachelor's sitting room chair or snub him in the street until he enlisted. Southern women also sustained faith in the ideals of martial honor. In April 1861, at a typical send-off for troops about to leave their communities, a Texas belle, selected for her beauty, addressed a regiment. She proclaimed that she and all the local virgins would always acknowledge the soldiers' coming sacrifices. The trials of battle would result, she continued, in their achieving immortal glory and the undying gratitude of their homeland in the fight against the Yankee fanatics. She then handed their commander a handsome, emblematic banner sewn by the young women's delicate fingers.

In contrast, the Loyal Publications Society took quite a different approach. The Union author contrasted the relatively calm and steadfast mood of Northern women with the unwomanly truculence of their honor-conscious Rebel counterparts. Women of the free states, he explained, held their emotions in check, abjured any kind of truculence, and considered their obligation to be more steadfast than impetuous. Loyal Northern women were likely to invoke the merits of duty to flag, country, and fellow soldiers. That term, "duty," was the watchword rather than "honor," because they, as well as their Union warriors, understood what it meant.

In the fighting itself, Southern women eagerly proclaimed the nobility of their fighting men. For many, that function exhausted their contribution,

apart from knitting socks, repairing uniforms, and other activities in the female realm. Some were compelled by circumstances to set aside the privileges and constraints of femininity when taking charge of farms, plantations, and businesses. To a lesser degree than the more self-assertive Northern women, some women even served as nurses in the medical wards, and they replaced men in state and Confederate administrative offices and in local classrooms. However, such activities only temporarily undermined the strict rules governing female life. When peace returned, they once more confined themselves to domesticity, albeit without their former reliance on slave labor and wealth. Throughout the conflict, there had been moments of elation and times of deep melancholy, but premonitions of defeat might well be followed by complete defiance. Upon hearing of antiwar riots in the North and some Confederate victories, a plantation matron rejoiced. She wrote a cousin that she felt absolutely murderous and yearned to get news from the North of widespread fire, ruin, and death.

In fact, when the end came, plantation women throughout the South felt the crush of defeat no less than the Confederate soldiers. For the most part, they had supported the effort fervently, even feverishly. A Georgia woman as late as January 1865 wrote that she and all others of her sex had sacrificed too much to contemplate surrendering to the Yankee hordes. Having lost a brother, she, like many other women, was certain that his spirit screamed for revenge. So long as any soldier was still in the field, the women at home should not give up. But even the stoutest feminine hearts had to admit that carrying on the war until the last infantryman had fallen would gain nothing. As the armies surrendered throughout the South, women mourned, like Hecuba in Euripides' *Trojan Women:* "So pitiful, so pitiful your shame and lamentation. I shall look no more on the bodies of my sons. No more." Defeat and the loss of wealth in goods, houses, and slaves were bound to bring misery, lamentation, and sense of futility. Honor was seemingly lost forever. Yet it was not long after Lee's surrender that ladies of the former Rebel states were immersed in the Lost Cause memorialization of the glorious heroes buried in the South's cemeteries. Once more the honor of the white race and woman's place in that ethical sanctuary flourished throughout a defeated and impoverished land. The determination to uphold the honor of white supremacy burned not just among the men but among the women as well, and it was manifest in the terrifying assaults on the post–Civil War freedmen who were seeking their own security and political voice.

Bertram Wyatt-Brown

See also Confederate Homefront; Confederate Soldiers, Motives; Flags, Regimental; Grimké (Weld), Angelina (1805–1879); Grimké, Sarah Moore (1792–1873); Nonslaveholding Southerners; Northern Women; Nurses; Religion; Slaveholding Women; Southern Women; Union Homefront; Union Soldiers, Motives.

References and Further Reading
Chestnut, Mary. 1981. *Mary Chesnut's Civil War,* edited by C. Vann Woodward. New York: Oxford University Press.
Clinton, Catherine, and Nina Silber, eds. 1992. *Divided Houses: Gender and the Civil War.* New York: Oxford University Press.
Culpepper, Marilyn Mayer. 2002. *All Things Altered: Women in the Wake of Civil War and Reconstruction.* Jefferson, NC: McFarland.
Faust, Drew Gilpin. 1996. *Mothers of Invention: Women of the Slaveholding South in the American Civil War.* Chapel Hill: University of North Carolina Press.
Rable, George C. 1989. *Civil Wars: Women and the Crisis of Southern Nationalism.* Urbana: University of Illinois Press.
Wyatt-Brown, Bertram. 1982. *Southern Honor: Ethics and Behavior in the Old South.* New York: Oxford University Press.
Wyatt-Brown, Bertram. 2001. *The Shaping of Southern Culture: Honor, Grace and War, 1760s–1880s.* Chapel Hill: University of North Carolina Press.

Hopkins, Juliet Ann Opie (1818–1890)

Juliet Opie Hopkins is known as the Florence Nightingale of the Confederacy because she made important contributions to Confederate medical care during the Civil War. Recognizing the need for hospital facilities to treat sick and wounded Alabama soldiers serving in the war's Eastern the-ater, Hopkins organized and managed several institutions in Richmond and other Virginia towns from 1861 to late 1863, when the government assumed control of all military hospitals.

Born in Jefferson County, Virginia, on May 7, 1818, Juliet Opie lived a life of wealth and privilege. She attended a prestigious Richmond academy until her mother's death in 1834, whereupon she returned to the family estate and helped her father manage his extensive land and slaveholdings. Though widowed at the age of twenty, Opie's second marriage to Arthur Francis Hopkins in 1854 proved more permanent. Hopkins, a prominent Alabamian, was the president of the Mobile and Ohio Railroad when the couple married, and they lived in Mobile when the Civil War began.

In the summer of 1861, the nascent Confederate government had made few preparations for hospital facilities to treat sick and wounded soldiers. Outbreaks of measles, typhoid fever, and other contagious diseases among troops stationed in Virginia, however, threatened to overwhelm the Confederate Medical Department during the war's early months. As sick soldiers flooded into every available space in Richmond and nearby towns, the area became one vast hospital. In June, Juliet Hopkins traveled to the Confederate capital to help alleviate the suffering of sick Alabamians. She secured a suitable building, hired several physicians and nurses, and purchased food and other supplies. When Hopkins opened the First Alabama Hospital in August, it was the first institution to treat Alabama troops serving in Virginia. By the fall of 1861, Hopkins had organized the Second Alabama Hospital in Richmond and others in Warrenton, Culpepper Court House, Yorktown, Bristoe Station, and Monterey, Virginia.

As a volunteer hospital organizer, Hopkins relied on private donations and appropriations from the Alabama state legislature. She served without salary and contributed an estimated $200,000 to staff and equip the hospitals. Known for her kindness and dedication to the patients, Hopkins was loved and respected by all. Her picture appeared on several denominations of Confederate Alabama currency, and she received numerous letters praising her devotion to the welfare of Alabama troops.

Juliet Opie Hopkins died on March 9, 1890 and was interred in Arlington National Cemetery. Scores of veterans attended her funeral, including former Confederate Generals Joseph E. Johnston and Joseph Wheeler.

Nancy Schurr

See also Hospitals; Nurses; Southern Women.
References and Further Reading

Faust, Drew Gilpin. 1996. *Mothers of Invention: Women of the Slaveholding South in the American Civil War.* Chapel Hill: University of North Carolina Press.

Griffith, Lucille. 1953. "Mrs. Juliet Opie Hopkins and Alabama Military Hospitals." *Alabama Review* 6: 99–120.

Schultz, Jane E. 2004. *Women at the Front: Hospital Workers in Civil War America.* Chapel Hill: University of North Carolina Press.

Sterkx, H. E. 1970. *Partners in Rebellion: Alabama Women in the Civil War.* Madison, NJ: Fairleigh Dickinson University Press.

Hopley, Catherine Cooper (ca. 1832–n.d.)

Though little is known of the pre– or post–Civil War life of Catherine Cooper Hopley, this Englishwoman authored one of the most significant accounts of the Confederacy written by a foreign observer, as well as one of the earliest published biographies of Confederate General Thomas J. "Stonewall" Jackson.

Born about 1832, Catherine Cooper Hopley, a schoolteacher, came to the United States around 1854. She visited relatives in different parts of the North and lived for a time with a sister in Indiana. Hopley traveled to Virginia in early 1860, where she worked as a tutor for a plantation family. She visited England in the summer of 1860 but returned to America by the fall of that year, at the time of Lincoln's election. Hopley resided in Richmond during the winter of 1860–1861 before again finding employment as a tutor and as an instructor at a seminary in Warrenton. In early 1862, she journeyed to Florida, where she worked as a teacher for Governor John Milton's large family.

Returning to Virginia in early August 1862, Hopley obtained a Confederate passport allowing her to cross into Union lines at City Point, Virginia. She then traveled to Baltimore and on through Pennsylvania before reaching her sister in Indiana. She remained in Indiana for a short time and then left for New York, where she boarded a steamer for England. By the end of 1862 she had prepared a manuscript of her Confederate experiences: *Life in the South from the Commencement of the War by a Blockaded British Subject: Being a Social History of Those Who Took Part in the Battles, from a Personal Acquaintance with Them in Their Own Homes.* The two-volume book was published in London the following year.

Hopley's account is unwaveringly sympathetic to the South and to the institution of slavery, which she contended had been unfairly portrayed by lies and misrepresentations. In addition, *Life in the South* offered a vivid portrait of the South at war. Hopley accurately detailed political and military events, and she described the impact of the war on the Southern population. She included comments on prominent politicians and military officers that she met during her travels. She concluded her work by proclaiming the South and the Confederacy a respectable and valuable nation. Confederate bibliographer E. Merton Coulter lavished praise on Hopley's work, commenting on her keen observations, knowledge of current events, and writing ability.

Hopley subsequently authored *"Stonewall" Jackson, Late General of the Confederate States Army. A Biographical Sketch, and an Outline of His Virginian Campaigns.* This laudatory biography of Jackson included a brief overview of his early years, including his service in the U.S.-Mexican War and as an instructor at the Virginia Military Institute. However, it focused primarily on his wartime exploits from the 1862 Valley Campaign through his wounding at Chancellorsville. Hopley concluded with an account of Jackson's final illness, death, and burial. Throughout the book, Hopley stressed Jackson's Christian nature. She contended that the general's glory would be appreciated by generations of Southerners.

Details of Hopley's subsequent life remain unknown. However, her written record of her experiences between 1860 and 1862 is one of the most valuable volumes written by a woman living in the Confederate states.

David Coles

See also Confederate Homefront; Chancellorsville, Battle of (April 29–May 6, 1863); Education, Southern; Immigrant Women; Wartime Literature.
References and Further Reading
Coulter, E. Merton. 1948. *Travels in the Confederate States: A Bibliography.* Norman: University of Oklahoma Press.
Hopley, Catherine Cooper. 1863. *"Stonewall" Jackson, Late General of the Confederate States Army. A Biographical Sketch, and an Outline of His Virginia Campaigns.* London: Chapman and Hall.
Hopley, Catherine Cooper. 1971. *Life in the South from the Commencement of the War by a Blockaded British Subject. Being a Social History of Those Who Took Part in the Battles, from a Personal Acquaintance with Them in Their Own Homes.* 2 volumes. New York: Augustus M. Kelley Publishers. (Orig. pub. 1863.)

Hospitals

Thousands of American women—Northern and Southern, white and black—served in military hospitals during the Civil War, making important contributions to the Union and Confederate war efforts. Though largely untrained and seen as the weaker sex, American women proved vital to the care of sick and wounded soldiers throughout the conflict.

In 1861, hospitals were rare because most nineteenth-century Americans cared for sick family members at home. Hospitals, or almshouses as they were frequently called, were regarded as asylums for the indigent and seen as a last resort for respectable people. At the war's outset, the Union army had only one military hospital, a forty-bed institution in Leavenworth, Kansas, while the Confederacy had no governmental facilities to care for sick and wounded soldiers. The outbreak of contagious diseases such as measles, malaria, and yellow fever, combined with the high casualties of the war's early battles, made the establishment and staffing of military hospitals a top priority for both sides.

Several Northern women volunteered to help the Union establish and staff military hospitals. On April 23, 1861, Secretary of War Simon Cameron appointed Dorothea Dix, a well-known antebellum crusader for improved care for the mentally ill, to the position of Superintendent of Female Nurses in the United States Army. Her duties included enlisting female nurses, supervising the organization of military hospitals, and requisitioning supplies from the homefront. A rigid disciplinarian, Dix carefully screened each female applicant and usually rejected those who were young, unmarried, or attractive. Though her authority was sharply curtailed in October 1863, Dix appointed at least thirty-two hundred nurses to Union military hospitals. In late April 1861, Elizabeth Blackwell—the first woman to receive a medical degree in the United States—and her sister Emily met with other Northern reformers to propose the training of women nurses for Union hospitals. This group established the Woman's Central Association of Relief and oversaw the selection and training of approximately one hundred nurses.

The United States Sanitary Commission (USSC) provided significant aid to the Union army's medical department. Formally established in June 1861, the USSC was a civilian-run, national relief organization that sent food, clothing, medical supplies, and white female nurses to military hospitals. Functioning as a centralized organization for funneling supplies and personnel where they were most needed, the USSC enlisted more female volunteers than any other Northern organization.

In the Confederacy, the supply and staffing of hospitals were less organized since prewar reform groups were extremely rare. Many of the first Confederate hospitals were civilian endeavors. Like their Northern counterparts, groups of elite women formed state and local hospital aid societies and sent food, blankets, and medicine to their state's sick soldiers. Enormous casualties resulting from the first battle of Bull Run, however, led aid society volunteers in new directions. Women, fired with patriotism and the desire to be useful, saw medical care as an appropriate outlet for their zeal. Members of the South Carolina Aid Association, for example, not only sent supplies but also provided nurses for the Palmetto State's patients recovering in Virginia. These efforts resulted in the creation of the South Carolina Hospital in Richmond and the Midway Hospital in Charlottesville.

Women's collective activity spread to other Virginia towns. When it became evident that additional

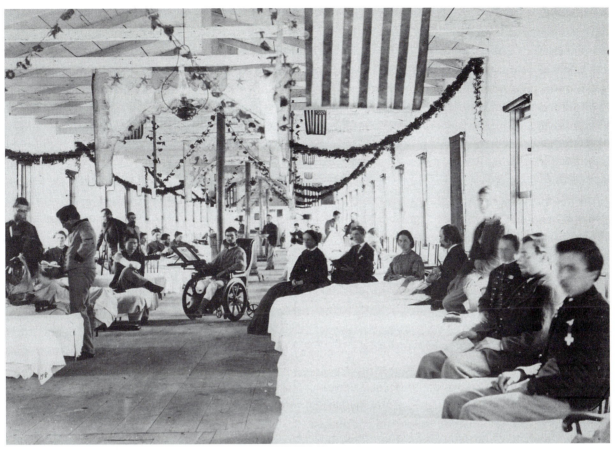

Patients receive treatment at Carver General Hospital in Washington, D.C. The Civil War brought with it a staggering amount of debilitating diseases and serious injuries that demanded advancements in the medical practices of the time. (Library of Congress)

hospital space was badly needed in Lynchburg, local women under the leadership of Lucy Mina Otey formed a hospital association and opened the Ladies' Relief Hospital in the former Union Hotel. Moreover, numerous groups of women in the war's Western theater organized private hospitals. The Southern Mothers' Home in Memphis, as well as the ladies' hospitals in Chattanooga, Tennessee, and in Greenville and Montgomery, Alabama, are examples of such local efforts.

The Confederacy's inadequate hospital preparations were further illustrated by the fact that a few elite Southern women, backed by socially prominent husbands or fathers, became self-appointed hospital organizers. Letitia Tyler Semple, the daughter of former president John Tyler, established one of the first Confederate hospitals, located on the grounds of the Female Seminary in Williamsburg, Virginia. Mary Martha Reid, the forty-nine-year-old widow of Florida's former territorial governor, established a hospital in late 1861 for Florida soldiers recovering in Richmond. After the first Battle of Bull Run, Sally Tompkins, the South's most famous hospital organizer, used her family's considerable influence in the Confederate capital to persuade Judge John Robertson to donate his home for hospital purposes. Tompkins's Robertson Hospital had a capacity of twenty-two patients and reportedly treated over twelve hundred patients during the war; it boasted one of the lowest mortality rates in the Confederate hospital system. Alabamian Juliet Opie Hopkins, wife of an influential lawyer and politician, organized several hospitals for her state's troops serving in Virginia. In late 1861, Governor

John Gill Shorter appointed Hopkins superintendent of all Alabama hospitals in Virginia.

By November 1862, the Confederacy suffered from a serious shortage of soldiers at the front, in part due to the hundreds of enlisted men detailed for hospital duty. As a result, the Confederate Congress passed the Hospital Act, which mandated the employment of civilians in military hospitals and subjected those so employed to military authority and discipline. Henceforth, medical officers were encouraged to hire women to serve as matrons, nurses, cooks, and laundresses. Thus, most Southern female hospital workers applied for jobs at specific hospitals, rather than through a centralized agency like the United States Sanitary Commission.

Though Northern and Southern women entered hospital service through different means, they faced similar challenges. Initially, army doctors demonstrated a distinct prejudice against female employees. Afraid that hospital work would upset women's delicacy and refinement, some medical officers opposed their presence in the wards. Yet many elite and middle-class white women successfully argued that their nurturing, self-denying natures specially qualified them for hospital work. Indeed, they envisioned the care of sick and wounded men as a natural extension of their roles as mothers. Many women formed strong bonds with their patients and attempted to create a home away from home for their charges. Decorating the wards with flowers and curtains, supplying patients with religious tracts and other reading material, and preparing special treats at Christmas were common activities for many female hospital workers.

Women from minority groups also participated—willingly and unwillingly—in military hospital care. At least six hundred nuns representing twelve religious orders nursed soldiers from both sides. Their hospital duties mirrored those of white Protestant nurses: They distributed supplies, cooked and served meals, dressed wounds, dispensed medication, and provided religious counseling. Nuns also encountered discrimination. In addition to the widespread anti-Catholic feeling in many areas, the sisters, more than one-half of whom were Irish or of Irish descent, faced anti-Irish sentiment. Historians have noted Dorothea Dix's wartime opposition to the use of sister nurses; as Superintendent of Female Nurses, Dix crusaded to establish a white, largely Protestant nursing corps. Dix and others also criticized the nuns for not forming relationships with the patients. Yet nuns' vows of chastity and the rules of their orders precluded them from conversing with men unless the conversations were religious in nature. Despite this criticism, Catholic nuns remained popular with medical officers on both sides. Citing their prewar training in private hospitals, their ability to obey orders, and their intense dedication, many surgeons in charge of hospitals specifically requested the services of sister nurses.

African American women—both slave and free—engaged in medical care during the Civil War. One historian estimates that free and contraband black women comprised approximately 10 percent of female employees in Union hospitals. The majority of these women worked as cooks and laundresses supervised by white middle-class matrons. In Union hospitals, African American women earned between $6 and $10 per month, compared to the $12 wage earned by white women. Although incomplete records preclude a reliable statistical analysis of Confederate hospital workers, it is clear that, in many institutions, blacks outnumbered whites. In the South, elite white supervisors assigned black women backbreaking, often dangerous work. At a Chattanooga hospital, for example, matron Kate Cumming reported that slave laundresses washed the bedding and clothes of patients infected with smallpox. While these and other slave workers received a daily ration, the proceeds of their labor—usually between $20 and $25 per month—went directly to their owners. Moreover, whether they worked in Union or Confederate hospitals, African American women confronted racial antagonism. Many white workers refused to socialize with black women, and most opposed the quartering of black and white women in the same room. Although white and black women were working toward the same goal—to heal sick and wounded soldiers—the racial barrier precluded whites from envisioning blacks as sisters in common cause.

Nancy Schurr

See also African American Women; Blackwell,
Elizabeth (1821–1910); Catholic Women;
Confederate Homefront; Cumming, Kate (ca.
1835–1909); Dix, Dorothea Lynde (1802–1887);
Hopkins, Juliet Opie (1818–1890); Northern
Women; Nurses; Southern Women; Tompkins, Sally
Louisa (1833–1916); Union Homefront; United
States Sanitary Commission; Women's Central
Association of Relief.

References and Further Reading

Abel, Emily K. 2000. *Hearts of Wisdom: American
Women Caring for Kin, 1850–1940.* Cambridge,
MA: Harvard University Press.

Brown, Thomas. 1998. *Dorothea Dix: New England
Reformer.* Cambridge, MA: Harvard University
Press.

Cumming, Kate. 1987. *Kate: The Journal of a
Confederate Nurse,* edited by Richard Barksdale.
Baton Rouge: Louisiana State University Press.
(Orig. pub. 1959.)

Faust, Drew Gilpin. 1998. "'Ours as Well as That
of the Men': Women and Gender in the Civil
War." In *Writing the Civil War: The Quest to
Understand,* edited by James M. McPherson
and William J. Cooper Jr., 228–240. Columbia:
University of South Carolina Press.

Giesberg, Judith Ann. 2000. *Civil War Sisterhood:
The United States Sanitary Commission and
Women's Politics in Transition.* Boston:
Northeastern University Press.

Maher, Sister Mary Denis. 1989. *To Bind Up
the Wounds: Catholic Sister Nurses in the
U.S. Civil War.* Westport, CT: Greenwood
Press.

Rable, George C. 1989. *Civil Wars: Women and the
Crisis of Southern Nationalism.* Urbana:
University of Illinois Press.

Schultz, Jane E. 2004. *Women at the Front: Hospital
Workers in Civil War America.* Chapel Hill:
University of North Carolina Press.

Hospital Ships

Hospital ships were vessels dedicated to the care of sick or wounded soldiers. Following the first major battles of the Civil War, the United States navy and relief organizations realized the need to move the wounded and sick away from the front as rapidly as possible. Military officials responded by developing systems to transport the wounded and found women to provide care for the men. Although nothing about the naval hospital system was permanent

during the years of the Civil War, the experiments led to establishing the naval medical corps.

Even before the Peninsula campaign in the spring of 1862, it was apparent that the injured needed to be removed from the battlefields as soon as possible to save more of them. Initial attempts were haphazard. Individual commanders sometimes put their wounded on the decks of rams (a type of warship) and transports that had just delivered troops or supplies, but these vessels had few supplies for the care of the injured or ill.

Beginning at the time of the Peninsula campaign, specific transports were assigned to carry the wounded away. Crews rigged canvas awnings on decks to protect the men from weather conditions, the sun being as harmful as rain or snow. Space was dedicated for amputations, and small kitchens were provided.

Volunteers from towns near battlefields came on board to provide what aid they could; the national relief societies, such as the United States Christian Commission (USCC) or the United States Sanitary Commission (USSC) as well as religious orders offered their services. To help the men combat shock, the volunteers turned out kettles of broth or warm drinks containing alcohol, and they washed the men and their wounds. The arrangements were temporary, with each vessel returning to its regular duties as soon as the men were unloaded or as battle conditions required. The system depended on women volunteers who carried out a kind of triage. Some of them stayed on the deck to greet the wounded being brought aboard, and they sent those needing surgery to an area near the working doctors. They made those considered too badly injured to survive as comfortable as possible and concentrated their efforts on the others.

Steamers served as the earliest rescue boats because no ships were dedicated to such work in either army. Nor did the military have any experts in providing immediate relief. Consequently the transport system was put under the control of the USSC, which used donated funds and materials to outfit the steamers with comfortable beds and efficient, if small, kitchens. In addition, the USSC provided bedding, dressings, instruments, and medicines. Despite

United States hospital boat *Red Rover* at Vicksburg on the Mississippi River. (Miller, Francis Trevelyan and Robert Sampson Lanier, *The Photographic History of the Civil War,* vol 7, 1911)

the objections of the navy, women volunteers provided nursing care. During the Peninsula campaign, the transport system dealt with as many as eight hundred sick and wounded soldiers at a time and moved as many as four thousand men in one three-day period. Despite the success, control of the transports returned to the army at the end of the campaign. A similar experiment was successful in the West. There the Western Sanitary Commission operated transports that helped to save lives at the Battle of Shiloh, also known as Pittsburgh Landing.

Ships had to be fitted out one at a time as appropriate vessels were located. Some were rented from private owners. For instance, Cornelius Vanderbilt provided his side-wheeled steamer *Ocean Queen.* The vessel had room for berths for four hundred men, and Frederick Law Olmsted, the USSC official in charge of the project, believed as many as one thousand men could be put aboard her.

Throughout this endeavor, volunteers had to deal with naval surgeons who often had ideas that conflicted with USSC plans. Naval officers opposed using female nurses, who they thought were too delicate and ill equipped for the treatment of soldiers. Although Olmsted understood their objections, he bowed to reality and was astounded at the quality of care the women provided and how much work they put in on their jobs.

By the summer of 1862, naval leaders decided to create a permanent hospital ship. The U.S.S. *Mound City* seized the C.S.S. *Red Rover* during the fighting around Island No. 10. It was officially transferred to the navy on October 1, 1862, and recommissioned as the U.S.S. *Red Rover* for service in December of that year. The *Red Rover* was supposed to be a temporary hospital for the summer months. However the ship's services were needed so much, that it was refitted for use all year. The ship was state-of-the-art, according to naval officials. This hospital transport ship was initially supplied to provide for two hundred men for a period of three months, but hundreds more than that received care aboard the *Red Rover*. The ship had a laundry facility, an amputation room, nine bathrooms with two on each deck, gauze on the windows to keep cinders from blowing into open wounds, and multiple kitchens. The nursing corps came from the Sisters of the Holy Cross. Because the women were dedicated to a life of religion and service, they were acceptable to military officials.

Although the commissioning of the ship and the acceptance of the female nurses provide historical beginnings for the naval medical service, the trend was not a steady one. The *Red Rover* had regular military duties in addition to its medical responsibilities. The vessel regularly steamed the waters of the West carrying men and supplies. However, when necessary, it was used in military actions, and the tables used to track the numbers and positions of ships during the Civil War did not always identify the *Red Rover* as a hospital ship. Although the nuns worked throughout the war, their nursing duties were taken up by men or hired nurses following the conflict.

Karen A. Kehoe

See also Aid Societies; Catholic Women; Domesticity; Hospitals; Northern Women; Nurses; Olmsted, Frederick Law (1822–1903); Religion; Separate Spheres; Union Homefront; United States Christian Commission; United States Sanitary Commission.

References and Further Reading
Censer, Jane Turner, ed. 1986. *The Papers of Frederick Law Olmsted*, Volume IV: *Defending the Union*. Baltimore, MD: Johns Hopkins University Press.

Giesberg, Judith Ann. 2000. *Civil War Sisterhood: The U.S. Sanitary Commission and Women's Politics in Transition*. Boston: Northeastern University Press.

Ginzberg, Lori D. 1990. *Women and the Work of Benevolence: Morality, Politics, and Class in the Nineteenth-Century United States*. New Haven, CT: Yale University Press.

Ross, Kristie. 1992. "Arranging a Doll's House: Refined Women as Union Nurses." In *Divided Houses: Gender and the Civil War*, edited by Catherine Clinton and Nina Silber, 97–113. New York: Oxford University Press.

House (Fletcher), Ellen Renshaw (1843–1907)

A young and single Southern woman during the Civil War, Ellen Renshaw House remained a defiant Confederate in occupied East Tennessee.

House was born in Savannah, Georgia, on August 10, 1843. Her father, Samuel, came from South Carolina and her mother from Philadelphia. When Ellen was born, her father worked as a customs collector and trade commissioner. When the family moved to Marietta, he became a small planter. By 1850, Samuel owned seven slaves and employed two white servants. A year before the Civil War, the House family sold their slaves and reestablished themselves in Knoxville, Tennessee. Samuel became a bookkeeper and the family lived a middle-class existence.

The Civil War divided Knoxville just as it split most of East Tennessee. Despite the unionism in their midst, Ellen and her family became ardent Confederates. One brother went to work as a clerk in the Confederate government. Two brothers enlisted in the Confederate army, and both wound up in Union prison camps. After his release, one of Ellen's brothers was murdered by robbers on the East Tennessee homefront in an act likely unrelated to the war.

When Union troops under the command of General Ambrose Burnside occupied Knoxville, Ellen's animosity toward the North increased. Union soldiers evicted her from her parents' home so that they could occupy the house themselves, and she otherwise experienced the shortages and privations common on the Southern homefront. Despite her personal difficulties, she remained an ardent Confederate. Unlike the rest of her family, she refused to take the loyalty oath. In addition, she spent much of her time and energy caring for Confederate prisoners housed in the city, visiting them often and donating many personal items to assist them. In an act of solidarity, she orchestrated a group of women to wave handkerchiefs as Confederate prisoners were marched through Knoxville.

On several occasions, House verbally abused the occupying Union soldiers. Her willingness to voice her displeasure with the occupying Union army eventually got her into trouble. In April 1864, she insulted the wife of a Union officer who was quartered in her parents' home. In response, Ellen was evicted from the city and forced to move behind Confederate lines. She would spend the rest of the war in exile, staying at the homes of family friends in Abington, Virginia, and Eatonton, Georgia. She remained in Georgia until the end of the war, avoiding the invasion of William Tecumseh Sherman's army.

After the war, House remained hostile to Yankees and unionists. She returned to Knoxville, where she met her future husband, James Washington Fletcher. They married in November 1867 and had four children, the first of whom they named after Ellen's murdered brother. Ellen Renshaw House Fletcher died on May 19, 1907.

Andrew K. Frank

See also Confederate Homefront; Diaries and Journals; Loyalty Oaths; Military Invasion and Occupation; Refugees; Slaveholding Women; Southern Women.
References and Further Reading
Sutherland, Daniel E., ed. 1996. *A Very Violent Rebel: The Civil War Diary of Ellen Renshaw House*. Knoxville: University of Tennessee Press.

Howe, Julia Ward (1819–1910)

Author of "The Battle Hymn of the Republic," Julia Ward Howe was also a women's rights advocate, an abolitionist, and a reformer.

Born in New York City on May 27, 1819, to Julia Rush Cutler and Samuel Ward, Julia Ward Howe was raised in a wealthy household. Her mother died when Julia was five years old. The well-educated girl displayed a keen intellect and an interest in philosophy, theology, and literature. Early in life she decided to become a writer. Her father, a Wall Street banker, died in 1839 when Julia was twenty years old.

In 1841 she met Samuel Gridley Howe, a noted reformer and head of the Perkins Institute for the Blind in Boston. The two were married in 1843 and Julia gave birth to six children between 1844 and 1859. Because her husband disapproved of married women having a life outside the home, Julia spent most of this period raising her children while writing and publishing anonymously. Her relationship with her husband was never serene and almost led

to divorce in 1854 and again in 1857. However, they remained married until Samuel's death in 1876.

The Howes played active roles in the abolitionist movement beginning in the early 1850s. She had helped her husband publish a newspaper supporting the Free Soil Party, and she was a friend of many of Boston's leading abolitionists, including Elizabeth Palmer Peabody, Charles Sumner, and William Lloyd Garrison. The Howes continued their work for abolitionism as the war began.

With the onset of the Civil War, the Howes involved themselves in the aid of the Union. Julia worked for the New England Sanitary Commission. In November 1861 she accompanied her husband on an inspection trip of Union army camps in the Washington, D.C. area. The authorities had asked her husband to investigate health issues among the tens of thousands of troops encamped around the nation's capitol. By this time, Julia had already taken an active role in war work, having participated in soldiers' relief. With the Sanitary Commission, she had prepared bandages and made clothes for Union troops. However, she later admitted that her lack of domestic skills made these activities frustrating for her, and she felt helpless to contribute further to the cause.

The inspection trip offered her a new outlet for her energies. After a particularly active day touring military camps with Samuel, Julia awoke in the middle of the night having received what she later believed to be a divine inspiration. She claimed that the lyrics to "The Battle Hymn of the Republic" had come to her so freely that almost no editing was required. She submitted the poem to *The Atlantic Monthly*, where it was published in February 1862. The poem was soon set to the music of the popular abolitionist marching song, "John Brown's Body." While it never became as popular among the troops as "John Brown's Body," "Battle Hymn" captured the imagination of the Northern civilian population. The poem reflected the changing war aims—a war originally declared to save the Union had been transformed into one to free slaves. "The Battle Hymn of the Republic," with its imagery of a militant deity leading a struggle for justice and freedom, became a powerful symbol of the new war aims.

Julia Ward Howe, author of "The Battle Hymn of the Republic," in 1861. (Miller, Francis Trevelyan and Robert Sampson Lanier, *The Photographic History of the Civil War,* vol 9, 1911)

In the late 1860s, Julia joined with noted abolitionist and women's rights activist Lucy Stone to lead the American Woman Suffrage Association, one of two national suffrage organizations that resulted from a Civil War–related schism in the women's movement. In 1871 Howe organized a Woman's Peace Congress in London.

After her husband's 1876 death, Julia became even more active in social causes, necessitated in part by the depletion of her inheritance as a result of Samuel's poor management of the family's finances. She immediately embarked on her first national speaking tour to promote the national women's club movement. In 1881 she was elected president of the Association for the Advancement of Women, an organization that promoted educational and professional opportunities for women.

"The Battle Hymn of the Republic" brought celebrity to Julia Ward Howe and transformed her life. In 1908 she was the first woman elected to the American Academy of Arts and Letters, her membership sponsored by Mark Twain. Despite her husband's opposition to her public role, after "Battle Hymn" assured her a place in the American imagination, she began lecturing and developed an enthusiasm for oratory that remained with her for the rest of her life. She used the poem's popularity and the unexpected fame it brought her to advance her reformist agenda until her death. Despite the prominence that "Battle Hymn" has assumed in her life's history, Howe's most substantial contributions came from her career in the American women's movement.

Julia Ward Howe continued to write books, articles, and poems and to give lectures, and she remained active in leadership positions in the women's clubs and suffrage movements until her death on October 17, 1910, at the age of ninety-one.

Robert D. Bohanan

See also Abolitionism and Northern Reformers; Aid Societies; Fiction Writers, Northern; Peabody, Elizabeth Palmer (1804–1894); Poets, Northern; Stone, Lucy (1818–1893).

References and Further Reading
Clifford, Deborah Pickman. 1978. *Mine Eyes Have Seen the Glory: A Biography of Julia Ward Howe.* Boston: Little, Brown and Company.

Grant, Mary H. 1994. *Private Woman, Public Person: An Account of the Life of Julia Ward Howe from 1819 to 1868.* Brooklyn, NY: Carlson Publishing.

Ream, Debbie Williams. 1993. "Mine Eyes Have Seen the Glory." *American History Illustrated* 27: 60–64.

Williams, Gary. 1999. *Hungry Heart: The Literary Emergence of Julia Ward Howe.* Amherst: University of Massachusetts Press.

Hunter, David (1802–1886)

A career soldier and Civil War general, David Hunter is best-known for his unauthorized emancipation of slaves in three Southern states in 1862 and his order to burn sections of the Shenandoah Valley in 1864. People throughout the Confederacy condemned him for his disregard for civilian property and women's spaces during the Shenandoah Valley campaign.

Born on July 21, 1802, Hunter graduated from West Point in 1822. Commissioned a second lieutenant, he was assigned to various frontier posts. While at Fort Dearborn, Hunter met Maria Indiana, whom he later married. Maria Hunter followed her husband to his various postings, remaining with him for his entire life. Hunter briefly resigned from the army but returned and served as a paymaster, rising to the rank of major.

Despite his age, fifty-eight in early 1861, and his lack of experience as a field commander, Hunter was given an infantry division at the start of the Civil War. He led his troops during the First Battle of Bull Run, where he was wounded in action. Following his recovery and promotion to the rank of Major General of Volunteers, Hunter awaited a permanent assignment, eventually finding himself in charge of the Department of the South, where the Union army controlled limited areas on the coastline of South Carolina, Georgia, and Florida. Fearing that he was outnumbered by Confederate troops, Hunter requested reinforcements from Washington. When his request was denied, the general considered other ways of filling the ranks.

On May 9, 1862, Hunter declared all enslaved persons within his department freed, and urged blacks to take up arms to fight for their freedom. He formed the First South Carolina Volunteer Infantry, a unit comprised of black soldiers and white officers. Even though President Abraham Lincoln repealed Hunter's emancipation order, reserving for the commander in chief the right to free slaves, Northern newspapers reacted in outrage to this radical act. The Confederate government branded Hunter an outlaw, accusing him of encouraging slave rebellion.

In 1864 Hunter was ordered to capture Lynchburg, Virginia, a crucial rail junction. Marching through the Shenandoah Valley, Hunter destroyed railroads and various military buildings. His soldiers also ransacked personal homes that they encountered along their route, enraging women throughout the region. In Lexington, Hunter ordered the destruction of the Virginia Military Institute and the home of former governor John Letcher. Approach-

David Hunter, an officer for the Union, issued an emancipation proclamation to slaves in North Carolina, Georgia, and Florida in 1862, only to have his proclamation annulled by Abraham Lincoln in an effort to maintain executive authority. Hunter also organized one of the Union army's first negro regiments. (Library of Congress)

ing Lynchburg, Hunter's force was driven off by Confederate troops. Hunter so poorly planned his retreat that he left the Shenandoah Valley open for a Confederate advance on Washington, D.C. Despite varying estimates of the extent of the damage, Hunter certainly caused a great deal of hardship for civilians, mostly women, who lost their homes during the campaign. Confederate women across the Shenandoah Valley branded him a barbarian for his destructive actions.

Following the war, Hunter served on the military commission that investigated the assassination of

President Lincoln. He retired from the military having spent forty-three years in uniform and died on February 2, 1886, at the age of eighty-three.

Kanisorn Wongsrichanalai

See also Bull Run/Manassas, First Battle of (July 21, 1861); Destruction of Homes; Destruction of Personal Property; Sheridan, Philip Henry (1831–1888); Sheridan's Shenandoah Valley Campaign (1864).

References and Further Reading

Miller, Edward A. 1997. *Lincoln's Abolitionist General: The Biography of David Hunter.* Columbia: University of South Carolina Press.

I

Immigrant Women

Although immigration soared in the years before the war and, despite the fact that many of the new arrivals were women, their stories have often been neglected in general accounts of the great European migrations of the mid-nineteenth century. Only recently have historians begun to document the lives of the many women who joined immigrant men on the farms and in the factories, mills, and sweatshops. Immigrant women's work in the textile and garment industries kept clothing on the backs of soldiers and civilians. In large part, the agricultural and industrial labor of immigrant women freed men to go to war.

To replenish the civilian workforce and to drum up military volunteers, the administration of Abraham Lincoln encouraged immigration with legislation such as the Homestead Act. Many immigrants enlisted or were drafted into the military. For women whose husbands were in the service, the burdens of keeping home and family together were enormously increased. Military pay could be lower than the wages the men had earned before the war, and the threat of being widowed, deserted, or left to care for a wounded husband loomed large for immigrant women, as it did for all women on the Civil War homefronts. Frequently, immigrant women were dependent on men whose lives were at risk almost daily. To make ends meet, many immigrant men took on perilous jobs that native white men refused or that slave owners were unwilling to let valuable black slaves perform.

Every immigrant's tale was unique, but most came to America to escape hardships in their native countries. The women who came to America usually arrived as part of a family migration—with husbands or fathers. Others however, especially the Irish, came singly. Some women came willingly, some reluctantly, but most were looking for an opportunity to improve the material conditions of their lives. Whether alone, in groups with other women, or as the daughters or wives of immigrant men, the majority who made the journey were young and, as a result, gave their most productive years to their adopted land.

The new immigrants generally settled in Northern cities where jobs in factories or opportunities for domestic service were plentiful and where there were already established immigrant enclaves. The migration of Europeans to the South made up a small percentage of the overall immigrant population. Conditions in the South were not as hospitable for immigrants, and opportunities were not as plentiful as they were in the North. Slave labor provided most of the South's agricultural manpower, and the lack of industrialization drove immigrants to seek work in the North. The immigrants who went south settled mostly in Louisiana and Texas or in the South's few cities, including Charleston.

Large numbers of immigrants headed west, where there was abundant farmland. For many immigrants, especially those from the Scandinavian countries or the German-speaking areas of Europe, the opportunity to own large tracts of land beckoned them to the rural areas of New York, Pennsylvania, and the upper Midwest. German-speaking women tended to arrive in family groups and channeled their efforts into saving money for land and building family farms. Scandinavian women also concentrated on farming in rural areas of the upper Midwest. Women toiled in the fields as well as in the home, and they usually had the responsibility for tending livestock in addition to their other duties. Clearing land and establishing homesteads, though the fulfillment of a dream for many immigrants, made for backbreaking, isolating, and often heartrending work.

Irish women comprised the largest group of female immigrants. Great numbers arrived unmarried and typically found positions as domestic servants in the large Northern cities, especially in New York and Boston. The life of the domestic servant was difficult, and native women who could choose other occupations did so; work in a factory may have been dirty and exhausting, but many immigrants believed it was preferable to working, and usually residing, in the private home of one's employer. In any event, many Irish women were willing, if not delighted, to have the domestic jobs. The pay for domestic work was often higher and the work less dangerous than that of factory work. In addition, saving money on housing, clothing, and transportation was a decided incentive for Irish women to take on domestic labor. Most women sent earnings home to help families they had left behind or to provide passage for relatives.

While immigrants from German-speaking lands and Great Britain predominated, other women migrated in much smaller numbers. Jewish women from Europe sometimes traveled alone or with other family members, but more often they arrived as the wife of an already established immigrant. They tended to work in family businesses as they raised their families. In addition, Italian immigration did not occur in large numbers until after 1870, and Asian and Eastern European immigration was very limited in the years surrounding the Civil War.

Though they came from many countries and different walks of life, once in America, immigrant women found a society quite unlike those they had left behind. Adjustments were often painful and the obstacles were daunting. A new language, a new culture, prejudice, and poverty confronted them. The challenges of bearing and raising children without the familiar network of family and neighbors made life stressful and often lonely. The war's effects rippled into every city, and many resources that might have helped immigrant families were diverted. Moreover, antiforeign hostility did not fade. Despite the difficulties, many thousands of women raised families and helped build social, cultural, and religious networks that eased the transition for other newcomers, as they served their own communities and their new country. Although often silent participants, immigrant women, many of whose lives were cut short through illness, childbirth, and overwork, played a significant role in the growth and development of the nation during the nineteenth century.

Yvette Florio Lane

See also Catholic Women; Civilian Life; Factory Workers, Northern; Farm Work; Jewish Women; Northern Women; Religion; Rural Women; Southern Women; Urban Women, Northern; Urban Women, Southern; Western Women.

References and Further Reading
Diner, Hasia R. 1983. *Erin's Daughters in America: Irish Immigrant Women in the Nineteenth Century.* Baltimore, MD: Johns Hopkins University Press.
Gabaccia, Donna. 1994. *From the Other Side: Immigrant Life in the U.S., 1820–1990.* Bloomington: Indiana University Press.
Mahin, Dean B. 2002. *The Blessed Place of Freedom: Europeans in Civil War America.* Washington, DC: Brassey's.
Weatherford, Doris. 1986. *Foreign and Female: Immigrant Women in America, 1840–1930.* New York: Schocken Books.

Impressment

Impressment is the seizure of private property for use by the government. During the Civil War, agents of the Confederate and Union governments and armies impressed a wide variety of edible and non-edible agricultural products, livestock, wagons, and even slaves to aid in the war effort. Property owners received either receipts, paper currency, or occasionally gold in exchange for impressed goods. Though most of the civilians affected by impressment were, by virtue of geography, Southerners, both armies seized private property for military use during their short forays onto Union soil.

Impressment was not the only means by which the Confederate and Union governments obtained private property for army use. The Confederate tax-in-kind placed a tithe on agricultural goods, which was collected and forwarded to the armies at regular intervals throughout the war. The Confederacy also instituted property confiscation to punish Southerners who remained loyal to the Union or publicly objected to Confederate policies, although it is unclear how often the government invoked this prerogative. The United States government also created a series of Confiscation Acts, giving Union armies the authority to seize property used to aid the Confederate war effort without compensating property owners. In 1871, the United States Congress created the Southern Claims Commission, providing Southerners who had remained loyal to the Union with the chance to receive payment for some of the property Union soldiers had seized during the war.

Most of the impressment of Southern property, however, occurred at the hands of Confederate impressment agents. The first Confederate impressment legislation concerned cotton. The Davis administration created a Cotton Bureau to impress cotton at a uniform national price and to carry on all trade in cotton, particularly with foreign buyers. Impressed cotton also served as collateral in the Confederacy's only large international loan. In March 1863, the Confederate Congress gave army commanders the authority to impress food and to forage from local farmers, legislating and legitimizing what had already been in practice for well over a year. Congress also insisted that the War Department institute a price schedule to ensure that farmers received fair compensation for all impressed goods.

This legislative action created a lengthy debate over whether Southern farmers should receive the market value for impressed goods. Many cited the impracticality of determining market value at various points in the country, particularly as scarcity and inflation caused prices to spiral upward at rapid rates. Others suggested that not providing adequate compensation would simply encourage farmers to hide goods from impressment agents, thus jeopardizing the Confederate army's ability to obtain sufficient food. Not surprisingly, representatives from areas of the homefront closest to the armies—and thus most prone to impressment—called most strongly for compensation at market value. In practice, the Confederate War Department's price schedules always lagged behind market prices, and the paper currency they distributed quickly depreciated. Most farmers, moreover, received no immediate compensation for impressed goods but were instead given receipts that became completely worthless once the Confederate armies surrendered.

The Confederate government also began impressing slave labor in March 1863, once again creating order out of an ad hoc form of impressment that had been ongoing since the beginning of the war. The legislation called for able-bodied male slaves between the ages of eighteen and fifty-five to work on Confederate fortifications, usually for a period of two or three months. Florida, Virginia, Alabama, Louisiana, and Mississippi already had state legislation in place to impress slave laborers, and the War Department sought the cooperation of state legislatures in these states to enact slave impressments in the other Confederate states. In the other six Confederate states, state and military officials had called for short-term levies of black labor prior to the national legislation, but the scale of the War Department's actions was unprecedented. As with the impressment of agricultural goods, of course, the burdens of slave impressment fell the hardest on communities closest to the Confederate armies.

Jaime Amanda Martinez

See also Civilian Life; Confederate Homefront; Destruction of Homes; Destruction of Personal Property; Food; Foraging, Effects on Women; Military Invasion and Occupation; Morale; Northern Women; Politics; Rural Women; Shortages; Slaveholding Women; Southern Women; Union Homefront.

References and Further Reading

Blair, William A. 1998. *Virginia's Private War: Feeding Body and Soul in the Confederacy, 1861–1865.* New York: Oxford University Press.

Grimsley, Mark. 1995. *The Hard Hand of War: Union Military Policy toward Southern Civilians 1861–1865.* New York: Cambridge University Press.

Rable, George. 1994. *The Confederate Republic: A Revolution against Politics.* Chapel Hill: University of North Carolina Press.

Thomas, Emory M. 1979. *The Confederate Nation, 1861–1865.* New York: Harper & Row.

Thomas, Emory M. 1991. *The Confederacy as a Revolutionary Experience.* Columbia: University of South Carolina Press.

Imprisonment of Women

Nineteenth-century gender conventions greatly impacted the treatment of women in Civil War prisons. Because society denied that women could be independent political actors, officials faced a difficult decision in holding women responsible for their actions, and individual officers had significant leeway in how they treated women prisoners. Nevertheless, in almost all cases, officials allotted little or no time in prison for women they arrested. Rather, they preferred to punish women with a stern lecture, house arrest, or banishment behind enemy lines. Moreover, if women did spend time incarcerated, the material conditions of their confinement were likely to be better than those faced by male prisoners, and their experience could make them local and sometimes national celebrities.

The most celebrated and best documented cases of women's imprisonment involved female spies. Despite regulations stipulating that no distinctions should be made between male and female spies and that spying was a capital crime, there is no evidence that any woman was executed for spying. Perhaps the closest any officer came to executing a woman was when Nathan Bedford Forrest sentenced Pauline Cushman, a Union spy, to hang. The timely arrival of Union forces, however, prevented Forrest from having to decide if he would carry out the sentence. Union officials arrested Belle Boyd several times for spying in 1862. The first time, they released her, and the second time they incarcerated her for a week at a hotel. Only after her third arrest did she enter Old Capitol Prison, a three-story dingy brick structure in Washington, D.C. Even there, she received special treatment. While guards verbally abused her (with Boyd responding in kind) and confined her to a room, the door and windows were kept open. As the summer heat and humidity increased, Union officials released her after only one month in the prison. Upon her fourth arrest in 1863, Boyd was sent to Carroll Prison for three months and then banished to the Confederacy.

Other women spies experienced similar treatment. Union officials put Rose O'Neal Greenhow, her eight-year-old daughter, and two of her couriers under house arrest in August 1861. With the addition of other women prisoners, including Eugenia Phillips, a prominent critic of the Lincoln administration, the house became known as Fort Greenhow. Confinement did not prevent Greenhow from trying to continue her intelligence work, and, as a result, in January 1862, she and her daughter were sent to Old Capitol Prison for five months until they were exiled to the Confederacy. Phillips suffered house arrest, placement in Fort Greenhow, and then banishment to New Orleans. There, further conflict with Union General Benjamin Butler over her public laughter during a funeral led to her three-month confinement on Ship Island at the mouth of the Mississippi River.

The physical conditions faced by imprisoned women varied greatly depending on the military officials in charge of their cases. Phillips most likely exaggerated when she spoke of the filthy rooms and soiled beds in the attic of the Greenhow house. Other sources described her accommodations there as a plush apartment. Even in prisons, women lived in better sheltered and less cramped conditions than men did. Some women, however, faced difficult conditions. For instance, at Ship Island, Phillips lived in an abandoned boxcar, battled insects, and ate stale, rancid food. Elsewhere, in a St. Louis jail, women lived without heat, had to bribe guards to secure adequate food, saw their letters of protest burned, slept in rags, and were possibly forced into prostitution. Mary Walker, a Union army surgeon captured in April 1864, spent four months in a Confederate prison. The filthy conditions and poor food caused her long-term health problems, with one of her relatives claiming that Walker had lost half her body weight during her incarceration.

Class combined with gender to shape the treatment of arrested women. Wealthy women received benefits not accorded to their poorer sisters, particularly the possibility of house arrest rather than incarceration. In Richmond, Virginia, as many as one hundred women, charged with crimes such as treason, disloyalty, and other minor offenses, spent time in the city's dreaded Castle Thunder prison. While women of modest means suffered in prison, Mary Allan, an elite woman accused of being a spy, was first housed in a convent. After paying $100,000 for bail in February 1864, her attorney managed to secure a sufficient number of trial postponements so that her case remained untried at the end of the war. Elsewhere, even the Beast, Benjamin Butler, permitted Phillips to bring an Irish maid with her to Ship Island.

As the war progressed, the treatment of civilians by both armies worsened. Consequently, the probability that women would be imprisoned both for their own actions and for the actions of their male relatives increased. In areas where the Union army faced Confederate guerrillas, women could be arrested as bushwhackers or taken as hostages. In Kansas City, Missouri, five women held in this manner died when their rickety jailhouse collapsed in 1863. These deaths possibly contributed to the unrestrained violence of Quantrill's raid on Lawrence, Kansas, which took place only a week later. In some areas, Confederates jailed Southern women who helped their husbands dodge the draft or desert from the army. Ironically, in other instances when officers tried to maintain a sense of prewar gender

distinctions, men could be arrested for their wives' verbal threats or physical attacks on soldiers.

A limited number of women entered the army disguised as men. Of these, a still smaller number were captured by enemy forces and recognized to as women. Because both armies officially prohibited women's enlistment, neither army's regulations stipulated what to do with female prisoners of war. Instead, the armies dealt with these women on a case-by-case basis with releasing the prisoner being the most frequent choice. Generally, a woman's gender was discovered upon capture, but unsubstantiated stories tell of women whose gender was allegedly discovered only upon their giving birth in prison. Although rarely requesting special consideration, most female prisoners of war received separate accommodations and more lenient treatment than their male counterparts.

John M. Sacher

See also Boyd, Belle (1844–1900); Butler, Benjamin F. (1818–1893); Cushman, Pauline [Harriet Wood] (1833–1893); Domesticity; Female Combatants; Female Spies; Greenhow, Rose O'Neal (ca. 1814–1864); Northern Women; Phillips, Eugenia Levy (1819–1901); Separate Spheres; Southern Women; Walker, Mary Edwards (1832–1919).

References and Further Reading

Blanton, DeAnne, and Lauren M. Cook. 2002. *They Fought Like Demons: Women Soldiers in the American Civil War.* Baton Rouge: Louisiana State University Press.

Clinton, Catherine, and Nina Silber, eds. 1992. *Divided Houses: Gender and the Civil War.* New York: Oxford University Press.

Leonard, Elizabeth D. 1999. *All the Daring of the Soldier: Women of the Civil War Armies.* New York: W. W. Norton & Company.

Speer, Lonnie R. 1997. *Portals to Hell: Military Prisons of the Civil War.* Mechanicsburg, PA: Stackpole Books.

J

Jackson, Mary Anna Morrison (1831–1915)

Anna Jackson was the wife of Thomas Jonathan "Stonewall" Jackson and one of five sisters who married Confederate officers or officials.

Born July 31, 1831, in Mecklenburg County, North Carolina, Mary Anna Morrison was the third daughter and fourth child of Reverend Robert Hall Morrison and Mary Graham. Her childhood was spent at Davidson, where her father was president of Davidson College and at the family's Lincoln County plantation, Cottage Home. Anna was educated at Salem Academy.

In 1851, Anna Morrison met Major Thomas J. Jackson through her sister Isabella Hill, wife of Major D. H. Hill. Both men taught at colleges in Lexington, Virginia. In 1853 Jackson married Elinor Junkin, who died fourteen months later. In 1856 Morrison and Jackson met again after having not seen each other for several years. The two were married July 16, 1857, in Lincoln County, North Carolina, where her family lived after Robert Morrison's retirement. Before the Civil War called the major to duty, the Jacksons lost their first daughter, Mary Graham. During the war, Anna lived in Charlotte in her sister's home. She delivered her second daughter, Julia, in November 1862. Anna was visiting in Richmond when she received the news that her husband had been wounded at Chancellorsville. She traveled to Guiney's Station, Virginia, where he had been moved and was with him when he died on May 10, 1863.

Anna Jackson remained at her father's house in Lincoln County until about 1873, when she moved to Charlotte. There she provided a good life for her daughter and divided her time between her church, First Presbyterian, and two ancestral societies, the Stonewall Jackson Chapter of the United Daughters of the Confederacy and the Mecklenburg Chapter of the Daughters of the American Revolution, both organized in 1898. She also wrote a book about her husband, published in 1892 and another about her daughter, published in 1910. Julia Jackson, who died in 1889, had married William Edmund Christian and had had a son and daughter.

Anna Jackson was beloved not only in North Carolina but in all the former Confederate states. Veterans visited her throughout her life, and she was often referred to as the First Lady of the Confederacy after Varina Davis died in 1906. Anna Morrison Jackson died March 24, 1915, of pneumonia and received military honors at her funeral. As a sign of respect, the Charlotte City Hall and other businesses were closed the day after she died and on the day of the funeral. She is buried in Lexington, Virginia, next to her husband.

Debra A. Blake

See also Southern Women.

References and Further Reading

Gardner, Sarah E. 2001. "'A Sweet Solace to My Lonely Heart': 'Stonewall' and Mary Anna Jackson and the Civil War." In *Intimate Strategies of the Civil War: Military Commanders and their Wives*, 49–68. New York: Oxford University Press.

Herran, Kathy Neill. 1997. *They Married Confederate Officers: The Intimate Story of Anna Morrison, Wife of Stonewall Jackson and Her Five Sisters.* Davidson, NC: Warren Publishing.

Jackson, Mary Anna. 1892. *Life and Letters of General Thomas J. Jackson.* New York: Harper and Brothers.

Jacobs, Harriet Ann [Linda Brent] (1813–1897)

Born into slavery, Harriet Jacobs escaped in 1842. In 1861, she published her autobiography, *Incidents in the Life of a Slave Girl,* which detailed the horrors of slavery, especially those peculiar to slave women. Although the beginning of the Civil War muted the initial impact of *Incidents,* it remains an important source of information on life in slavery for women. The book was never reprinted in Jacobs' lifetime and its authorship was often debated. However, Jacobs maintained her dedication to African American causes throughout her life. She remained an active champion of rights for freedpeople until her death in 1897.

Harriet Jacobs was born in 1813 in Edenton, North Carolina, to Delilah, a slave of Margaret Horniblow, and Daniel Jacobs, a slave of Andrew Knox. Like many young African Americans, Harriet did not realize she was someone's property until the age of six, when her mother died. When Harriet was a child, Horniblow taught her to read and sew, but Horniblow died in 1825, bequeathing Harriet to her three-year-old niece, Mary Matilda Norcom. Jacobs moved in with the Norcom family, where she was subjected to repeated sexual advances from Mary's father, physician James Norcom.

Jacobs's grandmother, freed slave Molly Horniblow, encouraged Jacobs to leave the Norcom residence and offered to help. Jacobs was frightened, however, and would not leave. Instead, in 1829, she began a relationship and had two children, Joseph and Louisa, with white attorney Samuel Tredwell Sawyer. Jacobs's behavior infuriated Norcom, who sent her to one of his plantations to work as a field hand. Terrified that her children would be forced to follow the same path, Jacobs ran away. After staying with various neighbors both black and white, she moved into a tiny crawlspace above a storeroom in her grandmother's house in 1835. She hoped that her absence would prompt Norcom to sell her children to their white father. Norcom, as expected, posted a reward for Jacobs's capture and return.

Jacobs remained in hiding in the crawl space for almost seven years. The space was nine feet long and seven feet wide, and had no light or ventilation. During those years, Jacobs emerged only for brief periods at night to exercise. She spent her time sewing, reading the Bible, and sending letters to Norcom to confuse him as to her whereabouts. Sawyer purchased their children but did not emancipate either one of them. He moved them to a house nearby, and Jacobs could sometimes watch them through a peephole she had made as they played outside.

When Sawyer won a seat in the United States House of Representatives in 1837, he moved to Washington, D.C., without the children. Instead he sent Louisa to Brooklyn to work as a house servant.

In 1842, Jacobs escaped by boat and headed to Brooklyn in search of Louisa. Although free from her life as a slave, she lived in constant fear of recapture. For the next ten years, Norcom continued to search for her. Jacobs found a job for herself as well as a place for her to live with both of her children. She worked as a nursemaid in Boston for Mary Stace and abolitionist poet Nathaniel Paker Willis. In 1849, Jacobs began eighteen months living above the Rochester, New York offices of Frederick Douglass's antislavery newspaper, *The North Star.* In Rochester, she worked with her antislavery lecturer brother, John S. Jacobs, also a fugitive slave. She traveled frequently between Boston and New York, becoming an active member of a group of antislavery feminists, including Amy Post, who encouraged Jacobs to share her story with the public.

In 1852, the Willises purchased Jacobs and freed her. She then began working on her autobiography, *Incidents in the Life of a Slave Girl.* She wrote at the Willises' home, Idlewood, an isolated, fourteen-room writers' retreat on the shore of Moodna Creek. By day, Jacobs tended to the Willis children, and by night she worked on her memoirs in secret. Jacobs's letters to Post reveal a connection between her decision to tell her story and the recent death of her grandmother, Molly Horniblow. Jacobs felt that she could never share the sordid details of her life while her grandmother still lived; she feared that the sexual realities of her life as a slave would horrify her grandmother. In addition, Jacobs initially hoped that Harriet Beecher Stowe, author of the recently released *Uncle Tom's Cabin*, would make a good partner in the effort. Although this collaboration did not materialize, Jacobs's belief in the relationship between her own life's story and Stowe's fictional antislavery work indicates Jacobs's understanding of her potential contribution to the growing canon of slave literature.

Jacobs's work on her autobiography initially took the form of several anonymous letters to *New York Daily Tribune*, where they were published in 1853. Jacobs's published letters tackled central issues from her life story and addressed head-on the sexual abuse of slave girls and the efforts of their mothers to protect them. Her account of her sexual abuse shocked the American public and ultimately made it difficult for Jacobs to find a publisher. By the summer of 1857, Jacobs had completed her account of her life as a slave. She then enlisted the help of antislavery author Lydia Maria Child to get her story into print. Jacobs contracted with the Boston publishing house Thayer & Eldridge to publish the book, but the publisher went bankrupt. Undeterred, Jacobs and her antislavery friends had *Incidents in the Life of a Slave Girl* published in late 1860 by a Boston printer. It was published in London in 1861 as *The Deeper Wrong; Or, Incidents in the Life of a Slave Girl.* In both editions, Jacobs used a pseudonym, Linda Brent.

The first fugitive slave narrative written by a woman, *Incidents* received praise from antislavery circles in the United States and Britain. It revealed the horrors of slavery from a woman's point of view and highlighted the sexual perversion of the South's peculiar institution. Abolitionists hoped the book would incite others, especially women, to oppose slavery based on its corrupting sexual aspects. In an era that stressed women's proper roles, as well as the proper treatment of women by white men, a detailed account of how slavery denied women protection shocked many readers.

In *Incidents*, Jacobs never revealed her true identity. She instead maintained the alias Linda Brent and similarly renamed other actors in her life's story. Jacobs later stated that her primary motive was to address white women of the North on behalf of thousands of slave mothers and to appeal to their common identities as women and mothers. She also hoped to arouse the sympathy of her readers by showing herself as a victim of horrible circumstances that she could not control. She emphasized, however, the parts of her life that she could control. Throughout her autobiography, Jacobs portrayed herself not as a victim but as an active agent in her story, controlling her own sexuality by choosing to take a white lover while risking the wrath of her master and pursuing her own freedom.

Throughout the Civil War, Jacobs involved herself in relief efforts in the Washington, D.C. area. In particular, she aided the former slaves who had become wartime refugees, nursed African American troops, and taught the freedpeople. In 1863, she and her daughter founded the Jacobs Free School in Alexandria, Virginia, to train African American teachers for the freedpeople. When Jacobs and her daughter headed to Savannah, Georgia, in 1865, they moved the school with them. Jacobs returned to Edenton in 1867, where she promoted the welfare of former slaves. She remained in the South, working to aid her fellow freedpeople until racial violence finally drove her out.

In the postwar era, Jacobs continued her aid efforts. In 1868 she and Louisa raised money in London for an orphanage and home for the aged in Savannah, Georgia. Then the two returned to Massachusetts where, in 1870, they opened a boarding house in Cambridge. By the mid-1880s, Jacobs had settled in the District of Columbia with Louisa. In Washington, Jacobs worked at newly formed black schools and later at Howard University. Soon before her death, she was involved in the organizing meetings of the National Association of Colored Women.

Harriet Jacobs died in Washington, D.C., on March 7, 1897, at the age of eighty-four. She is buried next to her brother, John, in Cambridge's Mt. Auburn Cemetery.

Eloise E. Scroggins

See also Abolitionism and Northern Reformers;
African American Women; Child, Lydia Maria
Francis (1802–1880); Contrabands; Domesticity;
Douglass, Frederick (ca. 1818–1895); Slave Families;
Stowe, Harriet Beecher (1811–1896); Teachers,
Northern; Teachers, Southern.

References and Further Reading

Garfield, Deborah, and Rafia Zafar, eds. 1996.
*Harriet Jacobs and 'Incidents in the Life of a
Slave Girl': New Critical Essays.* New York:
Cambridge University Press.

Jacobs, Harriet A. [1861] 1987. *Incidents in the Life
of a Slave Girl,* edited by Jean Fagan Yellin.
Cambridge, MA: Harvard University Press.

Yellin, Jean Fagan. 2004. *Harriet Jacobs: A Life.*
New York: Basic Civitas Books.

Jewish Women

During the American Civil War, Jewish men and
women were divided in their political and social
alliances. Although most Jewish families lived in the
North and supported the Union, many Southern
Jews supported the Confederacy.

Like women of all faiths, Jewish women supported the war efforts by urging their men to enlist
and assisting the war through various social organizations. According to one estimate, at least seven
thousand Jewish soldiers fought for the Confederacy and the Union. In addition, Jewish communities
organized to support the war from behind the battle
lines. In addition to synagogues, which orchestrated
many wartime relief efforts, Jewish women formed
and joined various religious and nonreligious welfare organizations and took active roles as individuals in the support of the Union and Confederacy.
Across the country, Jewish men and women minis-
tered to the wounded, the widowed, and the
orphaned. In establishing communal charitable
societies, Jewish women organized and raised
money to support impoverished families. Jewish
women in the North and South held weekly meetings in local synagogues and private homes to discuss further involvement in the war relief effort.
With the money they raised through public events,
Northern women bought medical supplies, clothing,
stationery, and food to send to the United States
Sanitary Commission for soldiers.

Even though Jews on both sides of the battle suffered from a wartime shortage of kosher foods,
especially during Passover, they continued to celebrate their traditional holidays. Many found additional meanings in wartime holidays, comparing
their situation to that of their ancestors. In addition,
every Jewish holiday was utilized to help in the war
effort. The largest sum collected by any congregation for the Sanitary Commission came from
Shearith Israel Congregation in New York City
from their 1864 Purim carnival.

In some Northern cities, Jewish women established organizations to aid both the Union cause as
well as the people left behind on the homefront. In
Philadelphia, for example, Rebecca Gratz founded
a number of Jewish women's organizations, including the Female Hebrew Benevolent Society, the
Philadelphia Orphan Society, and the Jewish Foster
Home. Gratz's active participation in the war effort
came even though she was deeply distraught that
her family members held opposing loyalties to the
North and the South.

Jewish women in the South were similarly supportive of their own war effort, often taking on dangerous
responsibilities. For example, an antebellum philanthropist who had married at age sixteen, Rosanna
Dyer Osterman served as a Confederate nurse and a
spy during the war. In 1838, the couple had moved
from Baltimore to Galveston, Texas, to establish their
business. While Union forces besieged Galveston,
Rosanna nursed the wounded, both Union and Confederate, in her home. When Galveston fell to Union
forces, she secretly delivered strategic information to
Confederate officers in Houston. Aided by this military intelligence, Southern forces recaptured Galveston on New Year's Day in 1863.

Eugenia Levy Phillips followed a similar path to
wartime prominence. A native of Charleston, South
Carolina, she married prominent lawyer Philip
Phillips and moved with him to Alabama. When he
was elected to Congress, they decided to reside permanently in Washington, D.C. Shortly after the war
broke out, Eugenia, her two daughters, and her sister were put under house arrest, suspected of spying
for the Confederacy. They fled to New Orleans after
their release. From there, Eugenia delivered a

Eugenia Levy Phillips, Confederate spy (1820–1902). (Clay-Clopton, Virginia, *A Belle of the Fifties: Memoirs of Mrs. Clay, of Alabama, Covering Social and Political Washington and the South, 1853–1866*, 1905)

coded message from Confederate spy Rose O'Neal Greenhow to President Jefferson Davis. Phillips's loyalty to the Confederacy caused her to clash with General Benjamin Butler, the Federal commander of New Orleans, and she was imprisoned again and sent to Ship Island in the Gulf of Mexico.

Phillips's sister, Phoebe Yates Levy Pember, served as the matron of the Chimborazo Military Hospital in Richmond, Virginia. The hospital had one hundred and fifty wards, and by the end of the war seventy-six thousand Southern soldiers had been treated there. In her memoirs, *A Southern Woman's Story* (1879), Pember, one of the first women to infiltrate the male-dominated discipline of nursing, described the difficulties that wartime women nurses faced.

Many women in the Union and Confederacy kept diaries during the war to record the momentous events around them. Jewish women were no different. For example, in her journal and letters,

Emma Mordecai, a member of several affluent Jewish families, narrated the travails of daily life during the war and gave details about the fall of Richmond and the capture of Jefferson Davis. In New Orleans, Clara Solomon, who was sixteen when the war started, kept a diary from June 1861 to July 1862. Commenting on the daily news and current events from a pro-Confederate viewpoint, Clara repeatedly declared her belief in the imminent victory of the Southern states.

Despite these notable exceptions, primary sources describing the war from a Jewish female perspective are not abundant. The majority of the extant sources come from assimilated Southern Jewish women of the upper class. The surviving manuscripts and documents, mainly memoirs, journals, and letters written by Jewish women, depict numerous tales of immeasurable suffering, self-sacrifice, and acts of bravery.

Dina Ripsman Eylon

See also *Confederate Homefront;* Diaries and Journals; Enlistment; Female Spies; Greenhow, Rose O'Neal (ca. 1814–1864); Letter Writing; Northern Women; Nurses; Religion; Pember, Phoebe Yates Levy (1823–1913); Phillips, Eugenia Levy (1819–1901); Solomon, Clara (ca. 1845–1907); Southern Women; Union Homefront; United States Sanitary Commission.

References and Further Reading

Korn, Bertram W. 1961. *American Jewry and the Civil War.* New York: Meridian Books and Jewish Publication Society.

Simonhoff, Harry. 1963. *Jewish Participants in the Civil War.* New York: Arco Publishing.

Solomon, Clara. 1995. *The Civil War Diary of Clara Solomon: Growing Up in New Orleans 1861–1862,* edited, with Introduction, by Elliott Ashkenazi. Baton Rouge: Louisiana State University Press.

Spiegel, Marcus. 1985. *Your True Marcus: The Civil War Letters of a Jewish Colonel,* edited by Frank L. Byrne and Jean Powers Soman. Kent, OH: Kent State University Press.

Wolf, Simon. 1972. *The American Jew as Patriot, Soldier and Citizen,* with new Introduction and Preface by George Athan Billias. Boston: Gregg Press.

Young, Mel. 1991. *Where They Lie: The Story of the Jewish Soldiers of the North and South Whose*

Deaths—Killed, Morally Wounded or Died of Disease or Other Causes—Occurred During the Civil War, 1861–1865. Lanham, MD: University Press of America.

Johnson, Ann Battles (1815–1866)

A free woman of color during the Civil War, Ann Battles Johnson experienced the ambiguities experienced by black slaveholders.

Born a slave in Natchez, Mississippi, in 1815, Johnson obtained her freedom in 1826. She joined a sizable free black community in the town's relatively small urban community. She was already literate, and she had free and slave family members in and around Natchez.

At the age of twenty, she married William T. Johnson, a successful barber, businessman, and free man of color in Natchez. After their marriage, he purchased a small cotton plantation with as many as eight slaves, whom he managed as an absentee owner. The couple had eleven children, nine of whom lived to adulthood. Ann spent most of her time in their Natchez home, taking on all of the responsibilities of a free slaveholding woman. Early in their marriage, Ann performed many household chores, including taking care of a large garden, tending to livestock, and providing well-rounded educations to their children. Ann also taught her daughters how to become talented seamstresses. As they became more prosperous, Ann became a manager of household slaves who were purchased to help.

William Johnson was murdered in 1851 as the result of a land dispute with Baylor Wynn, another free man of color. Although Johnson named his assassin before his death, Wynn avoided conviction by claiming that a black man could not testify against him because he falsely claimed he was white. William's death and Wynn's acquittal were devastating to Ann.

As a widow, Johnson took control of an estate estimated to be worth more than $25,000. For the next fifteen years, she administered the properties and businesses left to her. She sold her agricultural holdings and began renting rooms in her Natchez home. She added rooms to her home and built a building in Main Street to augment her rental income. She also continued to manage William's barbershops, make small loans to family and friends, and use slaves to bring her goods to and from the marketplace.

During the war, Johnson experienced financial difficulties common in the urban South. More concerned with survival than with the meaning of the war, she found the war unsettling. With money in short supply and Union troops occupying New Orleans, rents and occupancy rates fell. She also suffered from the economic loss of her slaves, many of whom ran away to Union lines. Now reliant on free labor in an economically depressed region, Johnson struggled to feed her family. When the war ended, she began to rebuild her life as an African American landowner in the postemancipation South.

Johnson did not live to see how her family would survive in the postwar South. She died in August 1866, at the very outset of Reconstruction.

Andrew K. Frank

See also African American Woman; Confederate Homefront; Free Blacks; Shortages; Slaveholding Women; Southern Women; Urban Women, Southern.

References and Further Reading

Gould, Virginia Meacham. 1998. *Chained to the Rock of Adversity: To Be Free, Black, and Female in the Old South.* Athens: University of Georgia Press.

K

Keckley, Elizabeth Hobbs (ca. 1818–1907)

Former slave, seamstress, and organizer of the Contraband Relief Association, Elizabeth Keckley became Mary Todd Lincoln's dressmaker and confidant. She published her memoir, *Behind the Scenes, or Thirty Years a Slave and Four Years in the White House*, in 1868.

The exact birth date and parentage of Keckley have been a mystery. Recent scholarship has established that she was born a slave in February 1818, in Dinwiddie Courthouse, Virginia, the daughter of Agnes Hobbs. Her father has been variously identified as George Pleasant, a slave from a nearby plantation, or Colonel Armistead Burwell, a white master. She later gave birth to a son by another master, Alexander Kirkland. Loaned to one of Burwell's daughters, Anne Garland, she moved to St. Louis and worked as a dressmaker for the seventeen members of this family for two years. Sometime around 1852, she married James Keckley, an emancipated slave. During the early 1850s, she convinced the Garlands to allow her to buy her freedom and that of her son, George. Her dressmaking customers finally raised the funds, and she was issued a deed of emancipation in 1855. In 1860, she separated from James and went to Washington, D.C., establishing a dressmaking business there.

She sewed for politicians and their wives, including Jefferson and Varina Davis, Adele Cutts Douglas, Stephen Douglas's widow, and Ellen Stanton, wife of the secretary of war. On March 3, 1861, First Lady Mary Todd Lincoln hired Keckley as her dressmaker.

Keckley's son, George, whose light complexion allowed him to pass as white, volunteered for the First Missouri Volunteers of the Union army. He was killed during the Battle of Wilson Creek, Missouri, in August 1861.

In 1862 Keckley founded the Contraband Relief Association, a group that assisted freedmen in the Washington, D.C. area. It was later named the Freemen and Soldiers' Relief Fund. On behalf of this group, she collected contributions from Frederick Douglass, Mary Lincoln, and anti-slavery societies in England and Scotland.

Keckley consoled Mary Lincoln after the death of her son William Wallace "Willie" Lincoln and later, following President Lincoln's assassination. After the Civil War, Keckley accompanied Mary to Chicago to help market some of the former first lady's wardrobe, a project that ended in disaster. Keckley returned to Washington, D.C., and reopened her dressmaking business.

G. W. Carleton published Keckley's memoir, *Behind the Scenes*, in 1868. The volume has also been variously attributed to James Redpath, Hamilton Busbey, and Jane Swisshelm. Originally written to help Mary Lincoln financially, it contained many confidential letters Keckley had not intended for publication. For matters of identity, she consistently signed her formal name as Elizabeth Keckly; when signing her first name only, she wrote Lizzy, not Lizzie as Mary Lincoln had done.

Elizabeth Keckley died on May 26, 1907, in the National Home for Destitute Colored Women and

Children in Washington, D.C. Francis Grimké, husband of Charlotte Forten Grimké and uncle to Angelina Grimké, delivered the eulogy.

Ralph Hartsock

See also African American Women; Contraband Relief Association; Davis, Jefferson (1808–1889); Davis, Varina Banks Howell (1826–1906); Douglass, Frederick (ca. 1818–1895); Forten (Grimké), Charlotte L. (1837–1914); Grimké (Weld), Angelina (1805–1879); Lincoln, Mary Todd (1818–1882); Slave Families; Swisshelm, Jane Grey (1815–1884); Union Homefront.

References and Further Reading

Fleischner, Jennifer. 2003. *Mrs. Lincoln and Mrs. Keckly.* New York: Broadway Books.

Keckley, Elizabeth. 1988. *Behind the Scenes, or Thirty Years a Slave and Four Years in the White House.* New York: Oxford University Press.

Kelley, Abby (1811–1887)

Raised as a Quaker in Worcester, Massachusetts, Abby Kelley became a radical abolitionist and feminist who spoke out for social change in antebellum America.

Abby Kelley was born to a farming family of strict Quakers. She attended Quaker schools and decided to teach for a living. After attending a female seminary, she accepted a teaching position in Lynn, Massachusetts, in 1836. There, Kelley was exposed to the growing abolitionist movement. The values of this movement—the equality of the races and ending slavery—appealed deeply to her. She joined the Lynn Female Anti-Slavery Society, quickly became a leading member, and began attending state and national female antislavery conventions as well.

When Kelley heard the Grimké sisters, Angelina and Sarah, speak in 1837, she realized that giving abolitionist speeches was a worthy vocation. She first addressed a mixed group (male and female) of abolitionists in 1838 and was encouraged to become a public speaker. She returned to her family home in Connecticut and began talking to small groups about the evils of slavery.

Once on the lecture circuit, Kelley confronted many people who believed that women had no place in the public sphere. Kelley found herself defending not only abolitionism, but also her right as a woman to speak in public. She often faced hostile crowds but bravely persevered. For a number of years in the 1840s, Kelley was one of a very few women who spoke in public to mixed groups.

The issue of women giving public lectures led in part to the 1840 split in the antislavery movement. In fact, Kelley's appointment to the business committee of the American Anti-Slavery Society, traditionally a male group, was the immediate cause of this split. The conservative members—who opposed women's leadership in the movement—left to form the American and Foreign Anti-Slavery Society. William Lloyd Garrison led the more radical members in the original group.

Members of Kelley's religious faith similarly opposed her participation in the radical abolitionist movement. In 1840, the Quakers disowned Kelley for her radical activism. Despite the position of the church on her activities, Kelley maintained many Quaker ways of thinking and behaviors.

Kelley followed a standard routine on her speaking tours. She usually went to a place that knew little about antislavery principles. She gave between three and six speeches over the course of a week, leaving only to return a few weeks later to give more lectures. At the conclusion of her lectures, Kelley sold subscriptions to abolitionist newspapers. She found this practice most effective in gaining long-term converts to the movement.

In the early 1840s, Kelley lectured across Ohio, where she met Lucy Stone and persuaded her to become involved in the antislavery movement. Throughout her career with the abolitionist movement, Kelley recruited people, including Susan B. Anthony and Ernestine Rose. She married fellow radical abolitionist lecturer Stephen Foster in 1845 and gave birth to daughter Alla in 1847. Kelley kept her maiden name.

The passage of the Fugitive Slave Law in 1850 gave new strength to the abolitionist movement. As the 1850s progressed and the country grew more sectionalized, antislavery activists became less marginalized, but the formation of the Republican Party again split the abolitionists. Many, such as Garrison, welcomed this mainstream political group. However, more radical abolitionists, led by

Abby Kelley, abolitionist and advocate of women's rights (1810–1887). (Cirker, Hayward and Blanche Cirker, eds., *Dictionary of American Portraits*, 1967)

the Fosters, distrusted the Republicans, complaining that the party was not against slavery as a whole, but merely opposed the *extension* of the institution into the territories.

Kelley did not support the Civil War. She distrusted President Abraham Lincoln, whose stand against slavery she saw as weak. Despite her misgivings about the war, she worked for the National Women's Loyal League, which petitioned Congress to pass the Thirteenth Amendment.

When the Civil War ended, Abby Kelley and her husband helped prevent the disbanding of the American Anti-Slavery Society, using it to help freedmen fight for their civil rights. Although Kelley was a strong advocate for women's rights, ill health prevented her from taking too active a role in this movement.

Ellen H. Todras

See also Abolitionism and Northern Reformers; National Women's Loyal League [Women's National Loyal League]; Northern Women; Quaker Women; Union Homefront.

References and Further Reading

Sterling, Dorothy. 1991. *Ahead of Her Time: Abby Kelley and the Politics of Antislavery.* New York: W. W. Norton & Company.

Venet, Wendy Hamand. 1991. *Neither Ballots Nor Bullets: Women Abolitionists and the Civil War.* Charlottesville: University of Virginia Press.

Kemble (Butler), Frances "Fanny" Anne (1809—1893)

British-born actress and writer Fanny Kemble became an outspoken abolitionist after spending time on her husband's Georgia plantation. She achieved acclaim on the stage in her youth and later as a reader of Shakespeare, and she wrote plays, poetry, and other works. Her published journals of America, particularly her exposé of life under the slavery system, *Journal of a Residence on a Georgian Plantation,* reveal the horrors of life in slavery and offer a window into nineteenth-century life.

Known familiarly as Fanny, she was born on November 27, 1809, into the famous Kemble family of actors; her uncle was John Philip Kemble, the leading authority on Shakespeare, and her aunt, Sarah Siddons, was the greatest actress of her time. Her father, Charles Kemble, himself a talented Shakespearean actor, assumed management of Covent Garden Theatre after John Philip's retirement. Fanny's sister, Adelaide, became an opera star.

The Kemble family was beset by financial difficulties, and creditors took possession of the theater. Fanny, having previously been deemed to have no acting talent, was given a strenuous crash course in the theatrical arts, and she made her debut as Juliet on October 5, 1825. She was a success with both her audience and her critics; the *Times* pronounced her debut the most triumphant they could remember. She was thrust into a whirlwind of performances and social engagements, and, although she enjoyed acting, she grew to hate the publicity the profession entailed.

Fanny's success on the London stage, however, proved to be not enough to rescue the theater, and her father decided to take her on a two-year profes-

Frances Ann Kemble, actress, writer, and abolitionist (1809–1893). (Library of Congress)

sional tour of the United States. Fanny abhorred the idea, calling America a "dreadful" place, but consented to go. The two set sail on August 1, 1832. Fanny became a sensation in America, starting fashion trends, causing mobs at the box office, and attracting the attention of dignitaries. She received an audience with several prominent leaders, including President Andrew Jackson. On the whole, however, Fanny was unimpressed with the young republic, and she kept a journal of her observations, including comments on tobacco spitting and on servants who did not know their place.

Fanny also attracted male admirers, the most persistent of whom was Pierce Butler of Philadelphia. Butler came from a prominent Georgia family who owned two plantations on Butler and St. Simon's Islands, with the second largest slave population in the state. He and his brother (who died in 1848) were set to inherit the estates upon the death of their maiden aunt. Pierce's devoted attentions to Fanny and her family and the promise of a secure and comfortable existence away from the celebrity she despised caused Fanny to fall in love with him.

She married him in Philadelphia on June 7, 1834. The marriage proved to be a prolonged, bitter struggle, with cycles of feuds and reconciliations that ultimately led to heartbreak, divorce, and public scandal. Fanny expected to continue life the way she had lived it, free to attend the theater, participate in intellectual society, and express her views, whereas Pierce and his family expected her to retire into what they believed to be a respectable life of quiet domesticity. Furthermore, each expected the other to come around to his or her own views on slavery.

To provide for her aunt's heirs, Fanny published her American journal against Pierce's express command, because it contained material he thought embarrassing to his family. Her sharp and witty *Journal of America* (1835) outraged national pride and was criticized by both the American and the British press, even as it became an instant best seller. She gave birth to their first child, Sarah, that year, and to their second child, Frances ("Fan"), in 1838.

Kemble was deeply opposed to slavery even before she met Pierce. When he inherited his estates in April of 1836, she pleaded with him to be allowed to accompany him to Georgia, and he consented. Fanny kept a travelogue of this experience from December 1838 to April 1839.

Although she admired the natural beauty of the land, especially on St. Simon's Island, Fanny was shocked by the primitive and poverty-stricken condition of the South, attributing it to the degrading influence of a slave economy. She criticized the aristocracy with its "ignorance," "sensuality," and "cruelty," and she regretted that Southern courtly manners could charm her native countrymen far more than those of the egalitarian Yankees. But the greatest impact of her journal was in her observations of the wretched conditions and miserable complaints of the plantation slaves. She deeply sympathized with them, especially the women, who were put to hard work, violated sexually, and sometimes even beaten while pregnant. Although she was in Georgia for only four months, Fanny established a slave's hospital and nursery, rewarded cleanliness, and paid her personal servants wages. She also carried pleas and complaints to her husband, although he inevitably refused to listen to them.

Back in Philadelphia, Fanny circulated her journal among her abolitionist friends, although Pierce forbade her to so. Butler and even her friends the Sedgwicks treated her as if her mental health was failing.

On December 1, 1840, the couple sailed for London with their children after hearing that Charles Kemble had fallen ill. Fanny's father recovered, but Butler prolonged their stay, wasting money on gambling and extravagances. Kemble found letters in 1843 that contained evidence of Butler's infidelity, and she sought legal counsel. The following March, Butler was challenged to a duel for having an affair with a friend's wife.

Butler presented her with a contract for a formal separation, and Kemble left for England in October of 1845. She once again took up acting when Butler reneged on his promise of support. Learning of her return to the stage, he began divorce proceedings; after two years he could claim desertion on her part.

Kemble found success performing readings of Shakespeare, which she preferred to acting on the stage. Learning of Butler's actions to divorce her, however, she returned to America in September 1848. She bought a house called The Perch, in Lenox, Massachusetts, and toured the country, performing. They were divorced September 22, 1849, with Fanny being allowed to see her children for two months each year, but Butler did not honor his promise of support due to financial difficulties. Fanny had to continue her readings for income, and Butler was forced to sell half of his slaves.

Sarah Butler married Owen Wister in 1859. They had one son, Owen Jr., author of *The Virginian*.

With the coming of the Civil War, Fanny predicted a Union victory and the end of slavery. Her two daughters held opposing views. Sarah was supportive of the Union and against slavery, like her mother, and Fan showed sympathies more aligned with those of her father. During the war, Butler was imprisoned for a time by the Federal government on suspicion of disloyalty, causing the girls much anxiety.

While in England in 1862, Kemble became alarmed at the growing sympathy there for the Confederacy. The Union was facing setbacks on the battlefield, and the blockade was hindering the British textile industry. The prime minister, Henry John Temple, Third Viscount Palmerston, spoke in favor of acknowledging and aiding the South, which would have resulted in war between the United States and Britain. Kemble decided the times required the publication of her Georgian journal, and she published it, braving yet more condemnation and possible estrangement from her daughters, particularly Fan.

How influential the book, published in May 1863, was on British policy has been debated, but after the Union victory at Antietam and the announcement of the Emancipation Proclamation, British popular opinion strongly favored the North, making the government's break from neutrality impossible. Kemble's journal, among other abolitionist works, helped bolster antislavery sentiment from cotton factories to the floor of the House of Commons.

After the war, Butler returned to his lands in Georgia to rebuild his estate, accompanied for a time by his daughter Fan, who wrote a journal of her experiences. Kemble remained in Europe, occasionally visiting the United States and keeping busy during her last decades with her readings, writing memoirs and other works, and receiving illustrious friends, like Henry James. In 1867, Pierce Butler died of malaria. Fan Butler married an Anglican minister, James Leigh, and moved to England with him after they had struggled unsuccessfully to manage the Butler Island plantation. Fanny Kemble lived with them in London until her death on January 15, 1893.

Gabrielle Bruns

See also African American Women; Civilian Life; Diaries and Journals; Domesticity; Plantation Life; Rape; Separate Spheres; Slave Families; Slaveholding Women.

References and Further Reading

Blainey, Ann. 2001. *Fanny and Adelaide.* Chicago: Ivan R. Dee.

Clinton, Catherine. 2000. *Fanny Kemble's Civil Wars.* New York: Simon & Schuster.

Furnas, J. C. 1982. *Fanny Kemble: Leading Lady of the Nineteenth-Century Stage.* New York: Dial Press.

Kemble, Frances Anne. [1863] 1961. *Journal of a Residence on a Georgian Plantation: 1838–1839*, with Introduction by John A. Scott. Athens: University of Georgia Press.

Simmons, James C. 2000. *Star Spangled Eden.* New York: Carroll and Graf Publishers.

Knapp, Frederick Newman (1821–1889)

Frederick Newman Knapp was a Harvard-trained Unitarian minister and an important member of the United States Sanitary Commission (USSC). Noted for his tact, thoroughness, and sensitivity, Knapp worked to help organize and maintain the USSC, provided immediate care for soldiers of the Union armies, and bridged the gap between commission officials and the women who supplied needed materials and money.

Knapp supervised the Department of Special Relief. He cared for discharged soldiers traveling to their homes and supervised special homes opened up to care for such men. He helped inspect hospitals, observed the operation of the military medical department, and wrote detailed reports about the care of the men by the armies and by the USSC and other civilian workers. Because of his work, he became known as one of the best men in the country for handling emergencies. Along with his other duties, Knapp attended leadership committee meetings held in Washington every six weeks.

As a director, Knapp was also actively involved in carrying many of the commission's plans into action. Because of his responsibilities as commissioner of special relief, he rushed into the field when a battle was reported and, with his team of aid, provided immediate care for the soldiers, a practice started after the first battle at Bull Run. His messages from that battle were among the first to indicate the shocking lack of care for the wounded. The reports he composed following the action included critiques of the medical system, the military, facilities, and supply systems—both civilian and military. His careful, professional notations helped motivate the important work of the commission and convinced commission leaders to begin the operation of hospital ships.

Knapp's inspection tours included careful interrogation of the people he met. He was particularly careful to speak with the women of the aid societies and to maintain correspondence with them. Unlike many of the commission's officials, Knapp had a deep respect for their work and included praise for women's efforts in his reports.

His observations of soldiers in transit motivated him to try to change the kinds of care veterans received. Knapp became convinced that large numbers of discharged and unemployed soldiers posed a threat to middle-class society. He advocated that the commission support and enlarge on the work of local aid societies like those of Milwaukee, Wisconsin, which had created refuges for soldiers making their way home. In that way, the men could slowly re-enter civilian life. The commission failed to embrace the idea, and Knapp found the last months of his service with the group filled with conflict because of his convictions.

Following the war, Knapp undertook a number of ventures. He opened several short-lived schools for boys. He also tried his hand as a cranberry farmer. Knapp died suddenly in 1889.

Karen A. Kehoe

See also Aid Societies; Northern Women; Nurses; United States Sanitary Commission.

References and Further Reading

Maxwell, William Quentin. 1956. *Lincoln's Fifth Wheel: The Political History of the United States Sanitary Commission.* New York: Longmans, Green & Company.

Jeanie Attie. 1998. *Patriotic Toil: Northern Women and the American Civil War.* Ithaca, NY: Cornell University Press.

L

Ladies' Memorial Associations

At the end of the Civil War, Southern women who had been active in wartime soldiers' aid societies found a new purpose—memorializing the Confederate dead. In communities across the South, they formed ladies' memorial associations whose activities consumed the lives of elite Southern white women in the decades immediately following the war. No longer caring for the needs of the living, these memorial associations took responsibility for the fallen—removing the dead from battlefields, burying them in designated Confederate cemeteries, and erecting monuments to the dead in the same cemeteries. Most important, ladies' memorial associations were responsible for the springtime ritual of decorating the graves with flowers and Confederate flags on what eventually became known as Memorial Day.

In many ways, women's wartime experiences had prepared them to assume their postwar memorialization tasks. Confederate women's experience as nurses, laborers in munitions factories, and members of soldiers' aid societies gave them the necessary skills and confidence to meet the social and cultural needs of the region in the aftermath of defeat. Furthermore, memorializing Confederate men did not threaten prescribed gender patterns and was generally accepted as an extension of women's domestic role as caretakers. Their memorial activities enabled elite Southern women to play a significant role in the creation of the New South. They became influential public figures, but under the guise of preserving the integrity and honor of their men.

Carrie Hale, a member of the memorial association in Fayetteville, North Carolina, offered a recollection of women's activities in her hometown. The activities she detailed mirror those that took place elsewhere in the South. She described how the women of Fayetteville recovered the remains of local soldiers killed in battle, reinterred their bodies in the local cemetery, and then built a monument to these men and other Confederate soldiers.

The first Confederate holiday established in the South was Memorial Day, also referred to as Decoration Day, the term more generally applied to the same commemoration in the North. Memorial Day was an outgrowth of the activities of ladies' memorial associations that emerged in the region immediately after the Civil War. Many communities lay claim to being the first to have begun Confederate Memorial Day, making it clear that the ritual developed simultaneously in several places throughout the South, as memorial associations emerged in various communities. More significant, however, is how the holiday developed, what rituals were observed, and what differentiated the South's Memorial Day from the North's Decoration Day

It was important to white Southerners that the South received credit for the national celebration. Articles in the *Confederate Veteran*, the official organ of Southern heritage organizations like the United Confederate Veterans and the United Daughters of the Confederacy, went to great pains to document the development of Memorial Day, explaining that it was only after General John A. Logan of the Grand Army of the Republic (GAR) witnessed Southern women in Richmond and its environs decorating the graves of Confederate soldiers that the idea of a national holiday emerged.

Having witnessed how the South honored its dead, Logan, also a congressman from Illinois, proposed the resolution to make May 30 Memorial Day for decorating the graves of the Civil War dead. That resolution, which passed on May 5, 1868, established Memorial Day to specifically honor Union war dead. Known as Decoration Day, it marked a divergence from Confederate Memorial Day, and the two evolved along different trajectories.

Rhetorically, the day was intended as a point of sectional reconciliation to honor all the dead. However, separate commemorations offered proof that white Southerners were unwilling to relinquish or compromise their belief that they originated the holiday. Although Northerners and Southerners celebrated differently and often on different days, both sections agreed that Memorial Day was a holiday to honor the common soldier.

Although May 30 was commemorated as Memorial Day in the North, Southerners observed memorial days on different days from state to state. The varying dates depended partially on when each state's flowers were in bloom, but also on the days an individual state imbued with significance. The two most common dates were April 26 and May 10, the day of Joseph E. Johnston's surrender and the anniversary of Stonewall Jackson's death, respectively. June 3 was chosen as Memorial Day in Louisiana in honor of Jefferson Davis's birthday.

Ladies' memorial associations remained active in the South through the early twentieth century. In 1900, they were organized into one overall organization known as the Confederated Southern Memorial Association (CSMA), headed by Katie Behan of New Orleans, Louisiana. Under the CSMA, women's memorial work continued but quickly became obsolete as the last of Confederate veterans died and new generations of women, with no personal attachment to the war, lost interest in the activity. Moreover, the United Daughters of the Confederacy (UDC), founded in 1894, superseded the organization in influence.

Karen L. Cox

See also Monuments; Southern Women; United Daughters of the Confederacy.

References and Further Reading

Cox, Karen L. 2003. *Dixie's Daughters: The United Daughters of the Confederacy and the Preservation of Confederate Culture.* Gainesville: University Press of Florida.

Whites, LeeAnn. 1995. *The Civil War as a Crisis in Gender, Augusta, Georgia, 1860–1890.* Athens: University of Georgia Press.

Larcom, Lucy (1824–1893)

Though much of the poetry written during the American Civil War focused on military subjects, Lucy Larcom explored civil matters and patriotism on the homefront in her work. In her writing, Larcom's doubts about the war and slavery surfaced. She believed that both went against God's wishes.

Lucy was born in Beverly, Massachusetts, on March 5, 1824, to Lois Barrett and Benjamin Larcom, a sea captain turned shopkeeper. The ninth of ten children from her father's two marriages, Lucy primarily entertained herself by reading and exploring the outdoors. One of her aunts taught her to read when she was two years old. She could read on her own by the time she was three, and she wrote her first poem when she was eight.

After her father's 1835 death, the family moved to Lowell, Massachusetts. There her mother ran a boarding house for the town's mill workers. Eventually, Lucy joined her sisters working in the mills as a doffer. When Lucy was thirteen, her mother made her quit school to work full-time in the mills, where she worked until she turned twenty-one.

Her early poems were published in *The Lowell Offering*, a magazine published by the mill girls. The magazine was one of the few that women controlled and contributed to. After leaving the mills, Larcom taught for many years before turning her full attention to a literary career.

Larcom found that the outbreak of war intensified her feelings for the United States and its flag. In addition, the war deepened Larcom's apprecia-

Lucy Larcom was a nineteenth-century poet, teacher, and editor who wrote about her experiences in the Lowell mills. (Cirker, Hayward and Blanche Cirker, eds., *Dictionary of American Portraits*, 1967)

tion of everyday beauty and her connections to family and friends. In October 1861, she knit socks for soldiers and sewed quilts for hospitals, but she expressed that she felt more like a looker-on and wanted to give more. Throughout the war, Larcom felt that patriotism united everyone.

During the Civil War, several of Larcom's poems appeared in *The Atlantic Monthly:* "The Rose Enthroned," "Waiting for the News," and "A Loyal Woman's No." Her poetry during this period reflects her patriotism, her sentimentalism, and her impulse to make sense of the war. In "A Loyal Woman's No," published in December 1863, Larcom countered a distant beau's pro-South sentiment, thus making her personal beliefs known in a public forum. Toward the end of the war, she edited a children's periodical, *Our Young Folks: An Illustrated Magazine for Boys and Girls.*

Her most important work was not poetry but her memoir, published in 1889, *A New England Girl-*

hood. Her description of working in the Lowell mills captured important facets of everyday life of the period. Larcom died in Boston on April 17, 1893, and was buried in Beverly, Massachusetts.

Rebecca Tolley-Stokes

See also Abolitionism and Northern Reformers; Education, Northern; Factory Workers, Northern; Northern Women; Poets, Northern; Sewing Bees; Teachers, Northern; Union Homefront; Wartime Literature.

References and Further Reading

Marchalonis, Shirley. 1988. "Lucy Larcom." *Legacy: A Journal of American Women Writers* 5 (1): 45–52.

Marchalonis, Shirley. 1989. *Worlds of Lucy Larcom, 1842–1893.* Athens: University of Georgia Press.

LeConte, Emma Florence (1847–1932)

Diarist Emma Florence LeConte spent the Civil War in Columbia, South Carolina, where she experienced firsthand the shortages and hardships of wartime, as well as General William T. Sherman's campaign in the Carolinas. Emma's diary reveals her constant dedication to the Confederacy and to the ideals of the Old South despite repeated military defeats and the Union invasion of the homefront.

The eldest child of Caroline Elizabeth "Bessie" Nisbet and prominent scientist Joseph LeConte, Emma was born in Athens, Georgia, during her father's tenure on the faculty of the University of Georgia. The LeContes left Athens in 1856 when Joseph took a job at South Carolina College, now the University of South Carolina, in Columbia. There, the family grew with the births of three more daughters, one who died in childhood. A son joined the family in 1870. Emma grew up surrounded by the luxuries common to planter-class families.

Emma became her father's constant companion and student. The rigorous curriculum he designed for Emma included the study of Latin, Greek, French, German, modern languages, and mathematics. Although Emma sometimes attended school, she received most of her education at home through her father's tutoring.

Like those of other Southerners, the LeContes's lives were turned upside down by the Civil War.

Joseph left Columbia and the college, which closed during wartime, to help the Confederacy. He produced medicines and worked at the niter works. As did most women, seventeen-year-old Emma remained at home with her mother and sisters. She spent her time sewing and otherwise helping Confederate soldiers, reading, worrying about her father and other family members, visiting friends and family, and dealing with wartime shortages and realities.

Emma's brief but descriptive journal illuminates homefront life in South Carolina's capital between December 31, 1864, and August 6, 1865. Throughout her journal, Emma reaffirmed her loyalty to the Confederacy and her confidence in its ultimate success. She, like many other elite white women, spent the war making items for Confederate soldiers and sacrificing luxuries for the cause. She celebrated U.S. President Abraham Lincoln's assassination and despaired at news of Confederate President Jefferson Davis's capture. She also continued to uphold the tenets of slavery.

In particular, Emma's journal offers insight into Southern women's reactions to Sherman's March. As Union soldiers marched out of Georgia after their capture of Savannah, Emma and other South Carolinians correctly assumed that they were headed toward their state. Despite her fear of Union soldiers, Emma remained at her home on the college campus and continued her studies and wartime work. She even attended the city's bazaar to raise funds for Confederate soldiers as Sherman's troops neared the state. She described in detail the evacuation of much of the city as the enemy approached, the preparations for the arrival of Sherman's troops, their invasion of the city, and the desolation the enemy soldiers left behind.

The end of the war and of the South's bid for independence left Emma depressed but determined. She resumed her studies and attended local dances with the returned soldiers. In 1869, Emma married Confederate veteran and fellow Georgian Farish Carter Furman. The couple moved to the Furman farm near Milledgeville, Georgia. After the birth of stillborn twins, Emma gave birth to two daughters, Katherine Carter (1872) and Elizabeth Nisbet (1874). Emma sorely missed her father, who had moved with the rest of the family to Berkeley, California, in 1869.

Emma ran the farm after Farish's 1883 death from malaria. She also took over the education of their daughters. After the turn of the century, she moved to Macon, Georgia, to live with her youngest daughter, Elizabeth, and her son-in-law, Nicholas Talley. During World War I, Emma began another diary, once again recording her observations on military events and the homefront. As she had done during the Civil War, during this war Emma worked with women's aid societies to help the soldiers. Her diary also discusses her involvement in the suffrage movement and her work in a school for African American children.

Emma LeConte Furman died in 1932.

Lisa Tendrich Frank

See also Civilian Life; Columbia Bazaar (January 17–21, 1865); Confederate Homefront; Diaries and Journals; Fairs and Bazaars; Girlhood and Adolescence; Military Invasion and Occupation; Morale; Sherman's Campaign (1864–1865); Shortages; Southern Women.

References and Further Reading

LeConte, Emma. 1987. *When the World Ended: The Diary of Emma LeConte*, edited by Earl Schenck Meirs, with Foreword by Anne Firor Scott. Lincoln: University of Nebraska Press.

Lee, Elizabeth "Lizzie" Blair (1818–1906)

A daughter of the politically prominent Blair family and the wife of Rear Admiral Samuel Phillips Lee, Elizabeth Blair Lee is primarily remembered for her correspondence, rich in historical value. She knew many prominent figures of the Civil War era, and her hundreds of private letters provide a civilian insider's view of affairs in Washington during these times.

Elizabeth was born in Frankfort, Kentucky, on June 20, 1818, the daughter of Eliza and Francis Preston Blair, a member of Andrew Jackson's kitchen cabinet, editor of the Democratic *Washington Globe*, and a founding member of the Republican Party. In her youth she transcribed documents for both Jackson and her father. Her father remained a powerful figure in Washington; her older brother Montgomery served as postmaster general to Abraham Lincoln and her younger brother Frank became a Missouri congressman, major general, and senator. The Blairs had two homes: a farm six miles from Washington called Silver Spring and a house on Pennsylvania Avenue across from the White House.

On April 27, 1843, against her parents' wishes, Lizzie Blair married Samuel Phillips Lee, a young naval lieutenant. Lee was third cousin to Robert E. Lee, albeit from a less privileged branch of the family. The couple faced initial opposition, but eventually his wife's family embraced Lee, with Preston Blair working with his daughter to secure promotions for Lee while he served.

The couple promised to write one another every day while Lee was at sea, and his wife remained faithful to her promise, often writing her letters in journal style, with dated segments. While her husband was on duty, Lizzie lived with her parents, and many military and political officials frequented both her parents' home and her own. She reported the news to her husband, often with her own analyses. Presumably due to loneliness and boredom while Phil was away, she worked at the Washington City Orphan Asylum, joining its board in 1849. On August 9, 1857, their first and only child was born, Francis Preston Blair Lee.

Lizzie continued to write to her husband during the Civil War, while he fought for the Union. He commanded the North Atlantic Squadron and the Mississippi Squadron, and he was promoted to rear admiral after the war. Her letters to him contained, along with more domestic news of their son, items such as news about the Battle of Bull Run, thirty miles away, and about fleeing Washington for a time for safety. She also wrote of her family's clash with the Frémonts and the struggle in the Republican Party as it grew more radical.

Elizabeth Blair Lee died on September 13, 1906.

Gabrielle Bruns

See also Bull Run/Manassas, First Battle of (July 21, 1861); Letter Writing; Northern Women; Politics; Union Homefront.

References and Further Reading

Laas, Virginia Jeans, ed. 1991. *Wartime Washington: The Civil War Letters of Elizabeth Blair Lee.* Urbana: University of Illinois Press.

Laas, Virginia Jeans. 2001. "'A Good Wife, the Best Friend in the World': The Marriage of Elizabeth Blair and S. Phillips Lee." In *Intimate Strategies of the Civil War: Military Commanders and Their Wives,* edited by Carol K. Bleser and Lesley J. Gordon, 225–242. New York: Oxford University Press.

Lee, Mary Anna Randolph Custis (1808–1873)

A member of the Virginia aristocracy, Mary Custis Lee was the wife of Confederate General Robert E. Lee. During the Civil War, she suffered the loss of family members as well as her beloved home, Arlington. A staunch supporter of the Southern cause, she was considered the model Confederate woman for her unwavering faith in military victory as well as for her tireless work on behalf of the army. In spite of her own poor health, she devoted herself to nursing gravely ill relatives during the conflict. After the war, Mary Lee was a vocal advocate of Lost Cause ideology.

Mary Anna Randolph Custis was the daughter of Mary Lee Fitzhugh and George Washington Parke Custis and a great-granddaughter of Martha Washington. Her father, the grandson of Martha and her first husband, had been raised by the Washingtons. George Custis built Arlington House to serve as an early American memorial to President Washington. Mary inherited from her father her devotion to country, love of history, and reverence for her Washington ancestry. Her mother instilled in her a deep religious faith, a dedication to family, and her conviction that the Arlington slaves should receive a rudimentary education and eventual emancipation.

In 1831, Mary Custis and Lieutenant Robert E. Lee were married at Arlington House. For the next thirty years the couple divided their time between Arlington and Lee's duty stations. Between 1832 and 1846, Mary gave birth to seven children, all of whom survived childhood. When Robert traveled to remote locations, Mary and the children often remained at home with her parents. Following her parents' deaths, Mary inherited Arlington.

As the Civil War approached, Mary viewed the political crisis with despair. She initially criticized secession and even expressed her willingness to lay

Mary Custis Lee, wife of General Robert E. Lee and staunch Confederate (1808–1873). (Library of Congress)

down her own life to preserve the Union. After Virginia seceded in April 1861, Robert resigned from the United States Army and soon became a Confederate officer. His decision would ultimately cost Mary her home. In May she reluctantly abandoned Arlington.

The war exacted a heavy toll from Mary Lee. In 1862, her two infant grandchildren died and her daughter Annie succumbed to typhoid fever. Despite devoted nursing on her part, Mary suffered the loss of her daughter-in-law after a period of illness. In 1863, her cousin was executed as a Confederate spy. Throughout the war she rose above her personal tragedies. Her faith in the Confederate cause strengthened morale in Richmond, and she was highly esteemed for her production of immense amounts of clothing for the army's soldiers.

While religious faith enabled Mary Lee to accept the deaths of loved ones, nothing reconciled her to the loss of Arlington. The Federal army had occupied her estate in 1861. Unable to comply with a wartime practice that required the personal payment of property taxes in insurrectionary districts,

Mary saw her property confiscated by the government. In 1864, it was converted to a national cemetery for Union war dead. Mary viewed this use of Arlington as the ultimate desecration of her home. The demise of Arlington was the one wartime loss from which she never recovered.

In 1865, the Lees moved to Lexington, Virginia, where Robert became president of Washington College. Mary led an isolated existence, confined to a wheelchair by rheumatoid arthritis. She spent her time fundraising for the local Episcopal Church and publishing a new edition of her father's memoirs. She remained a staunch advocate of the Lost Cause. After Robert's death in 1870, Mary became her husband's chief defender. She played a crucial role in Lee's apotheosis through her collaboration with his biographers.

In her final years, Mary found happiness in her grandchildren and church work, but the loss of Arlington remained her greatest torment. In 1873, she returned to her former home. The acres of graves and the absence of everything familiar underscored that the home she loved was gone forever. In her last months, Mary's anguish over Arlington increased. Her grief affected her mind, and she imagined herself back there with her young children. Mary Custis Lee died on November 5, 1873. Although overshadowed by her illustrious husband, she remains a seminal figure of the American Civil War.

Karen Kinzey

See also Confederate Homefront; Lee, Robert Edward (1807–1870); Southern Women.
References and Further Reading
MacDonald, Rose. 1939. *Mrs. Robert E. Lee.* Boston: Ginn & Company.
Perry, John. *The Lady of Arlington: The Life of Mrs. Robert E. Lee.* 2001. Sisters, OR: Multnomah Publishers.

Lee, Mary Greenhow (1819–1907)
Mary Greenhow Lee was an avowed Confederate sympathizer in battle-torn Winchester, Virginia. Her actions aiding Southerners and Southern armies led to banishment from her home by the Union army, a rare punishment for an elite woman during the Civil War.

Mary Greenhow was born to a prominent Richmond family in 1819 and solidified her class status by marrying Hugh Holmes Lee in 1843 and moving to his home in Winchester. After her husband died in 1856, Lee continued to live in Winchester with her two sisters-in-law, two nieces, two nephews, and five slaves. At the onset of war her nephews joined the Confederate army, leaving only women in the Lee household.

Near the border of Maryland, Winchester's transportation network made it highly desirable to both armies. Over the course of the war, six battles took place nearby. In addition, the town changed hands thirteen times and served as headquarters to one occupying army or the other for most of the war. Because of the constancy of the war in these townspeople's lives, Winchester's men were as likely to join one army as the other. Because the remaining men of conscription age were arrested by the Federal Army during one of its occupations in 1862, Lee's household was not unique in being female-only.

Living in a battle zone led to opportunities for Winchester's women to engage in activities that would strengthen their own army and weaken the enemy's. While many in the town were pro-Union, Lee's extended family had vociferously supported secession from the beginning, and her sister-in-law, Rose O'Neal Greenhow, would become one of the most famous Confederate spies in Washington, D.C. By the first year of the war, Lee had clearly dedicated herself to doing whatever she could to support the Confederate cause. Thus, when Southern forces held the town, Lee opened her home to the officers, provided food and supplies to the soldiers, and assisted in caring for the wounded. When Union forces occupied Winchester, Lee hid food to keep the enemy from appropriating it. She also took advantage of Union occupations to buy or steal as much food and provisions as possible to smuggle to or to save for Confederate soldiers. She refused to house Union soldiers or officers, and, when forced to do so, she treated them with as much disrespect as possible. Her house served as a Confederate information headquarters, and she was able to pass on much valuable information, gathered by shrewd observation, to the Confederate armies, including troop strength and movements. Additionally, she ran an illegal underground Confederate postal service.

However, not until the final Union occupation of Winchester in 1865 did Major General Philip H. Sheridan take action to stop Lee's activities by banishing all the white women in the Lee home. Despite the myriad of seriously treasonous activities she had participated in, Lee was convinced that the primary reason for her banishment was her refusal to interact socially with Union officers. Her last act of preserving her power as a Southern lady had been to snub Northern gentlemen, whom she felt were beneath her.

In the course of her banishment Lee traveled to Staunton and Richmond, still collecting and delivering information to the Confederate armies to the utter frustration of Union forces. After the Civil War, Lee bought and ran a series of boardinghouses in Baltimore, Maryland. Although some of her family from Winchester stayed with her for a time, she lived out the latter part of her life primarily with boarders. In 1895, she became a charter member of the Baltimore chapter of the United Daughters of the Confederacy and served as secretary of the organization in 1896. A secessionist until her death, Mary Greenhow Lee died in Baltimore in 1907, finally returning to Winchester for the first time since her banishment to be buried next to her husband.

Angela Boswell

See also Greenhow, Rose O'Neal (ca. 1814–1864); Sheridan, Philip Henry (1831–1888); Southern Women; United Daughters of the Confederacy.

References and Further Reading

Delauter Jr., Roger U. 1992. *Winchester in the Civil War.* Lynchburg, VA: H. E. Howard.

Faust, Drew Gilpin. 1996. *Mothers of Invention: Women of the Slaveholding South in the American Civil War.* Chapel Hill: University of North Carolina Press.

Odendahl, Laura. 2003. "A History of Captivity and a History of Freedom." In *Searching for Their Places: Women in the South across Four Centuries,* edited by Thomas H. Appleton Jr. and Angela Boswell, 122–143. Columbia: University of Missouri Press.

Phipps, Sheila R. 2004. *Genteel Rebel: The Life of Mary Greenhow Lee*. Baton Rouge: Louisiana State University Press.

Lee, Robert Edward (1807–1870)

Robert E. Lee commanded the Army of Northern Virginia and became the most renowned Confederate general. Although the general of a defeated nation, Lee remains one of the most venerated of Civil War figures.

Born into a prominent Virginia family, Robert entered West Point in 1825 and graduated with an impressive record as a cadet. He joined the elite Corps of Engineers and saw considerable action during the Mexican War. By 1861 he was seen as one of the most capable and respected officers in the United States Army. The firing on Fort Sumter, Lincoln's call for volunteers to suppress the rebellion, and Virginia's subsequent secession led him to resign his commission and offer his services in the defense of Virginia and the Confederacy.

By the spring of 1862, Lee took command of what would soon be known as the Army of Northern Virginia. Lee and his soldiers dominated the Virginia theater of operations well into 1864, despite setbacks like the loss at Gettysburg in July 1863. In the end, Lee's army was beaten at Petersburg, and he surrendered his command to Ulysses S. Grant at Appomattox Court House in April 1865.

Women always played a very important role in Lee's life. His mother, Anne Hill Carter, had a major impact on his emotional development in his pre–West Point years. In 1831, he married Mary A. R. Custis, a descendant of George Washington. From his wife he gained an elevated status in Virginia society as well as the considerable Custis estate, which included the Arlington plantation and its slaves. The Lees had four daughters, who competed with their brothers for an often absent father's attention and love. None of Lee's daughters ever married, and the speculation is that they did not because no potential husbands could ever measure up their legendary father.

Lee enjoyed the company of women and kept up a considerable correspondence with female friends

Confederate General Robert E. Lee, pictured here shortly after the surrender at Appomattox Courthouse in Virginia on April 9, 1865. (National Archives and Records Administration)

and family members during his life. His popularity as a Confederate hero attracted a legion of female admirers. Although never totally comfortable with being a celebrity, Lee enjoyed the attention given to him by Southern, and sometimes Northern, ladies. After his death, this veneration increased as organizations like the United Daughters of the Confederacy worked tirelessly to memorialize Lee. Such activities continued well into the twentieth century and are a major part of the mythology of the Lost Cause.

Robert E. Lee spent his last years as the president of Washington College. His reputation as a soldier, gentleman, and Southerner continued to grow after his death in 1870.

Robert A. Taylor

See also Lee, Mary Anne Randolph Custis (1808–1873); Monuments; United Daughters of the Confederacy.

References and Further Reading
Connelly, Thomas L. 1977. *The Marble Man: Robert E. Lee and His Image in American Society.* New York: Alfred A. Knopf.
Coulling, Mary P. 1987. *The Lee Girls.* Winston-Salem, MA: John F. Blair.
Fellman, Michael. 2000. *The Making of Robert E. Lee.* New York: Random House.
Thomas, Emory M. 1995. *Robert E. Lee.* New York: Random House.

Letter Writing

Widespread literacy and a well-established postal system ensured that letters played an integral part in the Civil War in both the North and the South. Women were deeply involved in all aspects of wartime correspondence: as recipients of letters from soldiers in the field; as amanuenses in war hospitals and prisons for those who could not write; and as writers of letters that serve as a record of their own activities as participants in a country at war.

Despite paper shortages and the cost of postage, millions of letters were exchanged during the Civil War. More than a billion 3¢ stamps were produced, and most were used. By 1860 there were 28,498 postal stations in the United States. Although more than one hundred thousand pieces of mail were not delivered to the South by the U.S. Post Office following secession, one of the first acts of the Confederate States of America was the establishment on February 21, 1861, of the Post Office Department of the Confederate States of America, under the administration of a former United States congressman, John Henniger Reagan. Northern blockades, difficulties in obtaining stamps, and severe paper shortages, which forced individuals to use everything from ledger paper to wallpaper as stationery, impeded letter writing in the South but never ended it.

Mothers, wives, sisters, and sweethearts were frequent recipients of combatants' letters. Often these letters were part of a true dialogue, in which letters served to develop new relationships and maintain existing ones. Sometimes, however, the women addressed in soldiers' letters seem less important individually than as a way for a soldier to focus on more personal, nearly private, reportage and reflection. Similarly, in their responses and in the letters they originated, women wrote not only to share news but also to create a kind of journal or diary, exploring their feelings and the changes in their lives.

Women volunteering in war hospitals and visiting prisons often served a secretarial function, ensuring that those who were ill or wounded had the necessary materials and help for writing letters. Women serving as nurses, as well as those who wanted to help but had not yet developed nursing skills, were expected to take dictation from those who, because of illness, injury, or illiteracy, could not write themselves. It is not always possible to know how authentic these letters are and how often the women who served as amanuenses polished and added to the words of those for whom they wrote.

Finally, women were active initiators of correspondence. Those at home wrote of their fears and of their pride in their new accomplishments. Those in the field wrote their own accounts of the war, often with an eye to eventual publication. Louisa May Alcott's first book, *Hospital Sketches*, was assembled from her letters home while she nursed the wounded. She was not unusual in planning on the publication of her letters. In the years that followed the Civil War, nurses, spies, and other women used their letters to create reminiscences and histories of the war.

JoAnn E. Castagna

See also Alcott, Louisa May (1832–1888); Wartime Literature.

References and Further Reading
Decker, William Merrill. 1998. *Epistolary Practices: Letter Writing in America before Telecommunications.* Chapel Hill: University of North Carolina Press.
Nelson, Michael C. 1997. "Writing during Wartime: Gender and Literacy in the American Civil War." *Journal of American Studies* 31 (1): 43–68.

Lewis, Edmonia (ca. 1843–ca. after 1909)

African American and Native American sculptor Edmonia Lewis's depictions of historical and literary figures received international attention. Many of her subjects, like Robert Gould Shaw and John Brown, played prominent roles in the Civil War.

Born Mary Edmonia Lewis near Albany, New York, the exact dates of the artist's birth and death, as well as her parentage, are unknown. Lewis claimed that her mother was African American and Chippewa. Her father, Samuel Lewis, was a freed slave who worked as a valet. After her mother's death in 1844, Edmonia lived with her father until he died in 1847. Her brother, Samuel, who prospered during the California gold rush, sent Edmonia to New York Central College at McGrawville. In 1859, she attended the Ladies' Preparatory Division at Oberlin College in Ohio, which featured strong abolitionist activity.

After studying drawing and other subjects, Lewis decided to become a sculptor. In 1862, while still in Ohio, she was accused of poisoning the drinks of Maria Miles and Christina Ennes, two young white women at the college with whom she was friends. A white mob dragged Edmonia into the streets where she was harshly beaten. African American attorney John Mercer Langston represented Edmonia in court and she was acquitted of all charges.

Her brother Samuel encouraged her to move to Boston, where William Lloyd Garrison introduced Edmonia to local sculptors. Lewis studied with Edward A. Brackett and became friends with Lydia Maria Child, a novelist, activist, and friend of Garrison's. In early 1864, Lewis produced a medallion featuring the head of abolitionist John Brown. Lewis funded a trip to Europe for the next year with the proceeds she earned from selling the medallion, along with one hundred copies of a bust she made of Colonel Robert Gould Shaw, Bostonian leader of the Fifty-fourth Massachusetts, the first all–African American regiment.

Lewis joined the expatriate British and American artist community in Italy that included Anne Whitney, Harriet Hosmer, and Charlotte Cushman. Instead of hiring Italian stoneworkers to transfer her plaster carvings into marble, Lewis carved her own marble to dispel any rumors that she was a fraud. Her heroic figures, which blended neoclassicism with realism and naturalism, were in high demand. As a result, her studio became a trendy stop on many

Americans' grand tour of Europe. Her work based on Biblical scriptures was popular, but Lewis also depicted scenes and personages from Greek and Roman mythology. However, her most powerful pieces were drawn from her heritage: themes of slavery and emancipation, as well as Native America.

Lewis received national acclaim for "The Death of Cleopatra," which was unveiled at the Philadelphia Centennial Exposition in 1876. For most of her life, Lewis lived in Rome, returning to the United States for visits when her sculptures were shown. The last year that anyone saw Lewis alive was 1909. The circumstances of her death are unknown, and her body was never found.

Rebecca Tolley-Stokes

See also African American Women; Child, Lydia Maria Francis (1802–1880); Education, Northern; Free Blacks; Native American Women.
References and Further Reading
Richardson, Marilyn. 1995. "Edmonia Lewis's 'The Death of Cleopatra.'" *The International Review of African American Art* 12 (2): 36–52.

Lincoln, Abraham (1809–1865)

Abraham Lincoln served as president of the United States during the Civil War. His administration resulted in the preservation of the Union and the emancipation of slaves.

Born in Kentucky, Lincoln lived there and in Indiana before finally settling on the Illinois frontier. He slowly rose above his hardscrabble beginnings, serving as a soldier in the Black Hawk War and becoming a successful attorney, despite almost no formal education. His legal career soon led him into politics. Lincoln was elected to the Illinois state legislature in 1834. He won a term in the U.S. House of Representatives 1847 as a Whig. His opposition to the war with Mexico cost him re-election. However, by 1854 Lincoln re-entered politics in the wake of the controversial Kansas-Nebraska Act, casting his lot with the new Republican Party. After losing an 1858 U.S. Senate seat to Stephen A. Douglas, Lincoln became a leading contender for his party's 1860 presidential nomination. Lincoln won the election with less than 40

Abraham Lincoln served as president of the United States during the turbulent years of the American Civil War. Lincoln's crucial role in abolishing slavery in the U.S. in 1863 has earned him the informal title of the Great Emancipator. (Library of Congress)

percent of the popular vote. His election fueled sectional tensions that resulted in the ultimate secession of eleven slaveholding states.

President Lincoln faced the daunting challenge of putting down the rebellion of Southern states and restoring the Union. He had to contend not only with determined Confederates on the battlefields, but also with Northern homefront opposition to many of his policies. He skillfully built an administration that he guided to accomplish his primary war goal: saving the Union. When Lincoln issued the Emancipation Proclamation on January 1, 1863, he added another war aim: the end of slavery. This document effectively ended any real chance of European intervention on the Confederate side and led the way to Union recruitment of African American soldiers. Throughout the war, Lincoln found himself physically and mentally taxed by the tasks of keeping the Union armies fighting. He persevered and won a second term in 1864. A visibly exhausted Lincoln had plans for reconstructing the nation, but fell to assassin John Wilkes Booth's bullet in April 1865 as the war ground to a halt.

Lincoln was never truly comfortable in the company of women, though at times he felt particularly close to his stepmother. He always preferred the sort of rough male society he knew from his days in Illinois, and he had few serious female relationships. In 1842, he married the well-to-do Mary Todd after a stormy courtship. Their marriage was at times rocky, but it endured. The Lincolns suffered through the deaths of a child, relatives, and friends as the Civil War swirled around them. The president often helped his grieving wife in her attempts to use spiritualists to contact the deceased. To calm Mary's fear of losing another child, he refused their oldest son Robert's pleas to be allowed to enlist until the war was all but over.

Lincoln was sensitive to the special agony that mothers faced during wartime. Their petitions to the president often resulted in discharges or the commutation of death sentences for sons charged with crimes like desertion or sleeping on guard duty.

Female guests were common in the Lincoln White House, but not all such visits were cordial. Jessie Frémont, wife of explorer and Union General John Frémont, came to see Lincoln in 1861 to defend her husband's activities in Missouri. After a stormy discussion, the president dismissed her with a curt comment. Lincoln's meetings with women like antislavery activists Harriet Beecher Stowe and Sojourner Truth went much better. Lincoln realized the importance of women to the Northern war effort and to his larger goal of restoring the nation. He highly praised women's efforts in his address to the Washington Sanitary Fair in 1864.

Abraham Lincoln died on April 15, 1865, from a close-range gunshot wound. The first president to be assassinated, his death shocked the nation. Millions of Americans, male and female, turned out to mourn their slain leader.

Robert A. Taylor

See also Election of 1860; Election of 1864; Emancipation Proclamation (January 1, 1863); Family Life, Union; Frémont, Jessie Benton (1824–1902); Lincoln, Mary Todd (1818–1882);

Politics; Secession; Stowe, Harriet Elizabeth Beecher (1811–1896); Truth, Sojourner [Isabella Baumfree] (1797–1883); Union Homefront.

References and Further Reading

Baker, Jean H. 1987. *Mary Todd Lincoln: A Biography.* New York: W. W. Norton & Company.

Burlingame, Michael. 1994. *The Inner World of Abraham Lincoln.* Urbana: University of Illinois Press.

Davis, William C. 1999. *Lincoln's Men: How President Lincoln Became Father to an Army and a Nation.* New York: Free Press.

Donald, David Herbert. 1995. *Lincoln.* New York: Simon & Schuster.

Oates, Stephen B. 1977. *With Malice toward None: The Life of Abraham Lincoln.* New York: Harper & Row.

Mary Todd Lincoln, First Lady of the United States and wife of President Abraham Lincoln. (Library of Congress)

Lincoln, Mary Todd (1818–1882)

The wife of President Abraham Lincoln and the Union's first lady during the Civil War, Mary Todd Lincoln was a devoted politician's wife, supporting and encouraging her husband's political ambitions and reveling in the status that her husband's presidential success brought to her. Charming, ambitious, outspoken, and often controversial, Mary's life was one of extreme joys and sorrows. As one of the most socially and politically active first ladies of the nineteenth century, controversy and conflict often surrounded her. Sorrows came with the loss of those nearest to her, especially with the assassination of her husband and the deaths of three of her sons.

Mary Todd was born in December 1818, in Lexington, Kentucky, the third daughter of Eliza Parker Todd and Robert Smith Todd. The Parker and Todd families had founded Lexington in the 1770s, and Mary grew up among the privileged classes in the town. She received ten years of formal education and developed a keen interest in politics, especially in the Whig Party, at an early age.

In the spring of 1837, Mary traveled to Springfield, Illinois, to visit her sisters. There she met a young attorney, Abraham Lincoln. Following her brief employment as a schoolteacher, the two began courting in earnest in 1840. After a sometimes tumultuous courtship, the two married in November 1842. Although the two were opposites in many respects, their differences served more as complements than as obstacles in the relationship. Mary worked to refine her husband's frontier mannerisms and to promote his political ambitions, and his political connections offered Mary the social status she desired. The couple eventually had four sons, and Mary devoted much of her energy to motherhood. She also enjoyed being a hostess and had plenty of opportunities to act as one, as her husband's political status rose throughout the 1840s and 1850s.

Mary frequently advised her husband on political personalities and party patronage. She vigorously campaigned for him through letter writing when he was nominated for president in 1860. Her political involvement never extended to a firm stance on prevailing issues of the day or to an advocacy of women's issues, such as the vote, but rather manifested itself in the public persona of first lady and White House hostess throughout Lincoln's administrations. She was often criticized for aggressively blending political and social ambition. Her harshest wartime critics rebuked her for overspending her four-year $20,000 allotment for White House furnishings in the first year of the administration. She also spent a lot on clothes, seeing it as a vital symbol of her status; some viewed this expenditure as too extravagant during wartime. Other critics contended that Mary's sympathies were with the Confederacy; this was untrue, and the rumors stemmed from the wartime divisions within the Todd family. All three of Mary's half brothers fought and died for the Confederacy, and her half sister, Emilie Todd Helm, was a vocal pro-Confederate supporter, who once visited the White House during the war and was married to Confederate General Benjamin Hardin Helm.

The deaths of loved ones and corresponding feelings of abandonment pervaded Mary's life. When Mary was six years old, her mother died following childbirth. Poor relations with her stepmother made the loss of her father and of her beloved grandmother Parker in 1849 all the more painful. In 1850, the Lincolns lost their son Eddie, and, while they were in the White House, another son, Willie, died. Mary felt each loss severely, including the death of a third son, Tad, in 1871, but none compared to the assassination of her husband in April 1865. Following Abraham's death, Mary assumed a permanent mourning lifestyle, never surrendering the dark clothes of a grieving widow. Her belief in spiritualism, specifically the ability to communicate with the dead, brought her some comfort and a lingering connection to lost loved ones, but a sense of personal abandonment and loneliness remained a lasting part of her emotional state.

Her life after her husband's death focused on developing Lincoln's legacy as an American hero and on asserting her uniqueness as First Lady. In addition, much of her time was devoted to securing her own financial status, which would eventually lead to controversy in Congress over a political widow's pension and to a bitter and devastating conflict with her only surviving son, Robert. Finally, she spent much of the remainder of her life traveling throughout the United States and Europe in search of relief for her physical ailments. Eventually, her health problems overtook her, and Mary died on July 16, 1882, following a stroke.

Kristen Streater

See also Lincoln, Abraham (1809–1865); Northern Women; Pensions, Union Homefront; Union Widows; Politics; Widows, Union.

References and Further Reading

Baker, Jean H. 1987. *Mary Todd Lincoln: A Biography.* New York: W. W. Norton & Company.
Donald, David Herbert. 1995. *Lincoln.* New York: Simon & Schuster.
Turner, Justin G., and Linda Levitt Turner, eds. 1987. *Mary Todd Lincoln: Her Life and Letters.* New York: Fromm International Publishing Corporation.

Livermore, Mary Ashton Rice (1820–1905)

Born in Boston in 1820, Mary Ashton Rice Livermore rose through the ranks of Chicago's voluntary associations to serve as an Associate Manager of the Northwestern Branch of the United States Sanitary Commission during the Civil War. Although an experienced writer and leader of women's organizations, Livermore's wartime work proved seminal. During the war she met many people, learned new skills, and took up the cause of women's rights. In the postwar years she became a nationally known public speaker and published *My Story of the War.*

Livermore shared the office of associate manager with two men and Jane Hoge, a friend who divided with Livermore the massive workload and inspired her with confidence. To countless visitors, the two women became the faces of the commission. Many times each day they sold the agency's merits to skeptical would-be donors. In addition, they oversaw the sorting of tons of donated goods, packing and sealing boxes to be sent to the front lines. Both had children of their own and functioned as surrogate mothers to convalescing soldiers. They recruited nurses to serve at army posts and, in their spare minutes, handled a voluminous correspondence among local aid societies, family members, and the rank and file of the army. Finally, they planned and led two huge fairs in Chicago that raised money, eventually disbursing more than $1 million in relief.

Mary Livermore made an important contribution as an organizer of medical relief services for the Union army during the Civil War. An ardent supporter of women's rights, she also co-founded the American Woman Suffrage Association. (Library of Congress)

Besides office responsibilities, Livermore's wartime activities involved a fair amount of travel. She visited sites ranging from Washington, D.C., to the battle lines in the Western theater, meeting such people as President Abraham Lincoln and General Ulysses S. Grant. Following an early 1863 visit to the armies camped outside Vicksburg, Livermore helped prevent an outbreak of scurvy there by collecting and shipping more than one thousand bushels of fresh potatoes, onions, and other vegetables to the troops. Moreover, she represented the commission to a wide range of people, encouraging the exhausted members of aid societies to keep up their labors, telling them what the armies needed and why they should make their contributions through the Sanitary Com-

mission. Finally, in an era when women who spoke to mixed audiences were considered promiscuous, Livermore learned to present brilliant and compelling speeches before large groups of men and women.

Livermore's wartime work made her aware of the restrictions that society imposed on women. In 1863, a builder refused to sign a contract with her and Hoge because they were women, even though they were agents of the Sanitary Commission and had in their possession both the money and the lumber necessary to construct the building they needed. In the decade following the war, righting wrongs against women became one of Livermore's most important causes. She wrote articles for various magazines, helped organize the Illinois Woman Suffrage Association, and in 1869 briefly published a magazine that she entitled *The Agitator.* For this effort, Livermore won the admiration and praise of the suffrage movement's national leaders, including Elizabeth Cady Stanton and Susan B. Anthony.

While Livermore continued to maintain a presence among woman suffragists, by 1870 she had begun shifting her priorities toward launching a speaking career. She moved to Boston, merged *The Agitator* with the *Woman's Journal,* edited by Lucy Stone, and began giving popular lectures. Livermore eventually enjoyed a nationwide speaking career, giving thousands of lectures, including more than eight hundred presentations of "What Shall We Do with Our Daughters?"

Still being printed today, Livermore's *My Story of the War* sold approximately sixty thousand copies in its first decade. It offers a woman's perspective on the Civil War, gives details about military hospitals and relief work, describes her encounters with prominent Union officials, and provides glimpses into the operations of the United States Sanitary Commission. She was a nationally known figure by the time she died in Boston in 1905.

Nancy Driscol Engle

See also Fairs and Bazaars; Hoge, Jane Currie Blaikie (1811–1890); Northern Women; Nurses; Societies; Union Homefront; United States Sanitary Commission.

References and Further Reading

Brockett, Linus P., and Marcy C. Vaughan. 1867. *Woman's Work in the Civil War,* with an introduction by Henry W. Bellows. Philadelphia, PA: Zeigler, McCurdy & Co.

Henshaw, Sarah Edwards. 1868. *Our Branch and Its Tributaries.* Chicago: Alfred L. Sewell & Co.

Livermore, Mary A. 1889. *My Story of the War.* Hartford, CT: A. D. Worthington and Company.

Livermore, Mary A. 1899. *The Story of My Life.* Hartford, CT: A. D. Worthington and Company. (Reprinted 1974. New York: Arno Press.)

Long, Ellen Call (1825–1905)

The daughter of Richard Keith Call, Andrew Jackson's protégé and future Florida territorial governor, Ellen Call Long published her fictionalized memoir of the Civil War, *Florida Breezes*, in 1883.

According to some sources, Ellen Call was the first white child born in Florida's new territorial capital on September 9, 1825. Her father farmed, practiced law, and engaged in land speculation before eventually becoming involved in territorial politics. He eventually served two terms as governor, first as a Democrat and later as a Whig.

During her youth, Ellen attended schools in Maryland and Pennsylvania. She was ten years old in 1836 when her mother, Mary Letitia Kirkman Call, died. After finishing her schooling Ellen returned to Tallahassee in 1843. One year later she married local lawyer Medicus A. Long, and the couple had four children. Medicus's activity in Democratic politics put him in opposition to his father-in-law, by that time an ardent Whig. At some point in the 1850s, Medicus left Ellen and his children for Texas, perhaps for health reasons. Though the couple evidently never divorced, they never reunited.

Long's father remained a staunch Unionist during the secession crisis, which led to much criticism from his former constituents. In her later writings, Ellen defended her father and attacked Floridians who took the state out of the Union. Brokenhearted with the outbreak of war, Richard Call died at the family estate, The Grove, in 1862. Remaining in Tallahassee throughout the war, Ellen supported, if not enthusiastically, the Confederate war effort, helping to organize a ladies' benevolent association.

Her son served in the Confederate army and her brother-in-law, Theodore Brevard, rose to high military rank. As the war ended, Long was relieved at the return of peace, but angry and humiliated at the Confederate defeat.

In the postwar years, Long became involved in various patriotic activities, including serving as a delegate in 1876 to the Philadelphia Centennial Exposition. Before suffering financial difficulties later in life, she traveled regularly and was active in Tallahassee social circles. In the 1880s she received criticism for her support of a black man to serve as the local postmaster.

Always a regular letter writer and diarist, Long became a formal author after the war. In 1883, she published *Florida Breezes; or, Florida, New and Old*, a memoir of life in antebellum and Civil War Florida. The volume consists of two sections. In the first, Long tells her story through a fictional character, Harry Barclay, a Northerner who visits Florida for two years during the 1830s and who subsequently corresponds with a Florida friend after returning north. The book's second section offers a number of letters written between Barclay and Ruth, the niece of his Tallahassee friend, during the secession crisis and the war years. Though Call's decision to use fictional characters in *Florida Breezes* somewhat limits its usefulness as a reference, it still provides unique details on the Second Seminole War, slavery, dueling, and antebellum and Civil War events in Florida. While offering a romanticized view of life in the Old South, *Florida Breezes* also displays the author's contempt for the Southern extremists who prevailed during the secession crisis of 1860–1861.

In addition to *Florida Breezes*, Call authored a number of magazine and newspaper articles, as well as the book *Silk Farming in Florida* and the pamphlet *The Battle of New Orleans: Jackson and Packenham*. She also wrote a biography of her father and a history of Florida, but both of these remain unpublished.

Ellen Call Long died in Tallahassee on December 18, 1905. She was buried at The Grove beside her father.

David Coles

See also Aid Societies; Confederate Homefront; Nationalism, Confederate; Nationalism, United States; Secession; Southern Women.

References and Further Reading

Long, Ellen Call. [1882] 1962. *Florida Breezes; or, Florida, New and Old.* Gainesville: University Press of Florida.

Revels, Tracey J. 2004. *Grander in Her Daughters: Florida's Women during the Civil War.* Columbia: University of South Carolina Press.

Loyalty Oaths

From the beginning of the war, President Abraham Lincoln's administration concerned itself with measuring or defining the loyalty of citizens and Southerners. In April 1861, Lincoln ordered all civilian employees in the executive branch to take a loyalty oath. Congress quickly followed by demanding a similar pledge from its employees and went on in December 1861 to draft the Ironclad Test Oath. The Ironclad Oath, which took effect in July 1862, required professions of both past and future loyalty to the Union, disqualifying Confederates and their supporters from voting or office holding.

Loyalty oaths spread throughout the South, particularly in Louisiana, Tennessee, and Missouri. As areas came under Union military control, oaths were administered in an attempt to build a critical mass of loyal citizens to bring states back into the Union. Union soldiers also administered oaths to Southerners who sought to travel into Union-controlled territory, necessitating some intellectual and moral gymnastics on the part of Confederates. Many Confederates who took the oath justified their actions to themselves and others by arguing that an oath taken under coercion was not binding and that it could therefore be violated with impunity. Much as children cross their fingers to negate a promise, Confederate oath takers held their breath and put thoughts of perjury and dishonor out of their heads in order to tolerate what they believed to be an intolerable predicament.

Loyalty oaths also played a significant role in the struggles between Lincoln and congressional Republicans over the shape of wartime Reconstruction. Lincoln's Ten Percent Plan had a low standard of loyalty, requiring only a pledge of future allegiance to the Union, while the congressional Wade-Davis bill called for the more stringent Ironclad Oath. Oaths served to disfranchise many Southern whites during the elections of 1864 and 1868, ensuring Republican control of the presidency.

Anne Sarah Rubin

See also Civilian Life; Confederate Homefront; Military Invasion and Occupation; Northern Women; Reconstruction (1865–1877); Southern Women; Union Homefront.

References and Further Reading

Hyman, Harold Melvin. 1954. *Era of the Oath: Northern Loyalty Tests during the Civil War and Reconstruction.* Philadelphia: University of Pennsylvania Press.

M

Maury, Elizabeth "Betty" Herndon (1835–1903)

During the American Civil War, Betty Herndon Maury, who was pregnant with her second daughter, started a two-volume diary documenting her wartime experiences from 1861 to 1863.

Born in Charlottesville, Virginia, on June 25, 1835, Elizabeth "Betty" Herndon Maury was the eldest daughter of Ann Hull and Matthew Fontaine Maury, a brilliant scientist at the United States Naval Observatory and later Secretary of the Navy for the Confederate States of America. Betty married Judge William Arden Maury before the Civil War began.

Maury's Virginia family was sharply divided by the war. Her diary details these divisions as well as the tensions in her marriage that resulted from her husband's initial reluctance to leave his post in Washington, D.C., to join the Confederate army. It also documents her experience as a refugee, after her mother's familial home in Fredericksburg was invaded and occupied by Federal troops. Although Maury was at heart a patriotic Southern woman who volunteered her time sewing clothing and tents for Confederate soldiers, she often felt conflicted between her patriotism and her concern for the safety of her father, husband, and brothers, all of whom served the Confederate cause. A confirmed Southerner, Maury was equally critical in her writings on the Union and Confederate administrations and on their ineptness at prosecuting the war. Her daughter, Alice Mary Parmalee, who was born in

May 1863 when Maury's diary came to a close, later donated the diary to the Library of Congress.

Betty Herndon Maury died in 1903.

E. Susan Barber

See also Aid Societies; Civilian Life; Confederate Homefront; Diaries and Journals; Nationalism, Confederate; Politics; Refugees; Southern Women.

References and Further Reading

Caskie, Jacquelin Ambler. 1928. *The Life and Letters of Matthew Fontaine Maury*. Richmond, VA: Richmond Press, Inc.

Lewis, Charles Lee. 1927. *Matthew Fontaine Maury: The Pathfinder of the Seas*. Annapolis, MD: U.S. Naval Institute.

May, Abigail Williams (1829–1888)

As the chairperson of the United States Sanitary Commission (USSC) in 1862, Abigail Williams May distributed more than $1 million in supplies to Union and Confederate soldiers, and she traveled aboard a hospital transport ship to gain personal knowledge of wartime conditions to ameliorate the shortages and suffering of soldiers on the front. She directed the USSC until it was disbanded in 1888 but was called Chair the rest of her life due to her leadership of the commission and her reform efforts in Boston, Massachusetts. May's leadership bridged the gap between women's political efforts at the local level and the growth of concerted efforts on behalf of women at the national level.

The product of two prominent New England families, the Mays and Goddards, Abigail May was born in Boston on May 21, 1829, as the third of Samuel J.

and Mary (Goddard) May's seven children. Her parents were involved in the abolitionist movement. Their example served May well; she too found her life's work in reform efforts, including freedmen's aid, woman suffrage, and women's education.

Besides her parents' influence, May's lifework was informed by the ideas of several people. The preaching of several Unitarian ministers, including Theodore Parker, her brother Samuel J. May, Jr., and her first cousin Samuel Joseph May, also influenced her passion for philanthropic endeavors. May was first cousin to the social worker Abigail May Alcott and a close friend of Louisa May Alcott. Brought up believing that women should be educated and work outside the home to prevent future poverty and hardship, May attended Boston's private schools and the Boston School of Design, which she later shepherded as part of its governing committee.

Prior to her involvement with the USSC, May founded and served as secretary of the Obstetrics Clinic of New England Female Medical College in 1859. Her USSC efforts began in 1861 at the local level in Boston where she served as secretary of the New England Women's Auxiliary Association, a branch of the USSC. She worked in this capacity until, at age thirty-two, she coordinated the war relief efforts for the entire New England region. Then, in 1862, May became chairperson of the USSC, the only civilian relief organization to receive official government sanction. Its women solicited supplies from localities for national distribution, offered battlefield support, and consulted with the Union army on medical matters. Given women's traditional role as nurses in the home, meeting the commission's objectives allowed women to expand their endeavors into public areas, prove their mettle as leaders, and address social and health needs. May strove to create a strong network of local relief organizations that would eventually meld into a larger, national movement.

May never married; her love of and dedication to public work and service outweighed any notions she had of being a man's helpmeet. Her family's financial support, coupled with the emotional support of her steadfast female friends, sustained her work. May died from an ovarian cyst at Massachu-setts Homeopathic Hospital in Boston on November 30, 1888.

Rebecca Tolley-Stokes

See also Abolitionism and Northern Reformers; Aid Societies; Alcott, Louisa May (1832–1888); Livermore, Mary Ashton Rice; Northern Women; Schuyler, Louisa Lee (1837–1926); Separate Spheres; Union Homefront; United States Sanitary Commission.
References and Further Reading
Giesberg, Judith Ann. 2000. *Civil War Sisterhood: The U.S. Sanitary Commission and Women's Politics in Transition.* Boston: Northeastern University Press.

McCord, Louisa Susana Cheves (1810–1879)

Proslavery writer and poet, Louisa Susana Cheves McCord ran a hospital for Confederate soldiers, formed a soldiers' aid society, and used her plantation to provide food for the wounded during the Civil War. She published her defenses of slavery and Southern paternalism in antebellum newspapers.

Born in Charleston, South Carolina, on December 3, 1810, to Mary Dulles and Langdon Cheves, Louisa was the fourth of ten Cheves children who survived infancy. Her family's prominence and wealth—her father was a lawyer, planter, and politician—allowed Louisa rare opportunities for education and travel. Although she learned housekeeping from her mother, Louisa felt closer to her father, and he may have helped foster her love of intellectual pursuits. Her formal schooling prepared her for life as a wife and mother, but she managed to gain a more intellectual education on her own.

Louisa married David McCord in 1840, and the couple had three children. Unlike most women of her time, upon her marriage Louisa maintained control of the plantation she brought to the marriage. Between 1848 and 1856, Louisa published a volume of poems, a play, essays, book reviews, and a translation of a book on political economy. In her work, she offered a vehement defense of slavery and she promoted women's proper place in society.

A widow when the war began, Louisa became a fervent supporter of secession and the Confederacy. After her son and two brothers enlisted in the Confederate army, she found ways to help the sol-

Louisa Cheves McCord, staunch Confederate and author (1810–1879). (Duyckinck, E.A. and George L. Duyckinck, eds., *Cyclopaedia of American Literature*, 1855)

diers. She formed a local soldiers' aid society and outfitted her son's regiment. In addition, she became the matron of the hospital at South Carolina College (now the University of South Carolina). She used her plantation to supply food not only to her family, but also to her patients. The loss of her son, a brother, and several nephews did not dampen Louisa's support for the Confederacy.

When Union General William Tecumseh Sherman and his troops arrived in Columbia in 1865, Louisa and her family remained. They gained some protection from the looting when their home became General Oliver O. Howard's headquarters, but the presence of the enemy in their home did not please anyone in the family. The end of the war found Louisa clinging to the idea of an independent Southern nation; Louisa put on a mourning dress when, out of necessity, she signed the oath of allegiance to the United States.

After the war, Louisa helped commemorate the Lost Cause, becoming the president of the South Carolina Monument Association. Depressed by the loss of so many things and ideals that she held

dear, she left for Canada in 1871 and did not return until 1876.

Louisa Cheves McCord died in Charleston on November 23, 1879.

Lisa Tendrich Frank

See also Aid Societies; Confederate Homefront; Domesticity; Education, Southern; Food; Hospitals; Loyalty Oaths; Nurses; Poets, Southern; Politics; Separate Spheres; Sherman's Campaign (1864–1865); Southern Women.

References and Further Reading

Fought, Leigh. 2003. *Southern Womanhood and Slavery: A Biography of Louisa S. McCord, 1810–1879.* Columbia: University of Missouri Press.

Fox-Genovese, Elizabeth. 1988. *Within the Plantation Household: Black and White Women of the Old South.* Chapel Hill: University of North Carolina Press.

McDonald, Cornelia Peake (1822–1909)

Confederate diarist Cornelia Peake McDonald kept a detailed record of her war experiences. Her journal, which runs from her husband's departure for the battlefield in March 1862 through the summer of 1863, describes life in occupied Winchester as well as life as a Confederate refugee.

Cornelia Peake was born June 14, 1822, in Alexandria, Virginia, to Anne Linton Lane and Humphrey Peake. She spent some of her childhood in Missouri. She married Angus W. McDonald III in 1847 and raised her family, which would eventually include nine children, in Winchester, Virginia.

When the Civil War started and Virginia seceded in 1861, Cornelia and her husband were devoted Confederates. Cornelia had never viewed slavery as a positive institution, and she expressed concern for her own slaves' conditions. However, she bemoaned the loss of slaves, especially after the Emancipation Proclamation, and she maintained the racial views of other middle- and upper-class Southern women of the era. Angus volunteered for Confederate military service, eventually securing a post in Richmond. As he left in the spring of 1862, he asked his wife to keep a record of her wartime experiences. Cornelia remained alone in Winchester to provide for her family and to secure their home against invading armies.

Cornelia's wartime experiences were difficult. Throughout much of 1862 and 1863, Union troops occupied the town, and Union commanders frequently approached her and demanded the use of her home for their headquarters or hospitals. She persistently resisted the invasions and was generally successful in keeping most Union troops out of her home. However, her family's land, animals, and supplies were constantly susceptible to passing troops, making basic survival a challenge. Purchasing food was difficult, not only because of Confederate currency's depreciated value, but also because many shopkeepers would not sell to anyone who had not taken the oath of allegiance to the Union, something Cornelia was unwilling to do. Bartering with others, including Union soldiers, with the supplies she had allowed Cornelia to feed her family through much of the war.

In the face of renewed Union aggression in the area in the summer of 1863, Cornelia abandoned her home. She and her children became refugees for the remainder of the war. They eventually secured a home in Lexington, Virginia, but continued to face economic hardship. Her husband came home briefly, but, as Union troops invaded the state, he was forced to leave again in the summer of 1864. Following a protracted illness, exacerbated by his capture by Union forces, he died in December of that year. Now left completely alone, Cornelia taught drawing lessons to Lexington girls to provide for her family. After the war, the family remained in Lexington until 1873, when they moved to Louisville, Kentucky, where Cornelia penned many of her reminiscences of the war. She died in Louisville on March 11, 1909.

Kristen L. Streater

See also Confederate Homefront; Diaries and Journals; Loyalty Oaths; Military Invasion and Occupation; Refugees; Shortages; Southern Women; Teachers, Southern.

References and Further Reading
Faust, Drew Gilpin. 1996. *Mothers of Invention: Women of the Slaveholding South in the American Civil War.* Chapel Hill: University of North Carolina Press.

McDonald, Cornelia Peake. 1992. *A Woman's Civil War: A Diary, with Reminiscences of the War, from March 1862,* edited by Minrose C. Gwin. Madison: University of Wisconsin Press.

McEwen, Henrietta (Hetty) Montgomery Kennedy (1796–1881)

Hetty McEwen gained a reputation as a fearless Unionist by flying a homemade United States flag from the chimney of her Nashville, Tennessee house while Confederates held the town during the first several months of the Civil War. Ignoring Rebel orders to remove the flag, Hetty threatened to shoot anyone who attempted to tamper with it. Even after Tennessee's Confederate governor, Isham G. Harris, dispatched soldiers to collect civilians' guns, Hetty resisted relinquishing hers, vowing that should the governor come in person to remove her weapons, he would risk his life. When violent secessionists threatened to burn her house, she publicly announced she would guard it with her shotgun. Federal occupancy in early 1862 preempted a confrontation with Harris. Nashville's Union commander presented her a silk flag in recognition of her staunch patriotism.

Hetty was born July 29, 1796, to Ester and Robert Campbell Kennedy, both of Scot-Irish ancestry. Several members of Kennedy's family fought at the Battle of King's Mountain during the Revolutionary War. Raised in Washington County, Virginia, Kennedy moved from East Tennessee to Nashville in 1786. Nearly twenty years later, he settled in Lincoln County, Tennessee, and began farming and operating a mill. Hetty and some of her siblings attended Valladolid Academy in Nashville. In 1815, Hetty married Robert Houston McEwen, a first cousin of Sam Houston, who had served with her brother William in the War of 1812. The McEwens began married life in Fayetteville where McEwen owned a dry goods store. He opened a new one in Nashville when the family moved there in 1828. The McEwens had seven children who survived to adulthood. McEwen was Tennessee's first state superintendent of public schools, holding this position between 1836 and 1840. Subsequently he was a collector for Eastern Merchants, Brokers, & Bankers.

Although Hetty came from a slaveholding family, by the eve of war her household included only one occupant listed as a servant, a young woman born in Ireland. Hetty's brother William had sent numerous slaves to Liberia through his membership in the Colonization Society. Some of Hetty's extended family supported secession, and others wanted to preserve the Union. After the war, Hetty continued charitable work through the Presbyterian Church and the Nashville Protestant School of Industry. She died January 19, 1881, in Augusta, Georgia. She and her husband are buried in Mt. Olivet Cemetery, Nashville.

Nancy L. Adgent

See also American Colonization Society; Confederate Homefront; Nationalism, United States; Southern Unionists; Southern Women.
References and Further Reading
Moore, Frank. 1866. *Women of the War: Their Heroism and Self-Sacrifice.* Hartford, CT: S. S. Scranton & Co.

McGuire, Judith White Brockenbrough (1813–1897)

A diarist and refugee in Richmond, Virginia, during the Civil War, Judith White Brockenbrough McGuire was born into an elite family on March 5, 1813, near Richmond, Virginia.

The fifth child of William Brockenbrough and Judith White Brockenbrough, Judith grew up in luxury. Her father served Essex County in the Virginia House of Delegates and in 1834 became a judge on the Virginia Supreme Court of Appeals. On November 26, 1846, she married the Reverend John Peyton McGuire, a rector in Essex County and later principal of the Episcopal High School in Alexandria, Virginia.

As ardent Confederates, John and Judith McGuire fled Alexandria in 1861 when Federal troops threatened to occupy the city, and they remained refugees for the rest of the war. After spending the rest of 1861 with friends and family in Winchester and other parts of northern Virginia, the McGuires finally settled in Richmond in February 1862 and remained there for the rest of the war. Like many refugees, the McGuires encountered financial hardships and diffi-culty finding affordable housing in overcrowded Richmond. Both found it necessary to earn money to support themselves. John worked as a clerk in the post office and then as a hospital chaplain, while Judith obtained a position as a clerk in the Confederate Commissary Department.

Judith McGuire began a diary in 1861 and kept it faithfully throughout the war. Intended originally to be a record of the war for future family members, she was persuaded, perhaps because of financial straits, to publish it in 1867 as the *Diary of a Southern Refugee during the War.* McGuire's diary clearly shows the upheavals and hardships the war caused for elite families. She describes the scarcity of housing, food, and clothing items that pervaded Richmond and affected all classes of people. In particular, she notes the toll that the war took on women, who were often left without financial support as widows, orphans, and refugees. McGuire carefully follows the war news and chronicles battles and troop movements, the death of important leaders such as Stonewall Jackson, and events in Richmond itself, including the Bread Riots in April 1863. Throughout her narrative, McGuire remains fiercely supportive of the Confederate cause.

After the war, the impoverished McGuires ran a small school in Essex County, Virginia. After her husband died in 1869, McGuire continued to run the school herself until 1880. In 1873, during her widowhood, she completed a second book, intended for the use of her scholars, called *General Robert E. Lee, the Christian Soldier,* and donated the profits to her church. McGuire died in Richmond on March 21, 1897, and was buried beside her husband in Essex County.

Amy Minton

See also Bread Riots; Confederate Homefront; Diaries and Journals; Refugees; Southern Women; Teachers, Southern; Urban Women, Southern.
References and Further Reading
McGuire, Judith W. 1995. *Diary of a Southern Refugee during the War, by a Lady of Virginia,* with Introduction by Jean V. Berlin. Lincoln: University of Nebraska Press.
Weathers, Willie T. 1974. "Judith W. McGuire: A Lady of Virginia." *Virginia Magazine of History and Biography* 82 (1): 100–113.

McKay, Charlotte Elizabeth Johnson (1818–1894)

Union field nurse Charlotte McKay aided wounded soldiers, often in close proximity to the battlefields. Receiving no pay for her services, she felt a moral obligation to perform her nursing duties. She was awarded the Kearny Cross by her brother's regiment for her brave work in a field hospital within three miles of the Battle of Chancellorsville.

Charlotte Johnson was born in 1818 in Maine, one of seven children and the daughter of a successful physician. As an adult, she married and had a daughter. Her husband died in 1856, only two years after they married, and in 1861 their only child died. Stricken with grief, McKay devoted herself wholeheartedly to nursing.

In the spring of 1862 she moved to Frederick, Maryland, and found work at a hospital, caring for the wounded from the battles of Winchester, Second Manassas, and Antietam, as well as distributing supplies to the troops. The Union troops abandoned Frederick in September 1862, but she stayed there for a short time helping wounded Confederate soldiers, expressing in her memoirs surprise at finding them gentlemanly. She also wrote in her memoirs about how the soldiers suffered from their wounds and the lack of food.

In January 1863, McKay became a field nurse and was stationed near Falmouth. She rode on boxcars and supply wagons to get supplies and food to the troops. In May of that year, she worked in a field hospital not three miles away from the fighting at Chancellorsville, crossing the Rappahannock on a pontoon to get there. As the line of fire eventually drew near to them, the medical staff retreated to Fredericksburg, 13 miles away, with the wounded soldiers.

Around this time, McKay's brother, a lieutenant in the Seventeenth Maine, was mortally wounded. In May 1863, McKay was awarded the Kearny Cross, which was presented to her by the Seventeenth Regiment's Maine volunteers.

When the Army of the Potomac moved into Pennsylvania in pursuit of Robert E. Lee's Army of Northern Virginia, McKay accompanied them. She nursed soldiers wounded at the Battle of Gettysburg, doing her duties about five miles from the battle. Here she also cooked for the men, dealing with a shortage of food and utensils. McKay continued her nursing duties in 1864 and 1865, serving at the battles of the Wilderness, Spotsylvania Court House, and Cold Harbor. After March 1865, she no longer nursed, but she remained in Virginia for over a year teaching the freed slaves how to read and write.

When her work with the freedmen ended in 1866, McKay moved to Massachusetts. She had no military pension; in fact most, if not all, of her nursing work during the war had been without pay. It is likely that she may have relied on her siblings and other family members during this time for financial support. It was in Wakefied, Massachusetts, that she wrote her memoirs, publishing them in 1876.

In the 1890s, McKay moved to San Diego. She died there in 1894 at the age of seventy-five.

Sigrid Kelsey

See also Antietam/Sharpsburg, Battle of (September 17, 1862); Bull Run/Manassas, Second Battle of (August 29–30, 1862); Chancellorsville, Battle of (April 29–May 6, 1863); Education, Southern; Gettysburg, Battle of (July 1–3, 1863); Northern Women; Nurses; Teachers, Northern.

References and Further Reading

McKay, Charlotte E. 1876. *Stories of Hospital and Camp.* Philadelphia, PA: Claxton, Remsen & Haffelfinger.

Shultz, Jane E. 2004. *Women at the Front: Hospital Workers in Civil War America.* Chapel Hill: University of North Carolina Press.

Meriwether, Elizabeth Avery (1824–1916)

Novelist, playwright, journalist, public speaker, and crusader for temperance and woman suffrage, Elizabeth Avery Meriwether is best known for her memoir, *Recollections of 92 Years*, which offers an intimate and often frank look at the life of a white Southern woman struggling against female subordination.

Born and raised in West Tennessee, Elizabeth Avery was largely self-educated. She married civil engineer Minor Meriwether of Kentucky in 1852, and bore three sons.

Before the outbreak of the Civil War, she participated pseudonymously in discussions of issues of the day in local newspapers, always from a feminist standpoint.

While her husband served as an engineer officer in the Confederate army, Meriwether sought to maintain her household of children and a few slaves, lending her voice to secession and Southern nationalism. Expelled from Memphis by Union commander William T. Sherman in late 1862, she gave birth to her third son, author and journalist (Minor) Lee Meriwether, while seeking refuge in Mississippi. The family spent most of the war in Tuscaloosa, Alabama. To help support herself, she wrote "The Story of a Refugee," which received a monetary prize and in 1864 was serialized in the exiled newspaper, *The Sunday Mississippian*. Drawing on incidents in her life in Memphis under Federal occupation, she hinted at some of the themes—the feminine nature of the South versus the masculine, militaristic North, and the injustice of the legal disabilities placed on women in both regions—that she would treat at greater length in postwar works.

The most notable of these, besides her memoir, is her novel, *The Master of Red Leaf*. Set on a Louisiana plantation during the Civil War, this work posits both the benignity of the slave system (in the proper hands) and the malignity of a social structure that subordinated women to men. A typical Victorian potboiler in many ways, replete with coincidence and disguise, some of the main female characters are much more than they seem.

After the war, the Meriwethers returned to Memphis, where Minor become a successful lawyer. Elizabeth herself became an expert on coverture, the legal subordination of wives to husbands, and became known as a public speaker, as well as the publisher and editor of a short-lived newspaper. In one famous incident, she insisted on casting a ballot (which was accepted but not counted) in the 1872 election. By the1880s the family had relocated to St. Louis. Elizabeth became an associate and ally of Elizabeth Cady Stanton and Susan B. Anthony, with whom she made a speaking tour.

Unlike many elite Southerners of the era, the Meriwethers were fairly openly skeptical of religion. Elizabeth Avery Meriwether died in late 1916, after the serialization of her *Recollections* in regional newspapers had begun.

Ed Frank

See also Fiction Writers, Southern; Nationalism, Confederate; Refugees; Southern Women.
References and Further Reading
Meriwether, Elizabeth Avery. 1880. *The Master of Red Leaf.* New York: E. J. Hale & Son.
Meriwether, Elizabeth Avery. 1958. *Recollections of 92 Years.* Nashville: Tennessee Historical Commission.

Methodist Women

Like many other religious groups, those of the Methodist faith divided along regional and racial lines prior to and during the American Civil War.

The first American Methodists were strongly antislavery, but by the mid-nineteenth century the church had adopted positions that accommodated its Southern adherents. Although Methodists moderated their views about slavery, rising abolitionist sentiment in the North during the 1830s and 1840s again brought the issue to the center of denominational life. The greatest schism in the Methodist ranks occurred in 1845 when Methodists in the Southern and border states created the Methodist Episcopal Church, South (MEC South) in which the ownership of slaves was acceptable. Although Union victory encouraged Northern Methodists to attempt to win back the Southern churches by force, white Southerners resisted and maintained their ecclesiastical independence after 1865. The rift was not healed until 1939.

Official Methodist tepidity on the slavery issue resulted in a number of additional schisms prior to the Civil War from impatient Northern factions. Notable were the Wesleyan Methodist Connection, founded in upstate New York in 1843, and the Free Methodist Church, organized in 1860 in the same area. The Wesleyan Church, as the denomination is now called, and the Free Methodist Church were strongly influenced by the Holiness movement and its leader Phoebe Palmer. Palmer instructed thousands at a time when women were not generally granted positions of leadership or authority in America, and she became the spokesperson for a powerful religious impulse that would wield world-wide influence.

A third schism in the Methodist denomination occurred much earlier in the century over the issue of race relations. The African Methodist Episcopal Church (AME) was formed in 1816 after two decades of friction between white and black Methodists in Philadelphia. By the outbreak of the Civil War, the AME had nearly twenty-three thousand members, had founded the first African American magazine in America (1841), and had acquired Wilberforce University in Ohio (1856). A similar controversy in New York led its African American members to found the AME Zion Church in 1821. As Union armies moved into the South, both of the AME churches began missions among the freedmen that they sustained during Reconstruction. By 1896 the denominations together claimed nearly one million members.

In all of these Methodist denominations, women played a vital role during the Civil War. Methodist women formed church aid societies that provided soldiers and freedpeople with necessary articles of clothing and food. Women like Annie Turner Wittenmyer and Laura Smith Haviland participated in aid societies outside the confines of the local church. Wittenmyer helped organize local soldiers' aid societies in Keokuk, Iowa, and briefly served as the state sanitary agent of Iowa. Wittenmyer's most important contribution to the war was the creation of a system of special diet kitchens for the sick and wounded in hospitals. By the outbreak of the Civil War, Haviland, a Wesleyan Methodist, had already devoted many years to the abolitionist cause, assisting fugitive slaves through the Underground Railroad. During the war, she directed the Raisin Institute in Michigan Territory, a school she and her husband founded in 1837 that taught white and African American male and female students. In 1863 she became a leader of freedpeople's relief in the South and in Kansas. During the last years of the war, she traveled throughout the South assisting Union prisoners and inspecting refugee camps and hospitals.

Methodist women supported with special vigor the Methodist Society, the largest and most active agency for supplying literature to the Confederate troops. In the South, Methodist women cared for the wounded in hospitals located in homes and churches. As the war wore on in the South, many churches stopped holding services because ministers enlisted or served as chaplains in the military or because the churches had been destroyed. In response, women organized their own prayer services and increasingly turned to their Bibles for inspiration and instruction.

African American Methodist women of remarkable talent and fortitude participated in the war effort as well. Fanny Jackson Coppin, wife of Levi Coppin, the pastor of Philadelphia's Mother Bethel Church (the first AME church), was a leading educator of the nineteenth century and the first black woman to receive a full-fledged collegiate education from Oberlin College. During the war, she remained at Oberlin and set up night classes for the hundreds of newly freed men and women who arrived in town. In 1865, she took a position at the Institute for Colored Youth in Philadelphia and four years later was the school's principal, the first African American woman in the country to occupy such a position. She was also a founder of the national Association of Colored Women. During the 1880s she became a leader in the Home and Foreign Missionary Society of the AME and served a number of terms as its president. After thirty-seven years of teaching, she resigned in 1902 to become a missionary, traveling with her husband to South Africa.

One of the most widely known nineteenth-century African American women was Frances Ellen Watkins Harper. Harper did not serve in the Civil War, but she wrote a novel about it. *Iola Leroy* (1892) was the best-selling novel by an African American in the nineteenth century. It is the story of educated, light-skinned, free blacks who are sold into slavery. Iola and her brother join the Union army as a nurse and a soldier, and then they reunite, older and much wiser, after the Civil War. Harper's first career was as a teacher at Union Seminary in Ohio, a school organized by the AME Church. Both the AME Church and the Unitarians have claimed Harper as a member. Indeed, she joined the First Unitarian Church in Philadelphia in 1870 but never broke ties with the AME Church. Harper, in fact, was reluctant to choose between the two. The AME was the church in which she had been raised. She published numerous short sketches in the AME Church publication, *The Christian Recorder,* and continued to teach Sunday school at Mother Bethel Church in Philadelphia throughout the 1870s.

By the end of the Civil War, the MEC South had lost about a third of its members, the majority of whom were former slaves who joined the Northern Methodist or the AME Church. Within fifteen years, however, the MEC South had doubled its membership. As a custodian of the Lost Cause, it quickly regained the dominant place in Southern life. With the coming of peace, the church went separate, segregated ways in the North and South. The Colored (now Christian) Methodist Episcopal Church was formed in the South in 1870, and in 1866 the Northern Methodist church organized a separate African American conference with its own bishop. North and South reunited in 1939. Although many African Americans participate in the Methodist tradition, the large majority belong to one of the three major black Methodist denominations: AME, AME Zion, and Christian Methodist Church.

Karen Fisher Younger

See also Aid Societies; Coppin, Fanny Jackson (1837–1913); Harper, Frances Ellen Watkins (1825–1911); Haviland, Laura Smith (1808–1898); Religion; Wittenmyer, Annie Turner (1827–1900).

References and Further Reading

Ahlstrom, Sydney. 1972. *A Religious History of the American People.* New Haven, CT: Yale University Press.

Campbell, James. 1998. *Songs of Zion: The African Methodist Episcopal Church in the United States and South Africa.* New York: Oxford University Press.

Massey, Mary Elizabeth. 1994. *Women in the Civil War.* Lincoln: University of Nebraska Press. (Orig pub. 1966 as *Bonnet Brigades.*)

Miller, Randall M., Harry S. Stout, and Charles Reagan Wilson, eds. 1998. *Religion and the American Civil War.* New York: Oxford University Press.

Mitchell, Maria (1818–1889)

Pre-eminent American astronomer and strong advocate for women's rights, Maria Mitchell grew up on Nantucket Island. She became famous in 1847 after discovering a comet. She was one of the first professors at Vassar College, the first post-secondary institute for women in the United States.

Mitchell credited her upbringing for much of her later success. Nantucket's isolation from the continent secluded the residents from many contemporary influences. People on the island prized learning, and Mitchell's Quaker upbringing stressed hard work, a quiet demeanor, and, in many respects, equal opportunities for women.

Mitchell was the first of ten children in her family, nine of whom survived childhood. Her father was a banker and astronomer and her mother a librarian. From her early years, Mitchell loved to go up on the house's catwalk at night to practice astronomy with her father. By the time she was in her twenties, she led these expeditions to view the stars. In 1836 she assumed the position of librarian at the newly built Athenaeum. The job suited her

American astronomer and women's rights advocate Maria Mitchell (seated) in 1889. (Special Collections, Vassar College Libraries)

well, because she could pursue her own studies when not helping someone.

In 1843, after much deliberation, Mitchell left the Quaker faith. She could not bear its distrust of color and beauty, and she disliked its harsh punishments for members whose infractions were, in her opinion, relatively mild. Nevertheless, she continued to hold onto Quaker attitudes, such as valuing simplicity and directness.

On October 1, 1847, Mitchell noticed the appearance of a strange fuzzy body through her telescope that she had never seen before. She called her father who identified it as a comet. He immediately reported the discovery, which turned out to be the first viewing ever of that particular comet. Maria Mitchell became an overnight sensation for her discovery. In 1848 she became the first woman member of the American Academy of Arts and Sciences, the first of many honors. In 1849, Mitchell began working for the *American Euphemeris and Nautical Almanac.*

In 1857, a wealthy Chicago banker invited Mitchell to chaperone his young daughter through the South and then abroad to Europe. Mitchell saw this as a great opportunity to view the world and kept a journal of her experiences in the South. In her journal, Mitchell discussed the issue dominating the nation: slavery. She visited a slave market in New Orleans, heard white Southerners' defense of slavery, and observed related Southern attitudes about Northern "intrusions" into Southern affairs. As a result of her trip, Mitchell concluded that slavery was at least as great an evil for the master as for the slave.

One of Mitchell's brothers, Andrew, commanded a Union merchant ship in Mobile Bay during the Civil War. Another brother, Forster, went to the South to educate freedmen and later became a missionary.

After the war, Maria Mitchell took a position teaching astronomy at Vassar College in Poughkeepsie, New York. Throughout her twenty-three-year tenure there, she was a strong supporter of and role model for women's rights. She died on June 28, 1889, in Lynn, Massachusetts.

Ellen H. Todras

See also Northern Women; Teachers, Northern.
References and Further Reading

Albers, Henry, ed. 2001. *Maria Mitchell: A Life in Journals and Letters.* Clinton Corners, NY: College Avenue Press.
Kohlstedt, Sally Gregory. 1978. "Maria Mitchell and the Advancement of Women in Science." *New England Quarterly* 51: 39–63.
Wright, Helen. 1949. *Sweeper in the Sky: The Life of Maria Mitchell, First Woman Astronomer in America.* New York: Macmillan.

Monuments

The women of both the North and the South led or aided efforts to build thousands of Civil War monuments in cemeteries, battlefield sites, parks, city streets, and town squares. Grateful citizens also erected memorials to individual women and to groups of women for their efforts and sacrifices during the war. Southern women played a larger role in monument building than did their Northern counterparts. Women's efforts at monument building began before the Civil War concluded and continued into the 1930s.

Northerners began erecting monuments to their soldiers before the war ended. For example, a citizens' committee in Detroit, Michigan, began planning a monument in 1861. The town of Berlin, Connecticut, claims to have built one of the first Civil War monuments in the nation. A local reverend, Charles B. Hilliard, and sculptor Nelson Augustus Moore provided much of the impetus in the fundraising for the monument that Berlin's citizens dedicated on July 28, 1863.

Local Grand Army of the Republic chapters and leading men of the communities dominated postwar monument building in the North. The Women's Relief Corps, an auxiliary of the Grand Army of the Republic, instigated some monument building on their own, including a memorial to the unknown Union dead in Baltimore and a soldiers' monument in Cumberland, Maryland. However, in the case of most monuments, Northern women served in supporting roles, unlike their Southern counterparts who initiated and led much of their local monument building activity.

Southern women were more active in monument building than Northern women for several reasons. First, immediately after the war and during the Reconstruction era, military officials and newly elected Republican politicians curtailed large gatherings of ex-Confederate veterans or displays of the Confederate flag. The authorities found it more acceptable for women to form processions and gather in cemeteries to honor their fallen heroes, so Southern women became the accepted memorializers. Furthermore, Southern women's participation in monument building was a natural progression from the more accepted feminine roles of caring for and mourning the dead. The Federal government paid for a massive effort to re-bury and mark the graves of the thousands of Yankee soldiers buried throughout the South, but it was left to the former Confederate states and localities to pay for the proper burial and memorialization of their soldiers. Southern women took the leading role in the reburial effort.

The early efforts were typical of the local efforts to memorialize the dead Southern soldiers. The monuments were a natural extension of local women's efforts to mark and bury the dead in the immediate vicinity. For example, the Ladies' Memorial Association in Cheraw, South Carolina, erected what is likely the first monument to the Confederate dead. The women, led by Mrs. D. B. McLeod, met in the summer of 1866 and proposed building a memorial to mark the graves of sixty-two Confederate soldiers buried in the town. The ladies unveiled the monument, a thirteen-foot pillar of marble, on July 26, 1867. In contrast to later Confederate monuments, the inscription on the Cheraw memorial contains no mention of "Our Confederate Dead." The captain of the local Federal garrison did not want the inscription to glorify the Confederate cause but did not object to the more generic inscription "To Our Heroic Dead."

Similarly, the women of Fayetteville, North Carolina, led by Ann Kyle and Maria Spear, dedicated an early Confederate monument in Cross Creek Cemetery on December 30, 1868. Kyle and a group of women met to discuss their plans soon after Union General William Tecumseh Sherman left Fayetteville in March 1865. They saw to the rebur-ial of approximately thirty soldiers who had been hastily interred throughout the town. The women also determined to build a monument in memory of the fallen soldiers. Before they could proceed, they had to raise the money to build the proposed monument, a simple obelisk topped by a cross. At the suggestion of Spear, the women sewed a quilt and sold raffle tickets with the quilt as a prize. They sold $300 worth of tickets and had the monument built. In a show of continued loyalty to the failed Confederate nation, the winner of the quilt presented it to former Confederate President Jefferson Davis.

Honoring the fallen soldiers of the Lost Cause contained an inherent political element. In the years immediately following the Civil War, Southern women had more freedom than men did to participate in the commemoration of the Confederacy and its soldiers. However, the withdrawal of Federal troops from the former Confederate states and the re-enfranchisement of former Confederate leaders did not end Southern women's role in erecting monuments and memorializing lost soldiers. The decades from 1890 to 1920 saw an increase of monument building throughout the South as ex-Confederates and conservative whites began to flex their political muscle in a more public way. The unveiling ceremonies often drew thousands of spectators and featured politicians of note as well as former Confederate officers as orators.

During this period, Southern women formalized their monument associations into chapters of the United Daughters of the Confederacy (UDC). They still used the fundraising methods pioneered by the early monument builders, such as selling their handicrafts and holding dances. Southern women, who were assumed to be, as women, apolitical, also began lobbying their state assemblies for matching funds to commemorate fallen soldiers.

Most of the Civil War monuments built during this period were statues of a standing soldier. This common style is visible on hundreds of Southern courthouse lawns and town squares. In some instances, Southern women commissioned local or nationally prominent sculptors to craft the statues for their community. Far more common, however, were monuments mass-produced by companies that aggressively marketed their products through advertisements in *Confederate Veteran* and with elaborate catalogs touting easy payment plans. Although early monuments had been erected primarily in cemeteries, they began to be placed in more public spaces. The change in venue illustrated the change in the message of the memorials from one that stressed the remembrance of dead Confederate soldiers to one that highlighted the importance of passing on the legacy of the soldiers' noble cause and sacrifices to succeeding generations. Another marker of the change in focus came with the inclusion of children in prominent roles in dedication ceremonies.

Many onlookers saw the unveiling of the Confederate monument in Arlington National Cemetery on June 4, 1914, as a vindication of the United Daughters of the Confederacy's earlier memorial building efforts and as a symbol of national reconciliation. To erect the monument, the UDC raised money nationally with time-tested methods such as ice cream socials and Confederate bazaars. In addition, the innovative idea of selling Confederate Christmas seals enabled the organization to raise the $50,000 necessary to build the monument.

Women not only built monuments, but they were also honored with them. During the 1890s, veterans of the Confederate army began efforts to build monuments to the women of the South. The monuments were intended to acknowledge women's perseverance and sacrifice during and after the Civil War. A joint committee consisting of members of the United Confederate Veterans and the Sons of Confederate Veterans decided in 1909 to choose a common design for the monument and then let states purchase casts of it for their state capital grounds. The committee decided on a design by Belle Kinney, a native Tennessean and daughter of a Confederate veteran. In the end, only two states, Tennessee and Mississippi, used the chosen design, which featured a woman placing a palm of glory on a dying Confederate soldier while an allegorical figure of fame placed a crown of palms on her head.

Ultimately, seven of the eleven former Confederate states erected monuments to their women. South Carolina unveiled the first state monument to Confederate women on April 11, 1912. Their monument depicted an angel and two winged, cherubic children honoring a seated woman and was erected on the grounds of the new State House. North Carolina's 1914 monument and Florida's 1915 effort shared similar designs, featuring a seated woman reading to children the "true" history of the Civil War from an open book. Arkansas and Maryland dedicated their respective monuments in 1913 and 1918. Individual communities also erected monuments to their women. In 1934, the citizens of Wadesboro, North Carolina, dedicated a monument to the community's Confederate women. The Wadesboro monument featured two bas relief sculptures: one panel depicted a hoopskirted Southern belle sending a man off to war, and the other showed the same lady handing an infant to a stereotypical mammy figure.

The Northern states had no regional effort to specifically honor their Civil War women as a group. The headquarters building of the American Red Cross, dedicated in Washington, D.C., in 1917, was originally intended to honor the women of the North and their sacrifices during the Civil War. Former Union General Francis C. Barlow spearheaded the original effort of building a monument to these women, in part to honor his wife, Arabelle Wharton Barlow, who had died in 1864 of a fever she had contracted while working as a nurse at a Union hospital. Congress passed a bill to fund the building in 1913. However, in its final form, the bill stated the building was intended to honor women of both the North and the South.

In many cases, however, grateful Northern citizens erected monuments to individual women who played vital roles in the Civil War. For example, on September 9, 1962, the Maryland Civil War Centennial Commission dedicated a plaque on the Antietam battlefield to Clara Barton, the Civil War nurse and founder of the American Red Cross. The town of Frederick, Maryland, similarly dedicated a monument in 1914 to Barbara Fritchie. This legendary heroine of the poem by John Greenleaf Whittier supposedly waved an American flag in defiance as Confederate Brigadier General "Stonewall" Jackson and his men marched through the town.

Other Northern monuments honor the women who served as nurses. In Washington, D.C., at the intersection of M Street and Rhode Island Avenue, sits a memorial honoring the nuns who nursed the wounded during the Civil War. In 1906, the citizens of Galesburg, Illinois, dedicated a monument to Mary Ann Ball "Mother" Bickerdyke, a Civil War nurse and postwar advocate for veteran's pensions. The monument shows Bickerdyke kneeling and tending to a wounded soldier. The statue sits on the courthouse lawn, an area usually reserved for the commonplace standing soldier statues.

Thomas Vincent

See also Barton, Clara (1821–1912); Bickerdyke, Mary Ann Ball "Mother" (1817–1901); Mourning; Northern Women; Southern Women; United Daughters of the Confederacy.

References and Further Reading

Blair, William. 2004. *Cities of the Dead: Contesting the Memory of the Civil War in the South, 1865–1914.* Chapel Hill: University of North Carolina Press.

Cox, Karen L. 2003. *Dixie's Daughters: The United Daughters of the Confederacy and the Preservation of Confederate Culture.* Gainesville: University Press of Florida.

Foster, Gaines M. 1987. *Ghosts of the Confederacy: Defeat, the Lost Cause, and the Emergence of the New South.* New York: Oxford University Press.

Mills, Cynthia, and Pamela H. Simpson, eds. 2003. *Monuments to the Lost Cause: Women, Art, and the Landscapes of Southern Memory.* Knoxville: University of Tennessee Press.

Neff, John R. 2005. *Honoring the Civil War Dead: Commemoration and the Problem of Reconciliation.* Lawrence: University Press of Kansas.

Piehler, G. Kurt. 1995. *Remembering War the American Way.* Washington DC: Smithsonian Institution.

Tinling, Marion. 1986. *Women Remembered: A Guide to Landmarks of Women's History in the United States.* Westport, CT: Greenwood Press.

Moon, Charlotte "Lottie" (1829–1895)

Lottie Moon was the elder of a pair of sisters who served as spies, couriers, and smugglers for the Confederacy during the Civil War.

Born Cynthia Charlotte in Danville, Virginia, on August 10, 1829 to Dr. Robert S. and Cynthia Ann (Sullivan) Moon, Moon was independent and strong-minded from an early age. Her natural proclivity for horsemanship, marksmanship, and acting served her well in her activities on behalf of the Confederacy in later years. Moon's brothers Robert and William served in the Confederate army and Navy respectively, while she and her sister Ginnie did their part on the homefront.

Before marrying Peace Democrat Judge James Clark on January 30, 1849, Moon was betrothed to Ambrose Burnside who later became a general with the Union army. She and Burnside met while she visited Brownsville, Indiana, and he courted her, bringing small gifts to her younger sisters Ginnie and Mary, at her family's home at Oxford, Ohio. On their wedding day, June 21, 1848, Moon arrived at the altar and said that she had changed her mind and would not marry Burnside.

As the South withdrew from the Union, Clark avowed states' rights and supported secession. Moon's subterfuge began when she pretended that her son Frank was ill and ordered medical supplies, which she then delivered to wounded Confederate soldiers. Clark's and Moon's Jones Station home became the central hub of anti-Union activities in Butler County.

Her first mission was in the summer of 1862. Walker Taylor, a nephew of Zachary Taylor, arrived at Jones Station, Ohio, with a message from General Sterling Price to Colonel Edmund Kirby Smith in Lexington, Kentucky. Taylor was too recognizable to carry the message, so Lottie volunteered. Disguising herself as an Irish woman, she easily passed the papers to a Confederate officer who placed them in Kirby's hands.

On another mission in October 1862, she traveled to Canada disguised as a British woman, and she carried letters from Reverend Stuart Robinson, who tried to convince Jefferson Davis that the Confederacy should unite with the Knights of the Golden Circle. Her acting abilities, flair for costume, and ear for accents coupled with her uncommon skill at knocking her joints out of place eased her crossing of lines and supposedly landed her in President

Abraham Lincoln's party—though one account places her in his carriage—when he reviewed the Army of the Potomac. She allegedly met Secretary of War Edwin M. Stanton on that occasion.

Finally recognized by General Ambrose Burnside, Moon was caught and her usefulness to the Confederacy ended. Some scholars suggest that Moon exaggerated her exploits because her movements were logistically impossible and that she was never captured by Burnside, but created a fictionalized account based on her sister Ginnie's capture.

After the Confederacy's fall, Clark and Moon moved to New York City where she became a war correspondent for the *World* during the Franco-Prussian War. Returning to Manhattan, she wrote novels under the pseudonym Charles M. Clay. She died of cancer at her son's home in Philadelphia on November 20, 1895.

Rebecca Tolley-Stokes

See also Davis, Jefferson (1808–1889); Female Spies; Imprisonment of Women; Lincoln, Abraham (1809–1865); Moon, Virginia "Ginnie" (1844–1925); Southern Women.

References and Further Reading

Marsh, Thomas O., and Marlene Templin. 1988. "The Ballad of Lottie Moon." *Civil War: The Magazine of the Civil War Society* 21: 40–45.

Marvel, William. 1991. *Burnside.* Chapel Hill: University of North Carolina Press.

Smith, Orphia. 1962. *Oxford Spy: Wed at Pistol Point.* Oxford, OH: Cullen Printing Co.

Moon, Virginia "Ginnie" (1844–1925)

Ginnie Moon was the younger of a pair of sisters who served as spies, couriers, and smugglers for the Confederacy. She was also the most noted female spy working in Memphis, Tennessee.

Ginnie was born Virginia Bethel in Oxford, Ohio, on June 22, 1844 to Dr. Robert S. and Cynthia Ann (Sullivan) Moon. Unlike the stereotypical Southern belle, Moon was independent and noted for carrying a pearl-handled pistol in her skirts.

When her family moved to Memphis at the beginning of the war, Ginnie stayed behind at Oxford Female College. She soon got around the school rule prohibiting young women from leaving the college unescorted. The school expelled her for shooting the stars out of an American flag flying on campus, and she joined her family in Tennessee.

In Memphis, Moon comforted sick and wounded Confederate soldiers in many ways, including becoming engaged to sixteen of them. She prepared bandages and helped in other efforts. When the city fell to Union forces in 1862, Ginnie's beauty and charm beguiled many Union soldiers and officers who revealed information that she passed to Confederate officials. In the winter of 1863, Ginnie, like her sister Lottie, acted as a courier for General Sterling Price, carrying his message from Jackson, Mississippi, to her brother-in-law, Judge James Clark, of Jones Station, Ohio. A young, charming woman, Moon easily slipped into and out of Union territory with sensitive information.

Detained by Union officials as she traveled aboard the *Alice Dean* from Cincinnati to Memphis on April 3, 1863, Moon drew her Colt revolver on Captain Harrison Rose when he tried to search her without anyone else in the room. After Ginnie threatened to kill him if he touched her and to report his behavior to General Ambrose Burnside, Rose left her in the cabin. She removed sensitive dispatches relating to the Northwest Conspiracy from her corset, wet them, and swallowed them. As Rose accompanied her to the Custom's Office, the clanking of her hoop-skirt gave her away. Quilted within her clothing were vials of morphine, opium, and camphor, and Moon was charged with smuggling.

Burnside, an old family friend and spurned beau of Lottie's, kept informed of Ginnie's case and released her into her mother's custody. They stayed in Cincinnati for three weeks until Union officials transferred Ginnie to Fort Monroe, Virginia, where she was imprisoned for several months. Eventually, she was paroled to Jones Station, Ohio, home of her sister and brother-in-law.

Moon's version of the events leading to her arrest and detention at Fort Monroe differs significantly from published accounts. In April 1864, she, her sister-in-law Lizzie, along with Lizzie's two children and their nurse, boarded the *Flag of Truce* at Richmond bound for Newport News. They planned to take the steamer to Baltimore and then go on to Europe to join Moon's brother in Liverpool, England. General Benjamin Butler detained the party before they boarded the steamer, demanding that they swear an oath of allegiance to the Union; Ginnie refused. The provost marshall walked her two blocks to Fort Monroe where she stayed a little over a month. Her mother had not known that Ginnie was imprisoned until she returned to Danville, Virginia, where she corresponded with Confederate President Jefferson Davis. At Danville, Ginnie took charge of a ward at the General Hospital, overseeing the care of fifty soldiers. On one occasion, a seriously wounded charge would not eat the hospital food, so Moon downed two robins, had them cooked, and brought them to him. Before he died, he asked that Moon get his cap and pistol to his family in Kentucky upon his death. Moon attended his funeral as his chief mourner. The soldier's father came for his son's body after the war and heard of Moon's ministrations. In the summer of 1866, the soldier's father visited Memphis to take her to Kentucky to live as his adopted daughter. Ginnie refused, but she visited the family when coming home from a trip north.

Moon devoted her life to helping others and is remembered in Memphis as the heroine of the yellow fever epidemic of the early 1870s. She appeared in several movies after moving to California to pursue her interests in acting and aviation. Eventually settling in Greenwich Village, New York, she died on September 11, 1925.

Rebecca Tolley-Stokes

See also Davis, Jefferson (1808–1889); Female Spies; Imprisonment of Women; Moon, Charlotte "Lottie" (1829–1895); Nurses; Southern Women.

References and Further Reading

Kinchen, Oscar A. 1972. *Women Who Spied for the Blue and the Gray.* Philadelphia, PA: Dorrance & Company.

Leonard, Elizabeth D. 1999. *All the Daring of the Soldier: Women of the Civil War Armies.* New York: W. W. Norton & Company.

Marvel, William. 1991. *Burnside.* Chapel Hill: University of North Carolina Press.

Moon, Virginia B. No date. "Experiences of Virginia B. Moon, during the War between the States."

Moon Collection. Oxford, OH: Smith Library of Regional History.

Smith, Orphia. 1962. *Oxford Spy: Wed at Pistol Point.* Oxford, OH: Cullen Printing Co.

Morale

Maintaining morale over the course of four years of war taxed both the material and emotional resources of Confederate and Union women. Wartime morale was directly related to patriotism, loyalty, and military success. Nineteenth-century conceptions of wartime morale were highly gendered. Men demonstrated their commitment to war aims primarily by volunteering to serve in the armed forces and then by re-enlisting to continue their service to their respective nations until war's end. For women, supporting the war effort required sustained self-denial and sacrifice, demonstrated by encouraging male kin to do their duty by enlisting, by contributing their time and resources to supply the armies, and by providing emotional support through letters and stoicism. Morale on both the Union and Confederate homefronts surged and plummeted, responding to military defeats and victories, political missteps and initiatives, and economic circumstances across seasons.

At the outbreak of the war, women of the Confederacy and Union witnessed the eagerness with which their male kin and neighbors volunteered for military service. They lent support by encouraging the men who did not readily enlist to do so and by providing uniforms, flags, and other supplies to local companies heading off to defend home and country. However, women's assistance was moderated by their fears regarding male relatives' battlefield deaths and the potential for their family's economic instability. Even so, women were expected to endure soldiers' leave-taking with smiles, kisses, and approval rather than with tears, fears, and doubts.

Confederate women earned high regard as they were swept up in the excitement of the South's declaring war and hearing about the early victories in the fall of 1861 through the summer of 1862. Demonstrating their faith in the Confederate cause through patriotic verse, prose, and plays, with letters to absent men, and by grieving stoically for fallen soldiers, women attempted to reinforce positive attitudes about the war and the sacrifices that both they and their male kin made on the Confederacy's behalf. These efforts to maintain morale were generally accepted because they adhered to expectations regarding Southern white womanhood rather than challenging them. Confederate women also pursued less socially acceptable ways of demonstrating patriotism by engaging in activities that threatened perceptions of their femininity and purity. These included volunteering as nurses, criticizing or questioning political and military decisions and actions, and developing an increasing sense of independence through managing farms and plantations. Forming volunteer organizations, like the Charleston Soldiers' Relief Association or more informal neighborhood groups, to collect and make items to send to local military units gave Southern white women a greater sense of purpose and a way to contribute materially to the war effort. Gathered together in one another's homes, churches, and town halls, they were able to reaffirm their commitment to the cause individually and collectively, as well as provide emotional support to each other in the event that they received bad news from the battlefield.

Despite Northern women's efforts to organize local soldiers' aid societies, sew flags, collect lint, and roll bandages in unprecedented numbers and to wave as their soldier kin boarded steamboats and railroad cars, they were criticized by some for not committing themselves as fully to the Union war effort as had their Confederate counterparts. Southern women were held up as the model of female patriotism, whereas Northern women did not meet that standard, according to newspapers and political leaders. In spite of, and sometimes in response to, these complaints, many Union women dedicated themselves to improving soldiers' physical environment, comfort, and spirits. They did so formally as agents of the United States Sanitary Commission or as nurses employed by the Federal government, as well as informally through visits to military camps and the delivery of care packages containing items from home. Soldiers consistently reported that women like Clara Barton and Mary Ann "Mother" Bickerdyke raised their spirits by providing personal care and spreading cheer among the wounded and weary.

Fundraising fairs, bazaars, and performances sponsored by women's volunteer organizations in both the Confederacy and the Union generally garnered public approbation. In cities like New York City and Chicago, Columbia and Atlanta, these activities attracted large numbers of people willing to contribute items for sale or auction as well as generous sums of money. In towns and villages, people attended ice cream socials, dances, and lyceums to share war news from local units and to visit with soldiers on furlough. Displaying festive decorations and banners and offering patriotic music and speeches, these gatherings, both large and small, were public exhibitions intended to reinvigorate civilian morale, especially as the war stretched from months into years.

Some women were reticent about the war, if not unsupportive. From the beginning of the war Fannie Chamberlain, wife of Union Gettysburg hero Joshua Lawrence Chamberlain, resented her husband's war career, especially after he received a life-threatening wound; she also eschewed women's soldiers' aid organizations and activities. Although neither her diffidence nor his poor health undermined her husband's commitment to the war, other wives' ambivalence toward their male kin's war service and their criticism of the military as well as the political leadership did have an adverse effect on their soldiers' morale, especially as the war casualties rose and letters requesting, pleading, and then demanding men's return increased in the last two years of the war. Some soldiers wrote home to persuade women of the worthiness of their military service and of the need for women's loyalty, attempting to boost the morale of their wives and mothers.

Socioeconomic class distinctions strained women's commitment to the war effort and willingness to sacrifice their male kin and the family's well-being. The Union government, with its superior resources and established bureaucracy, increasingly responded to women's economic hardships by issuing incentives like bounties and pensions to alleviate some of the economic distress faced by working-class soldiers' families. In addition, the government

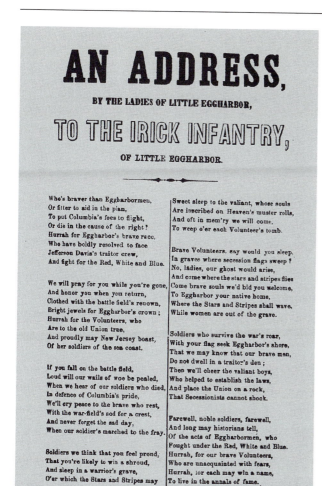

An address, by the ladies of Little Eggharbor to the Irick Infantry of Little Eggharbor, New Jersey, 1861. (Library of Congress)

offered expanded employment opportunities for women as nurses or clerks as another form of financial assistance. Some soldiers' relief societies directed their funds and supplies to poor women whose male breadwinners were away serving in the war, leaving their families without means of support.

On the other hand, some commentators glorified poor women's suffering and suggested that wealthy women should emulate their sacrifice. In the cash-poor Confederacy, with inflation spiraling out of control, many women and children hovered at the edge of subsistence and poverty. With their husbands no longer providing for and protecting them, white women looked to Confederate leaders to assume the role of provider and protector; however, the government was ill equipped to ameliorate their plight. By the spring of 1863, the dire economic conditions led to bread riots, instigated by women protesting merchants' extortionist prices and the government's inability to offer assistance. Their wealthy counterparts communicated their waning support for the Confederate cause through hosting extravagant parties and purchasing luxury items instead of donating to support the war effort.

Before 1863, Northern African American women organized supplies to send to Southern slave families rather than to white Union troops. Escaped slave women in Union army military camps offered their services as laundresses and cooks, sometimes as a way to aid the army but most commonly as a means to support themselves. Their labor clearly improved soldiers' and officers' morale, however, as they benefited from clean uniforms and well-cooked meals. African American women experienced a marked increase in their dedication to Union war efforts after the Emancipation Proclamation of January 1, 1863, and they actively engaged in recruiting for the new black regiments. Abolitionist Sojourner Truth spoke at rallies to boost support for the Republican Party in 1864, and other black women involved themselves in relief efforts for escaped and newly freed slaves. African American women faced fears that extended beyond those experienced by white soldiers' wives because of Confederate policy to kill or enslave black Union soldiers. In addition, unequal pay and benefits to black soldiers had adverse effects on their wives and children; they therefore endured economic hardship, which then caused their men's morale to decline.

Following the Union victories in the summer and fall of 1863 and then the military stalemate in the winter of 1864–1865, war weariness had set in on both sides of the Civil War, although it was much more pronounced in the Confederacy. Enduring the many economic hardships, labor problems, and loss of male relatives and neighbors, Confederate women's morale fell to an all-time low. Sacrifice and suffering, once the foundation of women's patriotism, prompted some women, their morale exhausted, to beg their husbands to desert the army and return to their families. Some historians suggest that Confederate women's waning support for the war contributed significantly to the Confederacy's loss. Many Union women, too, urged soldiers either not to re-enlist at the end of their three-year term of service or to leave the army before their enlistment term expired, despite the indications that the war would result in a Union victory. After Abraham Lincoln's death and with the war's conclusion imminent, Northern women varied in their assessment as to whether the war merited their four years' worth of sacrifices and losses. The Civil War's cost to both Union and Confederate women physically, materially, and emotionally far exceeded their expectations.

Andrea R. Foroughi

See also African American Women; Aid Societies; Barton, Clara (1821–1912); Bickerdyke, Mary Ann Ball "Mother" (1817–1901); Bread Riots; Camp Followers; Chamberlain, Frances Caroline "Fannie" Adams (1825–1905); Columbia Bazaar (January 17–21, 1865); Confederate Homefront; Contrabands; Domesticity; Emancipation Proclamation (January 1, 1863); Enlistment; Fairs and Bazaars; Family Life, Confederate; Family Life, Union; Flags, Regimental; Food; Fundraising; Hospitals; Letter Writing; Nationalism, Confederate; Nationalism, United States; Nonslaveholding Southerners; Northern Women; Nurses; Plantation Life; Politics; Rural Women; Separate Spheres; Sewing Bees; Shortages; Slaveholding Women; Southern Women; Truth, Sojourner [Isabella Baumfree] (1797–1883); Union Homefront; Wartime Employment.

References and Further Reading

Cashin, Joan. 2002. "Deserters, Civilians, and Draft Resistance in the North." In *The War Was You and Me: Civilians in the American Civil War*, edited by Joan E. Cashin, 262–285. Princeton, NJ: Princeton University Press.

Faust, Drew Gilpin. 1996. *Mothers of Invention: Women of the Slaveholding South in the American Civil War.* Chapel Hill: University of North Carolina Press.

Faust, Drew Gilpin. 1998. "'Ours as Well as That of the Men': Women and Gender in the Civil War." In *Writing the Civil War: The Quest to Understand*, edited by James M. McPherson and William J. Cooper Jr., 228–240. Columbia: University of South Carolina Press.

Silber, Nina. 2005. *Daughters of the Union: Northern Women Fight the Civil War.* Cambridge, MA: Harvard University Press.

Smith, Jennifer Lund. 2001. "The Reconstruction of 'Home': The Civil War and the Marriage of Lawrence and Fannie Chamberlain." In *Intimate Strategies of the Civil War: Military Commanders and Their Wives*, edited by Carol K. Bleser and Lesley J. Gordon, 157–177. New York: Oxford University Press.

Whites, LeeAnn. 1992. "The Civil War as a Crisis in Gender." In *Divided Houses: Gender and the Civil War*, edited by Catherine Clinton and Nina Silber, 3–21. New York: Oxford University Press.

Morgan, Sarah Ida Fowler (1842–1909)

Sarah Morgan of Baton Rouge was nineteen in 1862 when she began what was to be one of the most important diaries of the Civil War years, chronicling her experience of the dislocation and devastating personal loss experienced by many families in the South. She wrote with wit and insight, and so well that the published version required little editing.

Born in New Orleans on February 28, 1842, Sarah was the daughter of Judge Thomas Gibbes Morgan and Sarah Hunt Fowler. Her father had migrated before 1820 from Pennsylvania to Baton Rouge, where he practiced law and married into the local plantation aristocracy. All the Morgan children except for Sarah and her younger brother Jimmy were born in Baton Rouge on the site subsequently occupied by the state capitol. Judge Morgan was appointed collector for the Port of New Orleans, and it was there Sarah was born. The Morgans returned to Baton Rouge in 1850. Sarah was educated almost entirely at home and read widely on her own. She was introduced to New Orleans society in 1860.

Sarah's journal begins with a retrospective of the April 1861 death of her brother Harry in a duel and of Judge Morgan's fatal illness six months later. She adopted the political views of her father, a Southern Whig who favored preserving the Union but, upon secession, became a loyal Confederate. Three of Sarah's remaining brothers fought for the Confederacy. Philip was a Union supporter and sister Lavinia married a Union officer, complicating but not diminishing Sarah's fervent Confederate patriotism. In 1862, shelling from Union gunboats drove the Morgans out of Baton Rouge and their home was looted. Much of Sarah's narrative chronicles the family's experiences as refugees, Sarah's flirtations with Confederate officers, her convalescence after a serious back injury in a November 1862 buggy accident, and the family's mourning for the two brothers who died in Confederate service.

After the war, Sarah and her mother lived with brother Jimmy in South Carolina. She was courted by the influential Charleston newspaper editor Francis Warrington Dawson, who encouraged her to begin writing for his paper in 1873. Sarah's anonymous columns were very popular and afforded her modest financial independence. After marrying Dawson on January 25, 1874, she wrote only occasional book reviews. The Dawsons had three children, one of whom died in infancy.

Sarah's life was shattered in 1889 by her husband's murder. Subsequent financial difficulties led her to write stories for magazines, but few were published. In 1899 she moved to France to live with her son. *Les Aventures de Jeannot Lapin* (1903), a French version of the Brer Rabbit stories, was her greatest literary success.

Sarah Morgan Dawson died in Paris on May 5, 1909, and is buried next to her husband in Charleston.

Nancy Gray Schoonmaker

See also Civilian Life; Confederate Homefront; Diaries and Journals; Refugees; Southern Women.
References and Further Reading
East, Charles, ed. 1991. *The Civil War Diary of a Southern Woman.* New York: Simon & Schuster.

Mosby's Rangers

Officially known as the Forty-third Battalion of Virginia Cavalry, Mosby's Rangers were Confederate troops who disrupted Union supply operations in several northern Virginia counties during the Civil War. Commanded by Colonel John Singleton Mosby, the Rangers were known for their daring exploits. Gathering information, supplies, and support from the local populations, the Rangers came into close contact with many civilians. Their proximity and reliance on Southern civilians, however, led Union forces to target these non-military allies as well.

The Rangers' success can be credited to the exploits of their famed leader. Not only did he give his name to the command, but Mosby also recruited, coordinated, and led his men on various raids and attacks. Born in 1833, John Singleton Mosby attended the University of Virginia and was practicing law when the Civil War broke out. Mosby served in the First Virginia Cavalry as a scout and a picket. He eventually joined the staff of famed Confederate cavalry general James Ewell Brown "J.E.B." Stuart.

In January 1863, Stuart approved Mosby's request to lead a small band of men in guerrilla operations behind Union lines. To sustain the thousands of troops in the field, the Union army needed a secure depot and a reliable supply train that could connect the main army with its base. The farther the Union army advanced, the longer and more vulnerable these supply lines became. Mosby suggested that he and his guerrillas might be able to disrupt these lines and keep many Union troops from joining the main army because they would have to be detailed to protect their supply trains.

Aside from professional soldiers, most of the men Mosby recruited were in their twenties and thirties. Many of them were lured by the belief that raiding Union trains on horseback was a romantic and adventurous ideal. As men with families in the immediate area, they could also remain close to home and kin while serving the Confederacy. From its beginnings as a small group of about fifteen men, Mosby's command eventually grew to several hundred. By the end of the war, nineteen hundred men had served under his command at one time or another.

Mosby's Rangers operated mainly in the northern Virginia counties of Fauquier and Loudoun, but they also struck Union troops in surrounding counties, sometimes crossing into the Shenandoah Valley as well. Their favorite stomping grounds soon became known as Mosby's Confederacy. The Rangers relied on agility, coordination, and surprise to overcome the Union's numerical superiority. They struck camps, broke into garrisons, raided wagon trains, and even held up a locomotive. After a raid, the troopers would disappear, blending in with the civilian population, until they were summoned again. Perhaps Mosby's most daring exploit was the capture of Union General Edwin Stoughton as he slept in a Union-held town. For a period, Union defenders were even concerned that Mosby—nicknamed the Gray Ghost—might sneak into Washington to kidnap President Abraham Lincoln.

The Rangers relied heavily on a friendly civilian population. As members of the community, they could count on shelter and food from many civilians. Men and women in the area who were loyal to the Confederate government sought to help their soldiers and protect them from capture. Furthermore, earning local support allowed Mosby an intricate knowledge of the forests, farms, and roads in the region. Many women served as spies, passing information they had gained from Union troops back to Mosby. Mosby created a network for passing along information, which helped him pinpoint Union columns as they entered the region, seeking to capture or destroy his forces.

All raids had the potential for disaster, and many Rangers fell wounded or were captured during the course of their various operations. Mosby himself was severely wounded during a nasty skirmish. The Rangers faced many determined Union commanders. Among the most vicious were the troops under Union General Philip Sheridan, who operated against Mosby from the late summer of 1864 to the early months of 1865. Charged with clearing out the Shenandoah Valley, Sheridan could not allow Mosby's Rangers to threaten his supply base. Consequently, he ordered thousands of cavalrymen to ride into known guerrilla territory to destroy any supplies that might be used by the partisan fighters. The contest between these two opposing sides escalated when Mosby threatened to hang a Union prisoner for each of his Rangers who was captured and executed by the Union commander.

Since Mosby's men blended in seamlessly with the local population, Union authorities concluded that they must target Mosby's civilian supporters. To this end, various Union raids netted old men and young boys who, they suspected, were aiding the guerrillas.

In addition, they arrested some women for allegedly giving aid and information to Mosby's men. During the most vicious period of war between Mosby and his Union counterparts, barns and outbuildings, where the guerrillas might have hidden, were burned, and livestock were butchered or hauled away so that they could not be used to feed the Rangers. These Union raids destroyed millions of dollars in property, all in the name of capturing or chasing away Mosby's men.

Despite the harsh tactics, Union countermeasures never fully halted Mosby's operations. Even though they did force the guerrillas onto the defensive from time to time, Union commands could never capture Mosby himself or curtail his activities. In the same vein, although Mosby's men were a great annoyance and brought fear to Federal troops garrisoned in northern Virginia, they had limited success in derailing the main Union operations in the field. Mosby never surrendered his command, choosing instead to quietly disband it at the end of the war.

Kanisorn Wongsrichanalai

See also Civilian Life; Confederate Homefront; Destruction of Homes; Destruction of Personal Property; Family Life, Confederate; Female Spies; Food; Foraging, Effects on Women; Honor; Guerrilla Warfare; Morale; Southern Women.

References and Further Reading
Ashdown, Paul. 2002. *The Mosby Myth: A Confederate Hero in Life and Legend.* Wilmington, DE: Scholarly Resources.

Ramage, James A. 1999. *Gray Ghost: The Life of Col. John Singleton Mosby.* Lexington: University Press of Kentucky.

Wert, Jeffry D. 1990. *Mosby's Rangers.* New York: Simon & Schuster.

Mott, Lucretia Coffin (1793–1880)

A Quaker minister, leader in the abolitionist movement, and women's rights activist, Lucretia Mott organized the Philadelphia Female Anti-Slavery Society and ran a station on the Underground Railroad at her Philadelphia home. She worked with Frederick Douglass and William Lloyd Garrison in the fight against slavery.

Lucretia was born on January 3, 1793, in Nantucket, Massachusetts, to Anna and Thomas Coffin. Raised in the Society of Friends, Lucretia's views on slavery and women's rights were set at an early age. The Coffin family moved to Boston in 1804, and the children attended public school so that they would be familiar with all types of people. In 1806 Lucretia was sent to the Quaker boarding school at Nine Partners, New York, where she eventually became an assistant teacher. She was unhappy to learn that the female teachers made only a fraction of the salary of the male teachers. In 1809, the family moved to Philadelphia, where Lucretia remained for the rest of her life.

On April 10, 1811, Lucretia married James Mott, whom she had met at Nine Partners. Together, they had six children, some of whom would actively participate in their parents' abolitionist activities.

In 1821 Lucretia was designated as a minister in the Society of Friends, and by 1829 she was preaching against slavery in the colored churches in Philadelphia. In general, the Quakers did not take a strong antislavery stand, and Lucretia's views were met with animosity by her fellow church members. Undeterred, Lucretia made her first prominent appearance at an antislavery convention in Philadelphia in 1833, where she delivered a speech that was met with both praise and vilification. At one point, the Society of Friends discussed dissolving Lucretia's membership with the church.

Around this time Lucretia organized the Philadelphia Female Anti-Slavery Society. She served as the organization's first secretary and then as its president for many years. This group labored for thirty-six years, and its membership included Lucretia's daughters Anna Mott Hopper and Maria Mott Davis. In 1840 the Philadelphia society elected Lucretia as a delegate to attend a world antislavery convention in London. No women were allowed to speak at the convention, however, and those who were allowed to attend were seated as visitors. Lucretia met Elizabeth Cady Stanton at the convention in London, a meeting that eventually led to the Equal Rights Convention at Seneca Falls, New York, in 1848.

After the 1850 passage of the Fugitive Slave Act, Lucretia continued speaking publicly against slav-

As a Quaker minister, abolitionist, and women's rights advocate, Lucretia Mott played a major role in the early American reform movement. (Library of Congress)

ery and engaged in further antislavery and nonresistant activities such as the Underground Railroad. Lucretia worked closely with other antislavery advocates, such as Frederick Douglass and William Lloyd Garrison. When the Civil War broke out in 1861, Lucretia, an advocate of nonviolence, denounced the war. However, she hoped the war would end slavery. Lucretia served as vice president of the Pennsylvania Peace Society, which raised money for the education of free blacks and those who had become newly free.

After the war, Lucretia served as the first president of the American Equal Rights Association, an organization devoted to securing the vote for former slaves. Because women had no participation in politics, Lucretia's energies were attracted to the organization and maintenance of freedmen's associations to relieve the acute demand for food and to promote industry and self-support among blacks.

Mott and other female proponents of equal rights initially opposed the Fourteenth Amendment because they wanted it to include votes for women. However, they met with much derision and had to accept that black men would get their rights first. Mott and other women's rights activists hoped that voting rights for women would follow in the not too distant future.

Lucretia's husband James died on February 26, 1868. Lucretia quietly lived out the remainder of her life, never wavering in her beliefs on equality for all people. Her last public address was made in May 1880 at the Philadelphia yearly meeting of the Society of Friends. She died at home on November 11, 1880.

Gwen Thomas Mays

See also Abolitionism and Northern Reformers; Douglass, Frederick (ca. 1818–1895); Fourteenth Amendment; Garrison, William Lloyd (1805–1879); Northern Women; Quaker Women; Stanton, Elizabeth Cady (1815–1902); Union Homefront.

References and Further Reading

Bacon, Margaret Hope. 1980. *Valiant Friend: The Life of Lucretia Mott.* New York: Walker & Company.

Cromwell, Otelia. 1958. *Lucretia Mott.* Cambridge, MA: Harvard University Press.

Greene, Dana, ed. 1980. *Lucretia Mott, Her Complete Speeches and Sermons.* Lewiston, NY: Edwin Mellen Press.

Moulton, Louise Chandler (1835–1908)

One of the most popular American women writers of her time, both in the United States and abroad, Louise Chandler Moulton sponsored two salons, which became gathering places for eminent literary figures in Boston and London. Her poetry received praise from authors such as Robert Browning and Thomas Hardy, and her short stories and novels were popular as well.

Born April 10, 1835, in Pomfret, Connecticut, Louise Chandler was the only child of Louisa Rebecca Clark and Lucius Lemuel Chandler. She grew up in a strict Calvinist household, receiving her education at a Pomfret school and later at Emma Willard's Female Seminary in Troy, New York. At fourteen, Louise first submitted poetry to a newspaper and continued writing for periodicals under the name Ellen Louise. At eighteen, her first book, *This, That and the Other,* a collection of her newspaper and magazine writings, was published. It quickly sold over twenty thousand copies.

Following the publication of her book, Louise enrolled at Mrs. Willard's, graduating after one year. On August 27, 1855, she married William Upham Moulton, editor and publisher of the *True Flag,* a Boston literary journal to which she had regularly contributed. The couple had one daughter. During the 1850s, Moulton contributed to magazines such as *Godey's Lady's Book* and *Peterson's Magazine,* common venues for literary work at the time. Her second book, *Juno Clifford,* published anonymously in 1855, achieved great popularity.

Moulton's writing during the Civil War shared themes encouraging women to support their husbands and sons in the war effort. Morally didactic, her stories of this time contain women bravely and generously seeing the men in their lives off to war. "Buying Winter Things," for example, features a young woman's struggle to be brave and to busy herself with work to ease her wait for war's end. A widow in "Captain Charley" has to decide whether to let her son enlist, and "Kitten" and "My Thanksgiving" have women with sweethearts in the war.

From 1870 to 1876, Moulton was the Boston literary correspondent for the *New York Tribune.* In 1876, she made her first trip to Europe, staying abroad for close to two years. Henceforth, she visited England almost every summer, and London soon became her second home. She became friends with Robert Browning and met celebrated writers like Alfred Lord Tennyson and Dante Gabriel Rossetti. Moulton, popular for both her writing and her recitations, was well received in England.

Moulton entertained her literary contemporaries, including Ralph Waldo Emerson, James Russell Lowell, Henry Wadsworth Longfellow, Oliver Wendell Holmes, and Robert Browning, at her "salons" in Boston and London. She was noted for her charming personality and kindness.

In 1877 her first book of poetry, *Swallow Flights,* was published in America; the English edition was

Louise Chandler Moulton, popular American writer (1835–1908). (Library of Congress)

published in 1878. She continued writing into the 1890s, publishing two books for children. Her trips to Europe ceased for two years after her husband William's death on February 19, 1898.

Louise Chandler Moulton died in Boston on August 10, 1908, following a lengthy illness.

Sigrid Kelsey

See also Fiction Writers, Northern; Northern Women; Poets, Northern; Union Homefront; Wartime Literature.

References and Further Reading

Moulton, Louise Chandler. 1909. *The Poems and Sonnets of Louise Chandler Moulton.* Boston: Little, Brown and Company.

Sizer, Lyde Cullen. 2000. *The Political Work of Northern Women Writers and the Civil War, 1850- 1872.* Chapel Hill: University of North Carolina Press.

Whiting, Lilian. 1910. *Louise Chandler Moulton: Poet and Friend.* Boston: Little, Brown and Company.

Mountain Charley [Elsa Jane Guerin aka Charles Hatfield] (n.d.–n.d.)

Mountain Charley was the name used by Elsa Jane Guerin, a woman who dressed as a man to find work, go westward during the gold rush, and eventually enlist in the Union army. In 1861 she published an autobiography of her pre–Civil War life, *Mountain Charley, or the Adventures of Mrs. E. J. Guerin, Who Was Thirteen Years in Male Attire: An Autobiography Comprising a Period of Thirteen Years Life in the States, California, and Pike's Peak.* Information about her wartime activities was later published in a series of articles in the *Colorado Transcript.*

In *Mountain Charley,* Guerin explained how her early life influenced her strange choice in careers. Her lack of a regular family, her time away at school, and her marriage and young widowhood meant that she had long depended on herself. Widowed with two young children to raise, Guerin searched for a way to survive. She understood the difficulties she would face as a young woman, so she decided to dress as a man to get a job.

Charley soon discovered both the economic and social benefits of being male. She gained freedom as a man who could go wherever he wanted and do as he wished. In the spring of 1855, Charley joined a party of sixty men who were bound for California, the Land of Gold. By 1859 she was running a bakery and saloon in Colorado, and, although several people now knew that she was a woman, she continued dressing as a man. She married her barkeeper, H. L. Guerin.

Although her book ends before the Civil War began, Mountain Charley corresponded with an old friend, newspaper publisher George West, with specific details about her wartime activities. She explained that she had enlisted in Iowa as Charles Hatfield and had served in Western units. In Missouri, she had persuaded the generals that she could spy on the Confederate camp disguised as a woman. She successfully fooled not only the enemy, but even some former friends, now also serving in the war, who had known her as a man but who did not recognize her as a woman. At one point Charles was wounded and her sex discovered, but surprisingly the doctors did not reveal her secret to military officials. She was eventually promoted to first lieutenant and served until the end of the war. Charley delighted in her ability to move back and forth between gender identities.

Although Mountain Charley's adventures were unique, accounts of other Civil War cross-dressers appeared quite regularly in wartime literature, newspapers, and memoirs. It is estimated that as many as four hundred women dressed as men to fight in the Civil War.

Tiffany K. Wayne

See also Female Combatants; Female Spies; Western Women.

References and Further Reading
Guerin, Elsa Jane. *Mountain Charley, or the Adventures of Mrs. E. J. Guerin, Who Was Thirteen Years in Male Attire: An Autobiography Comprising a Period of Thirteen Years Life in the States, California, and Pike's Peak.* 1968, with Introduction by Fred W. Mazzulla and William Kostka. Norman: University of Oklahoma Press.

Mourning

One in five of the more than 31 million people living in the United States in 1860 had died in service to the Union or the Confederacy by the time the Civil War ended in 1865. During and after the war, people of the North and South looked to belief in the justness of their cause and in God's promises of reunion and eternal life to cope with the sacrifice of sons, brothers, and husbands. Religion was mainly the province of women in the nineteenth century, as were mourning and its rituals. The war resulted in more mourning women than battle dead. Over half of all military fatalities during the Civil War were the result of illness, but almost every dead soldier was survived by a bereaved mother, wife, or sister.

Before the disruptions of the war, death and mourning in Victorian culture were ritualized observances with the home at their center. Loved ones died in their own beds, surrounded by family, who cherished the last sentimental details of parting and often clipped a lock of the deceased's hair as a token of remembrance. Crepe was hung on the front door to announce a death. Bodies were prepared for burial and laid out in the parlor. The family watched over the body and received condolences as the community filed through the parlor to pay its respects. A funeral in the parlor was followed by a graveside service. The family wore black—crepe hatbands for the men and the women in head-to-toe "deepest mourning" garb. The roles of family members and the responses of close friends and the larger community were formulaic. If one were not properly brought up to read and respond to the cues of the family—or to deploy them after one's own loss—popular advice manuals were available to help.

Death and ritualized mourning customs loomed large in the antebellum public imagination. Mourning manuals delineated strict periods of successively lighter mourning and the appropriate attire and accessories for each, down to the width of the black borders on handkerchiefs and stationery. Men wore crepe hatbands and armbands to mark the loss of members of their fraternal and civic organizations, and they composed testimonials affirming the worthiness of the deceased's character and the inestimable loss to his family, friends, and community. Women wore black, curtailed their activities, and tended the graves.

There were clear guidelines for acceptable mourning attire. In deepest mourning, a woman wore only the most somber fabrics, especially dull crepe, merino, and bombazine; she swathed herself in a heavy black crepe veil when she left the house. After six months she might add a white collar to signify that she was beginning to emerge but was still mourning, and after a year she could move into somber purples and lilacs. Advice manuals detailed the length of each phase of mourning in remembrance of husbands, siblings, children, and other relations and described the attire and activities appropriate to each stage. Manuals admonished that the entire family, down to the youngest child, must observe these guidelines. Whole emporiums in large cities catered to the "black trade" and fed the demand for an ever wider array of mourning accessories. The death of Prince Albert, husband of Britain's Queen Victoria, in late 1861 sparked renewed interest in mourning as a becoming and fashionable mode of dress.

At the dawn of the Civil War, most people adhered to the dictates of custom, but many had begun to openly criticize this formalized public expression of private grief. Publications such as *Godey's Lady's Book*, which reached one hundred and fifty thousand women in the North and South in 1860, both reinforced and questioned mourning customs, reflecting the extent to which they were both important and problematic. Antebellum Americans cherished sincerity and pure sentiment. Critics decried the increasing commercialization of the "trappings of woe" and pointed out that the manuals' rules to govern emotions and sentiments were at best arbitrary and artificial. At worst, they allowed those who were not truly grieving to pretend to be and to lay claim to sympathy and empathy they did not deserve.

For Christians, whose beliefs were pervasive in public discourse, the rituals surrounding death derived much of their meaning from their religious significance. Christians were admonished to bear their losses without a murmur as the will of divine Providence and to console themselves with the promise of blissful eternal togetherness for all who professed their faith. Carried to what some saw as a logical conclusion, grieving for one who was in Heaven with God was blasphemous.

The Civil War swept away most of these prewar critiques. For families whose soldiers died far from home, there were no tender deathbed scenes with professions of faith and loving leave-takings. Often there was no body, no funeral, and no grave to visit. Mourning attire became an important symbol of loss and for many the only ritualized observance of death the war allowed them. The ranks swelled of women wearing black—"putting on mourning"—in remembrance of a father, brother, or son sacrificed to the cause. A lady in black reminded the world of the real cost of the war, and that she had paid dearly.

Women of faith in the Union and Confederacy fretted about their unconverted men, who might die without professing their faith and ensuring eternal togetherness for the family. Families of soldiers who died far from home cherished letters from comrades or nurses describing the deaths and reassuring the bereaved that they were lovingly remembered at the end and that their soldier had died professing religious faith. Some even included a lock of hair.

The Civil War was the first war on American soil since the antebellum rural cemetery movement had made the grave a sacred site for religious meditation in an attractive, well tended cemetery. Embalming became a booming industry, especially in the Union; families yearned to have the remains of war dead shipped home for burial. When the war ended, undertaking was professionalized.

White women in the South were three times as likely to lose a son or husband in the Civil War as were those in the North. Their desire to dress in black in honor of their heroic dead was complicated by the Northern blockade of Southern ports, which by the second year of the war had slowed imports to a trickle. The war created shortages of all kinds, and the demand for black fabric and mourning accessories was acute. In early 1863, Confederate nurse Phoebe Yates Pember wrote to her sister that she could not find black merino. By November 1863, diarist Kate Stone complained that she would have to stop wearing mourning clothes for her brother because she could get nothing black to wear. Nearly every household, she noted, mourned someone.

In the early days of the war, senior officers who died in battle lay in state in public buildings and were given elaborate funerals; others were buried with appropriate military ceremony. Soon the number of dead far outstripped the ability of prewar military customs to adequately honor them. As casualties mounted and death became commonplace, the general public grew more and more numbed to the sorrow of others. In the South, war news crowded out published memorial testimonials, with the blockade making paper scarce. As the war ended, the assassination of Abraham Lincoln occasioned a state funeral and public expressions of mourning across the North. There was a general outpouring of grief; buildings were draped in black.

Public mourning for the Civil War dead continued after the war. In the spring of 1866 Southern women organized memorial observances and spruced up the gravesites of both Union and Confederate soldiers. Societies devoted to the erection of memorial monuments soon formed, especially in the defeated Confederacy. After Reconstruction, Memorial Day or an equivalent day of remembrance was observed North and South with speeches, reunions of soldiers, parades, picnics, and cemetery visits. Civil War veterans were buried with military pomp well into the twentieth century.

Nancy Gray Schoonmaker

See also Confederate Homefront; Domesticity; Monuments; Northern Women; Religion; Pember, Phoebe Yates Levy (1823–1913); Southern Women; Stone, Sarah Katherine "Kate" (1841–1907); Union Homefront.

References and Further Reading

Douglas, Ann. 1998. *The Feminization of American Culture.* New York: Farrar, Straus and Giroux. (Orig. pub. 1977.)

Farrell, James J. 1980. *Inventing the American Way of Death, 1830–1920.* Philadelphia, PA: Temple University Press.

Faust, Drew Gilpin. 1996. *Mothers of Invention: Women of the Slaveholding South in the American Civil War.* Chapel Hill: University of North Carolina Press.

Faust, Drew Gilpin. 2005. "'The Dread Void of Uncertainty': Naming the Dead in the American Civil War." *Southern Cultures* 11 (2): 7–32, 113.

French, Stanley. 1974. "The Cemetery as Cultural Institution: The Establishment of Mount Auburn and the 'Rural Cemetery' Movement. *American Quarterly* 26 (1): 37–59.

Halttunen, Karen. 1982. *Confidence Men and Painted Women: A Study of Middle-class Culture in America, 1830–1870.* New Haven, CT: Yale University Press.

Pike, Martha V., and Janice Gray Armstrong. 1980. *A Time to Mourn: Expressions of Grief in Nineteenth Century America.* Stony Brook, NY: Museums at Stony Brook.

Reveley, Bryce. 1993. "The Black Trade in New Orleans: 1840–1880." *Southern Quarterly* 31 (2): 119–122.

Taylor, Lou. 1983. *Mourning Dress: A Costume and Social History.* London: George Allen & Unwin.

Wilson, Charles Reagan. 1980. *Baptized in Blood: The Religion of the Lost Cause 1865–1920.* Athens: University of Georgia Press.

Murfreesboro, Battle of (December 31, 1862–January 2, 1863)

Also known as the Battle of Stones River, this Union victory allowed the Federal army to gain control of central Tennessee, and served to boost Northern morale after a withering defeat at Fredericksburg, Virginia, weeks earlier. It was also at this battle that the identity of one of the soldiers of the Second East Tennessee Cavalry, Frank Miller, was revealed to be a young woman named Frances Hook.

Major General William S. Rosencrans's Union Army of the Cumberland, with a force of nearly forty-five thousand men, secured Nashville, Tennessee, after Confederate forces had threatened it during the fall of 1862. Repairing the railroad line from Louisville, Kentucky, to Nashville enabled Rosencrans to resupply and reorganize his troops and to begin their movement south toward Murfreesboro, where Confederate General Braxton Bragg was entrenched. Rosencrans had taken over command of the Union forces in Kentucky from Brigadier General Don Carlos Buell, who had so far been unable to push Bragg from East Tennessee after his hasty retreat from Kentucky in early October.

On December 30, Rosencrans, with forty-three thousand men, moved into position across Stones River from Bragg, a point just northwest of the town of Murfreesboro, where the Nashville Turnpike and the Nashville & Chattanooga Railroad intersect near the river. Bragg, with thirty-seven thousand men, had been successful in evading Buell, and he was now entrenched along the eastern edge of the river a little north of the town.

Bragg took the offensive and, under the cover of heavy fog on December 31, struck Rosencrans's right flank in a predawn raid. Unprepared for the early assault, Rosencrans retreated three miles under heavy fire throughout the morning. Rosencrans's right center division commander, General Philip H. Sheridan, was prepared for the assault and, in heavy fighting, slowed the Confederate advance. The ensuing battle cost Sheridan three of his brigade commanders and a third of his men. Major General George H. Thomas held the center with artillery support from Colonel William B. Hazen, while Rosencrans reinforced a new right line.

Bragg ordered his division commander, John C. Breckinridge, to continue with a frontal assault, causing many casualties on both sides. According to eyewitnesses, the roar of constant fire was deafening and deadly, with Union soldiers and officers falling rapidly in the intense fighting. Rosencrans held his position, though both his right and left flanks were beaten back significantly. By nightfall, a confident Bragg cabled Richmond, announcing Rosencrans's impending retreat. Rosencrans, however, regrouped and stood his ground with a little advancement on New Year's Day.

The following day, January 2, Rosencrans advanced across Stones River to assault Bragg's communications base. Bragg ordered Breckinridge to advance on this division, and, though initially successful in pushing Rosencrans back to the river, heavy Union fire halted Bragg's advance. Breckinridge's men faced fifty-eight Union guns placed strategically on a hill above the river, and he lost two thousand men in twenty minutes. Buoyed by Breckinridge's hasty retreat and by Bragg's inability to reorganize his men for another assault, Rosencrans advanced again and by nightfall had claimed high land overlooking Murfreesboro. On the morning of the third, Rosencrans, fresh with reinforcements from Nashville, was now positioned on the east side of the river and poised to bombard Murfreesboro. That night, Bragg abandoned the town and retreated some twenty-five miles south to the Duck River.

Frances Hook, known as Frank Miller to the men of the Second Tennessee, had been wounded badly during the Union advance across Stone's River. While attending to her wounds, the army physician discovered her sex and reported her to Rosencrans. Though impressed with her bravery and skill as a soldier, he forced her to return to her parents in Pennsylvania. A seasoned war veteran, having served with several other regiments and having been taken prisoner on at least one occasion, Hook reenlisted with the Eighth Michigan, where, disguised again, she served throughout the rest of the war.

This Union victory boosted sagging Northern morale but at a heavy price. While both sides sustained nearly a third of their troop strengths in casualties, including killed, wounded, and captured, Rosencrans's army was so weakened he could not attempt another offensive movement for months. Later that year, under orders from General Ulysses S. Grant, Major General George H. Thomas relieved Rosencrans of his command of the Army of the Cumberland.

Bragg, already under fire for retreating from Kentucky, fought and argued with his division commanders, who by then were questioning his leadership. Bragg, expecting to be replaced as head of the Army of Tennessee, remained in his post because political infighting prevented the immediate appointment of another, more competent general. By the end of the year, however, poor leadership and continued complaints by Bragg's superiors and subordinates forced Jefferson Davis to relieve him of his command. After a stunning loss at Lookout Mountain, near Chattanooga, Tennessee, in November 1863, Davis appointed General Joseph E. Johnston to lead the Army of the Tennessee.

After Murfreesboro, one of the bloodiest battles of the war, tending to the thousands of wounded soldiers required immense resources. With over three thousand dead and sixteen thousand wounded, the United States Sanitary Commission rushed nurses and supplies to the battle area, but some soldiers lay on the battlefield for days before help could arrive. The nurses were overwhelmed by the devastation they encountered, and many remained stationed there for months tending to the injured, sick, and dying.

Kate Clifford Larson

See also Female Combatants; Northern Women; Nurses; Southern Women; United States Sanitary Commission.

References and Further Reading

Catton, Bruce, and James McPherson, eds. 1996. *The American Heritage New History of the Civil War.* New York: MetroBooks.
McPherson, James. 1988. *Battle Cry of Freedom: The Civil War Era.* New York: Oxford University Press.

Music, Northern

Northern Civil War music encompassed a broad range of published songs, military marches, minstrel tunes, and imported European opera and symphonies. Many of these were created or reinterpreted to present an idealized vision of Northern patriotism and unity while not alienating Southerners, since the fundamental Northern war aim was to restore the Union.

Military and civilian brass bands were pervasive throughout the Civil War. For the benefit of the Union armies, they played rousing marches and patriotic tunes like "The Star-Spangled Banner," "The Red, White, and Blue," and "Yankee Doodle." Patrick Gilmore, through his innovations as leader of all Massachusetts military bands, made lasting contributions to the development of American instrumental music. Brass bands were also common features at public events throughout the North.

Northern patriotic songs were popular for enlistment rallies, parades, and other army functions. The earliest patriotic songs sought to rally Northerners around the Union cause and therefore contained frequent references to the American Revolution, the strength of the Union, and glory on the battlefield. The most popular Union rallying song, George Frederick Root's "The Battle Cry of Freedom," was published in the summer of 1862, in response to President Abraham Lincoln's call for three hundred thousand new troops, and it employed a dual rhetoric of Union and liberty. In addition, Northern patriotic songs often sought to glorify the contributions of individual soldiers and were less likely than Southern patriotic songs to contain favorable references to high-ranking officers. The most prominent expressions in Northern patriotic songs drew on common rhetoric of political liberty, the Union as a family of the living and the dead, the obligations of soldiers toward their comrades and the Federal government, and the justice and holiness of the Union cause.

While the patriotic songs appear most often in twentieth-century compilations of Civil War music, sentimental ballads generally formed the core of both the soldiers' and the civilians' song repertoire. The sentimental songs of the Civil War, often composed for performance in minstrel shows but also for purchase by amateur musicians, helped personalize the conflict for soldiers and civilians alike. These songs allowed the singer to imagine the reaction of a single soldier—or his mother, sweetheart, child, or brother—to the impersonal effects of the war. Thus, they were often performed by a single person instead of a large group. Many Northern sentimental songs were popular in both the Union and the Confederacy because they generally eschewed obvious statements of national identity.

Sentimental war songs also usually involved female characters, departing from the masculine rhetoric of the rallying songs and creating a crucial link between the battlefield and the home. Mothers were particularly prominent in Northern sentimental songs like Root's "Just Before the Battle, Mother" and Charles Carroll Sawyer's "Who Will Care for Mother Now?" Both of these songs, though published in the North, were also available from Southern publishers. Other female characters also appeared regularly in wartime sentimental songs. Moreover, young middle-class women were the primary consumers of the sheet music for these songs, which fit easily into the broader genre of parlor music.

Northern women were not merely consumers of wartime music, they also played key roles in the production of both sentimental and patriotic songs. Female composers and lyricists took part in a contest to create a new national hymn in the summer of 1861. More famously, Julia Ward Howe penned new lyrics to the Methodist hymn "Say, Brothers Will You Meet Us?" which had already been reworded once as "John Brown's Body," and created the rousing and elegiac "Battle Hymn of the Republic." Ethel Lynn Eliot Beers of Massachusetts wrote a poem entitled "The Picket-Guard," which eventually became the popular song "All Quiet along the Potomac Tonight." In the realm of art music, Northern opera singers Clara Louise Kellogg and Isabella Hinckley tailored their performances to bolster Union patriotism, and women were largely responsible for keeping philanthropic symphony societies alive during the war.

Jaime Amanda Martinez

See also Civilian Life; Morale; Music, Southern; Union Homefront.

References and Further Reading

Crawford, Richard. 1977. *The Civil War Songbook.* New York: Dover Publications.

Elmira Cornet Band, Thirty-third Regiment, of the New York State Volunteers in July 1861. (Library of Congress)

Fahs, Alice. 2001. *The Imagined Civil War: Popular Literature of the North and South, 1861–1865.* Chapel Hill: University of North Carolina Press.

Heaps, Willard A., and Porter W. Heaps. 1960. *The Singing Sixties: The Spirit of Civil War Days Drawn from the Music of the Times.* Norman: University of Oklahoma Press.

Kelly, Bruce C., and Mark A. Snell, eds. 2004. *Bugle Resounding: Music and Musicians of the Civil War Era.* Columbia: University of Missouri Press.

Olson, Kenneth E. 1981. *Music and Musket: Bands and Bandsmen of the American Civil War.* Westport, CT: Greenwood Press.

Music, Southern

Southern Civil War music, whether for performance by military bands or for publication and purchase by civilians, was central to the construction and maintenance of Confederate national identity.

General Robert E. Lee's oft repeated exclamation that he could not have an army without music could be extended to the entire country; Southern music idealized Confederate unity by iterating key themes like liberty, protection of the home, and the legacy of the American Revolution.

The Confederate music publishing industry was not well developed at the outset of the war, but enterprising Southerners quickly realized the necessity for publication of new Southern songs. Acknowledging the fundamental importance of patriotic music in the support of a new nation and its war effort, they produced music that helped in the process of creating a Confederate national identity. This music highlighted the major themes of Confederate nationalism, such as liberty, rights, honor, protection of the home, and adherence to Revolutionary ideals. The most famous Confederate song, however, espoused none of this rhetoric, for "Dixie" predated the war and was written by the Ohio minstrel performer Daniel Decatur Emmett. Two new Southern songs emerged to solve this problem, although they failed to fully surpass "Dixie" in popularity. The first, Harry Macarthy's "Bonnie Blue Flag," contained frequent assertions of Southern rights, particularly property rights, and Southern unity. The second, "My Maryland," with lyrics by Baltimore native James Ryder Randall, encouraged residents of Maryland to join the Confederacy by cataloguing examples of Union tyranny and recalling Maryland's participation in the American Revolution. In addition to these rallying songs, Southern publishers produced many purely instrumental waltzes, polkas, and marches dedicated to famous Southern officers, particularly in the first year of the war.

Although the patriotic songs appear most often in twentieth-century compilations of Civil War music, sentimental ballads formed the core of both the soldiers' and the civilians' song repertoire. Composers altered preexisting musical forms to create new genres of sentimental songs tailored to the needs of the Southern wartime population—farewell songs, letter songs, camaraderie songs, remembrance songs, and deathbed songs. The sentimental songs of the Civil War, often composed for performance in minstrel shows but also for purchase by amateur musicians, helped personalize the conflict for soldiers and civilians alike.

Many Northern wartime sentimental songs were popular in the Confederacy as well because they generally eschewed obvious statements of national identity, but Southern sentimental songs were often as clear in their national allegiance as the patriotic rallying songs. Macarthy's "The Volunteer," for example, mixed Southern wartime rhetoric of honor, Northern treachery, and the country's cause with sentimental musical flourishes and the individual medium of a soldier's farewell to his wife. Interestingly, while Northern composers most often addressed sentimental songs from the soldier to his mother, Southern composers wrote more songs in which the soldier

addressed his wife or sweetheart. This seems to be a general trend, but there were obviously many deviations on both sides.

Sentimental war songs usually involved female characters, departing from the masculine rhetoric of the rallying songs and creating a crucial link between the battlefield and the home. Southern women also participated in the wartime music industry as consumers, performers, and producers of popular songs. Lottie Macarthy stood on stage with her husband, waving a Confederate flag, as he performed his songs "The Volunteer" and "The Bonnie Blue Flag." Constance, Hetty, and Jennie Cary of Baltimore first turned Randall's poem "My Maryland" into a song by wedding the lyrics with the Christmas carol "O Tannenbaum." Catherine Ann Warfield of Kentucky wrote the ferociously patriotic song "You Can Never Win Us Back," creating a powerful statement of Southern resolve to fight, Confederate racial ideology, and the religious imagery with which Southerners justified their war effort. Southern women in urban areas like Richmond and Charleston also regularly patronized performances of opera and other forms of European art music.

Jaime Amanda Martinez

See also Civilian Life; Confederate Life; Morale; Music, Northern.

References and Further Reading

Abel, E. Lawrence. 2000. *Singing the New Nation: How Music Shaped the Confederacy, 1861–1865.* Mechanicsburg, PA: Stackpole Books.

Crawford, Richard. 1977. *The Civil War Songbook.* New York: Dover Publications.

Fahs, Alice. 2001. *The Imagined Civil War: Popular Literature of the North and South, 1861–1865.* Chapel Hill: University of North Carolina Press.

Harwell, Richard. 1950. *Confederate Music.* Chapel Hill: University of North Carolina Press.

Kelly, Bruce C., and Mark A. Snell, eds. 2004. *Bugle Resounding: Music and Musicians of the Civil War Era.* Columbia: University of Missouri Press.

Olson, Kenneth E. 1981. *Music and Musket: Bands and Bandsmen of the American Civil War.* Westport, CT: Greenwood Press.

N

National Women's Loyal League
[Women's National Loyal League]

A group of reformers who wanted to play an active political role in the outcome of the American Civil War organized the National Woman's Loyal League (NWLL) in 1863.

After President Abraham Lincoln issued the Emancipation Proclamation freeing slaves in the rebel states, effective January 1, 1863, abolitionists and women's rights activists Susan B. Anthony and Elizabeth Cady Stanton issued a "Call for a Meeting of the Loyal Women of the Nation" and organized women to urge Congress to pass a Constitutional amendment permanently ending slavery everywhere. The resultant NWLL first met in New York on May 14, 1863, and its primary work over the next year and a half of its existence was to collect signatures in support of such an amendment. By August 1864, the League had approximately five thousand members and had collected and presented to Radical Republican allies in Congress some four hundred thousand signatures. The Thirteenth Amendment to the Constitution, abolishing slavery throughout the United States, was ratified after the war in 1865.

The founders and officers of the NWLL had been prominent women's rights leaders before the war. While the war temporarily slowed the efforts of the organized women's movement, many reformers from both the women's rights and the antislavery movements continued their efforts on behalf of the emancipation of slaves while emphasizing the need for an expanded role for women. At the first meeting of the NWLL, Stanton articulated women's desire to make a contribution to the war beyond sacrificing their sons, nursing, and supplying soldiers with clothes and food. Although society had given men the ability to act on the battlefield while women primarily remained on the homefront, Stanton emphasized that women had a vital part to play in the war.

In their effort to include the concerns of women, Stanton and Anthony revived the issue of the vote—of women's right to equal citizenship—as one of the goals of the war. In a special resolution at the first meeting of the League, they declared that the peace and survival of the nation required equal rights and voting for all women and African Americans. Not all League members agreed with the demand for suffrage, however, with the opposition declaring the idea of giving the vote to women as well as blacks would endanger the League's larger goal of gathering support for immediate abolition. Newspapers reported on this debate and controversy within the NWLL by criticizing the fact that a group that had been created with exemplary patriotic motive to end slavery had instead transformed into a radical movement for women's rights. The woman suffrage resolution passed, but membership in the League declined after that point.

Although supportive of the Union cause, NWLL leaders such as Stanton and Ernestine Rose were publicly critical of President Abraham Lincoln for not demanding full emancipation as a stated goal of the war. For this political boldness, these women faced criticism by some newspapers, including the *New York Herald,* which cynically suggested that perhaps the women might take over national politics themselves. The NWLL met weekly in New York, even during the week of the July 1863 draft riots, and all of the major newspapers covered the proceedings of this "great uprising" of Northern women.

Thinking that their Republican congressional allies at least would agree with their aims, the women must have been disappointed when Charles Sumner thanked them for their work in collecting signatures but expressed dissatisfaction that women felt called to engage in the masculine field of politics. In the end, the relative success of the women's efforts in gathering and delivering their petitions was more a function of the public's perception of the wartime political participation of women as a function of extraordinary circumstances, not as a desirable model for women's continued political action. After the war, and especially after black men were granted the vote in 1870 with the Fourteenth Amendment, white women of the National Women's Loyal League and their allies returned to a reorganized women's rights movement now focused exclusively on securing the vote for women.

Tiffany K. Wayne

See also Abolitionism and Northern Reformers; Anthony, Susan B. (1820–1906); Draft Riots and Resistance; Emancipation Proclamation (January 1, 1863); Fourteenth Amendment; Lincoln, Abraham (1809–1865); Northern Women; Politics; Stanton, Elizabeth Cady (1815–1902); Thirteenth Amendment; Union Homefront.

References and Further Reading

Ryan, Mary. 1990. *Women in Public: Between Banners and Ballots, 1825–1880.* Baltimore, MD: Johns Hopkins University Press.

Venet, Wendy Hamand. 1991. *Neither Ballots Nor Bullets: Women Abolitionists and the Civil War.* Charlottesville: University Press of Virginia.

Nationalism, Confederate

With the formal creation of the Confederacy came an urgent need to define the new nation and thereby val-idate its claim for independence. Recognizing this, white Southerners quickly set about crafting cultural and intellectual scaffolding for their new nation. They lacked most of the usual markers of national distinctiveness, such as a unique language or religion, an exclusive past, or a clearly demarcated territory. Even so they were able to fashion the beginnings of a national identity and a sense of shared national purpose, retaining the major features of United States nationalism and adding a Southern twist by emphasizing the defense of slavery, conservative social and religious values, and a purported return to the original political vision of the Founding Fathers. Confederate nationalism was more a variation on American nationalism than a rejection of it.

White Southern women were crucial participants in the creation of Confederate nationalism. They were most visible in their supporting or symbolic roles: cheerfully waving off the departing soldiers and patiently enduring hardship and sacrifice. But the exigencies of war, combined with the need for united national resolve, opened up more active opportunities to serve the nation and to shape its character. In the end, significant female dissatisfaction with the Confederate bid for independence contributed to its failure, demonstrating the central role that white women played in all stages of Confederate nationalism.

The disintegration of the United States and the formation of the Confederacy sent waves of exhilaration across the white South. Southern women had never in fact been detached from the supposedly male domains of politics and war, but the enormity of the events of 1860 and 1861, permeating not only all areas of the South but also all areas of Southern life, increased their interest in public affairs. Talk of secession and the transfer of loyalties from the United States to the Confederacy filled newspapers, conversation, and the letters and diaries of both men and women. Nationality was now an issue for urgent and open discussion; ordinarily unspoken assumptions about identity and allegiance became explicit as white Southerners weighed the claims of the old United States and the new Confederacy.

In these early days of Confederate independence, Southern women as well as men consciously

Confederate women send their men to war (*Frank Leslie's Illustrated Newspaper*, May 23, 1863). Southern women demonstrated their commitment to their nation by encouraging their men to enlist in the Confederate army. (Library of Congress)

reflected on the meaning of the new nation and on the nature of their attachments to it. Most understood the Confederacy not as a departure from American nationality, but rather as a new chapter of it, one in which white Southerners would rescue the American experiment of republican self-government from Northern perversions and restore its original promise. Thus the Confederacy's constitution, flag, and even stamps all bore strong similarities to their United States equivalents. The major difference, of course, was slavery, the sine qua non of the new nation. But even as most white Southerners positioned slavery at the heart of the Confederacy, they began to construct around it a broader intellectual justification for their political separation; they began to create an expansive Confederate nationalism. Many made claims for a distinctive Southern identity—so distinctive as to warrant sep-

arate national status—with reference to fundamental differences of character and even of morality between Northerners and themselves. Confederates also defined their new nation as a religious community, one whose very existence was mandated by God. Imbuing the new nation with religious meaning helped smooth many Southerners' transition from the United States to the Confederacy and lent a powerful spiritual dimension to their national attachments.

As has been true of most instances of nationalism, gender was an important element of Confederate nationalism. Formal citizenship was understood to be an all-male concern. From the Confederacy's earliest days, men displayed their citizenship and therefore their dedication to the new nation by volunteering for military service—a path closed to women, except for the few who disguised themselves as men. But, even though many Confederate men imagined the national community as an exclusively male comradeship, the important symbolic and supporting roles played by women and femininity were held in high esteem. Furthermore, women took advantage of the new opportunities, made possible by the pressures of war and by the urgent need to defend Confederate nationhood, to participate more actively in the making and remaking of Confederate nationalism.

Female contributions to Confederate nationalism were most often glorified to the degree that they bolstered male nationalism. Reports of public festivities in 1860 and 1861 portrayed white women waving handkerchiefs as the men paraded about displaying their devotion to the cause in appropriately "manly" ways. The women's function in flag presentations to departing troops was also defined as being emphatically supportive. In towns and communities across the South, local women presented flags to departing soldiers in emotional and symbolic ceremonies. Speeches that were, revealingly, delivered by a man even if they in fact had a female author, pledged women's devotion to and appreciation for "their" men, who were so bravely risking their lives by fighting in defense of their family, community, state, and nation. Women's prescribed roles as the supporters of male patriotism and as the domestic embodiments of the national cause that men fought to defend were publicly enacted across the South.

The female sacrifice that these rituals emphasized became a permanent staple of Confederate nationalism. White Southerners slotted the image of the ideal Confederate woman into a long-standing mythic tradition of wives, mothers, sisters, and sweethearts who support the national cause by loyally supporting their men. This tradition stretched back to the women of Sparta, but it drew more immediately on the memory of the American revolutionary generation—the women of '76, celebrated in the popular imagination as stoic matrons who had willingly sacrificed their male relatives and the material well-being of themselves and their families. Similar images of devoted and sacrificing Confederate women were celebrated in newspaper reports, songs, and poetry, as well as throughout Confederate culture. In addition to providing many women with a model through which to make sense of their national obligations, these idealized images also helped sustain men's commitment to the Confederate cause. They persisted as the dominant representation of Confederate women for decades after the war.

Even as Confederate culture emphasized women's supporting roles in Confederate nationalism, there were many opportunities for more constructive contributions. Because the Confederacy was at war for almost its entire existence, ordinarily everyday activities were imbued with nationalist meaning and purpose. The domestic production of cloth, for instance, took on new import because of the blockade and the material deprivations of war; consequently, both the making and the wearing of homespun carried nationalistic implications. Sexuality, too, could be deployed on behalf of the nation. Stories circulated throughout the Confederacy of young women denying their favor to men who did not volunteer for the military, thereby holding men accountable for their gender-specific national obligations. By encoding even everyday activities with national meaning, women shaped the evolving Confederate nationalism.

For many women, the new nation offered new opportunities in normally restricted activities. The general atmosphere of political ferment encouraged women to intervene in both private and public discourse about political, military, and other national events. Newspapers across the Confederacy printed letters and poems written by women, many connected to the shaping of Confederate nationalism.

Opportunities for female participation in the process of nationalism were amplified by the exigencies of war. At the same time as men were performing their national citizenship with military or political service, white women performed their commitment to the nation—developing their own version of citizenship—with service of other kinds. The massive mobilization of Confederate men meant that women increasingly filled teaching positions, for instance, and the constant barrage of battlefield casualties drew many women into nursing. Both pursuits could be characterized as service to the nation. Other positions could be found in the government bureaucracy in Richmond, which connected women's work even more directly to the national cause. The most common form of involvement in national affairs, though, was through sewing clubs and soldiers' aid associations. White women formed over one thousand such organizations across the Confederacy, opening up new experiences in public life and new opportunities to perform their Confederate nationalism. In these and other ways, the demands of war and the need to develop new forms of national belonging enabled women to play crucial roles in both the war effort and the shaping of Confederate nationalism.

Of course, some Southern women did not wish to participate in Confederate nationalism at all. African American women had little reason to support or celebrate the new nation, and, insofar as they felt themselves to be a part of a nation at all, it was almost certain to be the United and not the Confederate States. A significant number of white women, too, retained their national allegiance to the United States, especially those with less material investment in the defense of slavery. Unionist men and women across the South kept up their American nationalism in a variety of forms throughout the war.

Even for those who identified with the Confederacy, the hardships of war could strain newly created national loyalty and purpose. The absence of working-age men meant that women had to perform traditionally male economic roles in addition to their own. These difficulties were only exacerbated by the general deterioration of the Confederate economy. Apparent inequities of material contributions to the war effort generated class conflict, much of it involving women on the homefront, and they fed into a more general disaffection with the war itself. Women wrote directly to government officials, demanding either changes in policy or the release from military service of male relatives who were needed at home to perform crucial economic functions. Officials very rarely agreed to such requests, leaving the most disaffected soldiers with little choice but to desert illegally. The sentiments of women on the homefront influenced some desertions and contributed to a decline in Confederate morale as the military situation became less and less hopeful. Accordingly, some historians have placed considerable responsibility for the eventual failure of the Confederacy's bid for independence on the declining commitment of women. Although not all Confederates, whether women or men, had given up on the Confederacy by 1865, the general pattern was one of declining commitment to the goal of national independence. This trend, as well as the fact that Confederate nationalism developed more as a variant of American nationalism than as a rejection of it, made reintegration into the United States psychologically acceptable—though not typically pleasurable—for the majority of white Southerners.

Even so, a strong white Southern identity, based on the shared experience of war and defeat, persisted long after 1865. White Southern women played a vital role in defining the memory of the Confederacy in the decades after Appomattox. Through organizations such as the United Daughters of the Confederacy, women celebrated the South's attempt at national independence and upheld the idealized image of loyal Confederate women who sacrificed all and who patiently supported their men's failed military endeavor. In emphasizing women's supportive function, such narratives minimized women's more constructive participation in the Confederacy's bid for independence. Nevertheless, white women's central role in the memorialization of Confederate nationalism fittingly reflected the crucial contributions they had made to its making and remaking during the war itself.

Paul D. H. Quigley

See also African American Women; Aid Societies; Civilian Life; Confederate Homefront; Desertion; Diaries and Journals; Domesticity; Enlistment; Fiction Writers, Southern; Flags, Regimental; Morale; Music, Southern; Nationalism, United States; Nurses; Politics; Religion; Secession; Separate Spheres; Southern Unionists; Southern Women; Treasury Girls; United Daughters of the Confederacy; Wartime Employment; Wartime Literature.

References and Further Reading

Bonner, Robert E. 2002. *Colors and Blood: Flag Passions of the Confederate South*. Princeton, NJ: Princeton University Press.

Faust, Drew Gilpin. 1988. *The Creation of Confederate Nationalism: Ideology and Identity in the Civil War South*. Baton Rouge: Louisiana State University Press.

Faust, Drew Gilpin. 1996. *Mothers of Invention: Women of the Slaveholding South in the American Civil War*. Chapel Hill: University of North Carolina Press.

Gallagher, Gary. 1997. *The Confederate War: How Popular Will, Nationalism, and Military Strategy Could Not Stave Off Defeat*. Cambridge, MA: Harvard University Press.

Rable, George C. 1989. *Civil Wars: Women and the Crisis of Southern Nationalism*. Urbana: University of Illinois Press.

Rubin, Anne Sarah. 2005. *Shattered Nation: The Rise and Fall of the Confederacy*. Chapel Hill: University of North Carolina Press.

Nationalism, United States

Before the Civil War, nationalism in the United States was limited; Americans identified mostly with their local communities or states. The power of regional loyalties trumped any connections to the larger national community. The slow development of a cohesive nationalism prior to 1861 resulted from several factors, including the lack of industrialism, the absence of external enemies, differences between the North and South, and the Federal government's inability to spread patriotism. While antebellum nationalism was weak, the Civil War marked an important turning point in the construction of national identity. During and after the war, citizens of the United States developed a sense of what it meant to be an American, and regional identities became less dominant. The rise of American nationalism after 1865 may have resulted, in part, from industrialization, the role of political elites, socialization, communications, and activities of the federate government. However, women's roles in the growth of American nationalism must be considered.

From 1861 to 1865, many women developed a strong sense of national identity and circulated these ideas as they participated in various activities. They crafted messages of nationalism and created forums where these ideas could be spread throughout the North. Some became public speakers or writers, touring the North as they sought to peddle their view of American nationalism. Several themes were embedded in their messages to the public, such as loyalty to the Union, volunteerism, and Christianity.

One of the most common themes that Northern women focused on during the Civil War was loyalty to the Union. Prior to the war, there was little sense of loyalty to the country or patriotic fervor, because most people were instead tied primarily to their local communities or regions. During the Civil War, however, Northern women helped develop this aspect of American nationalism through numerous sanitary fairs. These fundraising events were designed to lift the spirits of the troops and the nation, as well as to promote a sense of national patriotism. Sanitary fairs encouraged people to donate money and supplies to the Union cause, and spurred them to partake in events designed to demonstrate their loyalty.

Women, who were the central organizers of these events, used sanitary fairs to influence the cultural direction of the nation. After the first sanitary fair was held in Chicago in 1863, women across

TO THE
Patriotic Women of Philadelphia.

A meeting of the Ladies of the City of Philadelphia will be held this day, at 4 o'clock, P.M., at the School Room, in Tenth Street, One door above Spring Garden St., west side, to devise means to give aid and comfort to our noble Soldiers, who have volunteered for the defence of our outraged Flag.

Contributions will be thankfully accepted of such materials as may be found useful to the Volunteers.

In times like these, when our Husbands, Fathers, Sons and Brothers are doing battle for the honor of our common country, let the women be not behind-hand in bestowing their aid and sympathy.

MANY LADIES.

KING & BAIRD, Printers, 607 Sansom Street, Phila.

An 1861 call for the "patriotic women of Philadelphia" to attend a ladies' aid society meeting to help Union soldiers. Women throughout the United States demonstrated their loyalty to their nation through participation in aid societies. (Library of Congress)

the United States began to organize local events in other parts of the North, collecting donations and supplies for the war effort. Not only did ladies' aid societies gather items for Union soldiers, but these forums also socialized visitors to think about the country from a patriotic perspective. Sanitary fairs acted as a tribute to the nation, extolling its virtues and creating virtual museums where artifacts of the nation's history were displayed. At the fairs, American art, agricultural wares, and historical documents were made available to the public to examine for the first time. Items were presented in a manner that made Northerners contemplate a sense of what it meant to be American. Consequently, women who arranged these fairs created a narrative of the United States that helped construct its identity.

Women also helped foster United States nationalism through their participation in numerous volunteer activities, including nursing, sewing soldiers' uniforms, and developing organizations to inspect hospitals. Their participation in aid societies and activities, as well as their encouragement of others to participate, allowed Northern women outlets for their patriotic fervor. These were not, however, the only acts of volunteerism that allowed women to show their loyalty. Some Northern women also sewed American and regimental flags. In addition, a small number of Northern women secretly joined the army and fought in battles to show their patriotism. Volunteerism was a vital indicator of women's nationalism during the war. By donating their time and energy, women demonstrated their commitment to the Union and to its struggle against the Confederacy. Furthermore, civil society was important to these women because it was the main vehicle through which they spread their patriotic messages. Northern women pursued these acts of volunteerism to express their commitment to the American nation.

Religion has played an important role in the political and social life in the United States throughout the nation's history, and the Civil War was no exception. During the Civil War, Northern women helped foster this aspect of the American nation by promoting the Union as Godlike and favored by Divine inspiration. Northern women used Christianity in their wartime nationalistic endeavors, infusing religion into the nationalist message that they spread throughout the North. In particular, they sought to show that God was on the Union's side. This message gained prominence at sanitary fairs across the North, eventually displacing discussions of slavery and states' rights as central themes of the war effort. While religion was a part of America's founding and influenced ideas like Manifest Destiny, women of the North buttressed the idea of the United States as a Christian nation as they planned their wartime aid activities. They helped steer the country to its religious foundations and highlighted Christianity and piety.

Scholars have offered several interpretations of wartime Northern women and United States nationalism. One interpretation asserts that political elites and various commentators pressured Union women to take steps to foster nationalism. In the early years of the conflict, women were accused of not sacrificing for the cause and were blamed for the Union's lackluster performance against the Confederacy. Southern women, some argued, put forth much more effort to help their husbands, sons, and fathers in the conflict than did their Northern sisters. These iconic images of Southern women continue to color interpretations of wartime women's roles, and scenes from *Gone with the Wind* permeate American perceptions of the war and highlight Southern women's selflessness. Scholarly discussions of this image highlight the role of Northern magazines and newspapers in promoting this propaganda in urging Union women to take up the call and to volunteer to help their soldier. Women writers also participated in the effort to shame Northern women into action. Much like the calls to action received by Southern women, Northern women were admonished to relinquish their desire for luxury and instead champion the Union in its fight against the Confederacy. As a result of this pressure, this interpretation holds, Northern women ultimately picked up the pace of their activities and volunteered their time.

Others have offered a somewhat more sympathetic interpretation of the motivations behind Northern women's wartime actions and patriotism. While still accepting that some women were pressured into wartime service, these scholars argue that Federal government officials exploited Northern women during the war. For instance, some historians contend that the United States Sanitary Commission, which sought to organize volunteerism during the war, used women in a way that exploited their labor without adequate compensation or recognition; these women's free labor permitted the government to fight the war without spending additional revenue. Furthermore, the nature of women's wartime work may have benefited the national government by ensuring that women, busy with volunteer work, could not obtain positions that might further women's rights. Their treatment by officials led many women to create their own organizations that would free them from interacting with the Federal government.

Women's role in the development of United States nationalism did not end with the Civil War. Several years after the war, women pursued different activities designed to show their nationalist spirit, one of which was the creation of a holiday commemorating the war dead. Women played a role in shaping the perceptions of the country by promoting the observance of Memorial Day. The women who worked to institute this holiday were seeking to create a day for Americans to remember those who sacrificed their lives for the nation, thereby promoting the reinforcement of nationalism and patriotism. This day of contemplation and remembrance permitted citizens the opportunity to recall the sacrifices made in the Civil War and to think of their country as a community, helping to foster the solidification of American nationalism. Northern women also worked to create cultural habits that would foster nationalism. In addition to helping establish Memorial Day, women sought to institute the Pledge of Allegiance as a regular ritual in public schools, hoping this would build a sense of national pride among the nation's youth.

Women's traditional household and family duties were incorporated into their wartime roles and reinforced in the process. The image of women sacrificing for the cause, through material or physical means, provided a reference point for Northern politicians seeking to gain the moral high ground in the war. By highlighting the patriotism of pure and virtuous women, political elites in the North claimed a level of superiority that they claimed their enemies did not possess. This imagery also created a perspective of American nationalism that invited Northerners to think about women in terms of purity, charity, and sacrifice for the common good. Although it gained attention for women's impressive war efforts, this approach had its drawbacks for women. Because they were framed in a pious and pure manner, ladies had to restrict their activities to what the larger society deemed as acceptable, or feminine, forms of behavior. These expectations pushed women into sewing, prayer, and fundraising rather than into political and military roles. Even as their image was used to buttress patriotism, the actions of women were simultaneously proscribed by gender stereotypes. Portrayals of women as the protectors of morals and the caretakers of the household framed the acceptable limits of their participation in the Civil War.

Even though Northern women helped forge American nationalism, their role in the nation was not secure following the Civil War. Despite their service to the country in various capacities—including as fair organizers, fundraisers, nurses, spies, and soldiers—they were not granted equal status with men. While many of them pushed to have women's rights included in the Fourteenth and Fifteenth Amendments, women were unsuccessful in this endeavor; politicians instead focused solely on the freed slaves and their plight. Instead of gaining equal status with men, many women were forced to return to their homes and serve their husbands and families. Although American society embraced other ideas espoused by women, such as loyalty to country, volunteerism, and Christianity, it rejected notions of gender equality as being part of the country's political creed. As a result, women continued to struggle to gain rights as citizens of the nation that they helped construct. Yet their efforts during the war created a legacy that would serve as a model for future generations of women.

Even though women did not receive equal rights following the war, their patriotism and commitment to the Union were important to its victory. Not only did women help build nationalism and raise needed equipment and money for the troops, but their actions also lifted the morale of their husbands, fathers, and sons who were fighting in the war. Women further helped focus the country's attention on the national community and weaken attachments to local and regional identities, thereby buttressing American national identity.

Scott N. Cole

See also Aid Societies; Civilian Life; Domesticity; Fairs and Bazaars; Family Life, Union; Female Combatants; Female Spies; Fifteenth Amendment; Flags, Regimental; Fourteenth Amendment; Fundraising; Morale; Music, Northern; National Women's Loyal League [Women's National Loyal League]; Nationalism, Confederacy; Northern Women; Nurses; Politics; Religion; Separate

Spheres; Sewing Bees; Union Homefront; United States Sanitary Commission; Wartime Employment; Wartime Literature; Women's Central Association of Relief.

References and Further Reading

Attie, Jeanie. 1998. *Patriotic Toil: Northern Women and the American Civil War.* Ithaca, NY: Cornell University Press.

Blanton, DeAnne, and Lauren M. Cook. 2002. *They Fought Like Demons: Women Soldiers and the American Civil War.* Baton Rouge: Louisiana State University Press.

Lawson, Melinda. 2002. *Patriot Fires: Forging a New American Nationalism in the Civil War North.* Lawrence: University Press of Kansas.

Schultz, Jane E. 2004. *Women at the Front: Hospital Workers in Civil War America.* Chapel Hill: University of North Carolina Press.

Silber, Nina. 2005. *Daughters of the Union: Northern Women Fight the Civil War.* Cambridge, MA: Harvard University Press.

Native American Women

Native Americans are often overlooked in studies of the American Civil War. Members of sovereign nations within the United States, American Indians had to make hard choices about participation in the national conflict. Some of the indigenous nations engaged extensively in the conflict, others peripherally, and most not at all. Those living close to contesting states found it difficult to escape the war's influence. Women in Native communities, who played as large a role as females in mainstream white culture—and sometimes a larger one—lived through all the hardships and turmoil of the Civil War. Nineteenth-century white culture relegated American Indian women to a double minority status through accepted ethnic and gender biases. This twofold minority status created a unique wartime experience. Their national or tribal identity strongly shaped the particular role Native women would play in the Civil War.

Women living in a Native society structured on a matrilineal (female-centered) system enjoyed a power and an influence unknown to their white and black sisters. Matrilineal social organization gave women ownership of household goods and agricultural fields, control of children, and important influ-

ence in the family. The emphasis on women as producers of life, as both mothers and agriculturalists, granted females respect and authority within the communal society. This position affected the experience of Native women during the Civil War. Those who had retained elements of a matrilineal society found themselves in a better position to deal with wartime difficulties than women raised in paternal systems. Less dependent on men for economic and social survival, traditional matrilineal women coped well with the changed landscape around them: They were already supporting and controlling homes and families. However, as the government's "civilization" program made headway in the nineteenth century, many Native groups moved toward a mirroring of the patrilineal, paternalistic structure of Euro-Americans. Women whose societies had weakened their roles in this way experienced the war in a manner more similar to that of white women. However, the influence of matrilineal traditions ebbed and flowed over time, and in some areas the upheaval of war prompted a return to traditional gender roles. Two Native groups who fought in the Civil War—Cherokees and Iroquois—serve as examples of women's roles.

Residing on the border of Union and Confederate Territory, the Cherokees could not ignore the conflict brewing but initially maintained neutrality by the end of 1861 they had allied themselves with the Confederacy. However, rival factions within the nation quickly produced competing military regiments enlisted with the Confederate army. The situation devolved into an internal civil war as the Cherokees split into opposing governments by 1863, one remaining within the Confederacy and the other renouncing the earlier treaty of alliance to the South to support the Union. The Cherokee Nation was now at war both as part of the national struggle and, perhaps more damagingly, with itself.

Apart from the actual fighting, women bore the brunt of the hardships of war. Cherokee women lived in an incredibly unstable area. Their experience is most like that of women in the Border States, where conflicting loyalties split churches, sundered kin groups, and shattered the deepest community ties. Both Confederate and Union forces rode through the Cherokee Nation at various times. In addition, numerous groups of armed men operating outside traditional military discipline roamed the region, such as the infamous guerrilla Quantrill and his men. In such an atmosphere, the protection of family quickly became the primary focus of everyone's efforts. With men away in military service, the burdens of maintaining home and hearth fell on women. Cherokee women struggled to stay out of the reach of threats they could not necessarily identify. Because fellow Cherokees could easily be enemies, almost no one could be trusted. Shortages of every type of foodstuff plagued the region. Mills fell in smoking ruin, leaving nowhere to process any grain that might be obtained. Spinning wheels fell silent as cotton and even cards became scarce. Simply holding a family together and meeting basic necessities became a nearly insurmountable challenge for even the best connected women like Sarah Watie, wife of Confederate General Stand Watie. The challenges of providing moral instruction, education, and physical support to dependents seemed impossible in the midst of a bloody civil strife. The losses of the war took a heavy toll on Cherokee women, leaving one-third of them as widows and one-fourth of their children as orphans.

Women throughout the country had to adjust to the challenges brought on by four years of warfare. Northern women rarely dealt with destruction caused by invading armies, but rather they found their lives altered by economic changes. As men went to fight, farms needed planting and harvesting, stores required tending, and women of all ages and classes had to fill in the gaps left by absent males. The concerns of Native American women in Northern areas tended to follow these patterns. Iroquois women were one such group. Traditional Iroquois have often been used as an example of women empowered by matrilineal social structure. Older women governed the longhouse and their families with enviable authority. However, by the mid-nineteenth century, their roles had been altered by the influx of Western ideas, particularly the opinions of missionaries. Other changes had

moved the Iroquois toward a market economy, creating jobs primarily filled by men. When these men went off to fight in the Civil War, Iroquois women stepped into the void, and they did well. The war years saw an increase of both crops and livestock on the reservation in western New York. This bounty was produced despite the ravages of smallpox that swept Iroquois communities during the war. However, positive aspects such as empowerment due to a return to matrilineal traditions or involvement in economic production generally waned after the war, and Native women were left to reconstruct lives often immeasurably altered by the conflict.

Clarissa W. Confer

See also Family Life, Confederate; Family Life, Union; Northern Women; Shortages; Southern Women.

References and Further Reading

Dale, Edward Everett, and Gaston Litton. 1939. *Cherokee Cavaliers.* Norman: University of Oklahoma Press.
Gaines, W. Craig. 1989. *The Confederate Cherokees: John Drew's Regiment of Mounted Rifles.* Baton Rouge: Louisiana State University Press.
Hauptman, Laurence. 1993. *The Iroquois in the Civil War: From Battlefield to Reservation.* Syracuse, NY: Syracuse University Press.
Johnson, Carolyn Ross. 2003. *Cherokee Women in Crisis: Trail of Tears, Civil War, and Allotment.* Tuscaloosa: University of Alabama Press.
Perdue, Theda. 1999. *Cherokee Women.* Lincoln: University of Nebraska Press.
Taylor-Colbert, Alice. 1997. "Cherokee Women and Cultural Change." In *Women of the American South,* edited by Christie Anne Farnham, 43–55. New York: New York University Press.

Nonslaveholding Southerners

Nonslaveholders, who comprised 75 percent of the households in the antebellum South, were both the mainstay of the Confederacy and the main white body of opposition to the new nation within the South. Despite the popular image of poor white Southerners protesting a "rich man's war and a poor man's fight," most nonslaveholding whites willingly, and even enthusiastically, joined the Confederacy. Politics, economics, culture, and racial identity all gave nonslaveholding whites strong incentives to support breaking away from the Union. And, although the longevity and the destructiveness of the conflict tested the commitment of the middle and lower classes in the South, most white Confederates supported the nation until its collapse in April 1865. Of the minority of Southern whites who opposed secession from the beginning or who developed an animosity to the Confederacy during the war, many were poor whites who found that the new nation's policies no longer matched their interests. The experience of nonslaveholding Southern whites during the war reveals the diversity of experiences and beliefs in a community that is often perceived as monolithic.

Political leaders in the antebellum South justified secession primarily in terms of the damage that would be done to the Southern economy and society if Republicans prohibited the growth of slavery in the Western territories and eventually enacted full emancipation, as white Southerners anticipated they would. The economic disaster that would result from a Republican administration in Washington, D.C., would not only affect the wealthy, they argued; nonslaveholding whites would see their own livelihoods deteriorate and their communities collapse. Nonslaveholding whites took this threat seriously. Emancipation presaged several serious economic problems for all members of Southern society. Many nonslaveholding workers drew their wages from jobs sustained by slave-based agriculture. Iron forges, tobacco factories, railroads, and most of the Southern commercial sector depended on the production of raw goods by slave labor. For white workers on the bottom of the economic ladder, the threat of competing against black workers loomed large. The example of the North, where immigrant workers undercut American workers by accepting lower wages for unskilled and dangerous jobs, seemed to foreshadow the conflict that would engulf the South upon emancipation. Even nonslaveholding farmers feared the disruption of local trade and production that would follow from such an event. Although political leaders often exagger-

ated their argument about the vulnerability of nonslaveholders, to judge from the broad and deep support given to the Confederacy in the early months of the war, most nonslaveholders recognized the underlying truth to their arguments.

The main problem for nonslaveholders was that the Civil War itself seemed to facilitate the destruction of the Southern economy. As the war extended in time, the Southern economy steadily weakened, and no group in society felt this change more acutely than nonslaveholders. Four factors combined to accelerate inflation: the profusion of printed money; the Union blockade of the Confederate coastline, which increased the scarcity of goods; the reduction of usable land for agriculture; and the breakdown in transportation. With fewer economic resources to draw on, nonslaveholding whites experienced increasing hardships in the search for food. First luxuries and then necessities were priced out of the reach of average Southerners. By 1865, a barrel of flour was selling for $1,200 in Richmond, Virginia. In the face of this problem, many Southerners returned to barter as a system for exchanging the few goods they were able to grow or produce. Most of the burden for feeding families fell on women. One event in particular revealed the depth of their dissatisfaction with how the Confederate government was administering the economy. On April 2, 1863, a group of several hundred middle- and lower-class Virginians, mostly women, began rioting in Richmond. The riots, in which women broke into bakeries and government warehouses where flour was stored, reflected popular dissatisfaction with the escalating price for bread and a deep sense that the burdens of the war were not being borne equally. The crowd dispersed, but only after Jefferson Davis called out a phalanx of regular troops and ordered them to fire on the protesters unless they returned home. Similar bread riots occurred around the Confederacy that year.

The political problem of distributing the costs of the war evenly demanded attention from Confederate leaders precisely because white men had accumulated significant political authority in the antebellum South. When those men and their wives expressed public displeasure with certain policies during the war, the government could not afford to ignore them. During the 1840s and 1850s, a number of Southern states democratized their political processes, eliminating property ownership qualifications for voting or holding office and making more offices elective rather than appointed. These changes and the growth of mass political parties drew all white men into a vibrant political culture and promised them a substantive role in the administration of their society. The politics of the antebellum South also tied nonslaveholders to their slave society since political leaders and thinkers explained the necessity of slavery as the basis for true republicanism. Alexander Stephens articulated this connection most clearly in his inaugural address as Confederate vice president, known later as the Cornerstone Speech. Most nonslaveholding whites would have immediately understood his celebration of the Confederacy as the "first" true republic in human history because it honestly and openly based white liberty on black slavery.

The drawback of creating a responsive political system in which all white men were invested was that the system had to remain responsive during the war. The first conflict came with the draft. The Confederacy, like the Union, enlisted its initial group of volunteers for one year, and most of these men planned to return home in the spring of 1862. However, because the Confederacy would have collapsed without experienced soldiers to resist the anticipated Union invasion, the government implemented a draft. An unprecedented action in United States history, the Confederate draft made all white males, aged eighteen to thirty-five, eligible for three-year terms of service. The upper age limit was moved to forty-five and then to fifty-five during the course of the war and the lower limit decreased to seventeen. The legislation creating the draft also automatically re-enlisted all one-year volunteers as three-year men. Exemptions existed for civil servants, teachers, clergy, and men working in war industries. More problematically, the Confederacy also offered one exemption for every twenty slaves a man owned. Since only the wealthiest Southern-

ers owned this many slaves, most Confederates perceived this as grossly unfair legislation that favored the people whom the war was already designed to protect. Substitution, an old American tradition, was included, although this practice was abolished in 1864. The draft generated significant opposition among the soldiers, and the Confederacy experienced a spike in desertion following its enactment. Soldiers perceived their one-year enlistment agreements as contracts violated by the draft. Although the Confederacy needed the draft to ensure that it could field armies to resist Federal troops, conscription became the source of much dissatisfaction among nonslaveholding Southerners.

The Confederacy undertook other centralizing measures as well. These policies, like the draft, angered poor Confederates and alienated some to the extent that they considered abandoning the nation altogether. The 1863 tax-in-kind, a 10-percent tax in key foodstuffs, hit yeomen hard and they complained bitterly about it. Likewise, the policy of impressment, which beginning in late 1863 allowed the Confederate government to seize from civilians whatever items were needed for military use, created a climate of fear. Because civilians were reimbursed for impressed items in Confederate scrip, largely devalued by the persistent inflation, they perceived impressment as arbitrary. Even as poor Confederates complained about the inequity of the system, citing laws like impressment and the tax-in-kind, they applauded the actions of the Confederacy when it, or state or local governments, aided the poor and destitute. The tax-in-kind and impressment both brought food into the coffers of the Confederate government, which could then be redistributed to needy Southerners. The control that the Confederacy exercised over the South angered many yeomen committed to the idea of states' rights, but it was an essential tool for ensuring the nation's ability to feed its families and to preserve itself.

The extent to which nonslaveholding whites rejected the Confederacy and actively aided the Union war effort is hard to measure. Ample evidence exists to show that, in certain places across the South, nonslaveholding men rejected the Confederacy and assumed a stance of active rebellion against the government. In Jones County, Mississippi, in Lawrence County, Alabama, and in Floyd County, Virginia, bands of deserters and draft dodgers reigned supreme by 1864. But the motivations varied among these and other communities that turned against the Confederacy. In some places, prewar conflicts manifested themselves as wartime hostilities. In other places, a strong political Unionism prevailed. In others, poor Southerners abandoned the cause when they felt their government had abandoned them through policies that unfairly punished nonslaveholders. The extent of desertion in the army, where such a loss of faith would have had the most effect, is hard to measure because few reliable quantitative studies have been conducted. Over the course of the war, the rate of desertion among Confederate troops probably paralleled that of Northern troops—about 10 percent. But even desertion cannot be reduced to a simple act of dissatisfaction with Confederate policies. Few deserters left explanations of their actions, and, when those actions can be recreated, it appears that local events and immediate problems, like a lack of proper supplies or food or incompetent officering, had as much to do with high rates of absenteeism as did any abstract shift in loyalty. Equally hard to measure is the degree of noncompliance with Confederate civilian policies. Certainly, many people hid goods from impressment officers and cheated on their tax-in-kind applications, but opposition to the state's policies did not necessarily equal opposition to the state. Most nonslaveholding whites remained committed to Confederate victory until the war's end.

This commitment remained intact throughout the war partly because the Confederacy promised to maintain the existing racial order. Many nonslaveholding Southerners were drawn into the conflict to prevent the collapse of that order under Republican rule. The effort to sustain the racial hierarchy of the antebellum South became increasingly difficult as the war progressed, but Southerners did not abandon their efforts. The Army of Northern Virginia acted as a giant slave patrol, arresting escaping slaves and sending them back to their masters. As Lee's army marched into the North in 1862 and 1863, it seized African Americans and sent them back to the South and into slavery. By functioning as state-sanctioned slave catchers and kidnappers, Confederate soldiers proved their commitment to the institution throughout the conflict. The Emancipation Proclamation elicited scorn, derision, and anger among nonslaveholders; all perceived it to be a vile attempt to incite slaves to murder, and some suspected that it would be successful. More problematic even than the Emancipation Proclamation itself was the use by the North of black soldiers. Condemned as barbarism by Confederates, the deployment of the United States Colored Troops throughout the South, as active participants in battles and as garrison troops, inspired Confederates to fight harder against Northern victory and fused the interests of slaveholding and nonslaveholding Southerners.

For nonslaveholding Southerners, the war was physically and psychologically debilitating. The sacrifices made on behalf of the Confederacy yielded little tangible benefits. At war's end, the Southern economy was ruined, much of the region's industrial and agricultural infrastructure destroyed, and its political system nonexistent. Defeat challenged Southern notions of masculinity, autonomy, and racial hierarchy. Nonslaveholders, in particular, suffered a great deal and left them uniquely embittered toward both the Union and the old Confederate government.

Aaron Sheehan-Dean

See also Confederate Homefront; Conscription; Desertion; Enlistment; Factory Workers, Southern; Impressment; Politics; Rural Women; Southern Women; Wartime Employment.

References and Further Reading

Blair, William. 1998. *Virginia's Private War: Feeding Body and Soul in the Confederacy, 1861–1865.* New York: Oxford University Press.

Bynum, Victoria. 2001. *The Free State of Jones: Mississippi's Longest Civil War.* Chapel Hill: University of North Carolina Press.

Escott, Paul D. 1978. *After Secession: Jefferson Davis and the Failure of Confederate Nationalism.* Baton Rouge: Louisiana State University Press.

Groce, W. Todd. 1999. *Mountain Rebels: East Tennessee Confederates and the Civil War, 1860–1870.* Knoxville: University of Tennessee Press.

McCurry, Stephanie. 1995. *Masters of Small Worlds: Yeoman Households, Gender Relations and the Political Culture of the Antebellum South Carolina Low Country.* New York: Oxford University Press.

Owsley, Frank Lawrence. 1949. *Plain Folk of the Old South.* Baton Rouge: Louisiana State University Press.

O

Olmsted, Frederick Law (1822–1903)

Although Frederick Law Olmsted is best-known as the landscape architect of New York's Central Park, he also served as the general secretary of the United States Sanitary Commission (USSC) from its inception in June 1861 until his resignation in September 1863. In this capacity, Olmsted was instrumental in promoting the value of women's contributions to the war effort, both on the homefront and close to the battlefield.

In the early 1850s, Olmsted's interest in civic issues and his reputation as a writer convinced the *New York Daily Times* to commission him to travel through the South and record his impressions of slavery there. His two trips led to the publication of three books: *A Journey in the Seaboard Slave States* (1854), *A Journey through Texas* (1856), and *A Journey in the Back Country* (1860). These books were well received in the North and established Olmsted as something of an authority on slavery in the South. As a result of his observations, Olmsted believed that slavery was an unhealthful institution and should not be extended to the territories—a key issue, ultimately, in the contentious election of 1860.

After war broke out in April 1861, women across the North mobilized to help the soldiers in any way they could. The Women's Central Association of Relief for the Sick and Wounded in the Army (WCAR), based in New York City, was perhaps the largest group of this sort. Concurrently, influential Northern men formed the United States Sanitary

Frederick Law Olmsted (1822–1903) served as the general secretary of the United States Sanitary Commission from June 1861 until September 1863. (Library of Congress)

Commission (USSC) to act as an aid and advisory group for the Medical Bureau of the United States War Department. Although the goal was not specified, the USSC also acted to organize the efforts of women involved in groups such as the WCAR. Ultimately, the WCAR became a branch of the USSC.

As general secretary of the USSC, Olmsted was an organizational genius. In its first months of existence, the USSC oversaw the health of soldiers in the volunteer part of the Union army, developed a system for inspecting camps and hospitals, and lobbied to modernize the Army Medical Bureau. In October 1861, Olmsted also wrote an open letter to the "Loyal Women of America," describing how the Sanitary Commission would channel supplies to the army and suggesting ways for women to help in this effort. Over forty thousand copies of this letter were distributed across the North.

It was Olmsted, more than any other USSC official, who advocated greater responsibilities for women in the war effort. He agreed to provide salaries for such female organizers as Mary Livermore, and he believed that women would serve admirably as nurses to wounded soldiers. Both of these beliefs were instrumental in breaking down the barriers preventing women from doing work equal to their capabilities.

During the Peninsular campaign in the spring of 1862, an opportunity arose to prove these beliefs in women's abilities. The USSC determined to help the Union army by using ships as floating hospitals to transport wounded soldiers from the battlefields of eastern Virginia to hospitals in the North. Olmsted decided to employ women as nurses on the boats that carried the wounded northward. He remained on the peninsula for months to direct this venture personally. Although Olmsted imagined that these women would be shielded from the horrors of the battlefield on the hospital ships, just the opposite turned out to be the case. As thousands of wounded arrived at river landings, women often worked for several days without sleep. Sometimes they cleaned and fed soldiers who had lain out on the battlefield for days with untended wounds. Female volunteers assisted doctors in amputating shattered limbs. Most of them proved themselves up to the challenge, and many reported that nursing allowed them to be the most alive they had ever felt. Olmsted wholeheartedly praised the women; they, too, were devoted to him.

Once back from the Peninsular campaign, Olmsted again addressed a general appeal to Northern women. He emphasized the necessity of the aid societies and their role in preserving the Union, urging women to forgo local concerns for the greater national good. This appeal coincided with intense military engagement; just a month earlier, the Battle of Antietam, the bloodiest single day of the war, had been fought in Maryland. Northern women responded resoundingly to Olmsted's appeal, and the USSC was at its peak in the fall of 1862.

The hospital transports and other USSC endeavors were so successful that, over time, they merged with the Army Medical Bureau. As the influence of the Sanitary Commission waned, Olmsted began to feel that his presence was no longer necessary. Despite urgings from other Sanitary Commission officers, Olmsted resigned from the position of general secretary in 1863. He and his family moved to California, where he assumed the position of manager of the Mariposa Mining Company. He died August 28, 1903, in Waverly, Massachusetts.

Ellen H. Todras

See also Hospital Ships; Livermore, Mary Ashton Rice (1820–1905); Northern Women; Peninsular Campaign; Union Homefront; United States Sanitary Commission; Wartime Employment; Women's Central Association of Relief.

References and Further Reading
Attie, Jeanie. 1998. *Patriotic Toll: Northern Women and the American Civil War.* Ithaca, NY: Cornell University Press.

Giesberg, Judith Ann. 2000. *Civil War Sisterhood: The U.S. Sanitary Commission and Women's Politics in Transition.* Boston: Northeastern University Press.

Rybczynski, Witold. 1999. *A Clearing in the Distance: Frederick Law Olmsted and America in the Nineteenth Century.* New York: Scribner's.

United States Sanitary Commission. [1864] 1972. *The Sanitary Commission of the United States Army: A Succinct Narrative of Its Works and Purposes.* New York: Arno Press and New York Times.

Young, Agatha. 1959. *The Women and the Crisis: Women of the North in the Civil War.* New York: McDowell, Obolensky.

P

Parsons, Emily Elizabeth (1824–1880)

Union nurse Emily Elizabeth Parsons supported the efforts of the United States Sanitary Commission during the Civil War.

Born in Taunton, Massachusetts, on March 8, 1824, and educated in Boston, Parsons lived with her family in Cambridge. She refused to let vision and hearing impairments limit her ambitions or activities. When war broke out, Parsons began training as a nurse at Boston's Massachusetts General Hospital. In October 1862, she offered her services to the United States military.

Parsons received a position at Fort Schuyler's MacDougall Hospital on Long Island Sound, but her father's concern about the health risks led her to resign. Parsons moved to New York City to seek a new appointment. She contacted the prominent reformer Dorothea Dix but failed to obtain a position. Soon she became acquainted with Jessie Benton Frémont, wife of Union General John C. Frémont. In January 1863, Jessie Frémont used her connections in the Western Sanitary Commission to get Parsons an assignment at the Lawson Hospital in St. Louis, Missouri. After less than a month, Commission officials gave Parsons the prestigious assignment as head nurse on the steamboat *City of Alton*. In this capacity, she accompanied sanitary stores to Vicksburg. During the voyage on the Mississippi River, Parsons contracted malarial fever, which weakened her and plagued her for the rest of the war. After recuperating, Parsons became superintendent of female nurses at Benton Barracks Hospital, St. Louis, the area's largest hospital. Here Parsons nursed both white and black soldiers, as well as a large number of escaped slaves. Within six months, Parsons suffered another fever attack and went home to Cambridge to recuperate. Although she returned to St. Louis, ill health forced her to resign in August 1864.

Parsons remained active during the last year of the war, working from her East Coast home where she collected and sent supplies to the Western Sanitary Commission for the freedmen and refugees in St. Louis. She also supported Chicago's Northwestern Sanitary Fair in May 1865.

Parsons maintained her commitment to hospital work during the postwar years. In 1867, she established a charity hospital for Cambridge's poor women and children. Within two years the institution closed, but Parsons urged citizens to help create a new facility; Cambridge Hospital opened in 1871. Parsons, who never married, spent the rest of her life supporting the hospital and advocating for the poor.

Emily Elizabeth Parsons died on May 19, 1880. Her father, Theophilus Parsons, published a selection of her wartime letters to raise funds for her causes. Her letters show a collegiality often missing in other Civil War hospital accounts and reflect Parson's deep satisfaction and pride in her wartime contributions.

Kelly D. Selby

See also Dix, Dorothea Lynde (1802–1887); Fairs and Bazaars; Frémont, Jessie Benton (1824–1902); Fundraising; Hospitals; Hospital Ships; Letter

Writing; Northern Women; Nurses; Union Homefront; United States Sanitary Commission; Wartime Employment.

References and Further Reading
Brockett, L. P., and Mary C. Vaugh. 1867. *Women's Work in the Civil War: A Record of Heroism, Patriotism and Patience*. Philadelphia, PA: Zeigler, McCurdy & Co./Boston: R. H. Curran.
Parsons, Theophilus. 1880. *Memoir of Emily Elizabeth Parsons*. Boston: Little, Brown and Company.
Schultz, Jane E. 1992. "The Inhospitable Hospital: Gender and Professionalism in Civil War Medicine." *Signs* 17 (2): 363–392.

Peabody, Elizabeth Palmer (1804–1894)

Transcendentalist, educational reformer, and author Elizabeth Palmer Peabody is considered the first woman publisher in the United States.

The eldest of seven children, Elizabeth was raised in Salem, Massachusetts, by her dentist father, Nathaniel Peabody, and her schoolteacher mother, Elizabeth Parler Peabody. She and her siblings were educated by their mother, and she ultimately taught in the family school before embarking on her own career as teacher and educational reformer.

In 1834 Peabody worked as a teacher and assistant at Bronson Alcott's alternative Temple School. In 1836 she published her notes on the experiment as *Record of a School*. Peabody's publication created controversy about Alcott's methods, and he was later forced to close the school. Her reputation linked with Alcott's, Peabody then turned from teaching to reform work and publishing. In 1840 Peabody opened a bookstore in Boston that became the center of Transcendentalist activities throughout the decade. Peabody also became the publisher for many Transcendentalist and reform essays and books, publishing writings by Henry David Thoreau and her brother-in-law Nathaniel Hawthorne, among others.

Peabody herself authored or edited ten books and more than fifty articles, most of them related to education and educational reform, her primary interest after 1859. In 1860 she was inspired—along with her sister, Mary Peabody, who was married to educational reformer Horace Mann—to

Elizabeth Peabody, first woman publisher in the United States (1804–1894). (Library of Congress)

establish the first kindergarten in the United States. Elizabeth also founded a journal of the kindergarten movement and promoted the idea throughout the remainder of the century. In the 1880s Peabody joined with former Transcendentalist colleagues and lectured on early childhood education at Bronson Alcott's Concord School of Philosophy.

Although not active in abolitionist organizations and activities before the Civil War, Peabody claimed that, like many of her reform colleagues, she had always been antislavery. Peabody's efforts often focused more on promoting other writers and reformers, and to this end she worked to garner support and enthusiasm for writer Mattie Griffith's 1856 book, *Autobiography of a Female Slave*. Griffith was in fact a white woman who presented this slave narrative as part of her own antislavery crusade and as an effort to raise money to free slaves she herself had inherited, but the book went largely unnoticed outside of abolitionist circles.

In 1859 Peabody came to the defense of another crusader, Aaron Stevens, who had participated alongside John Brown in the unsuccessful raid on Harper's Ferry. Like many progressive Massachusetts reformers, Peabody followed the trial of radical abolitionist Brown. After Brown's celebrated capture and execution, Peabody traveled to Virginia to help appeal, unsuccessfully, the execution of Stevens as well. During the Civil War, Peabody met Abraham Lincoln twice and was present in the House of Representatives when the Thirteenth Amendment to the Constitution abolishing slavery was passed.

Elizabeth Palmer Peabody died on January 3, 1894.

Tiffany K. Wayne

See also Abolitionism and Northern Reformers; Education, Northern; Northern Women; Teachers, Northern; Thirteenth Amendment; Union Homefront.

References and Further Reading
Marshall, Megan. 2005. *The Peabody Sisters: Three Women Who Ignited American Romanticism.* Boston: Houghton Mifflin Company.
Ronda, Bruce, ed. 1984. *Letters of Elizabeth Palmer Peabody, American Renaissance Woman.* Middletown, CT: Wesleyan University Press.
Ronda, Bruce. 1999. *Elizabeth Palmer Peabody: A Reformer on Her Own Terms.* Cambridge, MA: Harvard University Press.

Pember, Phoebe Yates Levy (1823–1913)

Phoebe Levy Pember's *A Southern Woman's Story* (1879) chronicles her work as matron at Richmond's Chimborazo Military Hospital from December 1862 until after the end of the war. The book is a rich source of information about Civil War medical care, Richmond gossip, and the common soldiers of the Confederacy.

Phoebe Yates Levy was born into privilege on August 18, 1823, the daughter of Charleston businessman Jacob Clavius Levy and British native Fanny Yates. The Levy family had six daughters and one son; Phoebe was the middle child. There is no record of her education, but her book, surviving letters, and stories suggest it was excellent. Around 1850, Jacob Levy moved his family to Savannah.

Phoebe married Thomas Pember of Boston, who died of tuberculosis shortly after the war began, and Phoebe returned to her parents' home in Savannah. In 1862 the family left the blockaded city and settled in as refugees in Marietta, Georgia. Sister Eugenia Levy Phillips was twice arrested and imprisoned by Federal officials for her vehement support of the Confederacy. Nearing forty, Phoebe wanted independence. Through the influence of the wife of Confederate Secretary of War George W. Randolph, she was offered a salaried appointment as the first matron at Chimborazo Military Hospital Number Two.

Pember worried about the social stigma of hospital work but reported for work at the hospital in December 1862 with energetic determination. No provision had been made to house women, so she converted an outbuilding into her quarters and slept on a straw mattress. She was responsible for the six hundred men in the hospital. Although actual nursing care was discouraged, from the start she washed wounds and assisted surgeons with amputations when there was an influx of battle casualties. The 1862 hospital bill passed by the Confederate Congress specified that a matron keep the hospital clean and in good order, procure and prepare special foods for patients, and dispense the hospital's luxuries such as medicinal whiskey as prescribed by physicians. All these responsibilities presented challenges. She did not understand that she had the authority to hire a staff—including assistant matrons, cooks, and laundresses—until she had been there for several days. Dr. James B. McCaw, Chimborazo's chief surgeon, found her peeling potatoes and asked where her cooks were.

Confederate hospitals faced chronic shortages of food, personnel, and medical supplies. Pember described the whiskey barrel as a symbol of authority in the power struggles between male and female staff members. The monthly barrel of whiskey resided with the apothecary, and there was never enough to meet patients' needs. She demanded that McCaw put it under her control as the law stipulated. She kept it under lock and key, and throughout the war hospital staff tried all manner of ploys to gain access for their own use.

Chimborazo was built on a high bluff on the outskirts of Richmond. Pember had once been accused of taking up hospital work to find romance, so she was careful not to fraternize with the staff. In 1863 she moved to rooms in the city, and the evenings she spent with Richmond's elite raised her spirits. Pember remained devoted to her work and her patients. Making rounds twice a day, she wrote letters for patients and learned recipes to tempt homesick convalescents. Dressed in homespun because of the blockade, her maternal presence provided comfort to the sick and wounded. When Richmond fell, Union officers took charge of the hospital and began bringing in their own wounded. She stayed on to care for her patients until the last had died or was on the mend. By early June, Chimborazo became a school for freed slaves and Pember rejoined her family in Georgia.

A serialized version of her hospital journal was published in *The Cosmopolite* in 1866. Revised, it was issued as *A Southern Woman's Story* in 1879. *The Atlantic Monthly* printed one of her short stories that year, and two appeared in *Harper's New Monthly Magazine* in 1880. She traveled widely and was living in Pittsburgh when she died in 1913.

Nancy Gray Schoonmaker

See also Confederate Homefront; Homespun; Hospitals; Letter Writing; Nurses; Phillips, Eugenia Levy (1819–1901); Refugees; Southern Women.
References and Further Reading
Green, Carol C. 2004. *Chimborazo: The Confederacy's Largest Hospital.* Knoxville: University of Tennessee Press.
Pember, Phoebe Yates Levy. [1974] 2002. *A Southern Woman's Story,* with Introduction by George C. Rable. Columbia: University of South Carolina Press.
Schultz, Jane E. 2004. *Women at the Front: Hospital Workers in Civil War America.* Chapel Hill: University of North Carolina Press.

Peninsular Campaign (April–July 1862)

The Peninsular Campaign of April to July 1862 represented an attempt to take the new Confederate capital at Richmond, Virginia, via the Chesapeake Bay. It the wake of its failure, the campaign fostered the growth of the Confederate hospital complex in Richmond.

In the late summer of 1861, Union Army of the Potomac commander Major General George B. McClellan began to formulate a plan to by-pass the Confederate fortifications in Northern Virginia to mount an offensive on Richmond, and thereby end the war.

After transferring his army and equipment from Northern Virginia to Virginia's Tidewater region, McClellan commenced his advance toward Richmond on April 4. The next day, the discovery of Confederate General James Magruder's Confederate fortifications in Yorktown convinced McClellan to deploy his army into a siege mode in the hopes of forcing the Confederates out of their entrenchments. The month-long siege gave Confederate General Joseph E. Johnston time to pull his troops from Northern Virginia, and transport them by rail to Magruder's positions. On April 16, McClellan's army attempted to break through the enemy's lines, but was forced to pull back.

On May 3, Johnston retreated from his works in front of Yorktown. McClellan pursued and later struck at the Confederate rear guard in the indecisive Battle of Williamsburg. McClellan dispatched an infantry division by naval transport up the York River to cut off the Confederate retreat. Unfortunately, the Federal division commander allowed Johnston's force to slip by at Eltham's Landing. During this period, a Union attempt failed to take Confederate occupied Norfolk, but the attack forced an evacuation of the city and the destruction of the *C.S.S. Virginia*. Hoping to capitalize on the destruction of the Confederate ironclad, the Union Navy tried to push up the James River to Richmond, but was blunted by Confederate batteries at Drewry's Bluff on May 15. By the end of the month, the Union army had moved within view of the Confederate capital.

With Johnston's retreat from Yorktown, a period of panic fell upon the Confederate capital. Many citizens feared that Richmond would soon be captured. Portions of the Confederate government prepared to evacuate, and the Confederate Congress went into recess. Confederate President Jefferson Davis sent his wife and their children by rail to Raleigh, North Carolina. This move would open Varina Davis to criticism for abandoning her husband and the nation's capital during its time of crisis. President Davis finally allowed his family to return to home by the end of August 1862.

Despite efforts directed toward evacuation, Richmond began to grow as a hospital complex for the Confederate war effort in Virginia. The wounded and sick from the campaigns on the Peninsula began to flood the Confederate capital. The initial wave of wounded into Richmond came to nearly 7,000 men during May 1862. Citizens, especially women, created additional spaces for patients after the military hospitals were filled to capacity. Wounded soldiers were housed in public and private buildings. Women, like Sallie Putnam, cooked meals and washed bandages, clothing, and linens for the suffering men. For the Union forces, the medical director of the Army of the Potomac, Dr. Charles S. Tripler, was completely overwhelmed by the influx of casualties from the fighting. Fortunately, the United States Sanitary Commission dispatched ships and female nurses to help in the treatment of the wounded. Tripler initially disapproved of the commission and its nurses, but they later proved to be invaluable in dealing with the influx of wounded from the Peninsula battlefields.

Johnston's retreat back to Richmond increased the pressure by the Confederate president for a counterstrike. The swollen Chickahominy River split the Union forces in half, and Johnston saw an opportunity to defeat McClellan's army. Johnston attacked elements of the army that were isolated south of the river at Seven Pines and Fair Oaks on June 1, 1862. His attacks were poorly coordinated, and were generally indecisive. Johnston, however, was seriously wounded during the engagement, and General Robert E. Lee, who was President Davis's military advisor, took command of the Confederate forces.

In accordance with his president's wishes, Lee prepared to strike McClellan's Union forces. He ordered Major General Thomas "Stonewall" Jackson to move his troops from the Shenandoah Valley to Richmond and he ordered his cavalry to probe McClellan's right flank. His cavalry commander, Brigadier General J.E.B Stuart, rode around the Union army, thereby alerting McClellan to his isolated position. McClellan then consolidated his army and changed his base of operations from the York River to the James River.

On June 25, Lee launched a series of attacks which have been called the Seven Days' Battles. These assaults initially attempted to isolate and destroy one of the Union corps on the Chickahominy River, but they were changed into an offensive push to drive the Union forces back to the James River. McClellan pulled his army back from the gates of Richmond, and he continued to retreat until his army arrived at Harrison's Landing on the James River. With his back against the river and supported by the U.S. Navy, McClellan drew up into a fortified position on Malvern Hill on July 1. General Lee attempted to strike and overrun this position in hopes of shoving McClellan's forces into the river. After a number of costly attacks, Lee withdrew from the field, and eventually allowed the Federals to evacuate their position.

William H. Brown

See also Davis, Varina Banks Howell (1826–1906); Hospitals; Military Invasion and Occupation; Nurses; Putnam, Sarah "Sallie" Ann Brock (1831–1911); Southern Women; Wounded, Visits to.

References and Further Reading
Dowdy, Clifford. 1964. *The Seven Days: the Emergence of Lee.* Boston: Little, Brown.
Freeman, Douglas Southall. 1942–1944. *Lee's Lieutenants: A Study in Command.* 3 vols. New York: Scribner's.
Sears, Stephen W. 1988. *George B. McClellan: The Young Napoleon.* New York: Ticknor &Fields.
Sears, Stephen W. 1992. *To The Gates of Richmond: The Peninsular Campaign.* New York: Ticknor & Fields.
Schultz, Jane E. 2004. *Women at the Front: Hospital Workers in Civil War America.* Chapel Hill and London: University of North Carolina Press.
Wheeler, Richard. 1986. *Sword Over Richmond: An Eyewitness History of McClellan's Peninsular Campaign.* New York: Harper.

Pensions, Confederate Widows

From the end of the Civil War until the 1880s, indigent Confederate widows had been limited to making it on their own—relying on friends, relatives, or charitable institutions for relief—or finding new husbands in their efforts to make ends meet as manless women. Beginning in the 1880s, a new option arose throughout the South. They could turn to their state governments for support in the form of Confederate widows' pensions.

Although Southern state governments had provided financial assistance to soldiers' wives and widows throughout the war, such state-sponsored aid was unavailable during the tumult of Reconstruction. The financial ramifications of the war and an economic depression in the 1870s, combined with Republican administrations who were uninterested in rewarding the sacrifices of their recent enemies, coincided to stymie such aid. It was not until the very late 1870s that state-sponsored economic aid to widows began to emerge in the South. The first state to offer Confederate pensions to widows was Georgia in 1879. During the 1880s, North Carolina (1885), Alabama (1886), South Carolina (1887), Virginia (1888), Mississippi (1888), Florida (1889), and Texas (1889) all followed suit. Louisiana instituted widows' pensions in 1898, and Tennessee (1905), Kentucky (1912), Oklahoma (1915), and Arkansas (1915) all did so after the turn of the century. Missouri was the only former Confederate state that never offered pensions to its Confederate widows.

Although the implementation dates of widows' pensions, the methods of distribution (some states used county court systems whereas others had pension examining boards or a pensions commissioner), and the amounts offered varied significantly, each Southern state established roughly the same requirements to guide its pension distribution to widows. First, a widow could collect a pension based only on her husband's service if she had been married to him during the war. As time passed, some state legislatures altered this requirement to include widows who had married veterans immediately after the war's end and eventually to include those who married veterans years after the war. Second, a widow's husband had to have been honorably discharged. Third, she must be indigent. Although the definition of indigence varied across the states, generally the standards were meant to include, not to exclude. Fourth, the widow must not have remarried. Many states changed this regulation so that, if a widow had remarried after her husband's death, she could apply if her second husband had abandoned her or left her widowed. Finally, a widow must have been a resident of the state to which she was applying for a pension for a specific period of time. For states that used the county system to distribute pension funds, applicants were also required to be a resident of their county for a specific length of time. With most application forms, widows were required to provide minimal evidence that what they claimed on the form was true. Such evidence could include affidavits from various sources including neighbors or ministers to verify the marriage and the residence of the applicant; comrades or physicians to verify the wound, disease, or death of the husband; and local officials to attest to the applicant's property and income. Over time the qualifications to receive a Confederate widow's pension changed. Generally, state legislatures relaxed requirements, making it easier for a widow to acquire a pension.

Another similarity among Confederate state pensions was their generosity or the limits of their generosity. Though pension amounts varied from state to state, widows generally, though not always, received less than veterans. Additionally, state-disbursed Confederate widows' pensions were not nearly as generous as those provided to Union widows by the United States government. Under the 1862 pension law passed by the United States Congress, Union widows received anywhere from $8 to $30 per month, depending on the rank of their deceased spouses. Per year, then, Union widows could receive anywhere from $96 to $360. Additionally, after 1873 Union widows were entitled to an additional $2 per month per child under the age of sixteen. In the Southern pension systems, a widow's pension amounted to an average of only $25 to $30 per year.

Although the individual amount of each Confederate pension paled by comparison to those of the

Federal system, proportionately Southern states and citizens expended significantly more on pensions than did the Federal government. At the same time that Southern citizens contributed to the Union pension system through indirect taxes, they also contributed to Southern state pension systems through indirect and direct taxes including sales, property, and the infamous poll taxes designed to keep African Americans from voting in the South. Few complaints about funding Southern pension systems arose. In states like Georgia, where pensions had to be approved by a vote of the citizenry, pension legislation passed easily. Additionally, during the years of the Depression, many Southern states began to feel the financial pinch of the economy and responded by withholding pension checks from their veterans and widows. Soon thereafter, legislators faced public pressure to keep pension payments steady. Similarly, attempts to place Confederate veterans and widows on old age assistance programs rather than pension programs also instigated public outcry. Pension proponents roundly opposed these efforts because of the stigma attached to old age aid. Whereas Southern society considered Confederate pensions a right earned by an individual because of immense sacrifice for the cause, old age assistance was merely a privilege afforded elderly poor people. Eventually, opponents prevailed, and Confederate pensions remained independent of old age assistance programs. The last Confederate widows' pensions were distributed in the late twentieth century.

Jennifer Lynn Gross

See also Courtship and Marriage; Pensions, Union Widows; Southern Women; Widows, Confederate.
References and Further Reading
Gorman, Kathleen. 1999. "Confederate Pensions as Southern Social Welfare." In *Before the New Deal: Social Welfare in the South, 1830–1930*, edited by Elna C. Green, 24–39. Athens: University of Georgia Press.

Gross, Jennifer Lynn. 2001. *"Good Angels": Confederate Widowhood and the Reassurance of Patriarchy in the Postbellum South.* Ph.D. diss., University of Georgia, Athens.

Rodgers, Mark E. 1999. *Tracing the Civil War Veteran Pensions System in the State of Virginia: Entitlement or Privilege.* Lewiston, NY: Edwin Mellen Press.

Young, James R. 1982. "Confederate Pensions in Georgia." *Georgia Historical Quarterly* 62: 47–52.

Pensions, Union Widows

Women were significant beneficiaries of the Federal Civil War pension system, established in 1862. The original intention of Congress was to provide regular payments to disabled Union veterans and to the survivors of men who died in Union service. Under subsequent postwar legislation, eligibility for pensions broadened and the generosity of the system increased to the point that, by the 1890s, over 40 percent of the Federal budget was being spent just on Civil War pensions.

The bulk of survivors' pensions went to the widows of Union soldiers and sailors. Under the 1862 Act, or General Law, widows could collect $8 per month, paid quarterly, plus an additional $2 per month for each child under sixteen years of age. To be approved for a pension, a widow had to prove that her husband's death was service-related and that she had been legally married to the man in question at the time of his death. Legal marriage could be proven by government records or by the testimony of two people who either witnessed the marriage ceremony or could state the couple lived together as husband and wife. The latter provision was established to assist the widows of common law marriages, ex-slaves, and Native Americans, for whom no record of a ceremony existed. The U.S. Pension Bureau, which administered Federal military pensions, used relevant state law in deciding the legality of marriages, deferring to a long tradition of state primacy in domestic law. Hence, a marriage that was legal in one state could conceivably be judged by Federal bureaucrats not legal in another state, even if the circumstances of the marriage were identical.

The first significant change in the General Law, specifically pertaining to widows, came in 1882. In a law passed on August 7 of that year, Congress mandated that "the open and notorious adulterous cohabitation of a widow who is a pensioner shall operate to terminate her pension from the commencement of such cohabitation." Evidently, some widows were living out of wedlock to enter into new relationships and keep their pension, which by law would be terminated upon a remarriage. The U.S. Pension Bureau energetically investigated charges of Union widows living in "open and notorious adulterous cohabitation." Their vigor not only reflected Victorian morality, but also the fact that, through Civil War pensions, the Federal government effectively was standing in for a dead soldier or sailor in supporting his widow, and it expected the same fidelity.

Another change in the pension laws affecting Union widows and other pensioners was the so-called 1879 Arrears Act. This legislation allowed people who had not already made pension claims to collect a lump sum for payments back to the date they would have been initially eligible, not to the date they had first applied as had previously been the case. Hence, if a widow of a Union soldier had never applied for a pension, the woman could now collect all the pension payments she would have been entitled to from the date of her husband's death. Because over a decade had passed since the end of the war, the back payments, or arrears, could amount to well over $1,000, a significant sum of money at the time. While the law benefited many widows who for one reason or another had not applied for a pension at the time of their husband's death, it also prompted specious claims from women purporting to be Union widows and hoping for a financial windfall. There also were charges that the husbands of remarried widows lay behind some claims, hoping to benefit from the ability of their wives to collect arrears from the date their soldier husband died up to the date of their remarriage.

Women were also greatly affected by the single biggest change in Union pension legislation on June 27, 1890. Better known as the 1890 Law, this legislation opened pension eligibility to Union veterans disabled for any reason, not just from war-related causes. As administered by the Pension Bureau, the 1890 law enabled just about every surviving Union veteran who was not in perfect health to collect a Federal pension. It also opened pension eligibility to the widows of veterans of the Union army and navy who had died since the end of the war, provided their husband had served at least ninety days and had an honorable discharge. This change affected an enormous number of women because by 1890 about half the men who had served the Union during the Civil War had died. The only significant limitation to the 1890 Law as it pertained to widows was the requirement that they must have married their husband prior to the passage of the law. This condition seemed aimed at preventing women, especially young women, from marrying veterans subsequent to the passage of the law in the hopes of collecting a widow's pension after his death. Congress softened this provision of the 1890 law in 1916 by opening eligibility to widows who had married veterans in or before 1905.

As the 1916 law shows, Congress was willing to amend pension legislation to offer Union widows greater fairness. It made these gestures individually as well as collectively. Women were the beneficiaries of many special pension laws, congressional acts granting pensions to specific individuals. The intent of the congressmen who introduced such bills, as they pertained to widows, seems to have been to assist deserving women who, because of their inability to prove a legal marriage or some other justifiable reason, were not able to obtain a pension via normal bureaucratic channels. Regardless of how they got them, women represented an increasing percentage of Civil War pensioners as the years went by; partly because the female lifespan was longer and partly because men were marrying younger partners, women increasingly replaced men on the pension rolls. In fact, although the last Union veteran died in 1955, the last verified Union widow, Gertrude Janeway, died in January 2003, at the time of her death collecting a pension of $70 per month as a Union widow.

Donald R. Shaffer

See also Courtship and Marriage; Domesticity; Northern Women; Separate Spheres; Widows, Union.

References and Further Reading

Holmes, Amy. 1990. "'Such Is the Price We Pay': American Widows and the Civil War Pension

System." In *Toward a Social History of the American Civil War: Exploratory Essays*, edited by Maris Vinovskis, 171–195. Cambridge, UK: Cambridge University Press.

McClintock, Megan J. 1996. "Civil War Pensions and the Reconstruction of Union Families." *Journal of American History* 83: 456–479.

Regosin, Elizabeth. 2002. *Freedom's Promise: Ex-Slave Families and Citizenship in the Age of Emancipation.* Charlottesville: University Press of Virginia.

Shaffer, Donald R. 2004. *After the Glory: The Struggles of Black Civil War Veterans.* Lawrence: University Press of Kansas.

Skocpol, Theda. 1992. *Protecting Soldiers and Mothers: The Political Origins of Social Policy in the United States.* Cambridge, MA: Belknap/Harvard University Press.

Petersburg Campaign (June 1864–April 1865)

The Petersburg campaign was the longest siege in American warfare, bringing the effects of the war to Confederate women and children near the end of the war. The residents of the town suffered from food and fuel shortages as well as from the other vagaries of war.

In May 1864, with the presidential election looming on the horizon, the Union Army of the Potomac, under the leadership of General Ulysses S. Grant, attempted to capture Richmond by direct assault. After a bloodbath at the battle of Cold Harbor, Grant turned his focus toward the town of Petersburg, an important supply line 25 miles south of Richmond.

On June 9, while Grant disengaged his troops from Cold Harbor, Union General Benjamin F. Butler sent a force of sixty-five hundred infantry and cavalry toward Petersburg. The few Confederate troops under General Pierre G. T. Beauregard protected the northeastern side of the line, while the town's militia, comprised primarily of elderly men and young boys, defended the southern end. The Union army probed the southern end of the line and pushed them back toward town. There, the Southern militiamen, with support from the regular Confederate soldiers, forced the Federals to retreat.

Within a week, Confederate and Union forces reached a stalemate and the Union put the town under siege. In the following months, Grant methodically strained Confederate manpower and military resources by attempting to break the line between Petersburg and Richmond. This tactic eventually cut Lee's supply lines to the south. In the meantime, during the prolonged trench warfare, soldiers on both sides of the line spent endless days of tedious enemy shelling, military drills, thick mud, exposure to the elements, and poor food. Confederate hopes that the North would tire of the war crumbled when President Abraham Lincoln was re-elected in November. Union General William Tecumseh Sherman's devastating push through the Southern homefront also hastened the deterioration of Confederate resolve to continue the fight. Letters from impoverished families, combined with the horrific conditions in the trenches, caused a number of desertions from the Confederate army throughout the winter of 1864–1865. By early February 1865, Lee had only sixty thousand troops remaining to face Grant's one hundred and ten thousand.

Meanwhile, the residents of Petersburg suffered alongside the Confederate troops. Filled with many refugees from elsewhere in the Confederacy, Petersburg was hardly prepared for a long siege. Matters worsened as the town was in range of the Yankee guns, causing more than five hundred residential and commercial buildings to be damaged by artillery barrages. Entire sections of the city were uninhabitable. Short supplies of fuel, high food prices, and rising crime rates created extreme misery among the citizens that winter. Some women resorted to burning wood from a nearby bridge to keep warm in the winter. These conditions forced some women and children to beg for food from the soldiers.

During the course of the nearly nine-and-a-half-month siege, the armies would clash in six major battles, eleven engagements, forty-four skirmishes, six assaults, nine actions, three expeditions, and one affair. These included the bloody Battle of the Crater and the last major Confederate offensive of the war at Fort Stedman. Casualty figures for the campaign were about forty-two thousand soldiers for the Union and approximately twenty-eight thousand for the Confederacy. Finally, on April 1, 1865, the stalemate at Petersburg concluded when the Union crushed the Confederates at Five Forks. The next day, the Union army renewed the assault and the Confederate right flank crumbled. Only a last stand at Fort Gregg saved the retreating Confederates from immediate defeat. The collapse of the Confederate line at Petersburg resulted in the evacuation of Richmond, and it forced Lee to eventually surrender his troops to Grant on April 12, 1865 at Appomattox Courthouse.

Kristina K. Dunn

See also Civilian Life; Confederate Homefront; Confederate Surrender (1865); Lee, Robert Edward (1807–1870); Letter Writing; Sherman's Campaign (1864–1865); Shortages; Southern Women.

References and Further Reading

Alexander, Edward Porter. 1989. *Fighting for the Confederacy: The Personal Recollections of General Edward Porter Alexander*, edited by Gary Gallagher. Chapel Hill: University of North Carolina Press.

Horn, John. 1993. *The Petersburg Campaign: June 1864–April 1865*. Conshohocken, PA: Combined Books.

Trudeau, Noah Andre. 1995. *National Parks Civil War Series: The Siege of Petersburg*. Fort Washington, PA: Eastern National Park and Monument Association.

Phelps, Elizabeth Stuart (Ward) [Mary Gray Phelps] (1844–1911)

Elizabeth Stuart Phelps's first novel, *The Gates Ajar* (1868), offered a comforting vision of heaven as the perfection of earthly domesticity to a grieving nation that found the consolation of traditional religion inadequate after the Civil War. Its success gave rise to a genre of novels about the afterlife, including Phelps's *Beyond the Gates* (1883) and *The Gates Between* (1887). *The Gates Ajar* was second only to *Uncle Tom's Cabin* (1852) in sales of a novel by a nineteenth-century woman. Phelps's literary career reflected, in complex and revealing ways, her rejection of strict Calvinism and male domination of women.

Born Mary Gray Phelps in Boston on August 31, 1844, the author was the daughter and granddaughter of eminent Calvinist theologians and dutiful ministers' wives. Her parents, Elizabeth Wooster Stuart and Austin Phelps, moved to Andover when

Elizabeth Stuart Phelps, nineteenth-century genre novelist (1844–1911). (Library of Congress)

she was three. Her brother Moses Stuart was born in March 1849, and Mary's first memory was of her mother reading stories she had written and illustrated for her children. Using a pseudonym, her mother began writing novels about ministers' wives; these books gained immediate popularity and sold well. However, the strain of being a writer, wife, and mother was debilitating; Elizabeth Phelps died on November 29, 1852, a few months after the birth of her second son, Amos Lawrence.

Young Mary strongly identified with her mother. By the time she completed her studies at Abbott Academy and entered Mrs. Edwards's School for Young Ladies, she was using the name Elizabeth Stuart Phelps and she began to write.

Phelps's beau, Samuel Hopkins Thompson, died of wounds received at the Battle of Antietam, and she drew on this experience in her writing. "A Sacrifice Consumed," her story of a seamstress whose fiancé was killed at Antietam, appeared in the January 1864 *Harper's New Monthly Magazine*. The responsibility of helping to raise her brothers fed Phelps's desire for independence. To increase her income, she wrote books for Sunday schools, as had her mother, as well as books for young girls. Meanwhile, she had begun *The Gates Ajar* (1868).

Phelps's bereavement and the inability of patriarchal religion to comfort her were experiences shared by thousands of women after the Civil War. *The Gates Ajar*, with its vivid descriptions of reunions in heaven, immediately became a best seller. It drew heavily on contemporary Utopian and Spiritualist themes, and it raised the ire of conservative clergymen. Its sequel, *Beyond the Gates*, conceived in 1868 but not written until 1883, depicted a heaven with supportive men and women seeking personal fulfillment.

The Gates Ajar gave Phelps financial independence. She continued to write, exploring themes of female independence and the burdens of marriage and motherhood as constraints on women's creativity. To the surprise of many, she married Herbert Dickinson Ward, a man seventeen years her junior, on October 20, 1888. Collaborative novels in the early years of the marriage were unsuccessful, and Herbert began spending less and less time at home. Phelps wrote about invalid women and wandering husbands in her last years, and she died January 28, 1911 in Newton, Massachusetts.

Nancy Gray Schoonmaker

See also Family Life, Union; Fiction Writers, Northern; Mourning; Northern Women; Religion; Union Homefront; Wartime Literature.

References and Further Reading
Baym, Nina. 2000. "Introduction." In *Three Spiritualist Novels*, by Elizabeth Stuart Phelps, vii–xxiii. Urbana: University of Illinois Press.

Kelley, Mary. 1984. *Private Woman, Public Stage: Literary Domesticity in Nineteenth-Century America*. New York: Oxford University Press.

Kelly, Lori Duin. 1983. *The Life and Works of Elizabeth Stuart Phelps, Victorian Feminist Writer*. Albany, NY: Whitston Publishing Company.

Kessler, Carol Farley. 1982. *Elizabeth Stuart Phelps*. New York: Twayne Publishers.

Sizer, Lyde Cullen. 2000. *The Political Work of Northern Women Writers and the Civil War, 1850–1872*. Chapel Hill: University of North Carolina Press.

Phillips, Eugenia Levy (1820–1902)

Eugenia Levy Phillips, wife of prominent Washington, D.C. attorney Philip Phillips, was an outspoken proponent of secession. Her indiscreet partisanship earned her the distinction of being arrested and confined twice by Federal authorities during the war. She was a sister of Phoebe Yates Pember, matron at Chimborazo Military Hospital and author of *A Southern Woman's Story: Life in Confederate Richmond*.

Eugenia Levy was born in Charleston, South Carolina, in 1820, to prosperous Jewish businessman Jacob C. Levy and British-born Fanny Yates Levy. Eugenia and her five sisters enjoyed a life of privilege, including a good education. She was married September 7, 1836, to Philip Phillips, the son of prominent Jewish Charlestonians. Born in 1807, Phillips had established a successful legal practice in Mobile, Alabama. The couple lived in Mobile for eighteen years, and seven of their nine children were born there. Phillips was chairman of the state Democratic Party and served two terms in the state legislature. When he was elected to the United States Congress in 1853, the family moved to Washington, D.C.

Eugenia, beautiful and witty, enjoyed Washington's social life. After one term in Congress, Philip decided to practice law there and prospered in the years before the war. When hostilities began, Unionist Phillips and his family remained in Washington.

On August 24, 1861, Eugenia, daughters Caroline and Fanny, and sister Martha were placed under house arrest by Federal detectives and later moved to the home of Rose O'Neal Greenhow, another suspected Confederate spy. Through appeals to influential friends, Mr. Phillips managed to secure his family's release on September 18. Banished, they traveled to Richmond. According to her daughter's memoir, Eugenia gave Confederate officials a coded message from Greenhow, smuggled out in a ball of yarn. The family settled in New Orleans, which was occupied by Union forces under General Benjamin F. Butler by the following summer.

Eugenia soon ran afoul of Federal authorities. General Butler, known as Beast Butler to Southerners for his infamous Woman Order, had Eugenia arrested for laughing as a Yankee soldier's funeral passed below her balcony. Butler ordered her imprisoned on Ship Island in the Gulf of Mexico but allowed her to take her maid. Months of inadequate rations, heat, insects, and close confinement led to illness for both women. Philip secured their release and the family left Union territory, eventually settling in Georgia. For the rest of her life, Eugenia fancied herself a Confederate heroine.

Philip resumed his successful law practice in Washington after the war, and he died in 1884. Eugenia Levy Phillips lived until 1902.

Nancy Gray Schoonmaker

See also Butler, Benjamin F. (1818–1893); Confederate Homefront; Female Spies; Imprisonment of Women; Jewish Women; Pember, Phoebe Yates Levy (1823–1913); Southern Women; Woman Order (General Order Number 28).

References and Further Reading

Jacobs, Joanna. 1988. "*Eugenia Levy Phillips vs. The United States of America.*" *Alabama Heritage* 50: 22–29.

Morgan, David T. 1984. "Eugenia Levy Phillips: The Civil War Experiences of a Southern Jewish Woman." In *Jews of the South: Selected Essays from the Jewish Historical Society*, edited by Samuel Proctor and Louis Schmier with Malcolm Stern, 95–106. Macon, GA: Mercer University Press.

Saxon, Elizabeth Lyle. 1905. *A Southern Woman's War Time Reminiscences, by Elizabeth Lyle Saxon, for the Benefit of the Shiloh Monument Fund.* Memphis, TN: Press of the Pilcher Printing Co.

Pickens, Lucy Petway Holcombe (1832–1899)

The "uncrowned Queen of the Confederacy," an advocate of women's rights, and the only woman to have her image engraved on Confederate Treasury notes, Lucy Petway Holcombe Pickens served as the vice-regent representing South Carolina for the restoration of Mount Vernon.

Born June 11, 1832, at La Grange, Tennessee, to Beverly Lafayette and Eugenia Dorothea Hunt Holcombe, Lucy was the second of five children. She received her early education and instruction in music from her mother and a governess. In 1846, Lucy and her older sister, Anna Eliza, were sent to the Moravian Female Seminary in Bethlehem, Pennsylvania, to receive a classical education. Lucy excelled in literature and languages. In 1849 the sisters returned to La Grange, adept in the classics, arts, conversation, and flirting. Unhappy in the role of a Southern belle, Lucy sought recognition for her intelligence, maintaining that a woman of intellect with knowledge of the social graces should take a stand for the betterment of society.

In 1850, the Holcombe family suffered financial losses and moved to Marshall, Texas. There Lucy's father farmed and built Wyalusing, a plantation home. Although Lucy had many suitors, she rejected all matrimonial offers, believing marriage would relegate her to the kitchen and the nursery. She took an interest in politics, writing, and giving speeches for presidential candidates. In 1851 she championed General Narciso López in his filibuster attempt to liberate the Cubans from Spanish rule. The attempt failed and Lucy, age nineteen, wrote a novel castigating the American government for not coming to the aid of the filibusters. *The Free Flag of Cuba, or the Martyrdom of General Lopez* was published in 1856 under the pseudonym H. M. Hardimann. Not satisfied with the success of her novel and her many published poems, Lucy looked to someone of political standing who might further her ambition for recognition as an intellectual.

In 1857 she met Francis Wilkinson Pickens, a wealthy and influential congressman from Edgefield, South Carolina. Although Pickens was a widower twice her age with seven children, Lucy agreed to marry him if he obtained a high position in government. After President James Buchanan appointed Pickens minister to the royal court of Russia, Lucy and Francis were married at Wyalusing, in Marshall, Texas, on April 26, 1858. They left for Russia May 29, 1858.

With her natural beauty and intelligence, Lucy created a sensation throughout Europe. At the

Russian imperial court, Czar Alexander II paid particular attention to this American beauty and showered her with gifts and jewels, causing considerable gossip. Although Lucy enjoyed the czar's attentions and those of the royal courtiers, she became increasingly homesick. In 1859 she gave birth to a daughter christened by royalty as Francis Eugenia Olga Neva Pickens. The Russians added the name Douschka, the Russian diminutive meaning Little Darling, a name by which Lucy's daughter was forever known.

The Pickens family returned to the States on the eve of Abraham Lincoln's election to the presidency, November 6, 1860. Francis was chosen governor of South Carolina, the first state to secede from the Union. Lucy backed her husband's decision and, after the firing on Fort Sumter, sold jewels and precious gifts given her by the czar to finance a Confederate legion named in her honor, the Holcombe Legion.

As the wife of the governor and an avid supporter of the Confederacy, Lucy gave speeches, reviewed troops, encouraged men to enroll, helped the wounded, and gave freely of her time, talent, and money. For her considerable help, the Confederacy honored her by engraving her image on Confederate $1 and $100 Treasury Notes issued in 1862–1863 and 1864.

Devastated by the untimely death of her daughter, Lucy, with her faithful former slave, Lucinda, raised three grandchildren, kept Edgewood as a haven for all in need, and promoted the memory of those who fought for the Confederacy. Lucy Petway Holcombe Pickens died of a stroke in 1899 and is buried in the Pickens' family plot in Edgefield, South Carolina.

Elizabeth Wittenmyer Lewis

See also Confederate Homefront; Fiction Writers, Southern; Southern Women.
References and Further Reading
Burton, Georganne B. and Orville Vernon Burton, editors. 2002. *The Free Flag of Cuba, The Lost Novel of Lucy Holcombe Pickens.* Baton Rouge: Louisiana State University Press.
Greer, Jack. 1975. *Leaves from a Family Album.* Waco: Texian Press.
Lewis, Elizabeth Wittenmyer. 2002. *Queen of the Confederacy, the Innocent Deceits of Lucy Holcombe Pickens.* Denton: University of North Texas Press.

Pickett, LaSalle Corbell (ca. 1843–1931)

The wife of Confederate General George E. Pickett, LaSalle Corbell Pickett was a prolific writer, poet, and public speaker who appealed to Lost Cause mythologists for sectional reconciliation and nationalism in the late nineteenth and early twentieth centuries.

Sallie Ann Corbell was probably born on May 16, 1843, but may have been born as early as 1841. Her parents, John David and Elizabeth Phillips Corbell, were planters in Nansemond County, Virginia. Sallie grew up in modest circumstances and wrote that she met her future husband, George Pickett, in 1852, when she claimed to be only six years old. She married Pickett in September 1863, two months after the bloody charge at Gettysburg that made his name famous. Sallie later claimed to be age fifteen at the time of the marriage. George Pickett died in 1875. Sallie never remarried and outlived her husband by fifty-six years.

In those fifty-six years, she mixed devotion to her husband with plagiarism and fiction to create a heroic, mythological George Pickett much different from the historical figure. In doing so, she applied the basic tenets of the Lost Cause myth, including an idealized version of the Old South and the unfailing courage of its soldiers. She also appealed to the growing feelings of reconciliation and nationalism, most notably in her fabricated story of her husband's friendship with Abraham Lincoln.

She published her first book, *Pickett and His Men,* in 1899. Much of it was plagiarized from the history of Pickett's division written by Walter Harrison, one of Pickett's staff officers. In 1913 she published her most infamous work, *The Heart of a Soldier.* She claimed the contents were Pickett's wartime letters to her, some of them dated from the field at Gettysburg. Readers accepted these letters as genuine until the late 1950s. Since then, analysis of both the content and writing style has convinced most scholars that Sallie wrote them herself. Many have questioned LaSalle Pickett's motives. The simplest explanation is her devotion to her husband and to the Old South, combined with her necessity to generate an income as an independent woman.

In death, LaSalle Corbell Pickett became more controversial than she was in life. The debate over the authenticity of her writings was accompanied by a long struggle by her descendants to have her buried next to her husband in the venerated soldier's section of Hollywood Cemetery in Richmond. Finally, in 1998 she was reburied next to her husband, the man whose memory she had created.

Robert D. Bohanan

See also Letter Writing; Poets, Southern; Southern Women; Widows, Confederate; Widows, Union.
References and Further Reading
Gallagher, Gary. 1986. "A Widow and Her Soldier: LaSalle Corbell Pickett as Author of the George E. Pickett Letters." *The Virginia Magazine of History and Biography* 94: 329–444.
Gordon, Lesley J. 1998. *General George E. Pickett in Life and Legend.* Chapel Hill: University of North Carolina Press.
Gordon, Lesley J. 2001. "'Cupid Does Not Readily Give Way to Mars': The Marriage of LaSalle Corbell and George E. Pickett." In *Intimate Strategies of the Civil War: Military Commanders and Their Wives*, edited by Carol K. Bleser and Lesley J. Gordon, 69–86. New York: Oxford University Press.

Plantation Life

The plantation was a crucial theater of the Civil War where important battles were waged by enslaved women and their female owners. While they both experienced the physical and emotional hardships of war, female slaveholders and bondswomen struggled against each other in their efforts to preserve and destroy the peculiar institution. The growing resistance of plantation slaves during the war testifies to the deplorable conditions of the homefront, slaves' dogged commitment to obtaining their freedom, and the decreasing power of slaveholders. Combined, these factors undermined some slaveholding women's dedication to the war effort, strengthened female slaves' resolve

to be free, and contributed significantly to the collapse of both slavery and the Confederacy.

Both slaveholding women and bondswomen approached the Civil War with mixed emotions. Among Southern women, female slaveholders had the most invested in the antebellum social and economic system of slavery; so their initial reaction to secession and war was to support the Confederacy. Despite fears of being left alone on their plantations and of losing loved ones in battle, most slaveholding women followed the directives of the Confederate government and press, and they encouraged their male kin to enlist in the army and defend their way of life. Not content to watch from the sidelines, many plantation mistresses desired an active role in the conflict. Those who remained on their plantations found an outlet for their patriotism in the donation of goods or money and, even more important, in the production of blankets and clothes for Southern soldiers.

While many female slaveholders knitted and sewed items for the Confederate army themselves, most of this work was put on the shoulders of slave women. An increased emphasis on domestic production disrupted the working routines of female slaves and gave them additional cause for resistance. Slave women were well aware of the potential consequences of the Civil War and had no desire to assist the Confederacy. When ordered to produce goods for the army rather than for their own families and slave communities, many bondswomen expressed their discontent by slowing down their work. Eager to hasten the end of slavery but often forced by the remoteness of their location to wait for the end of the war, female slaves began to challenge their bondage with increasing uncooperativeness.

Aside from changes in domestic production, life for black and white women on most Southern plantations remained relatively unchanged at the start of the war. Unlike yeoman women who had few resources at their disposal, plantation mistresses could rely on their wealth and slaves to maintain plantation production. Moreover, plantations located in states that did not have a Federal military presence faced few outside challenges to the slave system. Initially, slaveholders in unoccupied areas

Sucklers. —

Sucklers are not required to leave their houses until sun-rise, when they leave their children at the children's house before going to field. The period of suckling is 12 mo. Their work lies always within 1/2 a mile of the quarter. They are required to be cool before commencing to suckle — to wait 15 minutes, at least, in summer, after reaching the children's house before nursing. It is the duty of the nurse to see that none are heated when nursing, as well as of the Overseer & his wife occasionally to do so. They are allowed 45 minutes at each nursing to be with their children. They return 3 times a day until their infants are 8 mo. old — in the middle of the forenoon, at noon, & in the middle of the afternoon: 'till the 12th mo. but twice a day, missing at noon during the 12th mo. at noon only. On weaning, the child is removed entirely from its mother for 2 weeks, & placed in charge of some careful woman without a child, during which time the mother is not to nurse it at all.

Remarks — The amount of work done by a Suckler is about 3/5 of that done by a full-hand, a little increased toward the last.

Old & Infirm. —

Those who from age & infirmities are unable to keep up with the prime hands are put in the sucklers gang.

Pregnant. —

Pregnant women, at 5 mo., are put in the Sucklers gang. No plowing or lifting must be required of them.

Sucklers, old & infirm, & pregnant receive the same allowances as full-work hands.

Plantation manual of James Henry Hammond that gives instructions for treatment of "Sucklers," "Old and Infirm," and "Pregnant" slaves. (Library of Congress)

were able to keep their operations running normally. Disruptions, however, were not far off.

Four major changes on Southern plantations interrupted the regular course and quality of life for bondswomen and plantation mistresses: the exodus of white men, the increased resistance of slaves, the material shortages of the homefront, and the eventual presence of Union troops.

One of the first and most consequential changes to take place on Southern plantations during the Civil War was the removal of white men for military service. As the husbands, overseers, and adult sons of slaveholding women enlisted in the war, the planter class began to demand special consideration from the government. Slave management, which was crucial to the maintenance of the Southern economy and society, was now largely the responsibility of white women. Yet contemporary gender conventions held that their delicate nature was antithetical to this kind of work, for mastery was understood to be a uniquely masculine characteristic. Slaveholding men and women alike feared the repercussions of leaving plantation mistresses solely responsible for crop production and slave supervision, both of which could make or break the Confederacy. Government officials, who shared these concerns, responded by passing a law that exempted from service one white male on plantations with twenty or more slaves. Although the law set planters' minds at ease for a moment, pressure from nonslaveholding whites and the need for military manpower undermined the legislation.

Slaveholding women soon found that their greatest challenge as plantation managers was the supervision of slaves. Although some female slaveholders had experience managing plantations in their husbands' absences before the war, they did so with the assistance of male overseers who handled the direct supervision and discipline of slaves. Those who lost their overseers to the war effort had to find ways to assert their command over slaves on their own. Most employed a variety of tactics. Although violence was not a sanctioned part of white womanhood, some plantation mistresses threatened and exacted corporal punishment on their slaves. Those who were afraid of retaliation or desertion tried to cajole loyalty and good work from their bondspeople with acts of kindness and charity. Others relied on slaves' sympathy or pity and resorted to begging. No matter the method of management, female slaveholders were desperate to control their slaves because they feared the consequences of not doing so.

Although plantation mistresses continued to speak of their steadfast trust in their slaves during the war, the numerous stories of slave rebellion, violence, and disloyalty that circulated throughout the South touched a nerve. Southern whites worried about the repercussions of leaving slaveholding women alone in the company of restive bondspeople, even though few instances of violent resistance by slaves were substantiated. Female slaveholders were usually confronted with nonviolent but effective acts of defiance. Plantation slaves acknowledged the increased opportunities that they had to challenge the system of slavery during the war and they took advantage of them. Exercising traditional methods of resistance such as slowing down production, stealing, and feigning illness, as well as bolder practices like direct confrontation or running away, Southern bondspeople grew more independent and more committed than ever to breaking free from the chains of bondage.

One of the most powerful wartime incentives for slave resistance was the rapid deterioration of their quality of life, due primarily to the limited availability of food and supplies in the Southern states. The Union blockade prevented most goods from coming in and most crops from going out, so slaveholders had not only fewer opportunities to purchase supplies, but also restricted funds with which to procure them. Moreover, the material goods and foodstuffs that were available for purchase were overpriced because inflation hit the Southern market. Civilians' demands for clothing, among other necessities, created an unprecedented need for domestic production, and it was the South's female slaves who carried the burden of this necessity. Plantation mistresses and planters put tremendous pressure on their bondswomen to spin, weave, and sew, even if this meant taking them out of the fields or putting them to work after a full day of agricultural labor. The dearth of manufactured goods increased female slaves' workload because they had to make clothing and supplies for their own families as well as for their owners' families.

Although even the wealthiest Southerners experienced the hardships of material deprivation, their struggle was hardly comparable to that of their slaves. The quality of life in the slaves' quarters declined steadily as slaveholders cut back on their distribution of provisions. Making due with meager rations of food, clothing, and blankets, bondspeople were plagued by malnutrition and disease. Yet despite the terrible conditions in which they were living, most slaves stayed on their owners' plantations during the war. Concerns for the safety and well-being of their families most often discouraged them from escaping. However, the wartime living conditions for slaves on some plantations were so unbearable that numerous individuals decided it would better for their families if they risked running away. Unprecedented numbers of female slaves and their children made the difficult decision to escape. Although most fugitive slaves tried to leave with their families, many had to decide whether freedom was worth a potentially permanent separation from their loved ones—something that was always a possibility in slavery, too. Moreover, they faced sale, imprisonment, or even execution if they were recaptured. Notwithstanding these risks, thousands of African Americans took a faithful leap toward freedom during the Civil War.

Slaveholders often struggled to understand why their slaves left. It was particularly hard for plantation mistresses when the slave in question was a favorite domestic servant or childhood playmate. Believing their own paternalistic rhetoric, female slaveholders frequently felt abandoned upon the loss of such slaves and were incensed at what they perceived as disloyalty. Aside from their personal feelings, slaveholding women's anger was due to the loss of valuable workers. White women commonly relied on trusted male slaves to keep order on the plantation in the absence of their husbands and white overseers, and domestic slaves made it possible for them to avoid household chores. The absence of these individuals gave some white women a taste of what life was like without slaves.

In an effort to check escalating slave resistance, slaveholding women pleaded with Confederate officials to release their husbands or sons from service so that they could help control their bondspeople. The difficulties these women faced were less a result of their inability to manage effectively than a consequence of a changing system of slavery in which slaves increasingly challenged whites' ability to keep them in bondage. When the government and military neglected to heed their call for assistance, many slaveholding women began to withdraw their support of the Southern war effort and, when possible, employed harsher means of discipline on their plantations. Those who had overseers on hand ordered more stringent punishments for disobedience, including time in jail, public beatings, and even sale. Yet these efforts also proved to be futile as the war progressed, as slaves grew more resistant, and as Union troops drew near.

The presence of the Federal army compounded the economic and social problems on Southern plantations. Hearing stories of Northern soldiers who commandeered, pillaged, and destroyed the Southern homes that lay in their path, many slaveholding women attempted to hide their valuables underground, in their slaves' cabins, and even in their own hoopskirts. Moreover, when confronted by enemy forces, some white women demanded that the soldiers treat both them and their property with the respect due to "ladies." Their claims to ladyhood may have protected some female slaveholders from personal violation, but they usually

did not prevent the theft and destruction of their property.

Believing that bondspeople owned no property, Northern soldiers also ravaged slaves' cabins and gardens, dispossessing them of their few items. Some individuals did not stop at robbery and vandalism; slave women were often the victims of rape and abuse at the hands of Federal troops. Yet not all Union soldiers behaved in such deplorable ways. Indeed, their presence on and in the vicinity of Southern plantations more often than not helped slaves realize their dreams of freedom. Moreover, they sent a message to slaveholders that slavery's days were numbered.

Slaves made their last push for emancipation near the end of the war by exercising more blatant and forceful acts of resistance that undermined power relations on the plantation. As a result, some female slaveholders pressured their husbands and sons to abscond from the military, unwilling to continue sacrificing their well-being or that of their families for a goal that no longer seemed attainable. As such, plantation mistresses and their bondswomen delivered a deadly blow to the Confederacy.

Nikki Berg Burin

See also African American Women; Aid Societies; Confederate Homefront; Destruction of Personal Property; Letter Writing; Military Invasion and Occupation; Rape; Rural Women; Sheridan's Shenandoah Valley Campaign (1864); Sherman's Campaign (1864–1865); Shortages; Slaveholding Women; Southern Women.

References and Further Reading

Clinton, Catherine. 1995. *Tara Revisited: Women, War, and the Plantation Legend.* New York: Abbeville Press.

Edwards, Laura. 2000. *Scarlett Doesn't Live Here Anymore: Southern Women in the Civil War Era.* Urbana: University of Illinois Press.

Faust, Drew Gilpin. 1996. *Mothers of Invention: Women of the Slaveholding South in the American Civil War.* Chapel Hill: University of North Carolina Press.

Rable, George. 1989. *Civil Wars: Women and the Crisis of Southern Nationalism.* Urbana: University of Illinois Press.

Schwalm, Leslie A. 1997. *A Hard Fight for We: Women's Transition from Slavery to Freedom in South Carolina.* Urbana: University of Illinois Press.

Weiner, Marli F. 1998. *Mistresses and Slaves: Plantation Women in South Carolina, 1830–80.* Urbana: University of Illinois Press.

Pleasant, Mary Ellen (1814–1904)

Called the mother of civil rights in California, Mary Ellen Williams Smith Pleasant's legacy has been obscured by rumor and public scandal. A study in contradictions, Mammy Pleasant, as she was popularly known, is revered by many for her work as an abolitionist, activist, and feminist, but she was reviled by critics as a con artist, madam, and voodoo practitioner. She is reported to have donated $30,000 to aid John Brown's raid at Harper's Ferry in 1859, and, in 1866, she won a lawsuit that effectively desegregated San Francisco streetcars. Pleasant's life has been recreated and mythologized in plays, novels, magazine articles, and a silent film, most of whose content relies on rumor and legend.

Pleasant's biographical details are a subject of open debate. Her abolitionist activities demanded secrecy, and she neither confirmed nor denied the speculations surrounding her business and personal activities. She claimed she was born free to a black mother and Hawaiian father in Philadelphia, Pennsylvania, on August 19, 1814. However, her African American contemporaries believed she was born a slave in Augusta, Georgia, before being sent to Philadelphia and then to Nantucket, Massachusetts, where a Quaker family named Hussey raised her. In the 1830s, Pleasant moved to Boston, where she married abolitionist James Smith and befriended notable figures such as Frederick Douglass and William Lloyd Garrison. Historians believe Pleasant inherited a large estate from Smith upon his death in the mid-1840s. Pleasant remarried in the late 1840s to John James Pleasants (the "s" was later dropped), another abolitionist. In 1852, they moved to San Francisco. A brilliant entrepreneur, Pleasant invested her wealth in banks, real estate, and mining, but she also worked as a cook for prominent wealthy families, owned a string of laundries, and ran several boardinghouses.

Pleasant offered refuge to fugitive slaves on the Underground Railroad and mobilized resources to aid in escaped slaves' court trials. She lived for a short time in Chatham, Ontario, a hotbed of abolitionist activity and the site of her meetings with John Brown, but she returned to San Francisco just before the Civil War. During the war years, Pleasant used litigation to fight for black voting rights and desegregation of schools and transportation.

In 1877, she built a thirty-room mansion on San Francisco's Octavia Street, which she cohabited with her business partner, Thomas Bell, the Scottish vice president of the Bank of California. Locals were scandalized and dubbed the mansion the House of Mystery. Bell later married, but his family remained in the house with Pleasant. Seven years after Bell's 1892 death, his son Fred unsuccessfully accused Pleasant of murdering Bell by pushing him down the stairs. Bell's heirs engaged in a protracted legal battle to divest Pleasant of her wealth, claiming rightful ownership. Pleasant was also involved in the sensationalized divorce trial of United States Senator William Sharon in the 1880s; Sharon claimed the plaintiff, his alleged wife Sarah Althea Hill, was really a prostitute and Pleasant, her madam.

Pleasant died January 11, 1904, and she is buried in the Sherwood family cemetery in Napa, California. In 1965, the San Francisco Negro Historical and Cultural Society fulfilled a request Pleasant had made during her lifetime by marking her grave with a plaque reading, "She was a friend of John Brown." In 2005, the city of San Francisco declared February 10 Mary Ellen Pleasant Day in honor of her civil rights work.

Jennifer Jane Nichols

See also Abolitionism and Northern Reformers; African American Women; Douglass, Frederick (ca. 1818–1895); Garrison, William Lloyd (1805–1879); Western Women.

References and Further Reading

Cliff, Michelle. 1993. *Free Enterprise: A Novel of Mary Ellen Pleasant.* New York: Dutton.

Holdredge, Helen. 1953. *Mammy Pleasant.* New York: G.P. Putnam's Sons.

Hudson, Lynn M. 2003. *The Making of "Mammy" Pleasant: A Black Entrepreneur in Nineteenth-Century San Francisco.* Urbana: University of Illinois Press.

Poets, Northern

Northern poets, like their Southern counterparts, played an active role in shaping public responses to the Civil War. Poetry was seen as a largely public and social discourse in the nineteenth century, and nineteenth-century poets often saw the personae of their poems as voices speaking for the nation, culture, or community in shared grief, glories, and values.

In recent years, scholarly attention has been given to women writers and popular literature, offering insight into social moods and discourses in time of war. Scholars have evaluated the place of public poetry in nineteenth-century America as valuable political and cultural discourse. Scholars have noted that the Civil War produced a social crisis for American women, who searched for a way to meaningfully contribute to the war effort. Some used poetry and songwriting as an outlet for ideas and commentary on events.

The more canonical Northern male poets of the Civil War era, including William Cullen Bryant, John Greenleaf Whittier, Oliver Wendell Holmes, James Russell Lowell, and Henry Wadsworth Longfellow, all wrote war pieces. In addition, Walt Whitman and Herman Melville each wrote an entire volume of poems on the topic. Whitman's *Drum-Taps* (1865) contains nearly all of his poems on the war. Whitman focused on the impact of individuals' heroism and the poignant horrors of the battlefield. Melville's *Battle Pieces* (1866), written during and after the war, explores the irony of war as an instrument of righteous justice. A variety of viewpoints present the more disturbing questions of the war: whether the massive destruction was necessary for victory, whether the Rebels should be punished, and whether reconciliation was possible.

Widely read were the works of popular male poets, including Francis Miles Finch ("The Blue and the Gray"), Bret Harte, Augustine J. H. Duganne, Henry Howard Brownell ("The Bay Fight"), and Thomas Buchanan Read ("Sheridan's Ride"). In addition, many of the song lyrics, written by George F. Root, Henry Clay Work, Charles Carroll Sawyer, and others, had great impact on the public perception of the war's meaning.

Writing in seclusion in Amherst, Massachusetts, in the mid-nineteenth century, poet Emily Dickinson (1830–1866) wrote more than half of her works during the Civil War (1830–1886). (Cirker, Hayward and Blanche Cirker, eds., *Dictionary of American Portraits*, 1967)

Women were also heavily involved in the nineteenth-century surge of publishing. Their works often dealt with hearth-and-home matters, but they made a strong impact on political and intellectual discourse. In addition to fiction and poetry, women wrote essays and editorial pieces, reflecting their high engagement in social issues.

Much of Northern women's wartime poetry followed a few basic themes: rallying support to the cause, calling for emancipation, and giving voice to the anguish of war's waste and the missing loved one. Women's poetry often had a sentimental and didactic style and tone. However, these pieces reached a large audience, and they had powerful political and social impact. Women's poems reinforced patriotic values, championed moral steadfastness, and condemned injustices.

The most influential and well-known work of Northern wartime verse was Julia Ward Howe's "The Battle Hymn of the Republic," which was published first as a poem in *The Atlantic Monthly* in February 1862 and later by Oliver Ditson as a song. The song became widely popular. Howe wrote other war poems, including one of forgiveness for the Confederates ("Pardon") and a tribute to Robert E. Lee. However, "Battle Hymn" is the best remembered.

Wartime poets did not always focus on the war in their work. Massachusetts poet Emily Dickinson remained oddly untouched by the war, despite her relatives' and friends' participation as soldiers. The early part of the 1860s was her most productive period, however, and she frequently focused on death. "Success Is Counted Sweetest" (67), may have been composed in 1859, yet alludes to one who dies in battle. "My Portion Is Defeat" (639), written perhaps in 1862, continues on that theme, referring to the dead on the field, the blank looks in their eyes, and how bitter the trumpets of victory are to the defeated. "It Feels a Shame to Be Alive" (444) and "They Dropped Like Flakes" (409) may also have been inspired by the war.

Others dealt directly with contemporary issues. Popular poet Lucy Larcom's "Call to Kansas" was a plea for resistance to proslavery depredations. In addition, she published other war-related poems, including "Re-enlisted," "Waiting for News," "The Sinking of the Merrimack," and "The Flag." In "The Nineteenth of April," she compared the Civil War to the American Revolution.

Wartime poetry also included a prolific subgenre on the missing picket: a soldier shot on picket duty who died alone. For example, Northerner Ethel Lynn Beers (Ethelinda Eliot) wrote "The Picket Guard," which ironically was set to music by Southern composer John Hill Hewitt. As the song "All Quiet along the Potomac Tonight," her poem became one of the most popular of the war. She also penned "Across the Lines," about a mother's search to find her slain son in enemy territory.

Publishing as Howard Glyndon, Laura Redden Searing of Missouri became an accomplished war correspondent, observer of Washington politics, and poet. Her widely published poems and essays covered a broad range of topics. Her volume of war poems, *Idyls of Battle and Poems of the Republic,*

included "Belle Missouri," a poem set to music as an anthem for Missouri Unionists. Her "After Vicksburg" mourned the sacrifice of war and questioned its efficacy.

Other women also contributed to the growing catalog of wartime poetry. Nantucket Quaker Phebe Ann Coffin Hanaford wrote poems and essays about the Union cause. She and Mary J. Webber published a collection of various poets' war-related works in *Chimes of Freedom and Union* (1861). Novelist Harriet Beecher Stowe's "Consolation: Written after the Second Battle of Bull Run" (1862), published in *The Liberator,* encouraged public morale. In addition, poet, satirist, journalist, and critic Gail Hamilton (Mary Abigail Dodge) wrote several war pieces, including "Battle Song for Freedom" (1865), urging Northern men on to victory. Popular poets Alice and Phoebe Cary of Ohio, later leaders of a New York literary salon, wrote a few wartime pieces in *Poems of Faith, Hope, and Love* (1868). Alice also published "Song for Our Soldiers" (1864). Many other female poets of the time, including Rose Terry Cooke, Caroline Atherton Mason, Martha Remick, Phila Henrietta Case, Ella Ellwood, Edith M. Clarke, Sylvia A. Speery, Lottie Linwood, Sarah Warner Brooks, Augusta Cooper Kimball, and Mary A. Lee, were published and widely read.

The majority of mid-nineteenth-century poets, most of them women, published in popular weeklies and monthlies and were neither credited nor paid. The poets' relative anonymity makes it difficult to measure fully the impact of Northern women's Civil War poetry.

Randal Allred

See also Abolitionism and Northern Reformers; Dickinson, Emily (1830–1886); Dodge, Mary Abigail [Gail Hamilton] (1833–1896); Domesticity; Howe, Julia Ward (1819–1910); Larcom, Lucy (1824–1893); Northern Women; Politics; Separate Spheres; Union Homefront; Wartime Literature.

References and Further Reading
Aaron, Daniel. 1987. *The Unwritten War: American Writers and the Civil War.* Madison: University of Wisconsin Press.
Bennett, Paula Bernat. 2003. *Poets in the Public Sphere: The Emancipatory Project of American*

Women's Poetry, 1800–1900. Princeton, NJ: Princeton University Press.

Coultrap-McQuin, Susan. 1990. Doing Literary Business: American Women Writers in the Nineteenth Century. Chapel Hill: University of North Carolina Press.

Fahs, Alice. 2001. The Imagined Civil War: Popular Literature of the North and South, 1861–1865. Chapel Hill: University of North Carolina Press.

Sizer, Lyde Cullen. 2000. Political Work of Northern Women Writers and the Civil War, 1850–1872. Chapel Hill: University of North Carolina Press.

Wilson, Edmund. 1962. Patriotic Gore: Studies in the Literature of the American Civil War. New York: Farrar, Straus and Giroux.

Poets, Southern

The role of wartime Southern poets, like that of Northern poets, was to help rally patriotic support and voice sectional solidarity. Overtly sensitive to their status as a new nation, Southern poets tended to be defensive of the new Confederate enterprise. There was a prolific response to the war from women poets in the South, who produced much of the popular poetry. Poetry had a highly civic and therefore political role in public discourse about the war.

When the Civil War began, the South did not have a highly developed publishing industry. Most Southern poetry was published in periodicals, and most newspapers and magazines in the South simply went out of business for lack of Northern markets, paying customers, advertising revenue, and materials. Despite the shortages, popular poems and songs were common, and an upsurge in women's writing activity resulted. Several Southern periodicals, including the Southern Literary Messenger, DeBow's Review, Southern Literary Companion, and Southern Illustrated News, managed to remain in business throughout most of the war.

Much wartime poetry, by men and women, called upon Southerners to fight. William Gilmore Simms, a strong champion of Southern culture and tradition and the most renowned literary figure in the antebellum South, produced little during the war years. However, one of his few war pieces, "Ode——Do Ye Quail?" called on Carolinians to resist the Northern "heathen." Similarly, poet and editor Paul Hamilton

Hayne's "Charleston—at the Close of 1863," promised that Carolinians would spurn the would-be invaders, and "Vicksburg—A Ballad" characterized the Mississippi fortress as a Christian citadel assailed by the fiends of hell. Georgian Sidney Lanier, who fought in the Seven Days' Battles, allowed little of the war in his poetry other than "The Dying Words of Stonewall Jackson."

Poetry also encouraged patriotism and dedication to the Confederacy. Baltimorean James Ryder Randall wrote the most famous of the call-to-arms poems, "Maryland, My Maryland." Henry Timrod supported neither secession nor slavery, but his "Carolina" echoes "Maryland, My Maryland," calling on Carolina's sons to spurn the invasion of the Northern barbarians. John R. Thompson, the influential editor of the Southern Literary Messenger and the Southern Illustrated News, contributed a number of patriotic poems, including "On to Richmond," "Lee to the Rear," "The Burial of Latane," and a lyrical elegy to Virginia cavalryman Turner Ashby. Physician Francis Orray Ticknor wrote the popular "Little Giffen" in tribute to the brave young soldier he had healed who was later killed in battle. Abram Joseph Ryan, a Catholic priest and chaplain in the army, wrote a number of poems; his popular "The Conquered Banner" lamented the bitterness of defeat.

Women's popular poetry flourished in the South, for many of the same reasons it did in the North. Primarily, writing allowed women an acceptable outlet for supporting their country. Women's need to participate in the war effort produced many pieces on homefront issues, such as bereavement, material sacrifice, patriotic duties, motherhood, and the support of the men on the battlefields. In addition, Southern women's wartime writing was often openly patriotic, martial, and defiant of Federal coercion.

Women wrote many of the popular lyrics in the South. Many of these verses lamented the tragedy of the dying soldier, including Mollie E. Moore's "Chickamauga," Fanny Falks's "The Little Drummer Boy," and Mary Ashley Townsend's "A Georgia Volunteer." In addition, Marie Ravenal de la Coste's "Somebody's Darling," another poem in the dying soldier genre, was set to music by John Hill Hewitt.

Elite women contributed to the wealth of female wartime poetry. Well-known wartime poet and sister-in-law of Stonewall Jackson, Margaret Junkin Preston, wrote about the soldier's life rather than of political matters. Her "The Bivouac in the Snow" honored the hardiness of the soldiers, and "The Shade of the Trees" paid homage to her famous brother-in-law. Preston's "A Grave in Hollywood Cemetery, Richmond," "Slain in Battle," and "Only a Private" all paid tribute to the dying soldier. Many of her short poems were excerpted from her book-length poetic work, *Beechenbrook: A Rhyme of the War* (1865). Other women also contributed to the wartime literary scene. Mary Bayard Clarke of North Carolina published a number of war poems, including "The Battle of Manassas," "The Battle of Hampton Roads," and "The Rebel Sock." The wife of a planter, her poems showed strong support for the Confederate cause, as in "The South Expects Every Woman to Do Her Duty."

Many women wrote poems of spirited support for the Confederacy and celebrated the sacrifice necessary to support it. For example, Carrie Belle Sinclair's "The Homespun Dress," boasted of Southern ladies' refusal to wear Yankee silk. Catherine M. Warfield's "Manassas" also glorified the Southern cause. Poems like "The Southern Mother's Charge" expressed political values; the narrator counseled her son to go and fight to the death.

Not all Southern poets celebrated the Confederacy. Frances Ellen Watkins Harper, born to free black parents in Baltimore, was one of the most popular poets of her time. Also a journalist, novelist, speaker, essayist, and activist, Harper published her first volume of poems in 1845 and another in 1854. Poems such as "The Slave Mother," "The Slave Auction," and "Bury Me in a Free Land" openly contested the slave system. In "Songs for the People," the narrator calls for poems that did not celebrate war but raised the hopes of the people. "An Appeal to My Countrywomen" warned Southern women to mourn not for atrocities and suffering, but for their own sons who soon would go off to war to pay for the sins of their slaveholding fathers.

As in the North, Southern women wrote a large percentage of the anonymously published wartime poems.

Randal Allred

See also Confederate Homefront; Domesticity; Harper, Frances Ellen Watkins (1825–1911); Homespun; Poets, Northern; Politics; Separate Spheres; Southern Women; Wartime Literature.

References and Further Reading

Aaron, Daniel. 1987. *The Unwritten War: American Writers and the Civil War.* Madison: University of Wisconsin Press.

Fahs, Alice. 2001. *The Imagined Civil War: Popular Literature of the North and South, 1861–1865.* Chapel Hill: University of North Carolina Press.

Perry, Carolyn, and Mary Louise Weeks, eds. 2002. *The History of Southern Women's Literature.* Baton Rouge: Louisiana State University Press.

Rubin, Louis D. Jr., ed. 1985. *The History of Southern Literature.* Baton Rouge: Louisiana State University Press.

Wilson, Edmund. 1962. *Patriotic Gore: Studies in the Literature of the American Civil War.* New York: Farrar, Straus and Giroux.

Pond, Cornelia "Nela" Jones (1834–1902)

A member of the Confederacy's social elite, Cornelia Jones Pond lived the life of a Southern belle until General William T. Sherman's March to the Sea destroyed her idyllic lifestyle.

Cornelia Jones was born into a prominent rice-planting family near the Georgia coast. Known as Nela, she grew up on Tekoah, a plantation located in Liberty County, Georgia. Her parents—William and Mary Jane Robarts Jones—owned nearly one hundred slaves and were among the wealthiest people in the county. Two of her relatives served in the United States Senate, and she was related by marriage to many of the region's social elite.

Born and socialized to embrace the life of the plantation, Nela grew up with the luxuries afforded to the South's social elite. Her family lived an opulent lifestyle, enjoying lush gardens, wearing expensive and stylish clothing, and throwing extravagant parties. They also enjoyed the conveniences provided by house slaves. As a privileged daughter,

Nela was well educated, receiving formal schooling at Montpelier Institute in Macon, Georgia, and at the Methodist Female College in Madison, Georgia. Both schools were Christian institutions, reflecting the religiosity of her parents.

In 1853, Nela married Thomas Goulding Pond, a close friend and groomsman of her brother. For the next few years, Thomas worked as a professor of mathematics at schools in Georgia. During these years, the couple had five children. In 1861, their infant daughter died of scarlet fever.

For most of the Civil War, Nela lived comfortably on her parents' plantation, where she had moved for safety. There she participated in many domestic activities that were common on the homefront. She spun cotton, knitted socks, and made palmetto hats, dyes, and candles. Although she dealt with some shortages and the effects of blockades, in 1863 the Jones family still had the resources to throw an elegant albeit somewhat subdued wartime wedding for Nela's sister.

General Sherman's arrival brought an immediate end to Pond's luxurious lifestyle. Union soldiers on the March to the Sea foraged their way through Pond's home in December 1864. She and her family tried to hide valuables from the soldiers, but their efforts were betrayed by one of their slaves. In addition to freeing slaves, many of whom remained in the region until the war's conclusion, Union troops took or destroyed most of Nela's personal possessions. Despite these losses, the war left Pond untouched in one significant way: all of her brothers and her father survived the war.

After the war, her family turned to freedpeople to perform the field labor and housework. Neither Nela's father nor her husband remained in cotton agriculture for long. In 1867, her father moved to Athens to teach at the University of Georgia and to publish the *Southern Cultivator.* Her husband turned to the ministry and took work as an Episcopalian minister. They lived in Alabama for four years and returned to Georgia in 1875.

Cornelia Jones Pond died on May 13, 1902.

Andrew K. Frank

See also Confederate Homefront; Destruction of Personal Property; Education, Southern; Homespun; Military Invasion and Occupation; Sherman's Campaign (1864–1865); Shortages; Slaveholding Women; Southern Women.

References and Further Reading

MacKethan, Lucinda H. 1998. *Recollections of a Southern Daughter: A Memoir by Cornelia Jones Pond of Liberty County.* Athens: University of Georgia Press.

Port Royal

Bordered by Hilton Head Island to the south across Port Royal Sound and by St. Helena Island to the North, Port Royal is part of the Sea Islands along the southeast coast of South Carolina. It was founded first by Spanish explorers during the sixteenth century; then English colonizers, who mostly came from the aristocracy of the British West Indies where large plantation systems built on slave gang labor defined economic and social life, permanently settled the area by the early eighteenth century. By the start of the Civil War, a small number of powerful landholding families controlled both the economy and slavery in this district, owning eleven thousand slaves, or 83 percent of the area's total population. Long staple cotton and rice production dominated the region's agriculture.

On November 7, 1861, the Union naval fleet captured two forts at the mouth of Port Royal Bay in a surprise battle that lasted only four hours. Confederate forces and most white civilians fled the area, leaving behind plantations, storehouses, and thousands of slaves. Capturing the Sea Islands, including Port Royal, Hilton Head, Ladies, and St. Helena's islands, Union forces claimed a vital position from which to launch offensive raids throughout the region. From here, Federal forces were able to control much of the coastline south to St. Augustine, Florida, a military zone called the Department of the South.

Many of the thousands of slaves left behind, as well as those who ran away when their owners abandoned their plantations in the Port Royal district, sought shelter behind Union lines. Early in the war, wherever Union troops were encamped, slaves from surrounding communities often attempted to flee to the protection of Federal forces. Although fleeing slaves were not officially considered contraband of war until March 1862, they were protected by the Union under war resolutions permitting the confiscation of rebel property. Major General David Hunter, a staunch abolitionist who had been assigned early command of the Department of the South in Port Royal, went one step further and in mid-April declared all slaves in his jurisdiction free. President Abraham Lincoln revoked Hunter's order, and, though Hunter effec-

tively ignored it, Lincoln's policy remained in effect until the Emancipation Proclamation freed all slaves in rebel states on January 1, 1863.

In Port Royal, the needs of the thousands of newly freed slaves overwhelmed government forces. Appeals from the military went out to Northern churches, as well as to antislavery and relief societies, for clothing, books, money, supplies, and volunteers. Boston, New York, and Philadelphia set up educational and relief associations within weeks of each other in the early months of 1862. Port Royal attracted the participation and support of some of the nation's most powerful abo-

African Americans prepare cotton for the gin on Port Royal Island, South Carolina, in 1862. (Library of Congress)

litionists, teachers, businesspeople, and missionaries from New England, New York, Pennsylvania, and beyond.

Much of the early military and private efforts in Port Royal targeted the dismantling of the plantation slave labor system by replacing it with a wage-based system, a difficult task given the hundreds of years of forced labor that had denied education and economic opportunity to thousands of Sea Island slaves. This early effort, called the Port Royal Experiment, hoped to help former slaves learn to function in a free, capitalist economy. This wartime environment also offered a new opportunity in expanded civil rights, rights that remained contested even in some Northern states. In Port Royal, newly freed people were experiencing legal, social, and civil rights, such as testifying against whites in court, attending integrated schools, entering into contracts, and buying land, rights not fully enjoyed by African Americans elsewhere. These expanded rights, along with programs to promote for-profit farming and free labor practices, became the model for later Freedmen's Bureau programs and Reconstruction efforts after the Civil War.

The Port Royal Experiment also provided opportunities for black and white women of the North who were eager to put their skills into service for the Union. They came as teachers, nurses, doctors, domestics, and relief organizers. The Boston Education Commission, one of the first relief organizations formed, sent its first group of civilian workers to Port Royal in March 1862. Twelve women were among the first group of fifty-three to embark for South Carolina. Some male organizers believed the women would not fare well and in fact be more trouble than help.

Charlotte Forten Grimké, Lydia Maria Child, Elizabeth Botume, Frances D. Gage, Susie King Taylor, Elizabeth Hunn, Lucy McKim, Laura Towne, and Harriet Ware were among the scores of women who devoted their time and energy to teaching, nursing, and organizing the distribution of thousands of dollars of food, clothing, books, and medicine. In addition, Harriet Tubman arrived in Port Royal to serve the Union as a scout, spy, nurse, cook, and teacher of domestic arts. These women

proved the doubters wrong, and their contributions to the Port Royal Experiment became a successful proving ground for postwar women's expanded participation in the public sphere.

During the spring of 1862, Hunter began building a regiment of black soldiers, the First South Carolina Volunteers, made up of newly liberated slaves in the Port Royal District. Lincoln, however, was not ready to outfit a regiment of black troops and ordered Hunter to dismantle his fledgling regiment. Hunter ignored the order. Later, General Rufus Saxton, military governor of the Department of the South, under the direction of Secretary of War Edwin Stanton, formally authorized the creation of five regiments of black troops in late August 1862. Hunter's First South Carolina Volunteers, officially organized under the command of Massachusetts abolitionist Thomas Wentworth Higginson, was ready to go in November of that year. Additional regiments filled quickly, marking the beginning of the participation of two hundred thousand African American soldiers in the Civil War.

Hospitals were also set up in the town of Beaufort, Port Royal, and on other islands to accommodate the mounting numbers of sick and dying civilians and soldiers, who were ill not only from battle wounds, but also from contaminated water and food, poor sanitation, and the particular natural environment found in the Port Royal area. Home to innumerable swamps, marshes, creeks, and irrigation and drainage ditches, Port Royal and the surrounding islands were an ideal breeding ground for disease. Many Northerners, whether soldiers or volunteers, fell victim to the outbreaks of smallpox, dysentery, measles, malaria, scarlet fever, typhoid, pneumonia, yellow fever, and other infections that eventually weakened and killed thousands.

Port Royal continued to play an important role in military efforts to capture Charleston, South Carolina, to the north, which would eventually fall in February 1865.

Kate Clifford Larson

See also African American Women; Aid Societies; Antislavery Societies; Camp Followers; Child, Lydia Maria Francis (1802–1880); Contrabands; Disease; Education, Southern; Forten (Grimké), Charlotte L.

(1837–1914); Freedmen's Bureau; Hospitals; Reconstruction (1865–1877); Taylor, Susie Baker King (1848–1912); Teachers, Northern; Towne, Laura Matilda (1825–1901); Tubman, Harriet [Araminta Ross] (1822–1913).

References and Further Reading

McPherson, James. 1988. *Battle Cry of Freedom: The Civil War Era.* New York: Oxford University Press.

Rose, Willie Lee. 199. *Rehearsal for Reconstruction. The Port Royal Experiment.* Athens: University of Georgia Press.

U.S. War Department. 1882. *The War of the Rebellion: A Compilation of the Official Records of the Union and Confederate Armies.* Records and Pension Office. Washington, DC: U.S. Government Printing Office.

Presbyterian Women

Like the Baptist and Methodist denominations, the slavery issue divided the Presbyterian Church in the antebellum years. These divisions became permanent with the start of the Civil War.

The first division came in 1837 between Old and New School Presbyterians. The division was not entirely a result of the slavery issue but is considered the first great ecclesiastical South–North separation. The Old School's most solid support lay in the Deep South, while the New School claimed most of the Presbyterians who were evangelicals. Initially the New School was only slightly less conservative on slavery than the Old School. Yet the New School's great numerical strength in areas where abolitionism was strongest, together with its very small Southern constitution, guaranteed that the group would take steps toward an antislavery position. In 1857, the New School General Assembly officially repudiated slavery, and the few remaining Southern New School members withdrew to form a separate church.

The most dramatic split, however, took place in 1861. As the nation separated into two nations, so did the Presbyterian Church. The Civil War produced the United Presbyterian Church in the United States of America (UPCUSA), popularly known as the Northern Presbyterian Church, and the Presbyterian Church in the Confederate States of America (PCCSA), commonly called the Southern Presbyterian Church and renamed the Presbyterian Church of the United States (PCUS) after the Civil War.

The Presbyterian Church in both the North and the South served as the focal point, catalyst, and meeting place for many wartime group activities of women: military aid societies, other benevolent activities, and prayer meetings. Records of wartime activity, however, are relatively scant. One of the few mentions of the war in the Southern Presbyterian synod records asked Alabama women to organize weekly prayer meetings for the church, soldiers, and country. Presbyterian women supplemented the rations of soldiers by sending food packages to camps and hospitals. Mary Russell McIlwain led the women of the Presbyterian Church in Valley Creek, Alabama, in feeding and clothing Alabama soldiers. The women who participated in the Ladies' Aid Society of Philadelphia were mostly members of Tenth Presbyterian Church. The group organized a system of relief that included eighty-six auxiliaries in Pennsylvania and supported E. H. Harris, the secretary of the aid society, who visited hospitals with donations from the society and then served as a nurse at various Potomac hospitals as well as in the western theater.

Often, the war intruded abruptly into church life. Ministers joined Union and Confederate armies as chaplains, leaving women to carry on the church activities. Church life was further disrupted as Presbyterian church buildings were damaged, destroyed, or put to use as hospitals. In the South, the unavailability of church buildings, the absence of ministers who were away at war or arrested by Union forces, and the difficulty of transportation resulted in a shift from church services led by ministers to home services conducted by women. Female-led prayer services in homes reflected a larger trend that encouraged Southern women to embrace leadership roles as a wartime measure.

A few Presbyterian women took volunteer action to remarkable levels. Some entered the traditionally male occupation of nursing. Compelled by missionary zeal, Louise Wotring Lyle went off with a clergyman brother-in-law to nurse soldiers, roll bandages, and make hospital supplies. After the war, Lyle became one of a handful of female physicians and later, with the help of Pittsburgh's most prominent Presbyterian women, founded The Presbyterian Hospital of Pittsburgh.

A few became important administrators. Eliza Barber, member of First Presbyterian Church in Akron, Ohio, was a director of the Middlebury Soldiers Aid Society. Jane Blaikie Hoge was a leader in the United States Sanitary Commission. In late 1861, Hoge was appointed an agent of Dorothea Dix, Superintendent of the United States Army Nurses, to recruit nurses for service in hospitals in the Western theater. In March 1862, she and her friend Mary A. Livermore made a tour of army hospitals in Cairo and Mound City, Illinois, in St. Louis, Missouri, in Paducah, Kentucky, and elsewhere. In December 1862, Hoge was appointed an associate director of the Chicago branch. In this position she oversaw the work of upward of a thousand local aid societies throughout the Northwest in collecting and forwarding clothing, medical and hospital supplies, food, and other materials. During 1863, Hoge made three trips to the front in the Vicksburg, Mississippi campaign, combining her inspection of the logistics system with the nursing of soldiers. Hoge's account of her wartime experiences was published as *The Boys in Blue* (1867). After the war, Hoge headed the Woman's Presbyterian Board of Foreign Missions in the Northwest.

The Civil War propelled Presbyterian women toward a new independence and into an enlarged participation in religious affairs, and it opened up new opportunities for women in the secular world regardless of religious denomination.

Karen Fisher Younger

See also Aid Societies; Baptist Women; Confederate Homefront; Dix, Dorothea Lynde (1802–1887); Hoge, Jane Currie Blaikie (1811–1890); Hospitals; Livermore, Mary Ashton Rice (1820–1905); Methodist Women; Northern Women; Nurses; Religion; Southern Women; Union Homefront; United States Sanitary Commission.

References and Further Reading

Ahlstrom, Sydney. 1972. *A Religious History of the American People.* New Haven, CT: Yale University Press.

Massey, Mary Elizabeth. 1994. *Women in the Civil War.* Lincoln: University of Nebraska Press. (Orig pub. 1966 as *Bonnet Brigades.*)

Miller, Randall M., Harry S. Stout, and Charles Reagan Wilson, eds. 1998. *Religion and the American Civil War.* New York: Oxford University Press.

Rikard, Marlene Hunt, and Elizabeth Wells. 1997. "'From It Begins a New Era': Women and the Civil War." *Baptist History and Heritage* 32 (3): 59–73.

Young, Agatha. 1959. *The Women and the Crisis: Women of the North in the Civil War.* New York: McDowell, Obolensky.

Prescott (Spofford), Harriet E. (1835–1921)

With a literary career spanning over sixty years, Harriet Prescott Spofford is best known for her short stories published in popular monthlies and weeklies of the time, such as *The Atlantic Monthly* and *Harper's Weekly.* In addition to short stories, she wrote novels, poetry, and domestic fiction.

Born April 3, 1835, in Calais, Maine, Harriet Prescott was the daughter of Sarah Jane Bridges and Joseph Newmarch Prescott. Shortly after Harriet's father moved to Oregon to seek his fortune when she was fourteen, she and her mother moved to Newburyport, Massachusetts, where she attended school, first at Putnam Free School for three years and later completing her formal education at Pinkerton Academy. Thomas Wentworth Higginson noted Prescott's abilities while she studied at Putnam, and he encouraged her to pursue a writing career. When her father returned from the West ill and penniless, Harriet began writing for newspapers and periodicals to help with household expenses. She remained largely unnoticed until the February 1859 *Atlantic Monthly* publication of "The Cellar" launched her literary career. The following year, she published her first novel, *Sir Rohan's Ghost.*

On December 19, 1865, she married Richard Smith Spofford Jr., a lawyer from Newburyport. Together they had one son, who died in infancy. In 1874, they moved to Deer Island in the Merriman River, where she continued to enjoy a long writing career made easier financially by her husband's success.

Harriet E. Prescott Spofford, prolific writer (1835–1921). (Library of Congress)

Spofford grew into a prolific writer, publishing numerous short stories and novels. Her writing, characterized by romantic details before the war, took a turn to simpler prose and realism after the war. Sympathetic to but not active in reformist movements, Spofford published many works in *The Atlantic Monthly,* considered at the time to be a liberal reformist publication.

A number of her postwar stories center on racial issues, especially in connection with the North and the Civil War. For example, her October 1865 *Atlantic Monthly* story, "Down the River" is the story of a foolish slave girl, devoted to her owner and not wishing for freedom, who is by the end of the story convinced to gain her freedom. The conclusion of the story could imply that the Northerners rescued the slaves from slavery and in fact from a nature that prevented them from rescuing themselves.

After her husband died in 1888, Spofford associated with a circle of women writers, including Sarah Orne Jewett and Louise Chandler Moulton, living in Boston at the time. Much of the associated liter-

ature of the time centers on Civil War themes. Postwar Washington, D.C., is a setting for Spofford's 1906 collection of stories, *Old Washington,* where many of the characters made their homes after being displaced by the Civil War.

In her later life, she spent some winters in Boston, mostly remaining in New England but venturing to Europe twice. Harriet Prescott Spofford died at Deer Island on August 14, 1921.

Sigrid Kelsey

See also Fiction Writers, Northern; Moulton, Louise Chandler (1835–1908); Northern Women.
References and Further Reading
Sizer, Lyde Cullen. 2000. *The Political Work of Northern Writers and the Civil War, 1850–1972.* Chapel Hill: University of North Carolina Press.

Primus, Rebecca (1836–1929)

The daughter of a prominent African American family in Hartford, Connecticut, Rebecca Primus served as a teacher to free Southern blacks during Reconstruction. Letters between her and domestic servant Addie Brown provide a wealth of insight into black female relationships during the Civil War.

Primus was born in 1836 as the eldest of four children to Holdridge Primus, a clerk in a well-known Hartford grocery company, and Mehitable Jacobs Primus, who worked occasionally as a seamstress. The family owned their own home on Wadsworth Street, where Rebecca eventually became a teacher. In 1866, after the Civil War, Rebecca traveled to Royal Oak, Maryland, where, with the help of the Hartford Freedmen's Aid Society, she helped found a school to teach newly freed slaves. The school was later named the Primus Institute in her honor. Primus returned to Hartford in 1869.

Letters between Primus in Maryland and her close friend and domestic servant in Hartford, Addie Brown, reveal an intimate female friendship during the Civil War era. Exactly how and when the two met is unknown, but in 1859, when Brown's letters to Primus begin, Brown was eighteen and Primus was twenty-three. Brown wrote one hundred and fifty letters from Hartford, Farmington, and Waterbury, Connecticut, and from New York

City between 1859 and 1868. The letters paint a vivid portrait of a flirtatious and sexual friendship. Several letters from Brown to Primus indicate that, when together, they shared a bed along with hugs, embraces, and kisses. In April 1868, while in her late twenties, Addie Brown married. She died on January 11, 1870.

Primus also sent accounts of her time in Maryland to her family in Hartford. She discussed her confrontations with Southern prejudice, her struggle to educate the freedmen, the practical effects of the politics of Reconstruction, and the everyday events of life in Royal Oak.

Sometime between 1872 and 1874, while in her middle to late thirties, Primus married a man she met in Maryland, Charles Thomas. Throughout her life, she was a member of the Talcott Street Congregational Church and was much beloved in the small black community in Hartford. She died in 1932 after an extended illness.

Eloise E. Scroggins

See also Aid Societies; Brown, Addie (1841–1870); Letter Writing; Teachers, Northern.

References and Further Reading

Griffin, Farah Jasmine, ed. 1999. *Beloved Sisters and Loving Friends: Letters from Rebecca Primus of Royal Oak, Maryland, and Addie Brown of Hartford, Connecticut, 1854–1868.* New York: Alfred A. Knopf.

Hansen, Karen. 1995. "'No Kisses Is Like Youres': An Erotic Friendship between Two African American Women during the Mid-Nineteenth Century." *Gender and History* 7 (2): 151–182.

Prostitution

Prostitution, or the sale of sexual services for money or goods, has a history dating long before the American Civil War began. During the war, however, this occupation—previously a clandestine one practiced behind closed doors and in dark alleys—took on a public presence in many Northern and Southern communities.

In the North, the deployment of thousands of American men into Southern territory meant the depletion of an available client base for many Northern prostitutes, necessitating their migration southward. Southern officials often greeted this influx of unwelcome sex workers into their communities with contempt.

However, not all prostitutes were from Northern communities. Although little has been written about Southern women and prostitution, the occupation flourished there long before the Civil War began. In many antebellum Southern cities, including Richmond, Virginia, Charleston, South Carolina, and Nashville and Memphis, Tennessee, many types of prostitutes, including brothel workers, mistresses, and streetwalkers—or "strolling strumpets"—practiced their profession. In New Orleans, Louisiana, brothel owners developed a "fancy girl" business that provided light-skinned African American prostitutes for elite white men.

During the Civil War, Northern and Southern prostitutes experienced not only an unprecedented regional shift in their client base, but also an increased demand for their services. In seeking to satisfy these increased demands, Southern sex workers, in particular, frequently invaded the public spaces, including theaters, hotels, municipal parks, and public conveyances such as carriages and hacks, thus making these public locations less acceptable for respectable Southern women. Union General Benjamin Butler's infamous General Order 28, issued May 13, 1862, exacerbated these concerns about well-bred Southern women being mistaken for prostitutes. It stated that any Southern woman seen disrespecting a Union soldier on the streets of occupied New Orleans, Louisiana would be treated like a prostitute practicing her trade.

As prostitutes' numbers and visibility increased, theater owners and municipal leaders attempted to contain their spread by relegating prostitutes and their clients to theater balconies, by enforcing vagrancy laws, and by enacting increasingly stringent regulations against tippling houses where sex workers often plied their trade in a private room set aside for sexual liaisons.

As a result of these efforts, local courts were sometimes clogged with cases involving women and men engaged in sexual commerce, but there was a class element to the sex trade. White prostitutes and brothel owners who catered to an elite white clientele often fared better before the bar of justice than their dark-skinned counterparts. Their cases were often not prosecuted, or they resulted simply in the payment of a fine, whereas black prostitutes and madams faced the possibility of a prison sentence or a public whipping.

Women who engaged in prostitution often did so because the income they were able to generate was much higher than what they could earn for any other traditional form of women's work. In the South, some women who fled their homes in advance of an invading enemy force found themselves working in refugee brothels in their new communities. Evidence on the exact numbers of women engaged in prostitution during the American Civil War is difficult, if not impossible, to obtain. Prostitutes become visible only when they have violated public space and have come to the attention of civil authorities. Thus the numbers often indicate only those who ran afoul of the law. A study of several hundred antebellum and Civil War prostitutes in Richmond, Virginia, indicates that their ages ranged between thirteen and fifty-five, although most women were in their late teens or their twenties. Evidence also suggests that there was occasionally a generational pattern to prostitution, with mothers socializing their daughters into the profession. Sometimes whole families of women were involved, and married women occasionally operated brothels with their husbands. Although many Richmond brothels were segregated by race, at least a few contained both white and black sex workers and clients, suggesting that Southern brothels might have been places where sexual activity between white women and black men could occur without public recrimination or overt violence.

Civil War brothels were very dangerous places for prostitutes and their clients. Soldiers who were denied admittance after the brothels had closed sometimes broke down doors, destroyed furnishings, and assaulted the residents. Brawls occasionally broke out between soldiers who were competing for the services of a particular prostitute. These outbursts usually ended in injury and occasionally in the death of one or more of the participants. In a few cases, drunken men attempted to force their way into houses of prostitution on horseback.

As Union armies made their way throughout the South, prostitutes also traveled with the military, sometimes posing as wives of the men who were their clients. When the armies were encamped, cross-dressing prostitutes donned male garb in an attempt to slip into the camps undetected by the military guard. The records of the Judge Advocate General's Office for the U.S. Army contain information about soldiers and officers, for example, who were court-martialed for keeping prostitutes in their quarters. Some scattered evidence suggests that a few commanders, however, may have viewed prostitution as a necessary evil that protected respectable women from predations by an occupying military force. In Alexandria, Virginia, for example, military commanders routinely sent a team of soldiers to inspect the city's seventy-five brothels.

The majority of military officials, however, were concerned about the effects of prostitution on their fighting forces. Southern military leaders dispatched hundreds of Confederate chaplains to visit the camps, preaching about the evils of unregulated sex. These concerns were not unfounded since, during the Civil War, at least 11 percent of the Confederate soldiers confined to hospitals as unfit for duty were suffering from venereal disease. In Memphis and Nashville, Tennessee, Union military officials imposed a licensing system for prostitutes similar to the system for identifying and licensing British prostitutes who provided sexual services—and many believed, gonorrhea—to British sailors. This plan appears not to have spread to other Southern regions. Despite the danger they posed, prostitutes at times provided invaluable information about enemy troop movements or various forms of criminal activity. In Richmond, Virginia, for example, testimony from prostitutes helped uncover a counterfeiting ring at work in the Confederate capital.

Civil War prostitutes often were economic opportunists who submerged their political beliefs in favor of earning an income. At the war's end, many Northern prostitutes who had migrated southward in search of work returned to their original communities. Other Northern and Southern prostitutes followed the U.S. Army westward, providing services to military units engaged in Indian wars on the western frontier. As they did, the demographics of prostitution became more complex because white and black prostitutes competed with Mexican and Chinese sex workers for the trade. Other Southern prostitutes simply awaited the arrival of Union occupation forces, whose presence shifted their client base from loyal Southern soldiers clad in butternut gray to Northern invaders wearing Union blue.

E. Susan Barber

See also Abolitionism and Northern Reformers; Butler, Benjamin F. (1818–1893); Camp Followers; Civilian Life; Confederate Homefront; Disease; Morale; Northern Women; Refugees; Southern Women; Union Homefront; Urban Women, Northern; Urban Women, Southern; Wartime Employment; Woman Order (General Order Number 28).

References and Further Reading

Barber, E. Susan. 2002. "'Depraved and Abandoned Women': Prostitution in Richmond, Virginia, across the Civil War." In *Neither Lady Nor Slave: Working Women of the Old South*, edited by Susanna Delfino and Michele Gillespie, 155–173. Chapel Hill: University of North Carolina Press.

Burnham, John C. 1971. "Medical Inspection of Prostitutes in American in the Nineteenth Century: The St. Louis Experiment and Its Sequel." *Bulletin of the History of Medicine* 45: 203–218.

Butler, Anne M. 1985. *Daughters of Joy, Sisters of Misery: Prostitutes in the American West, 1865–90*. Chicago: University of Chicago Press.

Guilfoyle, Timothy. 1992. *City of Eros: New York City Prostitution and the Commercialization of Sex, 1790–1920*. New York: W. W. Norton & Company.

Hill, Marilyn Wood. 1993. *Their Sisters' Keepers: Prostitution in New York City, 1830–1870*. Berkeley: University of California Press.

Jones, James Boyd. 1985. "A Tale of Two Cities: The Hidden Battle against Venereal Disease in Civil War Nashville and Memphis." *Civil War History* 31 (3): 270–276.

Kampmeier, Rudolph H. 1982. "Venereal Disease in the United States Army, 1775–1900." *Sexually Transmitted Diseases* 9 (2): 100–108.

Stansell, Christine. 1986. *City of Women: Sex and Class in New York, 1789–1860*. New York: Alfred A. Knopf.

Walkowitz, Judith R. 1980. *Prostitution in Victorian Society: Women, Class, and the State*. Cambridge: Cambridge University Press.

Pryor, Sara Agnes Rice (1830–1912)

A prominent Southern woman and the wife of a Virginia congressman, Sara Rice Pryor published a memoir of her experiences during the Civil War.

In the 1850s, the Pryors lived in Washington, D.C., where Roger Pryor was the editor of a newspaper. In 1859, he was elected a congressman from Virginia. Sara Pryor fit well into the Washington social scene. Although she loved the United States and considered herself a patriot, Pryor staunchly supported the South's premises for war, and the family headed South when the Civil War began. Roger Pryor became an officer in the Confederate army. During his wartime absence, Sara lived in various places in Virginia.

In 1904, Sara published a memoir of her wartime experiences, *Reminiscences of Peace and War*. This book, although somewhat sentimentalized, provides insight into the experiences of a Southern woman at this cataclysmic time. In her book, Pryor described how Southern women responded to the war. Although the South's relief effort was less centralized than the North's, women participated enthusiastically in aid efforts for the soldiers. Women gathered locally to make or embroider sewing kits, razor cases, and other items for the soldiers. Like many Southern women, Pryor tried to settle wherever her husband was stationed. At times, her desire to be near her husband placed her very near the battlefield.

During the Seven Days' Battle in 1862, Sara volunteered as a nurse at a field hospital. She fainted upon seeing a soldier with an amputated arm but returned the next day, ultimately acclimating herself to the horrors of hospital life. She felt she truly redeemed herself when she brought a basket of bandages made from her family's linens to the hospital.

As the war progressed, conditions in the South deteriorated. Pryor described the starvation and emotional depression in the South. In her memoir, Pryor included a letter from a friend in Richmond that described the bread riot of 1863. Pryor also described her return to the destroyed family home. Her husband became a prisoner of war in the last year of the war, and, when he finally returned home, they were immobilized for months, having no idea what to do.

The Pryors moved to New York City after the war to re-establish themselves, Sara selling her remaining jewels to finance the trip. Roger became a successful lawyer and judge, and Sara supported various charitable causes. She also founded the National Society of the Daughters of the American Revolution.

Ellen H. Todras

See also Bread Riots; Confederate Homefront; Nurses; Southern Women.
References and Further Reading
Campbell, Edward Jr., and Kym S. Rice. 1996. *A Woman's War: Southern Women, Civil War, and the Confederate Legacy.* Richmond, VA: The Museum of the Confederacy.
Faust, Drew Gilpin. 1996. *Mothers of Invention: Women of the Slaveholding South in the American Civil War.* Chapel Hill: University of North Carolina Press.
Pryor, Sara Rice (Mrs. Roger A.). 1905. *Reminiscences of Peace and War.* New York: Grosset & Dunlap.

Putnam, Sarah "Sallie" Ann Brock (1831–1911)
Born in Madison County, Virginia, on March 18, 1831, Sallie Brock Putnam became an author and a resident of Richmond, Virginia, during the Civil War.

Putnam was the daughter of Ansalem Brock and Elizabeth Beverley Buckner. Her father was a tutor and later a hotel owner, moving the family to Charlottesville around 1850 and then to Richmond in 1858. Putnam was raised in a genteel manner and gained an education that allowed her to become a tutor herself, an occupation she was pursuing in King

In 1904 Sara Pryor published a memoir of her experience as a Southern woman during the Civil War. (Library of Congress)

and Queen County in 1860. When the Civil War broke out in 1861, Sallie returned to her family in Richmond and helped run the household. A Southern partisan, she remained in Richmond throughout the war.

In 1865, Putnam moved to New York, where she began to write a memoir of her wartime experiences in the Confederate capital, which she published in 1867 as *Richmond during the War: Four Years of Personal Observation.* Putnam's narrative revealed the social and economic upheavals that the residents of the Confederate capital experienced. She described changed social roles and attitudes as poverty, food shortages, overcrowding, and escalating inflation gripped the city, forcing formerly genteel women into paying jobs simply to make ends meet and leaving people scrambling for whatever food and housing they could get. Putnam and the city residents she described remained fiercely loyal to the Confederacy throughout the war, and she detailed the sacrifices of men, comforts, luxuries, and even basic necessities that women made in the name of patriotism and the war effort. Against the narrative of social turmoil, Putnam included accounts of battles and military operations, illustrating how closely connected Southern civilians were to the ebb and flow of events on the battlefields.

After the publication of *Richmond during the War,* Putnam continued to pursue her writing career. In 1869, she collected poems written about the Confederacy and the Civil War into a volume entitled *The Southern Amaranth: A Carefully Selected Collection of Poems Growing Out of and in Reference to the Late War,* including among the poems several of her own. In the following years, Putnam wrote a number of pieces for literary magazines and drafted several novels. She wrote under pseudonyms, including one, Virginia Madison, that referred to her birthplace. In 1882, while in her fifties, she married Richard Fletcher Putnam, an Episcopal minister, in Richmond and went to live with him in Brooklyn, New York. She died March 22, 1911, and was buried beside her husband in Richmond's Hollywood Cemetery.

Amy Minton

See also Confederate Homefront; Southern Women.

References and Further Reading

Putnam, Sallie Brock. 1996. *Richmond during the War: Four Years of Personal Observation.* Lincoln: University of Nebraska Press.

Q

Quaker Women

Quaker women, the most activist group of nineteenth-century American women, did much to propel the antislavery and women's movements forward.

In the seventeenth and eighteenth centuries, the Quakers, or Society of Friends, constituted a highly controversial sect of the Protestant Reformation. The group's marginal position resulted from many of its positions, not the least of which was its view of women. The Society of Friends allowed women, as well as men, to be ministers. The Quaker belief system liberated women in other ways, too: women conducted affairs at their own meetings, took part in economic activity, gained education, and became politically active.

As Separatists, the Quakers kept themselves apart from other colonists in the nation's early years. Although few Quakers fought in the Revolutionary War—they believed in nonviolence—the war brought many of them into American everyday life. After witnessing the devastation of war on individuals, Quakers began to provide relief to needy civilians and soldiers. Historians see this activity as the beginning of the Quaker tradition of relief work, which often was women's work. The Revolutionary War also marked the beginning of Quakers' public opposition to slavery. As early as 1688, Friends in Germantown, Pennsylvania, urged other Quakers to free their slaves. By the 1770s and 1780s, various Meetings began to disown Quakers who owned slaves.

As the Quaker faith grew in the early 1800s, a schism divided the Society. The split centered on Elias Hicks, a minister who opposed slavery and downplayed literal interpretations of the Bible in favor of the inner light, or the primacy of Christ inside the believer. Determined that theirs was the correct way, the Hicksites broke off from the Orthodox Quakers, who saw Hicks's preachings as heresy. The Hicksites' views on women differed from those of other Quakers as well. Hicksite women were more assertive than other women and did not ask the brethren for approval once they had decided on a course of action.

Quaker women's assertiveness allowed them to pursue reform, some focusing on the cause of antislavery and pursuing it diligently. In 1806, Alice Lewis, of the Philadelphia Women's Yearly Meeting, was the first to urge her Quaker sisters to boycott slave-produced goods such as sugar and cotton.

Other Quaker women focused on education. In 1833, Connecticut Quaker Prudence Crandall allowed a black girl to attend her Canterbury Female Boarding School. When the parents of other girls threatened to withdraw their daughters, Crandall closed the school but reopened it two months later with twenty black girls in attendance. Crandall was arrested and convicted but later freed. She closed the school after a mob attacked it.

In 1833, Philadelphia men formed the American Anti-Slavery Society. Four days later, Quaker Lucretia Mott and other women founded the Female American Anti-Slavery Society. They opened their society to Quakers and non-Quakers, as well as to blacks and whites. Female antislavery societies sprung up throughout the North, and women honed their organizational skills as they opposed the South's peculiar institution.

Two years later, South Carolina sisters Sarah and Angelina Grimké joined the Philadelphia Female Anti-Slavery Society and helped promote its goals. Despite their membership in the Orthodox Quaker sect, whose elders roundly criticized them for their public activities, the Grimké sisters took on prominent roles in the abolition movement. The American Anti-Slavery Society published a pamphlet by Angelina, in which she appealed to her Southern sisters to end slavery. The Grimké sisters' firsthand experiences with slavery gave them credence and made them authorities in the eyes of Northern antislavery activists. They began giving lectures to other women and then, as their fame spread, to men as well. Their public speaking engagements ended in 1838, but by then they had inspired another young Quaker woman, Abby Kelley, to continue their work.

Women's antislavery activities provoked controversy about women's roles. The debate over the realm of women in turn led to the formation of a women's rights movement. Quaker Lucretia Mott, along with Elizabeth Cady Stanton, organized the first women's rights convention in Seneca Falls, New York, in 1848. In addition to Mott, many other Quaker women—Susan B. Anthony among them—carried forward the battle for women's suffrage throughout the nineteenth century.

During the Civil War, many Quaker women held to their nonviolent principles. For example, Mott supported young Quaker men who, as conscientious objectors, refused to enlist or fight when drafted. Other Quaker women, such as Cornelia Hancock and Amanda Way, nursed soldiers in the field and in city hospitals throughout the war. In addition, female Friends continued in their antislavery efforts, aiding the freedmen. As the war progressed, Laura Haviland, founder of the first antislavery society in Michigan and an effective conductor on the Underground Railroad, refocused her efforts. Haviland traveled in Mississippi and Louisiana, working for the Freedman's Aid Commission distributing relief supplies to former slaves. Abby Hopper Gibbons served as a nurse and aide to freed slaves in Washington, D.C., for more than three years.

Some Quaker women took their activism into the political spheres. Anna Dickinson began speaking on the cause of women's rights and abolitionism in 1860, at the age of eighteen. Her charisma and popularity as a speaker led the Republican Party to seek out Dickinson's services in 1863. Dickinson began stumping for Republican candidates across the North. She praised the Emancipation Proclamation and the use of African American soldiers in the fight against the Confederacy. Although Dickinson saw President Abraham Lincoln's antislavery stance as weak, she supported him in the 1864 presidential election.

Quaker women joined the Freedmen's Bureau's efforts to educate and aid the former slaves. Quaker Lucy McKim accompanied her father to the South Carolina Sea Islands during the war to prepare former slaves for freedom. McKim recorded the slave songs that she heard there and eventually published them in 1867 as *Slave Songs of the United States*.

Countless Quaker women worked for the passage of the Thirteenth, Fourteenth, and Fifteenth Amendments during the war and immediately afterward. Many continued this work even when it became clear that women would not get suffrage along with black men. They continued to come to the South to educate freed slaves too, many staying long after the war ended.

Ellen H. Todras

See also Abolitionism and Northern Reformers; Anthony, Susan B. (1820–1906); Antislavery Societies; Dickinson, Anna Elizabeth (1842–1932); Education, Northern; Education, Southern; Election of 1864; Emancipation Proclamation (January 1, 1863); Fifteenth Amendment; Fourteenth Amendment; Freedmen's Bureau; Gibbons, Abigail (Abby) Hopper (1801–1893); Grimké (Weld), Angelina (1805–1879); Grimké, Sarah Moore (1792–1873); Hancock, Cornelia (1839–1926); Haviland, Laura Smith (1808–1898); Kelley, Abby (1811–1887); Mott, Lucretia Coffin (1793–1880); Northern Women; Nurses; Port Royal; Stanton, Elizabeth Cady (1815–1902); Teachers, Northern; Thirteenth Amendment; Union Homefront.

References and Further Reading

Bacon, Margaret Hope. 1896. *Mothers of Feminism: The Story of Quaker Women in America.* New York: Harper & Row.

Brown, Elizabeth Potts, and Susan Mosher Stuard, eds. 1989. *Witnesses for Change: Quaker Women over Three Centuries.* Piscataway, NJ: Rutgers University Press.

Silber, Nina. 2005. *Daughters of the Union: Northern Women Fight the Civil War.* Cambridge, MA: Harvard University Press.

Todras, Ellen. 1999. *Angelina Grimké: Voice of Abolition.* North Haven, CT: Linnet Books.

Quantrill, William Clarke (1837–1865)

William Clarke Quantrill was one of the most notorious Southern guerrillas of the Civil War.

Born in Canal Dover, Ohio, on July 31, 1837, Quantrill headed west in 1857 to the Kansas Territory, where he began a life of crime, including kidnapping freed African Americans and cattle thieving. At the opening of the Civil War, Quantrill joined the Confederate cavalry in Texas where he served with distinction in battle. Soon after leaving the army and returning to Missouri, he became entangled in the border wars. By January 1862, Quantrill had a well-established band of guerrilla raiders that actively terrorized pro-unionist citizens, jayhawkers (antislavery guerrillas), and the regular Union army.

Union General Thomas Ewing responded to the guerrilla attacks by deciding to arrest the wives and sisters of the bushwhackers and place them under guard in Kansas City. In August 1863, a building where some of the women were being held collapsed and killed five of them, including Bloody Bill Anderson's sister, Josephine Anderson. Another one of his sisters, sixteen-year-old Mary, was severely wounded. Jesse and Frank James's two cousins, Sue Vandiver and Armenia Gilvey, were also in the building. In retaliation, Quantrill rallied these Southern bushwhackers and others to join him in destroying the abolitionist town of Lawrence, Kansas. Riding into town, the guerrillas slaughtered 182 unarmed men and boys and burned 185 buildings.

Taking advantage of Unionist outrage at Quantrill's actions, Ewing made a sweeping move to destroy the guerrilla home base. Four days after the events at Lawrence, Kansas, General Ewing issued General Order Number 11, which forcibly removed approximately twenty thousand citizens from four counties along the Kansas–Missouri border. Citizens had fifteen days to evacuate the area and the edict was ruthlessly enforced.

After the raid on Lawrence and the subsequent disavowal of the action by the Confederate government, many of the guerrillas realized that Quantrill lacked the support of the official Confederate military. Feeling disillusioned with events in Missouri and desiring to rediscover their former glory, Quantrill and a handful of followers left for Kentucky. Disguised in Federal uniforms, Quantrill and his men crossed the Kentucky border during January 1865. Almost immediately, events went sour for the guerrilla leader. In early skirmishing, Quantrill lost several friends and his trusty warhorse, Old Charley. Quantrill established his base at the Wakefield farm in Spencer County. Although local Southern sympathizers joined his ranks, Quantrill never regained his cohesive fighting force.

On May 10, the Union army finally caught Quantrill and shot him in the back while he was trying to escape. The bullet lodged in his spine, paralyzing him from the waist down. He remained conscious and was transported to Louisville, where he received well-wishers until his death on June 4, 1865.

Kristina K. Dunn

See also Guerrilla Warfare.

References and Further Reading

Castel, Albert. 1999. *William Clarke Quantrill: His Life and Times.* Norman: University of Oklahoma Press.

Goodrich, Thomas. 1995. *Black Flag: Guerilla Warfare on the Western Border, 1861–1865.* Bloomington: Indiana University Press.

R

Rape

Rape was an ever present possibility during the American Civil War, especially in areas with high concentrations of soldiers. Occasional references to sexual assaults can be found in women's diaries, but more prevalent in their writings were concerns about the possibility of rape. In areas where an invasion was imminent, some women banded together for protection, arming themselves and putting on multiple layers of clothing. Despite these precautions, rape occurred, although the number of actual rapes is extremely difficult—if not impossible—to ascertain. Although occasional cases of rape and attempted rape were tried in civilian courts, there is no discrete body of evidence in civilian records documenting the crime during the Civil War period. Some historians therefore have concluded that the Civil War was a low-rape war.

There are records of rapes and attempted rapes, however, in the Union courts-martial. Civilian crimes such as rape were not part of either the Union or Confederate Articles of War at the start of the conflict. In March 1863, the United States Congress militarized, or brought into the army's legal jurisdiction, rape and attempted rape, along with other civilian crimes such as murder, arson, theft, and assault and battery, and the Union army appears to have taken these accusations seriously. As a result, the United States Army prosecuted more than two hundred Union soldiers and civilians in courts-martial or military commissions for the crime of rape or attempted rape during the course of the war. By doing so, the Union military courts effectively provided a venue for white and black women to bring accusations of sex crimes before the bar and to achieve a measure of justice for them, something that was often impossible to achieve in civilian courts during this period.

The Confederate Congress did not militarize civilian crimes in the Confederate Articles of War. It did, however, extend jurisdiction over civilian crimes to permanent military courts that it established in 1862 and that were attached to the various Confederate armies. The jurisdiction over civilian crimes was obtained only when the armies were outside the Confederacy. There is no evidence, however, that these permanent military courts ever invoked jurisdiction over civilian crimes, and there is little evidence that Confederate courts-martial prosecuted sexual crimes.

During much of the nineteenth century, rape was a civilian crime that was defined by the laws of the states as unwelcome heterosexual genital contact. There was no Federal definition of the crime. Women who brought accusations of rape or attempted rape, in either civilian or military courts, had to demonstrate that they had not consented to the act, that they had physically resisted with all their might, and that they were of virtuous character. Typically, Union courts-martial brought accusations of sexual crimes quickly to trial, often in a matter of days. Woman reported these offenses either to the local provost marshal or to the commanding officer of the military unit stationed in the region.

In some instances, a physician was summoned to examine the victim. Occasionally, women were asked to identify soldiers from a lineup. Trials usually lasted one or two days with testimony presented before a panel of five to thirteen officers in courts-martial; in the case of military commissions that were empanelled to try civilians, the panel consisted of three officers. Of the more than two hundred cases tried by the Union army, 179 of the defendants were soldiers and forty-three were civilians attached to the military. Of those executed, nine were white and fifteen were black. Once a sentence was rendered, a defendant had no opportunity of a direct appeal, but all cases were reviewed by superior officers. Sentences mandating execution or lengthy prison terms were reviewed by Judge Advocate General Joseph Holt and by the president of the United States.

White and black women who brought accusations of rape and attempted rape before Union courts-martial ranged in age from five to eighty-two. They included both slave and free women from all social classes, although most were of the poor or working class. Those most vulnerable to assault were women and children who lived in the vicinity of an encampment, were contrabands, or worked in the camps as cooks, laundresses, and hospital matrons. At least seventy women were assaulted during home invasions that often included robbery or the destruction of private property. Another twenty-six assaults were perpetrated on female relatives of other soldiers; one, the mother of a wounded soldier, was assaulted by the soldier assigned to protect her. Since the age of consent in most states at the time of the Civil War was ten, girls over that age were often required to provide testimony refuting the charge that the sex was consensual.

The purpose of military justice was primarily to discipline soldiers for crimes that threatened military order, such as desertion, insubordination, sleeping on post, being drunk and disorderly, and other similar behavior. Punishments, especially executions, were frequently public spectacles designed to impress the troops with the importance of conforming to military order. By militarizing civilian crimes such as murder and rape, the U.S. Congress made it possible for the military justice system to prosecute soldiers who committed crimes against the civilian population. Congress instructed the Union military courts to follow the laws of the state in which the crime was committed. In regard to prosecutions of sexual crimes, however, the military courts frequently disregarded the state law. In particular, the military courts admitted the testimony of black witnesses in Southern states, where blacks were prohibited from testifying against whites in court. Thus, black women were able to bring sex crime accusations against white assailants with the expectation that their complaints would be heard and that the trial would result in a guilty verdict. The military courts also routinely ignored the sentencing guidelines, sometimes meting out harsher punishments than those stipulated by state law. In this way, the Union military managed to achieve some degree of sexual justice amid the chaos of war.

E. Susan Barber and Charles F. Ritter

See also African American Women; Confederate Homefront; Courts Martial; Destruction of Homes; Destruction of Personal Property; Military Invasion and Occupation; Northern Women; Sheridan's Shenandoah Valley Campaign (1864); Sherman's Campaign (1864–1865); Southern Women; Union Homefront.

References and Further Reading
An Act for Enrolling and Calling Out the National Forces, and for Other Purposes. 1863. HR 125, 37th Congress, 3rd Session. *Statutes at Large of the United States*. Vol. 12. Boston: Little, Brown and Company.

Bunch, Jack A. 2000. *Military Justice in the Confederate States Armies*. Shippensburg, PA: White Mane Publishing Co.

Corbin, D. T. 1866. *Digest of Opinions of the Judge Advocate General of the Army*. Washington, DC: U.S. Government Printing Office.

Dehart, William C. 1869. *Observations on Military Law and the Constitution and Practice of Courts Martial*. New York: D. Appleton & Co.

Everett, Robinson O. 1956. *Military Justice in the Armed Forces of the United States*. Harrisburg, PA: Military Service Publishing Company.

R.G. 153. No date. Records of the U.S. Army, Office of the Adjutant General. Washington, DC: National Archives and Records Service.

Sommerville, Diane M. 2004. *Rape and Race in the Nineteenth-Century South.* Chapel Hill: University of North Carolina Press.

Tucker, St. George, ed. 1803. *Blackstone's Commentaries* New York: Augustus M. Kelley Publishers. (Reprinted 1969. South Hackensack, NJ: Rothman Reprints.)

Ratcliffe, Laura (1836–1923)

Confederate nurse and spy Laura Ratcliffe aided Colonel John Singleton Mosby and his men.

Laura Ratcliffe was born on May 28, 1836, and attended school in Fairfax, Virginia. After her father died, the family moved to her mother's hometown, a crossroads in Fairfax County only ten miles west of Washington known as Frying Pan. Due to its location, Frying Pan was an area fraught with civil strife and military encounters during the war. Laura began nursing Confederate soldiers and serving as a spy for Mosby; one of her efforts saved the colonel and his men from a dangerous Federal ambush near Frying Pan.

Laura's devotion to the Confederate soldiers she nursed drew the attention of General J.E.B. Stuart, and they began a friendship. When he departed, he left several precious items in her possession, and two poems that he had written and dedicated to her. Stuart trusted Ratcliffe completely, and he introduced her to Mosby as someone who would be a valuable ally in the conduct of the war in that highly contested area of Virginia.

Mosby frequently used the Ratcliffe farm for his headquarters and for storing confiscated Yankee materials until they could be transferred to Confederate authorities. At Laura's suggestion, the Confederates used a large rock on the property, nicknamed Mosby's rock, to hide money and important documents or to move messages among troops in the area. In addition, Laura often delivered information in a false-bottomed egg basket. The Federals repeatedly searched the farm and questioned Laura, but to no avail.

Ratcliffe saved Mosby's life in February 1863. Federal and Confederate cavalry troops were jockeying for supremacy around Frying Pan. Mosby, who set off to engage a Federal picket posted near Frying Pan, walked into a Union trap. Hiding in the pines behind the picket was the First Virginia waiting to kill or capture him and his men. Fortunately for him, a talkative young soldier, who had stopped at Laura's home for milk, had bragged about the trap, dismissing her as a woman who could do no harm. Laura ran to alert her neighbors to watch for Mosby and warn him, but she found him herself and told him about the trap.

Impoverished after the war, Laura and her sister were befriended by an older Yankee gentleman, Milton Hanna, who lived nearby. He built them a new home so that he could watch over them and, after her sister died, he married Laura. Milton died seven years later, leaving Laura alone and wealthy. She used her inheritance to help the poor and to support local churches. She also took an active interest in managing her estates until an accident left her bedridden for the last nine years of her life.

Laura Ratcliffe Hanna died at the age of eighty-seven in 1923.

Donna Cooper Graves

See also Confederate Homefront; Female Spies; Nurses; Southern Women; Wartime Employment.

References and Further Reading

Bakeless, John. 1970. *Spies of the Confederacy.* Philadelphia, PA: J. B. Lippincott Co.

Eggleston, Larry G. 2003. *Women in the Civil War: Extraordinary Stories of Soldiers, Spies, Nurses, Doctors, Crusaders, and Others.* Jefferson, NC: McFarland.

Markle, Donald E. 2000. *Spies and Spymasters of the Civil War*, rev. ed. New York: Hippocrene Books.

Massey, Mary Elizabeth. 1994. *Women in the Civil War.* Lincoln: University of Nebraska Press. (Orig pub. 1966 as *Bonnet Brigades.*)

Simkins, Francis Butler, and James Welch Patton. 1936. *The Women of the Confederacy.* Richmond, VA: Garrett & Massie.

Ream, Vinnie (1847–1914)

In addition to her position as the first women to serve the Federal government as a clerk in the Dead Letter Office of the United States Postal Service during the Civil War, Vinnie Ream overcame gender discrimination to became the first woman and the youngest artist to receive a commission from the United States government for a statue.

Vinnie Ream at work upon her Lincoln bust which rests upon the stand she used in the White House while President Lincoln posed for her (1847–1914). (Library of Congress)

Born in Madison, Wisconsin, in 1847 to Robert Lee and Lavinia (McDonald) Ream, she and her younger sister Mary attended the St. Joseph Female Academy and later the Christian College in Columbia, Missouri, where the family moved when she was ten. At the outbreak of the Civil War, the family lived in Kansas, where her father was involved in land surveying and mapping as the clerk to the surveyor general of Kansas. Dismissed from his post because he supported the fight for Kansas to be admitted to the Union as a free state, Robert Ream brought his family east, by way of Fort Smith, Arkansas, where Robert Ream Jr. stayed, eventually joining the Confederacy.

In 1862, the family traveled through Confederate lines to Washington, D.C., where the War Department hired Robert as a cartographer. He called on his connections and found a $600-a-year post office clerkship for Vinnie. Civil service positions were open to women due to wartime shortages of workers, and all three Ream women took advantage of this opportunity.

In addition to her postal work, Ream clerked for James Rollins, the Missouri congressman who helped her family procure wartime appointments. Vinnie's wartime efforts included writing letters to men in Union and Confederate prisons, sewing shoulder straps and epaulets onto uniforms, collecting writing materials for the troops through her work with the Ladies Great National Sanitary Fair in 1864, and singing for the wounded at the Lincoln General Hospital. Ream's public singing netted her an extra $150 a year.

In 1863 Rollins introduced Ream to the self-taught and preeminent American sculptor Clark Mills, and she became his part-time student. In 1864, she asked President Abraham Lincoln if she could sculpt him. After first refusing, Lincoln allowed her to set up a studio in the corner of his White House office where he sat for Ream for half an hour a day for five months. Critics were impressed by Ream's skill and praised the bust.

The Lincoln bust attracted attention from other politicians who, once taken by her charm, youth, intelligence, and beauty, commissioned busts and medallions. Heartened by her reception as a sculptor, Ream successfully sought the $10,000 commission offered by Congress in 1866 for a full-length marble statue of Lincoln.

After the war, Ream studied in Rome and Paris. She earned $20,000 for a bronze statue of Admiral David G. Farragut in 1875. After marrying Richard L. Hoxie of the U.S. Army Corps of Engineers in 1878, her artistic labor ceased upon his request that she end her career. She died in 1914 of uremic poisoning.

Rebecca Tolley-Stokes

See also Fairs and Bazaars; Government Girls; Letter Writing; Lincoln, Abraham (1809–1865); Lewis, Edmonia (ca. 1843–ca. after 1909); Monuments; Wartime Employment.

References and Further Reading

Cooper, Edward S. 2004. *Vinnie Ream: An American Sculptor.* Chicago: Academy Chicago Publishers.

Jacob, Katherine Allamong. 2000. "Vinnie Ream: The 'Prairie Cinderella' Who Sculpted Lincoln and Farragut—And Set Tongues Wagging." *Smithsonian* 31 (5): 104–115.

Reconstruction (1865–1877)

Women of all regions, classes, and races played significant roles in the Reconstruction era. The Federal government's quest to reform and reunite the nation after the destructive Civil War led to new policies and altered the course of the United States. Reconstruction was not only a political process, but also a cultural refashioning of the nation that had to take into account the 4 million newly freed slaves. Many women took an active role in the redefinition of citizenship, affecting the freedmen's transition from slavery.

The first postwar dilemma resulted from the struggle over whether the executive or legislative branch would control Reconstruction. The debate began even before the end of combat. During the war, President Abraham Lincoln and the United States Congress bantered back and forth about the control of Reconstruction. The end of the war and Lincoln's assassination spawned one of the greatest American political conflicts of the era. The discord between newly inaugurated President Andrew Johnson and the Republican Congress created tensions that not only led to his impeachment, but that also detrimentally affected Reconstruction as a whole, the freedmen, and the United States.

Johnson and Congress split over how best to bring the Union back together. Johnson's plan of Reconstruction highlighted a policy of reconciliation. The Southern-born president wanted to bring the seceded states back into the Union peacefully; he disagreed with plans that involved Federal interference, African American rights, or punishing Confederates for treason. On the other side, Congress wanted to assure secession would never occur again. Legislators believed that, to do so, the Federal government had to punish Confederates for taking up arms against the nation as well as give political and civil rights to the freedmen. The inability of the president and congress to agree on a plan of Reconstruction led to a plethora of conflicts and the near conviction of a president.

Conflict arose over the role of the Bureau of Refugees, Freedmen, and Abandoned Lands. More commonly known as the Freedmen's Bureau, this military-run organization handled a wide variety of tasks associated with the newly freed African Americans. The Freedmen's Bureau dealt with land redistribution, setting up a court system, passing out Union pensions to former black soldiers, establishing hospitals and staffing them with nurses, many of whom were women, and negotiating labor contracts between the former slaves and their former owners. The Freedmen's Bureau also established schools and hired teachers to educate the freedpeople. Northern women became involved in and aided this effort by becoming teachers and helping raise funds for the new schools.

Education created the biggest impetus for future change during the Reconstruction era. As both as teachers and students, women made large advances for themselves and the freedpeople. Without white and black Northern women's efforts as teachers, missionaries, and social reformers, progress toward assimilating freedmen into society would have been greatly retarded. The Bureau provided the buildings for the schools, and Northern religious groups, such as the American Missionary Association, provided the teachers. The other large missionary organization, the American Freedmen's Union Commission (AFUC), also used many female teachers but excluded women from its leadership positions. Though denied positions in the AFUC leadership, women formed most of the Commission's aid societies. Women also created a few of their own missionary societies to aid the freedpeople. Founded by women, the National Freedmen's Relief Association began during the Civil War and remained active during Reconstruction.

The job of educating freedpeople began quickly. By the end of 1865, the Bureau employed 1,134 teachers, many of whom were women, to teach 90,589 students in 740 schools across the South and in the Border States. Women filled most of the teaching positions in freedmen's schools, making up

75 percent of all Northern teachers in the schools. All missionary societies had more applications than positions, but teacher tenure lasted an average of just under two years. Nevertheless, the freedmen's schools helped establish the path to public schools in the South as well as women's roles as teachers.

The primary goals of Reconstruction-era teachers went well beyond teaching reading, writing, and arithmetic. Their goals were also political and religious. The initial wave of missionary teachers consisted mostly of white middle-class women in their twenties who were unmarried, educated, and evangelical Christians. These teachers of faith, whose applications for service far outpaced funding or positions, sacrificed mostly for the greater rewards they believed they would receive in Heaven.

In addition, heading south as teachers liberated these women, however briefly, from their domestic roles. This experience exposed them to a different culture and made them actors in the fight for social justice—including their own. These women broke from the cult of domesticity that was so long practiced by white women in the nineteenth century.

Also during Reconstruction, many women served as teachers on Indian reservations as part of President Ulysses S. Grant's policy of placing missionaries in the West to Christianize and pacify America's Native peoples. Northern women took their faith not only south, but west as well.

Initially, only about 5 percent of Freedmen's Bureau teachers in the South were black and less than half were women. The lack of black teachers changed, however, largely due to the establishment of Freedmen's Bureau colleges that educated future teachers who would go south. The Freedmen's Bureau helped establish colleges such as Hampton, Howard, and Fisk, among others. All were coeducational, an uncommon occurrence in the nineteenth-century South. The curricula at these schools led to the growing number of black instructors in the South. By 1869 black teachers in the South outnumbered whites.

Female teachers, whether white or black, faced several obstacles. For example, Isabella Gibbons, a freedwoman in Virginia, had never taught before and had little idea of how to do so. She had students read the Bible and emphasized behaviors that she believed would gain the respect of others for her students. As an African American woman, she faced both race and gender prejudices.

Reconstruction allowed educational advances for black women who took advantage of the new opportunities. In 1872, African American Charlotte E. Ray became Howard University's first female law school graduate, as well as the first woman in the United States, white or black, to graduate from an accredited, nonprofit law school. That same year, the first female faculty member joined the Howard Medical School in defiance of the American Medical Association's code of ethics.

Like the colleges established by the Freedmen's Bureau, the Bureau's Southern schools included both men and women. When confronted in 1866 by a white North Carolinian who did not believe in educating freedwomen, General Oliver Otis Howard, commissioner of the Freedmen's Bureau and namesake of Howard University, responded that white Northern women had succeeded through education and so could African American women. Howard then took the man on a tour of a school full of black women. The man was "converted" according to Howard.

Freedmen's teachers of all races and sexes faced many obstacles in the course of performing their duties. White Southerners often subjected them to violence and ostracized them, and the teachers had a difficult time finding places to board during their tenures in the former Confederacy. Freedmen's teachers, white and black, were regularly intimidated, flogged, driven away, and murdered by white Southerners. After one teacher's murder, Howard urged others to stand strong, keep their faith, and continue to aid the freedmen. He advised them to be bold and take on a role he believed the government could not fulfill.

Freedmen's Bureau teachers faced violence throughout the South. As late as 1868, General J. J. Reynolds told Howard not to send women to Texas because he could not protect them against abuse there, where women made up 75 percent of Northern teachers. A Northern white female teacher readied herself for admission and baptism into a Baptist church in Louisville. However, when the white congregation discovered that she had taught in a freedmen's school and had lived at the home of a black pastor, she was denied admission to the church. Despite such treatment, African American students and teachers, as well as white teachers, persevered. A female missionary teacher in Raleigh could not comprehend the sacrifices freedmen took to send their children to school.

Reconstruction transformed freedwomen more than it did white Southern women. Freedom allowed African American women the opportunity to reunite their families, often divided by slavery, and to become full-time parents. As the war ended, black women sought to legitimize marriages and otherwise to take control of their lives. Like their male counterparts, freedwomen who worked outside the home faced discrimination and violence from white Southerners. The postwar changes in the black family, as well as the creation of Freedmen's schools, greatly disrupted the Southern labor force. African American children, who as slaves had been forced to work in the fields from sunup to sundown, now depended on their parents and went to school.

Freedwomen's rights did not advance as rapidly as did their educational opportunities. The Freedmen's Bureau and the Freedmen's Homestead Act designated the man as the head of the family, making it difficult, if not impossible, for female heads of household to claim land. In addition, the Fifteenth Amendment did not include women in the granting of suffrage to citizens, regardless of race. As a result, African American women, like their white counterparts, did not gain many of the new civil rights, such as serving on juries, which black men had recently attained. Despite these roadblocks, black women, like their white counterparts, refused to exclude themselves from political activity. For example, when they went to their jobs in white homes, many black maids wore presidential campaign buttons supporting Ulysses S. Grant. Taking political activity further, former slave Sojourner Truth worked tirelessly for women's suffrage and

had waged a campaign for it even before emancipation. In 1870, Truth gained an introduction to President Grant to discuss suffrage. She, like prominent suffragist Susan B. Anthony, would not live to vote.

African American women, including Truth, traveled the country raising money to aid freedmen. Some of this money was used to help the former slaves move from the former Confederacy. Many black women served in the Freedmen's Bureau or worked to promote it. Black women also worked as employment agents to help freedmen find work outside of overcrowded areas, particularly the nation's capital. One woman's report noted that General Howard thought the women who encouraged freedmen to leave the capital filled one of the Bureau's most important roles. Truth gave speeches to raise money, petitioned Congress for support, and traveled to Kansas in December 1870 to encourage westward settlement. Two other women, Emily Howland of Virginia and Cornelia Hancock of South Carolina, bought land to sell and rent to former slaves.

Southern white women often took roles as resistors to Reconstruction. They, no less than their male counterparts, often resented the freedom of African Americans and longed for a return to antebellum race and labor relations. They refused to treat the freedpeople as equals, socially or politically. In the face of postwar poverty, many former slaveholding women also blamed the freedpeople for their plight.

The Civil War and Reconstruction led to changes that would ultimately alter the lives of all Southerners, including white women. During this period, more women went to school than had in the antebellum years. In addition, poverty forced many women to venture into the public sphere to do tasks that servants had previously performed as well as to find employment for themselves. White women also had to perform their own domestic service, or they had to compete with freedwomen for scarce job opportunities. Elite white Southern women continued to hold antebellum ideals in high esteem while becoming more publicly visible, better educated, and more politically active.

Reconstruction activity intersected with the women's reform movement. Women's inability to hold key positions in the freedmen's aid movement demonstrated society's fear of the expansion of women's power outside the home. Nevertheless, Northern women's activity in aiding freedpeople through charity and utilizing Federal power was revolutionary. As a result, white Northern women, freedwomen, white Southern women, and America were impacted by women's roles in Reconstruction.

Scott L. Stabler

See also African American Women; Anthony, Susan B. (1820–1906); Domesticity; Education, Southern; Freedmen's Bureau; Hancock, Cornelia (1839–1926); Northern Women; Politics; Rape; Separate Spheres; Sherman Land (Special Field Orders, Number 15); Southern Women; Teachers, Northern; Truth, Sojourner [Isabella Baumfree] (1797–1883).

References and Further Reading

Butchart, Ronald E. 1980. *Northern Schools, Southern Blacks, and Reconstruction: Freedmen's Education, 1862–1875.* Westport, CT: Greenwood Press.

Censer, Jane Turner. 2003. *The Reconstruction of White Southern Womanhood, 1865–1895.* Baton Rouge: Louisiana State University Press.

Edwards, Laura F. 1997. *Gendered Strife and Confusion: The Political Culture of Reconstruction.* Urbana: University of Illinois Press.

Faulkner, Carol. 2004. *Women's Radical Reconstruction: The Freedmen's Aid Movement.* Philadelphia: University of Pennsylvania Press.

Foner, Eric. 1988. *Reconstruction: America's Unfinished Revolution, 1863–1877.* New York: Harper & Row.

Jones, Jacqueline. 1992. *Soldiers of Light and Love: Northern Teachers and Georgia Blacks, 1865–1873.* Chapel Hill: University of North Carolina Press.

Whites, LeeAnn. 2005. *Gender Matters: Civil War, Reconstruction, and the Making of the New South.* New York: Macmillan.

Refugees

The Civil War created a massive movement of refugees around the South and in other parts of America. Refugees, primarily women and their children, left their homes to avoid an approaching army or battle, to leave Union-occupied territory, or to create a new, permanent life beyond the reach of the war. The refugee experience had a tremendous impact on Southern civilians during the Civil War.

As the war began, so too did the flight of civilians from their homes, especially in the South. Because nearly all adult Southern men served in the Confederate military, their wives and daughters who remained at home made up most of the South's refugees.

The flight of women and their dependents was a response to the incredible devastation visited on the South. Historians estimate that roughly two hundred thousand Confederates became refugees at some point during the war. Among the earliest were the residents of northern Virginia, who quickly found that battles like Bull Run and the movement of armies across a relatively small piece of territory could be incredibly destructive and dangerous. They began therefore to remove themselves from the affected areas. Some streamed into Virginia cities like Richmond and Petersburg, while others went to rural areas west or south of the main fighting.

By the later years of the war, northern Virginia's population had endured extensive troop movement and numerous battles, and thousands had taken to the roads in attempts to avoid the carnage, settling with relatives and friends or anywhere they thought they could find safety. They sometimes found, however, that their new destinations placed them in as much danger as their previous homes. Petersburg, for example, became the stopping point of many refugees early in the war. However, the city itself came under a lengthy siege in 1864 and 1865.

Civilians became no less migratory in the Western portions of the Confederacy, though battles and the movement of troops in this region were spread over a larger area than in the East. Many women in the Deep South and Western states of the Confederacy never saw an army, whether Union or Confederate, but those who lay in the path of the armed forces often found removal to be the wisest course. Along the Tennessee River, near New Orleans, Baton Rouge, and Vicksburg, around Chattanooga, Atlanta, and Sherman's wide path to the sea and northward, women fled the destruction that threatened to destroy their farms and bring danger to their families.

As more and more of the Confederacy came under the control of Union forces, many women decided to forsake their homes in favor of protecting their lives. They chafed under the prospect of enemy occupation and feared the depredations of a hostile army. Numerous women fled to areas still under Confederate control, where they could express their political allegiances openly and live in what they viewed as their own nation.

Some Confederate civilians were forcibly expelled from occupied territories by Union authorities. Wives of important Confederates and women who refused to take an oath of loyalty to the United States could find themselves thrust into the Confederacy. Although many did not mind the change of government that such a move entailed, they bemoaned the loss of their homes and the need to start rebuilding their lives in a new area.

Civilians in the Border States and territories also encountered the need to flee, and the experience for them often proved especially brutal. In addition to the difficulties created by the movement of Union and Confederate armies in the area, the border regions were also torn apart by fierce guerrilla warfare, of which civilians often became the targets. Kentucky, Missouri, and Kansas all saw considerable violence that pushed many civilians out of their homes.

The Indian Territory was also torn apart by incredibly brutal conflicts that exacerbated existing schisms stemming from the removal treaties of the 1830s. Tribes split over the question of supporting the Union or the Confederacy, and, as in the Border States, civilians were both the participants in and the targets of vicious fighting. Thousands of Union and Confederate supporters fled the carnage. Confederate refugees from these areas often went to Texas, whereas Union sympathizers traveled to Kansas.

For civilians in Louisiana, Mississippi, Arkansas, Missouri, and the Indian Territory, Texas beckoned as an especially attractive destination. The trek to Texas was not too arduous, and the state was generally beyond the reach of Union forces. Thousands of women and their families made the journey, set-tling thickly in eastern Texas. There they, like refugees in other areas, tried to create the semblance of stability by finding new homes and developing ties to new people and places.

For some women in the Western portion of the Confederacy, becoming a refugee meant more than leaving home to avoid the violence of a battle or the depredations of an army. Instead, these women intended to recreate their plantation society in Texas, where they hoped the Union army would never arrive. Some planters, for example, moved all or part of their agricultural operations to Texas, marching slaves and livestock overland. They rented or bought land and began to plant, determined to make a living. Some prospered, but, as they struggled through the final years of the war, most found the obstacles overwhelming: a harsh climate, the Union blockade that prevented the export of cotton and other agricultural products, a lack of startup capital and the opposition of slaves who resented being uprooted and sensed that the war could potentially destroy slavery.

The life of a refugee was difficult, and women had to fight to support themselves and their families. Many families left their homes quickly upon hearing that battle or the arrival of an army was imminent, and they often packed hurriedly. Hasty, often panicked, packing, combined with the economic devastation of the war years and the privations caused by the Union blockade, ensured that women left home without the resources necessary to ensure a comfortable stay in a new location. Women who had family to stay with fared best, though an extended refugee period could wear on the patience and resources of even the most supportive relatives. Other women, arriving in a new area with no connections and little hard currency, found innumerable hardships. Housing was often in short supply, inflation was staggering, and, especially in urban areas, acquiring food could be difficult. Finding themselves in dire straits, many refugee women sold their clothing, jewelry, and anything else of value in a desperate attempt to feed and house their families.

In the process, they often faced a hostile reception in their destination. Civilians already struggling to survive amid the hardships of war and blockade rarely welcomed the influx of more homeless, jobless, hungry families to their area. They resented and sometimes took advantage of the desperate newcomers, charging exorbitant prices for food and housing.

While many refugees left home for only a short period of time, returning home after the immediate danger had passed, others stayed away for months or years. Either by design or the course of events, some women found that they could not return home. Whether they lived as refugees for a few days or years, however, women feared, with good reason, what they might find upon returning home. They were likely to discover destroyed fields, looted homes, and slaughtered livestock. The passage of an army, even friendly Confederates, through an area brought considerable destruction; fences were pulled down for fires, and fields and barns were stripped for food. The coming of a vengeful Union army or a battle in the area compounded the damage, and many women found that they had nothing left to which they and their families could return.

While the vast majority of Civil War refugees were Confederates, some Union women and their families also had to flee. Some Unionists left the South, especially the states of the upper South, at the outbreak of hostilities. The choice to leave the Confederacy was a painful one for many Union supporters, who grieved for the disintegration of their nation as well as for the loss of their homes. Furthermore, they dreaded the prospect of starting over in a new area. While they may have hoped for a brief exile, many Unionist women feared that they might never see their Southern homes again. Some Northern women also fled their homes in advance of Confederate invasions into Maryland and Pennsylvania.

By the end of the war, many women began to bring their families home. Others, however, settled permanently in their new location, either because they had grown to like the area or because they discovered that they had nothing left at home. Whether after an absence of a few days or at the end of the war, the return home could be wrenching. Women often arrived to find their homes looted, burned, or occupied by squatters and their farms in disarray. They were faced with the task of rebuilding when they had little money. They also faced a severe shortage of labor caused by the erosion of the slave system and the absence, maiming, or death of white male Southerners in the war.

African American women and their families also became refugees, often to escape bondage or harassment. Thousands of African American refugees made their way to Union camps during the war. Although many of the refugees were male, women and children also left their homes for the relative safety and freedom that Union camps offered. Upon arrival, they found crowded, unsanitary conditions, frequent outbreaks of disease, and military leadership that was both unprepared for their presence and unwelcoming. Many women took up work in the Union camps, washing and cooking to support themselves and their families. Northern churches and charities provided education, medical care, and other services, and they helped ameliorate the deplorable conditions, but camp life continued to offer considerable hardships to refugee women and their families.

Other African American women found refuge in the South's urban areas or in the Northern states. Some Northern churches and charitable organizations sponsored refugees, helping them create new lives in the North. Even with assistance, however, refugee life was often difficult for freedwomen and their families. They struggled to find work and support themselves in the face of poverty and racism.

The most famous African American refugees were those who followed Union General William T. Sherman through southern Georgia. The group grew into the thousands, including men, women, and family groups. Frustrated by their presence and eager to be rid of them, Sherman issued Field Orders Number 15 in January 1865, which allocated to the African American refugees a huge swath of abandoned land in coastal South Carolina, Georgia, and Florida. Many former slaves settled on the land and began working it, but by the end of the year President Andrew Johnson had reversed the order and returned the land to its former Confederate owners.

Julia Huston Nguyen

See also African American Women; Aid Societies; Atlanta, Evacuation of (Special Field Orders, Number 67); Border States; Camp Followers; Civilian Life; Confederate Homefront; Contrabands; Destruction of Homes; Destruction of Personal Property; Disease; Family Life, Confederate; Family Life, Union; Food; Foraging, Effects on Women; Loyalty Oaths; Northern Women; Sherman Land (Special Field Orders, Number 15); Sherman, William Tecumseh (1820–1891); Sherman's Campaign (1864–1865); Shortages; Southern Unionists; Southern Women; Union Homefront; Urban Women, Northern; Urban Women, Southern.

References and Further Reading

Faust, Drew Gilpin. 1996. *Mothers of Invention: Women of the Slaveholding States in the American Civil War.* Chapel Hill: University of North Carolina Press.

Massey, Mary Elizabeth. 2001. *Refugee Life in the Confederacy.* Baton Rouge: Louisiana State University Press. (Orig. pub. 1974.)

Rable, George. 1989. *Civil Wars: Women and the Crisis of Southern Nationalism.* Urbana: University of Illinois Press.

Reid, Mary Martha (1812–1894)

The widow of former Florida territorial governor Robert Raymond Reid and the daughter of Florida developer and Civil War blockade runner Samuel Swan, Mary Martha Reid established a Richmond, Virginia hospital for Florida's Confederate soldiers and spent the war caring for these men.

Mary Martha Swan was born in St. Mary's, Georgia, on September 29, 1812. As a young child, she moved with her parents to Florida, and in 1836, while visiting St. Augustine, Mary met and married Robert Raymond Reid, then a judge of the United States Superior Court. Together they had two children. One died in infancy and the other, Raymond Jenckes Reid, lived long enough to serve in the Civil War.

Three years after their marriage, Robert Reid was appointed governor of the Florida territory. He died in 1841, shortly after leaving office. The widowed Mary taught school to provide for herself and her son. Upon the outbreak of the war, Reid became a nurse at a military hospital in Lake City, Florida. Her son enlisted in the Second Florida Infantry, which left for Virginia in July 1861. Her son's wartime absence undoubtedly contributed to Reid's decision to assist in the establishment of a hospital for Florida troops in Virginia.

In the summer of 1862, Reid and several other prominent Floridians began urging the state government to create a Florida hospital in Richmond. Officials selected an old tobacco warehouse as the location of the new Florida Hospital, also known as General Hospital Number 11. Floridians donated supplies for the hospital, and the state provided additional funding. Florida Governor John Milton appointed Dr. Thomas Palmer as superintendent and director, and Reid became head matron. She left Lake City in July 1862 for the journey to Richmond.

Reid's patients treated her with an affection bordering on adoration. Numerous accounts describe Reid's devotion to the hospital and its patients. Statistics for the hospital's first year of operations show that the facility treated 1,076 patients with a mortality rate of less than 5 percent. A Richmond paper credited the hospital's surgeons and also the devotion of its matron, Reid, whom her patients called the *buena madre*.

In late 1863, the Confederate government moved to reorganize the administration of its military hospitals in Richmond and to close many of the small facilities, including the Florida Hospital. Reid then worked at Howard's Grove Hospital, where one of the wards was reserved primarily for Floridians. In the spring of 1864, Reid suffered a tragic personal loss when her son was mortally wounded at the Wilderness; his grieving mother supervised his burial in Hollywood Cemetery. An obituary lauded Jenckes Reid's wartime service, as well as that of his mother.

Reid continued her work at Howard's Grove until the end of the war. She fled Richmond on the same train that carried President Jefferson Davis from the city. Returning to Florida, she stayed briefly at the home of her "honored friend," Dr. Palmer. In 1866 the state legislature passed an act granting Reid an annual pension of $600. She taught for a time after the war before eventually moving in with a relative and living with his family until her death on June 24, 1894. The first Florida United Daughters of the Confederacy chapter was named for

Mary Reid, as was a dormitory at the University of Florida.

David Coles

See also Confederate Homefront; Hospitals; Mourning; Nurses; Pensions, Confederate Widows; Politics; Southern Women; Teachers, Southern; United Daughters of the Confederacy.
References and Further Reading
Revels, Tracy J. 2004. *Grander in Her Daughters: Florida's Women during the Civil War.* Columbia: University of South Carolina Press.

Remond, Sarah Parker (1826–1894)

African American antislavery activist Sarah Parker Remond promoted abolitionism in the Civil War era and better conditions for the freedpeople after the war. Remond raised money and lectured in both the United States and Great Britain, publishing many of her speeches, as well as some of her other writings. Remond's life clearly reflected her commitment to social activism and, more important, to self-determination, which she exhibited throughout her life.

Born in Massachusetts to successful and affluent free black parents who valued education, Sarah attended public schools in Salem while young, but she was primarily self-educated. Her parents were members of the social and financial black elite of New England, and they participated extensively in the Massachusetts antislavery society, the Underground Railroad, and other national abolitionist organizations. Sarah's mother also taught her to pursue liberty legally and that being African American was not a crime. Sarah's brother, Charles, was one of the first African American speakers on the antislavery circuit.

Charles first encouraged Sarah's entry into antislavery activities and then helped shape her performance on the speakers' platform. For about a decade starting in 1859, Remond intermittently gave lecture tours in England, Ireland, and Scotland, sponsored by British antislavery societies. Remond's speeches focused on raising money for American Anti-Slavery Society activities and on raising English consciousness about attitudes toward blacks in their Caribbean colonies. All who heard Remond's lectures praised her style of rhetoric and presentation. From a typically overemotional and sentimentalized nineteenth-century tone, she transitioned to straightforward, rational, and calmly presented lectures. Sarah believed that African Americans should speak out on their own behalf against slavery, especially since the American press had done such a poor job of it. She relied on facts and statistics to provide an arena in which her listeners were rationally convinced to see the injustices of slavery, rather than emotionally moved. The manner and substance of her work won her continued respect in Europe, where she lectured after the war against the discrimination and ill treatment of the freedpeople and raised money in England for their relief.

Her family background made Sarah well aware of the horrors of slavery and the efforts to end the institution. It also affected Sarah's reaction when she personally experienced racial discrimination. After purchasing a ticket to the opera in New York City and being seated with friends, Sarah was injured while being forcibly removed from her seat. She sued the theater managers and won her case in the mid-1850s. While touring for the American Anti-Slavery Society, Sarah and Charles encountered insults and discrimination in accommodations. When in England in the mid-1860s, Remond applied for a visa to visit France and was turned down by an American embassy agent asserting that African Americans were not citizens of the United States. The British Foreign Secretary later approved her request.

On her extended stays in England, Sarah attended college classes in London and visited not only the countries of the British Isles, but France and Italy. Her move to Florence, Italy, became permanent in 1866 when she entered medical school at the Santa Maria Nuova Hospital; she received a diploma in 1871 and practiced medicine in Florence for twenty years. She married a Sardinian man and resided in Italy until her death in 1894. She is buried in Rome.

Donna Cooper Graves

See also Abolitionism and Northern Reformers; African American Women; Antislavery Societies; Education, Northern; Free Blacks; Freedmen's Bureau; Northern Women; Union Homefront.

References and Further Reading

Massey, Mary Elizabeth. 1994. *Women in the Civil War.* Lincoln: University of Nebraska Press. (Orig pub. 1966 as *Bonnet Brigades.*)

Peterson, Carla L. 1995. *"Doers of the Word": African-American Women Speakers and Writers in the North (1830–1880).* Piscataway, NJ: Rutgers University Press.

Porter, Dorothy B. 1935. "Sarah Parker Remond, Abolitionist and Physician." *The Journal of Negro History* 20 (3): 287–293.

Remond, Sarah P. 1942. "The Negroes in the United States of America." *The Journal of Negro History* 27 (2): 216–218. Address delivered in 1862 before the International Congress of Charities, London.

Ricketts, Fanny (n.d.–1900)

During the Civil War, Frances "Fanny" Ricketts achieved a respectable notoriety for her dedicated nursing of her critically wounded husband after the Battle of Manassas. When her husband, Union Captain James Ricketts, was sent to a prisoner of war facility in Richmond, Virginia, Fanny became a voluntary captive and shared her husband's confinement. She prevented the amputation of his leg and successfully interceded when he was threatened with execution. Later, she opened her home to wounded soldiers, continuing her tradition of dedicated nursing.

Fanny Lawrence and James Ricketts were married in 1856. She accompanied him to the Texas frontier, where he was stationed with the First Artillery. Fanny developed a reputation as a compassionate nurse and a productive member of the garrison. In 1861, the couple traveled to Virginia when the First Artillery was transferred there in preparation for the impending war.

On July 21, 1861, James was severely wounded while commanding his battery at the Battle of Manassas. Fanny was determined to find him and nurse him back to health. To pass through Confederate lines, she drew upon her relationships with Confederate officers whom she had favorably impressed before the war. Colonel J.E.B. Stuart issued her a pass to travel through the Confederate lines, and General Joseph Johnston granted her permission to reach the battlefield.

On July 26, Fanny located her gravely wounded husband at a makeshift hospital. In her diary she recorded the horrible conditions she encountered. Amputated limbs littered the floor and gangrene ran rampant. Surgeons planned to amputate James's leg, but Fanny refused to allow it. For one week, she nursed him and other wounded captives.

In August, James was transferred to a Richmond hospital. When prison officials attempted to prevent Fanny from accompanying her husband, she appealed to General Johnston. In Richmond, the couple encountered grim conditions at the hospital. Fanny continued to nurse her husband, once even opening an infected abscess. She employed her diplomatic skills to obtain extra food from the wives of high-ranking Confederate officers.

In November, the Ricketts were transferred to Libby Prison where Fanny learned her husband had been selected as a hostage for captured Confederate privateersmen. Because the Federal government viewed the Confederate captives as traitors subject to execution, Confederate authorities threatened selected captives with the same fate. Fanny appealed to the wife of the Confederate adjutant and inspector general; her intervention played a role in the commutation of her husband's sentence.

Fanny's imprisonment ended in December when her husband was released. After his death in 1877, Fanny received a pension; when financial hardship forced her to seek an increase, former Union soldiers who had benefited from her nursing testified on her behalf. Fanny Ricketts died in 1900 and was buried with her husband at Arlington National Cemetery.

Karen Kinzey

See also Bull Run/Manassas, First Battle of (July 21, 1861); Imprisonment of Women; Northern Women; Nurses; Pensions, Union Widows.

References and Further Reading

Black, Linda. 1994. "A Wife's Devotion: The Story of James and Fanny Ricketts." *Blue and Gray Magazine* 11: 22–28.

Moore, Frank. 1866. *Women of the War: Their Heroism and Self-Sacrifice.* Chicago: R. C. Treat.

Ropes, Hannah (1809–1863)

Nurse, supervisor, author, feminist, abolitionist, free soiler, and reformer, Hannah Ropes lost her life in the service of her country and a cause about which she was unusually passionate.

Hannah Anderson Chandler was born June 13, 1809, in New Gloucester, Maine, to Peleg and Esther Parsons Chandler. She had nine siblings. Her father and two brothers were lawyers involved in Massachusetts politics. Through family and acquaintances, she became friends with politically powerful people like Charles Sumner and Nathaniel P. Banks. In 1834, she married William Henry Ropes, a teacher and farmer. The couple had four children, only two of whom survived childhood. William abandoned Hannah and the children some time between 1847 and 1855. They never divorced but apparently never saw each other again.

As a single mother, Hannah reveled in her new-found freedom and joined the abolitionist movement. In 1855 she challenged proslavery sentiments with her son, Edward Elson Ropes, in the tumultuous Kansas territory. In Lawrence, Kansas, she nursed the sick until 1856 when she returned to Massachusetts as the violence in Kansas escalated. That same year, she wrote a book detailing her experiences in Kansas called *Six Months in Kansas: By a Lady*. She remained involved in political issues and benevolent works, publishing a second book in 1859 entitled *Cranston House: A Novel*, a fictional work loosely based on events in her own life.

In June 1862, following her son's enlistment in the Second Massachusetts Volunteer Infantry Regiment, Hannah signed on as a nurse under the supervision of Dorothea Dix, superintendent of the United States army nurses. Hannah wanted a part in the war effort and turned to one of the few arenas open to women and for which she had talent: nursing. She had been strongly influenced by Florence Nightingale's *Notes on Nursing: What It Is, and What It Is Not*, and Nightingale's philosophy motivated her to fight for better conditions for wounded soldiers. She embraced the belief that it was her duty and honor to mother "her boys." She arrived in Georgetown, Washington, D.C., in June 1862 and began her work as matron of nurses at the Union Hotel Hospital.

Louisa May Alcott, one of the nurses working under Ropes, nicknamed the hospital the Hurly Burly House, given the chaotic and poor conditions. It was an old building, poorly ventilated, damp, and cold. Ropes oversaw ten nurses and four hundred patients. She immediately worked to improve the conditions, sanitation, and patient treatment. As a part of that work, she reported two officers—a chief surgeon and a steward—for malfeasance. She accused them of depriving patients of food, stealing from patients, selling supplies meant for patients, and treating patients cruelly. When the surgeon general ignored her complaints, she appealed to Secretary of War Edwin Stanton. The two men were arrested and imprisoned, and Stanton reassigned the administrators.

Tragically, in January 1863, both Ropes and Alcott fell ill with typhoid pneumonia at the hospital. Alcott survived, but Ropes died. She is buried in New Gloucester, Maine.

Paula Katherine Hinton

See also Abolitionism and Northern Reformers; Alcott, Louisa May (1832–1888); Disease; Dix, Dorothea Lynde (1802–1887); Hospitals; Northern Women; Nurses; Politics; Wartime Employment.

References and Further Reading
Alcott, Louisa May. 1863. *Hospital Sketches*. Boston: James Redpath.
Brumgardt, John R., ed. 1980. *Civil War Nurse: The Diary and Letters of Hannah Ropes*. Knoxville: University of Tennessee Press.
Schultz, Jane E. 2004. *Women at the Front: Hospital Workers in Civil War America*. Chapel Hill: University of North Carolina Press.

Roswell Women

In July 1864, Union General William T. Sherman forced the female factory workers employed at the textile mills in Roswell, Georgia, to leave. They and their families were deported north of the Ohio River.

In 1839, Roswell King founded the Roswell Manufacturing Company north of Atlanta along the banks of Vickery's Creek, which fed into the Chattahoochee River. The small industrial complex with its two textile mills, twenty dwellings, two churches, a slave chapel, and a schoolhouse soon became known as Roswell. During the Civil War, the King mills produced fifteen thousand yards of cloth every month for the Confederate government. Most of the workers were young, white Southern women who needed the money to support their families and most of whom had male relatives in the Confederate army. In 1864, as Union troops neared Roswell, James Roswell King transferred ownership to French weaver Theophile Roche in the hopes of protecting his grandfather's mills.

The Union army pushed Confederate troops across the Chattahoochee River on July 1, 1864, and continued on toward Roswell. When Sherman's soldiers arrived in Roswell, they found French flags flying over the Kings' residence and mills. Roche and several citizens demanded protection due to French neutrality. However, the presence of French flags and citizens did little to protect the mills or the town, and they may have even angered Union officials. Sherman had given orders for his men to destroy the factories for their role in producing Confederate uniforms. A quick inspection soon revealed Confederate cloth in the factories, and the discovery sealed their fate. Union troops burned all the factories on July 6, 1864.

The Union did not stop at the destruction of the factories and surrounding homes. On July 8, Sherman gave orders to treat everyone associated with the factories, male or female, as enemies and traitors. He further ordered his subordinates to round up Roswell's civilians and send them to Marietta, Georgia. Four to five hundred civilians were forced to Marietta, most in army transports, to await trains that would take them to Nashville, Tennessee.

By July 10, the refugees had gathered at Marietta, where other Georgia mill workers joined them. Soon thereafter, the nearly three thousand people traveled north by railroad to Nashville, Tennessee, Louisville, Kentucky, and Evansville, Indiana. The women remained destitute, while state and local officials argued over who was responsible for their care.

Little is known about the fate of the Roswell refugees. As poor women, they left few records. As a result, the exact number of women who remained north or returned to Georgia after the Civil War is unknown.

William H. Brown

See also Atlanta, Evacuation of (Special Field Orders, Number 67); Confederate Homefront; Destruction of Homes; Factory Workers, Southern; Sherman, William Tecumseh (1820–1891); Sherman's Campaign (1864–1865); Southern Women; Wartime Employment.

References and Further Reading

Bynum, Hartwell T. 1970. "Sherman's Expulsion of the Roswell Women in 1864." *Georgia Historical Quarterly* 54: 169–182.

Castel, Albert. 1992. *Decision in the West: The Atlanta Campaign of 1864.* Lawrence: University Press of Kansas.

Evans, David. 1996. *Sherman's Horsemen: Union Cavalry Operations in the Atlanta Campaign.* Bloomington: Indiana University Press.

Rural Women

Much of Civil War America was rural. Southern plantation owners' wives and slaves, as well as middle-class and poor subsistence farmers' wives in the antebellum North and South, all lived in rural settings.

The profile of rural communities changed when white men joined the wartime military. In the South, black females predominated the population, while in the North and West, white women made up the bulk of the rural population. By the end of the war, small farms dominated the Southern landscape, as they did in the North before and after the war, and women headed more households than they had prior to the war. During the war, masses of rural Southern women, black and white, congregated in cities for employment and safety, many remaining afterward. During the war, women's attitudes, expectations, and activities changed. Women's wartime occupations as teachers, nurses, office and shop clerks, factory workers, spies, smugglers, soldiers, and farm managers often led to postwar activities that continued their wartime independence. Women directed public pursuits for the public good rather than solely for their families. As a result of war, working women constituted a new demographic group composed primarily of former rural residents.

Rural women's wartime experiences varied depending on their proximity to troops and battles, as well as their socioeconomic status, race, political persuasion, and household composition. More is known about Southern women's lives because many elite women kept diaries and wrote memoirs, recording their own, their slaves', and other women's conduct. Many wealthy rebel women enthusiastically supported the war and encouraged loved ones to enlist. On the other hand, some poor women resented Confederate laws that allowed wealthy men to avoid service by hiring a substitute.

All women whose loved ones became soldiers lost antebellum protection and companionship. Southern women coped with more widespread and devastating deprivations than did Northern women for several reasons. First, most battles were fought on Southern soil. Second, because most Southerners lived on farms, a higher percentage of Southern white men were in the armed forces and nearly one-third of them died during the war. Third, military and refugee populations overwhelmed the South's food production capacity. Like their Southern counterparts, Northern farm women shouldered some of the manual labor that men had performed. However, few endured shortages of food, clothing, and heat; few lacked medical care and transportation; few saw their homes and possessions destroyed or appropriated; and few lived as refugees or faced a lawless society. Southern rural women rarely escaped hardship, especially after the Union initiated hard war policies in early 1863. Their diminishing ability to survive and aid the Confederacy influenced the war's outcome and society's recovery.

War intruded primarily on the residences, gardens, and fields of rural women who lived near main roads and towns, troop encampments, battlefields, or lines of march. In Virginia and Tennessee, where the majority of battles occurred, more women and land withstood depredation than in other states. Throughout the South, military and refugee popula-

tions increased concurrently as laborers, implements, and work animals vanished. Plantation mistresses grappled with the heightened insubordination of the few remaining slaves. Union soldiers saw subsistence farmers' wives pulling plows, but some fortunate middling farmers' wives employed an able-bodied slave, exempt white man, or a discharged veteran to help raise crops and food. Homefront efforts benefited the military, sometimes the enemy, more than they did individual families. Where armies occupied areas for extended periods, soldiers exhausted the supplies of surrounding farms and continually expanded their foraging to more remote and smaller homesteads. As they invaded the countryside, soldiers took or destroyed food, crops, fences, tools, and livestock. In the South, salt became so scarce that women dug dirt from smokehouse floors and boiled it to render the precious preservative. They also substituted sweet potatoes and other vegetables for coffee, another rare commodity. Occasionally their hidden sugar, ground corn, and other preserved food escaped soldiers' searches. When warfare moved into the Deep South and slaves fled to Union lines, plantation mistresses, accustomed to slaves producing cotton and food, found it difficult to grow even a vegetable garden.

When rural Northern women left their homes, the move was often voluntary, and they stayed with relatives only until their husbands returned. Unlike those of their Southern sisters, Northern women's homes and possessions primarily remained intact. Northern and Southern women who remained on their land frequently consolidated households for security, additional workers, and emotional solace. Whether freely or forced, women on both sides accepted soldiers as guests or boarders. Northern and Southern rural women sheltered poor families who offered essential skills such as weaving or carpentry. Because Southern women accommodated greater numbers of temporary residents, they often lived in cramped conditions or in former barns and outbuildings.

Before soldiers appeared, rural Southern families began altering their living arrangements and refugees abounded. Many of the wealthiest families sent their children to distant boarding schools. Avid Confederate supporters vacated their homes for places deemed safer, such as Atlanta, Mobile, and Texas, while Unionist families moved north. Planters with large slave populations protected their investments by either selling or sending them to live in Texas or other places where they would be unlikely to find Union forces. When Federals captured territory, they arrested vocal male secessionists and ordered their families to move behind Confederate lines. If time permitted, women sewed money, bonds, gold, jewelry, and documents into their clothing. Elite plantation women lived in relative comfort, even if they had to move several times, until the war's final months when basic necessities were so scarce that money mattered little. Although technically refugees, they experienced few of the afflictions that their poor sisters endured. As hostilities intensified, less well-to-do Southern Unionists living among Confederate sympathizers (and vice versa) fled out of fear of violence or from violence itself, becoming itinerant refugees. Other Southern females joined refugee ranks after their homes were destroyed or commandeered, if they were unable to combine households with relatives or neighbors, or when they or family members were elderly or sick. Escaping slaves formed another refugee group, and they considered themselves fortunate if they found a vacant building or boxcar for shelter. Most eventually arrived in Union-controlled areas, where they found freedom, food, and work.

Rural women devised countless ways to earn money for survival while aiding their nation's war effort. Many made clothing for the troops, but only a few were paid for their efforts. Until their own provisions dwindled, many Southern farm wives made money selling produce and baked goods to soldiers. Numerous white and some black women, Northern and Southern, left their farms to work in hospitals, taking on vocations previously reserved for men. Other Southern white women toiled in government offices, factories, or stores. Although the army employed cooks and domestics, many Southern whites considered these tasks to be beneath them. Destitute women gleaned battlefields for food, clothing, minié balls, and anything

else that could be used or bartered. The most desperate women turned to prostitution.

As difficult as wartime life became for rural white women, it was considerably worse for African American women. Escaping slaves risked being caught, returned, and beaten; free blacks were in danger of losing their freedom if captured. Nevertheless, when Union forces neared, slaves left en masse. In rural areas, untold numbers of Northern and Southern black women helped escaped slaves and captured black Union soldiers find their way to freedom via the Underground Railroad. Slave women signaled coded messages to fugitives by hanging quilts that offered hidden information. Notable Northern black women, including Harriet Tubman and Sojourner Truth, risked capture and death every time they guided escapees through waterways and secret paths.

During the Civil War, many slaveholders, unwilling or unable to clothe and feed their slaves, leased them. In addition, household servants, usually those owned by small farmers, often remained with their white families, assuming the most strenuous tasks. Neither Confederate nor Union soldiers considered raping black women a crime; thus sexual assaults against blacks were more commonplace than those against whites. Undeterred, slave women continued to flee to contraband camps, to Northern cities, and to the Federal Army, where some were hired as cooks, seamstresses, and laundresses. When the Union army began enlisting black men in 1863, they were isolated from their families, who were prohibited from visiting them, for months. Until the U.S. colored troops' boycott forced the government to rectify its unequal pay scale, their families, North and South, confronted starvation.

Regardless of race or region, rural women supported their soldiers. Northern and Southern church and community groups sold quilts and other handmade goods to raise money for their cause. As casualties mounted, women on both sides unraveled fabric to collect lint for bandages. Southern women sacrificed prized possessions, including wedding dresses to make regimental flags, and later they converted linens into clothing and carpets into shoes. In the South, the cotton shortage, the diversion of most textiles to military use, and the lack of firewood for winter heat increased the army and civilian demand for cloth production. Women who had previously depended on slaves to make clothing and bedding learned to spin, card, weave, quilt, and produce blankets and uniforms. In addition, adventurous Union and Confederate women spied, smuggled, hid soldiers, and led soldiers through unfamiliar territory. Some Union commanders recruited black women as spies in the knowledge that Southern whites often talked freely around them.

While Northern women traveled freely, rural Southerners in occupied areas had to obtain travel passes from Union officers. Despite restrictions, elite young belles visited relatives and friends and attended dances hosted by occupying commanders.

The war interrupted most of the social life in the South. Without a horse or buggy, most rural Southern women lost the antebellum emotional support they once gained through their social life and church. Churches, schools, and government did not operate in the rural South during most of the war. Churches split according to political views; Unionists were shunned at some churches and Confederates outcast from others.

In addition, many Northern and Southern rural communities divided during the Civil War. Neighbors reported others to Union authorities for suspected support of Confederates, or vice versa, depending on which side controlled the territory. Guerrillas of both persuasions retaliated against their political opponents. Until midwar, in Union-held Southern territory, soldiers protected Unionists' farms. Union sympathizers' property was exempt from confiscation unless necessary; then they received compensation. Neutral women received protection, but their houses and personal property could be appropriated without compensation. Known Confederate supporters were subject to arrest, forced removal to behind Confederate lines, harassment, and property confiscation or destruction if they stayed in Federal territory. As the war progressed, Union troops raided wealthy secessionist farms more extensively. In most Southern states, law enforcement and courts were discontinued, leaving women at the mercy of guerrillas,

opportunistic thieves, foraging and violent soldiers, and potential slave revolts. Rural women on both sides protected their homes and families as best they could, wielding axes and guns when necessary.

Border states weathered a war within the larger Civil War. In Missouri and Kansas, the antebellum dispute over admitting Kansas as a free state precipitated bloody guerrilla attacks. Rural women there saw their husbands killed or brutally assaulted and their homes destroyed. The violence continued with secession and the outbreak of war. Proslavery bushwhackers, eventually legitimized as Confederate units, and free state jayhawkers conducted a reign of terror against each other's supporters. The irregulars arrested or physically harmed women who aided the opposing side or who were suspected of doing so. Women in states that did not secede, particularly Ohio and Kentucky, suffered similar treatment from outlaw bands supporting the Confederacy. Those were isolated incidents, in contrast to the prevalent attacks that Southern Unionist and black women experienced. All rural women lived with one constant wartime companion: fear.

Nancy L. Adgent

See also African American Women; Aid Societies; Camp Followers; Confederate Homefront; Confederate Sympathizers, Northern; Destruction of Homes; Destruction of Personal Property; Diaries and Journals; Fairs and Bazaars; Family Life, Confederate; Family Life, Union; Female Spies; Flags, Regimental; Food; Foraging, Effects on Women; Fundraising; Guerrilla Warfare; Homespun; Impressment; Military Invasion and Occupation; Nonslaveholding Southerners; Northern Women; Nurses; Plantation Life; Prostitution; Rape; Refugees; Religion; Southern Unionists; Southern Women; Truth, Sojourner [Isabella Baumfree] (1797–1883); Tubman, Harriet [Araminta Ross] (1822–1913); Union Homefront; Wartime Employment.

References and Further Reading

Clinton, Catherine. 1995. *Tara Revisited: Women, War, and the Plantation Legend.* New York: Abbeville Press.

Culpepper, Marilyn Mayer. 1991. *Trials and Triumphs: Women of the American Civil War.* East Lansing: Michigan State University Press.

Edwards, Laura F. 2000. *Scarlett Doesn't Live Here Anymore: Southern Women in the*

Civil War Era. Urbana: University of Illinois Press.

Faust, Drew Gilpin. 1996. *Mothers of Invention: Women of the Slaveholding South in the American Civil War.* Chapel Hill: University of North Carolina Press.

Forbes, Ellen. 1998. *African American Women during the Civil War.* New York: Garland Publishing.

Gutman, Herbert G. 1976. *The Black Family in Slavery and Freedom, 1750–1925.* New York: Pantheon.

Jenkins, Wilbert L. 2002. *Climbing up to Glory: A Short History of African Americans during the Civil War and Reconstruction.* Wilmington, DE: Scholarly Resources.

Massey, Mary Elizabeth. 1964. *Refugee Life in the Confederacy.* Baton Rouge: Louisiana State University Press.

Massey, Mary Elizabeth. [1966] 1994. *Women in the Civil War.* Lincoln: University of Nebraska Press.

S

Safford [Stafford], Mary Jane (ca. 1831 or 1834–1891)

Civil War nurse Mary Jane Safford was known for her tireless and dedicated service. She later turned her natural love of medicine and care for others into a lifelong career of distinction and honor as one of the best female doctors of her era.

Safford was born in Hyde Park, Vermont, on December 31 of either 1831 or 1834 (the records vary). She grew up in Illinois near Joliet, subsequently working as a governess for a German family in Canada for a short while before returning to Illinois. Here, in the summer of 1861, she met Mary Anne "Mother" Bickerdyke, a famous nurse who had come to Cairo, Illinois, to take care of the Union soldiers. When an epidemic of several infectious diseases broke out among the troops, Safford saw the need and volunteered as a nurse. She had long admired Bickerdyke and relished the opportunity to work with her. Safford could have remained at the hospital to care for the wounded, but her heart was with the soldiers languishing in the many camps. Soon she earned the name of Angel of Cairo for her tender care of the soldiers and her refusal to give up.

Traveling from camp to camp, overworked and exhausted, Safford fashioned a truce flag from a broomstick and white petticoat so that she would not be accidentally shot as she moved among the tents. She was a familiar figure on the fields near Fort Donelson in Tennessee and Belmont, Missouri, among others. After leaving Fort Donelson,

Civil War nurse Mary J. Safford [Stafford] became a doctor in 1869. (Brockett, Linus Pierpont & Mary C. Vaughan, *Woman's Work in the Civil War: A Record of Heroism, Patriotism and Patience*, 1867)

she went to work aboard two different transport boats, the *City of Memphis* followed by the *Hazel Dell*. In Tennessee, she also served with General Ulysses S. Grant at Shiloh and again with Bickerdyke in the camps at Savannah. Safford hurt her back severely and had to be confined to bed for several months. She returned to her brother's home in Illinois and then traveled to Europe to complete her recovery.

After the war, Safford realized she wanted to become a doctor. She threw herself into her studies with the same fervor and attention that she had given the soldiers, and she graduated from the Medical College for Women in New York in 1869. She traveled to Austria and studied at the General Hospital in Vienna before attending the University of Breslau in Germany. In Breslau, she became the first woman to perform an ovariotomy. In 1872, she opened a private practice in Chicago where she met and married James Blake, but the marriage ended in divorce in 1880. Safford spent the latter years of her career as a professor of women's diseases at the Boston University School of Medicine and as a staff doctor at the Massachusetts Homeopathic Hospital.

Mary Jane Safford retired to Florida where she died in Tarpon Springs December 8, 1891.

Jay Warner

See also Bickerdyke, Mary Ann Ball "Mother" (1817–1901); Disease; Hospitals; Hospital Ships; Northern Women; Nurses; Wartime Employment.

References and Further Reading
Cazalet, Sylvain. 1866. *History of the New York Medical College and Hospital for Women*. New York: University of the State of New York.

Schuyler, Louisa Lee (1837–1926)

Social reformer Louisa Lee Schuyler helped lead the United States Sanitary Commission during the Civil War.

She was born in New York City to a socially prominent and affluent family. Her great-grandfathers were Revolutionary War Generals Phillip Schuyler and Alexander Hamilton. Despite her privileged background, she dedicated her life to public service, which had long been a tradition in her family. As a young woman, Schuyler was active in the Children's Aid Society of New York.

Shortly after the Civil War erupted, Harry Raymond, founder of the *New York Times*, placed an advertisement in his newspaper asking for women to join his wife in compiling and preparing supplies for wounded soldiers. Women throughout the North responded by gathering in private homes and churches to produce the necessary items for Union soldiers. On April 26, 1861, Schuyler organized a meeting of four thousand women in New York City and founded the Women's Central Association of Relief for the Sick and Wounded of the Army. She wanted her organization, which was modeled after the British Sanitary Commission created during the Crimean War to combat the unsanitary conditions that caused disease, to be national in scope.

Schuyler attempted to get the Federal government to recognize her organization, but initially there was little interest. President Abraham Lincoln believed that the organization would be difficult to administer. However, on June 13, 1861, he reluctantly signed an order officially establishing the United States Sanitary Commission. By 1863, there were over seven thousand local commissions throughout the North. Schuyler served as chairman of the Committee on Correspondence and Publicity for the Commission. She wrote reports and letters, spoke to the local commissions, and gave public lectures on the Commission's work. Schuyler, along with other members of the Commission, inspected Union army camps and prison camps operated by the Confederate army, and she wrote detailed reports for the government on the unsanitary conditions she found there.

Thousands of women volunteered with the Sanitary Commission. Under Schuyler's leadership, the women collected food, clothing items, and medical supplies for Union soldiers. Over twenty-five thousand packages were sent to Union troops, and amazingly only one package was lost. The women served as nurses in army hospitals and camps. They used their homes to provide sleeping quarters and meals for soldiers traveling to and from the warfront. The Commission supplied and operated steamships, provided by the government, that were used as floating hospitals, and it pioneered the use of trains as mobile hospitals and a field ambulance corps. Schuyler helped to organize sanitary fairs in many large cities. The fairs were operated by the women volunteers and attracted the public by selling baked goods and handmade crafts, among other items. Over the course of the Civil War, the Sanitary Commission collected and distributed nearly $6 million.

After the war, Schuyler devoted the rest of her life to promoting social welfare. She founded the New York State Charities Aid Association in 1872. This organization inspected homeless shelters and made recommendations to improve the standards of care.

Louisa Lee Schuyler died in 1926.

Gene C. Gerard

See also Aid Societies; Fairs and Bazaars; Fundraising; Hospitals; Hospital Ships; Northern Women; Nurses; Union Homefront; United States Sanitary Commission; Women's Central Association of Relief.

References and Further Reading

Attie, Jeanie. 1998. *Patriotic Toil: Northern Women and the American Civil War.* Ithaca, NY: Cornell University Press.

Giesberg, Judith Ann. 2000. *Civil War Sisterhood: The U.S. Sanitary Commission and Women's Politics in Transition.* Boston: Northeastern University Press.

Secession

The idea of secession was based on the Constitutional theory of states' rights, a belief that citizens acting through their states were superior to the Federal government. This belief held that citizens could nullify, or choose not to enforce, Federal laws that violated the Constitution and, in the most extreme case, could choose to voluntarily leave the Union. These theories stretched back at least to 1798 and to the Kentucky and Virginia Resolutions, and they were discussed and debated in the press and by politicians across the country. The mechanism for nullification or secession was a special convention of the people—the ultimate source of sovereignty—modeled on those used to ratify the Constitution.

Only in South Carolina had voters actually tested the theory of states' rights, nullifying a Federal tariff law in 1832; an ambiguous compromise that resolved the crisis allowed both supporters and critics of states' rights to claim victory.

After the South Carolina nullification crisis, many white Southerners considered states' rights and secession to be their ultimate weapons in the battle to protect slavery. From the 1830s to 1860, the secession movement was rooted in the sectional disagreement about the future of slavery in the United States. White Southerners considered slavery the foundation of their social order and culture, and they believed that only its survival would preserve their civilization and ensure their safety and prosperity. Thus, when Southerners spoke of defending slavery, they understood it broadly to encompass their slave-based way of life. The majority of white Southerners, male and female, ultimately supported secession in 1860 and 1861 in order to protect slavery and all that it represented in their lives.

Before the 1850s, Southerners often discussed secession as a means to protect slavery, but, as long as the direct threat to the institution remained slight, secession was too radical for the great majority of voters. However, support for disunion grew in the aftermath of the Mexican War. Unexpectedly vigorous Northern opposition to the expansion of slavery surfaced before and during the war—evidenced by the overwhelming support for David Wilmot's free soil proviso—and shocked Southerners. Most Southerners believed free soil was a threat to the long-term viability and health of slavery; as support for free soil grew among Northern voters, white Southerners became increasingly anxious.

The most important development in the movement for secession was the formation and success of the free soil Republican Party. Most Republicans were not abolitionists, and probably just a minority had real moral misgivings about slavery itself; many, in fact, were racists who wanted to exclude all non-whites from the territories. For a great variety of reasons, though, Republicans were united in their commitment to stop the spread of slavery. This defining program presented Southerners with a double threat. First was the tangible danger that free soil presented to slavery. Unable to expand, most white Southerners believed, slavery would become increasingly unstable, ending finally with widespread rebellion, as whites were outnumbered by the growing slave population, or with what Southerners called racial amalgamation. Southerners would also lose power in the national government as they became an ever shrinking minority in the country, perhaps ending with a constitutional amendment to abolish slavery. Finally, without fresh land to develop, the market value of slaves would decline since they were only as valuable as what they produced. Thus, most white Southerners believed free soil to be just as unacceptable as abolition. In addition, more and more Republicans were actual abolitionists, and these so-called radicals gained strength in New England throughout the 1850s. For all these reasons, the overwhelming majority of Southern whites believed that the Republican Party presented a clear and immediate threat to Southerners' peculiar institution and to their entire way of life.

Beyond the real threat to slavery's future in the nation, Southern whites resented the Republicans' claim of Northern superiority. This insult to their honor was a challenge to Southerners' personal and collective reputations, and it questioned their equality as good Christians and Americans. Emphasizing these threats to slavery, the insult to Southern honor, and the challenge to manhood, the secessionist movement gained strength rapidly after 1856, when Republicans carried a majority of Northern states in the presidential contest. Southern voters denounced the sectional party and presented a more and more unified front in state and national elections in the late 1850s.

The presidential campaign of 1860 gave new urgency to the movement for disunion, and it energized secessionists, male and female, across the South. The possibility of a Republican victory appalled most white Southerners, and those who had worked actively for secession considered the election an opportunity to push their agenda: many rooted openly for Lincoln to win. Although not the only issue, secession and a possible civil war dominated the campaign, and Southerners debated whether a

Republican victory, by itself, would justify secession. The Southern Democratic Party—formed when the national organization split over the selection of a candidate—endorsed secession if Lincoln won, although their candidate, John C. Breckinridge, did not. The newly created Constitutional Union Party made no definitive statement about secession, and Northern Democrat Stephen Douglas opposed any sort of disunion. Republicans carried several key Northern states, including Pennsylvania, Ohio, and Indiana, in early October, virtually assuring their victory and suggesting that many voters who backed the Southern Democrats indicated their endorsement of secession. A strong majority of voters in the Deep South eventually supported Breckinridge, who carried eleven slave states.

Lincoln's victory, with essentially no Southern votes, prompted secessionists in every slave state to move quickly and attempt to capitalize on the widespread public outrage. While the majority of white men in the Deep South expressed support for secession, leaders of the movement took few chances. Vigilance committees, Minute Men clubs, and other local organizations held rallies, calling on men to do their duty and defend the South's honor. Many Unionists were intimidated, some drifted to the secessionist cause, and others just gave up when it became obvious that secession had widespread support.

Secessionists had dreamed of the moment when they could lead their states out of the Union. Although it had never been tried, most Southerners believed secession was legal. The mechanism, however, was less clear. Some favored a cooperative approach in which several states would secede together, but the majority held that logic dictated separate state secession: if each state was truly sovereign, then it should act alone. Nearly everyone who favored secession assumed that the individual states would unite to form a new slave-based nation.

Moved by their own feelings and popular pressure, governors and legislators in nearly all of the slave states called for special elections to choose delegates for conventions that would decide secession. These campaigns were characterized by low voter turnout and a mixture of candidates whose exact position on secession remained murky. Many ran as cooperationists but left open whether that meant cooperation within the Union to defend slavery or cooperative secession; in many counties, candidates ran unopposed. In each of the seven Deep South states, a large majority of prosecession delegates was elected. In the conventions, Unionists tried to stall the momentum by pushing for a cooperative movement that would take more time, during which postelection passions might calm. Others urged convention delegates to submit secession to the voters for a straight yes-or-no referendum. These delaying tactics, however, were defeated in most of the Deep South conventions; only in Texas did delegates submit their Ordinance of Secession to the voters, who approved it overwhelmingly. Beginning with South Carolina, on December 20, 1860, seven states declared themselves independent nations: Mississippi (January 9, 1861), Florida (January 10), Alabama (January 11), Georgia (January 19), Louisiana (January 26), and Texas (February 1). As the vast majority of delegates and voters expected, these states came together and formed the Confederate States of America in February 1861. At the news of each state's secession, elite white women cheered the decision and vowed to support the cause of Southern independence.

Secession was defeated, temporarily, in the Upper South, where a majority of residents did not believe that the simple fact of Lincoln's election warranted such a drastic step. Instead, so-called conditional Unionists urged patience and waited for Lincoln's inauguration, hoping for a compromise that would bring the other slave states back into the Union. The attack at Fort Sumter, however, made compromise impossible. When the Civil War started on April 12 and Lincoln subsequently called for volunteers to invade the South, four more states opted for secession: Virginia (April 17), Arkansas (May 6), North Carolina (May 20), and Tennessee (June 8). Each then joined the Confederacy. Secessionists in the Border States of Missouri, Kentucky, Maryland, and Delaware failed to lead their states out of the Union. Compared to the Deep and Upper South, fewer slaves and slaveholders and greater economic and family ties with the North

were the most important factors that influenced Border State voters to stay in the Union.

The secession movement across the Southern states was affected most evidently by the place of slavery in the economy and the extent of slave ownership. Slaves constituted a majority of the population in Mississippi and South Carolina and more than 45 percent in every other Deep South state except Texas; in the Upper South, slaves totaled between 25 and 40 percent. In the Border States, however, only Kentucky had a slave population that was central to its economy. The widespread ownership of slaves also translated into greater enthusiasm for secession. In Mississippi, for instance, most estimates suggest that over one-half of white households owned or rented slaves. The ownership and use of slaves was similarly common across the Deep South. Furthermore, the wild profits made from cotton in the 1850s undoubtedly caused many Deep South voters to feel particularly threatened by the Republicans' free soil platform. The prospect of military action by a Republican government against fellow Southerners convinced wavering Unionists that secession was necessary to protect slavery and to redeem regional honor.

White Southerners explained disunion by recounting a long list of what they referred to as Northern aggressions. Central to all Southern complaints, of course, was the Republican Party and its free soil ideology. Thereafter, prominent justifications for secession were the Republicans' entirely sectional appeal and support (including votes from black men in several New England states); Northern state laws that effectively nullified the Fugitive Slave Act; and Northerners' refusal to admit Kansas as a slave state in 1858 and their supposed support for John Brown and slave insurrection. Most of all, white Southerners labeled Republicans and Lincoln as abolitionists. According to Southerners, by electing a president with no Southern votes, Northerners had denounced slavery and elected a man that Southerners viewed as committed to the abolition of slavery. Finally, most Southern voters declared Lincoln's election—and all it symbolized—as an insult to the South and to their claim to equality within the Union. Over and over, Southerners used the same words to describe the Republican triumph: humiliating, insulting, and degrading. They consequently saw secession as the only action that would rescue and defend Southern honor. Secession and the formation of a new slave-based nation, even at the risk of civil war, was the solution that most white Southerners eventually supported.

Christopher J. Olsen

See also Election of 1860; Honor; Lincoln, Abraham (1809–1865); Nonslaveholding Southerners; Politics; Slaveholding Women.

References and Further Reading
Barney, William. 1974. *The Secessionist Impulse: Alabama and Mississippi in 1860.* Princeton, NJ: Princeton University Press.
Channing, Steven. 1970. *A Crisis of Fear: Secession in South Carolina.* New York: Simon & Schuster.
Crofts, Daniel. 1989. *Reluctant Confederates: Upper South Unionists in the Secession Crisis.* Chapel Hill: University of North Carolina Press.
Link, William. 2003. *Roots of Secession: Slavery and Politics in Antebellum Virginia.* Chapel Hill: University of North Carolina Press.
Olsen, Christopher. 2000. *Political Culture and Secession in Mississippi: Masculinity, Honor, and the Antiparty Tradition, 1830–1860.* New York: Oxford University Press.
Sinha, Manisha. 2000. *Counterrevolution of Slavery: Politics and Ideology in Antebellum South Carolina.* Chapel Hill: University of North Carolina Press.
Wooster, Ralph. 1962. *The Secession Conventions of the South.* Princeton, NJ: Princeton University Press.

Separate Spheres

Historians know from military records, diaries, and a host of other sources that women on both sides of the Civil War both challenged and conformed to their allotted sphere by serving as nurses, physicians, vivandières, sutlers, soldiers, and spies. Women provided soldiers with food, provisions, and liquor. They tended wounds, rolled bandages, and administered to the sick and injured in countless ways. Women organized fundraising events on the homefront, peddled goods and sex to soldiers on the frontlines, and even occasionally disguised themselves as men to fight as soldiers.

The concept of separate spheres was first identified in the early republic. Society began to associate the home and child rearing with women, as politics and other public activities became men's domain. As the young nation began to industrialize, production that was once in the home shifted to the workshop and then to the factory. Native-born American women competed with immigrants for factory jobs that they were expected to leave after marriage. Women in the rural South were more connected to the land and its work, and slave women were connected to their master's holdings. Even so, Americans felt the increased pace of life, and women found their new sphere defined as the home. White women of the South had their sphere defined by men as a part of the proslavery defense. Southern women generally avoided any claims that resisted patriarchal power. Most Southern women maintained traditional roles on Southern farms and plantations until economic circumstances mandated a change in their sphere.

African American women, both enslaved and free, found their sphere to have different meanings than that of white women. Free black women stayed in the workforce longer and were often forced by economic necessity and frequent separation from spouses to return to the workforce throughout their adult lives. Enslaved women found that their sphere held a double burden that included working for the master and then working for their families.

Working-class women of the North and slaves of the South could hardly expect to leave the workforce, but ruling the domestic space was strictly a woman's sphere. In the home, the doctrine of separate spheres celebrated the new status of middle-class women and highlighted their distinctive character where their role was dependent on their spouses' potential in the workforce. Women were urged by prescriptive literature, novels, and even sermons to reach for the Christian virtues of humility, submission, piety, and charity. These became quintessentially female traits that gave them a sphere of moral superiority.

The ideals of the domestic sphere and of what was called true womanhood enabled pious middle-class women to assist and uplift the war efforts.

Women had been at the forefront of peace, temperance, abolition, and moral reform movements during the antebellum years, and continuing this mission into the war years was a natural extension. Woman's sphere was a new social space that was limited and private but also an improvement over the colonial model of having no space at all. However, during the Civil War women were forced to take on new roles outside their "proper" sphere, and some women saw it as an opportunity for liberating growth.

Maneuvering within nineteenth-century society's idea of women's sphere, Sarah Josepha Hale, editor of the *Ladies Magazine* and later *Godey's Lady's Book,* called for women to take charge of the domestic sphere. Women were expected to remain in the home while their income-earning husbands worked in offices, stores, or professions. The woman's sphere, wrote Hale in the *Ladies Magazine,* was a "nobler" one, attuned to female values and character. It was the power base from which influence could emanate while moral superiority was preserved, uncorrupted.

Religion was one of the few activities beyond the home in which women could participate without seeming to violate their sphere. As a result, women provided many of the social services associated with the Civil War. In the name of Christianity, women organized sanitary fairs, rolled bandages, led prayer meetings, and organized a host of social events to raise money for their respective causes, using their sphere to advocate for increased benevolence and reform. Both Northern and Southern women founded orphanages, asylums, and other charitable organizations. Women extended the ideas of domesticity and feminine moral superiority by organizing sanitary fairs in order to ship medical aid, food, and suitable reading material to the front lines.

Many Civil War women found themselves challenging their sphere out of the necessity of taking over their husband's or father's work. Women were compelled to run farms and small businesses as the men left for the front. Northern industries, which had in many cases refused to hire women, suddenly found that women could provide a ready workforce for their factories. Working in a factory kept working-class women from idleness and taught them industriousness; so it was seen as acceptable. Furthermore, in most cases, society expected that women would return to full-time domesticity at the conclusion of hostilities.

In the South, women also took on a public role during wartime. Like their Northern counterparts, they rolled bandages and made clothes for their soldiers. Even young academy girls reported suspending studies to make Confederate uniforms. This type of work was taken up on plantations and in towns throughout the South by white and slave women. White Southern women also found themselves negotiating ideals of appropriate behavior in the face of pressing national needs and the needs of their own families. Southern women also took over farms, plantations, and small businesses, and they went to work in armories.

In both the North and South, tending to the sick had been well within a woman's sphere of domesticity. However, the vast numbers of wartime casualties took women out of home nursing and placed them in military hospitals, where nearly two thousand women on both sides of the conflict served as volunteers. Female nurses faced the horrors of the battlefield as they provided invaluable aid to sick and wounded soldiers. Although Louisa May Alcott recorded her nursing experience in a best-selling book, most women nurses toiled anonymously except for their names on muster roles. Among the first to respond to wartime needs with professionally trained nurses were the Sisters of Charity led by Elizabeth Ann Seton. Maintaining a strict code of neutrality, the sisters served on both sides of the war. But the two hundred and eighty nuns were quickly overwhelmed by the numbers of casualties, and the militaries were forced to rely on other women volunteers. In professionalizing the nursing corps, Dorothea Dix agreed with the army that nurses would conform to their sphere by emphasizing purity through plain dress. Other women took prominent medical roles on the battlefield. In addition to her own work on the front lines, Clara Barton raised funds to take women to the front lines in supporting roles, and, after the war, she established the American Red Cross.

One of the greatest challenges to a woman's sphere was from women in the medical profession. By midcentury, physicians' allopathic medical schools were beginning to replace preceptor training, so it is unclear how many women may have been trained as physicians by fathers or husbands. Women physicians were initially rejected by the military because of their sex. As a result, Dr. Mary Edwards Walker began her military service in the Union nursing corps because that was the only place for women. She was finally hired as a contract physician to an Ohio regiment, where she challenged her sphere by wearing men's clothing and working alongside male surgeons. Edwards also took advantage of her position, easily passing back and forth between the Union and Confederacy and reporting her findings to the Union army. Her dangerous exploits led Congress to award her the Congressional Medal of Honor after the war.

Civil War women challenged the ideals of the domestic spheres in other ways as well. Usually the wives and daughters of officers, vivandières performed hospitality functions. Although providing wounded soldiers with brandy in some ways conformed to the ideals of the domestic sphere, vivandières challenged their sphere by traveling in dangerous territory and occasionally fighting alongside men. These women traveled with soldiers for little or no pay, providing troops on both sides with supplies. They wore men's pants under a colorful knee-length skirt and military jackets often trimmed in lace. While most vivandières returned home during the winter months, many stayed at or near the front lines providing brandy, water, and food for soldiers. They became, in many cases, front-line nurses.

Women also became wartime entrepreneurs. Female sutlers followed the troops of both sides selling goods and sometimes sexual favors for cash and barter. These women both conformed to and challenged their sphere. Providing for the domestic needs of men had always been part of a woman's sphere, and accepting compensation for these services did not seem to violate anyone's sense of morality. Soldiers could pay sutlers for additional rations, mending of uniforms, cleaning of tents, and even sexual favors.

Women aided the war effort on both sides as spies, quickly earning a reputation for gaining and passing reliable information to military officials. Female spies used preconceived ideas about women and their domesticity to their advantage. For example, while conforming to her feminine sphere as a notable Washington hostess, Rose O'Neal Greenhow collected information for the Confederacy. In addition, women successfully smuggled information through the lines by hiding it in their skirts, bodices, hairdos, shoes, and other places that male soldiers were not likely to search. Southerner Elizabeth Howland, while stressing her role as a mother, placed information inside a ham bone and had her children carry it across the border. In Richmond, Unionist Elizabeth Van Lew entertained enemy officials and visited wounded soldiers and prisoners, gathering valuable information in the process, which she later delivered to Union officials.

African American women similarly used society's assumptions about their place and race to collect information. When performing their traditional duties as house servants, these women seemed harmless to those they served. However, some slave women listened in on strategic conversations between Confederate officers and then passed the details on to Union officials. Runaway slave Harriet Tubman, better-known for her activities on the Underground Railroad, worked as a Union cook and nurse during the Civil War. She organized African Americans in the areas in which she was stationed to report on Confederate troop movements.

The Civil War gave Northern and Southern women of all classes an opportunity to expand their horizons and broaden their domestic sphere. While maintaining the appearance of performing as "true women," women successfully took on new roles during wartime. They expanded their sphere and managed to run businesses and farms, care for casualties, and spy. After the war, many women used their newly acquired sense of independence to expand their concept of the domestic sphere to include the work of progressive reform, temperance, and women's suffrage.

Jill M. Nussel

See also African American Women; Aid Societies; Barton, Clara (1821–1912); Civilian Life; Confederate Homefront; Dix, Dorothea Lynde (1802–1887); Domesticity; Factory Workers, Northern; Factory Workers, Southern; Fairs and Bazaars; Family Life, Confederate; Family Life, Union; Farm Work; Female Combatants; Female Spies; Fundraising; Greenhow, Rose O'Neal (ca. 1814–1864); Hale, Sarah Josepha (1788–1879); Hospitals; Hospital Ships; Northern Women; Nurses; Politics; Prostitution; Slave Families; Teachers, Northern; Teachers, Southern; Religion; Southern Women; Treasury Girls; Tubman, Harriet [Araminta Ross] (1822–1913); Union Homefront; United States Sanitary Commission; Van Lew, Elizabeth (1818–1900); Vivandières; Walker, Mary Edwards (1832–1919); Wartime Employment; Wounded, Visits to.

References and Further Reading

Alcott, Louisa May. 1863. *Hospital Sketches.* Boston: James Redpath.

Attie, Jeannie. 1998. *Patriotic Toil: Northern Women and the American Civil War.* Ithaca, NY: Cornell University Press.

Degler, Carl. 1980. *At Odds: Women and the Family from the Revolution to the Present.* New York: Oxford University Press.

Forbes, Ella. 1998. *African American Women during the Civil War.* New York: Garland Publishing.

Genovese, Elizabeth Fox. 1988. *Within the Plantation Household: Black and White Women of the Old South.* Chapel Hill: University of North Carolina Press.

Leonard, Elizabeth D. 1999. *All the Daring of the Soldier: Women of the Civil War Armies.* New York: W. W. Norton & Company.

Ryan, Mary P. 1981. *Cradle of the Middle Class: The Family in Oneida County, New York, 1790–1865.* New York: Cambridge University Press.

Whites, LeeAnn. 1995. *The Civil War as a Crisis in Gender: Augusta, Georgia, 1860–1890.* Athens: University of Georgia Press.

Sewing Bees

Sewing bees, which during the antebellum era had served primarily as social gatherings for women, offered unique opportunities for women to participate in the Civil War. Both Northern and Southern women organized sewing bees in an effort to sew and knit uniforms, blankets, flags, and tents and to provide farewell feasts for their soldiers. As they gathered together to sew for their soldiers, women developed organizations that contributed to the support of their men in the Union and Confederate armies.

At antebellum sewing bees, women not only sewed and quilted but also discussed family affairs, cooking, and other life experiences. On certain occasions sewing bees functioned as community entertainment, where all gathered in a festive atmosphere and celebrated with singing and dancing. Women alternated between sewing and preparing the evening repast. Sewing bees also presented courtship opportunities and provided an opportunity for women to bond and neighbors to commune.

The Civil War changed the nature of sewing bees, which presented women an opportunity to participate in the war. Women wanted to contribute to the war effort and to support their embattled brethren, and, for many, needles became their weapons of choice. Most who participated in sewing circles came from upper- and middle-class households. Often officers' wives rallied community women to gather together to sew needed materials. In the South, members of sewing circles were women of the slaveholding elite. Frequently plantation mistresses delegated sewing duties to their slave women, to whom they assigned the most arduous task of sewing tents. Other than compulsory slave contributions, prominent sewing circles excluded black women from participation, even in the North.

Sewing circles began as intimate gatherings but quickly expanded during the war, spurring the development of women's organizations. Women's clubs and organizations had been prevalent in the antebellum North, and many women had experience in missionary organizations and moral groups. Accustomed to participating in official ladies' organizations and advocacy groups, Northern women quickly extended their organizational skills to their sewing circles. In the South, formal women's organizations were virtually nonexistent during the antebellum period. However, the Civil War significantly impacted the ability of Southern women to organize and work in unison for a united cause.

Sewing circles were transformed from minor establishments—in both the North and the South—to large-scale organizations with officers,

Sewing Circle during the Civil War making havelocks for the Volunteers. Engraving by Winslow Homer, 1861. (Bettmann/Corbis)

constitutions, and dues. While sewing circles welcomed women of all ages, a hierarchy existed, with matrons holding the leadership positions. Various ladies' aid associations, soldiers' friends' associations, and soldiers' aid societies were established across the North and the South, through which women provided support for their troops. They produced many necessary supplies. For example, women in Quincy, Florida, provided 420 blankets to a local company of soldiers. Additionally, between 1862 and 1863, Florida's sewing societies fashioned 3,735 pairs of cotton drawers, 2,765 cotton shirts, 169 woolen jackets and coats, 809 woolen pantaloons, and 1,000 pairs of cotton socks.

As the war progressed, soldiers' needs increased. The war's duration and devastation left raw materials such as wool and cotton in short supply, especially in the Confederacy. Members of sewing circles resorted to recycling household fabrics including tablecloths, napkins, towels, and carpeting from their own homes.

Ladies' aid societies expanded their services to meet the soldiers' needs. They hosted community fairs to raise funds for the purchase of supplies that could not be fashioned from raw materials or recycled. Women's organizations, both in the North and South, coordinated entertainment events featuring poetry readings and plays. They sold homemade crafts and foodstuffs. For example, the October 1863 Chicago Sanitary Fair raised $100,000, the June 1864 Pittsburgh fair raised $320,000, and the April 1864 New York Metropolitan Fair raised a record-breaking $2 million for Union hospitals and troops. Furthermore, local and state governments entrusted these women's organizations with supplies and money, knowing that they would distribute them to needy soldiers.

The experience women gained through their work in wartime organizations helped broaden their activism and participation in polity. For the first time, many women spoke in public, voiced their opinions, and rallied support for a common cause.

Dawn M. Sherman

See also Aid Societies; Confederate Homefront; Domesticity; Fairs and Bazaars; Fundraising; Northern Women; Separate Spheres; Southern Women; Union Homefront; United States Sanitary Commission.

References and Further Reading

Faust, Drew Gilpin. 1996. *Mothers of Invention: Women of the Slaveholding South in the American Civil War.* Chapel Hill: University of North Carolina Press.

Revels, Tracy. 2004. *Grander in Her Daughters: Florida's Women during the Civil War.* Columbia: University of South Carolina Press.

Silber, Nina. 2005. *Daughters of the Union: Northern Women Fight the Civil War.* Cambridge, MA: Harvard University Press.

Shaw, Sarah Blake Sturgis (1835–1902)

Abolitionist Sarah Blake Sturgis Shaw interacted with the intellectual and social elite of her time. Her son, Robert Gould Shaw, gained fame for his leadership of the United States' first colored unit, the Massachusetts Fifty-fourth Infantry Regiment.

Sarah Blake Sturgis was born in Massachusetts on August 13, 1815. The Sturgis family was one of

Massachusetts' most elite and wealthy families. Thus, Sarah received an excellent education and was exposed to many progressively minded individuals. On June 9, 1835, Sarah married Francis Shaw, another member of the Boston elite. Together, Francis and Sarah became active in promoting social changes through their involvement in the evangelical wing of the Unitarian Church. In 1838, they joined William Lloyd Garrison's radical abolitionist group, the American Anti-Slavery Society. They also provided aid to assist runaway slaves in establishing a free life in the North.

During the course of their marriage, Sarah and Francis had five children. In the 1840s, they moved their family to West Roxbury, Massachusetts. Their new property bordered the experimental and radical communal living establishment of Brook Farm. Their proximity to Brook Farm allowed the family to socialize with some of the most progressive intellectuals of their time. Sarah frequently attended lectures on abolitionism and women's rights, and she formed close friendships with Lydia Maria Child and Margaret Fuller.

In 1847, Sarah went to New York to receive medical treatment for her failing eyesight and overall poor health. She responded well to treatments and regained her vision. Due to her progress, the family decided to permanently relocate to Staten Island. After the family's European tour from 1851 to 1855, sectional turmoil in the United States increased Sarah's and Francis's involvement in the abolitionist movement.

When the Civil War began, Sarah and Francis's son, Robert Gould Shaw, enlisted in the Union army. After President Abraham Lincoln issued the Emancipation Proclamation in January 1863 and called for the formation of African American regiments, Francis utilized his connections to help establish the United States Colored Troops (USCT). To Francis and Sarah's delight, the army offered Robert a commission as colonel of the first African American regiment, the Fifty-fourth Massachusetts. To his parents' dismay, Robert initially declined the offer, but he quickly changed his mind and accepted the commission.

The Shaw family's elation over Robert's commission soon faded with the realities of wartime. In July 1863, Robert was killed while leading his men in an attack on South Carolina's Fort Wagner. Confederates unceremoniously tossed Robert's body into a mass grave with the African American soldiers he had led. This incident provided a rallying point for Northerners supporting the abolitionist causes of the war, and it promoted the heroics of the USCT. Sarah took comfort in the knowledge that her beloved son died as a martyr for the cause to which she had devoted much of her time and energy.

Sarah Shaw continued her activism for social progress with such causes as women's rights and anti-imperialism until her death on New Year's Eve in 1902.

Kristina Dunn

See also Abolitionism and Northern Reformers; Antislavery Societies; Child, Lydia Maria Francis; Emancipation Proclamation (January 1, 1863); Garrison, William Lloyd (1805–1879); Northern Women; Union Homefront; Unitarian Women.

References and Further Reading

Waugh, Joan. 1997. *Unsentimental Reformer: The Life of Josephine Shaw Lowell.* Cambridge, MA: Harvard University Press.

Sheads, Carrie (n.d.–1884)

During the Battle of Gettysburg, Carrie Sheads converted her school into a makeshift hospital and served as its superintendent. After the battle, she distinguished herself by providing constant nursing care for wounded soldiers. When a Union officer was threatened with execution, she successfully intervened on his behalf. In recognition of her dedicated service and contribution to the war effort, the Federal government awarded Carrie a clerk position after the Civil War. Carrie's family experienced devastating personal losses on behalf of the Union cause for which they were accorded special recognition.

Caroline Sheads was descended from John Troxell, Gettysburg's first settler and a proprietor of a tavern. A large extended family, the Sheadses played an important role in the development of the borough. In 1859, Carrie purchased three acres near the town's Lutheran Theological Seminary. She opened Oak Ridge Seminary, a school for girls, in a house built by her father. On July 1, 1863, the

Battle of Gettysburg erupted near the school. When the wounded began to flow in, Carrie and her family opened their home to the injured, treating over seventy severely wounded combatants.

Among the soldiers who found their way to Carrie's school was Colonel Charles Wheelock, commander of the Ninety-seventh New York Infantry. Surrounded by Confederates, Wheelock waved a white handkerchief in surrender. In the chaos of battle, Confederate infantry began to fire on him and his men. Carrie had provided the officer with a large white cloth, which allowed him to signify his intent to surrender. After the Union captives were confined inside the school, a Confederate officer demanded Wheelock's sword. Despite the threat of execution, the colonel adamantly refused. Carrie intervened and appealed to both of the officers, begging the Southern soldier to avoid further bloodshed and Wheelock to compromise his principles. During a moment of confusion, Carrie hid the sword and thus averted a tragedy.

Throughout the battle, Carrie and her family continued to nurse the wounded. When the Confederates began to remove their prisoners of war, Carrie appealed for assistance in caring for those under her charge. When the commanding officer offered her three of his captives as nurses, she successfully lobbied for five. For several weeks after the battle, Carrie continued to supervise her hospital.

Carrie and her family suffered many losses during the war. Her school suffered severe damage at the time of the battle. Four of her brothers served in the Union army: two perished during the war, one died of tuberculosis after his discharge, and one received a wound that shortened his life. Carrie's mother and sister died soon after the war. In recognition of her many sacrifices, Carrie Sheads received a clerkship in the Treasury Department after the war. She died in 1884 and was buried in the Sheads family plot in Evergreen Cemetery.

Karen Kinzey

See also Gettysburg, Battle of (July 1–3, 1863); Teachers, Northern.
References and Further Reading
Black, Linda. 1994. "Three Heroines of Gettysburg." *Gettysburg Magazine* 11:119–125.

Moore, Frank. 1866. *Women of the War: Their Heroism and Self-Sacrifice.* Chicago: R. C. Treat.

Sheridan, Philip Henry (1831–1888)

A professional soldier whose career spanned much of the nineteenth century, Philip Henry Sheridan is best known for his service during the Civil War and the Indian Wars. Given command of an army in the Shenandoah Valley in 1864, he defeated opposing Confederate forces but became infamous for his harsh treatment of civilians. Sheridan served in Louisiana during Reconstruction, advocating a hard hand against former Confederates. Transferred to the West, he planned ruthless campaigns against Native American tribes. Before his death in 1888, he was promoted to general of the army.

Born March 6, 1831, Sheridan graduated from West Point in 1853. He was assigned to duty on the frontier, where he led a small unit of dragoons and learned to track and fight Native Americans. Sheridan rose in the ranks at the start of the Civil War, eventually taking charge of an infantry division. He fought at the battles of Perryville, Stones River, Chickamauga, and Chattanooga in the Western theater.

In 1864, assigned to lead the Army of the Potomac's Cavalry Corps, Sheridan advocated the use of the mounted soldiers as a cohesive unit. Instead of guarding wagons, he reasoned, the cavalry should be a functional, fighting arm of the main army. Sheridan proved the success of his strategy when his cavalry corps scattered rebel defenders at the Battle of Yellow Tavern, a few miles north of Richmond and, in the process, mortally wounded famed Confederate General J.E.B. Stuart.

After Confederate General Jubal Early's raid into Maryland in July 1864, Sheridan bested him at the battles of Third Winchester, Fisher's Hill, and Cedar Creek. Aside from Early's army, Sheridan was greatly concerned with Confederate partisans behind Union lines. Ably led by John Singleton Mosby, the rebel guerrillas disrupted Union supplies, kidnapped officers, and killed Federal troops. Sheridan had little sympathy for civilians, men or women, who supported the Confederate guerrilla troops by supplying

Union General Philip H. Sheridan. (National Archives and Records Administration)

food, information, and shelter. Ordering the destruction of private property and the confiscation of available supplies in areas that the guerrillas were known to frequent, Sheridan believed that those who supported the war behind the lines should also feel its most direct consequences.

In 1865, Sheridan was instrumental in forcing Confederate general Robert E. Lee to surrender at Appomattox. After the war, Sheridan oversaw the reconstruction of the former Confederate states of Texas and Louisiana. His hard-line approach toward former Rebels earned him the enmity of many Southerners. Transferred west to fight Native Americans, Sheridan brought his harsh war measures to the Great Plains.

Philip Sheridan died on August 5, 1888, at the age of fifty-seven. He left many admirers as well as enemies.

Kanisorn Wongsrichanalai

See also Chickamauga, Battle of (September 19–20, 1863); Confederate Homefront; Destruction of Homes; Destruction of Personal Property; Lee, Robert Edward (1807–1870); Military Invasion and

Occupation; Mosby's Rangers; Reconstruction (1865–1877); Sheridan's Shenandoah Valley Campaign (1864); Southern Women.

References and Further Reading

Hutton, Paul Andrew. 1985. *Phil Sheridan and His Army.* Lincoln: University of Nebraska Press.

Morris, Roy. 1992. *Sheridan: The Life and Wars of General Phil Sheridan.* New York: Crown.

Sheridan's Shenandoah Valley Campaign (1864)

Always an important strategic base because of its location as well as its rich agricultural lands and railway lines that helped supply the Confederacy, Virginia's Shenandoah Valley proved to be a contested area throughout the Civil War. Home to many families, the valley changed hands multiple times during the course of the war. As a result, civilians constantly dealt with soldiers of both sides as well as with shortages and the dangers of living in a war zone. During the 1864 campaign, Shenandoah Valley civilians faced destruction on a new level.

Determined to permanently cut General Robert E. Lee off from the benefits of the Shenandoah Valley, Union General Ulysses S. Grant ordered a full-scale attack on the area in 1864. In early August 1864, Grant created the Department and Army of the Shenandoah. He put Philip H. Sheridan in charge, ordering him to destroy Confederate forces under Jubal A. Early. In addition, Grant urged Sheridan to devastate the Shenandoah Valley, which provided food and resources for Lee's Army of Northern Virginia; Grant wanted the valley laid barren. Sheridan and his soldiers took these orders to heart. Throughout the offensive, Sheridan's thirty-five thousand men burned crops and barns as they drove off the livestock. They also attacked Southern homes, seizing foodstuffs and personal property in the process. The nearly five-month campaign resulted in more than twenty-five thousand casualties.

Sheridan and Early met on the battlefield on several occasions in the fight for the Shenandoah Valley. Their men skirmished throughout August as both sides jockeyed for position and information on the other. When a Unionist Quaker schoolteacher in Winchester, Rebecca Wright, alerted Sheridan that Lee had recalled one of his divisions from the valley to help protect Richmond and Petersburg, Sheridan realized he had gained a two-to-one advantage over his enemy, and he prepared to attack. On September 19, the two armies clashed in Winchester, Sheridan's troops initiating the fighting with an attack on Confederate defenses. Although the Union forces initially struggled, partially due to a bungled order, after several days of fighting they ultimately drove the Confederates into a retreat. Both sides suffered casualties of approximately fifty-five hundred, a number more damaging to the Confederate forces that had begun the battle with only fifteen thousand men.

After defeating the Confederates, Sheridan's men moved through the Shenandoah Valley destroying all food, farming implements, livestock, and raw goods, fulfilling Grant's orders to devastate the valley. By October, Sheridan reported having destroyed more than two thousand barns and seventy mills with their contents of wheat, hay, flour, and farming tools. In addition, he estimated that he had driven out, issued to his troops, or killed more than four thousand head of stock and three thousand sheep. The soldiers' attack on homefront resources continued for as long as the troops remained in the area. Although orders held that men should burn only barns and public buildings, soldiers often burned homes as well.

In attacking Confederate food resources, Union troops also destroyed civilian property and food. Often before burning a home, they invaded it and destroyed valuable and sentimental property. They expanded their mandate to destroy anything that could assist the Confederate war effort and demolished or stole women's wardrobes, fine china, silver candlesticks, glass vases, private journals, sewing supplies, and fancy linens. In addition, to get to these personal items, Union soldiers often ransacked women's bedrooms and private chambers, unleashing the ire of many white Southern women. Although soldiers commented on the effect of their actions on female civilians, few sympathized with the plight of Rebel women. Like their commander, they believed that these women had brought the destruction upon themselves by supporting the Confederacy, its soldiers, and its government.

Civilians also faced the problems of living in an area frequented by Southern guerrillas who trailed behind the Union forces. Not only did these guerrillas burn Union wagon trains, but they also shot at teamsters, stragglers, and couriers. In addition, many guerrillas, as they moved through the valley, seized the personal property and foodstuffs of its residents. Sheridan sent a detachment to deal with the guerrillas, but they remained a persistent problem.

After destroying what resources remained in the Shenandoah Valley, Sheridan and his troops headed north in mid-October. Then, in the early morning hours on October 19, Early's troops attacked Sheridan's army, which was encamped at Cedar Creek. Sheridan, who was asleep miles away in Winchester when the fighting began, hurried to his men as soon as the noises and the news of the battle reached him. By the time Sheridan arrived, Union soldiers had been driven from their camps and were retreating. However, the general quickly reorganized and galvanized his men. They resumed the fighting and eventually defeated the Confederates. Early's retreat after Cedar Creek ultimately allowed Union forces to hold the Shenandoah Valley for the remainder of the war. Although Early and his troops attempted to drive Union forces from the Shenandoah Valley again in mid-November, they could not do so. The Shenandoah Valley remained in Union hands for the remainder of the war.

White Southern women who encountered and read about the defeats and destruction in the Shenandoah Valley refused to sit back and watch events unfold around them. For example, in December 1864, twenty-eight women in Harrisonburg, Virginia, wrote to Confederate Secretary of War James A. Seddon, offering to form their own regiment to fight the Union. They vowed to arm and equip women between the ages of sixteen and forty and to do anything to help the Confederacy.

Sheridan's victory in the Shenandoah Valley, combined with Union General William Tecumseh Sherman's capture and evacuation of Atlanta, helped secure Abraham Lincoln's re-election in November.

Lisa Tendrich Frank

References and Further Reading
Frank, Lisa Tendrich. 2005. "War Comes Home: Confederate Women and Union Soldiers." In *Virginia's Civil War*, edited by Peter Wallenstein and Bertram Wyatt-Brown, 123–136. Charlottesville: University of Virginia Press.
Gallagher, Gary W., ed. 2006. *The Shenandoah Valley Campaign of 1864*. Chapel Hill: University of North Carolina Press.
Grimsley, Mark. 1995. *The Hard Hand of War: Union Military Policy toward Southern Civilians, 1861–1865*. New York: Cambridge University Press.

See also Atlanta, Evacuation of (Special Field Orders, Number 67); Confederate Homefront; Destruction of Homes; Destruction of Personal Property; Domesticity; Military Invasion and Occupation; Separate Spheres; Sheridan, Philip Henry (1831–1888); Sherman's Campaign (1864–1865); Southern Women.

Sherman, Ellen Boyle Ewing (1824–1888)

Ellen Ewing was the wife of United States General William T. Sherman.

Born in Lancaster, Ohio, she was the daughter of leading Whig politician Thomas Ewing and his intensely religious wife Maria Boyle Ewing. It was primarily because of her mother that Ellen gained her intense devotion to Catholicism (her father never became a Catholic). Her religious zeal for the Catholic Church was the greatest influence in her life. When she and future husband William T. Sherman were courting in the 1840s, his inability to accept her faith caused much heartache in their relationship and came close to preventing their marriage. Even after their nuptials in 1850, she constantly badgered him about his lack of faith, once even telling him that the only thing that kept him from reaching perfection was his refusal to become a Catholic.

Throughout their married lives, Ellen Sherman was both an important support and a major burden. In addition to constantly battling her husband about his lack of Catholicism, she insisted, early in their marriage, that they live in Lancaster, close to her father, even pressuring her husband to become manager of a salt mine so that they could remain nearby. He wanted his independence, and, after leaving the army in 1854, he became a banker in San Francisco. She did not want to accompany him, and, as a compromise, she left their first-born daughter with her parents in Ohio to assuage their grief at her departure for California. After a time there, Ellen left her husband and two children behind, and she went home to Ohio for an extended visit. She also suffered from several chronic illnesses and regularly complained about them. Although William was a very sociable person, Ellen refused to attend social functions with him, usually insisting that her health problems prevented her from doing so.

When William Sherman suffered anxiety and depression over the military situation in Kentucky at the start of the Civil War and almost lost his generalship as a result, Ellen led the intensive family effort on her husband's behalf to convince Federal officials, including President Abraham Lincoln, to maintain their support of him. Throughout the war and even more obviously afterward, she gave her husband the freedom to live his life to the fullest, while she remained at home as his anchor, maintaining home and family. Theirs was a combative relationship but one that served them both. While he showed interest in several other women, he never thought of not being married to her. Their major marriage conflict in the postwar years, one that caused a temporary separation, was over their son becoming a Jesuit priest. Sherman saw this young man as future family head and blamed his wife for allowing her church to take him.

William T. and Ellen Sherman remained loyal to one another until the end. He expressed it best, as he rushed to her deathbed in the New York home he had bought for her. "Wait for me, Ellen, no one ever loved you as I loved you."

John F. Marszalek

See also Catholic Women; Northern Women; Sherman, William Tecumseh (1820–1891).
References and Further Reading
Marszalek, John F. 1993. *Sherman: A Soldier's Passion for Order*. New York: Free Press. (Paperback edition 1993. New York: Vintage.)
Marszalek, John F. 2001. "General and Mrs. William T. Sherman, A Contentious Union." In *Intimate Strategies of the Civil War, Military Commanders and Their Wives*, edited by Carol K. Bleser and

Lesley J. Gordon, 138–156. New York: Oxford University Press.

McAllister, Anna. 1936. *Ellen Sherman, Wife of General Sherman.* New York: Benziger Brothers.

Sherman Land (Special Field Orders, Number 15)

Special Field Orders, Number Fifteen established a land policy to deal with the growing numbers of runaway slaves who attached themselves to the Union armies. African American men could apply for forty acres of land—nicknamed Sherman Land for the author of the policy—on which to settle their families.

In November 1864, Union General William Tecumseh Sherman advanced his armies overland from Atlanta to Savannah, Georgia. Thousands of slaves took the opportunity to claim their freedom and to follow the army. The growing number of black refugees hindered the rapid movement of the troops and exposed them to possible Confederate attacks.

Former slaves following Sherman's army faced a tragedy in late 1864. On December 8, Union Brevet Major General Jefferson C. Davis ordered his troops to take up the pontoon train before the black refugees crossed over Ebenezer Creek, Georgia, with the military. Fearing capture by Confederate troops and a forced return to slavery, many refugees panicked and tried to cross the flooded creek. As a result, a number of them drowned, despite efforts of individual soldiers to save them. Reporters and soldiers sent home accounts of the deaths and of Sherman's and his commanders' careless attitudes toward black refugees.

On January 11, 1865, United States Secretary of War Edwin Stanton and Adjutant General Lorenzo Thomas arrived in Savannah to meet with Sherman and representatives of Savannah's black community. Their discussion focused on the affair at Ebenezer Creek and Union soldiers' attitudes toward blacks during Sherman's campaign.

To settle the matter of refugees following the armies and to cover the administration from any future damaging statements, Stanton, Sherman, and Thomas worked on an order to resettle the freedpeo-ple. Special Field Orders, Number Fifteen set aside the abandoned lands on the Sea Islands as well as the land stretching thirty miles inland from Charleston, South Carolina, to Jacksonville, Florida, for the settlement of freedpeople without white interference. Each black male head of household received forty acres within this territory. Freedpeople rushed to claim their land. Female heads of household, not an uncommon sight in wartime or slavery, found it difficult to stake their claim to the land because Union officials did not recognize their position as head of household. To assist families in settlement, officials promised extra mules for distribution to farmers and appointed Brigadier General Rufus Saxton Inspector of Settlements and Plantations.

Sherman may have seen the land allotments as a temporary measure, yet others viewed the so-called Sherman grants as an important step toward complete emancipation. "Forty acres and a mule" became a clarion call for future reparations to former slaves. Land allotments to freedpeople continued through the Freedmen's Bureau until 1866. However, when President Andrew Johnson pardoned former Confederates, he also returned land to white property owners. The repatriation of Confederates forced approximately forty thousand freedpeople from Sherman land.

William H. Brown

See also Abolitionism and Northern Reformers: African American Women; Freedmen's Bureau; Reconstruction (1865–1877); Sherman's Campaign (1864–1865); Sherman, William Tecumseh (1820–1891).

References and Further Reading

Foner, Eric. 1988. *Reconstruction: America's Unfinished Revolution, 1863–1877.* New York: Harper & Row.

Marszalek, John F. 1993. *Sherman: A Soldier's Passion for Order.* New York: Free Press.

McPherson, James M. 1988. *Battle Cry of Freedom: The Civil War Era.* New York: Oxford University Press.

Oubre, Claude F. 1978. *Forty Acres and a Mule: The Freedman's Bureau and Black Landownership.* Baton Rouge: Louisiana State University Press.

Sherman, William T. 1875. *Memoirs of General William T. Sherman.* 2 vols. New York: D. Appleton & Co.

Sherman's Campaign (1864–1865)

In late 1864 and early 1865, Union General William Tecumseh Sherman carried out what was termed a hard war campaign on civilians in Georgia and the Carolinas. Sherman and sixty thousand soldiers marched through the fertile plantation area of the South, living off the land and working to destroy the Confederacy's material as well as moral support. Throughout the march, Union soldiers confronted elite Confederate women who had remained in their homes and on their plantations.

After capturing Atlanta on September 2, 1864, Sherman established a command post in the city. His Special Field Orders, Number 67, issued on September 8, evacuated the city of its largely female civilian population. On November 15, Union troops left Atlanta, burning all places of military importance, including depots, factories, foundries, and machine shops. Southern reports asserted that the fires also engulfed many homes and much personal property. The destruction continued as Sherman's troops marched to Savannah and northward into the Carolinas.

Throughout the campaign, Sherman divided his men into two wings, spread them across a sixty-mile-wide path, and marched between ten and fifteen miles daily. This tactic forced Confederate armies to spread their resources thinly as they tried to guess the path of the enemy. The campaign had several skirmishes but few casualties. Union troops foraged for what they needed and destroyed whatever was left to keep it from the Confederates. Union troops left the Southern countryside strewn with twisted railroad ties, the remnants of burnt houses and crops, dead animals, and trampled land. Officials designated a group of men as foragers, called bummers, but units in the main columns as well as individuals also gathered their own food and war treasures. Soldiers took as souvenirs women's personal property: clothes, letters, diaries, linens, jewelry, silver, and household items. Southern women railed at the indignity of having their personal space invaded and their personal effects taken by enemy men. Soldiers often sent captured Southern "treasures" home to loved ones and dropped others on the side of the road when they became too cumbersome.

Marching across the lower South gave Sherman and his men the opportunity to witness and to affect slavery. The troops, often indirectly, freed the slaves that they encountered. African Americans cheered as Union troops passed, followed them as camp followers, and even became spies for Sherman's army. Not all Union soldiers embraced their roles as liberators. Many raped the black women whom they encountered, and others felt burdened by the African American camp followers. When Union General Jefferson C. Davis's troops crossed Ebenezer Creek, for example, they removed a pontoon bridge before African American escapees could cross with them. Many of the black camp followers drowned trying to cross the bridgeless creek.

Sherman's troops cut through most of Georgia by December 10, 1864. They demanded the surrender of Savannah on December 17, besieging the city until the Confederate army abandoned it on December 21. Union troops took control of the city, and Sherman sent President Abraham Lincoln a telegram offering Savannah as a Christmas present. Sherman used Savannah to demonstrate that peaceful surrender would protect Southerners from Union destruction. He opened his headquarters to visitors, allowed the local government to function, and brought food into the city. Sherman expressed surprise that his conciliatory attitude did little to soften that of Southern women, who still defiantly proclaimed Confederate loyalties. Many refused to walk under the United States flag wherever it hung or to speak with occupying soldiers. From Savannah, Sherman issued Special Field Orders, Number 15, granting freedpeople full control of the Sea Islands as well as coastal land thirty miles inland from Charleston to Jacksonville. Sherman and his troops left Savannah on February 1, 1865, and headed toward Columbia and Charleston, South Carolina.

Sherman's men took special care to punish the elite families in the Palmetto State for their role in secession. As they had in Georgia, Union soldiers primarily encountered women as they marched through South Carolina. They burned and ransacked many of the homes and towns they encountered. They entered Charleston and Columbia on February 17 and 18, 1865, destroying much of both cities. Debate continues over who began the fire in the state capital of Columbia, but Union soldiers recorded their satisfaction in seeing it burn. Charleston fared no better, perhaps because of the concentration of large slaveholding families there. Sherman's men continued their destruction as they marched north out of Charleston, burning Camden, Winnsboro, Lancaster, Chesterfield, and Cheraw.

Sherman instructed his commanders to deal fairly with North Carolinians, who were poorer than their neighbors and rumored to have Unionist tendencies. However, Union soldiers continued their destruction of the Southern landscape, setting fire to the pine forests and to the turpentine, tar, and rosin factories that they encountered. They also continued to raid and destroy the homes of many elite families. Sherman's troops left Fayetteville on March 15, 1865, and soon drove back the out-gunned and outnumbered Confederates in a small confrontation. Fighting continued in Averasboro on March 16 and again at Bentonville on March 19, forcing a Confederate retreat. Within two weeks of Sherman's April 13 entrance into Raleigh, Confederate General Joseph Johnston surrendered his troops at Durham Station.

Lisa Tendrich Frank

See also African American Women; Atlanta, Evacuation of (Special Field Orders, Number 67); Camp Followers; Civilian Life; Confederate Homefront; Destruction of Homes; Destruction of Personal Property; Military Invasion and Occupation; Rape; Sherman, William Tecumseh (1820–1891); Sherman Land (Special Field Orders, Number 15); Southern Women.

References and Further Reading

Campbell, Jacqueline Glass. 2003. *When Sherman Marched North from the Sea: Resistance on the Confederate Home Front.* Chapel Hill: University of North Carolina Press.

Fellman, Michael. 1995. *Citizen Sherman: A Life of William Tecumseh Sherman.* New York: Random House.

Frank, Lisa Tendrich. 2001. "To 'Cure Her of Her Pride and Boasting': The Gendered Implications of Sherman's March." Ph.D. diss. University of Florida.

Glatthaar, Joseph T. 1995. *The March to the Sea and Beyond: Sherman's Troops in the Savannah and Carolinas Campaigns.* Baton Rouge: Louisiana State University Press. (Orig. pub. 1985.)

Grimsley, Mark. 1995. *The Hard Hand of War: Union Military Policy toward Southern Civilians, 1861–1865.* New York: Cambridge University Press.

Kennett, Lee. 1995. *Marching through Georgia: The Story of Soldiers and Civilians during Sherman's Campaign.* New York: HarperPerennial.

Marszalek, John F. 1993. *Sherman: A Soldier's Passion for Order.* New York: Vintage.

Royster, Charles. 1991. *The Destructive War: William Tecumseh Sherman, Stonewall Jackson, and the Americans.* New York: Vintage.

Sherman, William Tecumseh (1820–1891)

William Tecumseh Sherman, Union general and postwar United States Army commanding general, is best known for his 1864–1865 march through Georgia and the Carolinas.

Born in Lancaster, Ohio, to Connecticut transplants, Charles and Mary Hoyt Sherman, he had an enjoyable childhood until he was nine years old and his father suddenly died. His mother could not maintain the large brood of ten children, so family members and neighbors took them in. Cump, as his family always called him, became the ward of Thomas Ewing, a leading Whig politician. Ewing's wife, Maria, insisted that Cump be baptized a Catholic, and the name "William" was added to his original "Tecumseh." Ellen Ewing, four years his junior, thus began a lifelong role in his life. As a child, she viewed him as her protector, but there was no spark of romance between them until he left home, graduated from West Point, and began army life in the South. The two married in 1850 and produced a family of eight children.

Sherman's fame primarily rests on his victory at Atlanta and his successful psychologically powerful marches to the sea and through the Carolinas. As his soldiers purposefully destroyed property to end the fighting as soon as possible with the least loss of life, stories about him spread. Unsubstantiated rumors abounded that there were large numbers of rapes of women in his army's path. If, on the other hand, Sherman's army spared a house or a locality, the explanation developed that the mercy occurred

Union General William T. Sherman is best known for his 1864–1865 march through Georgia and the Carolinas. This campaign helped bring about Confederate surrender. (National Archives and Records Administration)

others threw themselves at him, such as Mary Audenreid, the widow of a military aide. All their married life he remained loyal to Ellen, however, and, when she died in the late 1880s, he suffered a severe depression. In the end, Ellen remained the most significant female influence in his life. Yet their marriage was more combative than romantic.

John F. Marszalek

See also Atlanta, Evacuation of (Special Field Orders, Number 67); Sherman, Ellen Boyle Ewing (1824–1888); Sherman's Campaign (1864–1865); Sherman Land (Special Field Orders, Number 15); Southern Women.

References and Further Reading

Campbell, Jacqueline Glass. 2003. *When Sherman Marched North from the Sea, Resistance on the Confederate Home Front.* Chapel Hill: University of North Carolina Press.

Marszalek, John F. 1993. *Sherman: A Soldier's Passion for Order.* New York: Free Press. (Paperback edition 1993. New York: Vintage.)

Marszalek, John F. 2005. *Sherman's March to the Sea.* Civil War Campaigns and Commanders Series. Abilene, TX: McWhiney Foundation Press.

because a former girlfriend of the general lived there and that he held his soldiers back out of remembrance of a prewar romance.

Women in the path of Sherman's army reacted to the soldiers' presence in a variety of ways. Some were cowed to the point of writing their boyfriends, husbands, brothers, or sons in the Confederate army elsewhere, urging them to return home and fulfill their gender roles of providing protection against the invaders. Other women stood up to the general and his soldiers with verbal and sometimes physical abuse. When Sherman captured Savannah, several leading Confederate generals left their wives in his care, demonstrating that they did not believe the stories about his alleged maltreatment of civilians.

After the war, Ellen Sherman refused to attend social events with her husband, so he often had a daughter or a female friend on his arm at a dinner party or the theater. He constantly flirted with women and charmed some, but others found his attention offensive. He was clearly attracted to some women, notably sculptress Vinnie Ream, and

Shiloh, Battle of (April 6–7, 1862)

The war's largest and deadliest battle west of the Appalachian Mountains, the Battle of Shiloh took place at Pittsburg Landing on the Tennessee River in southwestern Tennessee on April 6–7, 1862. More than 109,000 combatants, including a handful of women, met on the battlefield, and 23,746 of them became casualties. Both the unprecedented size and the extraordinary bloodiness of the battle shocked citizens of both the North and the South. Although the Confederacy came close to prevailing on the first day of fighting, Shiloh was a key strategic victory for Union control of the Western theater.

In February 1862, the Union had taken Forts Henry and Donelson in northern Tennessee, followed by the capital city of Nashville. The next Western Confederate stronghold in Union sights was Corinth, Mississippi, a key hub for the Memphis and Charleston Railroad. In March 1862, forces under General Ulysses S. Grant massed along the Tennessee–Mississippi border, ready to move on Corinth, about twenty miles to the south, as soon as additional troops from General Don Carlos Buell's Nashville occupation force arrived. Early in April 1862, Confederate General Albert Sydney Johnston, in command at Corinth, decided to get to Grant before Buell did.

Johnston succeeded on April 6, surprising Grant's men with an early morning attack. As the battle raged that first day, there was great disorganization on the field and considerable hand-to-hand fighting. Most of the combatants were very young, and many were raw, particularly on the Confederate side. Nonetheless, the Confederates aggressively pushed the Union soldiers back almost to the Tennessee River. By the end of the first day, Johnston had bled to death after being shot in the leg, and Union troops had made a valiant but ultimately untenable stand in a heavily wooded area christened the Hornets' Nest. April 7 brought renewed carnage, as well as Buell's reinforcements. The Confederates, now under General Pierre G. T. Beauregard, retreated to Corinth at day's end.

Two women are known to have fought for the Confederacy at Shiloh: Loreta Velazquez and Mary Ann Pitman. Both survived and later served as Confederate spies. Fighting as Harry T. Buford, Velazquez briefly commanded the Arkansas Grays regiment she had helped raise the previous year. On the second day of the battle, she was wounded by shrapnel in the arm and shoulder while helping bury the dead. Pitman, a Tennessean who used the alias Rawley, had helped raise a company and served as a second lieutenant.

At least four women fought for the Union. Jane Short, who used the name Charley Davis, sustained a minor hand wound. Frances Hook survived the battle, but her only brother did not. Two other Unionist women who served at Shiloh remain anonymous. One was badly injured and went to the Ladies Home for the Friendless in Washington, D.C., to recover. Another perished, and her remains were discovered in a mass grave in 1934.

Several women, who were in the camp with their husbands when the battle broke out, quickly became involved with nursing the wounded. Belle Reynolds, newly married, was with her husband John in the camp of the Seventeenth Illinois Infantry when shells began to fall on April 6. Belle and another woman nursed the wounded aboard the steamer *Emerald* and then at another temporary hospital near the landing. Belle's efforts at Shiloh prompted Illinois Governor Richard Yates to give her an honorary major's commission and name her daughter of the regiment.

Ann Wallace, wife of Union General William H. L. Wallace, arrived at Pittsburg Landing for a surprise visit on April 6. Her husband suffered a mortal head wound while leading his men out of the Hornets' Nest along the Sunken Road. Ann took care of him until he died on April 10.

As news of Shiloh's horrific casualties spread, Confederate women made their way to Corinth to tend the wounded. These volunteer nurses included nuns from the Sisters of Charity and family members of men involved in the fighting. Kate Cumming left her home in Mobile, Alabama, even as her brother received his baptism of fire at Shiloh, his first battle. In Corinth, Kate worked in the temporary hospital established at the Tishomingo Hotel. As she recounted in the journal that she kept to record her nursing experiences, the horrors she witnessed quickly banished images of glorious military exploits from her head. Cumming gave out food and water, bathed wounds, wrote letters for soldiers, and passed out sermons to them. The valuable work of Cumming and other women among the wounded from Shiloh prompted Dr. S. H. Stout, a surgeon who became medical director of hospitals of the Department and Army of Tennessee, to support women's presence in Confederate hospitals.

In the years after the battle, women contributed to commemorative activities at the battlefield, including dedication ceremonies for the monuments erected in the national cemetery, established in 1866, and in the national military park, established in 1894. Chapters of the United Daughters of the Confederacy (UDC) in Alabama and Arkansas sponsored monuments to the fallen from those states in 1907 and 1911, respectively. In 1917, the national UDC organization funded a large, symbolic monument to all of the Confederate dead at the battlefield. The $50,000 memorial, located in the Hornets' Nest, represented the victory experienced by the Confederacy on the first day and the loss and death experienced on the second.

Antoinette G. van Zelm

See also Catholic Women; Cumming, Kate (ca. 1835–1909); Female Combatants; Monuments; Nurses; United Daughters of the Confederacy; Velazquez, Loreta Janeta [Harry T. Buford] (1842–1897).

References and Further Reading
Blanton, DeAnne, and Lauren M. Cook. 2002. *They Fought Like Demons: Women Soldiers in the American Civil War.* Baton Rouge: Louisiana State University Press.
Harwell, Richard Barksdale, ed. [1959] 1998. *Kate: The Journal of a Confederate Nurse.* Baton Rouge: Louisiana State University Press.
Daniel, Larry J. 1997. *Shiloh: The Battle That Changed the Civil War.* New York: Simon & Schuster.
Leonard, Elizabeth D. 1999. *All the Daring of the Soldier: Women of the Civil War Armies.* New York: W. W. Norton & Company.
Smith, Timothy B. 2004. *This Great Battlefield of Shiloh: History, Memory, and the Establishment of a Civil War National Military Park.* Knoxville: University of Tennessee Press.

Shortages

The absence of many common and luxury items from women's lives during the Civil War profoundly shaped the homefront experience. Confederate women felt wartime shortages more severely than their Union counterparts, largely due to the Confederate military needs and to the increasingly effective Union blockade of the Confederate coastline. Women survived without their usual products, such as coffee and new clothing, by creating substitutes from items on hand or in nature. Although shortages affected lower-class and African American women the most, few women of any class or race avoided facing economic hardships in their daily lives during the war.

The causes of wartime shortages varied from inflation, felt by women in both sections, to government policies, such as government impressment and the Union blockade. With a shortage of capital and an abundance of paper money, inflation caused prices to rise to extraordinary levels. Throughout the war, Confederate money became increasingly worthless, complicating women's ability to purchase the products that were available. Industrial production focused on military needs rather than on consumer demands, forcing women to find alternate sources for their needs. While often innovative in their ability to find substitutes or to produce their own food and clothing, Confederate women were never able to fulfill completely the homefront demands for basic supplies. Often what was produced was susceptible to Confederate taxes or military impressment policies. The crippling blow for Confederate women came as the Union armies invaded the region and the Union blockade tightened. As battles and armies destroyed the land and the blockade prevented importation, Confederate women and their families daily struggled for survival.

One of the most critical shortages Confederate women faced was that of food. The antebellum Southern economy had been driven by cotton and tobacco production, and conversion to widespread food production on farms and plantations was unsteady at best. As men left for the battlefields and slaves fled to freedom, Confederate women remained to farm for their families, a task many were unused to, further exacerbating food shortages. Much of the food produced was seized by the government to feed the armies, and the food that was available for purchase could be had only at inflated prices.

In April 1863, frustrated women in Richmond, Virginia, took to the streets to protest in a bread riot, seizing the supplies of food they thought shopkeepers were hoarding. Although similar riots occurred throughout the Confederacy during the war, most women resorted to substitutes rather than stealing for their culinary needs. Beef alternatives included both fish and fowl, but in desperate times women cooked rats, frogs, snails, dogs, cats, and mules. When they ran out of salt, which was vital for both seasoning and preserving food, women collected dirt from the smokehouse floor and boiled it to separate out the salt. Another staple, flour, frequently cost more than $1,200 a barrel, forcing women to use corn meal, rice, or white potatoes in their recipes. For sugar, women found sorghum, honey, and maple sugar acceptable. Coffee, the most popular beverage in the Confederacy, also became prohibitively expensive as the war progressed; so women experimented with parched okra, corn, rye, sweet potatoes, acorns, dandelion roots, peanuts, beans, or wheat to satisfy their thirst. Other women found tea substitutes in the leaves of raspberries, huckleberries, blackberries, currants, or vegetables. If women were successful in finding an extra bit of food or in creating an alternative recipe, they readily shared with family and friends, and newspapers would often publish their successes as well.

Replenishing clothing supplies also proved challenging. As with food, most of the manufactured clothing in the antebellum South had come from the North or from Europe. With the blockade preventing importation during the war, women again turned to their resourcefulness. Many middle- and lower-class women, as well as slave women, continued to make their own clothes as they had before the war, but upper-class women began to make their own homespun clothing for the first time. Difficulties developed in the absence of skill and materials, from needles and thread to cloth and cotton cards. Nonetheless, Confederate women persevered with what they could find. Women fashioned knitting needles from oak or hickory wood, and they used thorns for pins. Women often combined materials, such as cotton and animal fur, to stretch their material further. With new cloth in short supply, women recycled any bit of cloth available, including drapes and table linens, into new clothes. Old clothes were reused, with some women unraveling the stitching from an old dress to be reused in a new outfit. Materials for accessories, such as hats and buttons, were found in nature, with women using grasses, leaves, or straw for hats and wood or gourds, animal horns and bones, shells, waxed thorns, and persimmon seeds for buttons. Women also had to make their own shoes, using all variety of materials from animal skins and carpet to wood and newspaper.

Beyond the basic necessities of food and clothing, women experienced a host of other shortages in their lives. Women often smuggled medicines, such as quinine or morphine, through the Union lines or found substitutes in nature. Women fashioned candles by dipping a cloth into melted wax (beeswax, myrtle wax, turpentine, or rosin) and wrapping it around an old candlestick, corn cob, or hickory stick. They refilled their mattresses and furniture cushions with straw, cottonseed, or leaves, and they replaced blankets with carpets. With paper and ink expensive and difficult to obtain, women turned to wrapping paper, blank book pages, wallpaper, or old letters to write on. They also frequently practiced cross-writing—filling a page and then turning it ninety degrees and writing over the page again—to make the most of the supplies they had. Proven substitutes for ink included berries, tree bark, seeds, and rusty nails. If women were forced from their homes by approaching armies, finding a new residence often proved difficult, and women turned to vacant public buildings or an extra room in someone's home to shelter their families.

Kristen Streater

See also Bread Riots; Confederate Homefront; Homespun; Impressment; Northern Women; Southern Women; Union Homefront.

References and Further Reading

Culpepper, Marilyn Mayer. 1991. *Trials and Triumphs: The Women of the American Civil War.* East Lansing: Michigan State University Press.

Edwards, Laura F. 2000. *Scarlett Doesn't Live Here Anymore: Southern Women in the Civil War Era.* Urbana: University of Illinois Press.

Faust, Drew Gilpin. 1996. *Mothers of Invention: Women of the Slaveholding South in the American Civil War.* Chapel Hill: University of North Carolina Press.

Massey, Mary Elizabeth. [1952] 1993. *Ersatz in the Confederacy: Shortages and Substitutes on the Southern Homefront.* Columbia: University of South Carolina Press.

Slater, Sarah Antoinette (n.d.–n.d.)

Sarah Slater was likely the courier who, during the early months of 1865, carried communication and money between Richmond and Confederate operatives in Canada and who associated with John Wilkes Booth and other Lincoln assassination conspirators. A mysterious figure to this day, she was known as the Frenchwoman among the conspirators, always wearing a veil and speaking broken English. Federal investigators pursued her as a result of testimonies given at the assassination trials, suspecting her of being the vital link between Richmond, Montreal, and Booth in Washington. But by that time, she had disappeared without a trace.

The dates of her birth and death are unknown. Louis Weichmann, a witness at the trials, named the Frenchwoman as Sarah Slater. This woman was born in Connecticut and moved with her family to New Bern, North Carolina, in 1858. On June 12, 1861, she married dance instructor Rowan Slater. He joined the North Carolina Infantry, departing on June 23, 1861, and, though he survived the war, he never saw his wife again.

In January 1865, she went to Richmond to apply for a passport north. While there, Secretary of War James A. Seddon recruited her for espionage work. Her first mission was to carry papers to Canadian authorities. On October 19, 1864, men in civilian clothes attacked St. Albans, Vermont, as part of a Confederate strategy to cause the Union to divide its forces. Although the town repulsed the raiders, they managed to rob three banks before escaping into Canada. Canadian authorities arrested them, and the Federal government demanded they be handed over for the robberies. Slater was to carry documents to prove to them that the robberies were part of an authorized military operation. She was successful in her mission; the Canadian government released the prisoners and returned the bank money to them.

Slater was trusted with a second mission to Canada in late February and early March 1865. On her route to and from Canada and Richmond, she stopped in Washington and New York, staying in the boardinghouse of Mary Surratt, who would later be executed for her role in the Lincoln assassination plot. Slater was escorted in her missions first by Augustus Howell, and later by John Surratt, Mary Surratt's son.

Her last mission, on April 1, 1865, was to bring money, originally intended to fund the Canadian operations, to Montreal to be sent to London for private use after the war. Slater met Booth one last time in Washington, departing on April 4. After that, she and the money disappeared.

Gabrielle Bruns

See also Confederate Homefront; Female Spies; Southern Women; Surratt, Mary E. Jenkins (1823–1865); Union Homefront.

References and Further Reading

Leonard, Elizabeth D. 2004. *Lincoln's Avengers: Justice, Revenge, and Reunion after the Civil War.* New York: W. W. Norton & Company.

Markle, Donald E. 2004. *Spies and Spymasters of the Civil War.* New York: Hippocrene Books.

Tidwell, William A., James O. Hall, and David Winfred Gaddy. 1988. *Come Retribution: The Confederate Secret Service and the Assassination of Lincoln.* Jackson: University Press of Mississippi.

Slave Families

When the American Civil War broke out, enslaved blacks lived in a variety of family arrangements depending on where and at what they worked. In the upper South, many lived in extended family households that included relatives and so-called fictive kin, or people taken into the household as though they were family. More than a few slave households contained only single adults. In most cases, children lived in one-parent family households. The predominance of one-parent households resulted from the domestic slave trade, which probably destroyed one in every three slave marriages and separated 20 percent of all the slave children in the seaboard South from their families. In the lower South, on the other hand, on the eve of the Civil War, a slightly larger percentage of the enslaved lived in households with both parents.

Adult slaves respected family ties, knew about their family relations, gave their children family names as surnames without revealing the names to white owners, honored family elders, taught their children important survival lessons, and tried to establish as strong a family unit as possible under the devastating conditions of slavery. When they ran away, slaves frequently did so in desperate attempts to find the families from which they had been separated. Unlike their white owners, they tried not to marry cousins or close relatives, and they paid homage to marriage and family relations in slave wedding ceremonies and funerals in both secret and open services and rituals. Young women usually married when they became pregnant, and the enslaved families readily adopted the children left orphaned by the slave trade or other circumstances of slavery. Mothers typically taught their children to respect their fathers and other male figures in the immediate and extended family.

Slave mothers dominated many, and in some places a majority, of the family units in the antebellum South. In families whose women lived as mothers without their husbands present, the slave mother emerged as a tower of strength and wisdom. On small plantations and farms such as those typical in the upper South, slave mothers, as women essentially on their own without men in their daily lives, relied on a network of enslaved women to assist them in child rearing and in coping with slavery. In the lower South, a more viable slave community usually existed, especially on the large sugar and cotton plantations, with husbands and male relatives partaking of family life along with spouses and kin. In both cases, however, the slave mother was an independent force in the household.

For a variety of reasons, many husbands and fathers lived apart from their families. Fathers were sold away from their families, or they saw their wives and children carried off by slave traders and migrating planters. Many husbands on smaller plantations lived apart from their wives and children in so-called abroad marriages. These resulted when slaveholders separated families to better manage the various parts of their properties or farms. In other instances, small slaveholders owned slaves whose mates lived on neighboring farms.

Even in families, however, whose parents lived together, a patriarchal husband seldom dominated the household. The husbands and wives were more like equal partners in slavery—equal in their lack of power to affect fundamentally their lives or the lives of their children. Spouses worked at heavy field labor on equal terms, although men were assigned the heaviest tasks, such as handling plow animals. Unlike the white household, the slave husband had little real authority over his family members. He could not protect his wife and children, nor could he enforce his will on them unless it conformed to the will of the slaveholder.

When the Civil War swept over the Confederate states, the region's 4 million enslaved people valiantly moved to protect their families even as they courageously embraced freedom. From the start of the war until the Emancipation Proclamation took effect in 1863, enslaved blacks were considered as little more than a burdensome nuisance by the Union army and as potential traitors by Southern whites. Fearful that loyal slaveholders in the Border States might join the Confederacy if the Union defined the Civil War as a war of emancipation rather than as a war to preserve the Union, Federal authorities in the first months of the war returned runaway slaves to their owners and openly discouraged the slaves from breaking for freedom. However, little could be done to stem the tide of enslaved people leaving for Union lines or running away at the first opportunity. More important, as Union troops occupied southern territory in Virginia and along the coastal regions of North and South Carolina, tens of thousands of slaves fell into Federal hands as refugees. Federal authorities began treating the enslaved refugees as contraband of war (the property of the enemy), justifying this designation because the Confederate forces used enslaved workers in building war fortifications and as nurses and support workers for the military.

United States President Abraham Lincoln issued the Emancipation Proclamation in 1863 and called for black males to enlist as Union soldiers, partly to convince Europeans that support for the Confederacy meant support for slavery, partly to encourage resistance to slavery by blacks within the Confederacy, and partly because enslaved blacks all over the South already had emancipated themselves by refusing to continue as slaves and by running away. By the end of the war, over one hundred thousand black men had served as Union soldiers and sailors, and many more women and children and elderly blacks lived as refugees in camps and depots wherever Union forces were present. Nearly eighty thousand such refugees were on the roads and

Five generations of a slave family in Beaufort, South Carolina, in 1862. (Library of Congress)

adrift in the lower Mississippi Valley after the fall of Vicksburg in the summer of 1863. Thousands of other blacks lived on their own in makeshift communities and settlements within the Confederacy while they awaited the end of the war.

Faced with thousands of black refugees who flocked to Union lines, the Federal government began placing the blacks on abandoned plantations run by the army or leased to Union entrepreneurs. Most of these plantations, especially in the lower Mississippi Valley, were occupied principally by women, children, and the elderly who worked for fixed wages by planting cotton or by planting rice and sugar elsewhere. Most of these free workers lived in family cabins left over from slavery and tried to survive as best as possible while husbands

and fathers served in nearby army regiments. It was on these government plantations that the formerly enslaved people, especially women, began to experience the first taste of freedom, including negotiating with the army and private agents over such things as wages, supplies, and living conditions.

On the whole, the story of the black family throughout the course of the American Civil War is the story of severe hardship, perhaps even more arduous than that experienced in slavery. Husbands who left for freedom or to enlist in the Union armies often left behind enslaved women and their families. Frequently, black men set off for freedom on their own to try to break the path for their families to follow, but the precariousness of the war meant that women and children were often left behind to fend for themselves. Under these circumstances, the plight of black women and their dependent children during and immediately after the war was extremely difficult. In some cases, white slaveholders punished black women for the actions of their husbands who joined the Union army. Enslaved blacks who were left behind were forced to work even harder than before to make up for loss of male workers, not only because of the runaways but also for slaves commandeered by Confederate forces. Any sympathy for the Union cause could result in severe whippings, and some black women were executed for expressing joy at the presence of Union forces and for providing information to the Yankees. Others were taken deeper behind Southern lines and even into Texas by slaveholders trying to retain a hold onto as many of their slaves as possible, thereby disrupting black families even more.

Still, thousands of black women ran away to Union lines with their children in tow, a break for freedom that was itself fraught with danger. Fleeing women and children usually left with no provisions and with little idea of where they were going. What they found, once they made it to Union lines, were horrible living conditions in refugee camps, where thousands died from diseases such as small pox, yellow fever, and the like; physical and sexual abuse by Union soldiers; relocation to plantations to work at hard labor in the fields; and a Federal policy that treated them as unwanted obstacles to efficient military maneuvers, to say the least. Black soldiers were punished if they provided their families with provisions issued to them by the military, and the desertion of black troops to help provide for their families, which happened frequently, often resulted in jail and even execution in a few cases.

Black women and their families survived in such conditions by banding together in settlements on their own; growing food crops on plantations abandoned by their former masters; laboring as cooks, hospital workers, and washerwomen for black soldiers as they lived in refugee camps or in hastily constructed shelters near the military encampments; and by just hiding out in the woods as best they could. In the cities and towns, they tried to

work as seamstresses repairing uniforms. Some became prostitutes. As in slavery, the Civil War left the black woman as the primary caretaker of black children, but the conditions of war and emancipation made the burden more difficult even than in slavery. In some cases, mothers were forced to leave some of their children behind when they fled for their lives from abusive masters, hoping to return to rescue them in the future.

When the fighting ended, thousands of black refugees returned to the abandoned plantations on which they had lived as slaves to work the land on their own or as wage hands living in family units. When Southern whites tried to pass Black Codes that gave them parental authority over black children and forced African Americans to work in gang labor, freedmen and freedwomen refused to work under such conditions or even for their old masters. In the Reconstruction era, blacks throughout the South used their labor power to insist on a new system of labor based on the family household. Black husbands and fathers negotiated terms that allowed women to work at domestic tasks in the home rather than in the fields, families to live in family cabins scattered across the plantation lands in forty-acre plots, and family autonomy and independence from daily supervision by white overseers or by former slaveholders. In many cases, African American workers insisted that the old white slaveholders move off the plantation as a condition of agreeing to work. This system of labor eventually came to be known as sharecropping or share tenancy, in which blacks worked for a share of the crop for wages or paid a share of the crop for rent. Although this work arrangement quickly entrapped black farmers in a system of debt peonage controlled by the Southern supply merchant rather than the planter/landlord, it began as a way of protecting the family unit as the basis of work and living.

The freedmen and freedwomen also rushed to have their slave marriages recognized by the Union army and the United States authorities, demanded schools for their children, searched for families separated from them by the slave trade, and worked to establish neighborhood churches composed of families made stronger by the shared experiences of slavery and the Civil War. Indeed, historians estimate that 90 percent of rural black families lived in households with parents and children in 1870 and 1880. Within a few years after slavery, the simple family unit had become the norm for Southern blacks.

Joyce L. Broussard

See also African American Women; Border States; Camp Followers; Confederate Homefront; Contrabands; Courtship and Marriage; Disease; Emancipation Proclamation (January 1, 1863); Family Life, Confederate; Freedmen's Bureau; Hospitals; Impressment; Prostitution; Rape; Reconstruction (1865–1877); Refugees; Rural Women; Sherman Land (Special Field Orders, Number 15); Southern Unionists.

References and Further Reading

Berlin, Ira. 2003. *Generations of Captivity: A History of African-American Slaves.* Cambridge, MA: Harvard University Press.

Campbell, Edward D. C. Jr., and Kym S. Rice, eds. 1996. *Southern Women, Civil War, and the Confederate Legacy.* Charlottesville: University Press of Virginia.

Faust, Drew Gilpin. 1996. *Mothers of Invention: Women of the Slaveholding South in the American Civil War.* Chapel Hill: University of North Carolina Press.

Fox-Genovese, Elizabeth. 1988. *Within the Plantation Household: Black and White Women of the Old South.* Chapel Hill: University of North Carolina Press.

Gutman, Herbert G. 1976. *The Black Family in Slavery and Freedom, 1750–1925.* New York: Random House.

Kolchin, Peter. 2003. *American Slavery: 1619–1877.* New York: Hill and Wang.

Rable, George C. 1989. *Civil Wars: Women and the Crisis of Southern Nationalism.* Urbana: University of Illinois Press.

Slaveholding Women

The slaveholding women of the Confederate States of America assumed immense social, political, and economic significance during the Civil War. As Southern men fought the Union army on the battlefield, women waged a war of equal importance on the homefront. Battling the difficulties of crop production, slave management, shortages of food and clothing, inflation, and the presence of Federal armies, female slaveholders struggled to protect their families, their homes, and their way of life. At the start of the war, the majority of slaveholding women expressed an ardent patriotism that was best conveyed in their willingness to sacrifice both their men and their comfort for the Confederacy. But as the demands and horrors of warfare pressed on them and challenged the Southern social order, some women's devotion to the cause turned to disillusionment. Even though they risked forfeiting the antebellum lifestyle on which their identity rested, some slaveholding women ultimately undermined the Confederate effort and demanded an end to the conflict.

Although Southern society expected women to refrain from political discussion, the prewar secession debates and the bombing of Fort Sumter led many female slaveholders to shed their apolitical guise. As members of the wealthiest and most powerful social group in the Old South, they had more at stake in maintaining slavery and the region's hierarchical social order than other Southern women. As such, they encouraged the white men in their lives to defend their way of life by taking up arms against the encroaching Federal Army. Hoping to capitalize on this informal recruitment, Confederate officials and propagandists exploited the antebellum gender prescription of female sacrifice. Patriotic women were supposed to forsake male protection and give their husbands and sons to the Confederacy. Although countless female slaveholders feared running plantations on their own, commanding slaves, and possibly losing loved ones in battle, the ideal Confederate woman was expected to repress such feelings in support of the cause. Consequently, many women focused on the romance and glories of war, rather than on its potential trials and tribulations, and they proudly, if not hesitantly, sent their men off to battle.

The mass mobilization and departure of white men from Southern plantations had a profound impact on female slaveholders. While some followed their husbands to battle, moved back home with their parents, or relocated to nearby cities, most remained on their estates as long as possible.

Unlike yeoman women who had few resources at their disposal, wealthy female slaveholders escaped significant disruption in their lives at the outset of the war, for they had money to maintain their antebellum lifestyle and the slaves to maintain plantation production. This gave slaveholding women the leisure to ponder their role in the conflict. Many were frustrated with their seeming insignificance and began to resent the restrictions that their gender placed on them. Prohibited from joining the army, they found an outlet for their patriotism and growing restlessness in volunteer activities. Thousands of ladies' relief and aid associations emerged across the South as women searched for proper ways to contribute to the war effort. Female slaveholders remained within feminine boundaries by sewing uniforms, flags, and tents and by collecting or giving donations of money, food, and supplies to Confederate soldiers.

As the war progressed, slaveholding women's attention shifted from volunteer activities to the plantation affairs for which they were now accountable. Taking over sole responsibility for Southern plantations during the war was a trying experience for most female slaveholders. Although many absentee planters' wives had managerial experience prior to 1861, a woman's administration was usually intermittent and not the primary responsibility of most plantation mistresses. Even those who fulfilled a managerial role on a regular basis were not prepared for the unique administrative problems wrought by war, particularly those concerning slaves. No amount of managerial training could prepare white women for the wartime resistance put forth by their bondspersons.

Slave management was elite women's most important war responsibility and also their greatest challenge. Maintaining control over bondspersons was essential to the Confederacy, for slavery was the bedrock of the South—the institution on which the Southern economy and social order rested. Moreover, the Union blockade necessitated a Confederate reliance on Southern plantations and slaves for the production of food and supplies. Consequently, slaveholding women assumed tremendous political, economic, and social significance as the wartime protectors of the slave system. This role was a difficult one to fulfill, not only because of slaves' increasingly defiant attitudes toward female slaveholders and bondage, but also because of society's doubts and women's own insecurities about their managerial capabilities.

Prior to the war, most Southerners did not see or treat the plantation mistress as a master. Although white women could be, and occasionally were, ruthless and violent slaveholders, popular gender prescriptions demanded passivity on their part. Their presumed or actual weakness often encouraged slaves to act more autonomously in their presence than in that of white men and caused white society to question whether slaveholding women had the emotional and physical strength necessary to command bondspeople. Often female slaveholders feared the repercussions of being held exclusively responsible for slave management during the war. Much to their dismay, their fears of slave resistance were realized following the wartime exodus of white men from Southern plantations.

The problems accompanying slaves' subtle and blatant disregard for slaveholding women's authority in the prewar years were amplified as the war progressed and bondspeople encountered greater opportunities for freedom. Consequently, many women pleaded with their husbands to return home and assume control of plantation affairs. When military leaders denied discharges or furloughs, the wives of slaveholders sent thousands of requests to government officials imploring them to exempt their men from service. The Confederate Congress responded by passing the so-called Twenty-Nigger Law of 1862. While expanded conscription laws eventually curbed its terms, this legislation exempted from service one white man from every plantation where there resided twenty or more slaves. The law not only privileged the wealthy over the poor, as small slaveholders and nonslaveholding whites complained, but it also confirmed widespread assumptions about women's natural weakness and vulnerability.

Many slaveholding women held these assumptions themselves, for their petitions regarding their husbands' military exemption were usually couched in terms of their need for masculine protection, particularly from restive slaves. They were frustrated with their inability to make their slaves work effectively, and they also feared insolence, violence, rape, and even murder. Stories concerning lazy, disrespectful, and aggressive slaves circulated around the Confederacy and intensified female slaveholders' frustration and trepidation. Many women wrote to their husbands about their dread of nightfall, the time during which they most feared a revolt. Some even claimed that they went to bed fully dressed so that they would be prepared for any disturbance.

Such concerns reflected an important shift in many slaveholding women's belief in slavery as a paternalistic institution that fostered harmonious relations between black and white Southerners. Even when the war broke out and their husbands left home, some women claimed to have no fear of their slaves, for they believed them to be devoted to their owners. The pervasiveness of this fantasy among female slaveholders was evident in the shock and disbelief that they expressed when their favorite slaves fled for Union lines during the war. Unable to grasp the reasons for leaving, many plantation mistresses conveyed feelings of abandonment, despair, and anger to their husbands, all of which revealed the extent of their dependency on their bondspersons.

Female slaveholders used a variety of means to prevent or temper insubordination and desertion and to inspire hard work among their slaves during the war. Some ignored gender prescriptions that demanded feminine morality and passivity, and they inflicted violence on their slaves. Others tried to cajole or charm their bondspersons with flattery, kindness, and affection. Some even resorted to begging. As the war drew on, however, all methods of slave management became increasingly difficult and ineffective. As a result, many women started to see slavery as a burden and demanded relief from their husbands and the government. When their pleas went unanswered, their devotion to the Confederate war effort waned.

Although some female slaveholders' disillusionment with the war and with the Confederate cause originated in their troubles with slave management,

it burgeoned with wartime hardships that cut across class lines. Inflation, monetary shortages, and a lack of food and material goods compounded slaveholding women's problems on the homefront. Although the wealthiest slaveholders were able to maintain a comfortable standard of living much longer than less prosperous Southerners, their lives did not escape disruption. The Union blockade and Confederate restrictions on the production and export of cotton caused slaveholders' revenue to decline drastically. The money that they did have fell in value as inflation hit the South and as the prices of food and supplies soared. Added to these problems was the limited availability of necessities like cloth, shoes, and flour. Domestic production and ingenuity staved off a state of crisis for slaveholding women and their families for a while, but, by the end of the war, starvation and material deprivation shook even the most affluent households.

Desperate to feed and clothe their children, some slaveholding women entered the ranks of paid labor during the war, most often requesting salaried positions in government offices. Faced with a pressing need for employees and a dearth of male applicants, Confederate officials overlooked peacetime gender conventions and filled many vacant positions with women. The most desirable appointments, such as those in the Treasury Department, usually went to members of the slaveholding class. Because of this, government work was an attractive option for struggling female slaveholders as well as a source of class tension. The salary of clerical workers far exceeded that of other female government employees and that of army privates. Moreover, working conditions were more pleasant and safe in Confederate office buildings than in factories or makeshift hospitals—places of employment reserved almost exclusively for poor women.

While the majority of slaveholding women escaped the dangers of the hospital and factory, many faced the hazards of living in the path of the Union army. Those who resided near the battlefront risked having their property commandeered, stolen, or destroyed by Northern soldiers. Female slaveholders tried to protect their possessions from Federal troops in various ways. Some buried items of monetary and sentimental value. Others trusted favorite slaves with their goods, assuming that the Northern army would not bother searching or destroying bondspersons' cabins. Many women even concealed belongings on their person. Stories circulated throughout the country of Southern women who hid silver, china, and jewelry in their hoopskirts. Although slaveholding women's elite status could provide them with a modicum of protection, this was a dangerous strategy, for it increased the risk of sexual violation by looting soldiers. By drawing attention to their ladyhood, those who were lucky sometimes evoked a sense of honor and propriety in the men who searched their homes. However, in the act of protecting themselves, female slaveholders may have put other women who did not possess the shield of gentility at heightened risk of sexual and physical abuse.

The dangers that accompanied military occupation, combined with the stress of slave management, material deprivation, and starvation, led many slaveholding women to grow disenchanted with the Confederate cause. By the latter years of the conflict, their unmet demands for assistance and protection turned into pleas for their husbands' desertion from the army. Increasingly desperate and compelling cries from home shook the soldiers on the front and in some ways undermined the Confederate war effort. The value of women's material and emotional support to the Confederacy was no clearer than when it began to waver.

Nikki Berg Burin

See also Aid Societies; Civilian Life; Destruction of Homes; Destruction of Personal Property; Domesticity; Family Life, Confederate; Letter Writing; Morale; Nationalism, Confederate; Plantation Life; Shortages; Slave Families; Southern Women.

References and Further Reading

Campbell, Jacqueline Glass. 2003. *When Sherman Marched North from the Sea: Resistance on the Confederate Home Front.* Chapel Hill: University of North Carolina Press.

Clinton, Catherine. 1995. *Tara Revisited: Women, War, and the Plantation Legend.* New York: Abbeville Press.

Edwards, Laura. 2000. *Scarlett Doesn't Live Here Anymore: Southern Women in the Civil War Era.* Urbana: University of Illinois Press.

Faust, Drew Gilpin. 1996. *Mothers of Invention: Women of the Slaveholding South in the American Civil War.* Chapel Hill: University of North Carolina Press.

Rable, George. 1989. *Civil Wars: Women and the Crisis of Southern Nationalism.* Urbana: University of Illinois Press.

Roberts, Giselle. 2003. *The Confederate Belle.* Columbia: University of Missouri Press.

Whites, LeeAnn. 1995. *The Civil War as a Crisis in Gender: Augusta, Georgia, 1860–1890.* Athens: University of Georgia Press.

Smith, Caroline "Cassie" Selden (1837–1907)

Her marriage to Confederate officer Kirby Smith made Caroline "Cassie" Selden Smith the Bride of the Confederacy, and the letters the couple left behind reveal the effects of the Civil War on their personal lives.

Born in September 1837, Cassie Selden was the eldest of seven children born into a wealthy Episcopalian family in Lynchburg, Virginia. Although her father died when she was twelve, family finances enabled Cassie to attend the prestigious Georgetown Seminary. There, she received an education fitting her status as a prominent member of Virginia society.

In spring 1861, Colonel Edmund Kirby Smith, a thirty-four-year-old career military man, arrived in Lynchburg to train recruits for the Confederacy. During a social gathering, Smith teased some of Lynchburg's young ladies, telling them that the girl who made him the finest shirt would receive his romantic attention. Cassie, a self-described Virginia belle, stitched two shirts for the colonel. Smith accepted the gifts graciously and Cassie recalled that, by the time he left Lynchburg in late May, she had "sewn" love's seeds.

Smith had been promoted to brigadier general by the next time Cassie saw him in July 1861. As he recuperated from a wound suffered at Manassas, Cassie doted on him, listening to his stories and taking him to church on Sundays. Smith proposed after he recovered, and the two were married with full military pomp in Lynchburg on September 24. Smith's fame at Manassas prompted the press to dub Cassie the Bride of the Confederacy. The newlyweds honeymooned at Smith's family home in St. Augustine, Florida.

The couple returned to Virginia where Smith served until February 1862. He was promoted and sent to East Tennessee. Cassie remained behind and discovered that she was pregnant. During their separation, the couple began exchanging letters that reflected the personal dimensions of the Civil War. Cassie revealed her anxieties about the pregnancy as well as her longing for her days as a carefree Southern belle.

When Kirby was promoted to lieutenant general and assigned to the Trans-Mississippi in February 1863, Cassie and daughter Catherine accompanied him to Shreveport, Louisiana. After a yellow fever epidemic prompted the general to send his family to Marshall, Texas, he visited them frequently.

After the war, Kirby sought refuge in Mexico and Cuba, and he sent Cassie back to Virginia. In November 1865, Kirby took the amnesty oath and the family reunited in Lynchburg. Left destitute by the war, they settled in Sewanee, Tennessee, where Kirby taught at the University of the South. For the next two decades, Cassie and her husband opened their home to Confederate veterans.

After the general's death in 1893, Cassie became active in the newly formed Daughters of the Confederacy and attended meetings as an honored guest. Nevertheless, as a widow she suffered increasing financial hardships, and only donations from Confederate veterans kept her from poverty. She remained active in promoting the causes of Confederate veterans until her death in 1907.

Jeffery S. Prushankin

See also Letter Writing; Southern Women.
References and Further Reading
"Mrs. Edmund Kirby Smith." 1907. *Confederate Veteran* XV: 563.

Parks, Joseph H. [1954] 1982. *General Edmund Kirby Smith C.S.A.* Baton Rouge: Louisiana State University Press.

Prushankin, Jeffery S. 2005. *A Crisis in Confederate Command: General Edmund Kirby Smith, Richard Taylor, and the Army of the Trans-Mississippi.* Baton Rouge: Louisiana State University Press.

Smith, Cassie. 1945. *All's Fair in Love and War, or The Story of How a Virginia Belle Won a Confederate Colonel.* Nina Kirby-Smith Buck.

Solomon, Clara (ca. 1845–1907)

A member of the Jewish community in New Orleans, Clara Solomon experienced the Civil War and Union occupation as a teenager. Her surviving diary provides a glimpse of a life influenced by several different identities: Jewish, Southern, New Orleanian, and female.

Born to Solomon P. and Emma Solomon, Jewish migrants from South Carolina, Clara Solomon grew up in New Orleans's highly assimilated Sephardic community. The Civil War began when she was sixteen, and her diaries for the years 1861 and 1862 record the thoughts and experiences of a young woman coming of age in the midst of war and occupation.

The Solomon family shared the strong Confederate loyalties of their Catholic and Protestant neighbors. They were members of the Sephardic Dispersed of Judah Congregation, whose rabbi, James Gutheim, gave impassioned sermons in favor of secession and the Confederate cause. Clara and her sister were also avid readers of local newspapers, devouring them in search of war news and the fate of friends and relatives in Confederate service.

Clara recorded the impact that her father's position as a Confederate sutler stationed in Virginia had on his wife and six daughters, who remained in Louisiana. She also wrote about the toll that the Union blockade took on the population of New Orleans. The commercial activity of the city ground to a halt, which dealt a devastating blow to Solomon Solomon's dry goods store and left the family severely in debt. That, combined with his absence from home and uncertain income as a sutler, made supporting themselves a necessary task. While Clara remained at the Louisiana Normal School, she joined her mother and sister in making clothes for Confederate soldiers. The work let them aid the war effort while also earning a small, but much needed income. The Solomon women found that inflation and the blockade made obtaining food, cloth, and other necessary items increasingly difficult. For their Passover celebration in 1862, the family resorted to eating cornbread because of a scarcity of matzo.

Clara also chronicled her experiences in the early weeks of the Union occupation of New Orleans. She was horrified by the surrender of the city, deplored the censorship of the local newspapers, and expressed the hope that the occupation would be short-lived. She noted disapprovingly the ostentatious displays of patriotism by New Orleans women who wore black ribbons and Confederate flags on their dresses. Clara's diary ended in 1862, but the family continued to live in the city for the duration of the war.

After the Civil War, the family's financial position remained precarious. In 1866, Clara Solomon married affluent jeweler Julius Lilienthal, twenty years her senior, and, following his death, she married Dr. George Lawrence.

Julia Huston Nguyen

See also Diaries and Journals; Jewish Women; Southern Women.

References and Further Reading
Ashkenazi, Elliott, ed. 1995. *The Civil War Diary of Clara Solomon: Growing Up in New Orleans, 1861–62.* Baton Rouge: Louisiana State University Press.

Southern Unionists

Refuting the myth of a monolithic Confederate South, many Southern women and men remained loyal to the Union throughout the Civil War. These Southerners opposed secession and hoped for a restoration of the United States. The activities of Unionist women ranged from dissenting silently to sheltering their Unionist male relatives from the Confederate army or to helping Union prisoners of war escape.

Historians disagree on the exact number of Southern Unionists, especially because of disputes over the definitions of the terms "Southerner" and "Unionist." Some scholars count only whites from the Confederate states as Southerners, whereas others include whites and African Americans from all of the slave states. The question of what constitutes Unionism is even less clear. While some Southerners never strayed from loyalty to the United States government, others began the war as Confederates but left their new nation when they felt that it had failed them, and still others suddenly emerged as Unionists only when the Federal army occupied their towns. Additionally, many Unionists kept their loyalty secret, and consequently counting them is impossible.

Southern women chose Unionism for a variety of reasons. Women born in the North most likely continued their fealty to the national government. Other women simply considered secession to be an unnecessary and hasty response to Abraham Lincoln's 1860 election, and therefore, rather than choosing Unionism, these women rejected secession and the Confederacy. Not surprisingly, African American slaves in the South embraced Unionism, especially after the passage of the Emancipation Proclamation. Still other women did not begin the war as Unionists but transferred their loyalty back to the Union when they felt that the Confederacy had failed their families, especially as privation stalked the land. Some historians claim that the Confederate government's actions, particularly the conscription and impressment policies, which made the war appear to be a rich man's war and a poor man's fight, drove these lukewarm, nonslaveholding Confederate men and women to Unionism. Other scholars, however, deny that Unionism had a class aspect, and they depict wealthy women who refused to become Confederates. Nevertheless, probably the most common reason that Southern women became Unionists was that their husbands chose to remain loyal to the United States. Women had an impact on family loyalty decisions, and some husbands and wives divided over the issue of secession. Aware that Unionism could fracture families and expressing sympathy for secessionist women, the Georgia legislature made male service in the Union army sufficient grounds for divorce. Instead of leaving their spouses, however, women married to Unionist husbands more commonly became de facto Unionists.

Geography had an impact on Unionism, with higher concentrations of Unionists in the Appalachian mountain region (including eastern Tennessee, western North Carolina, and northern Alabama) and in the piney woods and swamps outside the South's plantation belts. Generally, these areas were more isolated from major transportation arteries, had a lower percentage of slaves in their population, and had less wealth than the rest of the South. Additionally, religion and ethnicity could influence Unionism, with Dunkards in Virginia and Texans of German descent remaining disproportionately loyal to the United States.

The actions of Southern Unionists varied. Some Unionists fled their homes when the war began or after the August 1861 passage of a law that gave those who refused to support the Confederacy forty days either to depart the South or to be treated as enemy aliens. Some went to the North, while others remained refugees for the duration of the conflict. For those who remained at home, in many regions, silence was the best policy; these Unionists maintained a false outward show of loyalty to the Confederacy, crying when they felt like celebrating and celebrating when they felt like crying. Others took symbolic action, canceling their subscription to Confederate newspapers, refusing to provide money to Confederate charities, singing "Hail, Columbia" and the "Star Spangled Banner," or displaying American flags in their homes.

Unionist women, sometimes taking advantage of their gender, aided the Union army and its soldiers. Some Unionist women served as spies or intelligence gatherers. These included Elizabeth Van Lew, a Richmond abolitionist who helped Union prisoners of war escape from Libby prison and provided information to Ulysses S. Grant's invading army. Other female spies gained access to Confederate army encampments in the guise of looking for their male relatives, or they engaged in seemingly innocuous flirtatious conversations to learn troop deployments. Other women smuggled food, money, and mail to Union prisoners of war in Confederate hospitals. Often possessing more freedom to travel than men and being less likely to have their bodies searched, Southern Unionist women operated as a vital cog in a long-distance communication network between Northerners and Southern Unionists.

These Unionists helped start a new Underground Railroad that transferred information, prisoners of war, or Southern Unionists who feared for their lives rather than escaped slaves.

Other Unionists felt less compulsion to remain furtive in their loyalty to the United States. In regions such as eastern Tennessee and western North Carolina, where Unionists were a majority or a significant minority, they felt less need to hide their allegiance. And, when the Union army occupied a region, Southern Unionists became even more vocal in their fidelity to the United States government. Here, Unionist women often hoped to fulfill the same romantic dream of meeting a handsome soldier that their Confederate counterparts had wished for at the beginning of the war. In Key West, Florida, Unionist women truly echoed their Confederate sisters by presenting Northern soldiers with a flag and raising money for their cause. Federal occupation and Federal policies, which rewarded pledges of loyalty, often made it hard to distinguish between true Unionists and Unionists of convenience, men and women who transferred allegiance to the stronger side. When the Union army moved on, true Unionist women, fearing for their safety, often followed the invading army, for which some provided cooking and washing services.

Slave women can also be viewed as Southern Unionists. Unlike their white counterparts, they, however, could not rely on their gender to shield them from retribution. Nevertheless, this risk did not prevent them from taking advantage of opportunities. Mary Elizabeth Bowser, a former slave working in the Confederate White House, acted as a Union spy and worked with Elizabeth Van Lew. Slave women, like their male counterparts, fled to Union lines, engaged in work slowdowns, and generally tried to accomplish as much as they could to weaken the Confederate cause. They also provided Union troops with information about Confederate armies and could serve as guides. Perhaps the most famous of these guides was the escaped slave and Underground Railroad conductor Harriet Tubman.

Family and community were important to all Unionists regardless of race. Networks of Unionists provided support, both tangible and emotional, to one another. They participated in secret organizations, with names such as the Order of the Heroes of America or the Peace Society, where they discussed how to undermine the Confederate war effort and where they could express their true feelings without fear of retribution. The importance of this community support and the nature of Unionism changed after the Confederacy enacted conscription in April 1862. Prior to the passage of this act, Unionist men could refuse to serve in the Confederate army, but after its enactment avoiding service became a treasonous act with vigilance committees and committees of public safety constantly on the look out for draft dodgers. Thus, many Unionist men went into to hiding to avoid forced service in Southern armies. Unionist women played a vital role in supporting these fugitives by smuggling food and supplies to these men and by warning them when conscript hunters approached.

Whether men or women, Unionists risked both financial and bodily harm. Confederate law provided for the seizure of property of those who aided the Union war effort. Women who provided for their husbands, sons, and others who resisted conscription into the Confederate army could be insulted, have their homes burned, be arrested, or be tortured into revealing the location of their male relatives. Women branded as Unionists, especially those whose husbands fought in the Union army, could be denied government rations, prevented from receiving local charity, or refused the use of local mills for their grain. Also, in several areas, conflict between Unionists and Confederates took the form of guerrilla warfare. Violence begat increasingly violent retaliations, with both sides not necessarily distinguishing between combatants and noncombatants. In those situations, brutality toward women increased, including imprisonment, rape, and murder. Thus, without—and even with—the support of other Unionists, Unionist women often found themselves trapped in precarious situations.

John M. Sacher

See also African American Women; Border States; Bowser, Mary Elizabeth (ca. 1839–n.d.); Confederate Homefront; Conscription; Destruction of Homes; Destruction of Personal Property; Female Spies; Loyalty Oaths; Military Invasion and Occupation; Rape; Refugees; Rural Women; Southern Women; Tubman, Harriet [Araminta Ross] (1822–1913); Urban Women, Southern; Van Lew, Elizabeth (1818–1900).

References and Further Reading
Bynum, Victoria. 1992. *Unruly Women: The Politics of Social and Sexual Control in the Old South.* Chapel Hill: University of North Carolina Press.

Dyer, Thomas G. 1999. *Secret Yankees: The Union Circle in Confederate Atlanta.* Baltimore, MD: Johns Hopkins University Press.

Inscoe, John C., and Robert C. Kenzer, eds. 2001. *Enemies of the Country: New Perspectives on Unionists in the Civil War South.* Athens: University of Georgia Press.

Revels, Tracy. 2004. *Grander in Her Daughters: Florida's Women during the Civil War.* Columbia: University of South Carolina Press.

Storey, Margaret M. 2004. *Loyalty and Loss: Alabama's Unionists in the Civil War and Reconstruction.* Baton Rouge: Louisiana State University Press.

Southworth, Emma Dorothy Eliza Nevitte (1819–1899)

E.D.E.N. Southworth, probably the most widely read female author of the nineteenth century, was described by a contemporary as a Southern woman with Northern principles. Through stories set in the plantation South, Southworth exposed slavery as damaging to all whites who condoned it. Her melodramatic novels often featured unconventional and independent heroines and a sharp critique of men's power over women's lives. Serialized in mass circulation weekly newspapers, her work enjoyed tremendous popular success from the early 1850s to the late 1880s in both the North and the South.

Emma D. E. Nevitte was born December 26, 1819, in Alexandria, Virginia. Her mother, Maria McIntosh, came from generations of landed Southern gentry and married Charles Lecompte Nevitte, an importer who owned a fleet of ships. Emma adored her father, who died when she was four, having never fully recovered from a wound received in the War of 1812. Emma remembered herself as a shy, awkward, unattractive child, with a pretty younger sister who was the family favorite. She grew increasingly isolated and withdrawn, and much of her lonely childhood was spent in the kitchen listening to the servants' ghost stories, legends, and tales of the family's bygone wealth. The Nevittes faced constant financial problems, but summers with her extended family in Maryland exposed Emma to the plantation life often depicted in her novels.

Emma's mother remarried to a schoolmaster in Washington, D.C. After being educated in his school, Emma taught there for five years. In 1840 she married Frederick Southworth, a New York inventor, and they moved to the Wisconsin frontier. After they returned to Washington, he abandoned Emma and their two children in 1844. She returned to teaching to support the children and began writing fiction to supplement her inadequate salary. Her first story appeared in the *Baltimore Saturday Visiter* in 1846, and others the next year in the *National Era*, the capital's abolitionist newspaper. Ill and despairing, with eighty pupils, a bedridden child, and editors to satisfy, she wrote her first novel, *Retribution*. Pouring her misery into her writing seems to have been good for her, and the tale captivated readers.

Retribution, serialized in the *National Era*, launched Southworth's prolific career as a writer of popular fiction. It ran for fourteen installments in 1849 and was so well received that Harper's published it in book form the same year. Drawn from her own abandonment and her firm antislavery convictions, it is the story of a heroine, working to free her slaves, with an unfaithful husband. Suddenly, people offered Southworth friendship and sympathy. She had found independence, respect, and a career. The *National Era* continued to feature her work, and she went on writing abolitionist fiction despite criticism from her family and the Southern press. The *National Era*'s editor wanted an even more damning and attention-getting portrayal of slavery and began installments of Harriett Beecher Stowe's *Uncle Tom's Cabin* in 1851. Southworth continued to write for the *National Era* and sold some pieces to the *Saturday Evening Post*. Throughout her long career, she produced about two novels a year.

Hard work brought financial success. She moved into Prospect Cottage on the Potomac Heights in

Popular nineteenth-century author Emma Dorothy Eliza Nevitte (E.D.E.N.) Southworth. (Cirker, Hayward and Blanche Cirker, eds., *Dictionary of American Portraits*, 1967)

Georgetown in 1853. Among the many guests she entertained there were her friends John Greenleaf Whittier and Harriet Beecher Stowe.

In 1857, Robert Bonner of the *New York Ledger*, the most widely read paper in America, signed Southworth to an exclusive contract, securing the right to serialize all her novels before they were published in book form. Southworth's novels were its chief selling point, dominating the front page and often continuing for six months. Each week's episode, eagerly awaited by readers, was accompanied by a dramatic woodcut illustration. *The Hidden Hand* first appeared in 1859 and was her most popular tale. It was serialized again in 1868 and 1883 before being released as a book in 1888. Some nineteenth-century critics found fault with her overblown language, extravagant and improbable plot contrivances, imperfectly drawn characters, and sensational treatment of race and sex, but the reading public could not get enough. Her work was widely translated and reprinted abroad.

Southworth sailed for England in 1859, remaining there until 1862. On her return, she firmly supported the Union despite her Southern roots. Her letters to Robert Bonner of the *Ledger* clearly express her anti-Confederate sentiments. She nursed wounded soldiers, and her cottage was several times used as an auxiliary hospital.

Because her work was serialized and issued as books with a variety of titles and publishers, estimates of the number of novels she produced between 1849 and 1886 vary from forty to sixty. An indication of Southworth's lasting importance is the attention focused on her life and work. Literary scholars initially categorized her with the "scribbling women" and sentimental literary domestics, who wrote novels for a female audience, because she spun melodramatic tales that often ended in a happy marriage. More recently, scholars interpret Southworth's fondness for heroines who are rewarded for their independence and rebellion against Victorian female passivity as providing a subversive outlet for the fantasies of repressed female readers. Because she adapted the romantic Southern genre of the plantation novel to her storytelling style and because her most successful novel, *The Hidden Hand*, was not as explicitly abolitionist as her earlier works, twentieth-century critical consensus accused her of abandoning her antislavery principles. However, in the years before the Civil War, the *National Ledger's* editorial policy stressed neutrality in the interest of circulation. Southern readers had grown increasingly sensitive to Northern attacks on slavery, and Bonner allowed nothing that would offend them. Southworth, practiced in lampooning gender conventions, applied the same subversive literary techniques to race in *The Hidden Hand*. Beginning with the sale of its white heroine into slavery as an infant, the novel is full of episodes demonstrating that race had looser boundaries and less significance than many whites believed.

E. D. E. N. Southworth died at Prospect Cottage on June 30, 1899.

Nancy Gray Schoonmaker

See also Abolitionism and Northern Reformers; Fiction Writers, Southern; Hospitals; Fiction Writers, Northern; Northern Women; Nurses; Southern Women; Stowe, Harriet Elizabeth Beecher (1811–1896); Wartime Literature.

References and Further Reading
Dobson, Joanne. 1986. "The Hidden Hand: Subversion of Cultural Ideology in Three Mid-nineteenth-century American Women's Novels." *American Quarterly* 38 (2): 223–242.

Hart, John S. 1852. "Emma D. E. N. Southworth." In *The Female Prose Writers of America, with Portraits, Biographical Notices, and Specimens of their Writing*. Philadelphia, PA: E. H. Butler & Co.

Jones, Paul Christian. 2001. "'This Dainty Woman's Hand . . . Red with Blood': E. D. E. N. Southworth's *The Hidden Hand* as Abolitionist Narrative." *American Transcendental Quarterly* 15 (1): 59–80.

Sizer, Lyde Cullen. 2000. *The Political Work of Northern Women Writers and the Civil War, 1850–1872*. Chapel Hill: University of North Carolina Press.

Southworth, Emma Dorothy Eliza Nevitte. 1997. *The Hidden Hand,* with Introduction by Nina Baym. New York: Oxford University Press.

Swisshelm, Jane Grey Cannon. 1970. *Half a Century*. New York: Source Book Press. (Orig. pub. 1880.)

Stanton, Elizabeth Cady (1815–1902)

Women's rights reformer and abolitionist Elizabeth Cady Stanton devoted her life to the fight for equal rights for women.

Elizabeth Cady Stanton was born in Johnstown, New York, to Margaret and Daniel Cady. She attended Johnstown Academy and Emma Willard's Troy Female Seminary. In 1840, Elizabeth married reformer Henry Stanton, a prominent abolitionist. After the wedding, the couple attended the World's Anti-Slavery Convention. Male participants questioned the credentials of the female delegates, and after some debate the men decided that women could sit in a screened-off section. The debate over whether to seat women outraged Stanton, who, along with Lucretia Mott, a Quaker preacher, agreed to hold a women's rights convention when they returned to the United States. Eight years later they helped to plan the first women's rights convention in the United States.

In 1848, Stanton, Mott, Martha Coffin Wright, Mary Ann McClintock, and Jane Hunt issued a call for a women's rights convention to be held in Seneca Falls, New York. Delegates signed the Declaration of Sentiments modeled after the Declaration of Independence. A woman suffrage resolution introduced by Stanton sparked debate at the conference and was passed by a small margin.

In 1851, Stanton met Susan B. Anthony, and together the two fought for women's rights in New York. Stanton, who had seven children by 1859 and a husband who was often away from home, relied on Anthony to build support for women's rights. Stanton authored the speeches given by Anthony and she drafted resolutions. Anthony circulated petitions, held meetings, and organized women. In 1860, their hard work paid off when the New York State Legislature passed the Married Women's Property Act.

The Civil War halted Stanton's work for women's rights, and she came to believe that woman suffrage organizers had to shift their priorities. Stanton believed that women would be made citizens and enfranchised at the end of the war if they committed themselves to war work. Unlike other Northern women, she did not serve as a nurse or work with the United States Sanitary Commission. She and Anthony had other plans.

Anthony and Stanton favored abolitionism and believed that the conflict must abolish slavery. Stanton believed that President Abraham Lincoln moved too slowly on the issue of freedom for slaves. Lincoln, who faced pressure to draw up an emancipation policy, had stalled on the issue. He drew up a proclamation in 1862 and waited for the right time to issue it. On January 1, 1863, Lincoln signed the Emancipation Proclamation, freeing slaves in the Confederate states but exempting areas that remained in the Union.

The proclamation did not please Stanton or other abolitionists. They believed that the Constitution needed to be amended to end slavery once and for all. Henry Stanton encouraged his wife and Anthony to take action. They began drafting plans for a Northern women's organization. They issued a call for a meeting of the women of the Republic, and they assembled in New York in May 1863.

As one of the more radical of the nineteenth-century suffragists and women's rights leaders, Elizabeth Cady Stanton sought above all else to free women from the legal obstacles that prevented them from achieving equality with men. (Library of Congress)

Those who attended the convention formed the Women's National Loyal League, the delegates electing Stanton president and Anthony secretary. The goal of the league was to distribute petitions and obtain signatures of those in favor of a Federal amendment to the United States Constitution to abolish slavery. Less than nine months later, the league submitted petitions to Congress bearing the signatures of one hundred thousand individuals. Convinced of its overwhelming public support, the United States Senate passed the Thirteenth Amendment in April 1864, but the issue went down to defeat in the House of Representatives that June. By August 1864, the league had gathered nearly four hundred thousand signatures. In 1865, the House voted in favor of the Thirteenth Amendment, and the amendment was ratified that same year.

In 1864, Lincoln's re-nomination for president was uncertain as war casualties increased, and he received little support from the Republican Party. Stanton and abolitionist Wendell Phillips endorsed the candidacy of General John C. Frémont, who had issued an edict freeing the slaves of those who supported the Confederacy in Missouri. To stir up interest in the Frémont campaign, she asked abolitionist William Lloyd Garrison for his assistance and also sent suggestions to Frémont's wife on how to call a dissident political convention. At the convention, held in May 1864, a small group of supporters nominated Frémont for president. He withdrew from the presidential race in September, and Lincoln was re-elected to a second term in 1864.

In 1865, Stanton began receiving drafts of the proposed Fourteenth Amendment, which would, for the first time, introduce the word "male" into the Constitution. The drafts offended Stanton who believed that the nation would extend citizenship rights to women to thank them for their war work. She insisted that the amendment include women, fearing that it would be even more difficult eventually to secure woman suffrage if the amendment excluded women. Abolitionists disagreed. They refused to support woman suffrage, calling the postwar period the Negro's hour and favoring black suffrage.

Disappointed, Anthony and Stanton held the first women's rights convention since the beginning of the Civil War. Delegates formed the American Equal Rights Association to secure universal suffrage (black and woman suffrage). In 1867, Stanton tried to secure universal suffrage in New York and Kansas. The campaign in Kansas was particularly bitter and helped to foster an independent feminist movement, as Stanton and Anthony began to recognize that abolitionists like Wendell Phillips, a previous supporter of women's rights, refused to champion the cause until black suffrage had been secured.

In spite of Stanton's opposition to the Fourteenth Amendment, the amendment was ratified and became part of the Constitution in 1868. When the Fifteenth Amendment was introduced in Congress, Stanton used racist and elitist arguments to oppose the amendment. The issue of black suffrage and the Fifteenth Amendment split suffragists into two camps: those who favored the Fifteenth Amendment and those who opposed it. This split led to the creation of two separate suffrage associations in 1869: the National Woman Suffrage Association

(NWSA) headed by Anthony and Stanton, and the American Woman Suffrage Association. The groups merged in 1890, and Stanton became the first president of the resultant National American Woman Suffrage Association.

Elizabeth Cady Stanton died in 1902.

Jennifer Ross-Nazzal

See also Abolitionism and Northern Reformers; Anthony, Susan B. (1820–1906); Emancipation Proclamation (January 1, 1863); Fifteenth Amendment; Fourteenth Amendment; Garrison, William Lloyd (1805–1879); Lincoln, Abraham (1809–1865); Mott, Lucretia Coffin (1793–1880); National Women's Loyal League [Women's National Loyal League]; Northern Women; Quaker Women; Thirteenth Amendment.

References and Further Reading

Banner, Lois W. 1980. *Elizabeth Cady Stanton: A Radical for Woman's Rights.* Boston: Little, Brown and Company.

DuBois, Ellen Carol. 1978. *Feminism and Suffrage: The Emergence of an Independent Women's Movement in America 1848–1869.* Ithaca, NY: Cornell University Press.

Griffith, Elisabeth. 1984. *In Her Own Right: The Life of Elizabeth Cady Stanton.* New York: Oxford University Press.

Lutz, Alma. 1940. *Created Equal: A Biography of Elizabeth Cady Stanton, 1815–1902.* New York: John Day Company.

Stephens, Octavia (Tivie) Bryant (1841–1908)

Diarist Octavia Bryant Stephens was the wife of a small planter in East Florida. Her and her family's wartime experiences typified those of small slaveholders throughout the South.

Born on October 21, 1841, while her parents were visiting family members in Massachusetts, Tivie was raised in Jacksonville and on an estate called White Cottage in Waleka, Florida. Her father was a well traveled lawyer who also worked as a merchant and newspaper editor.

As a teenager, Tivie began a courtship with Winston Stephens, a well-regarded small planter and slaveowner more than eleven years her senior. Tivie accepted his marriage proposal in 1856, but her parents prevented the union because she was not yet fifteen. In 1858, when Stephens returned after fighting in the Third Seminole War, the couple courted in secret. They married on November 1, 1859, just after Tivie turned eighteen. The couple moved into the Rose Cottage estate in Welaka, Florida. The following year, their plantation contained ten slaves and primarily grew short staple and long staple cotton.

During the secession crisis, Tivie and Winston both hoped they could silence the radical Democrats in the region. In the 1860 election, Winston ran unsuccessfully for office as a Constitutional Unionist. After the fall of Fort Sumter, the Bryant family, like much of Jacksonville, divided its loyalties. Tivie's father remained a staunch Unionist and fled to Cuba, but all but one of her brothers fought for the Confederacy. Winston enlisted in the Second Florida Calvary, and Tivie took control of the homestead.

Tivie and other East Floridians felt the full brunt of the Federal naval blockade. Out of necessity and Tivie's ingenuity, the Rose Cottage became more self-reliant. Throughout the Confederacy and especially in isolated East Florida, food shortages and a reliance on local produce and homespun clothes became the norm. When Union troops invaded and occupied Fernandina in 1862, the situation on the homefront worsened. Tivie and her neighbors buried their valuables and otherwise prepared for invasion by Union troops. Near the end of 1863, the surrender of Jacksonville and the Confederate abandonment of East Florida led Tivie to abandon the Rose Cottage and relocate her family near Thomasville, Georgia. Tivie also suffered personal losses during the war. Her infant daughter Isabella died in January 1862.

Tivie, like many women, was widowed by the war. Winston was killed by a Union sniper during a small skirmish near Cedar Creek on March 1, 1864. No longer living at the home that they created together, she would remain in Thomasville until the war's conclusion. She gave birth to Winston Jr, the last of their three children, months after her husband's death.

Tivie returned to Welaka with her two children in 1869. She lived there until her death on September 6, 1908.

Andrew K. Frank

See also Confederate Homefront; Courtship and Marriage; Diaries and Journals; Letter Writing; Military Invasion and Occupation; Refugees; Shortages; Southern Women; Widows, Confederate.

References and Further Reading

Blakey, Arch Fredric, Ann Smith Lainhart, Winston Bryan Stephens Jr., eds. 1998. *Rose Cottage Chronicles: Civil War Letters of the Bryant-Stephens Families of North Florida.* Gainesville: University Press of Florida.

Stone, Cyrena Ann Bailey (1830–1868)

Southern Unionist, Vermont native, and essayist Cyrena Ann Bailey Stone spent the Civil War in Atlanta. Her journal remained anonymous for more than a century.

The fifth child of Phinehas and Janette MacArthur Bailey, Cyrena was born in East Berkshire, Vermont, in 1830. Her father's position as a Congregationalist minister moved the family between Vermont and New York. Her mother died in 1839, her father remarried soon after, and the family moved back to East Berkshire in 1845.

Little is known about Cyrena's early life. She was most likely educated at common schools, but she may have also been educated at home by her father. Cyrena honed her writing skills, as evidenced by her published essays on spiritual, natural, and political topics.

Cyrena met lawyer Amherst Willoughby Stone, the son of a local farmer, in East Berkshire sometime before 1850. The two married in August 1850 and set up house near Atlanta in Fayetteville, Georgia. Their daughter died of consumption in August 1854, soon after her first birthday. Cyrena published an anonymous essay in an Augusta paper that reflected her grief over Jennie's death. The Stones left Fayetteville for Atlanta in 1854.

Atlanta offered many opportunities for the young couple. They soon became ensconced in the city's intellectual, social, and civic life. From Atlanta, Cyrena anonymously published religious essays in local papers. They built a house with several outbuildings on fifteen acres on the outskirts of town, and they owned six slaves. By the Civil War, the Stones lived a life of privilege, influence, and luxury, but in many ways they remained outsiders because of their New England backgrounds.

Much of what is known about Cyrena's wartime life comes from her half sister's novel, *Goldie's Inheritance,* which contains large excerpts of Cyrena's diary, including portions that seem to have been lost. The extant diary stretches from January 1, 1864, to July 22, 1864, and it details life for a Unionist in the Confederate city. Throughout the diary, Cyrena carefully disguises her identity, referring to herself as Miss Abby. She also hides the names of other Atlanta Unionists.

The two documents offer broad outlines of Cyrena's life. Throughout the secession crisis and war, she upheld her dedication to the United States. She anonymously published pro-Union essays, and she spent the war visiting and aiding Union prisoners and wounded in the city. In late August 1862, Confederate authorities arrested Cyrena and several other Unionists for their anti-Southern activities. Amherst's April 1863 departure left Cyrena, like other Southern women, alone to protect her property and fend for herself. She remained in Atlanta during the 1864 siege but left a few weeks after the city's capture. She traveled to Nashville to reunite with Amherst, and the couple went to New York City.

Cyrena Bailey Stone died December 18, 1868, in Sheldon, Vermont.

Lisa Tendrich Frank

See also Civilian Life; Confederate Homefront; Religion; Sherman's Campaign (1864–1865); Southern Unionists; Southern Women; Summerlin, Mary (ca. 1837–n.d.).

References and Further Reading

Dyer, Thomas G. 1999. *Secret Yankees: The Union Circle in Confederate Atlanta.* Baltimore, MD: Johns Hopkins University Press.

Whitney, Louisa M. 1903. *Goldie's Inheritance: A Story of the Siege of Atlanta.* Burlington, VT: Free Press Association.

Stone, Lucy (1818–1893)

Women's rights activist Lucy Stone began her public career as an abolitionist lecturer but quickly added women's rights to her repertoire of speeches. For almost fifty years, she played a key role in American women's struggle for equal rights. Stone gained fame for her work as an organizer, publisher, and strategist in the early women's rights movement.

Stone was born in West Brookfield, Massachusetts, to a hardworking farming family. They were devout Congregationalists and abolitionists, and Lucy embraced both sets of beliefs. Against her parents' wishes, Stone used money she had saved to attend Mount Holyoke Seminary in 1839. She had to leave school after only one year to attend to an ill sister.

Stone continued her education at Oberlin College in 1843. Oberlin, the first coeducational college in the United States, did not allow her to practice rhetoric or to take part in class debates or discussions. Frustrated by this restriction, Stone and Antoinette Brown organized a debating society for young women. The two became lifelong friends. From Oberlin, Stone wrote to abolitionists Abby Kelley and Stephen Foster, persuading them to address the student body on the subject of abolition. At this time Stone resolved to become a public speaker for women's rights. Stone graduated from Oberlin in 1847, the first Massachusetts woman to earn a bachelor's degree.

In December 1847, Stone gave her first public lecture on women's rights. She also began giving public lectures against slavery. By 1848 the Massachusetts Anti-Slavery Society had hired her as an agent, but she was criticized for speaking about women's rights on "company time." Stone arranged to lecture on abolitionism on weekends and on women's rights during the week.

Through the 1840s and 1850s, Stone was a highly popular speaker on both abolition and women's rights. Audience members noted that her pleasant appearance and melodic voice made her acceptable even to those who viewed women speakers as loud or unladylike.

Although early in her life Stone claimed that she never would marry, she met Henry Blackwell in 1853 and married him in 1855. She maintained her views on women's rights in her wedding vows. Their unique wedding vows protested the conventional position of women in marriage. Unusual for the time, Stone also refused to change her last name after she

Lucy Stone's involvement in the woman's rights and woman suffrage movements overshadowed her years of labor for the antislavery movement (1818–1893). (Library of Congress)

The differences between Stone's conservative feminism and the more radical position of Stanton and Anthony resurfaced when the Fourteenth and Fifteenth Amendments were moving through Congress. Stone believed that women must support these amendments for the freed slaves' sake even though they ignored women's issues. Stanton and Anthony disagreed, and the disagreement led to a split in the women's rights movement in 1869. Stanton and Anthony formed the National Woman Suffrage Association. Stone led the American Woman Suffrage Association, along with such moderates as Mary Livermore and Julia Ward Howe.

In 1867, Stone began publishing the *Woman's Journal,* a journal devoted to women's interests and their educational, legal, and political equality. She served as its editor from 1872 to 1882.

By 1890 the leaders of the two suffrage organizations realized that reunification would best serve women. The groups merged, becoming the National American Woman Suffrage Association. Stone chaired the executive committee, but failing health limited her activities. She died at her home in Dorchester, Massachusetts, in 1893.

Ellen H. Todras

See also Abolitionism and Northern Reformers; Anthony, Susan B. (1820–1906); Education, Northern; Fifteenth Amendment; Fourteenth Amendment; Kelley, Abby (1811–1887); National Women's Loyal League [Women's National Loyal League]; Northern Women; Stanton, Elizabeth Cady (1815–1902); Thirteenth Amendment.

References and Further Reading
DuBois, Ellen C. 1978. *Feminism and Suffrage: The Emergence of an Independent Women's Movement in America, 1848–1869.* Ithaca, NY: Cornell University Press.
Kerr, Andrea Moore. 1992. *Lucy Stone: Speaking out for Equality.* Piscataway, NJ: Rutgers University Press.
Venet, Wendy Hamand. 1991. *Neither Ballots nor Bullets: Women Abolitionists and the Civil War.* Charlottesville: University of Virginia Press.

married. The couple's only child, Alice Stone Blackwell, was born in 1857.

Through the 1850s, Stone was a strong member of the women's rights movement. She worked closely with leaders Susan B. Anthony and Elizabeth Cady Stanton. However, her relationship with the two grew strained as they discussed the agenda for the 1860 convention. Stanton wanted divorce reform to be an issue, but Stone opposed pursuing it, believing it to be too radical an issue. Divorce was introduced, and Stone did not attend the convention.

When the Civil War broke out, women's rights activists agreed to redirect their energies to the war effort. They formed the Woman's National Loyal League, which enabled women to work in the political sphere for the nation. Its goal was to gather signatures on a Mammoth Petition to Congress to abolish slavery. They collected almost half a million signatures and ultimately helped push Congress to enact the Thirteenth Amendment.

Stone, Sarah Katherine "Kate" (1841–1907)
Kate Stone's Civil War diary gives vivid glimpses of her family's comfortable plantation life and their

efforts to maintain the status quo despite wartime shortages. Her narrative also details refugee life in the Confederacy.

Kate was born in Hinds County, Mississippi, on January 8, 1841, one of ten children of William Patrick and Amanda Susan Ragan Stone. The Stones valued education, and a tutor lived with the family. Kate was a graduate of Episcopal Bishop Stephen Elliott's fashionable academy in Nashville. Kate's father died in 1855, leaving heavy debts. However, Amanda Stone purchased Brokenburn plantation and ran it with such skill that the proceeds of the crop of 1861 would have given her clear title. She was making long-range plans to give a plantation and slave workforce to each of her children.

The war changed everything. Leaving Brokenburn, the Stones joined thousands of Southern refugees seeking a safe place to wait out the war. Kate's family was one of many who settled in Tyler, Texas. The townspeople were initially hostile, but after several months Kate and her mother were invited to take part in a benefit to raise money for a soldiers' home. Amanda Stone's expertise in assembling fashionable entertainment quickly put Kate and her mother at the center of Tyler society. Kate noted that people had grown accustomed to death from a steady stream of casualty reports; people grieved but social life continued.

Kate began her journal with a description of the departure of her brother William, captain of the company of men he had raised to fight for the Confederacy. Kate wrote of slaves escaping to freedom behind Yankee lines, planters burning their cotton to keep it from falling into the hands of the enemy, and the arrival of Union troops. When armed blacks menaced their neighborhood, Kate's widowed mother made plans to flee to Texas. Forced to leave almost everything behind, the Stones learned that their former slaves had remained on the plantation looting what was left after the Yankees had removed their furnishings. Kate's mother had managed the plantation well and left with enough money to live carefully until the war ended.

At the end of the war, three of Kate's brothers were dead. Facing an uncertain future, the family returned to Brokenburn and tried to raise a crop but ended the year deeper in debt. By 1868, the family was forced to leave. On December 8, 1869, Kate married Henry Bry Holmes, a member of the family's circle of friends in Tyler. They lived in Tallulah and raised two children to adulthood. Kate was a leader in the town's social and religious activities, and she died there on December 28, 1907.

Nancy Gray Schoonmaker

See also Aid Societies; Confederate Homefront; Diaries and Journals; Fairs and Bazaars; Fundraising; Refugees; Slaveholding Women; Southern Women.

References and Further Reading

Anderson, John Q., ed. 1955. *Brokenburn: The Journal of Kate Stone, 1861–1868.* Baton Rouge: Louisiana State University Press. (Reprinted 1995 with Introduction by Drew Gilpin Faust.)

Wilson, Edmund. [1962] 1984. *Patriotic Gore: Studies in the Literature of the American Civil War.* Boston: Northeastern University Press.

Stowe, Harriet Elizabeth Beecher (1811–1896)

Abolitionist and author Harriet Beecher Stowe stirred up antislavery sentiment with her novel *Uncle Tom's Cabin; Or, Life among the Lowly.* The novel, first published in serial form beginning in 1851, railed against the cornerstone of the Southern plantation economy—slavery—and guaranteed Stowe a place in the historical and literary canon.

Born in Litchfield, Connecticut, on June 14, 1811, Stowe was the daughter of prominent Congregationalist minister Lyman Beecher and his first wife, Roxana Foote. Like her older sisters, she attended the Litchfield Female Academy, a progressive school for girls. At the age of thirteen, she enrolled at the Hartford Female Seminary, a school founded by her older sister Catharine. She later taught there. In 1832, she began teaching at Catharine's Western Female Institute in Ohio. In 1836, Harriet married Calvin Stowe, a biblical scholar and theologian who taught at Lane Theological Seminary in Cincinnati.

Harriet began writing early in her life. In April 1834, "A New England Sketch" was published in *Western Monthly Magazine,* a literature periodical.

The Mayflower (1843), a collection of stories and sketches, launched her career as an antislavery writer. Her earliest writing was modeled after Joseph Addison's *The Spectator*, utilizing Enlightenment rhetoric to inculcate moral lessons.

By the time she wrote *Uncle Tom's Cabin* at her kitchen table in Maine, Stowe was the mother of seven children. She drew partly on her experiences in Ohio and her contact with escaped slaves there to create the characters and situations in the book. The novel first appeared in serial form in the *National Era*, a Washington-based abolitionist newspaper, from June 5, 1851, to April 1, 1852. The forty-installment novel captured public attention. Its popularity in the papers led to its publication as a book and provided publicity for the book's release on March 20, 1852. The novel would spawn plays, songs, and games.

Like many women of her time, Stowe took up her pen as a weapon to fight injustices that she perceived to threaten the American family. Inspired by the fiends and giants in John Bunyan's *Pilgrim's Progress* (1678), Stowe's landmark narrative against slavery was driven by chiaroscuro, the interplay of light and dark or good and evil. The character of Marie St. Clare, a selfish and self-centered invalid who lived in luxury and used her ailment to avoid taking action, was for Stowe the personification of feminine evil. Her inaction prevents St. Clare from caring for weaker and more ignorant individuals in her household and fulfilling her role as a mother. In this and other situations, *Uncle Tom's Cabin* spotlighted the conflict between slavery and motherhood as a result of literary devices that Stowe employed to prompt sympathetic imitation among American women. For example, at one point Stowe's narrator asks readers if they have ever felt the loss of a child, hoping to direct them to imitate a sequence of emotions as if the characters were neighbors or friends.

Stowe was idolized for her novel in England and in the North, but vehemently criticized for it across the slaveholding Southern states. She had never traveled south of northern Kentucky and received criticism from Southerners who said she knew nothing about their peculiar institution. To counter this criticism and to add credence to her critique of Southern society, Stowe published *A Key to Uncle Tom's Cabin* (1853). This follow-up contained documentary evidence about slavery culled from graphic anecdotes in Southern newspapers. Her sources for these stories, gathered by Southern abolitionists Sarah and Angelina Grimké, were originally published in *American Slavery as It Is: Testimony of a Thousand Witnesses* (1839) by Sarah Grimké and her brother-in-law Theodore Weld. The documents illuminate the basis for many of Stowe's characters and storylines. For example, the character of Lucy may have been styled after Margaret Garner, a slave who escaped with four children, only to be returned to the South on a ship that went down. Garner, who had killed her three-year-old child in prison, drowned her infant and then refused to let herself be saved.

In all of her work, Stowe used real-life experience to explore common themes. She understood the emotional conflicts that arose in parenting and infused this ordinary, everyday drama into her writing. During a cholera epidemic in 1849, she lost her youngest child Charlie when he was eighteen months old. During his life, Charlie presented Stowe with challenges that contradicted the angelic fictional children presented in Victorian children's literature. She wrote *Our Charley, and, What to Do with Him* (1858), a children's book of short stories, that seemed to convey the simple sentimentalism of a grieving mother even as it presented a realistic and lovable boy character who vacillated between good and bad behavior without having the opportunity of full character development.

Charlie's death had a tremendous impact on Stowe's writing. She told friends that her loss of him helped her understand the horrors that slave mothers faced in the South. She, too, knew what it was like to have a child torn from her. Perhaps Stowe's mourning for her last-born, as well as her rage over changes in the Fugitive Slave Act, shaped her creation of the fictional character of Little Eva, a child redeemer endowed with an intuitive spiritual sensibility in *Uncle Tom's Cabin*.

In subsequent works, Stowe continued to write about what she considered her society's biggest problems. In 1856, Stowe published another antislavery

Connecticut-born Harriet Beecher Stowe is famous as the author of the best-selling antislavery novel *Uncle Tom's Cabin* (1852), which aroused Northern feeling against slavery in the United States. (National Archives and Records Administration)

novel, *Dred: A Tale of the Dismal Swamp.* In this book, she presented black characters who she thought would evoke the sympathy of her white middle-class readers. In this work, Stowe showed herself as a radical abolitionist who called for emancipation. However, she stopped short of integration and instead supported the colonization of freed slaves. In *The Minister's Wooing* (1859), she satirized Calvinism and demonstrated her frustration with married women's limitations under the law. However, Stowe, like her sister Catharine Beecher, tapped into the powerful ideology of female labor as a woman's duty, particularly in one passage suggesting that housework should be completed in the morning to leave the rest of the day free for social obligations, familial repose, and intellectual development.

Her unmarried sister, Catharine, freed Harriet from many domestic obligations throughout the 1840s and allowed her time to write. Embedded in *Uncle Tom's Cabin* was the benevolent female influence that Catharine promoted in her *Essay on Slavery and Abolition with Reference to the Duty of American Females* (1837) that encouraged women to appropriately assert their power of persuasion in the domestic sphere. This essay, a reproach on the radical abolitionism practiced by Sarah and Angelina Grimké, ignited a debate among American women. Angelina Grimké responded to the essay with her *Letters to Catharine Beecher in Reply to "An Essay on Slavery and Abolitionism," Addressed to A.E. Grimké* (1838).

After Abraham Lincoln announced the drafting of an Emancipation Proclamation in late September 1862, Stowe called on First Lady Mary Todd Lincoln in New York City to request an invitation to the White House. Stowe was granted an invitation for tea on December 2, 1862, but she was not impressed by the First Lady. When she and her children arrived in Washington, D.C., they visited hospitals and tourist destinations in the area. When Stowe met President Lincoln, he supposedly greeted her with the apocryphal comment, "So you're the little woman who wrote the book that made this great war." When news of the Emancipation Proclamation arrived on January 1, 1863, Stowe was attending a New Year's Jubilee celebration at the Boston Music Hall. Recognizing her book as a major influence in pushing the nation toward abolition, the crowd gave Stowe a standing ovation, repeatedly calling out her name.

Stowe kept busy during the Civil War. Her son Fred enlisted in the Union army, as did many of her husband Calvin's students at Phillips Andover. She published articles in the *Independent* that detailed the excitement around her. The war took a toll on the Beecher family, as it did on nearly every family in the Civil War North and South. Many of the men of Harriet's family who served were wounded, and some of the women came down with tuberculosis. In addition, Stowe's health had been compromised by closely spaced pregnancies and her father died in 1863. Harriet helped support her family during these difficult times.

The Pearl of Orr's Island (1862) was the only book Stowe published during the Civil War. As it had prior to the war, much of her work centered on domestic themes and women's issues. In *The Pearl*, Stowe embedded feminine logic in ordinary domestic experiences, creating an innovative gender schema. She subtly intertwined gender roles so that her female characters baked, sewed, and navigated boats while the male characters practiced the law and hung curtains, redefining gender.

During the war, Stowe also submitted articles that were serialized in *The Atlantic Monthly* and published in a bound volume as *Household Papers and Stories* (1865). She started working for *Hearth and Home Magazine* during the same year. After the Civil War, she captured the social life and customs of post-Revolutionary New England in *Oldtown Folks*, published in 1869. *Uncle Tom's Cabin*, an all-time best seller, made Stowe a literary success, but that success came without copyright protection. Stowe had received $10,000 for the first three months of sales for the work, but she felt that she was owed much more. Not having reaped the monetary benefits of a best seller, Stowe was forced to continue writing to support her retired husband, unmarried daughters, and a son who was driven to drink by his experiences during the Civil War.

Stowe had trouble defining herself as a writer once she became famous. In 1866, she began to publish articles and books under the pseudonym Christopher Crowfield to give herself the freedom to write without bias for her past work or her gender. Under the name Crowfield, her *House and Home Papers* was published in 1869.

Stowe collaborated with her sister Catharine, who could no longer afford a home of her own, on *American Woman's Home* in 1869. Stowe contributed ideas for practical design elements for the household while Catharine promoted the idea of female-headed households. *American Woman's Home* defined the American household as a Christian institution combining home, school, and church complete with illustrated designs for multifunction spaces.

Throughout her life Stowe remained keenly aware of her role in ending slavery as the author of *Uncle Tom's Cabin*. Stowe also knew that her book added a new female rhetoric to the national consciousness that would not be forgotten or over-

looked. This knowledge gave her great comfort in her later years. Late in life, she divided her time between Hartford and Florida, where she wrote children's stories and hymns.

Harriet Beecher Stowe died in Hartford, Connecticut, on July 1, 1896.

Meredith Eliassen

See also Abolitionism and Northern Reformers; Beecher, Catharine (1800–1878); Fiction Writers, Northern.

References and Further Reading
Fields, Catherine Keene, and Lisa C. Kightlinger, eds. 1993. *To Ornament Their Minds: Sarah Pierce's Litchfield Female Academy, 1792–1833.* Litchfield, CT: Litchfield Historical Society.

Kelley, Mary. 1984. *Private Women, Public Stage: Literary Domesticity in Nineteenth-Century America.* New York: Oxford University Press.

Lerner, Gerda. 1998. *The Grimké Sisters from South Carolina: Pioneers for Women's Rights and Abolition.* New York: Oxford University Press.

Sizer, Lyde Cullen. 2000. *The Political Work of Northern Women Writers and the Civil War, 1850–1872.* Chapel Hill: University of North Carolina Press.

Sklar, Katherine Kish. 1973. *Catharine Beecher: A Study in American Domesticity.* New Haven, CT: Yale University Press.

Stowe, Harriet Beecher. [1852] 2001. *Uncle Tom's Cabin, or Life among the Lowly*, with Introduction by Jane Smiley. New York: Modern Library.

White, Barbara A. 2003. *The Beecher Sisters.* New Haven, CT: Yale University Press.

Summerlin, Mary (ca. 1837–n.d.)

Unionist widow and single mother Mary Summerlin lived in Atlanta during the Civil War. She visited Empire Hospital regularly, bringing supplies and money to Union soldiers. She also helped a Union spy gather information and move within Confederate society. Confederate officials imprisoned her for her suspected involvement in espionage activities.

Born in Virginia, Mary and her family soon moved to Athens, Georgia. At the age of eight, Mary was sent to Vermont to live with relatives and to go to school. In 1855, she returned to Athens. She married a local storekeeper, W. T. Summerlin, and the two lived in Henry County, Georgia. The couple's only child, Ella, was born sometime before W. T. Summerlin's 1858 death. To support herself and her daughter, Mary settled in Atlanta. There she opened a dressmaking shop in her home, which was across the street from Empire Hospital.

During the Civil War, Mary visited the hospital frequently, often to give aid to wounded Union soldiers. As did other Unionist women, Mary visited the hospital under the cover of aiding the Confederate soldiers there. Once in the hospital, she would casually bring "leftovers" to the Union men in residence. She and sometimes her daughter also smuggled money and other supplies to Union men. In late August 1862, Mary, with at least seven other Unionists, was suspected of and arrested for aiding the Union. However, her arrest and short imprisonment did little to hamper her Unionist efforts.

In December 1862, Summerlin met and began aiding a Union agent called Tommy. She passed him off as her cousin, Tommy Burton, during an invited stay at her home in early 1863 as well as during a hospital supply-gathering trip. When Summerlin, Tommy, and, most likely, hospital matron Ella K. Newsom traveled to Charleston and Augusta to gather hospital necessaries, Tommy gathered information on forts, harbors, and other Confederate military details.

Tommy left Summerlin's home soon after their return to Atlanta, but he returned in the summer of 1863. This time, however, many Confederates became suspicious of his motives and background. He evaded capture, dressing in one of Mary's dresses to get from his hotel to Summerlin's home, where he hid in a large table for two weeks. Mary then smuggled Tommy out of Atlanta dressed as a woman.

Soon after Tommy's escape, Confederate officials arrested Summerlin on suspicion of harboring spies. During her six-month imprisonment, she fell ill, obtained a parole, and returned home. Both Mary and her home felt the effects of the Union's 1864 bombardment of Atlanta; the home was damaged and she was wounded. Yet she received permission from General William T. Sherman to remain in Atlanta after he ordered its evacuation in September 1864.

Lisa Tendrich Frank

See also Atlanta, Evacuation of (Special Field Orders, Number 67); Confederate Homefront; Female Spies; Imprisonment of Women; Northern Women; Nurses; Sherman, William Tecumseh (1820–1891); Southern Unionists; Southern Women; Stone, Cyrena Ann Bailey (1830–1868).

References and Further Reading

Dyer, Thomas G. 1999. *Secret Yankees: The Union Circle in Confederate Atlanta.* Baltimore, MD: Johns Hopkins University Press.

Surratt, Mary E. Jenkins (1823–1865)

Born and raised in Maryland, Mary Surratt's relatively obscure life as a Southern slaveholding woman dramatically changed when she was arrested for assisting John Wilkes Booth with his plans to assassinate President Abraham Lincoln. Tried, convicted, and hanged by a military tribunal at the close of the Civil War, Mary Surratt became the first woman ever to be executed by the United States government.

Born in Prince George's County, Maryland, in 1823, Mary Elizabeth Jenkins was the second of three children and the only daughter of Archibald and Elizabeth Anne Jenkins. When Mary was two years old, her father died unexpectedly, leaving Mary's young mother to support the family on their modest plantation near Calvert Manor in Waterloo. In 1835, Mary attended a private Catholic girl's boarding school, the Academy for Young Ladies, in Alexandria, Virginia. Within two years, Mary converted to Catholicism, rejecting the Episcopal faith of her mother and setting her own course.

When Mary was sixteen years old, she met John Harrison Surratt; they married in August 1840. Within four years, Mary had given birth to three children: Isaac, Anna, and John Jr. An alcoholic, John Sr. was undependable and frequently in debt. His excessive drinking and volatile behavior frightened Mary and the children; so she sought solace in her deepening faith and her local Catholic church.

In 1851, tragedy struck the Surratt household. Their home near Giesboro, Maryland, burned to the ground, and the Surratts barely escaped with their lives. A family slave suspected of the setting the fire eluded arrest. John Surratt Sr. determined then to leave the life of a farmer and to build an inn and tavern on land he had inherited from an uncle. Located at the junction of two major thoroughfares twelve miles from Washington, D.C., the tavern became an immediate success. With the proceeds of the sale of their farm properties, John paid off most of his debts and used the remaining funds to purchase rental property, a boarding house on H Street, in Washington, D.C.

John's drinking continued unabated, but the tavern's business flourished under Mary's control. During the 1850s, the Surratt Tavern became the local post office, and the crossroads on which it sat became known as Surrattsville. Its location proved to be essential to the tavern's importance in regional communication and social networks. During the Civil War, the tavern and hotel became a haven for Confederate spies, couriers, and smugglers. Although located in a state that had remained loyal to the Union, the tavern's position between Washington, D.C., and Virginia, as well as the Confederate sympathies of its owner and neighbors, secured its reputation among secretive rebels as a safe haven.

John Surratt unexpectedly died in January 1862, leaving Mary with many unpaid debts. Most of her slaves had been sold, and the rest had run away, so operating the tavern proved increasingly difficult. Seventeen-year-old John Jr. was now postmaster, and he continued many of the covert services his father provided to the Confederacy. Son Isaac went to Virginia and joined the Confederate army. By November 1863, local Union forces became suspicious of the Surratts' rebel sympathies, and John lost his position as postmaster. Unable to use the regular mail system to ferry messages back and forth between Northern operatives and Richmond, the Confederacy became dependent on couriers to keep the lines of communication open. Young John became an active courier himself, drawing the Surratts deeper into treasonous activity.

In the fall of 1864, Mary decided to lease the tavern to a neighbor, John Lloyd, and move her family to Washington, D.C., to the boarding house her husband had purchased a decade earlier. The empty house soon filled with paying boarders, some of

Mary Surratt, an alleged member of Booth conspiracy, was hanged after Lincoln's assassination (1820–1865). (Courtesy New-York Historical Society)

whom were involved in the assassination plot to kill not only President Lincoln, but also Vice President Andrew Johnson, Secretary of State William H. Seward, and General Ulysses S. Grant. John Jr.'s courier activities and loyalty to the Southern cause brought him to the attention of John Wilkes Booth. Together, they began to recruit like-minded individuals into their initial scheme to kidnap the president. Though Booth never boarded in the Surratt home, Mary became inextricably involved in his plans during the months leading up to Lincoln's assassination.

The plan to murder Lincoln evolved during the last days of the Civil War, as the Confederacy surrendered at Appomattox in early April 1865. While some of the conspirators balked at the idea of murder, they remained committed accomplices, ensuring their future fates on the gallows or in prison.

On April 14, 1865, the night Lincoln was killed, accomplice Lewis Payne attempted to assassinate Secretary of State Seward. After brutally stabbing and beating Seward and his two sons, but not killing them, Payne fled to Mary Surratt's house, where he had once boarded. Arriving late at night while Federal authorities were questioning Mary and searching her home, Payne claimed to be a common laborer hired to dig a ditch for her. Mary denied ever having met Payne, but suspicious agents arrested them both. Louis Weichmann, a boarder-turned-witness, testified that Payne had boarded at Mary's home during the prior six months, exposing her lie. Weichmann also revealed that coconspirator George Atzerodt had boarded with the Surratts as well and that Booth's secret group frequently held meetings there. President Andrew Johnson later remarked that Mary provided the "nest that hatched the egg."

Mary's assistance of Booth on several occasions compounded her precarious situation. Planning carefully for his hasty flight after he murdered the president, Booth needed supplies hidden along a planned escape route out of Maryland. Surratt's former tavern was the ideal place; not only was it close to Washington, but its new manager, John Lloyd, was a trusted Confederate sympathizer. Lloyd testified that Mary coordinated arrangements with him, delivering messages and the vital supplies Booth would need for his quick escape. In fact, Mary delivered some of the supplies on the day of Lincoln's assassination. Though she continued to claim her innocence, she never offered explanations to refute the damaging testimony against her.

The trial, held before a military tribunal rather than a civil court, lasted seven weeks. Daily newspaper reports gripped the nation. Eight of the accomplices, including Mary, were tried and convicted. Mary's supporters tried desperately to appeal the verdict to no avail. On the afternoon of July 7, 1865, Mary Surratt was hanged with three other conspirators. She was the first woman executed by the United States government.

John Surratt, Jr. was the only known accomplice to avoid conviction. Booth was shot and killed while hiding in a barn in southern Maryland. Four more accomplices faced life sentences.

During and immediately following Mary's trial and execution, many Southerners maintained the illusion that she was an innocent victim of a vengeful and vindictive Northern court. Her name rallied the cause of defiant Southerners who were reluctant to rejoin the Union. For decades, sympathizers carried on the call for justice and retribution for Mary's hanging, portraying her as the epitome of wronged Southern womanhood. Surviving witnesses and government officials linked to the trial were compelled to defend their roles in her conviction and execution. While historians now agree that Mary was indeed a willing accomplice, her execution remains hotly debated.

Kate Clifford Larson

See also Confederate Homefront; Female Spies; Lincoln, Abraham (1809–1865); Slaveholding Women; Southern Women; Union Homefront.

References and Further Reading

Leonard, Elizabeth D. 2004. *Lincoln's Avengers: Justice, Revenge, and Reunion after the Civil War.* New York: W. W. Norton & Company.

Steers, Edward. 2001. *Blood on the Moon: The Assassination of Abraham Lincoln.* Lexington: University Press of Kentucky.

Trindal, Elizabeth Steger. 1996. *Mary Surratt: An American Tragedy.* Gretna, LA: Pelican Publishing Company.

Swisshelm, Jane Grey (1815–1884)

Jane Grey Swisshelm was a journalist, feminist, and abolitionist.

Born December 6, 1815, Swisshelm worked and lived in Pennsylvania, Minnesota, Chicago, and Washington, D.C., over the course of her life. Swisshelm was highly influential during her lifetime, especially before and during the Civil War, and her writings touched people across the country.

Swisshelm's religious background as a member of the Covenanter (Presbyterian) Church, which opposed slavery and encouraged its members to take abolitionist action, was instrumental in her commitment to abolitionism. In her twenties, Swisshelm began to write, at first anonymously but soon under her own name, poetry and prose for newspapers and other periodicals. Her themes included the rights of women as well as abolition. An inheritance from her mother enabled her to begin publishing the *Pittsburgh Saturday Visiter* in 1847, making her one of the first women to publish and edit her own paper and certainly the first to focus primarily on politics rather than on literature and domestic life. The paper was not a financial success, but its articles were often cited or reprinted by other editors, and Swisshelm's views on slavery and women's rights became well known. She hired female compositors for the paper on an equal basis with men, extending her theoretical beliefs into her practical life.

In 1857, after the failure of the *Pittsburgh Saturday Visiter* and her marriage, Swisshelm moved to St. Cloud, Minnesota, where she started a new paper, the *St. Cloud Visiter.* Minnesota politics were far from genteel, and Swisshelm's disagreements with local Democrats ended with the destruction of her presses by vigilantes. Undeterred, she soon reopened, and, when a libel suit connected to the earlier problems forced her to close the *Visiter,* she started the *St. Cloud Democrat.* In these papers she continued to make the abolitionist argument and to work for political parties that pursued abolitionism. Swisshelm supported Abraham Lincoln.

Horrified by the 1863 Dakota War, Swisshelm moved to Washington, D.C., hoping unsuccessfully to influence governmental attitudes on frontier issues. She took a position as one of the first women in the War Department's quartermaster general's office. During her employment, Swisshelm wrote many private and public letters on women as civil service workers and continued to write general political articles for newspapers nationwide. She also became interested in the war hospitals, striving to improve the health of the wounded and the nursing practices of women volunteers. She devoted many pages in her autobiography to "an inside history of the hospitals during the war of the Rebellion."

After the war, Swisshelm began the *Reconstructionist,* a paper published in Washington, D.C. from 1865 to 1866. She then left to live with her daughter in Chicago. Later she moved back to Pennsylvania, where she continued to write for many publications and to give public lectures.

Jane Grey Swisshelm died on July 21, 1884.

JoAnn Castagna

See also Abolitionism and Northern Reformers; Hospitals; Northern Women; Nurses.

References and Further Reading

Hoffert, Sylvia D. 2004. *Jane Grey Swisshelm: An Unconventional Life, 1815–1884.* Chapel Hill: University of North Carolina Press.

Larsen, Arthur J, ed. 1934. *Crusader and Feminist: Letters of Jane Grey Swisshelm 1858–1865.* Saint Paul: Minnesota Historical Society Press.

Swisshelm, Jane Grey. 1880. *Half a Century.* Chicago: J. G. Swisshelm.

T

Taylor, Susie Baker King (1848–1912)

A Georgia slave when the war began, Susie Baker King Taylor gained her freedom in 1862. She worked as a laundress for a Union army regiment, nursed soldiers, and taught other freed slaves to read and write. As the only written recollection of a black woman who served during the Civil War, her memoir is unique in Civil War literature.

Taylor grew up in Savannah, Georgia, in the care of her enslaved grandmother, who lived much like a freed black. Despite laws against literacy for slaves, Taylor learned to read. Her first lessons came from a freed black woman who ran a secret school. Other teachers included a white girl and the son of her grandmother's landlord.

When the Union army attacked Fort Pulaski in Savannah Harbor in 1862, Baker fled behind Union lines with her uncle and his family. Such slaves were considered freed, although this predated the Emancipation Proclamation by more than eight months. Amazed at her ability to read and write, Union officers asked Taylor to teach other contrabands in their care, which she did for about a month. When some of the former slaves formed the First South Carolina Volunteer Infantry to fight for the Union, Baker became a laundress for the troops. She also continued to teach soldiers to read and write, and she nursed them through injury and illness. She later nursed soldiers for the Massachusetts Fifty-fourth Infantry Regiment, a colored unit.

Susie Baker King Taylor, an escaped slave from South Carolina, joined the 33rd U.S. Colored Troops as laundress, teacher, and nurse during the Civil War. (Library of Congress)

Susie married Edward King, a sergeant from the South Carolina regiment, in 1862. He died suddenly in 1866. She married Russell Taylor thirteen years later.

After the war, Susie King taught school in rural Georgia and then in Savannah. She later worked as a laundress and a cook. She moved North in the 1880s, where she worked for the Women's Relief Corps, a branch of the Grand Army of the Republic.

In 1902, Taylor published her memoir, *Reminiscences of My Life in Camp: With the 33rd United States Colored Troops, late 1st S.C. Volunteers.* It provides insight into the feelings of African Americans in the South during and after the Civil War. Particularly poignant is her discussion of the excitement among the slaves on the day the Emancipation Proclamation went into effect. She also detailed the unequal treatment of the races and the vast disrespect for blacks she experienced when she returned South for a visit in 1898. Taylor's memoir concluded with her faith that justice for African Americans would ultimately prevail.

Susie Baker King Taylor died in 1912.

Ellen H. Todras

See also African American Women; Confederate Homefront; Contrabands; Education, Southern; Nurses; Teachers, Southern; Wartime Employment.

References and Further Reading

Schultz, Jane E. 2004. *Women at the Front: Hospital Workers in Civil War America.* Chapel Hill: University of North Carolina Press.

Taylor, Susie King. 1988. *A Black Woman's Civil War Memoirs,* edited by Patricia W. Romero and Willie Lee Rose. Princeton, NJ: Markus Weiner Publisher. (Originally published 1902 as *Reminiscences of My Life in Camp: With the 33rd United States Colored Troops, late 1st S.C. Volunteers.*)

Teachers, Northern

During the antebellum period, Northern women, both black and white, took advantage of expanded educational opportunities to become teachers. Although the common school movement was well in place in the North by the mid-nineteenth century, free blacks generally attended separate schools. And, while the education of free blacks was not as strictly proscribed in the North as it was in the South, white teachers of free blacks confronted de facto segregation and racism. With the outbreak of war, Northern teachers, imbued with abolitionist politics and religious zeal, ventured south as teachers of the freedpersons and missionaries of the gospel. After experiencing the chaos and violence of the war and Reconstruction, most teachers returned to the North. A select few, however, remained to contribute to building a system of common schools in the South.

Although Northern states provided for the education of some free blacks, the idea of racially integrated schools was vehemently opposed. In 1831, Prudence Crandall opened a school for the daughters of elite families in Canterbury, Connecticut. In 1832, she was approached by Sarah Harris, a servant girl with white, Native American, and African American lineage. According to one account, Harris's purpose was to get an education so that she could teach black children. When Crandall admitted her to the school, outraged white parents quickly withdrew their daughters. After making several clandestine trips outside the community ostensibly to gather teaching supplies, Crandall returned to Canterbury with the financial support for a black school and subsequently dismissed the remaining white girls. In March 1833, she placed an advertisement in *The Liberator,* William Lloyd Garrison's abolitionist newspaper, for the opening of a school for "young ladies and little misses of color." It would become the first private boarding school for black girls in New England. Eventually, she enrolled approximately sixteen students. A system of persistent harassment began, and Crandall and her students were insulted, threatened, and stoned. Crandall herself was arrested and jailed three times, and in 1834 the school was vandalized by a mob. She finally had to close the school because she could not guarantee the safety of her students. Two of Sarah Harris's daughters became teachers in the Southern states after the Civil War. Another of Crandall's students—Julia Ward Williams—attended Noyes Academy, an integrated school in Canaan, New Hampshire until it was destroyed by a mob of white men in 1835. While at the Academy she met and subsequently married noted black abolitionist Henry Highland Garnet.

Crandall was a member of the Religious Society of Friends (Quakers), who traditionally valued education. Many women who were affiliated with Quaker meetings believed that education not only played a central role in the religious experience but that it was also vitally important to emancipation. The matter of racial tolerance was complicated, however. Although Quakers expressed a belief in the equality of races and sexes, there was often a distinction made between Quaker theoretical beliefs and nonracist attitudes, including abolitionism. Some Quaker meetings in Indiana and Ohio, for example, experienced a schism when members disagreed about the role of Quakers in the abolitionist movement. Nevertheless, Northern Quaker teachers, such as Crandall and Emily Howland, were prominent in the education of free blacks.

Emily Howland, who was raised in Sherwood, New York, studied classical education in Philadelphia in a school for women administered by Mary Robinson. In 1856, defying her family's wishes, Howland answered a call for teachers issued by a newly opened Quaker-funded school for free black girls in Washington, D.C. Founded by Myrtilla Miner, a Baptist, the school was supported by Philadelphia Quakers. Howland left before the school closed in 1860, but the experience was a prelude to Howland's work with black war refugees. In 1863, she coordinated relief efforts at the refugee camp in Washington, D.C. Afterward, she began teaching. She served for a year at Camp Todd, near Arlington, Virginia, before going home to Sherwood in 1865. In 1866, she returned to Washington and founded a new school for blacks and poor whites with the help of the Freedmen's Bureau and the Friends Freedmen Association of Philadelphia. Noting that her day students were instructing their elders at home how to cope with postwar business transactions, she put mathematics instruction first in the curriculum, followed by reading and writing. This curriculum allowed black students to communicate with family members who had been relocated by government order and also help them with business matters.

In addition to white women, Quakers hired African American women as teachers and administrators. Fanny Jackson Coppin and Mary Jane Patterson, the first two black American women to obtain full college degrees (both from Oberlin College, Ohio), served as principal and assistant principal of the Institute for Colored Youth of Philadelphia. Sarah Mapps Douglass, an abolitionist and member of the Society of Friends, served as principal of the preparatory department of the Institute. Harriet Brent Jacobs, born into slavery and author of *Incidents in the Life of a Slave Girl,* taught in several schools before and during the Civil War, supported by funding from Quaker organizations. Charlotte Forten Grimké, a member of a wealthy free black family in Philadelphia, joined Laura M. Towne and Ellen Murray as teachers in the Sea Islands in the Port Royal experiment.

Along with her husband Charles, Laura Smith Haviland established the first school in Michigan to accept black students years before the Civil War. They resigned from the Society of Friends because of their intense involvement in abolition issues, although Laura eventually reunited with them. In 1837, they opened the Raisin Institute, the first school for indigent black children in Michigan. Haviland worked as a Federal agent of the Freedmen's Bureau and visited Quaker schools for blacks in Virginia in 1865. In 1862, Tacy Hadley and her husband Job, both teachers residing in Hendricks County, Indiana, at the time, felt called to travel to Cairo, Illinois. Abolitionist Levin Coffin, who lived in New Garden, Indiana, before relocating to Cincinnati, Ohio, helped them to establish a school in Cairo that eventually had an enrollment of four hundred students. The Ohio Yearly Meeting Friends paid Job's niece, Hannah Hadley, for teaching in the school.

When the Civil War began, hundreds of Northern women went south to teach, preach, and assist in the relief effort. While teaching gave them a professional identity, they were civilians in an occupied territory. Sponsored by benevolent societies and religious organizations, they not only taught rudimentary skills in reading, writing, and arithmetic but also inculcated Christian beliefs and middle-class values among freedpersons. The so-called

Yankee Schoolmarms, many of whom espoused abolitionist beliefs, perceived their role to be nothing less than the induction of former slaves into free society. More than half of them hailed from New England, 75 percent were women, and the majority were unmarried, white, and middle class. Although idealistic, their motives were not entirely altruistic. Like Southerners, they feared the consequences of millions of freed slaves and thought that Christianity would have a civilizing effect on freedpersons. The living conditions were primitive, the pay was meager, and the risk of physical harm, disease, and exhaustion was ever present. In addition to instruction, they were charged with finding suitable space for schoolrooms and with providing books and supplies. Their letters and diaries speak of deprivation, fear, loneliness, and the constant threat of violence from the residents of a ravaged land who resented the invasion of another "army" of Northern, mostly white teachers. Although they were technically under the protection of the Union army, many soldiers resented having to protect the women.

Although army officials recognized that women filled the void created by men who were serving in the army or in support roles, they adhered to narrow nineteenth-century gender constructs. Military authorities preferred older, stable white women who would not challenge the orthodoxy or authority of the war department. Women, rather than men, were also preferred because it was assumed that women's talent lay with teaching young children. Since prevailing racial stereotypes portrayed slaves as childlike simpletons, the rationalization was that women would prove to be better teachers. In addition to being nurturing, women by nature were considered to be kind, patient, and content to perform routine instructional drills. In fact, it was thought that they possessed innate pedagogical skills that were relational rather than cognitive or behavioral in nature. Moreover, white women were held up as paragons of moral virtue and expected to instruct exslaves in regard to domestic matters and personal habits of cleanliness, industry, and godliness.

For their part, white women held racial and gender stereotypes of black women as well. Ignorant of the pathology of slave society, white women balanced sympathy for the freedpersons against a maternalism created by a sense of white, Christian, female superiority. Blending education with socialization, they stressed the importance of familial ties by attempting to reunite black families and urging couples to legalize their marriage. They taught domestic science to black women and criticized them for their inability to keep a middle-class Northern house correctly. Worse, they blamed black women who were subject to rampant sexual abuse by Union soldiers for lacking morals. No less than men, they subscribed to prevailing theories of black racial inferiority in regard to intelligence and behavior. And, as educated individuals, they were called on by army officials to explain contradictory policies such as the proscription of freedpersons for military duty.

For both men and women, the education of freedpersons during the Civil War foreshadowed a debate over what was called negro education that was later forcefully argued by black leaders Booker T. Washington and W.E.B. DuBois. For black women, the training in domestic science and homemaking perhaps found its purest expression in training programs at the traditionally black Tuskegee Institute and Hampton Institute, which prepared black women for domestic service. During the late nineteenth century, the program known as the Jeanes teachers would continue the emphasis on vocational training for black women. Started in 1907 by the philanthropy of Quaker Anna T. Jeanes, these teachers were black women who taught domestic science, housekeeping, and home economics to black women throughout the rural South. Almost always African American women, Jeanes teachers taught rural blacks how to run their households in a sanitary, productive, and efficient manner.

Black female teachers were received somewhat differently than their white counterparts. A free, black, professional woman in the South raised complicated issues of social position. Such was the case with Charlotte Forten, who came to St. Helena Island in 1862 as the first and only black teacher. Unlike white women, Forten and other black women were encouraged to spend their time recruiting black soldiers rather than teaching freedwomen and children. Some of the freedpersons were unwilling to work for her, white missionaries resented her, and white teachers were by no means free of prejudicial racial attitudes, no matter how idealistic they had been in the North. Eventually, however, the suspicions of the freedpersons, who had been denied educational opportunities by Southern slave codes and Border State black codes, gave way to a determination that education was prerequisite to full social, economic, and political equality.

During Reconstruction, relief efforts finally ended, and educational efforts were transferred to Southerners and secular Northern philanthropic foundations. Hundreds of women teachers were released by the many relief societies operating in the South that had employed and sponsored them. Those who chose to remain in the South joined the ranks of other sympathetic Northerners, who aided the advancement of Southern blacks by equipping them with the fundamental skills necessary to survive the harsh economic and political aftermath of the Civil War. In so doing, their efforts contributed to a system of common (public) education for both Southern blacks and whites.

Jayne R. Beilke

See also Abolitionism and Northern Reformers; Confederate Homefront; Coppin, Fanny Jackson (1837–1913); Education, Northern; Education, Southern; Forten (Grimké), Charlotte L. (1837–1914); Free Blacks; Freedmen's Bureau; Garrison, William Lloyd (1805–1879); Haviland, Laura Smith (1808–1898); Jacobs, Harriet Ann [Linda Brent] (1813–1897); Port Royal; Quaker Women; Rape; Towne, Laura Matilda (1825–1901); Union Homefront.

References and Further Reading

Cashin, Joan E., ed. 2002. *The War Was You and Me: Civilians in the American Civil War.* Princeton, NJ: Princeton University Press.

Hoffman, Nancy, ed. 1981. *Woman's "True" Profession: Voices from the History of Teaching.* Old Westbury, NY: Feminist Press.

Jones, Jacqueline. 1980. *Soldiers of Light and Love: Northern Teachers and Georgia Blacks, 1865–1873.* Chapel Hill: University of North Carolina Press.

Selleck, Linda B. 1995. *Gentle Invaders: Quaker Women Educators and Racial Issues during the Civil War and Reconstruction.* Richmond, IN: Friends United Press.

Teachers, Southern

Southern teachers during the Civil War were most often Northern women who ultimately contributed to a system of Southern schooling through a pedagogy comprised of basic skills instruction, socialization, and a belief in the emancipatory power of education.

The South had traditionally resisted the creation of state-sponsored common school systems for white children. This resistance was further exacerbated by planter fears that literacy would spur the desire for freedom on the part of the enslaved population. In response, during the early nineteenth century, all Southern states passed laws prohibiting slaves from becoming literate and punishing slaveholders for teaching them. Throughout most of the antebellum period, only informal opportunities for schooling were available to slaves through the slave system itself or through subterfuge.

Formal schooling for Southern whites was limited to old field schools, the academy, and private tutoring for the children of plantation owners. Children of planter families were also sent abroad, most often to England, for education. Old field schools were similar to the one-room district schools of the North, but they were not funded by local taxes. Instead, they operated on a subscription basis whereby the tuition rates and length of term were agreed on by the teacher and the subscribers. While old field schoolteachers taught elementary subjects, those who taught at academies (an early form of secondary school) taught moral education, Bible study, and practical skills such as surveying.

Despite its strong regional identity, the South was not monolithic with regard to education. By 1860 only four Southern states—North Carolina, Kentucky, Alabama, and Louisiana—and a few isolated communities had fledgling common school systems. Most wealthy Southerners instead preferred to send their children to private institutions. Educational ideology varied not only from state to state, but also within states according to the predominant type of agriculture, the number rural versus urban population centers, the ratio of plantations to small farms, and the interconnected ideology of slavery. Despite the South's diversity, in general, Southerners were more reluctant to tax property for school costs and to innovate state-level supervisory mechanism for common school systems than were Northerners. As the Civil War approached, Southerners increasingly resented the emulation of the Northern model of common schools. Critics warned against the reliance of the South on Northern teachers, Northern textbooks, and Northern colleges. Despite the rhetoric, the South was unquestionably dependent on the North for teachers, school supplies, and the organizational common school model. Southern urban systems such as those of Charleston, South Carolina, continued to import Northern teachers as late as 1857, and Southern enrollment at Northern colleges remained strong into the late 1850s.

The majority of teachers during the mid-nineteenth century were between eighteen and twenty-five years old, although some were as young as fifteen or sixteen. It was not unusual for students to be older than their teachers, since age grading was not yet a fixture in schools. Teachers received what little training they could get from academies and normal schools, and teaching examinations, consisting of written and oral questions, were developed by local school districts. Teaching was a low-status profession that drew men on only a temporary basis. Once the war began and men joined the armies, teachers became even scarcer. As a consequence of Southern resistance to common school reform, teacher training in the region lagged behind that of Northern states. Teacher institutes that were held annually, semi-monthly, or on alternate Saturdays helped teachers improve their skills.

Popular schoolbooks in Southern schools included *McGuffey's Eclectic Reader, Ray's Arithmetic,* and Webster's blue back *Speller.* School supplies and furniture were in short supply. The length of the school day and year varied as the community saw fit, and in 1860 the average length of the school term was five months and five and one-half days. At their schools, students of all ages could expect recitation, slate work, arithmetic, geography, and history.

Schoolbooks often revealed their regional bias. *Hilliard's Fifth Reader,* published in the North in 1863, contained such readings as "The Religious Character of President Lincoln" as well as the "Song of the Union." War poems were also common during this period. Southern teachers, once the war began, had less access to Northern texts due to the political climate and the Northern blockade. Lack of resources and the destruction of printing equipment made the Southern production of materials impossible. Notable exceptions were *The Dixie Primer: For Little Folks* and *The Dixie Speller: To Follow the First Dixie Reader,* authored by Marinda Branson Moore of North Carolina.

Northern teachers heading South during wartime had their work cut out for them. At the outbreak of the Civil War only about 5 percent of slaves were literate, as judged by the ability to write one's name. As Federal troops occupied an area and set the slaves free, many former slaves established schools to help others make the transition to freedom. Federal troops invading Savannah, Georgia, in 1864 discovered, however, a secret school for slaves that a black woman named Deveaux had operated since 1833. Will Capers, an ex-slave who was a cabinetmaker, told Laura Towne that he had operated a secret night school for male slaves. Union army officers eventually encouraged the educational work of Northern missionaries, whose efforts paved the way for the establishment of the Freedmen's Bureau of Refugees, Freedmen, and Abandoned Lands in 1865. Situated in a department of the army, the Freedmen's Bureau revealed the government's formal stance in regard to the education of former slaves.

Northern teachers who traveled to the South were deeply resented by many Southerners and overworked by the Northern agencies that sent them. However, their initial reception did not deter these teachers, who continued to arrive in small groups. Predominantly unmarried and white, Northern women teachers did not receive a salary from the relief associations that sponsored them until late in the war. When they finally were paid, they received less than their male counterparts.

Desolate surroundings, loneliness, hard work, and the cultural clash of Northern white Protestant middle-class life with the remnants of the Southern slave system took their toll. The religious fervor expressed in "shouts" and the expressive singing

During and immediately following the Civil War, many Northern women headed South to help educate the newly freed slaves. (Corbis)

and dancing of the freedpersons shocked the sensibilities of many Northern teachers.

For Northern women who went south during the Civil War to work with African Americans, however, teaching was about more than lessons in reading, reciting Bible passages, or instilling moral values. Leaving the relative comfort and security of the North, teachers like Harriet Ware went south to teach as part of a higher moral calling. Displaying race- and class-based maternalism, Ware and others like her believed that African Americans needed their help. For many, teaching the freed-people became an outgrowth of other domestic occupations associated with the war effort: providing medical aid and clothing, supervising black laborers on occupied plantations, and offering instruction in reading, writing, religion, sewing, and the proper habits of dress and punctuality.

Most women who became teachers in the South also embraced the principles of abolitionism. Like many educated women during the nineteenth century, Massachusetts schoolteacher Lucy Chase enthusiastically embraced Unitarianism and a multifaceted philosophy of self-improvement and reform. Chase was influenced by women's suffrage, abolitionism, temperance, mesmerism, and phrenology. She and her sister Sarah went south to educate the freedmen through the auspices of the various freedmen's aid commissions. During this early period, an emphasis was placed on teaching the idea that freedom from slavery had boundaries—that slaves were, in fact, not free to disobey civil law or incite mass anarchy. Teachers instructed their African American students on the ideas of self-reliance, female morality, and domestic order. As much socialization as education, the education of the freedpeople stressed the importance of marital bonds and instilled white Protestant middle-class values.

As support for their efforts increased, teachers in the South faced careful selection guidelines. The recruitment of women stemmed from the nineteenth-century belief in them as moral centers. When selecting female teachers, most male officials believed that older and more practically oriented women would prove better teachers than young idealistic women. As the war progressed, however, teachers and administrators throughout the occupied South asked for more women to join the ranks, and younger women took on the task. In any case, female teachers were expected to serve as moral models for their African American students.

Organizations also recruited women as teachers because of their willingness, availability, and affordability. As a whole, women were content with lower salaries than their male counterparts. In addition, Northern women often answered the call to serve as teachers in the South out of a sense of duty to their nation; men served on the battlefield while women served in the schools. Northern women were generally more willing to join the education effort than men, who did not consider teaching to be a worthwhile endeavor. In addition, blacks who had been victimized by white soldiers were more likely to trust women, even white women, who seemed to them less threatening than men.

Women teachers' work in regard to relief and domestic instruction transitioned to teaching reading and writing, which signaled to African Americans that the acquisition of learning was valuable in and of itself. Female teachers focused their time on bringing the freedmen closer to a condition of freedom through education, while male teachers often split their time between teaching and plantation management. Not only did the role of female teachers in the South change during the Civil War, but also the pedagogy changed. Teachers began to establish so-called industrial schools, including numerous schools for training black women in such pursuits as sewing. Teachers hoped to help black women develop a useful skill so that they would no longer be dependent on Northern charity. Lucy Chase planned to teach sewing and literacy simultaneously.

Northern teachers in the South faced many obstacles but often experienced great success. In 1862, Quaker sisters Lucy and Sarah Chase arrived in Norfolk, Virginia, as emissaries of the Boston Education Commission. They were assigned to work with two thousand contrabands on Craney Island, six miles from Norfolk. Frustrated by army bureaucracy, they scrounged for supplies and acted as teachers, nurses, mediators, and comforters. Additional Quakers joined them by 1864; so they relocated to Slabtown, a new village for four hundred black refugee families near Yorktown. Here they organized parties of black men to build a community center, a warehouse, and schoolhouses. Other work parties tended truck gardens for Slabtown's food supply. In 1865, within a week of the Confederacy's surrender, the Chase sisters visited Richmond, where they soon opened a school in Richmond's First African Church and enrolled one thousand African American children and seventy-five adults. They were joined by Sarah F. Smiley of Philadelphia, who started an industrial school for adults in Richmond as well as a teachers' home.

With the ratification of the Thirteenth Amendment abolishing slavery in the United States, the battle over black education in the South intensified. A new group of teachers—black and white—came south to open thousands of new schools in which they continued to instruct the former slaves in domestic arts,

personal hygiene, and self-sufficiency. Despite their intentions, many of these teachers remained unconvinced of the freedpeople's intellectual capacities. African Americans, however, continued to associate education with ultimate freedom and opportunity.

Jayne R. Beilke

See also Abolitionism and Northern Reformers; African American Women; Civilian Life; Confederate Homefront; Education, Northern; Education, Southern; Freedmen's Bureau; Military Invasion and Occupation; Northern Women; Plantation Life; Quaker Women; Reconstruction (1865–1877); Religion; Separate Spheres; Teachers, Northern; Thirteenth Amendment; Towne, Laura Matilda (1825–1901)

References and Further Reading

Cashin, Joan E., ed. 2002. *The War Was You and Me: Civilians in the American Civil War.* Princeton, NJ: Princeton University Press.

Kaestle, Carl. 1983. *Pillars of the Republic: Common Schools and American Society, 1780–1860.* New York: Hill and Wang.

Selleck, Linda B. 1995. *Gentle Invaders: Quaker Women Educators and Racial Issues during the Civil War and Reconstruction.* Richmond, IN: Friends United Press.

Swint, Henry L. 1967. *The Northern Teacher in the South, 1862–1870.* New York: Octagon Books.

Telegraph Operators [Telegraphers]

By the Civil War, the telegraph had become an important part of American life. Although it had been in service for fewer than twenty years, during the war it was put to widespread use for news reporting, business communications, personal notices, and military communiqués. In addition to creating a new industry, the telegraph created a new type of technical worker: the telegraph operator. The 1860 census lists approximately two thousand men who were employed as telegraph operators. About one hundred women were similarly employed, although it is difficult to estimate the number with any certainty, because the 1860 census did not break down occupations by gender. Women had, in fact, worked as telegraphers since the late 1840s; it was one of the first technical professions open to women. Over fifty women were employed as telegraphers in the Northeastern United States alone in the 1860s, earning annual salaries of $300 to $500.

Telegraphy became a critical occupation as the Civil War began. As male telegraphers left for the Military Telegraph Corps, women replaced them in many offices. As telegraphers, women received and transmitted vital information during the war. For example, Elizabeth Cogley, an operator for the Pennsylvania Railroad in Lewistown, Pennsylvania, was the first operator in Pennsylvania to receive President Abraham Lincoln's call for troops in 1861. In addition, Emma Hunter, an operator in West Chester, Pennsylvania, since the early 1850s, sent and received many messages related to the movement of troops and war materials.

In the Confederacy, women took charge of telegraph offices as men went off to war. Although even less is known about female Confederate operators than their Northern counterparts, it appears that women worked as telegraphers and office managers in Georgia, South Carolina, Louisiana, Florida, and Alabama during the Civil War.

A few women served in the Military Telegraph Corps; their names can be found in the roster of 1,079 military telegraphers appended to William Rattle Plum's history of the Corps, *The Military Telegraph during the Civil War in the United States*. The only woman telegrapher about whom Plum provided any information was Louisa E. Volker, whose intelligence activities on behalf of the Union army at Mineral Point, Missouri, put her at risk of capture during Sterling Price's invasion of Missouri in 1864.

As the Civil War came to an end and men began to return home, competition for telegraph operator jobs increased. The status of women in the telegraph industry was debated, sometimes hotly, in the pages of *The Telegrapher*, a trade paper that first appeared in 1864. Women operators had come to view themselves as technical professionals and were unwilling to abandon the skills they had acquired and return to more traditional domestic roles.

Military telegraphers, who were civilians under military command and not part of the regular army, sought to gain recognition for their service after the war. On January 26, 1897, Congress passed Senate Bill 319, An Act for the Relief of Telegraph Operators Who Served in the War of the Rebellion. This act recognized former military telegraphers, including women, as honorably discharged members of the United States Army. The only female Military Telegrapher other than Louisa Volker to receive a certificate of honorable service under the Congressional act was Mary E. Smith Buell, of Norwich, New York.

The entry of women into the profession of telegraphy during the Civil War established a pattern of women replacing men in the telegraph office that would recur in later wars. And, as would happen in later wars, the return of men from the battlefield generated a debate over the long-term role of women in telegraphy. By debating their opponents in print and insisting on their right to earn a living as telegraphers, Civil War–era women operators created their own identities as skilled workers, thereby paving the way for the employment of large numbers of women as telegraphers in the 1870s.

Thomas C. Jepsen

See also Civilian Life; Confederate Homefront; Domesticity; Female Spies; Northern Women; Separate Spheres; Southern Women; Union Homefront; Wartime Employment.

References and Further Reading
Andrews, Melodie. 1990. "'What the Girls Can Do': The Debate over the Employment of Women in the Early American Telegraph Industry." *Essays in Economic and Business History* 8: 109–120.

Jepsen, Thomas. 2000. *My Sisters Telegraphic: Women in the Telegraph Office, 1846–1850.* Athens: Ohio University Press.

Penny, Virginia. 1870. *How Women Can Make Money.* Springfield, MA: Fisk.

Plum, William R. 1882. *The Military Telegraph during the Civil War in the United States.* 2 volumes. Chicago: Jansen, McClurg & Company.

Thirteenth Amendment

The adoption of the Thirteenth Amendment, forever settling the status of slavery in the United States, marked the most significant departure from the Constitution as it was written in 1787; however, the amendment is often overshadowed either by the Emancipation Proclamation or the Fourteenth

Amendment. As historians are well aware, the Emancipation Proclamation did not free a single slave yet its implementation set in motion forces for the destruction of slavery. The Fourteenth Amendment, ratified in 1868, guaranteed African Americans due process and equality before the law. Thus, the common view has interpreted the passage of the Thirteenth Amendment as either a postscript to the Emancipation Proclamation or as a necessary prologue to the Fourteenth Amendment. Certainly, the Thirteenth Amendment guaranteed that the provisions of the Emancipation Proclamation could not be overturned by a future presidential administration, Congress, or the courts, and the amendment prepared the way for the expansion of civil rights for African Americans that were later guaranteed in the Fourteenth Amendment.

The passage of the Thirteenth Amendment followed a complicated process. Early in the process, President Abraham Lincoln exhibited a constitutionally conservative approach. Rather than calling for a constitutional solution to the abolition of slavery, Lincoln relied instead on confiscation acts and the Emancipation Proclamation. Even the president's initial plans for reconstruction after the war called for Southern states to abolish slavery through the adoption of revised state constitutions. However, the enactment of the Emancipation Proclamation on January 1, 1863, opened serious debates in the North about the slavery issue, and Lincoln recognized the contingency of the proclamation. Without a constitutional amendment, the lasting effect of the proclamation remained an open question.

In the wake of the Emancipation Proclamation, several versions of an antislavery amendment were considered. In January 1864, John Henderson, a Congressman from Missouri presented a draft proposal for such an amendment, and Charles Sumner, working with Northern abolitionists, also submitted a version. In the amendment debates, Congressman James Ashley of Ohio emerged as the leading spokesperson for a constitutional amendment to abolish slavery and to protect the rights of the ex-slaves. Ashley also argued that Congress had unrestricted amending power that allowed for the abolition of slavery. Ultimately, the amendment took

shape under the direction of the Senate Judiciary Committee led by Lyman Trumbull of Illinois. Rather than adopting the broad language of Sumner's version, the Senate committee instead used language similar to that of the Northwest Ordinance of 1787, which called simply for the prohibition of slavery. The committee believed their amendment accomplished everything that Sumner sought an antislavery amendment and yet avoided the anger and potential loss of support from the War Democrats. The Thirteenth Amendment passed the Senate in April 1864, but it died in the House of Representatives as Democrats rallied support against the amendment under the banner of states' rights.

Despite the failure of the House to pass the Thirteenth Amendment, the amendment's demise was far from certain. Popular support for abolition gained strength in the North as war casualties and resentment toward the South grew. The thirty-eight-to-six vote in the Senate in favor of the Thirteenth Amendment demonstrated the growing base of support for abolition among Democrats as well as the unity of Republicans on the issue. The fate of the amendment ultimately rested on the outcome of the 1864 elections and the course of the war.

In the 1864 campaigns, the Republicans adopted a broad platform that committed the party to an antislavery amendment. However, the Democratic platform pledged to recognize states' rights thus ensuring the right of states to determine the fate of slavery. The antislavery amendment was often overshadowed by other campaign issues, chief among which was miscegenation. Democrats argued that black freedom would lead to miscegenation, and Republicans argued that miscegenation was the result of slavery. Local issues and peace terms also overshadowed the amendment as an election issue. However, when Lincoln was re-elected by an overwhelming majority, he claimed the victory as a mandate on the abolition amendment.

Immediately, Lincoln and other Republicans began to push the lame-duck Congress for passage of the Thirteenth Amendment. Whereas many Democrats had lost their seats in the 1864 elections, thus ensuring Lincoln a Republican majority when the new Congress was seated in March 1865,

Lincoln preferred passage by a bipartisan majority as a sign of wartime unity. Lincoln used his prestige and influence in an attempt to persuade Democrats to reverse their votes. In some instances, the president even used the promise of government jobs to outgoing congressmen to gain the necessary support for the amendment. Equally important to the outcome of the House vote, however, were Northern Democrats' increasing desire to avoid the proslavery label and their new political vision of the Constitution as a document that could be modified without being destroyed. On January 31, 1865, the Thirteenth Amendment finally passed the House with the Republicans unanimously in favor of the amendment and a number of Democrats either reversing their position or absenting themselves, thus allowing the amendment to be adopted with two votes to spare.

State ratification quickly followed. Of the nonseceding states, only New Jersey, Kentucky, and Delaware—states carried by James McClellan in the recent presidential election—failed to ratify the amendment. Because the Lincoln administration had fought the war on the basis that states could not secede, Lincoln believed it necessary to get three-fourths of all states to ratify the amendment rather than requiring only a three-fourths majority of the Union states. Under Andrew Johnson's plan for the restoration of the states to the Union, seceding states were required to ratify the Thirteenth Amendment as a condition of readmission. By December 18, 1865, the requisite number of states had done so.

Julie Holcomb

See also Abolitionism and Northern Reformers; Emancipation Proclamation (January 1, 1863); Fourteenth Amendment; Lincoln, Abraham (1809–1865); Politics; Union Homefront.

References and Further Reading

Cox, LaWanda. 1985. *Lincoln and Black Freedom: A Study in Presidential Leadership.* Urbana: University of Illinois Press.

Hyman, Harold. 1973. *"A More Perfect Union": The Impact of the Civil War and Reconstruction on the Constitution.* New York: Alfred A. Knopf.

Paludan, Phillip S. 1975. *A Covenant with Death: The Constitution, Law and Equality in the Civil War Era.* Urbana: University of Illinois Press.

Vorenberg, Michael. 2001. *Final Freedom: The Civil War, the Abolition of Slavery, and the Thirteenth Amendment.* New York: Cambridge University Press.

Thomas, Ella Gertrude Clanton (1834–1907)

Wealthy Georgian Ella Gertrude Clanton Thomas chronicled her life as the child of a wealthy and indulgent Georgia planter, her education at Wesleyan Female College in Macon, her marriage, the war years, and the gradual dissolution of her family's property and social standing in the years after the Civil War. Her extensive journal, begun in 1848 and kept for forty years, illuminates the experience of many elite white women, who had to adjust to new labor relations with former slaves and who had to work to support their families. The diary follows Gertrude's intellectual and emotional evolution from carefree Southern belle, through the disillusionment and losses of marriage and war, to a mature and self-reliant woman.

Ella Gertrude Clanton was born near Augusta, Georgia, on April 4, 1834. Her father, Turner Clanton, had parlayed his inheritance into a sizable fortune and had served two terms in the Georgia state legislature by the time he wed Mary Luke, also from a prosperous local family. Gertrude's place in society was defined by her father's wealth and status. She gave careful attention to the details of her wardrobe and grooming, in readiness for paying calls or receiving guests. Correspondence, writing in her journal, and reading everything that came to hand filled most of her days. Like most women of the planter class, she defined herself as a Christian and judged her success as a woman by how well she lived the tenets of her faith.

In January 1849, a few months after she began her journal, Gertrude went to Macon, Georgia, to attend the Methodist-run Wesleyan Female College. Her studies included mental philosophy, natural philosophy, and astronomy, but not the more rigorous classical languages, science, and mathematics taught at men's colleges. A few weeks after her arrival, Gertrude and many fellow students were converted to emotional, evangelical Methodism during a revival. Her newfound piety included a vow to give up dancing.

Just before her graduation from Wesleyan in 1851, the brother of a school chum began courting Gertrude. J. Jefferson Thomas, son of a local planter family, was nearing graduation from Princeton and planned to become a doctor. He won her heart but only the grudging consent of her father. He gave up the study of medicine by the time they married in December 1852.

Upon her marriage, her father gave Gertrude a plantation, house, and a slave labor force valued at $30,000. Jefferson assumed management of her property, as was customary, but was unable to support Gertrude in the style to which she was accustomed. Her father helped financially, and the young couple began having children.

When the Civil War began in 1861, Jefferson joined the Confederate army. Soon Gertrude's fears overcame her patriotic enthusiasm, and she was relieved when he resigned his commission in 1862, hired a substitute, and joined the local militia. In 1864, General William Tecumseh Sherman's men sacked one of her family's plantations, and her beloved father died. Gertrude's belief in the Confederate cause was based in part on her acceptance of Bible-based proslavery arguments, which placed God on the side of the Confederacy. The South's defeat shook her faith.

Confederate surrender in 1865 meant emancipation, which, besides liberating most of their capital assets, proved the greatest immediate challenge for Gertrude and women like her who had never had to hire servants or do their own housework. The jubilance and perceived disloyalty of her former slaves angered her. For the rest of her journaling days, she grappled with issues of race, chiefly free labor and miscegenation—the two that most personally affected her.

Friends and relatives began to rebuild their lives and fortunes, but Jefferson went deeper into debt. Having their property seized and advertised for public sale was mortifying for Gertrude, as was learning that Jefferson had borrowed heavily from her share of her father's estate during her father's lifetime.

Gertrude's problems were not only financial. Her Christian code of morality was affronted by the possibility that her father had willed her a slave who was her half sibling. During these years, perhaps because of her husband's drinking, she became active in the Women's Christian Temperance Union (WCTU).

Teaching had become acceptable for women impoverished by the war, but until late in 1878 Jefferson Thomas refused to hear of his wife working. Also in 1878, some short pieces she had written to read before the Grange were published. By 1880, she declared herself a "public woman" and signed submissions to two newspapers as Mrs. Gertrude Thomas. She found it satisfying to help pay bills and provide for her children, but the inexorable loss of their property continued. In the WCTU she met and worked with Rebecca Ann Latimer Felton. Gertrude championed better education for girls, especially the Industrial School for Girls at Milledgeville, and new opportunities for women, including the right to speak in public. When the Georgia Woman Suffrage Association (GWSA) was founded, Gertrude joined.

In 1893, Gertrude and Jefferson moved to Atlanta to live with one of their sons, a practicing physician in Atlanta. Gertrude left only scrapbooks of the last years of her life. Active in church groups, the Wesleyan alumnae, and literary societies, she was elected president of the GWSA in 1899 and was a dedicated and much admired member of the United Daughters of the Confederacy.

Gertrude Thomas died on May 11, 1907, and is buried in Magnolia Cemetery, Augusta, Georgia.

Nancy Gray Schoonmaker

See also Confederate Homefront; Courtship and Marriage; Diaries and Journals; Education, Southern; Felton, Rebecca Ann Latimer (1835–1930); Methodist Women; Plantation Life; Reconstruction (1865–1877); Religion; Sherman's Campaign (1864–1865); Slaveholding Women; Southern Women; Teachers, Southern; United Daughters of the Confederacy.

References and Further Reading
Massey, Mary Elizabeth. 1973. "The Making of a Feminist." *Journal of Southern History* 39 (1): 3–22.
Painter, Nell Irvin. 2002. *Southern History across the Color Line.* Chapel Hill: University of North Carolina Press.

Thomas, Ella Gertrude Clanton. 1990. *The Secret Eye: The Journal of Ella Gertrude Clanton Thomas, 1848–1889*, edited by Virginia Ingraham Burr. Chapel Hill: University of North Carolina Press.

Tompkins, Sally Louisa (1833–1916)

Born on November 9, 1833, in Matthews County, Virginia, Sally Louisa Tompkins operated Robertson Hospital in Richmond, Virginia, during the Civil War. With the help of ten surgeons and two cooks, she cared for more than thirteen hundred sick and wounded soldiers from July 31, 1861, to June 13, 1865. Tompkins' strategy was to heal both the body and the spirit. Soldiers often described her as walking through the hospital with a medicine bag strapped to her waist and a Bible in her hand.

At the beginning of the war, a two-tiered hospital system existed in the South: a chain of military hospitals under the direction of the Chief Surgeon Samuel P. Moore and a series of private hospitals operated by women. In October 1862, the Confederate Congress passed legislation consolidating military hospitals and stipulating that soldiers could be treated only in hospitals under the direction of commissioned officers holding the rank of captain or higher. This measure effectively closed private hospitals operated by Southern women or required them to be subsumed into the Confederate military hospital system. Tompkins's hospital was so successful, however, that she was able to obtain an honorary commission as a captain in the Confederate army from Confederate President Jefferson Davis. The president's action allowed Tompkins to keep her hospital open until the war's end. Of the 1,333 men treated at Robertson Hospital, only seventy-three died, a success rate of 94.5 percent, a figure that was unequaled in any other Confederate hospital.

After the war, Tompkins never married, and she depleted her remaining financial resources with charitable works for Confederate veterans. On July 25, 1916, she died in the Home for Needy Confederate Women in Richmond, Virginia, and was buried there with full military honors. In 1961, St. James Episcopal Church in Richmond, of which she was a member, installed a stained glass window in Tompkins's honor.

E. Susan Barber

See also Aid Societies; Confederate Homefront; Hospitals; Nurses; Southern Women.

References and Further Reading
Holtzman, Robert S. 1959. "Sally Tompkins, Captain, Confederate Army." *American Mercury* 127–130.
Massey, Mary Elizabeth. 1994. *Women in the Civil War.* Lincoln: University of Nebraska Press. (Orig pub. 1966 as *Bonnet Brigades.*)
Sally Louisa Tompkins Papers. Eleanor S. Brockenbrough Library, Museum of the Confederacy, Richmond, VA.
Schulz, Karen. 1966. "Descendant of Woman Captain Remembers Heroine of Civil War." *Richmond News Leader* 21.

Towne, Laura Matilda (1825–1901)

Laura M. Towne dedicated her life to the abolitionist cause and to educating freedmen in the South Carolina Sea Islands.

Laura Towne was born in Pittsburgh, Pennsylvania, on May 3, 1825. She was the fourth child of John and Sarah Robinson Towne. Soon after Laura's birth, her mother died and John took the family to Boston, where the Towne family became exposed to the abolitionist movement. It was not until moving to Philadelphia and attending the First Unitarian Church, however, that Laura actively engaged in abolitionist activities. During this time, Laura also studied at the Woman's Medical College.

At the beginning of the Civil War, Laura was living in Newport, Rhode Island. Immediately, she began assisting soldiers in their preparations for war by sewing clothing and performing other necessary duties. Laura, however, wanted to do more to help the Union war effort. In 1862, she volunteered to assist the Federal government with the education of former slaves living on the South Carolina Sea Islands. Through her associations in Philadelphia, Laura was selected to act as an agent of the Freedmen's Aid Society of Pennsylvania. On April 9, 1862, Laura boarded the steamer *Oriental* and sailed from

New York to Port Royal, South Carolina. She was soon joined in the Sea Islands by her friend, Ellen Murray.

Laura and Ellen settled on Saint Helena Island, where they assisted the local freedmen population. The training that Laura received at the Women's Medical College in Philadelphia assisted her in providing medical aid to the former slaves. In September 1862, Laura received funding to open a school in the Brick Church on Saint Helena Island. The school proved successful, but it became overcrowded with eighty students enrolled for lessons. The Pennsylvania Freedmen's Association provided for the construction of a new schoolhouse, the Penn School, across from the Brick Church. The new schoolhouse provided the basis for the promotion of the educational, political, and economic advancement of freedmen in the Sea Islands. Laura also utilized her medical knowledge to assist the freedmen during outbreaks of disease.

After the Civil War, Laura and Ellen remained dedicated to their work in the Sea Islands. Eventually, they purchased a home and estate, Frogmore, on Saint Helena Island and made it their permanent home. Their Northern sponsors, however, became increasingly less concerned with the plight of the freedmen. When the Freedmen's Relief Association dissolved, it caused the near financial collapse of the Penn School. Dedicated to the school's mission, Laura paid teacher salaries and other school expenses out of her pocket until she finally secured permanent Northern charitable funding. Laura Towne died in 1901, but her spirit remained evident in the buildings and advancements made by the Penn School on Saint Helena Island.

Kristina K. Dunn

See also Abolitionism and Northern Reformers; Teachers, Northern.

References and Further Reading

Holland, Rupert Sargent, ed. 1969. *Letters and Diary of Laura M. Towne: Written from the Sea Islands of South Carolina, 1862–1884.* New York: Negro University Press.

Treasury Girls

Between 1862 and 1865, the Confederate government hired hundreds of women, known as treasury girls, to replace men who left their jobs to fight in the Confederate armies. In 1862 the Confederate Congress enacted compulsory conscription and civilian jobs were drained of their main source of employees. In an effort to continue government functions, the Confederate Congress called on the women of the South to fill clerical positions in the Treasury Department, the Quartermaster Department, the War Department, the Commissary General, and the Post Office Department.

During the antebellum period, Southern women were not employed outside the home and were not monetarily compensated for their domestic duties. They depended on their husbands, fathers, or other male family members for financial stability. As Southern men continued to be called to battle, their wives, mothers, daughters, and sisters were left with the burden of providing for themselves and other family members. When the Confederate government opened clerical positions to women, it received thousands of applications. Competition for positions was fierce. Although Congress specified that positions be filled by women with the most need for income, jobs were most often filled by women with the right connections who submitted letters of recommendation from Confederate officers or powerful politicians. Most of the women given the jobs were from the middle and upper classes, and many were teenage girls. The available jobs were also limited to those who lived nearest the seat of government, Richmond, Virginia, and Columbia, South Carolina.

Treasury girls were responsible for signing Confederate notes. Prospective candidates were required to pass an oral exam. Once hired, women worked five days per week, from 9 a.m. to 3 p.m. Note signers had to sign thirty-two hundred notes per shift. Although this was not arduous work, pristine handwriting was necessary. Clerks' salaries were garnished 10¢ for each note that was tarnished. In 1862 treasury girls earned $600 for the year, but they were underpaid in comparison to the $1,000 earned by men in the same position. By 1864, both men and women earned the same salary for this work, $3,000 per year. However, the rate increase did not compensate for the high rate of inflation and rising cost of living. Although the task of making ends meet was difficult, treasury girls were the highest paid workers in the Confederacy. When the war ended, men returned home and to their jobs. Women were forced to revert to their domestic realm, but they did so knowing that they were capable of providing their own financial independence.

Dawn M. Sherman

See also Civilian Life; Confederate Homefront; Conscription; Domesticity; Family Life, Confederate; Politics; Southern Women; Wartime Employment; Widows, Confederate.

References and Further Reading
Kaufman, Janet E. 1986. "Working Women of the South: 'Treasury Girls.'" *Civil War Times Illustrated* 25: 32–38.
Kessler-Harris, Alice. 1982. *Out to Work: A History of Wage-Earning Women in the United States.* Oxford: Oxford University Press.
Rable, George C. 1989. *Civil Wars: Women and the Crisis of Southern Nationalism.* Urbana: University of Illinois Press.

Truth, Sojourner [Isabella Baumfree] (1797–1883)

Most people are familiar with Sojourner Truth's work as an abolitionist, preacher, and early proponent of women's rights. However, Truth also participated in the Union war effort in a variety of ways. She worked hard to obtain much-needed supplies, to raise funds, to nurse the wounded and sick, and to help former slaves. She also gave numerous speeches in support of Abraham Lincoln and the war itself.

Sojourner Truth was born Isabella Baumfree in 1797 in Ulster County, New York. James and Betsy, her parents, were both slaves. Truth spoke only Dutch until she was eleven years old and suffered at the hands of several physically and sexually abusive owners. She was sold four times during her life and was forced to marry a slave named Thomas. The couple had five children together. In 1826, when her owner refused to honor a promise he had made to free her, she ran away with one of her children. She went into hiding with the help of a Quaker family named Van Wagenen, who eventually purchased her freedom after her owner had discovered her hiding place. During that time, Truth became very spiritual and found her calling as a Methodist preacher. A year later she successfully sued her former owner for custody of one of her children. In 1828 she moved to New York City where she worked as a maid and continued to preach.

Truth struggled during the next few years, the victim of a religious cult led by the charismatic and corrupt Robert Matthias. She lost her life's savings to the group and was physically and psychologically abused. She finally ended her association with them when Matthias was accused of murder and Truth was accused of attempting to poison two members of the cult. Once again, she turned to the courts for redress, successfully suing Benjamin and Ann Folger for slander.

The turning point in her life occurred in 1843 when she changed her name to Sojourner Truth and became a traveling preacher. Her new name symbolized her calling to travel the land, spreading the word of God. In Massachusetts, she joined the Northampton Association for Education and Industry, a utopian group, and began her association with abolitionists like Frederick Douglass, Olive Gilbert, and William Lloyd Garrison. In 1850, with the help of Gilbert—Truth could not read or write—she published her memoir, *The Narrative of Sojourner Truth.* Truth continued to tour the country, speaking on behalf of women's rights, abolitionism, religion, and temperance. In 1851 she spoke at the Second Annual Ohio Women's Rights Convention where she presented her famous "Ar'n't I a Woman?" speech.

At the start of the Civil War, Truth was living in Michigan. She spoke at pro-Union rallies and urged that blacks be allowed to enlist in the Union army. When the Federal army began accepting African Americans into the ranks in 1863, her grandson, James Caldwell, enlisted. In June 1861, Truth was arrested following a speech in Indiana where she had broken a rarely enforced law making it illegal

Sojourner Truth, a former slave, spoke out for the abolition of slavery and for women's rights in America. (Library of Congress)

for blacks to enter the state. She escaped a somewhat violent situation and returned to Michigan, motivated even more to continue her public work.

For Thanksgiving, she collected food for the First Michigan Regiment of colored soldiers stationed in Detroit, Michigan, in 1863. As she visited with the men, she noticed they lacked sufficient supplies, and so she worked to remedy that situation, procuring and delivering needed goods for the men and entertaining them with songs. In 1864 she left for Washington, D.C. Along the way, she delivered speeches in support of President Abraham Lincoln and the war and attempted, but failed, to convince Harriet Tubman that Lincoln was sincerely trying to help African Americans. In Washington, D.C., she met Lincoln and began working in the city. She was appointed to the National Freedmen's Relief Association and raised money

for the Freedman's Aid Society. Truth visited the former slaves at the Freedmen's Village, gave motivational speeches to them, and helped them adjust to their new lives of freedom. Finally, she helped organize the Freedman's Hospital and taught the staff there how to clean and dress wounds.

In 1865 Truth confronted another problem in the District of Columbia: segregation on the streetcars. She was instrumental in forcing authorities to enforce desegregation laws already in place. During several often violent confrontations, she remained adamant about her right to travel as whites were allowed. She also continued to raise money and deliver speeches on behalf of the Colored Soldiers' Aid Society.

Following the war, she petitioned Congress for land grants, urging the government to give former slaves land in the West to help them establish a new life for themselves. She also helped freed slaves find employment and continued to speak out in favor of women's rights and temperance. Truth died November 26, 1883, in Battle Creek, Michigan.

Paula Katherine Hinton

See also Abolitionism and Northern Reformers; African American Women; Aid Societies; Douglass, Frederick (ca. 1818–1895); Freedmen's Bureau; Food; Fundraising; Garrison, William Lloyd (1805–1879); Hospitals; Lincoln, Abraham (1809–1865); Northern Women; Nurses; Politics; Reconstruction (1865–1877); Religion; Tubman, Harriet [Araminta Ross] (1822–1913).

References and Further Reading

Bernard, Jacqueline. 1967 [1990]. *Journey toward Freedom: The Story of Sojourner Truth.* New York: Feminist Press at The City University of New York.
Mabee, Carleton, with Susan Mabee Newhouse. 1993. *Sojourner Truth: Slave, Prophet, Legend.* New York: New York University Press.
Painter, Nell Irvin. 1996. *Sojourner Truth: A Life, A Symbol.* New York: W. W. Norton & Company.
Truth, Sojourner. [1850] 1997. *Narrative of Sojourner Truth.* New York: Dover Publications.

Tubman, Harriet [Araminta Ross] (1822–1913)

Born into slavery on the Eastern Shore of Maryland, Harriet Tubman gained notoriety as an Underground Railroad operator, abolitionist, Civil War spy and nurse, suffragist, and humanitarian. After escaping from enslavement in 1849, Tubman defied legal restraints to battle slavery and oppression, dedicating herself to the pursuit of freedom, equality, and justice, earning her the biblical name Moses and a place among the nation's most famous historical figures.

Originally named Araminta Ross, Harriet Tubman was born in early 1822 on the plantation of Anthony Thompson, south of Madison in Dorchester County, Maryland. Tubman was the fifth of nine children of Harriet "Rit" Green and Benjamin Ross, both slaves. Edward Brodess, the stepson of Anthony Thompson, owned Rit and her offspring through his mother, Mary Pattison Brodess Thompson. Ben Ross, the legal property of Anthony Thompson, was a highly valued timber inspector who supervised and managed a large timbering operation on Thompson's land. Tubman's relatively stable family life was shattered around 1824 when Edward Brodess took Rit and her children to his own farm in Bucktown, Maryland. Brodess often hired young Harriet out to temporary masters, some of whom were cruel and brutal in their treatment of slaves. He also illegally sold other members of her family to out-of-state buyers, permanently fracturing her family.

Sometime during her young teen years, Tubman was nearly killed by a blow to her head from an iron weight, thrown by an angry overseer at another fleeing slave. The severe injury left her suffering from headaches, seizures, and sleeping spells for the rest of her life. During the late 1830s and early 1840s, Tubman worked for John T. Stewart, a Madison merchant and shipbuilder, bringing her back to the familial and social community near where her father lived and where she had been born. Around 1844 she married a local free black named John Tubman, and she shed her childhood name Araminta in favor of Harriet.

On March 7, 1849, Edward Brodess died on his farm at Bucktown at the age of forty-seven, leaving Tubman and her family at risk of being sold to settle his large debts. In the late fall of 1849, Tubman took her own liberty. She tapped into an Underground Railroad that was already functioning well on the Eastern Shore. Traveling by night and using the

North Star and instructions from white and black helpers, she found her way to Philadelphia. She found work as a domestic, and saved her money to help the rest of her family escape. From 1850 to 1860, Tubman conducted about thirteen escape missions, bringing away approximately seventy individuals, including her brothers, parents, and other family and friends, while also giving instructions to roughly sixty more who found their way to freedom independently. The Fugitive Slave Act of 1850 left most refugee slaves vulnerable to recapture, and many fled to the safety and protection of Canada. Tubman brought many of her charges to St. Catharines, Ontario, where they settled into a growing community of freedom seekers.

Her dangerous missions won the admiration of black and white abolitionists throughout the North, who provided her with funds to continue her activities. In 1858, Tubman met with the legendary abolitionist John Brown in her home in St. Catharines. Impressed by his passion for ending slavery, she committed herself to helping him recruit former slaves into his army for his planned raid at Harper's Ferry, Virginia. Illness may have prevented her from joining him when he conducted his attack in October 1859. That same year, Tubman purchased a home in Auburn, New York, from William Henry Seward, Lincoln's future secretary of state, where she eventually settled her aged parents and other family members. On her way to Boston in April 1860, Tubman helped incite a riot to rescue a fugitive slave, Charles Nalle, from the custody of United States marshals charged with returning him to his Virginia master.

At the urging of Massachusetts governor John Andrew, Tubman joined Northern abolitionists in support of Union activities at Port Royal, in the Hilton Head district of South Carolina in early 1862. On June 2, 1863, Tubman became the first American woman to plan and execute an armed expedition during wartime. Acting as an advisor to Colonel James Montgomery, Tubman led a raid from Port Royal 25 miles up the nearby Combahee River. Using communication networks that were the provenance of black mariners, Tubman's spy missions provided crucial details about rebel enforcements and heavily mined waters. Under the cover of darkness, Tubman and Walter Plowden, a local scout, directed three gunboats loaded with men from Montgomery's Second South Carolina Volunteer Infantry Regiment, a black unit, along the heavily mined river.

Montgomery and his men effectively dispersed Confederate gunners, set fire to several plantations, and confiscated thousands of dollars worth of rice, corn, and cotton. In addition, Montgomery sent small boats to the riverbanks to retrieve the hundreds of slaves fleeing their homes, but the boats were soon swamped by the frantic and desperate freedom seekers. Using her extraordinary voice, Tubman began to sing, encouraging the crowds to stay calm. People on the riverbanks starting singing, shouting, and clapping, easing the pressure on the small boats and the evacuation continued safely. The expedition successfully freed about seven hundred and fifty former slaves. A reporter from the *Wisconsin State Journal,* who witnessed the victorious return, wrote a lengthy article crediting Tubman with planning and directing the raid, calling her the Black She Moses.

Immediately after this raid, Tubman was called to testify at the court-martial trial of Private John E. Webster, who was charged with embezzling goods from the military stores, including selling brown sugar to Tubman and others. The unprecedented testimony of blacks against a white defendant marked an important moment in the Port Royal experiment. In this military district, freedmen were experiencing legal, social, and civil rights not enjoyed by African Americans elsewhere. Tubman's stature in the Union camps and among Union officers was a significant factor in weighing her testimony and convicting Webster.

Her services as a scout and spy were highly valued by Union officers, who recognized her great ability to extract intelligence from the local population of former slaves who had fled their Confederate masters. Tubman received about $200 from the government for her scouting services, but much of it was used to pay other scouts and spies for information, and some was used to build a washhouse to train local women to earn wages by providing laundry

Hailed as "the Moses of her people" because of her courageous rescues of hundreds of slaves through the Underground Railroad, Harriet Tubman was a living symbol of the resistance of African Americans to slavery in the United States. (Library of Congress)

services to Union officials. Her expenditures made it difficult for Tubman to support herself and to save money to send back to her ailing parents in Auburn, New York. She was not a soldier, officially, and her on-again, off-again role as a scout and a spy precluded any formal pay arrangement with the army.

Tubman witnessed the carnage inflicted on the all-black Fifty-fourth Massachusetts Infantry Regiment on July 19 during the battle of Fort Wagner. She later told an interviewer that she served the regiment's leader, Colonel Robert Gould Shaw, his last meal. Tubman's description of that fateful day is haunting in its vivid imagery. Tubman also recounted the dreadful conditions and the difficult environment in which she had to care for the wounded and dying soldiers felled during the Wagner assault: Swarming flies, festering wounds, raging fevers, and pools of blood dominated work in the field and in the hospital.

Over time, wounded and ill soldiers overwhelmed the hospitals at Beaufort, where Tubman worked day and night. Tubman's skill at curing soldiers stricken by a variety of diseases was also well known. At one point during the war, Tubman was called to Fernandina, Florida, by the Union surgeon in charge there. She prepared a medicinal tea made from roots and herbs found in the nearby swamps, which helped cure the men of debilitating and often deadly dysentery. A cook, nurse, and launderer one day, spy the next, Tubman continuously reinvented herself, adapting to and accommodating the immediate requirements of wartime crises. She never received any pay for her nursing services either; so she struggled to support herself by making and selling pies and root beer and by washing and sewing for the local Union officers.

Granted a furlough in June 1864, Tubman stopped in Boston where she met Sojourner Truth. Truth had long been an antislavery, women's rights, and African American civil rights activist. Born a slave and deeply religious, Truth had much in common with Tubman. They differed, however, in their assessment of Abraham Lincoln. Truth had campaigned for Lincoln and believed he had done much for the betterment of African Americans, but Tubman still did not care for Lincoln. Identifying herself with the thousands of black troops during the Civil War who were paid less than half of white soldiers were paid for the same service, Tubman also resented that Lincoln had been at first hesitant to enlist black men for military service.

During late spring 1865, Tubman was recruited by the United States Sanitary Commission to work in Union hospitals, where the need for her services was great. Arriving at Fortress Monroe at Hampton, Virginia, Tubman was angered by the lack of good medical care given to black soldiers, who were dying at a rate two and a half times that of white soldiers. Tubman personally complained to the U.S. Surgeon General, who then instituted more sanitary medical practices there.

By early fall 1865, Tubman headed back to Auburn to care for her elderly parents. While riding on a train from Philadelphia to New York on a government pass, she was ordered to the smoking car, where other African Americans were forcibly segregated. She refused and was violently thrown from the train by four white men, breaking her arm and several ribs. It would take her months to recuperate. Unable to work, Tubman and her family suffered greatly from hunger and cold that winter.

Tubman remained in Auburn the rest of her life. Committed to woman suffrage, Tubman was also a lifelong community activist and humanitarian, feeding, clothing, and housing anyone in need who came to her door. Illiterate her entire life, Tubman dictated part of her life story to Sarah Bradford, a local central New York author. Published in 1869, this short biography, *Scenes in the Life of Harriet Tubman*, brought brief fame and financial relief to Tubman and her family. She married veteran Nelson Davis that same year; her husband John Tubman had been killed in 1867 in Maryland. Though she and Davis operated a brick-making business and sold produce from their small farm, Tubman battled poverty for the rest of her life. Denied her own military pension, she eventually received an $8 widow's pension as the wife of Nelson Davis and later a $12 Civil War nurse's pension.

Her humanitarian work triumphed with the opening of the Harriet Tubman Home for the Aged, located on land abutting her own property in Auburn, which she transferred to the African Methodist Episcopal Zion Church in 1903. Tubman continued to appear at local and national suffrage conventions until the early 1900s. She died at the age of ninety-one on March 10, 1913, in Auburn, New York.

Kate Clifford Larson

See also Abolitionism and Northern Reformers; African American Women; Female Spies.

References and Further Reading

Bradford, Sarah H. 1869. *Scenes in the Life of Harriet Tubman*. Auburn, NY: W. J. Moses.

Bradford, Sarah H. 1886. *Harriet, The Moses of Her People*. New York: Geo. R. Lockwood & Son.

Guterman, Benjamin. 2000. "Doing 'Good Brave Work': Harriet Tubman's Testimony at Beaufort, South Carolina." *Prologue* 42 (3).

Humez, Jean M. 2003. *Harriet Tubman: The Life and the Life Stories.* Madison: University of Wisconsin Press.

Larson, Kate Clifford. 2004. *Bound for the Promised Land: Harriet Tubman, Portrait of an American Hero.* New York: Ballantine Books.

Turchin, Nadine [Nedezhda] Lvova (1826–1904)

Nadine Lvova Turchin's diary of 1863–1864 presents details of her travels with the Union army as a nurse and the wife of a commander. Conveying thoughts about military strategies, everyday life, and descriptions of the people she knew, her diary is unique in that it is written by an educated immigrant woman with a military background.

Born in Russia as Nedezhda Lvova in 1826, Nadine Lvova Turchin was the daughter of a colonel in the czar's army. She was brought up in military camps, and, as a member of the aristocracy, she received a solid education. Her husband, born Ivan Vasilvetich Turcheninov and known as John Basil Turchin in the United States, was a graduate of the military academy in St. Petersburg and a veteran of the Crimean War.

The couple immigrated to the United States in 1856, living briefly in Long Island and Philadelphia before settling in Mattoon, Illinois, in the late 1850s where John found work as a topographical engineer for the Illinois Central Railroad.

In 1861, John Turchin was appointed colonel, commanding the Nineteenth Illinois Infantry. Nadine went with him on his campaigns in Missouri, Kentucky, Tennessee, and Alabama. An 1862 account tells of John becoming ill and Nadine taking his place as head of the regiment while nursing him. In 1863, John was ordered to report to the commander of the Army of the Cumberland, where he commanded a cavalry division. Again, Nadine accompanied him, and, after she was designated as a nurse, she nursed the men on the front lines of battle.

The only diary of Nadine's that has been found begins May 26, 1863, and ends on April 26, 1864. Written in French, it provides accounts of battles such as Missionary Ridge, Chattanooga, and Chickamauga. It also conveys Nadine's thoughts about the war, her acquaintances, and the infantry. She often complained about the incompetence of the American army and the army marshals' ignorance of military operations, implying that her husband's military accomplishments were underappreciated. She also recorded her frustration at being dependent on commanders whom she saw as unqualified, even writing that the commanding general ought to make her his chief of staff or personal advisor. At other times, she wrote of the boredom and monotony of military life. Despite the complaints in her diary, accounts by the men in the army lauded Nadine for her loyalty to America and to the troops, as well as for her bravery.

The Turchins settled in Radom, Illinois, after the Civil War and little is known of their life there. Nadine died in Radom in 1904.

Sigrid Kelsey

See also Diaries and Journals; Immigrant Women; Nurses; Vivandières.

References and Further Reading
De Pauw, Linda Grant. 1998. *Battle Cries and Lullabies: Women in War from Prehistory to the Present.* Norman: University of Oklahoma Press.

Leonard, Elizabeth D. 1999. *All the Daring of the Soldier: Women of the Civil War Armies.* New York: W. W. Norton & Company.

McElligott, Mary Ellen, ed. 1977. "'A Monotony Full of Sadness': The Diary of Nadine Turchin, May, 1863–April 1864." *Journal of the Illinois State Historical Society* 70: 27–89.

U

Union Soldiers, Motives

The key motivation for most Northern soldiers was their desire to preserve the Union as an example of democratic self-government. They appealed to ideals of liberty, the free labor ideology, the memory of the Revolutionary generation, and the Constitution. Men also enlisted as a result of peer pressure or because they sought adventure or glory, although they often found boredom and fear as well. Finally, Northern soldiers fought for the preservation of what scholars call the primary unit, as well as for self-preservation.

Northern soldiers exalted the concepts of honor, duty, and Union as their motivation for enduring the discomforts of army life. In addition to their desire to protect the Union, volunteers focused on the rule of law, individual liberty, and righteousness. Self-government, democracy, and egalitarianism went together in the minds of most Northern soldiers, and to some they were exclusively Northern traits, for they posited a Southern society in which slavery had corrupted democracy as the primary reason for secession and the war. They expressed their reverence for democracy through their desire to participate in the political process. Participation in politics was a clear way for the soldier to reaffirm his status as a citizen. Celebration of the citizen volunteer and disgust for the mercenary were key components of the Revolutionary legacy that Union soldiers fought to protect, motivations they maintained even after the Union government instituted a draft in 1863.

In addition, Union soldiers symbolically constructed the Union government as a benevolent father figure, creating a persuasive metaphor in which Confederates had rejected not only governmental authority, but also paternal authority. The metaphor of family extended from the soldier's relationship to the United States government to the community of soldiers themselves. Beyond fighting for the preservation of the primary unit, Civil War soldiers fought to legitimize the deaths of their comrades. Duty to nation, family, and community combined to create a powerful motivation for Union soldiers. This sense of duty compelled many to reenlist in 1864.

When speaking of liberty, Northern soldiers most commonly meant the liberty of self-government as defined by the Founding Fathers. Few mentioned slavery as a reason for enlistment, especially in 1861 and 1862. White Union soldiers, however, gradually accepted emancipation in the limited terms that the Lincoln administration defined it—as a means to win the war and restore the Union. Moreover, the black men who enlisted in the Union armies after Lincoln's 1863 Emancipation Proclamation were conscious of their ability to help bring an end to slavery and to stake a claim to full citizenship for free blacks in the North.

Many Union soldiers described Southerners as backward, ignorant, indolent, and brutal. Their response to the physical characteristics of the region—farms, schools, and centers of business— was similarly unfavorable. In their reactions to the man-made landscape of the South, Northern soldiers expressed their own visions of a civilized society. They fought to vindicate and extend this vision of society.

Gender ideology and religion also led to men's enlistment in the Union army. Some soldiers joined the army to prove their manliness. The rhetoric of manhood also infused the desires of most volunteers to see battle as quickly as possible. After the first experience with battle, duty compelled these men to continue fighting, while their sense of honor and manhood, in addition to their understanding of Christianity, tended to quell expressions of fear. Soldiers confident in their faith were less afraid to die; they cherished beliefs of a heavenly reunion with families and friends. In addition, many Union soldiers accepted the pronouncements of Northern clergy, whose explanations for the war were built on the assumption that God had created the United States to act as a religious and political model for the rest of the world. Thus, religious ideology paralleled political ideology in motivating Northern soldiers to fight.

Jaime Amanda Martinez

See also Abolitionism and Northern Reformers; Conscription; Desertion; Enlistment; Family Life, Union; Honor; Politics; Religion; Sacrifice; Union Homefront.

References and Further Reading
Frank, Joseph Allan. 1998. *With Ballot and Bayonet: The Political Socialization of American Civil War Soldiers.* Athens: University of Georgia Press.
Hess, Earl J. 1997. *The Union Soldier in Battle: Enduring the Ordeal of Combat.* Lawrence: University Press of Kansas.
McPherson, James M. 1997. *For Cause and Comrades: Why Men Fought in the Civil War.* New York: Oxford University Press.
Mitchell, Reid. 1988. *Civil War Soldiers.* New York: Viking.
Mitchell, Reid. 1993. *The Vacant Chair: The Northern Soldier Leaves Home.* New York: Oxford University Press.
Wiley, Bell Irvin. 1952. *The Life of Billy Yank: The Common Soldier of the Union.* Indianapolis, IN: Bobbs-Merrill Company.
Woodworth, Steven E. 2001. *While God Is Marching on: The Religious World of Civil War Soldiers.* Lawrence: University Press of Kansas.

Unitarian Women

For the majority of Unitarians, immediate abolition was the ultimate social reform. With an overwhelming constituency in the New England, Northern Unitarians contributed powerfully to the abolition movement and war effort. Indeed, the emotional pull of the Civil War was so great that the calm, rational theological language of the Unitarian tradition gave way to emotionalism as prominent Unitarians interpreted the war through the lens of religion. Unitarians almost universally conceived the war as a holy war, thereby justifying the abandonment of pacifism.

The great majority of Southern Unitarians, however, remained dedicated to the Southern slave system and believed Northern Unitarians had fallen victim to fanaticism. For Southern Unitarians, abolition was not a denominational or Federal issue, only a state one. If slavery was to be abolished, it had to happen gradually, state by state. By 1861, Southern Unitarians had come to believe that secession was the best option for a peaceful solution to the slavery crisis.

Southern Unitarianism suffered serious declension in the 1850s as abolition and Unitarianism became integrally linked in the North and South. Arguing that Northern Unitarians had violated the theological tenets of traditional Unitarianism, Southern Unitarians declared their independence from the American Unitarian Association. But abolition and Unitarianism were so closely associated in the minds of most Southerners that Unitarian churches throughout the South eventually were forced to close their doors. At war's end, only two Southern Unitarian churches survived: one in Charleston, South Carolina, and the other in New Orleans.

Unitarian women participated in all aspects of wartime life. Julia Ward Howe gave to the war the inspiring "Battle Hymn of the Republic," set to the tune of "John Brown's Body." The daughter of a wealthy Episcopal banker, Howe became increasingly attracted to Unitarianism as an adult. After the Civil War, she championed the ordination of women and preached in Unitarian pulpits. Other notable Unitarian women involved in the abolition movement and the Civil War were Louisa May Alcott, Lydia Maria Child, Dorothea Dix, Elizabeth Palmer Peabody, and Lucy Stone. The two most distinguished female Universalists who participated in the Civil War were Clara Barton and Mary Livermore.

Closely aligned with Unitarians, Universalists were also instrumental in the abolitionist movement and the Civil War. The central Universalist contention is that God purposes to save the soul of every human being. Both Unitarians and Universalists pioneered the practice of ordaining women to the ministry. After the Civil War, both groups provided leading figures in the women's rights and the temperance movements. Not surprisingly, many of the most important female figures before, during, and after the war were Unitarians and Universalists.

Karen Fisher Younger

See also Abolitionism and Northern Reformers; Alcott, Louisa May (1832–1888); Antislavery Societies; Barton, Clara (1821–1912); Child, Lydia Maria Francis (1802–1880); Dix, Dorothea Lynde (1802–1887); Howe, Julia Ward (1819–1910); Livermore, Mary Ashton Rice (1820–1905); Northern Women; Peabody, Elizabeth Palmer (1804–1894); Religion; Stone, Lucy (1804–1894); Union Homefront.

References and Further Reading

Ahlstrom, Sydney. 1972. *A Religious History of the American People.* New Haven, CT: Yale University Press.

Macaulay, John Allen. 2001. *Unitarianism in the Antebellum South: The Other Invisible Institution.* Tuscaloosa: University of Alabama Press.

Massey, Mary Elizabeth. 1994. *Women in the Civil War.* Lincoln: University of Nebraska Press. (Orig. pub. 1966 as *Bonnet Brigades.*)

Miller, Randall M., Harry S. Stout, and Charles Reagan Wilson, eds. 1998. *Religion and the American Civil War.* New York: Oxford University Press.

United Daughters of the Confederacy

During the last two decades of the nineteenth century, numerous organizations were founded in the South to commemorate the Confederacy and its heroes. Both men and women participated in this commemorative activity, which was part of the postwar Confederate tradition or Lost Cause celebra-

tion. During the 1890s, the Lost Cause experienced significant change as women came to dominate the leadership of the movement and made vindication, not just commemoration, the goal. In addition to honoring the Confederacy and its heroes, these women placed critical importance on preserving Confederate culture and transmitting it to future generations.

At the head of this movement was the United Daughters of the Confederacy (UDC), founded in 1894 by Caroline Meriwether Goodlett of Tennessee and Anna Davenport Raines of Georgia. Goodlett and Raines were representative members of an organization of women from the elite ranks of Southern society. These women were related by blood or by marriage to leading men in their respective states and the region. Most were formally educated at private female seminaries and women's colleges.

The organization was founded in Nashville, Tennessee. The Daughters, as they were also known, established five primary types of objectives to define their responsibility in the Confederate celebration: memorial, historical, benevolent, educational, and social. They retained the Confederate memorial tradition established by their forebears in ladies' memorial associations, and they planned to continue building monuments. Because history had the potential of vindicating the war generation, the Daughters also had a keen interest in what was being written and published about the Confederacy. In its early years, the organization was also concerned about the care of surviving Confederate veterans and their widows, and they vigorously pursued plans to ensure the well-being of their aging and indigent Confederate fathers and mothers. Most of the UDC's activities also had a social component, for example chapters held some gatherings at the homes of their members.

The educational objectives of the Daughters, however, distinguished their work from that of other Confederate organizations. UDC members believed that it was their duty "to instruct and instill into the descendants of the people of the South a proper respect for . . . the deeds of their forefathers." Confederate organizations wrote tomes about the importance of teaching the younger generation the "true history" of the Confederacy; the UDC constitution implied that the Daughters intended to take further steps to actively instruct and instill in future generations of Southern white children the values of the Confederate generation.

The UDC experienced enormous growth in the first decades of its existence. What began as a group of about thirty-five women became one of one hundred thousand by World War I. It swiftly became a powerful and influential women's organization in the early twentieth century, not only in terms of its numbers, but also with its ability to accomplish goals on behalf of Confederate causes. The Daughters were invested in preserving the social structure and culture of the Old South and Confederacy, and the organization drew members on that basis. Women joined the organization to be with members of their race and class and to preserve their status in both.

The activity with which the UDC is often identified is monument building. Although this was only one of their activities as an organization, the Daughters' success in marking the Southern landscape with monuments is important to understanding their commitment to vindicating the Confederate generation.

It is no coincidence that Confederate monuments appeared on the Southern urban landscape at the same time that the UDC was growing in numbers and influence. According to the work of historical geographers, 93 percent of Confederate monuments were built after 1895. One-half of them were unveiled between 1903 and 1912. Concurrently, the UDC grew from a membership of thirty-five thousand in 1903 to nearly eighty thousand in 1912. The Daughters were the Southerners most committed to monument building; the UDC's growth therefore provides a key explanation for the marked increase in monument building in the region.

True history, the South's version of the Civil War and American history to be exact, was equally important to the UDC. Soon after its founding in 1894, the UDC became the Confederate organization most actively engaged in combating what one Daughter called the "wicked falsehoods" being perpetuated by Northerners. Many UDC leaders spoke about the importance of impartial history, but their organization's efforts to preserve history were also concrete and systematic. The Daughters collected artifacts for museums and supported their male counterparts in setting up state departments of archives and history. They gathered manuscripts and collected war reminiscences from veterans and Confederate women, some of the earliest examples of what has since become the field of oral history. The UDC encouraged the study of history by establishing essay contests for its membership, and many Daughters were active amateur historians. They wrote history for local newspapers, published articles in regional magazines, and even wrote historical novels and textbooks for use in Southern schools.

The UDC sought to correct what it believed were interpretive inaccuracies and in doing so offered an interpretation that suited its cause. Above all, the Daughters resented claims that the South fought the Civil War to defend slavery and that Confederate soldiers were traitors to the United States. UDC members, as well as their male contemporaries, wanted history to record that the South fought the war to defend states' rights, not slavery. They insisted that Confederate soldiers were American patriots because they were the true defenders of the Constitution—a reference to the Tenth Amendment protecting the rights of states. Moreover, the Daughters believed that correcting such errors was essential if Confederate men were to be vindicated.

Vindication for the Confederate generation was, of course, the overarching goal of the UDC from its founding in 1894. Every monument placed in a courthouse square, every veteran or widow cared for, every history book removed from a library or school for being biased against the South, and every chapter of the Children of the Confederacy formed was done to vindicate Confederate men and women.

Yet it was another war, World War I, that gave the UDC members their best opportunity to vindicate the Confederate generation, and they capitalized on it. The UDC's war relief efforts were impressive. UDC President General Mary Poppenheim of South Carolina hoped that her organization's wartime efforts would be worthy of the group's

Confederate background. The women did their best, and Poppenheim reflected on her organization's achievement by suggesting that the "touchstone of war brought out all the latent power" of the organization. Mrs. J. A. Rountree of Alabama, chair of the UDC's War Relief Committee, reported that, in the last year of the war alone, the UDC had endowed seventy hospital beds at the American military hospital in Neuilly, France; made 3.5 million hospital garments; wrapped 4.5 million surgical dressings; knitted 100,000 garments; donated $82,000 to the Red Cross; subscribed $9 million in liberty bonds; and supported 830 French and Belgian orphans for $20,000.

After World War I, the Daughters did not return to monument building with the same sense of purpose as they had before the war. In fact, the goals of monument building, as set out by the founders, were nearly met, and, by the 1920s, there were fewer and fewer Confederate men and women who needed the UDC's assistance. The Daughters' success, as much as the passage of time, led the UDC to a change in emphasis.

The UDC had earned respect as a national patriotic organization, as evidenced by their partnerships with Northern voluntary associations during World War I. The Daughters interpreted their success and Northern expressions of respect as vindication. White Southerners were praised for their patriotism during World War I without having to relinquish their belief that the Confederate cause had been a just cause. Indeed, the Daughters can take some credit for ensuring that national reconciliation was made effectively on the South's terms, since vindication was the white South's requirement for sectional reconciliation.

Today, the UDC has a membership of approximately twenty thousand members, most of whom are not active. It is no longer the influential organization it was in its early years. Yet its early history remains important to understanding how the New South was created and why the region struggled to disengage itself from its culture of segregation—a culture that was created, in part, by Southern women in the early twentieth century.

Karen L. Cox

See also Ladies' Memorial Associations; Monuments; Southern Women.
References and Further Reading
Cox, Karen L. 2003. *Dixie's Daughters: The United Daughters of the Confederacy and the Preservation of Confederate Culture.* Gainesville: University Press of Florida.
Whites, LeeAnn. 1995. *The Civil War as a Crisis in Gender, Augusta, Georgia, 1860–1890.* Athens: University of Georgia Press.

United States Christian Commission

The United States Christian Commission was a Union-wide philanthropic association created to provide religious, intellectual, and medical relief services to Civil War soldiers. Blossoming in the latter years of the war, by 1865 it was second in size only to the United States Sanitary Commission. Springing from the antebellum Young Men's Christian Association (YMCA) and built on that foundation, it was led and staffed by its veterans. During the war, five thousand short-term temporary or long-term permanent agents went to the field under its auspices to offer spiritual, intellectual, and physical relief services to the soldiers. Its agents, or delegates as they were called, distributed more than $5 million worth of scriptures, reading material, foods, and medical supplies to soldiers on both sides of the conflict. By the end of their war their presence was ubiquitous; they followed the troops on the march, by train, by foot, or with wagons filled with supplies, offering religious counseling and services and distributing needed supplies. They also developed systematic programs for traveling libraries, the delivery of periodicals, and special hospital kitchens to improve the diet of the sickest soldiers.

Evangelical Christian women, already active in the nation's churches, were particularly drawn to the work of this religious-based benevolent organization. Its work was fueled by their liberal donations. At the beginning of the war, the Christian Commission's leadership did not include women, and working as delegates was deemed inappropriate for women. As the war intensified, the need for the labor and donations of every interested individual led to a shift in such policies. By 1865 women were officially employed as administrators, traveled as fundraisers, staffed and led auxiliary societies, and served in the field as lady managers in a popular Special Diet Kitchen program. Through this organization, thousands of American women's work and donations improved the lives of soldiers, but their participation also had a transformational impact on their lives. Not content to remain quietly in the private sphere in the postwar era, female veterans of the Christian Commission participated in increasingly public ways in variety of religious and secular reform efforts, from temperance to woman suffrage.

When the war began, YMCAs in the North saw their members marching off to fight and so extended their efforts from city streets to camp, hospital, and battlefield. At first, individual associations sent representatives to the field to bring religious teachings and Bibles to the soldiers, but they soon recognized the need for a more coordinated effort in a war of unprecedented magnitude. At a meeting called on November 14, 1861, to consider the problem, the United States Christian Commission was born. Mirroring the structure of the national YMCA, it was led by a volunteer executive board of veteran YMCA worthies who loosely coordinated the work of army committees at YMCA branches. These were charged with gathering and processing gifts for the soldiers and sending delegates and supplies to the field.

American women were deeply concerned with the outcome of the struggle and the spiritual and physical well-being of the soldiers. Always the largest percentage of church members and substantial contributors to the success of the antebellum YMCAs, evangelical Christian women were plentiful, and they made good agents in the field and good administrative employees.

To recognize the significance of the contributions of women and to increase their gifts, in May 1864 the Commission proposed the formation of ladies Christian commissions. These auxiliaries would raise money for the central office, collect and produce relief supplies, and process them and send them to the field to be distributed to soldiers. In these organizations, women held leadership roles, including acting as the national executive secretary, heading local societies, and traveling as organizers. The activities of these groups were vital to the functioning of the Commission. In the last year of the war, 266 societies registered with the Commission, some from as far away as California and Hawaii. They provided considerable aid to the work of the Commission, sending over $200,000 to the central office and an unrecorded amount of supplies directly to the field.

The Christian Commission was reluctant to send single women to the field to work as delegates. Correspondence suggests that female volunteers were rejected by the central office when they applied for such service. Local army committees, such as the one in St. Louis, were more amenable to their applications. There women were employed as missionaries and sent to locations as far away as Memphis, Vicksburg, and Little Rock for periods ranging from one to three years. Women also served in the field alongside husbands and fathers. For example, Hannah Smith served in Nashville, Tennessee, with her husband, the Reverend E. P. Smith. There she ran the Christian Commission rooms and acted as a regional manager for the Special Diet Kitchen program. Some women, such as Mrs. James Fisher, died in Commission service.

Prior to 1864, women's participation in fieldwork was scattered and isolated. In the spring of 1864, Annie Turner Wittenmyer, a wealthy widow from Keokuk, Iowa, and a veteran relief worker, proposed a program that created a special niche for women in the Christian Commission service. Wittenmyer, reacting to a widely held concern that the recovery rate of soldiers in Union hospitals was being sabotaged by the unhealthy and inappropriate diet served them, suggested a strategy to improve the diet of the sickest hospital patients. Under her plan, the Commission would sponsor the creation of Special Diet Kitchens within hospitals. The kitchens would be administered by middle-class Christian women employed by the Commission. These women would craft menus that would appeal to the ailing soldier and train soldier cooks to prepare the food in an appetizing manner. In addition, the women would work as missionaries when not busy running the kitchens.

The program began in Nashville, Tennessee, in April 1864. Early lady managers, as the Special Diet kitchen administrators were called, faced considerable challenges when they arrived to set up kitchens. Hospital administrators often resisted the invasion of women, particularly as administrators, but the diet kitchen managers persevered and in the end prevailed. By the end of the war, the kitchens had spread across Union-controlled territory from Little Rock, Arkansas, to Washington, D.C. and from North Carolina to New Orleans. Employing over one hundred and fifty women, with kitchens in over sixty locations, this work—designed, administered, and staffed by women—was highly regarded by military and medical authorities.

On January 1, 1866, the work of the Christian Commission officially ended, but its impact lived on. As workers or fundraisers for ladies' Christian commissions, field agents, or diet kitchen mangers, thousands of American women had labored to improve the lot of the soldier. They gained significant experience and established that women were effective and highly economical workers. In the years to come, veterans like Annie Wittenmyer would use new skills and status to shape the postwar world.

Wittenmyer established a national reputation during the war. For the rest of her life, she continued her relief and reform efforts, as an organizational leader and as an author of works urging women to participate in evangelical crusades and to take an active role in society. From the presidency of the Women's Christian Temperance Union, the largest women's organization of the nineteenth century, to leadership in the Women's Relief Corps, the women's auxiliary to the Grand Army of the Republic, she would work to stamp out vice, build homes for soldiers' orphans and widows, and win pensions for Civil War nurses. She also remained active as a writer, lecturer, and reformer until her death. Women who had served as lady managers also participated in the temperance crusade, traveled to foreign lands as missionaries, and held leadership roles in the fight for women's suffrage.

Theresa R. McDevitt

See also Aid Societies; Northern Women; Wittenmyer, Annie Turner (1827–1900).

References and Further Reading
Attie, Jeanie. 1998. *Patriotic Toil: Northern Women and the American Civil War.* Ithaca, NY: Cornell University Press.
Bremner, Robert Hamlett. 1890. *The Public Good: Philanthropy and Welfare in the Civil War Era.* New York: Alfred A. Knopf.
Ladies' Christian Commission. 1864. *Ladies' Christian Commissions: Auxiliary to the U.S. Christian Commission.* Philadelphia: C. Sherman.
Leonard, Elizabeth. 1994. *Yankee Women: Gender Battles in the Civil War.* New York: W. W. Norton & Company.
McDevitt, Theresa R. 2004. "'A Melody before Unknown': The Civil War Experiences of Mary and Amanda Shelton." *Annals of Iowa* 63 (2): 105–136.
Moss, Lemuel. 1868. *Annals of the United States Christian Commission.* Philadelphia, PA: J. B. Lippincott Co.
Wittenmyer, Annie Turner. 1895. *Under the Guns: A Woman's Reminiscences of the Civil War.* Boston: E. B. Stillings & Co.

United States Sanitary Commission

The United States Sanitary Commission (USSC) was a privately run philanthropic organization established during the American Civil War to collect and distribute supplies, to assist the Federal government in the management of military hospitals, and to make inquiries and give advice on issues of sanitation and medicine. The USSC was the only civilian-run organization to receive official recognition from the Federal government. Middle- and upper-class men, who sought to reassert their social and political status after the expansion of the franchise and the advent of machine politics, comprised the executive board of the Commission. Northern women of various socioeconomic backgrounds comprised the leadership of the Commission branches and the bulk of the volunteers. The wartime relationship between these men and women provided much needed battlefield assistance, along with conflict over the place and value of women's work.

The USSC emerged from the Women's Central Association of Relief (WCAR) in response to the

United States Army's failure to maintain adequate sanitation and supply sufficient medicine in the aftermath of the Battle of Bull Run in the spring of 1861. Elizabeth Blackwell, the first female doctor in the United States, founded the WCAR in the spring of 1861 to manage relief work, communicate directly with the U.S. Army Medical Department, and select and train women nurses. WCAR Vice President Henry W. Bellows traveled to Washington, D.C., to establish political connections, but he shifted his thinking regarding the nature of a wartime relief organization after visiting army camps and military hospitals. Rather then presenting the proposal laid out by the WCAR, Bellows informed Secretary of War Simon Cameron that a wartime relief agency, based in the capital, would improve and maintain the physical and mental health of the army, manage the organization of military hospitals and camps, and advise the transportation of the wounded. The USSC received executive approval in June 1861.

The USSC had a hierarchical structure, with an executive board, inspectors, and field agents in Washington, D.C.; Commission branches located in major Northern cities; and soldiers' aid societies dispersed in smaller towns. Unitarian Minister Henry W. Bellows served as president, New York lawyer George Templeton Strong as treasurer, landscape architect Frederick Law Olmsted as general secretary, and architect Alfred J. Bloor as corresponding secretary. Due to exhaustion, disagreements with other board members, and money difficulties, Olmsted resigned in 1863 and was replaced by John Foster Jenkins. Bloor maintained connections with the Northern homefront through direct correspondence with regional branches and local aid societies. Unlike his colleagues on the executive board, Bloor was convinced that the Commission needed to respond to the needs of Northern women. He was let go from his position in October 1864.

The USSC was supported by the grassroots efforts of Commission branches, including the WCAR, and by localized soldiers' aid societies. In September 1862, the USSC recognized the WCAR as an auxiliary branch, but it continued to function independently from the parent organization. Twelve regional branches located in New York City, Boston, Philadelphia, Cincinnati, Louisville, Cleveland, Pittsburgh, Chicago, New Albany, Detroit, Buffalo, and Columbus supported the USSC throughout the war. The regional branches existed and functioned under the authority and direction of the USSC, but they also initiated programs accepted by the parent organization. The establishment of female associate managers, who communicated supply requests to the homefront and provided reports on the conditions of the homefront and battlefront, provided branch managers with more time for recruitment activities. Local soldiers' aid societies provided the bulk of the support for the USSC coming from the Northern homefront. By late fall 1862, over fourteen hundred soldiers' aid societies were associated with the USSC, and, over the course of the war, nearly seven thousand aid societies were created. Both the regional branch offices of the USSC and the local soldiers' aid societies were managed, worked, and sustained primarily by women.

To counter what the Commission saw as the inefficiency and confusion of Federal government action and the lack of order or benevolence at the local level, the USSC emphasized centralized efforts and philanthropy based on scientific principles to effectively carry out wartime needs. The USSC fulfilled this goal through fundraising, inquiries, advice, transportation, and distribution. One of the Commission's first tasks included raising the necessary money to hire field agents and to transport supplies to the front. Money initially came from insurance companies, businesses, and property holders. Early donations allowed the Commission to begin its work, but the organization would be plagued by a lack of sufficient funds and supply shortages throughout the war. The course of the war and Northern sympathy toward the war influenced the amount of money and supplies held by the USSC at any given moment. Inspectors thoroughly investigated and reported the conditions of camps and troops, including sewage disposal, cleanliness, clothing, cooking, and diets, and advisors made recommendations to the War Department. The USSC

Quarters of the United States Sanitary Commission ca. 1860–1865. (National Archives and Records Administration)

advised the War Department to improve the diets of soldiers to include greater nutritional variety, to reorganize the Medical Bureau to better care for the sick and wounded in hospitals, and to allow the Commission to participate in the transportation of supplies and of the wounded and sick to hospitals.

In the first year of the war, the USSC focused on persuading the government to reorganize the Medical Bureau, which the Commission saw as plagued by poor management, bureaucracy, and the demands of special interests. In April 1862, Congress passed a reorganization bill, which provided for an increase in the number of medical and nonmedical personnel, inspectors, an increase in the requirements in sanitation reports, as well as the dismissal of Dr. Clement Finely from the post of surgeon general and the appointment of William Hammond.

The USSC remained in communication with its branches to ensure the continual flow of supplies to the troops and the battlefront. Women on the Northern homefront provided over $15 million worth of supplies over the course of the war, including ice, bandages, lint, pens, paper, clothing, and food. When the USSC was unable to obtain supplies from local aid societies, they bought goods on the market. To keep the Northern homefront abreast of its supply and distribution activities, the USSC began publishing *The Sanitary Commission Bulletin* in November 1863, along with lecture tours in USSC regions. Both attempts at improved communication with the homefront were suggestions of female branch managers. The Commission used the publication to advance the organizational themes of centralization and scientific basis for philanthropy.

The *Bulletin* was published twice a month and circulated to local aid societies and troops.

Due to wartime cooperation with the Federal government and the Northern homefront, the USSC experienced conflict and controversy. Advice offered by the USSC to the Federal government was not always welcome. While the USSC criticized the Medical Bureau for failing in its duties to the troops, the Bureau believed the Commission exaggerated its concerns about sickness and sanitation. The appointment of Edwin M. Stanton as secretary of war in 1862 also placed strains on the Commission's influence in the War Department, since Stanton accused the Commission of engaging in trade rather than philanthropy. Although the Commission was called on by the armies of George. B. McClellan and John C. Frémont, in early 1864 General William T. Sherman refused to let the Commission use military transportation for supplies.

The USSC clashed with other philanthropic organizations, including the United States Christian Commission (USCC) and the Western Sanitary Commission (WSC). Both the USCC and the WSC were perceived by the Commission to be threats to its success in gaining the support and contributions of the homefront and in the push for centralized and efficient work. The USCC functioned as a philanthropic organization and provided religious tracts and materials to soldiers, while the WSC provided supplies for the trans-Mississippi region including Texas, Kansas, Missouri, Arkansas, Mississippi, Tennessee, Louisiana, and Kentucky. Unlike the USSC, the WSC relied on local leaders and solutions to meet supply and distribution needs. The executive board believed the methods of the WSC were inefficient, bred repetitiveness, and undermined the USSC's role as a national benevolent organization.

The women of the Northern homefront proved to be the Commission's most formidable foe during the course of the war. At the beginning of the war, the executive board believed that they could easily gain the support and participation of women and that women would naturally and dutifully carry out benevolent activity, while the structure and centralized organization of the USSC would bring direction and efficiency to their activities. The wartime assistance of women on the Northern homefront depended on local circumstances like child care, family illness, and community welfare. As became increasingly evident in branch-issued questionnaires, Northern women held both the USSC and the Federal government responsible for the requests for and the distribution of supplies. Women questioned why the Federal government was unable to provide the necessary supplies for war, particularly in light of rising taxes. They indicated their anger over supposed corrupt and fraudulent practices on the part of the USSC. Specifically, women feared that the supplies they provided were not getting to the battlefront or were being sold.

Certain activities carried out by the women on the Northern homefront went against the directions of the USSC and earned its dissatisfaction. Some women sent supplies directly to the battlefront, rather than to the USSC, as instructed. Sanitary fairs, which were successful fundraising activities for Commission branches, were seen by the Commission to be violations of its emphasis on centralization. Despite the success of sanitary fairs—the Northwestern Sanitary Commission's fair raised $100,000 in 1863—the Commission believed that the fairs benefited the parent organization very little and provoked unnecessary emotion and localized activity.

The USSC chose not to involve itself directly in the process of demobilization, although Commission women sought to continue their activities by assisting returning soldiers and families. At the conclusion of the war, the USSC informed branches to continue operating until July 4, 1865, after which they needed to forward remaining supplies and money to the Commission. The last official act of the USSC came with the publication of its official history in 1866, entitled *History of the United States Sanitary Commission.*

Sarah K. Nytroe

See also Aid Societies; Blackwell, Elizabeth (1821–1910); Fairs and Bazaars; Hoge, Jane Currie Blaikie (1811–1890); Livermore, Mary Ashton Rice (1820–1905); Nurses; Olmsted, Frederick Law (1822–1903); United States Christian Commission; Women's Central Association of Relief; Wormeley, Katharine Prescott (1830–1908).

References and Further Reading

Attie, Jeanie. 1998. *Patriotic Toil: Northern Women and the American Civil War.* Ithaca, NY: Cornell University Press.

Cassedy, James H. 1992. "Numbering the North's Medical Events: Humanitarianism and Science in Civil War Statistics." *Bulletin of the History of Medicine* 66 (2): 210–233.

Frederickson, George M. 1965. *The Inner Civil War: Northern Intellectuals and the Crisis of the Union.* Urbana: University of Illinois Press.

Giesberg, Judith Ann. 1995. "In Service to the Fifth Wheel: Katharine Prescott Wormeley and Her Experiences in the United States Sanitary Commission." *Nursing History Review* 3: 43–53.

Giesberg, Judith Ann. 2000. *Civil War Sisterhood: The U.S. Sanitary Commission and Women's Politics in Transition.* Boston: Northeastern University Press.

Leonard, Elizabeth D. 1994. *Yankee Women: Gender Battles in the Civil War.* New York: W. W. Norton & Company.

Maxwell, William Quentin. 1956. *Lincoln's Fifth Wheel: The Political History of the United States Sanitary Commission.* New York: Longmans, Green & Company.

Urban Women, Northern

The start of the American Civil War coincided with the peak of the nineteenth-century women's rights movement that had, by 1860, prepared Northern women in particular for a larger public role. Although in the South it was primarily the war itself that upset gender roles and that brought women into the public in new ways, in the North many urban women had been gaining experience organizing and engaging in a battle for a public presence and the right to political participation since at least the 1830s. The Civil War found many Northern women prepared for public roles in defense of their nation.

Wartime gave new meaning to women's traditional work. In both the North and the South, women contributed publicly to the war through their domestic efforts: sewing clothing and blankets for soldiers and organizing relief and nursing centers in numerous cities from Boston to New York to St. Louis. At the outset of the war in 1861, Northern middle-class women founded the United States Sanitary Commission for the purpose of helping the army attend to the health needs of soldiers. The women of the Sanitary Commission took pride in their work as "foot soldiers" in the war effort and in their executive talents, which were put to use in organizing food and medical supplies to be sent to troops in the field. Both white and black women worked for the Sanitary Commission and were mobilized by the war to set up organizations to collect and distribute supplies, even when it meant stepping outside their traditional roles.

Individual women across the Union took on new roles on behalf of their nation. For example, Josephine St. Pierre Ruffin took her commitment to the Union cause one step further by working to recruit black men as soldiers. Initially reluctant to visit the battlefield herself because of propriety, Clara Barton was eventually convinced to take her much needed supplies directly to the front, thus expanding women's presence and range of activities in the midst of war. Dorothea Dix, an active reformer on behalf of the mentally ill in Washington, D.C., before the war, used her reputation and connections to organize nursing care during the war at a time when nursing as a profession did not officially exist. Other urban women served in informal roles, bringing food and comfort items to war prisoners and hospital inmates.

Northern urban women also used their numbers, their reform connections, and their organizational skills to raise money for the war effort, including the money necessary to carry out their relief work. Newspapers reported on the "mass movements of the Ladies" gathering in public spaces and holding fundraising fairs. Under the auspices of the Sanitary Commission, reformer Mary Livermore planned a large fundraising bazaar in Chicago in 1863. Although their goal was to raise $25,000, the women took in almost four times that amount. Such activities also raised issues about women's public roles, however; Livermore and her colleagues were frustrated by the fact that, even though they were competent organizers and leaders of their local associations, as women they could not sign contracts and therefore manage their own business affairs. This aspect of her wartime work led Livermore, for one, to think more broadly about women's rights after the

Civil War, and she later spearheaded the suffrage movement in Illinois.

One of the less traditional ways that urban women participated in the war effort was through factory and government work. Women filled many new clerical and government positions created by the war. Although most of these jobs were temporary and women were consistently paid less than men, women employed by the Federal government in Washington, D.C., could earn better salaries than in any other professions available to women at the time. The presence of women in the workplace, even in the name of supporting the Union cause, still raised concerns for some Northerners about protecting the virtue of the so-called government girls.

In some instances, women had more to worry about than their reputations because war-related work could be dangerous. Both Northern and Southern cities suffered female civilian deaths due to factory explosions. In June 1864, a munitions factory explosion in Washington, D.C., killed twenty-three workers and wounded several others. More than one hundred women were employed at the factory assembling rifle cartridges, most of them young unmarried Irish women, and the accident sent shockwaves of grief throughout the civilian population, already wearied by mounting casualties so late in the war. The city was so brought together over the tragedy that even President Abraham Lincoln attended the memorial service.

Besides volunteer work and employment directly related to supporting the Union cause, wartime also saw an increase in urban women's participation in public discussions, demonstrations, and parades. These public events might include residents as well as nonresidents because wartime attracted a range of individuals to the cities, both men and women, looking for either paid employment or ways to participate in the war effort. Women, for example, were drawn to urban areas to work in hospitals, to take government or factory jobs, or to accompany their enlisted husbands. As the Southern states began to secede, even before hostilities broke out, Northern women gathered in cities to show their support for the Union. In the early years of the war, women from New York all the way to San Francisco came out to show their support for soldiers and for their leaders. It was reported that an "Immense Demonstration" in New York in the summer of 1862 brought almost as many women as men out to declare their undying support for the Union. At such events, women might wave banners from high-rise apartment buildings or crowd the sidewalks with their children in tow to show their support for the troops gathering and marching through the streets.

Not all public gatherings were necessarily celebratory, however. The cities also served as centers of public anger over the war and its effects on the civilian population, and women were often at the forefront of urban riots and protests. While many middle-class urban women found new opportunities for displaying their patriotism and for public roles related to the war effort, working-class women were more likely to be economically devastated by the war. Working-class and poor immigrant women were at the center of the draft riots in New York City in the summer of 1863, protesting the conscription of their men to fight to free the slaves. The *New York Herald* noted the significance of the presence of "a large number of workingmen's wives" and even blamed the women for the draft riots themselves. The racial and class tensions in the city meant that the riots in New York City were about more than the draft; the city's African Americans, in particular, became the targets of white anger over the purpose and impact of the war. White female rioters reportedly participated in an attack on a black orphanage, targeted black women for violence, and even turned their anger on white abolitionists.

A few months before the draft riots, however, women protestors had already taken to the streets over the even more immediate issue of feeding their families. Bread riots in April 1863 resulted from, as the *New York Times* reported, thousands of hungry women rioting in the streets. While the numbers of rioters may have been exaggerated, no doubt women throughout Northern cities were affected by the conscriptions and deaths of male breadwinners, the scarcity of food, and the drop in morale as the war raged on.

Tiffany K. Wayne

References and Further Reading

Furgurson, Ernest B. 2004. *Freedom Rising: Washington in the Civil War.* New York: Alfred A. Knopf.

Matthews, Glenna. 1992. *The Rise of Public Woman: Woman's Power and Place in the United States, 1630–1970.* New York: Oxford University Press.

Ryan, Mary. 1990. *Women in Public: Between Banners and Ballots, 1825–1880.* Baltimore, MD: Johns Hopkins University Press.

Urban Women, Southern

The Civil War increased the numbers of women living in cities as female refugees brought their families to the places that they thought could offer support and protection. As refugees flocked to urban centers looking for food, wages, and safety, the wartime population influx contributed to overcrowding and food shortages.

On a daily basis, urban Confederates dealt with many of the difficulties faced by their rural counterparts, including displacement, food shortages, impressment, conscription, and widespread disorder. In addition, like their rural counterparts, urban women participated directly in the Confederate war effort. They helped raise military regiments, took over businesses, worked for the government, formed female home guards, and lobbied politicians. Some men remained on the urban homefront, especially the industrial laborers, teachers, railroad and river workers, civil officials, and telegraph operators who took advantage of the exemptions they were given in the 1862 Conscription Law.

As did the Southern countryside, Confederate cities experienced demographic upheaval, growing tremendously as the rural areas lost residents. City populations increased at astounding rates as rural civilians took refuge from Union forces, rebellious slaves, hunger, and homelessness. Some came to the cities to escape the tedium of rural life, but most arrived out of necessity. These refugees saw the urban areas as the safest place to be during wartime. However, the large influx of people resulted in a myriad of difficulties. The wartime shortages of food, clothing, housing, and medicines that all Southerners faced were intensified in the cities and exacerbated by the cities' overgrown populations.

At the outset of the war, the South's five most populous cities were New Orleans, Louisiana; Charleston, South Carolina; Richmond, Virginia; Mobile, Alabama; and Memphis, Tennessee. All their populations increased significantly during the war. For example, Richmond's wartime population tripled to over one hundred and forty thousand. Thousands of wartime refugees, politicians, soldiers, and peddlers made their way to the capital, ultimately making it the most congested Confederate city. This drastic increase forced President Jefferson Davis to declare martial law five days after his inauguration in the hopes of controlling the chaos, violence, and rising crime in the city. The disorder continued, however, and in 1862 local officials banned the sale of liquor, established a pass system, and arrested the disorderly and criminal elements.

The infrastructures of the South's cities could not handle the wartime influx of people. The drastic population growth caused housing, food, and supply shortages. Houses, hotels, and other types of accommodations filled beyond capacity. In addition, in Richmond and other urban centers, the food shortage led families to extreme actions, including food riots. In April 1863, approximately three hundred women and children set upon the capital and demanded that the government sell them food at official prices. When these requests were refused, the women raided the business section, seizing food and other necessary goods. Women staged similar bread riots in cities around the Confederacy, including those in Georgia, Alabama, North Carolina, Tennessee, Louisiana, and Virginia.

Once in the Southern cities, some women found work in factories as well as in government offices. Others took up jobs as teachers, seamstresses, cooks, or laundresses. Although their pay was often meager, it helped these women support themselves and their families.

Despite the demographic plights in the cities, these communities generally supported the war effort. Urban women gathered together to make and gather supplies for the soldiers. They set up sewing and aid societies that met in church basements, created centralized centers to gather material and monetary contributions for the soldiers, and staged bazaars, plays, and other entertainments to raise money for the fighting men. The cities' larger populations and the centralized nature of that population allowed the women in these areas to gather regularly and work together in groups for the benefit of the troops.

Women's aid societies also fed the soldiers who passed through their areas. Women in several Southern cities formed groups who met troop trains and then fed the men with whatever food was available. In Columbia, South Carolina, for example, the aid society set up around-the-clock shifts to ensure that at least a few members met every train, regardless of when it arrived.

The Union occupation of cities also affected life in the South's urban centers. Early in the war, Union forces captured New Orleans, Memphis, Nashville, Norfolk, and Alexandria. By the end of the war, they controlled many more towns and cities, including Atlanta, Savannah, Charleston, Richmond, Vicksburg, and Wilmington. Although the United States government often improved the infrastructure of the cities it occupied, helping sanitation, water supplies, and street conditions, few Southerners appreciated the upgrades. Instead, many urban Confederates resented their occupiers, visibly demonstrating their contempt for the invading Yankees. Southern women often verbally and socially chastised the occupying troops. Confederate women in occupied cities repeatedly avoided Union soldiers on the roads, waved Rebel flags and cheered for Jefferson Davis in front of Northern troops, refused to speak to Northerners, and held their noses when passing Federal soldiers. After capturing Atlanta, Union General William Tecumseh Sherman evacuated the city of its civilian population, avoiding problems in the city but provoking the ire of Southerners around the Confederacy.

The population growth in Confederate cities allowed for some anonymity. Consequently, it accelerated the growth of prostitution. Some urban Southern women turned to prostitution for the first time as a way of surviving the vagaries of war, whereas others flourished in their trade of many years.

Other women used the close proximity of soldiers, both enemy and their own, to advance their espionage work. Female spies often flirted with soldiers, gaining valuable information that they then transmitted to the Union or Confederacy.

Lisa Tendrich Frank

See also Aid Societies; Atlanta, Evacuation of (Special Field Orders, Number 67); Bread Riots; Butler, Benjamin F. (1818–1893); Confederate Homefront; Factory Workers, Southern; Female Spies; Government Girls; Imprisonment of Women; Prostitution; Rape; Southern Women; Teachers, Southern; Treasury Girls; Wartime Employment; Woman Order (General Order Number 28).

References and Further Reading

Ash, Steven V. 1995. *When the Yankees Came: Conflict and Chaos in the Occupied South.* Chapel Hill: University of North Carolina Press.

Massey, Mary Elizabeth. 1952. *Ersatz in the Confederacy: Shortages and Substitutes on the Southern Homefront.* Columbia: University of South Carolina Press.

Massey, Mary Elizabeth. 1994. *Women in the Civil War.* Lincoln: University of Nebraska Press.(Orig. pub. 1966 as *Bonnet Brigades*)

Usher, Rebecca (1821–1919)

Rebecca Usher was one of twenty thousand women who served as nurses during the Civil War. Usher wrote extensive letters to her sisters while volunteering at the Union army's General Hospital in Chester, Pennsylvania. In her letters, Usher describes the other nurses, the soldiers, her duties, the physical appearance of the hospital, and the frustrations and joys she experienced during her nursing stint.

Rebecca Usher was born in 1821 in Hollis, Maine. Her mother was Hannah Lane, and her father was Ellis Baker Usher, a wealthy lumberman who was also a state politician. Rebecca was the oldest of four sisters, with whom she remained in close contact throughout her life. At the age of sixteen, Usher attended the Ursuline Convent at Three Rivers in Canada, where she studied and then taught French. At the age of twenty, Usher returned to Maine and her family.

Little is known about Usher's activities before she became a nurse for the Union army. However, she never married. As a single, middle-class, middle-aged woman, Usher was a prime candidate to fulfill the role of nurse because American Victorian ideals dictated that she was less likely than her younger counterparts to be influenced by immoral male soldiers.

Following the Battle of Antietam, hospitals increased their recruiting of female nurses. In October 1862, Usher received a letter requesting her services under the authority of Dorothea Dix, superintendent of the United States Army nurses. Usher instead responded to Adaline Tyler, matron of the Chester General Hospital, who had put out her own call for volunteer nurses. Usher joined the Chester hospital in late November.

By the second week of December, Usher was in charge of her own ward. She and the other female nurses did not participate in medical assistance as much as they provided caregiving to the soldiers. Usher's duties included supervising mealtimes,

mending clothing, distributing goods, and providing companionship to soldiers. Usher also wrote letters to her sisters, from whom she requested stockings, tobacco, and other supplies that were needed to make the soldiers' stay at the hospital more comfortable.

Usher took great pride in her work at the hospital and found the work fulfilling. When the Chester General Hospital closed in 1863, Usher was distraught but ultimately found nursing duties elsewhere.

In 1865 she continued volunteer work—as a nurse and relief worker—with the Maine State Agency at City Point, Virginia. With the agency, Usher focused on serving the Maine soldiers, visiting them in hospital wards as well as providing them with food, supplies, and shelter.

At the war's end, Usher returned to Hollis, Maine where she attended to her family estate until her death in 1919.

Jessie Wilkerson

See also Antietam/Sharpsburg, Battle of (September 17, 1862); Dix, Dorothea Lynde (1802–1887); Hospitals; Letter Writing; Northern Women; Nurses; Union Homefront.

References and Further Reading

Leonard, Elizabeth D. 1995. "Civil War Nurse, Civil War Nursing: Rebecca Usher of Maine." *Civil War History* 41 (3): 190–208.

V

Van Lew, Elizabeth (1818–1900)

A native Virginian who served as a Union spy in the Confederate capital of Richmond, Virginia, Elizabeth Van Lew was often referred to as Crazy Bet. Van Lew's efforts on behalf of the Union during the Civil War led to the escape of dozens of Union prisoners from Libby Prison in Richmond, the collection of vital intelligence on Confederate military positions in and around the city, and other successful activities of the Union underground throughout the war.

Elizabeth Van Lew was born October 15, 1818, in Richmond, Virginia, the first child of John Van Lew and Eliza Louise Baker Van Lew. In the 1830s her parents sent her to Philadelphia to live with relatives while she received her education. Although the Van Lews owned slaves, Elizabeth developed a strong abolitionist stance that provided a foundation for her actions during the Civil War. She not only believed that slavery had corrupted Southern society but also that its immoral nature made it a national sin.

As the war began, Confederate women in their Church Hill neighborhood asked Van Lew and her mother to join them in providing sustenance and supplies to the growing Confederate armies that flocked to Richmond. The Van Lew women refused the requests, creating suspicion about the family's loyalty that would follow them throughout the conflict. In an effort to deflect the criticism, occasionally Van Lew would minister to the Confederate wounded and encamped soldiers. She also became an accomplished hostess, entertaining Confederate officers and government officials in the family's home, as well as boarding a Confederate captain and his family for a time. She even explained her desire to visit Union prisoners as a reflection of a proper Confederate woman's Christian duty to minister to those deemed most unworthy. This public persona was simply a way for Van Lew to gain access to people and information that would further the Union cause while raising the least suspicion.

The public perception of her as crazy may have developed from the odd clothing she wore and nonsensical mutterings she uttered as she walked through the streets of the city during the war. However, the most recent biography contends that factual evidence does not exist to support such contentions; instead, resentment for her Unionism, her radical stance on slavery, and her lifelong spinsterhood and reclusive lifestyle may be more the cause of the nickname.

The majority of Van Lew's early war work related to providing for and assisting in the escape of Union prisoners held in Richmond. Both personally and with the aid of free blacks, slaves, and other Unionists, Van Lew sent prisoners messages that were hidden in the spines of books, in the false bottoms of food platters, in the soles of her servants' shoes, or in a hollow egg in a basket of eggs. She had her own encryption code, composed of letters and numbers, which she kept secure in the back of her watch, and she used the family property around the city as relay stations to pass on information to Union officials. She also used much of her family's finances to bribe Confederate guards and clerks.

Van Lew supervised an extensive spy network that may have included Mary Elizabeth Bowser, believed to be Van Lew's former black servant who gained a maid position in the Confederate White House and sent information back to Van Lew. Some doubt exists about her identity and relationship to Van Lew, but the extent and success of the Union underground led by Van Lew, including the 1864 escape of 103 prisoners from Libby Prison, makes the story plausible.

By 1864, Van Lew began to work as chief correspondent of the Unionist spy network, sending information to Generals George H. Sharpe (chief of the Secret Service), Benjamin F. Butler (Army of the James), George G. Meade (Army of the Potomac), and Ulysses S. Grant (overall Union commander). The information coming from Unionists in Richmond led to a failed raid by General Judson Kilpatrick and Colonel Ulrich Dahlgren to free more prisoners and to the successful final Union assault by Grant's forces on Richmond. Gratitude for her services during the war eventually led to a government payment of $5,000 in 1867 and her appointment as postmaster of Richmond by President Ulysses Grant in 1869, a post she held for eight years. Community resentment toward Van Lew continued for the remainder of her life due to her Republican politics, her advocacy for African American equality, and her perpetual association with Southern disloyalty and the conquering Union.

Elizabeth Van Lew died September 25, 1900, in Richmond, Virginia.

Kristen L. Streater

See also Bowser, Mary Elizabeth (ca. 1839–n.d.); Female Spies; Nurses; Southern Women.

References and Further Reading

Leonard, Elizabeth D. 1999. *All the Daring of the Soldier: Women of the Civil War Armies.* New York: W. W. Norton & Company.

Ryan, David, ed. 1996. *A Yankee Spy in Richmond: The Civil War Diary of "Crazy Bet" Van Lew.* Mechanicsburg, PA: Stackpole Books.

Varon, Elizabeth R. 2003. *Southern Lady, Yankee Spy: The True Story of Elizabeth Van Lew, A Union Agent in the Heart of the Confederacy.* New York: Oxford University Press.

Velazquez, Loreta Janeta [Harry T. Buford] (1842–1897)

Cuban-born Loreta Janeta Velazquez recounted the cross-dressed experiences of a Confederate woman soldier in her 1876 memoirs, *The Woman in Battle.* Velazquez followed her husband to the Confederate army and, after his death, joined the ranks as Harry T. Buford. She served as both a soldier and a spy.

Born into wealth in Havana in 1842, the seven-year-old Velazquez was sent to live with a relative in New Orleans where she would complete her education. At fourteen, she refused an arranged marriage and instead eloped with an American officer named William. By 1860, Velazquez had two toddlers and a third child on the way. As she settled into her traditional role as wife and mother, a series of events drastically altered the direction of Velazquez's life. That spring, her third baby died shortly after birth. That fall, her two remaining children died of fever. When war broke out a few months later, William resigned his Federal Army post to join the Confederacy, and Loreta decided to follow him.

William headed to Pensacola to train Confederate recruits, but, while drilling his men, his carbine exploded in his hands, killing him almost instantly. Desperate with grief and loss and emotionally fragile, Velazquez headed to the front lines disguised as a male officer, Harry T. Buford. She fought as a self-appointed officer and served the Confederacy as a secret agent. Velazquez's wartime activities took her all over the South, from Arkansas, where she recruited soldiers, to the battlefields of First Bull Run, Ball's Bluff, Fort Donelson, and Shiloh. Although in her memoirs she bragged about her bravery in the heat of battle, she also revealed her understanding of the sober realities of battlefield violence. Wounded at Shiloh, Velazquez spent time recovering in an Atlanta hospital. She was arrested twice during the war: once in Richmond for impersonating a male officer and once in New Orleans on suspicion of being a spy. However, she emerged from both incidents with relatively minor consequences.

Velazquez told her version of her story in her memoir, written ten years after the close of the war. At the time, she was living in Texas, separated from

Loreta Janeta Velazquez served as a Confederate spy and soldier under the name of Harry T. Buford (1842–n.d.). (Velazquez, Loreta Janeta, *The Woman in Battle: A Narrative of the Exploits, Adventures, and Travels of Madame Loreta Janeta Velazquez*, 1876)

her last husband and raising a son on her own. A literate and well educated Latina, fluent in Spanish, French, and English, Velazquez revealed herself as a brash, quick-witted, and unconventional person, who clearly chafed against the race and gender restrictions of her time. Published in 1876, her book titillated and shocked audiences with its descriptions of her love affairs with women and men. Unlike many other postwar Confederate memoirs that glorified the Confederacy, *A Woman in Battle* criticized it. Prominent Confederate General Jubal Early began a public campaign to discredit Velazquez as a liar and prostitute. Based almost exclusively on his testimony, her work and wartime experiences were considered a hoax for over a century.

Contemporary researchers have discovered newspaper articles about Velazquez's soldiering and arrests during the war, documents in the National Archives that refer to her, and two of her handwritten letters, which now reside in the Richmond Museum of the Confederacy. The existence of the men who staked their reputations to vouch for her in public has been substantiated, and many of her detailed descriptions of camp life and events have been corroborated. Postwar evidence of Velazquez shows her leading a failed expedition of exiled Confederates to Venezuela and, in 1878, meeting with Jubal Early to argue she was indeed a soldier in disguise. A speech signed in her name was presented to Congress. In addition, articles in various newspapers dating as late as 1884 detail Madame L. J. Velasques's continuing political involvement in New York and the capital, this time using antislavery arguments to push for American involvement in liberating Cuba from Spain. However, she subsequently disappeared from the historical record, leaving many questions for future generations. Historians continue to debate the details of her life.

María Agui Carter

See also Bull Run/Manassas, First Battle of (July 21, 1861); Confederate Homefront; Domesticity; Female Combatants; Female Spies; Hispanic Women; Immigrant Women; Separate Spheres; Shiloh, Battle of (April 6–7, 1862); Southern Women; Vicksburg, Siege of (May 18–July 4, 1863); Wartime Literature.

References and Further Reading

Blanton, Deanne, and Lauren M. Cook. 2002. *They Fought Like Demons: Women Soldiers in the American Civil War*. Baton Rouge: Louisiana State University Press.

Hall, Richard. 1993. *Patriots in Disguise: Women Warriors of the Civil War*. New York: Marlowe & Company.

Leonard, Elizabeth. 1999. *All the Daring of the Soldier: Women of the Civil War Armies*. New York: W. W. Norton & Company.

Velazquex, Loreta Janeta. 2003. *The Woman in Battle: The Civil War Narrative of Loreta Janeta Velazquez, Cuban Woman and Confederate Soldier*, edited by Jesse Aleman. Madison: University of Wisconsin Press.

Victor, Metta Victoria Fuller (1831–1885)

One of the most prolific and popular of the dime novelists, Metta Victoria Fuller Victor was well known as a writer and magazine editor before the Civil War. During the war, she and husband Orville

Victor gained prominence in the Northern publishing industry. As part of the firm of Beadle and Adams, they produced and helped distribute books that provided soldiers and the general public with fiction and nonfiction about the war and the issues facing the nation. Several of those books were written or cowritten by Metta Victor.

Born in Pennsylvania in 1831, Metta Fuller's family soon moved to Wooster, Ohio, a frontier community. Metta started writing to earn a living when still a teenager. She had some early success, including the support of the influential Rufus Griswold. She may also have had an early marriage; there are a number of mentions connecting her to a Dr. Morse. However, no conclusive evidence of this marriage has been found, and her early novels were written as Metta Fuller.

Fuller's most popular early works drew on prominent controversies of her day. She wrote two very popular temperance novels: *The Senator's Son* (1851, also published under other titles) and *Fashionable Dissipation* (1858). Fuller's temperance novels were a vehicle through which she also spoke to women about women as workers and as wives and in which she argued against some of the conventions of middle-class domestic fiction. Unlike the usual formula for temperance novels, Fuller's novels focused as much on the lives of the female characters as on male drunkenness, and they provide models of women who put their own lives first. Fuller's novel *Mormon Wives* (1856) was also based on prominent cultural issues: Mormonism (especially the practice of polygyny) and free love. Although the novel included a long appendix filled with quotations from Mormon sources, the plot and the novel's main incidents had little connection with reality, and the novel's success rested on the delight of readers looking for entertaining, sensational literature. In this novel, too, the female protagonist flouts convention and vigorously pursues her own desires.

In 1856, Metta Fuller married Orville Victor, and the two began a lifelong association with the firm of Beadle and Adams. After her marriage, Fuller's writings became slightly more conventional, though many of her stories and novels continued to feature active female heroines. In 1860, the couple traveled to England to promote abolitionism and to raise British support for the Union cause. Late in 1861, Metta Victor's novel, *Maum Guinea and Her Plantation "Children"; or, Holiday-Week on a Louisiana Estate. A Slave Romance*, was published both in the United States and in England. In America, *Maum Guinea* was published as a special Beadle double-sized volume that sold for 20¢, twice the usual cost. The enormously popular book went through several editions. Some contemporary observers suggested it rivaled *Uncle Tom's Cabin* in popularity. The Beadle Company shipped barrels of copies of *Maum Guinea* and other dime novels to soldiers on active duty, providing reading material that was often shared, even across battle lines. The next year, Victor's *The Unionist's Daughter. A Tale of the Rebellion in Tennessee* was published and read both by soldiers and by the general reading public.

Both novels combined stereotypical romance plots with episodes reflecting current and historical events. In *Maum Guinea*, Victor included a long flashback scene that retold the story of Nat Turner's rebellion; in *The Unionist's Daughter*, she drew on William Brownlow's already famous Union stand in the Confederate stronghold of Knoxville Tennessee. The historical materials Victor drew on and her use of current events provided a background in which Victor, like Fanny Fern, discussed how the war was changing the wider culture, as well as what women's lives would be like when the war was over.

In both novels, Victor also included romantic plots. *Maum Guinea* includes four different love stories, including one interracial romance that ends with a happy marriage, and in *The Unionist's Daughter* Eleanor Beaufort's romances are integral to the plot. Marriage, however, is not what Victor saw as the whole of women's future. Especially in *The Unionist's Daughter*, she recognized that women could look to work outside the home as a valuable and worthy choice. These novels also presented women—white and black, Northern and Southern—who think for themselves and who act from a consistent moral position. At the same time, Victor's novels are a product of her time and her own limits. While not overtly racist, they posited a caste system in which African Americans willingly subordinated themselves.

Metta Victoria Fuller Victor died in New Jersey on June 26, 1885.

JoAnn E. Castagna

See also Abolitionism and Northern Reformers; Fiction Writers, Northern; Northern Women; Stowe, Harriet Elizabeth Beecher (1811–1896); Wartime Literature; Willis, Sara Payson [Fanny Fern] (1811–1872).

References and Further Reading

Evans, Clark. 1994. "*Maum Guinea:* Beadle's Unusual Jewel." *Dime Novel Roundup* 63 (4): 77–80.

Johannsen, Albert. 1950. *The House of Beadle and Adams.* Norman: University of Oklahoma Press.

Simmons, Michael K. 1976. "*Maum Guinea:* or, A Dime Novelist Looks at Abolition." *Journal of Popular Culture* 10 (1).

Sizer, Lyde Cullen. 2000. *The Political Work of Northern Women Writers and the Civil War, 1850–1872.* Chapel Hill: University of North Carolina Press.

Streeby, Shelley. 2002. *American Sensations: Class, Empire, and the Production of Popular Culture.* Berkeley: University of California Press.

Vivandières

As women who accompanied the troops to war, vivandières were often called daughters of the regiment. They served as laundresses, nurses, and cooks, and they performed ceremonial functions. Some of the women took part in military actions along with the men, although most remained behind the lines and out of combat.

The position of vivandière, created by the commanders of Napoleonic armies, helped control the number of women who followed men to war. Camp followers, most often the wives and daughters of soldiers, were a constant source of concern because they stretched supply systems and military discipline. After receiving commissions from the officers, the women sold the men food, drink, and other supplies. They also did laundry and nursed the sick and wounded. Although not fully a part of the military, the women had status in the camps, wore uniforms, and received military rations.

When the Civil War began, military commanders from both sides used the European armies of the

Mary Tippee, sutler with Collis Zouaves (114th Pennsylvania). (National Archives and Records Administration)

Crimean War as models for organization. Among other things, they adopted the institution of vivandière. In towns across the county, young women stepped forward to volunteer to accompany men into service. The women were usually appointed to be daughters of the regiment and were given commissions for that role by state officials. Some simply served ceremonial functions, appearing in bright uniforms to march at the head of columns of men. It was believed that their presence increased the morale of the men, reminded them of proper moral behavior, and encouraged others to enlist. Many of the women took very traditional approaches to their work by making meals, washing clothing, and nursing the men back to health when necessary. Other women interpreted their roles in more unusual ways when they took up arms as full members of their units.

The women were easily visible among the armies of the Civil War. Almost all of them adopted a costume that was based on that worn by Amelia Bloomer (1818–1894). She advocated dress reform and designed a two-part costume consisting of loose-fitting trousers and a knee-length dress worn without the corsets and stays popular at the time. The vivandières wore a variety of jacket styles and their clothing was of no standard coloration. Some wore brown because that color would make it less obvious that their clothing was not always fresh and clean. On ceremonial occasions, the women donned clothing that appeared to be military and that frequently was based on the uniforms worn by the men around them.

Eliza Wilson of Menomonie, Wisconsin was only a teenager when her father organized a recruiting event in their small town in western Wisconsin. She eagerly volunteered to accompany the Fifth Wisconsin Regiment of volunteer infantry to the front. Her father gave her a pair of matched bay horses to make the trip. She also traveled with a cozy tent and a maid. Wilson's duties were largely of the ceremonial variety, and soldiers wrote home that her presence made them feel very happy and that she spread sunshine wherever she went. They carefully noted the smallest changes in her uniform. Her adventures ended when an officer, who was also a relative, sent her home.

Bridget Divers served with the First Michigan Cavalry during and after the Civil War. The Irish Biddy, as she was known, was especially lauded for her cooking and nursing. At one point in her career, she transported a wounded officer many miles to secure the best possible care for him, and then she returned to her unit in the field. She took her responsibilities very seriously, delivering water to the men in the heat of battle and taking the place of wounded men in the battle line when necessary.

Kady Brownell, who served with the Fifth Rhode Island Volunteers, interpreted her position the most radically. She trained with the musket and sword, and she was the flag bearer when the unit was engaged on the field. She returned to civilian life only when her husband's wounds dictated that the couple must leave the front.

Karen A. Kehoe

See also Brownell, Kady (1842–n.d.); Divers, Bridget (ca. 1840–n.d.); Nurses.
References and Further Reading
Brockett, Linus P., and Mary C. Vaughan. 1867. *Women's Work in the Civil War.* Philadelphia, PA: Zeigler, McCurdy & Co.
Chartrand, René. 1996. *Napoleonic Wars, Napoleon's Army.* Washington, DC: Brassey's.
Hurn, Ethel Alice. 1911. *Wisconsin Women in the War between the States.* Madison: Wisconsin History Commission.
Massey, Mary Elizabeth. 1994. *Women in the Civil War.* Lincoln: University of Nebraska Press. (Orig pub. 1966 as *Bonnet Brigades.*)

W

Wakeman, Sarah Rosetta [Lyons Wakeman] (1843–1864)

Sarah Rosetta Wakeman was one of the several hundred women who fought in the American Civil War disguised as men. Enlisting in a regiment of New York volunteers on August 30, 1862, under the name Lyons Wakeman, she fought undetected for nearly two years until her death from dysentery on June 19, 1864. The collection of letters to her family she left behind provides unusual insight into the experience of a disguised woman soldier. Unlike narratives prepared for publication by other women soldiers, including Sarah Emma Edmonds and Loretta Janeta Velazquez, Wakeman's letters present a simple and unembellished account of her experience.

Born on January 16, 1843, in Afton, New York, Wakeman was the oldest of Harvey Anable and Emily Hale Wakeman's nine children. After some schooling and work as a domestic, she left home in early August 1862. Masquerading as a man under the name Lyons Wakeman, she became a boatman on the Chenango Canal, but enlisted in the One hundred Fifty-third Regiment of New York State volunteers on August 30, 1862. Although Wakeman's letters do not indicate clear motivations behind her decision to take on the role of a man, the motivations of women soldiers could include patriotism, a search for adventure, the desire to stay close to a loved one, or economic pressures. Her letters, however, attest to her enjoyment of the soldier's life. She wrote, "I like to be a soldier very much" (Burgess 1995, 22). She also clearly appreciated the independence gained through army life, writing, "I am as independent as a hog on ice" (Burgess 1995, 42).

Mustered into the Union army in October 1862, Wakeman's regiment served guard duty in Alexandria, Virginia, and in Washington, D.C. The One Hundred and Fifty-third Regiment joined Major General Nathaniel P. Bank's Red River campaign in Louisiana in February 1864, and in April Wakeman had her first engagement with the enemy. Falling ill with dysentery during the retreat to Alexandria after the failure of the campaign, Wakeman was admitted to the regimental hospital on May 3, 1864. By May 22, 1864, she had been sent to a larger hospital in New Orleans, Louisiana. Although she lingered for nearly a month before her death on June 19, 1864, medical personnel never recorded the secret of her sex on her records, and her headstone in the Chalmette National Cemetery of New Orleans reads simply Lyons Wakeman.

Juliana Kuipers

See also Female Combatants.

References and Further Reading

Blanton, DeAnne, and Lauren M. Cook. 2002. *They Fought Like Demons: Women Soldiers in the American Civil War.* Baton Rouge: Louisiana State University Press.

Burgess, Lauren Cook, ed. 1995. *An Uncommon Soldier: The Civil War Letters of Sarah Rosetta Wakeman, Alias Private Lyons Wakeman, 153rd Regiment, New York State Volunteers.* New York: Oxford University Press.

Leonard, Elizabeth D. 1999. *All the Daring of the Soldier: Women of the Civil War Armies.* New York: W. W. Norton & Company.

Walker, Mary Edwards (1832–1919)

Born in New York on November 26, 1832, Mary Edwards Walker became a Civil War surgeon, prisoner of war, and Medal of Honor recipient.

The child of free thinking abolitionists, Walker had an unconventional childhood. Her parents raised her and her sisters to be as independent as their only son. The intellectual atmosphere surrounding Mary during her youth became heightened as a result of the Seneca Falls Convention on Women's Suffrage in 1848, John Humphrey Noye's Oneida Commune, and the bloomer movement, as well as the spiritualism awakening, temperance, and abolitionism movements. Mary attended Falley Seminary and taught at the Muretto Village a short distance from her home. Throughout his life, her father voraciously read medical books in search of a cure for his recurring illness. Years later, those same books prompted Mary to seriously consider medical school. Her parents prohibited the fashionable tight clothing, such as corsets, that restricted movement and circulation. They agreed with some medical professionals who believed that snug-fitting dress caused permanent and irreversible damage to women's bodies, sentiments Mary advocated her entire life. In addition, Mary found long hoopskirts and crinoline bothersome and unnecessary. After acceptance to Syracuse Medical College in December 1853, she experimented with clothing design, permanently deciding on a uniform of shortened skirt with trousers underneath. Due to her choice of garments, Mary endured a life of ridicule, police arrests, and taunting by the press. Mary graduated with her medical degree in June 1855 and a few months later married classmate Dr. Albert Miller.

The marriage had a rocky start. Ignoring traditional wedding attire at the ceremony, Mary donned her usual uniform, had the word "obey" stricken from the vows, and preferred to hyphenate her last name, never acknowledging the title of Mrs. After a few years of marriage and a shared medical practice, rumors of Albert's infidelities reached Mary. He confessed after she confronted him. Although she left him and set up her own medical practice, she could not secure a divorce until after the Civil War.

Having received her M.D. degree in 1855, Mary Walker sought a formal commission as a military surgeon when the Civil War broke out. When the Federal government agreed to hire her as a nurse, not a doctor, Walker volunteered her services instead. She tended to the sick and wounded first at the so-called Indiana Hospital, housed in the U.S. Patent Office, and later in the field at Warrenton, Virginia. (National Archives and Records Administration)

Caught up in the dress reform movement in 1857, Walker published articles in *Sibyl*, a fashion reform magazine. Additionally, she lectured about temperance and women's suffrage. Throughout her life she remained dedicated to women's rights, serving on boards, speaking, and confronting Congress on an array of issues including pensions for Civil War nurses. Walker authored two books: *Hit* and *Unmasked, or the Science of Immortality*. Both covered a variety of topics including marriage, social diseases, and women's health issues. She headed to Washington, D.C., a few months after the war began to answer the Union call for physicians in October 1861.

Walker initially served voluntarily as assistant surgeon for Dr. J. N. Green while she worked to secure a paid commission from the Union army. As assistant surgeon, she met ambulances, prescribed medications, made diagnoses, and administered treatment. Walker left Washington in January 1862 to attend medical classes, but in November she raced to Virginia to help General Ambrose Burnside and his troops. After escorting sick soldiers by rail to Washington, she headed for Fredericksburg to help in the field. In Washington, she established free lodging for women looking for wounded loved ones, escorted mortally wounded soldiers to their homes, searched for missing soldiers, and advocated against amputation when she deemed it unnecessary.

In January 1864, Walker received an official appointment to the Fifty-second Ohio Volunteer Infantry under General George H. Thomas at Gordon's Mills. On April 10, 1864, she was taken prisoner of war and incarcerated in Castle Thunder Prison for four months. Then, in October 1864, she obtained an official contract as acting assistant surgeon, United States Army. She served the rest of the war in a female military prison in Louisville. On January 24, 1866, Mary received the Congressional Medal of Honor from President Andrew Johnson for meritorious service, but the decoration was later rescinded by the United States Congress. Walker unsuccessfully petitioned Congress for reinstatement of the medal but failed. Refusing to return the award as requested, she defiantly wore the medal until her death on February 21, 1919. Congress reinstated Walker's medal posthumously on June 10, 1950.

Adriana G. Schroeder

See also Aid Societies; Fredericksburg, Battle of (December 13, 1862).

References and Further Reading

Graf, Mercedes. 2001. *A Woman of Honor: Dr. Mary E. Walker and the Civil War.* Gettysburg, PA: Thomas Publications.

Poynter, Lida. 1946. "Dr. Mary Walker, M.D. Pioneer Woman Physician." *Medical Woman's Journal* 53 (10): 43–51.

Snyder, Charles McCool. 1974. *Dr. Mary Walker: The Little Lady in Pants.* New York: Arno Press.

Western Women

As white men in both the North and the South wasted no time in volunteering for service in the Union and Confederate armies, white women of both sections sought ways to contribute to the war effort. Their activities were not limited to the Northeastern, Mid-Atlantic, and Southeastern states but occurred as far west as California and the New Mexico Territory and in the intervening prairie states and plains territories. Distance from the primary theaters of battle near the countries' capitals and along the Ohio and southern Mississippi River valleys neither deterred men from enlisting nor women from involving themselves in the war. Both black and white women living in areas torn apart by divided loyalties and guerrilla warfare experienced armed conflict directly primarily in Kansas, Missouri, and Arkansas. Local militia units, mounted raiders, deserters, and enlisted men confiscated supplies, found refuge, hunted for enemies, and sought revenge from women. Unique to the West were preexisting problems that erupted in local civil wars in the context of the larger one; these small-scale but intense battles profoundly affected American Indian women and white women in the new settlements, especially in Minnesota and Colorado.

Western women of the northern prairies and plains, like their Eastern counterparts, quickly offered their time and talents to aid in the war effort, especially in ways that directly helped soldiers. During the first year of the war, they organized local soldiers' aid societies and branches of the United States Sanitary Commission. Rolling bandages, sewing flags and uniforms, and hosting fairs or socials to raise funds, women in these volunteer organizations committed themselves to providing aid and comfort to soldiers, especially loved ones and community members from locally organized companies and regiments. Although not as formally organized, women in the Confederacy's Western states also did their part in creating and sending care packages to military camps. Small numbers of Western women without husbands and young children worked as nurses in military hospitals; more women in northern areas of the West were able to do so than those in the southern West because railroad transportation extended across the northern prairie states. Regardless of military loyalties, Western women wrote letters regularly to their absent male acquaintances and family members, supplying gossip, practical information about town politics or a county's economy, and copies of or excerpts from local papers that did not reach military camps.

Beyond these relatively accepted ways of contributing to the war effort, a few Western women donned military uniforms and joined regiments, either as daughters of the regiment or as soldiers. With their experience with firearms, horses, and outside work in difficult environments, Western women entered the army with skills and physical strength that they would rely on as soldiers. Most of these women disguised themselves as men; however, in companies that stayed in frontier areas, some women soldiers dispensed with deception and were accepted by their comrades and officers.

Rural women across the Union and Confederacy were faced with decisions about operating farms without the acknowledged head of household and with limited numbers of male farm laborers. Even more difficult in the newly settled areas of the West was the cash-poor economy in the aftermath of an 1857 financial panic that devastated the economy of the northwestern trans-Mississippi region. Many mortgaged farms were not yet fully productive and what profits could be made needed to go to money-lenders, who often questioned soldiers' wives' authority to act on behalf of their absent husbands. Among the financially strapped women maintaining households without husbands were those whose spouses left, often to avoid the military draft in 1863 and 1864, and sought wealth in Western gold rushes rather than glory on the battlefield. These wives anxiously waited for news and money from their absent husbands. Rather than remain in the West without their spouses, some women with families in the East returned there with their young children to wait for the war's end and their husbands' homecoming.

For women in the antislavery areas of Kansas Territory, a civil war of sorts had been under way since 1855, as proslavery Missourians and abolitionist New Englanders competed for control of the territory not only through political action but also by sacking towns and attacking farmsteads. The outbreak of the Civil War caused some men from Missouri, Kansas, and Arkansas to enlist in regiments recognized by the Confederate and Union governments and incorporated into their armies; however, other men formed mounted units, sometimes sanctioned at the national level but more commonly acting on their own without orders and sometimes targeting homes where deserters, political opponents, or prewar enemies sought refuge. These guerrilla bands wreaked havoc not only on places like Lawrence, Kansas, in August 1863—where eighty women were widowed—but also directly on women's bodies through rape or torture and on their physical well-being by the theft or destruction of material possessions.

In both Minnesota and Colorado, violence erupted between American Indians and white settlers during the Civil War, leading to Union army involvement in the crises. In 1862, frustrated Dakota Indians attacked white settlers along the Minnesota River to retaliate against unfair treatment by store-owners and the United States government, as well as against the intrusion of farmers onto tribal lands. Over one hundred white women and children were taken captive for six weeks until two of the state's Union army regiments forced the Dakotas to surrender. Soldiers and civilians were incensed that white women had been captives of Native men, fearing they had been raped or adopted as wives and therefore were morally suspect. Two years later, Colorado organized a regiment under Union auspices to fight against Cheyennes who attacked wagon trains traveling west. The soldiers invaded a camp, murdering nearly one hundred twenty Cheyenne women and children to prevent the birth of a new generation of Cheyennes. Although peripheral to the larger war, these conflicts presented very real threats to Indian, white, and mixed-race women's sense of security. For Western women, the Civil War offered new opportunities but also untold losses.

Andrea R. Foroughi

See also Aid Societies; Border States; Destruction of Homes; Destruction of Personal Property; Female Combatants; Guerrilla Warfare; Hospitals; Letter Writing; Native American Women; Northern Women; Nurses; Rape; Rural Women; Southern Women; United States Sanitary Commission.

References and Further Reading
Blanton, DeAnne, and Lauren M. Cook. 2002. *They Fought Like Demons: Women Soldiers in the American Civil War.* Baton Rouge: Louisiana State University Press.
Fellman, Michael. 1994. "Women and Guerrilla Warfare." In *Divided Houses: Gender and the Civil War,* edited by Catherine Clinton and Nina Silber, 147–165. New York: Oxford University Press.
Josephy, Alvin M. Jr. 1992. *The Civil War in the American West.* New York: Alfred A. Knopf.
Peavy, Linda, and Ursula Smith. 1994. *Women in Waiting in the Westward Movement.* Norman: University of Oklahoma Press.
Silber, Nina. 2005. *Daughters of the Union: Northern Women Fight the Civil War.* Cambridge, MA: Harvard University Press.

Widows, Confederate

While no completely accurate count of women widowed by the Civil War has ever been conducted, one can take an educated guess at their numbers. With two hundred sixty thousand Southern men between the ages of eighteen and forty-five killed during the war, it is reasonable to assume that at least half were married, making one hundred thirty thousand a reasonable, though perhaps low estimate. Regardless of their exact numbers, Confederate widows made up a new class of Southern women in the postbellum South. Having lost their husbands to the cause, these tens of thousands of Confederate widows were no longer part of traditional households. Accordingly, they had to become the moral, social, and economic leaders of their families in a society in which women were supposed to be helpmates, not heads of households.

In the Old South, the roles that young white women had respectably played were limited to the dependent positions of daughter, wife, and mother. Daughters relied completely on their fathers for their public identities, and this dependence transferred to their husbands upon marriage. A woman's legal, social, and economic identity was always attached to the man in her life. According to white Southern social rules, marriage was the only truly acceptable state for a woman. There was no guaranteed place for widows; they were expected to remarry, especially if they were young and still in their childbearing years. Those who remained widows in the antebellum South were anomalous to Southern gender ideals for women.

In the postbellum period, remarriage allowed some Confederate widows to reestablish themselves as wives, provided for and protected by husbands. Yet many Civil War widows could not avail themselves of this traditional solution to the widow problem: too many white Southern men had died in the war. Unable or unwilling to remarry, other widows thrived as single women, taking over their husbands' farms or businesses or even venturing to establish their own commercial enterprises. Many others became dependent on friends or family members for support. For the majority of Confederate widows, survival was all they could hope for as they struggled to provide for their families on their own.

Although every Confederate widow shared the pain and grief of losing a husband, there was no single experience of the social, legal, or economic ramifications of Confederate widowhood. Factors such as family wealth before the husband's death, inheritance laws and practices, opportunities for gainful employment, and the presence or absence of an outside support system all affected the strategies of a Confederate widow to weather her widowhood.

When the Civil War ended in 1865, widows began the often daunting task of rebuilding their lives. Though for many the shock and grief of suddenly losing their spouses were difficult to bear, it was not grief alone that complicated widows' lives. They also had to face new familial responsibilities and economic distress that varied according to the family's financial situation before the death of the household head. Generally speaking, in rural areas, the more real estate a family owned before a husband's death, the better off a widow would be if her husband died. Conversely, widows from families with small amounts of property often suffered extreme hardship and deprivation. Although there were extremely wealthy Southerners, most white Southerners, roughly 67 percent, fell among the yeoman classes, and another 20 percent were poor and less economically established. Both of these groups depended almost entirely on the husbands' labor for their support. Not surprisingly, then, the widows of poor men and yeomen suffered tremendous economic loss upon their husbands' deaths because they no longer had either the income from his labor or the means to perform his job in his absence.

Even if a woman had enjoyed economic stability before her husband's death through the ownership of land or a substantial plantation, the added complications of an economy devastated by the war and discriminatory estate laws could often leave her facing a harrowing economic situation. Large areas of the South lay in the path of one or both armies, and many Southerners suffered from confiscation, impressment, and wanton destruction. In addition to a devastated landscape, the economy had also bottomed out, and, with the end of slavery, all money invested in human property disappeared. Additionally, many widows had been forced to become refugees; so they could not necessarily rely on their land to provide financial security.

The existing legal system regarding estates and inheritances also threatened a widow's economic existence. If a woman's husband died without leaving a will, which most did because will writing was rare during this period except among men with large amounts of property, Southern estate laws limited a woman's access to and control over the family's possessions. Beginning with the founding of the colonies, Southern statutes had provided that, when a husband died without a will, his widow was entitled only to a dower portion of his property. Dower rights gave a widow only the use of the dower real estate during her lifetime, officially called life interest. This meant that she did not have the power to sell or give away the property or to alter it in any way. If a widow altered the dower property, even if it was in an effort to increase profits, the law considered this wasting another person's property, and the rightful heirs could sue her. From 1790 until about 1890, a widow's dower constituted only a one-third life interest in any real estate and one-third of any personal property that her husband had owned during their marriage. If there were children from the marriage, they received equal portions of the remaining two-thirds of the real and personal property. If the couple had no children, the widow still received only a one-third life interest in the real estate, but her share of the personal estate increased to one-half. Southern estate laws dictated that inheritance of the other two-thirds pass as follows: the eldest brother of the deceased received the entire two-thirds; if there were no brothers, it was divided equally among any sisters of the decedent; if there were no siblings at all, the inheritance passed to the children of the decedent's paternal grandfather, beginning with the eldest male. For a personal estate, the line was identical except the decedent's parents were considered heirs before the siblings. Under Southern estate laws, a widow was never entitled to all of her husband's property unless there were absolutely no legal kin whatsoever.

For Confederate widows whose husbands wrote wills, most were, at least theoretically, well provided for. The majority of will-writing men left their wives all of their property, at least for the duration of their lives if the couple had children. But even if a widow inherited her husband's entire estate, there was no guarantee that she could keep it. Many men included the stipulation that their widows would lose all claim to the estate if they remarried. Additionally, the estate was still beholden to the legal processes of estate settlement and to current property valuation rates, which were extremely low during and after the war. Estate laws throughout the South and throughout the nation, for that matter, dictated that, before a will could be probated and inheritances doled out, all property in the husband's name had to be inventoried, appraised, and sold if there were outstanding debts against the estate. For some widows, it was more economically astute to renounce their husband's will, guaranteeing themselves their dower third rather than accept a will that gave them all of their husband's estate including its debts.

The postwar period was trying for many Southerners, but widows faced especially daunting circumstances because inheritance laws discriminated against them. Perhaps more important, however, widows found themselves in dire economic straits in a region in which few options for survival were open to them. Widows who could do so chose the traditional solution to widowhood: remarriage. For these women, a new spouse provided the emotional support and economic stability that they would perhaps be unable to achieve on their own.

A woman's decision to remarry generally reflected a decision based on a combination of need, opportunity, and desire. Financial concerns overwhelmingly influenced many decisions to remarry. For women with little or no property, remarriage was a very attractive possibility. On the other side of the coin, wealth or a substantial inheritance might dampen some women's desire to remarry. A woman's age, along with the absence or presence of children from her first marriage and their ages, also affected her decision and opportunities regarding remarriage. Older widows had a much more difficult time than younger ones finding new husbands. If a widow was older and had adult children, she might be less likely to seek remarriage, expecting to rely instead on her adult children for support. By contrast, a young widow with small children might seek out a new spouse to provide for her family. Childlessness might also compel a widow to choose remarriage so that she could fulfill her "motherly instincts."

Deprived of their husbands' labor, left with reduced property holdings because of Southern estate laws, and unable or unwilling to remarry, most widows in the South found it necessary to enter the paid labor force. However, few jobs were open to women, and none of them paid very well. Additionally, there were significant differences in the opportunities available to women depending on where they lived. Women who lived in urban areas or large towns generally had more opportunities for paid employment than their rural counterparts. During and after the war, many urban widows found employment in the civil service, became teachers, or turned their homes into boarding houses. Women whose husbands had owned commercial enterprises were sometimes able to take over the management of those businesses.

Of course, even after the war, the South remained predominantly rural where there were fewer opportunities for government employment and other service industry occupations. Although women in rural areas could certainly work in the fields, as many yeoman wives had done on their own farms

before the war, most white Southerners considered hiring out for labor that was beneath them and their children. Widows could also obtain work as domestic servants or washerwomen, but these jobs were generally reserved for African American women because, like agricultural labor, the work was considered too indelicate for respectable white women. More acceptable ways for rural women to earn money were through the sale of food or other homemade products or by working in the traditional female occupations of seamstress or milliner.

Many widows who were unable to find employment and even some who did were still unable to support themselves and their children without assistance. For some widows, assistance meant reluctantly giving up their independent households to move in with parents, in-laws, siblings, children, or other relatives. Of those widows who moved in with relatives, most lived with adult children or their own parents.

In the 1880s, two new options for economic assistance arose for Confederate widows. They could turn to the government for support as one Southern state after another made small pensions available to their Confederate veterans and widows. They could also obtain assistance from Confederate memorial groups like the United Daughters of the Confederacy who doled out individual assistance and established group homes for needy Confederate women in states across the South. Though neither of these options provided Confederate widows with a great deal of money, for some it was a soothing balm for their economic insecurities and struggles.

Jennifer Lynn Gross

See also Confederate Homefront; Family Life, Southern; Pensions, Confederate Widows; Rural Women; Southern Women; Teachers, Southern; Urban Women, Southern.

References and Further Reading

Blom, Ida. 1991. "The History of Widowhood: A Bibliographic Overview." *Journal of Family History* 16 (2): 191–210.

Hoff, Joan. 1991. *Law, Gender, and Injustice: A Legal History of U.S. Women.* New York: New York University Press.

Lebsock, Suzanne. 1984. *The Free Women of Petersburg: Status and Culture in a Southern*

Town, 1784–1860. New York: W. W. Norton & Company.

Scadron, Arlene, ed. 1988. *On Their Own: Widows and Widowhood in the American Southwest, 1848–1939.* Urbana: University of Illinois Press.

Scott, Anne Firor. 1970. *The Southern Lady: From Pedestal to Politics, 1830–1930.* Charlottesville: University of Virginia Press.

Shammas, Carole, Marylynn Salmon, and Michel Dahlin. 1987. *Inheritance in America from Colonial Times to the Present.* Piscataway, NJ: Rutgers University Press.

Wood, Kirsten E. 2004. *Masterful Women: Slaveholding Widows from the American Revolution through the Civil War.* Chapel Hill: University of North Carolina Press.

Widows, Union

The American Civil War, with its more than six hundred thousand dead, was the bloodiest conflict in American history. Consequently, it almost certainly left more women widowed than did any other American conflict before or since. A modern historian has estimated that approximately one hundred eight thousand Union women may have been widowed during the Civil War itself, with tens of thousands of additional veterans' wives becoming widows upon the deaths of their husbands in the decades after the war. In 1890 the Federal government conducted a census of Union veterans and widows that recorded 145,359 widows living at that time.

Northern war widows found themselves in a nation changing at a rapid pace economically, culturally, and socially. Throughout the war, Northern women had to alter their domestic roles to deal with the new realities of life. The conflict helped create a climate of both economic and moral paternalism, which particularly affected women who suffered the loss of their husbands during the conflict. Northern women also had to contend with the wartime changes of the government. The rise of the Federal government required new allegiance from women, who were placed in a subordinate role and who offered help under a paternalist system of wartime employment and pensions.

During the Civil War, the Federal government had no notification system to officially contact the families of killed and wounded soldiers. Consequently, a woman widowed during the war often learned of her loss from a newspaper casualty list, in a letter from a chaplain or from one of her husband's comrades, or from a soldier returning home on leave. Women whose husbands had been listed as missing or captured faced constant uncertainty. Many women contacted Clara Barton, who late in the war established an Office of Correspondence with the Friends of the Missing Men of the United States Army, to compile and distribute information on missing Union prisoners. In her postwar lectures, Barton recalled meeting and hearing the heartrending stories of many Union widows, including one who had lost her husband and three sons during the conflict.

A woman who received widespread publicity on the manner in which she learned of her husband's death was Philinda Humiston, the wife of Amos Humiston of the One hundred Fifty-fourth New York Infantry. Amos died at Gettysburg on July 1, 1863. When a burial party discovered his unidentified body, they found in his hands a photograph of three young children. Publicity about the incident led to a nationwide search to identify the soldier and his children. Philinda viewed the image after its publication in a number of Northern newspapers, identifying her children Frank, Frederick, and Alice as those in the photograph, and thus learning of the death of her husband. Humiston, a seamstress, received some funds from reproductions of the image to help support her family. A poem, later put to music, entitled "The Children of the Battle Field," further immortalized the incident. After the war, Philinda Humiston received a pension from the Federal government and worked for three years at an orphanage established at Gettysburg. She remarried in 1869 and died in 1913.

The experiences of Sarah Knapp Pardington were more typical. She married John Pardington in Trenton, Michigan, on December 29, 1860. The couple had a daughter, Maria, who was born in 1862 shortly before her father enlisted in the

Twenty-fourth Michigan Infantry, part of the famous Iron Brigade. John took part in the battles of Fredericksburg and Chancellorsville before also being killed at Gettysburg. He frequently sent Sarah loving letters from the battlefield. After not receiving word from her husband after the battle, Sarah asked a friend to write to the regimental chaplain for information. He replied that he had no definite information but hoped that Pardington had been taken prisoner. Unfortunately the chaplain's information proved unfounded, and Sarah, like thousands of her countrywomen, was left a widow with a young child, a stack of letters, and a locket with her husband's picture.

For thousands of widows like Pardington, a Federal government pension represented the only regular source of income for themselves and their families. The expanded pension system enacted during the war created a much larger class of government dependents than had ever existed in American history. In July 1862, Congress adopted a new law that increased pension benefits for widows and orphans and that expanded the number of family members eligible to receive compensation. Pension benefits continued to increase throughout the decades after the war. In 1893, 40 percent of the Federal budget was being used to support those affected by the war: widows, orphans, elderly, and wounded veterans. Initially a soldier or widow had to present proof of a service-connected wound or disability to obtain government assistance. However, lobbying by the Grand Army of the Republic (GAR) and other veterans' organizations led to a loosening of these restrictions. In the late nineteenth and early twentieth centuries, these rules were liberalized. Consequently most surviving Union veterans or their widows received pensions from the Federal government. Meanwhile, by the late nineteenth century, the former Confederate states also began providing payments to former Southern soldiers.

Widows could continue to receive their pensions following the death of their husbands and until they remarried. Because some women avoided this provision by living with another man, Congress revised the pension law in 1883 to include cohabitation as a reason to terminate a widow's pension. Women, however, could again become eligible for a pension if they remarried a veteran and he subsequently died. The marriage of young women to much older veterans had become relatively common in the early 1900s. Following the deaths of their husbands, these younger widows might remain on the pension rolls for decades. African American widows applying for pensions faced a problem unique to their race. Many of them had to prove the legitimacy of marriages that occurred in the antebellum years when slave unions were not legally recognized in the Southern states.

In addition to obtaining pensions from the United States government, Union widows also received help from private organizations like the GAR or its auxiliary, the Woman's Relief Corps. GAR posts assisted widows in a variety of ways, including helping them in obtaining or retaining government jobs, providing aid to those who became unemployed or who were unable to provide for themselves or their families, and providing assistance in the collection of debts or the payment of bills. The GAR also helped widows with funeral expenses, attended services for deceased members, and, if requested, performed a nondenominational GAR service.

War widows played a prominent role in the postwar years, especially in the commemorization and memorialization of the conflict. In some instances, Union widows helped recover the bodies and rebury men hastily buried on battlefields. In addition, they aided in the internment and marking of veteran's graves and in the erection of regimental and other monuments. They also worked in the beginning stages of preserving Civil War battlefields. Of particular concern to Northern widows was the proper internment of United States soldiers buried in Southern states. By the end of the century, nearly eighty national cemeteries had been established in twenty-two states and the District of Columbia.

Many Northern widows struggled with the question of whether to keep their husband's remains buried on the battlefield or in an often distant national cemetery or to bring the bodies home. The fact that many soldiers lay in unmarked graves made positive identification and removal impossible, but even when a soldier's burial location was known, the cost of removal often prevented the return of a body to its family. One Pennsylvania widow could not afford the $100 it would cost to have her husband's body returned home, but she asked that his grave be marked so that she could find it in the future. Like many widows, she wished his grave was closer to home but could not make the arrangements to make it so.

In their effort to memorialize Union war dead, widows and other groups contributed to a change in the national perception of death and burial. Although, in the antebellum years mourning was a private family ritual, the large numbers of wartime dead publicized the experiences surrounding death. In addition, the fact that so many soldiers died so far from home forced families to share the death experience with outsiders. Battlefield clergy, nurses, and other soldiers often communicated with a widow about the final moments of her husband's life. Before the Civil War, widows were seen as sturdy women who could control their grief and get on with their lives while memorializing their dead husbands within the family. However, during and after the Civil War, views on how to honor the war dead changed. The growing numbers of fallen soldiers and widows led to a public memorialization. Consequently, widows, who had always played the primary role in preserving their husbands' memories, gained a role in the public remembrance of war dead.

In additional to the establishment of national cemeteries and the building of monuments, Civil War widows also played a prominent role in the establishment of Decoration Day as a holiday to remember the Union dead. Shortly after the war, observances sprang up at a number of locations North and South, with widows and the mothers of war dead taking part and often organizing the events. In 1868, GAR recognized May 30 as a day for its posts to memorialize Union war dead, and, in the 1870s through the 1890s, most Northern states recognized Decoration Day as a state holiday. This commemorative day eventually became Memorial Day.

As the number of Northern Civil War veterans and widows began to decline in the late 1800s and early 1900s, organizations like the Sons of Union Veterans of the Civil War, Daughters of Union Veterans of the Civil War, and Ladies of the Grand Army of the Republic took over many of the memorialization functions begun by Union widows. Although the last surviving Union veteran died in the 1950s, a number of widows survived into the 1990s, and at least one into the twenty-first century. The last two identified Union widows were Daisy Anderson, the widow of escaped slave Robert Anderson, who had served in the One Hundred and Twenty-Fifth United States Colored Infantry, and Gertrude Janeway, the widow of John Janeway of the Fourteenth Illinois Cavalry. Janeway had married her husband in 1927, when she was eighteen and he was eighty-one. Upon her death on January 17, 2003, she was the last known Union widow, although apparently at that time at least two Confederate widows still survived. The death of the last widow will mark the end of the direct connection between the America of the twenty-first century and the great national crisis of the mid-1800s.

David Coles

See also African American Women; Barton, Clara (1821–1912); Courtship and Marriage; Domesticity; Family Life, Union; Monuments; Mourning; Northern Women; Nurses; Pensions, Union Widows; Separate Spheres; Union Homefront; Widows, Confederate.

References and Further Reading
Lassen, Coralou Peel, ed. 1999. *"Dear Sarah": Letters Home from a Soldier of the Iron Brigade.* Bloomington: Indiana University Press.
McClintock, Megan J. 1996. "Civil War Pensions and the Reconstruction of Union Families." *Journal of American History* 83 (2): 458.
Neff, John R. 2005. *Honoring the Civil War Dead: Commemorization and the Problem of Reconciliation.* Lawrence: University Press of Kansas.
Silber, Nina. 2005. *Daughters of the Union: Northern Women Fight the Civil War.* Cambridge, MA: Harvard University Press.

Wilderness, Battle of (May 5–7, 1864)

The opening round of the last Union incursion into Virginia, the Wilderness resulted in a Union defeat but nearly destroyed Robert E. Lee's Confederate Army of Northern Virginia. When the fighting finally ended, after three days of struggle in the dense and trackless second-growth woods, Lee's counterattack had blunted Ulysses S. Grant's southward thrust and resulted in heavy losses. However, Grant changed the pattern of conflict in this theater by continuing to move South rather than retreat. The resulting series of battles, known as the Overland campaign, would cause Lee and the Confederate forces to back up against the defenses of Richmond and Petersburg, where they would remain pinned until the last days of the war. During the Battle of the Wilderness, women served as nurses and soldiers and otherwise witnessed the war firsthand.

The Army of the Potomac had fought Lee at the Battle of Chancellorsville on the same ground almost a year before the Battle of the Wilderness. The tactical problem for the Union in both battles was to move soldiers quickly through the Wilderness into the more open country south of it in order to bring the smaller Confederate army to battle. However, Lee's swift positioning of his troops allowed the Confederates to catch the Federals while they were still moving and to destroy pieces of their army without the Union's being able to deploy its superior numbers and artillery in the heavy growth. After crossing the river, Grant's one hundred and eighteen thousand Federals moved south through the Wilderness on two roads. Lee, whose army of sixty-two thousand was quartered west of the Wilderness, moved swiftly east on the parallel Orange Plank Road and Orange Turnpike, roads that bisected the North–South roads that Grant moved on, clashing with the Union forces in the middle of the Wilderness on May 5. The Union advance came to a halt, and the army's divisions and brigades struggled to wheel into line of battle facing west to meet the Confederate threat. But only the roads and a few cleared fields would allow the line-of-battle formation. Many units advanced in the woods to meet the Rebel assault, only to lose formation and contact with comrades on the flanks, to get lost, or even to be fired on by friendly troops in the murky forest.

General Richard Stoddert Ewell, with Lee's Second Corps, moved in on the left along the Orange Turnpike, and met Union General Gouverneur Warren with General George Meade's Fifth Corps and forced it into a defensive stance; General A. P. Hill, with Lee's Third Corps, moved in on the right, along the Plank Road, finding General Winfield Scott Hancock commanding the Federal II Corps, which had just swung in from the east to form the Union left flank. At first, Hill drove Hancock back, but Hill was soon struck with a Union counterattack, which drove him back into a defensive position. As Hancock pushed Hill's troops to the breaking point, Lee looked anxiously for the arrival of his best corps, the First, under James Longstreet. In the night, General Ambrose Burnside's Federal Ninth Corps came in on Hancock's right flank to reinforce the Union push.

When Longstreet arrived on May 6, he threw his troops up the Plank Road to blunt Hancock's and Burnside's advance, and he relieved Hill's worn-out forces. Longstreet's assault caught Hancock off balance, and the Federals were driven back, as Lee personally tried to lead the Texas Brigade forward but was prevented from doing so by his men. Longstreet then moved around to flank Hancock's now entrenched line, but toward dusk he was wounded, and his attack lost momentum. Even though General John B. Gordon of Ewell's corps later attacked the Union right flank with his division and pushed it back, there were no reserves to exploit the breach, and the Confederate attack halted. On May 7, more clashes occurred in the woods as Grant began to disengage his army and move south. He and Lee would resume the conflict at Spotsylvania a few days later.

The fighting in the thick woods and brush was confused and disjointed, leaving many wounded where they fell, without access to aid. The furious fighting also ignited the dry underbrush afire and burned hundreds of wounded to death.

At least five women served in the Overland campaign—two Union and three Confederate—and presumably they were present in combat operations at the Wilderness battle. One account tells of a female lieutenant in Federal uniform who was wounded in the shoulder and was brought in with some of her wounded comrades, who attested that there was no soldier braver. She had apparently enlisted with her lover. She was hospitalized afterward, where because of her gender she was discharged from the army.

Probably the best civilian eyewitness accounts of the battle was written by Katherine Crouse, a young woman who wrote a twelve-page detailed account in diary style of the battles of the Wilderness and Spotsylvania as they raged around her house. She described loud noises of sharp skirmishing, the cannon firing far and near, and even a Federal foraging party that raided their farm, even though she and her family were pro-Union. She described how the Rebels on one side and the Yankees on the other seem to have surrounded their farm and how the armies moved past them to the South.

The losses for both armies were heavy. The Army of the Potomac, by some estimates, lost as many as 17,666 killed, wounded, and missing. The Army of Northern Virginia lost 7,750 or more, in addition to several key officers, including Lee's right-hand man, James Longstreet. Many female nurses cared for the wounded from the Battle of the Wilderness. Cornelia Hancock and Annie Etheridge both served as nurses at the Wilderness. Perhaps most notably, Clara Barton nursed many of the wounded men evacuated from the Wilderness in a Fredericksburg hospital.

Randal Allred

See also Barton, Clara (1821–1912); Blair, Lorinda Ann [Annie Etheridge Hooks] (ca. 1840–1913); Female Combatants; Hancock, Cornelia (1839–1926); Nurses.

References and Further Reading

Blanton, DeAnne, and Lauren M. Cook. 2002. *They Fought Like Demons: Women Soldiers in the American Civil War.* Baton Rouge: Louisiana State University Press.

Cushman, Stephen. 1999. *Bloody Promenade: Reflections on a Civil War Battle.* Charlottesville: University of Virginia Press.

Gallagher, Gary W., ed. 1997. *The Wilderness Campaign.* Chapel Hill: University of North Carolina Press.

Rhea, Gordon C. 2004. *The Battle of the Wilderness May 5–6, 1864.* Baton Rouge: Louisiana State University Press.

Trudeau, Noah Andre. 1989. *Bloody Roads South: The Wilderness to Cold Harbor May–June 1864.* Boston: Little, Brown and Company.

Willis, Sarah Payson [Fanny Fern] (1811–1872)

Fanny Fern was one of the most popular and widely read authors of the antebellum and postwar period. Her opinions and commentary significantly influenced public opinion, especially Northern women's attitudes, both before and during the Civil War.

Fanny Fern was born Sarah Payson Willis on July 9, 1811. Willis's marital history—she was widowed and then divorced before a lasting third marriage to James Parton in 1856—and many of her decisions about her life and her work were considered by many as unacceptable choices for a woman of the middle class. However, as Fanny Fern she was highly successful. Her ability to combine her often iconoclastic opinions with the dominant sentimentalism of the period enabled her to reach and influence women and men. Fern established herself as an independent and audacious voice on women's issues and current events in her widely reprinted newspaper columns, which were gathered together in *Fern Leaves from Fanny's Portfolio* (1853), *Fresh Leaves* (1857), *Folly as It Flies* (1870), *Ginger-Snaps* (1870), and *Caper Sauce* (1872), as well as in her novels, *Ruth Hall* (1854) and *Rose Clark* (1856).

Before, during, and after the Civil War, Fern found her audience through her regular columns written for the *New York Ledger* and often reprinted in other papers, giving her a national audience. The *Ledger's* publisher, Robert Bonner, wanted the paper's writers to avoid taking any particular political positions, and Fern made some attempts to comply. At the same time, she was determined to express her ideas about and her critique of the society in which she lived. Fern came to her ideas about women and the war from a foundation of deep religious beliefs. She was an independent thinker who rejected much of the dominant theological thought of her time as it was expressed by male ministers. Instead, she developed what she called maternalist Christianity. She saw in Christ's love a model of women's love for their children, which she then extended to society as a whole. She saw a need for women to demand that material help and care be given to the poor, that economic opportunities become available for women, and that injustice be challenged, wherever it occurred.

As tensions increased in the country, Fern made her abolitionist sympathies clear in a number of *Ledger* columns, although she seldom discussed specific events. Her style varied. Sometimes she used satire; at other times her work exemplified the sentimental style of midcentury women writers. After the war began, she began to write more directly about the war, including columns that argued for enlistment and that expressed contempt for Northern men who would not support the Union cause or who tried to avoid conscription. A sincere abolitionist, Fern wrote admiringly about the colored troops and was clear that her support for the war was based on an understanding of the evil of slavery. She was friendly with Harriet Jacobs and opened her house to Jacobs's daughter, Laura, during 1856–1858. Fern's conversations with Jacobs undoubtedly contributed to her understanding of the issues facing African American women, but Fern did not use their friendship directly in her work.

Fern's columns also explored how the war affected women. The inequities of women's economic condition during and after the war were a deep concern. She argued that the economic conditions of the war would affect poor and working-class women more than any other group. She declared that women, as both consumers and workers, in both the North and the South, were involved not just in the Civil War, but in an ongoing conflict in which their antagonists were business owners and industrialists. She recognized, too, the loneliness, fear, and physical dangers that the war brought to women left without the protection of their fathers,

Sarah Payson Willis influenced readers before and during the Civil War with her commentary written under the penname of "Fanny Fern" (1811–1872). (Library of Congress)

husbands, and sons. At the same time, she had hopes that the war would offer new possibilities for women and that in the aftermath of the war women would have greater scope, including suffrage. She supported the United States Sanitary Commission, especially the work of women with the commission, as a model of what women could do.

Fern wrote three books for children, and in *The New Story Book for Children* (1864) she included a chapter on John Brown. This highly favorable biography was a further indication of her abolitionist attitudes and was well received by Northern abolitionist parents.

Fanny Fern died on October 10, 1872.

JoAnn E. Castagna

See also Abolitionism and Northern Reformers; Conscription; Enlistment; Fiction Writers, Northern;

Jacobs, Harriet Ann [Linda Brent] (1813–1897); Northern Women; Religion; United States Sanitary Commission; Urban Women, Northern.

References and Further Reading

Harker, Jaime. 2001. "'Pious Cant' and Blasphemy: Fanny Fern's Radicalized Sentiment." *Legacy* 18 (1): 52–64.

Sizer, Lyde Cullen. 2000. *The Political Work of Northern Women Writers and Civil War, 1850–1872.* Chapel Hill: University of North Carolina Press.

Tonkovich, Nicole. 1997. *Domesticity with a Difference: The Nonfiction of Catharine Beecher, Sarah J. Hale, Fanny Fern, and Margaret Fuller.* Jackson: University Press of Mississippi.

Walker, Nancy A. 1993. *Fanny Fern.* New York: Twayne Publishers.

Warren, Joyce W. 1992. *Fanny Fern: An Independent Woman.* Piscataway, NJ: Rutgers University Press.

Wittenmyer, Annie Turner (1827–1900)

Involved in temperance, education reform, and benevolent work, Annie Turner Wittenmyer also served as a tireless advocate for soldiers' aid and relief during and after the Civil War. Utilizing her political, administrative, and organizational skills, she fought sexism and local politicians to improve the situations of innumerable Americans.

Sarah Ann Turner was born August 26, 1827, in Sandy Springs, Ohio, to John G. and Elizabeth Smith Turner. In 1847, she married merchant William Wittenmyer and three years later moved to Keokuk, Iowa. Of the couple's four children, only one, Charles Albert, survived childhood. In March 1853, Wittenmyer began her life of benevolence, founding the first tuition-free school for underprivileged children. Because her parents had ensured that she received an education, she adamantly insisted other children should have the opportunity. William's 1860 death left Annie a single mother.

When the Civil War began, Wittenmyer joined the Union war effort as a nurse in the Estes House, a hotel converted to a hospital. The unsanitary conditions, inadequate food, and psychological turmoil the soldiers suffered horrified her. In 1861 the Keokuk Ladies' Soldiers' Aid Society (KLSAS) elected her corresponding secretary. In that capac-

ity she visited the hospitals in her region to determine their needs, gathered and distributed supplies, secured transportation for the wounded, and helped organize a coalition of women's groups. Her work was often impeded by the Iowa branch of the United States Sanitary Commission (USSC), run by local men with connections to state politicians. Tensions rose between the KLSAS and the USSC as both fought for relationships with women's groups in Iowa. To circumvent these problems, Wittenmyer eventually accepted a salaried position as one of the Iowa State sanitary agents. Once the state legislature approved her position in September 1862, she and the KLSAS gained official status. As a sanitary agent, she continued collecting and distributing food, medicine, bandages, clothing, and beds.

Despite working together, the KLSAS and the USSC continued to spar. Wittenmyer and the other women of the KLSAS argued that as women they were morally and emotionally better equipped for the work and far better organized than the USSC men. The KLSAS publicly challenged the Iowa Sanitary Commission, characterizing it as incompetent at best. The two groups eventually combined into the Iowa Sanitary Commission. Wittenmyer remained a sanitary agent for about six months but resigned in May 1864 to devote her energies elsewhere.

Wittenmyer gained nationwide fame through her establishment of over one hundred Special Diet Kitchens in Union army hospitals. A visit to her brother, a patient in one of the hospitals, revealed to Wittenmyer the inedible and inappropriate food fed to patients. She hoped to reorganize kitchens so that each patient would receive individualized doctor-prescribed menus, suitable for that patient's circumstances. Wittenmyer's model helped save countless lives as the wounded and ill began receiving healthier, more nutritious, and better tasting food. At her request, the United States Christian Commission agreed to help fund and organize these revolutionary kitchens, still utilized today. Wittenmyer hired the staff, appointed managers, and supervised the two hundred paid women working in the kitchens.

Wittenmyer had other concerns as well. She began organizing orphanages in Iowa for Union soldiers' children in the fall of 1863, with the first one opening in 1864. In 1865 she applied to Congress for and received barracks in Davenport, Iowa, where the Iowa Soldiers' Orphans' Home was built later that year. During the next three decades, Wittenmyer published several books and articles, and she served as editor for *Home and Country*.

Wittenmyer is perhaps best known as the founder and first president of the Women's Christian Temperance Union, organized in 1874. In 1889 she moved to Pennsylvania and was elected president of the Woman's Relief Work of the Grand Army of the Republic, a national organization dedicated to helping former Union hospital workers obtain homes and pensions. She helped ensure the passage of the Army Nurses Pension Law in 1892.

On February 2, 1900, Annie Wittenmyer died. She was buried in Edgewood Cemetery in Sanatogo, Pennsylvania.

Paula Katherine Hinton

See also Aid Societies; Food; Hospitals; Northern Women; Nurses; Union Homefront; United States Christian Commission; United States Sanitary Commission; Wartime Employment.

References and Further Reading

Holland, Mary Gardner. 1998. *Our Army Nurses: Stories from Women in the Civil War*. Roseville, MN: Edinborough Press.

Leonard, Elizabeth D. 1994. *Yankee Women: Gender Battles in the Civil War*. New York: W. W. Norton & Company.

Schultz, Jane E. 2004. *Women at the Front: Hospital Workers in Civil War America*. Chapel Hill: University of North Carolina Press.

Wittenmyer, Annie Turner. 1895. *Under the Guns: A Woman's Reminiscences of the Civil War*. Boston: E. B. Stillings & Co.

Woman Order (General Order No. 28)

Union General Benjamin Franklin Butler issued General Order Number 28, his infamous Woman Order, on May 15, 1862, in New Orleans, two weeks after Admiral David Farragut had taken the city and turned it over to Butler's administrative control. The order generated immediate controversy and threatened to topple respectable Southern ladies from their pedestal of protection and reduce their status to that of prostitutes if they continued to behave disrespectfully toward Union soldiers and officers. The threat implied by the order inflamed Confederate passions, garnered criticism from elsewhere in the Union and abroad, and earned the general lasting infamy throughout the South. In recent decades feminist authors have forged new interpretations of the Woman Order that suggest how the gender and class politics of the time made Butler's order effective and why it has achieved such lasting significance.

New Orleans's unrepentant and unruly rebel residents initially proved unwilling to submit to Federal authority when troops occupied the city in late April 1862. Butler soon took matters in hand and later recalled that he quickly had the men of New Orleans completely under control. He was dismayed, however, to find that the city's women, especially those of the upper class, continued to abuse and disrespect his men. The behaviors that Butler and his troops found so galling included ladies exiting streetcars and leaving churches when officers or soldiers entered, teaching and encouraging children to sing Confederate songs, displaying or pinning small Confederate flags to their clothing, and choosing to walk in the middle of the streets or turning their backs to avoid acknowledging their occupiers. In a small number of cases, ladies also reportedly spat on officers or allowed their children to do so, and, in one outrageous incident, Butler reported that one of them dumped a "vessel" of "not very clean water" on the head of Admiral David Farragut as he passed below her balcony (Butler 1892, 417). Many writers have suggested that this vessel was a chamber pot.

To stem the tide of the females' disrespect, Butler created an order that brilliantly manipulated the South's existing gender and class ideologies while also taking advantage of the city's well-known reputation for harboring and tolerating large numbers of prostitutes. General Order Number 28 stated that, despite their courteous treatment of civilians, "the officers and soldiers of the United States have been subject to repeated insults from the women (calling themselves ladies) of New Orleans." As a result, "it

Caricature of Benjamin Butler's behavior as military governor of New Orleans, May–December 1862. In response to harrassment from women toward the Union troops occupying the city, Butler issued General Order No. 28 (Woman Order), declaring that offending women be treated as prostitutes. (Library of Congress)

is ordered that hereafter when any female shall, by word, gesture or movement, insult or show contempt for any officer or soldier of the United States, she shall be regarded and held liable to be treated as a woman of the town plying her avocation."

Butler's order cut right to the heart of both the class privilege accorded to and the gender expectations demanded from upright, respectable Southern ladies. Confederates outside New Orleans howled with indignation about the sexual threat they perceived in the Woman Order. Southern political leaders, ranging from Louisiana's exiled governor to President Jefferson Davis, took exception to the order in formal statements. Davis also placed a

bounty on Butler's head and ordered his summary execution if he was ever captured. The predictable outrage in Confederate circles also spread to newspapers in France and England, where Butler's order was condemned on the floor of Parliament.

Butler denied that his order contained an implicit sexual threat and defended it in his autobiography, claiming that it was necessary in response to the treatment received by soldiers. He also claimed that the order did not lead to any arrests, but historical records indicate that at least two women were imprisoned for infractions covered by the order, most notably prominent Confederate sympathizer and diarist Eugenia Levy Phillips.

Butler continued to upset gender conventions throughout his occupation of New Orleans. He kept women in his figurative line of fire when he demanded that they, like male Confederates, sign loyalty oaths to stay in the city. Butler's offensiveness was not limited to ladies, nor was his administrative brilliance a match for his abrasiveness, inflexibility, and financial opportunism. Foreign consuls bristled at his insensitive treatment and complained to Washington. These complaints, accompanied by rumors that Butler was using his position to gain personal financial advantage, led to his dismissal and replacement by Nathaniel Banks in December 1862.

Alecia P. Long

See also Butler, Benjamin F. (1818–1893); Civilian Life; Confederate Homefront; Imprisonment of Women; Phillips, Eugenia Levy (1819–1901); Southern Women; Urban Women, Southern.

References and Further Reading

Butler, Benjamin F. 1892. *Autobiography and Personal Reminiscences of Major-General Benjamin F. Butler.* Boston: A. M. Thayer & Co.

Faust, Drew Gilpin. 1996. *Mothers of Invention: Women of the Slaveholding South in the American Civil War.* Chapel Hill: University of North Carolina Press.

Hearn, Chester. 1997. *When the Devil Came Down to Dixie: Ben Butler in New Orleans.* Baton Rouge: Louisiana State University Press.

Rable, George. 1992. "'Missing in Action': Women of the Confederacy." In *Divided Houses: Gender and the Civil War,* edited by Catherine Clinton and Nina Silber, 134-146. New York: Oxford University Press.

Ryan, Mary. 1990. *Women in Public: Between Banners and Ballots, 1825–1880.* Baltimore, MD: Johns Hopkins University Press.

Women's Central Association of Relief

The Women's Central Association of Relief (WCAR) was vital to providing health services and military provisions for Union soldiers during the Civil War. On April 26, 1861, in New York City, a large gathering of both female and male social reformers founded the WCAR. The association was the precursor and most active chapter of the United States Sanitary Commission (USSC), the largest benevolent wartime institution at that time. As a branch of the USSC, the New York–based, female-led WCAR had authority over aid societies in much of New York, New Jersey, Connecticut, and Massachusetts. Similar to other women's relief associations, the WCAR trained nurses, raised money, worked on the battlefields, and coordinated the collection and distribution of army supplies. It was the most active single philanthropic society for the Union cause, providing relief services to thousands of soldiers, women, and children on the war-torn homefront. Throughout the war, the WCAR remained the dominant branch of the USSC.

As the first shots of the Civil War rang out, hundreds of independent relief aid societies sprang up across the North, and thousands of women collected supplies and offered their services as nurses. However, there was no method for coordinating the women's activities. Elizabeth Blackwell, the first woman medical doctor of the United States, and her sister Emily, also a physician, called for a meeting of the lady managers of New York's Infirmary for Women and Children to create a soldiers' aid society. The Blackwell sisters had founded the infirmary to train female doctors and nurses as well as to provide health care for the poor. Close to one hundred of New York's wealthiest and most influential female citizens turned out. To garner more support, the women decided to broaden their base and have a public meeting. Advertising their cause in newspapers, the female reformers appealed to all of New York's citizenry and over four thousand women and men assembled to discuss the agenda and organization of a nongovernmental relief program. At the gathering, Blackwell and Henry Whitney Bellows, influential pastor of the All Souls Unitarian Church in New York, proposed a plan of centrally organizing the distribution of medical services and military supplies. The philanthropists resoundingly approved the suggestion, and the WCAR was officially established with a board made up of twelve women and twelve men.

To manage their civilian operation, WCAR members mapped out a plan that included running existing local charities, putting together a board for training nurses, and establishing a formal relationship with the United States army to determine military needs. Within a few weeks, Bellows and a group of sanitary reformers went to Washington, D.C., to seek government help. The exact circumstances surrounding the Washington trip remain unclear. In the end, the government replaced the WCAR as the preeminent relief society and created the United States Sanitary Commission. President Abraham Lincoln officially sanctioned the USSC with Bellows as president and nationally known medical reformer Dorothea Dix as Superintendent of Women Nurses for the Union army. The founding of the USSC eclipsed the authority of the WCAR and the status of Elizabeth Blackwell. On September 19, 1861, the WCAR became a branch of the USSC, though it continued largely as an autonomous charitable society.

In the summer of 1861, the WCAR took up residence in the Cooper Union in New York City. Working in small quarters with only two tables, one desk, six chairs, and a wall map, the reformers immediately embarked on their mission. Under the leadership of twenty-four-year-old Louisa Lee Schuyler, New York socialite with a family heritage going back to Alexander Hamilton, WCAR affiliates enlisted the assistance of women in local and regional relief groups, organized supply efforts in cities and villages, and recruited, selected, and trained nurses. In less than seven months, the female volunteers had collected 30,000 hospital garments, 15,147 pieces of bedding, 6,112 havelocks, and over 2,000 jars of jelly and preserves. They had also trained and placed thirty-two nurses in military hospitals. With the appointment of Dix, however, the WCAR ceased involvement in the recruitment of nurses and concentrated its efforts on benevolent activities. With the war's conclusion in 1865, the WCAR held its last meeting on July 7, 1865, and closed its doors that September.

E. Sue Wamsley

See also Aid Societies; Blackwell, Elizabeth (1821–1910); Nurses; Schuyler, Louisa Lee (1837–1926); Union Homefront; United States Sanitary Commission.

References and Further Reading

Attie, Jeanie. 1998. *Patriotic Toil: Northern Women and the American Civil War.* Ithaca, NY: Cornell University Press.

Garrison, Nancy S. 1999. *With Courage and Delicacy: Civil War on the Peninsula: Women and the U.S. Sanitary Commission.* Mason City, IA: Savas Publishing Company.

Giesberg, Judith Ann. 2000. *Civil War Sisterhood: The U.S. Sanitary Commission and Women's Politics in Transition.* Boston: Northeastern University Press.

Women's National Loyal League

See National Women's Loyal League

Woolsey, Jane Stuart (1830–1891)

Civil War nursing administrator Jane Stuart Woolsey wrote *Hospital Days* (1868), a memoir of her experiences after the war. She also continued to work to improve nursing care and to open the profession to women.

Woolsey grew up in England, Boston, and New York City, where her father owned a sugar-refining business. She was one of the seven daughters of the Woolsey family, all of whom volunteered to aid the Union cause. After her father died in an accident at sea in 1840, the family moved to New York City, where wealthy relatives helped them financially. The children received excellent educations in an atmosphere of culture. Woolsey's mother was a strict abolitionist, although her family came from Virginia.

When the Civil War began, the Woolsey sisters volunteered in many ways. They were part of the group of women who began the Woman's Central Association of Relief, which later became part of the United States Sanitary Commission. In addition, several of Jane's sisters went south to nurse in military hospitals. She stayed in New York, where she worked at a temporary war hospital for several years.

In 1863, Jane Woolsey became the assistant superintendent of the Army Hospital in Portsmouth Grove, Rhode Island. There she learned hospital management under the direction of Katharine Wormeley and her own sister, Georgeanna. Later that year, Jane and Georgeanna became superintendents of nursing at Fairfax Theological Seminary near Alexandria, Virginia. The seminary had been turned into a large Union hospital, and it remained so until the end of the war. Jane's nursing experience in Virginia formed the basis for *Hospital Days*. At the Virginia hospital, Woolsey revealed a genius for administrative and organizational work. She was able to act quickly and effectively to resolve problems. In addition, she developed forms that made hospital business proceed smoothly.

After the war ended, Jane spent several years teaching freed slaves at Lincoln Industrial School in Richmond, Virginia. Unlike other Civil War nursing memoirs, *Hospital Days* offers an administrator's perspective. The memoir analyzes the wartime hospital system, with chapters devoted to the role of the superintendent, the selection and training of nurses, and the relationship of the staff to the chief surgeon.

In 1872, Jane Woolsey became the resident directress at New York Presbyterian Hospital. She remained in that position until 1876, when ill health forced her to resign. Jane Stuart Woolsey died in 1891.

Ellen H. Todras

See also Abolitionism and Northern Reformers; Disease; Education, Northern; Hospitals; Letter Writing; Nurses; Union Homefront; United States Sanitary Commission; Urban Women, Northern; Wartime Employment; Women's Central Association of Relief; Wormeley, Katharine Prescott (1830–1908).

References and Further Reading

Austin, Anne. 1971. *The Woolsey Sisters of New York: A Family's Involvement in the Civil War and a New Profession (1860–1900).* Philadelphia, PA: American Philosophical Society.

Bacon, Georgeanna Woolsey, and Eliza Woolsey Howland. 2001. *My Heart toward Home: Letters of a Family during the Civil War,* edited by Daniel John Hoisington. Roseville, MN: Edinborough Press.

Schultz, Jane E. 2004. *Women at the Front: Hospital Workers in Civil War America.* Chapel Hill: University of North Carolina Press.

Woolsey, Jane Stuart. [1868] 2001. *Hospital Days: Reminiscence of a Civil War Nurse.* Roseville, MN: Edinborough Press.

Wormeley, Katharine Prescott (1830–1908)

Wealthy Rhode Islander Katharine Wormeley volunteered as a nurse and hospital administrator for the Union army in 1862 and 1863. She later wrote a history of the United States Sanitary Commission (USSC), as well as a memoir of her Civil War nursing experiences.

Wormeley was born in England in 1830 to a wealthy family. Her father had roots in Virginia, and the family moved to the United States after his 1852 death. They settled in Newport, Rhode Island, and wintered in both Boston and Washington.

When the Civil War began, the formation of the Women's Central Association of Relief inspired Wormeley to found a similar organization in Newport, the Woman's Union Aid Society. Wormeley also became the assistant manager of the New England women's branch of the Sanitary Commission. In 1861, recognizing the soldiers' need for clothing, Wormeley used donations to the society to hire unemployed seamstresses to make the necessary supplies. Her group generated fifty thousand army shirts in this manner from 1861 to 1862.

In May 1862 the secretary of the USSC, Frederick Law Olmsted, invited Wormeley to volunteer on the first hospital transport ship, which supported wounded Union forces during the Peninsular campaign. She oversaw the linens, bedding, feeding of patients, and general conditions of the hospital wards until that summer.

In September, Wormeley became the superintendent of the Women's Department of the Lowell General Hospital for convalescing soldiers in Portsmouth Grove, Rhode Island. Serving with her were women Wormeley had worked with on the hospital transport ships, including sisters Georgeanna and Jane Woolsey, their cousin Sarah Woolsey, and Harriet D. Whetten. Their positions at the Lowell General Hospital marked the first time that ladies served in such capacities in a general hospital.

A year later, Wormeley returned to private life in Newport, Rhode Island. Her history of the USSC, *The United States Sanitary Commission: A Sketch of Its Purpose and Work* (1863), was sold at sanitary fairs to raise money for the organization.

In 1889 Wormeley published a memoir of her experiences on the hospital transport ships. *The Other Side of War: With the Army of the Potomac* describes female nurses' experiences and reveals the class distinctions between women during the war. It also describes how some Civil War nurses lost their interest in politics, instead focusing only on the wounded in their care. After the war, in addition to continuing her volunteer work, Wormeley became an expert translator of French authors such as Balzac and Molière.

Ellen H. Todras

See also Aid Societies; Hospital Ships; Hospitals; Northern Women; Nurses; Olmsted, Frederick Law (1822–1903); Union Homefront; United States Sanitary Commission; Women's Central Association of Relief; Woolsey, Jane Stuart (1830–1891).

References and Further Reading
Austin, Anne. 1971. *The Woolsey Sisters of New York: A Family's Involvement in the Civil War and a New Profession (1860–1900).* Philadelphia, PA: American Philosophical Society.

Schultz, Jane E. 2004. *Women at the Front: Hospital Workers in Civil War America.* Chapel Hill: University of North Carolina Press.

Silber, Nina. 2005. *Daughters of the Union: Northern Women Fight the Civil War.* Cambridge, MA: Harvard University Press.

Wormeley, Katharine P. 1889. *The Other Side of War: With the Army of the Potomac.* Boston: Ticknor.

Wounded, Visits to

The hospitals of the Civil War era were filled with people who came to visit the soldiers, some for a brief time and some for long periods. Southern and Northern women who made visits were attempting to recreate the conditions of home. They wanted to provide traditional care, to complete their domestic circles, and to protect their social roles.

Before the Civil War, women had become the spiritual leaders of their families because society considered them to be less corrupted by the world than men. Because they learned to care "for the least"—the poor, the orphaned, the sick, and even the slaves—through prayer and churchgoing, they sought to extend their help to those God placed in their paths. The charity they learned required that they provide physical comfort for those in need. Prior to the war, women had become accustomed to responding to emergency situations by making donations of money and material needed by others. Those practices included visiting the ill in their homes or in institutions. Women who refused such responsibility were seen as out of touch with their spiritual natures. The Civil War allowed women to extend their efforts to military hospitals or to anywhere soldiers needed care.

It was not clear, in the face of war, exactly how to carry out traditional responsibilities. Some women sought to fulfill their duties by sending donations of money and material to national commissions, such as the United States Sanitary Commission (USSC), the United States Christian Commission (USCC), or local aid societies. Others sent servants or slaves to carry donations of food, books, clothing, newspapers, or anything they thought might be useful directly to hospitals. Those who lived near the temporary or permanent military hospitals often called in person with donations. Both Northern and Southern women tried to recreate the sense of comfort found in their homes by reading to the wounded, fanning them in warm weather, singing and praying with them, writing letters for them, bringing them treats, or simply sitting with those who were dying.

Other women traveled to the hospitals in the Union and Confederacy hoping that someone would hire them to nurse the sick, or looking for their sons, husbands, fathers, or brothers. When women found their relatives, they stayed in the hospital or nearby until they could find a better place to care for the men. They tried to provide the same kinds of cleaning, cooking, and laundering that the men would experience at home. However, the women did not necessarily understand or appreciate the procedures used in the hospitals and were frequently in conflict with hospital or military officials.

The women also tried to maintain peacetime familial relationships. Those who provided care for many men, rather than just their own families, were often rewarded with the title of "Mother" because they comforted the men as if they were sick boys. Others who came to the army tried to locate their male relatives. Communication between the homefront and the military, especially following battles, was undependable. To regain the sense of security they felt before the war, women sometimes traveled to the hospitals near the front. Some brought their children with them, and some gave birth while sitting with their sick or wounded husbands. While some of the families came and went in a few brief hours, others stayed for days and weeks. A few stayed with the armies for the course of the war.

Some who visited the wounded took on greatly expanded responsibilities. Although they sought to ensure that the soldiers were receiving appropriate care, a traditional role for women, they worked in official capacities. For example, Cordelia Harvey served as a state agent for Wisconsin when the governor appointed her to the position after her husband's death. In her official capacity, Harvey visited all Union hospitals south of Memphis. In every one of them, she looked for Wisconsin soldiers, noted their names and units, recorded their conditions, helped them with any problems they were having, and reported back to the governor on a regular basis. When she was not carrying out these duties, she provided practical nursing support.

Other women worked for the national commissions. Henrietta Colt of Milwaukee, Wisconsin, was typical of many. She headed the Wisconsin Soldiers' Aid Society, which was affiliated with the USSC. On two separate occasions, she toured Southern hospitals, visiting the wounded men and the officials who ran the institutions. She brought delicacies and supplies with her and helped the nursing staffs. She recorded her observations of the hospitals and used them in written materials designed to increase the morale of the civilian population and to motivate them to increase their donations for the men.

Southern women similarly cared for and visited the wounded in their areas, and they traveled to help care for injured or ill family members. Without the auspices of an organization like the USSC, Confederate women's efforts were primarily locally based. Local aid societies often scheduled daily visits to nearby hospitals or to soldiers recuperating in homes around town. The supplies and care that these women provided did not go unnoticed by the soldiers or Confederate officials.

The military was not prepared to care for the civilians who came to the front. Many visitors slept on the floors or in supply rooms. Nurses gave up their own sleeping quarters for especially frail visitors and scavenged to provide for children and infants who toddled about the wards. Those who had no practical experience dealing with the sick and dying often became patients themselves when they fainted from the sights or smells of the hospital. Inexperienced women, dressed in impractical and inappropriate clothing, tried to move through overcrowded and blood-drenched wards in their hoop skirts, lace, and ribbons. No matter how annoying the visitors were, no one could bear to kick them out. For many, the tasks ended when the women accompanied a fallen soldier home for burial.

Karen A. Kehoe

See also Aid Societies; Camp Followers; Confederate Homefront; Domesticity; Family Life, Confederate; Family Life, Union; Hospitals; Northern Women; Nurses; Southern Women; Union Homefront; United States Christian Commission; United States Sanitary Commission.

References and Further Reading

Ginzberg, Lori D. 1990. *Women and the Work of Benevolence: Morality, Politics, and Class in the Nineteenth-Century United States.* New Haven, CT: Yale University Press.

Stearns, Amanda Akin. 1909. *Lady Nurse of Ward E.* New York: Baker & Taylor Company.

Z

Zakrzewska, Maria [Marie Elizabeth] (1829–1902)

Polish physician Maria, or Marie Elizabeth, Zakrzewska attended medical college in the United States and, during the Civil War, founded the New England Hospital for Women and Children in Boston.

Zakrzewska was born in Berlin, Germany, to Polish parents. Both her mother and grandmother practiced medicine—her grandmother as a veterinarian and her mother as a midwife. Her mother, Frederika Urban Zakrzewska, had begun midwifery study at the Royal Charite Hospital in Berlin, and, as a teenager, Marie lived at the hospital with her mother and accompanied her on her midwifery rounds. At age twenty, Marie enrolled in formal midwifery studies at the same hospital. Midwifery was the primary field of medical training available to women, and Zakrzewska went on to become a teacher in the program. She was promoted to head midwife in 1852 but quit after six months and emigrated, along with two of her sisters, to the United States to continue her medical training and career.

Zakrzewska was one of only a handful of women to enroll at Cleveland's Western Reserve College before the Civil War, receiving her medical degree there in 1856. With few opportunities available for women doctors professionally, immediately upon graduation, Zakrzrewska opened a small office next to that of Elizabeth Blackwell who, in 1849, had become the first woman to earn a medical degree in the United States. In May 1857, Zakrzewska joined with sister physicians Elizabeth and Emily Blackwell in founding the New York Infirmary for Women and Children. Their goal was to provide health services to women and children, but also to establish a hospital to train and employ female physicians.

In 1859, Zakrzewska moved to Boston, where she had been offered a position as professor of obstetrics and women's health at the New England Female Medical College. There she led efforts to expand the medical training curriculum and employment opportunities for female students beyond midwifery. She resigned in 1862 and founded the New England Hospital for Women and Children in Boston, the second American hospital to be operated by female physicians. Zakrzewska was committed to providing female patients with the highest level of medical care and to providing women students the same general education and broad medical training as male physicians received at other schools. The New England Hospital for Women and Children survived as a major training ground for women physicians and nurses well into the twentieth century and continues to operate today as the Dimock Community Health Center.

Though her primary work throughout the Civil War era was as a physician and an advocate of women's education and professional opportunities, Zakrzewska was also involved in a variety of American reform efforts. She was close friends with the leading antislavery activists of the day and supported woman suffrage and other causes. After the Civil War, Zakrzewska promoted black women's medical education and their access to the nursing profession. Maria Zakrzewska died on May 12, 1902.

Tiffany K. Wayne

See also Abolitionism and Northern Reformers; Blackwell, Elizabeth (1821–1910); Domesticity; Hospitals; Northern Women; Separate Spheres; Union Homefront; Wartime Employment.

References and Futher Reading

Dall, Caroline, ed. 1860. *A Practical Illustration of "Woman's Right to Labor;" or, A Letter from Marie E. Zakrzewska.* Boston: Walker, Wise & Co.

Vietor, Agnes C., ed. 1972. *A Woman's Quest: The Life of Marie E. Zakrzewska, M.D.* New York: Arno Press. (Orig. pub. 1924.)

Primary Sources

Harriet Beecher Stowe, *Uncle Tom's Cabin; Or, Life among the Lowly* (1852)

Prior to the Civil War, most Northerners were apathetic to the plight of African American slaves. This began to change after the publication of Harriet Beecher Stowe's Uncle Tom's Cabin. *This fictional account of the slave South was originally published as a serial in the* National Era. *It was immediately republished as a book that became a best seller. Within five years, it had sold more than 2 million copies. Stowe would obtain national recognition for her vividly brutal depictions of slavery and Southern planters. In the following excerpt, George describes the cruelty of slave owners and his resolve to risk his life rather than remain in bondage.*

"It was only yesterday," said George, "as I was busy loading stones into a cart, that young Mas'r Tom stood there, slashing his whip so near the horse that the creature was frightened. I asked him to stop, as pleasant as I could,—he just kept right on. I begged him again, and then he turned on me, and began striking me. I held his hand, and then he screamed and kicked and ran to his father, and told him that I was fighting him. He came in a rage, and said he'd teach me who was my master; and he tied me to a tree, and cut switches for young master, and told him that he might whip me till he was tired;—and he did do it! If I don't make him remember it, some time!" and the brow of the young man grew dark, and his eyes burned with an expression that made his young wife tremble. "Who made this man my master? That's what I want to know!" he said.

"Well," said Eliza, mournfully, "I always thought that I must obey my master and mistress, or I couldn't be a Christian."

"There is some sense in it, in your case; they have brought you up like a child, fed you, clothed you, indulged you, and taught you, so that you have a good education; that is some reason why they should claim you. But I have been kicked and cuffed and sworn at, and at the best only let alone; and what do I owe? I've paid for all my keeping a hundred times over. I *won't* bear it. No, I *won't!*" he said, clenching his hand with a fierce frown.

Eliza trembled, and was silent. She had never seen her husband in this mood before; and her gentle system of ethics seemed to bend like a reed in the surges of such passions.

"You know poor little Carlo, that you gave me," added George; "the creature has been about all the comfort that I've had. He has slept with me nights, and followed me around days, and kind o' looked at me as if he understood how I felt. Well, the other day I was just feeding him with a few old scraps I picked up by the kitchen door, and Mas'r came along, and said I was feeding him up at his expense, and that he couldn't afford to have every nigger keeping his dog, and ordered me to tie a stone to his neck and throw him in the pond."

"O, George, you didn't do it!"

"Do it? not I!—but he did. Mas'r and Tom pelted the poor drowning creature with stones. Poor thing! he looked at me so mournful, as if he wondered why I didn't save him. I had to take a flogging because I wouldn't do it myself. I don't care. Mas'r will find out that I'm one that whipping won't tame. My day will come yet, if he don't look out."

"What are you going to do? O, George, don't do anything wicked; if you only trust in God, and try to do right, he'll deliver you."

"I an't a Christian like you, Eliza; my heart's full of bitterness; I can't trust in God. Why does he let things be so?"

"O, George, we must have faith. Mistress says that when all things go wrong to us, we must believe that God is doing the very best."

"That's easy to say for people that are sitting on their sofas and riding in their carriages; but let 'em be where I am, I guess it would come some harder. I wish I could be good; but my heart burns, and can't be reconciled, anyhow. You couldn't in my place,—you can't now, if I tell you all I've got to say. You don't know the whole yet."

"What can be coming now?"

"Well, lately Mas'r has been saying that he was a fool to let me marry off the place; that he hates Mr. Shelby and all his tribe, because they are proud, and hold their heads up above him, and that I've got proud notions from you; and he says he won't let me come here any more, and that I shall take a wife and settle down on his place. At first he only scolded and grumbled these things; but yesterday he told me that I should take Mina for a wife, and settle down in a cabin with her, or he would sell me down river."

"Why—but you were married to *me*, by the minister, as much as if you'd been a white man!" said Eliza, simply.

"Don't you know a slave can't be married? There is no law in this country for that; I can't hold you for my wife, if he chooses to part us. That's why I wish I'd never seen you,—why I wish I'd never been born; it would have been better for us both,—it would have been better for this poor child if he had never been born. All this may happen to him yet!"

"O, but master is so kind!"

"Yes, but who knows?—he may die—and then he may be sold to nobody knows who. What pleasure is it that he is handsome, and smart, and bright? I tell you, Eliza, that a sword will pierce through your soul for every good and pleasant thing your child is or has; it will make him worth too much for you to keep."

The words smote heavily on Eliza's heart; the vision of the trader came before her eyes, and, as if some one had struck her a deadly blow, she turned pale and gasped for breath. She looked nervously out on the verandah, where the boy, tired of the grave conversation, had retired, and where he was riding triumphantly up and down on Mr. Shelby's walking-stick. She would have spoken to tell her husband her fears, but checked herself.

"No, no,—he has enough to bear, poor fellow!" she thought. "No, I won't tell him; besides, it an't true; Missis never deceives us."

"So, Eliza, my girl," said the husband, mournfully, "bear up, now; and good-by, for I'm going."

"Going, George! Going where?"

"To Canada," said he, straightening himself up; "and when I'm there, I'll buy you; that's all the hope that's left us. You have a kind master, that won't refuse to sell you. I'll buy you and the boy;—God helping me, I will!"

"O, dreadful! if you should be taken?"

"I won't be taken, Eliza; I'll *die* first! I'll be free, or I'll die!"

> Harriet Beecher Stowe, *Uncle Tom's Cabin; Or, Life among the Lowly* (Boston: John P. Jewett & Company, 1852), 61–64.

Varina Howell Davis (1861)

Many women moved as a result of the war. Some were refugees or camp followers; others used mobility to claim their freedom from slavery. For Varina Howell Davis, mobility came as a result of her position of political privilege. In March 1861, she moved to Montgomery after her husband, Jefferson Davis, was inaugurated as the president of the Confederacy. Her change of residence from Mississippi to Alabama required some sacrifice. In the following excerpt from her memoir, Davis recalls the sadness that accompanied the beginning of the war.

It was necessary to close up our home and abandon all we had watched over for years, before going to Montgomery; our library, which was very large and consisted of fine well-chosen English books, was the hardest to relinquish of all our possessions. After all was secured in the best manner practicable, I went to New Orleans en route to Montgomery, and remained a few days at my father's house. While there, Captain Dreux, at the head of his battalion, came to serenade me, but I could not command by voice to speak to him when he came on the balcony; his cheery words and the enthusiasm of his men depressed me dreadfully. Violets were in season, and the captain and his company brought several immense bouquets. The color seemed ominous. Perhaps Mr. Davis's depression had communicated itself to me, and I could not rally or be buoyed up by the cheerfulness of those who were to do battle for us. My journey up the Alabama River to join Mr. Davis in Montgomery was a very sad one, sharing his apprehensions and knowing our needs to be so many, with so little hope of supplying them. . . .

When he reached the hotel where the President was temporarily lodged, the Provisional Congress had assembled, he had been inaugurated, and the day of my arrival the Confederate flag had been hoisted by the daughter of Colonel Robert Tyler, and the granddaughter of the ex-President. . . .

The house chosen for us was a gentleman's residence, roomy enough for our purposes on the corner of a street and looking toward the State Capitol. There were many charming people there, who were all intent on kind services to us, our memory of Montgomery was one of affectionate welcome. . . .

Varina Howell Davis, *Jefferson Davis: A Memoir by His Wife* (New York: Belford, 1890), 34–37.

Enlisted Female Soldiers Discovered (1861)

At least several hundred women dressed as men to fight as members of the Union or Confederate army. In many instances, women were able to shield their sex by binding breasts, smoking tobacco, dressing appropriately, and otherwise acting masculine. For many women, their ability to pass for men ended when medics and soldiers had to tend to their war wounds. Early in the war, before the creation of the so-called colored units, some African Americans tried to pass for white to enlist in the Union army. The following article discusses the discovery of a black woman passing for a white man and reveals nineteenth-century attitudes about race and gender.

THE FEMALE SOLD-UIER

Our readers may remember the case of Jasper, a correspondent of the Daily Rimes, driven from Charleston awhile ago; and his wonderful escape, under many disguises, may not be quite forgotten yet. If Jasper's story was true—and we sincerely hope that it was—he is certainly one of the seven wonders of the world; but alas for human fame! He has been thrown completely in the shade by a more recent discovery.

An exchange, published somewhere in the country, fills of a column with this sublime statement:

A slave woman has been discovered in one of the Ohio regiments. She was discharged.

That is all. Clear, quiet, and simple in language, thrilling in meaning, and totally incomprehensible of understanding, we present it to our readers just as we find it. Our eyes do not deceive us.

A black woman has passed herself off as a white soldier. Shade of Jasper! What a metamorphosis. Was she whitewashed? Did she "paint an inch thick" to come "to that complexion?" How did she pass the medical examination unsuspected? What was her object? Did she wear a beard? The more questions we ask, the more profound our mystification grows. Is it an enigma, a conundrum? What-Is-It? We give it up. But, if this sort of thing is prevalent, what regiment is safe from these female Ethiopian Jaspers? How do we know that our army, which we have loved and esteemed so much, is not largely composed of negro wenches! Can anybody swear that Brigadier-General Pierce is not a colored maiden in disguise? If he is, let him also be discharged and speedily.

Seriously, it doesn't seem likely that this can be a very common case. Jasper's was not, and Munchausen's adventures were unique. Let us hope that the Ohio regiment is the only one in whose ranks a

Chloe or a Phyllis has found even a temporary asylum, and let us rejoice that in that case "she was discharged." It is probable that McAron's army alone boasts of an organization of "light quadroons;" and that we can put down a rebellion better than by "Putting it Down in Black and White."

Vanity Fair 4, no. 81 (July 13, 1861): 16.

The Woman Order in New Orleans (1862)

The Union occupation of New Orleans brought Confederate women and Union soldiers face to face. Although many of the city's women acted with civility or refrained from interaction altogether, many did not. In one notable exchange, a woman in New Orleans dumped the contents of a chamber pot onto the head of David Farragut. Major General Benjamin F. Butler, who was in charge of the occupying force, responded with the following order on May 15, 1862. In what became known as the Woman Order, Butler declared that any defiant woman in the city should be treated as a prostitute. Southerners gave Butler the nickname Beast in response to this order.

GENERAL ORDERS,
HDQRS. DEPARTMENT OF THE GULF,
No. 28.
New Orleans, May 15, 1862.

As the officers and soldiers of the United States have been subject to repeated insults from the women (calling themselves ladies) of New Orleans in return for the most scrupulous non-interference and courtesy on our part, it is ordered that hereafter when any female shall by word, gesture, or movement insult or show contempt for any officer or soldier of the United States she shall be regarded and held liable to be treated as a woman of the town plying her avocation.

By command of Major-General [Benjamin F.] Butler.

United States War Department, *The War of the Rebellion: A Compilation of the Official Records of the Union and Confederate Armies*, Series 1 (Washington, DC: Government Printing Office, 1880–1901), 15: 426.

A Northern Newspaper Supports Butler's Woman Order (1862)

Major General Benjamin F. Butler's Woman Order shocked many Southerners for its willingness to treat defiant Confederate women not only as the enemy, but also as prostitutes. The policy seemed to betray the standards of treatment typically reserved for female civilians under occupation. As a result, many Southerners began to refer to the Union leader as Beast Butler. The Woman Order surprised some Northerners as well. In the following article, Vanity Fair *declares its support for the order and for Butler.*

OUR CHIEF BUTLER

The bottled spirits of New Orleans are finding themselves in a tight place now that the BUTLER has taken to looking after them himself. Neither the Crescent nor the Cross have found the slightest favor from that stern chief, who has promptly suppressed both of them—the one represented by a newspaper, the other by the "ladies" of the city, if not of the town. BUTLER is not the man to stand any nonsense; and it is now well understood at New Orleans that ladies who contort their faces in defiance of Union soldiers, must serve out a term of imprisonment in a place called the "Calaboose." This may be considered by some as an aboose of the authority vested in General BUTLER's hands, but that depends upon what you call aboose. It may be remarked that as there are no cellars at New Orleans, our BUTLER must find himself rather astray there; but people will do well to remember that the Port of that city was never in better order than it has been since it came into his keeping.

Vanity Fair 5, no. 128 (June 7, 1862): 272.

Confederate Spy Belle Boyd Recalls Her Arrest (1862)

Women served as spies for both the Union and Confederacy. They often took advantage of their femininity to appear harmless and to coax information out of male informants. Belle Boyd was one of the most famous Confederate spies. She provided information to General Thomas "Stonewall" Jackson dur-

ing the 1862 campaign in the Shenandoah Valley. She was arrested in July 1862, only to obtain her freedom as part of a prisoner exchange. She was arrested again in June 1863. In the following excerpt from her memoir, Boyd recalls her first arrest.

It was on a lovely Wednesday evening that our firm and valued friend Lieutenant Preston, my cousin Alice, and myself were standing on the balcony, watching the last rays of the setting sun as it sank behind the western hills.

Our conversation turned upon the divided and unhappy state of our country. We recalled the peaceful scenes and joyous days of the past, which were so painfully contrasted by the present, and we were forced to agree that we had nothing to expect from the future but a continuance, if not an augmentation, of our calamities.

In such gloomy forebodings, and in the interchange of apprehensions and regrets, we passed some time, and the twilight was fast deepening into gloom when we heard the sound of horses' hoofs; and, straining our eyes through the darkness, we discerned a large body of cavalry approaching the house.

I immediately conceived the idea that it was a scouting-party on their way to the mountains with the design of surprising Major Harry Gilmore's cavalry, and feared that their enterprise would prove successful unless the Confederate officer should leave timely notice of his danger. I ran at once to my room and wrote a hasty note, in which I communicated my suspicions to Major Gilmore, and warned him to be on his guard.

This note I transmitted in the manner I have described in a previous chapter, by my "underground railway [an old slave]." After this feat I retired to bed, and slept quietly, undisturbed by any dream or vision of my approaching captivity.

Next morning I rose early, and soon after breakfast I went to the cottage door, where I daily spent much of my time, watching the movements of the persons who, for various purposes, frequented head-quarters. I had not been long at my post when I observed several Yankee soldiers go into the coach-house. They immediately proceeded to drag out the carriage, and pull it up at the door of head-quarters, where they put to the horses.

There was nothing very extraordinary in all this; but in these anxious days the minds of all were in a perpetual state of tension, and a slight incident was sufficient to cause alarm.

This may account for the strange feeling that came over me—an irrepressible desire to ascertain who was to be the occupant of the carriage, which was on the point of starting for a destination of which I was ignorant.

I walked out upon the balcony; and, looking up and down the street, I saw that it was thronged with cavalry, the men dismounted, lounging about, and conversing with each other, in groups of twos and threes, evidently waiting for the expected order to mount.

While I stood looking at this scene, not without interest and curiosity, one of the servants came to me and said—

"Miss Belle, de Provo' wishes to see you in de drawing-room, and dere's two oder men wid him."

I immediately went down-stairs, and, upon entering the room, I found the Major, whose face wore an expression of excitement and nervousness. There were, as the servant had said, two other men in the room with him: one, a tall, fine-looking man, was introduced to me by the name and title of Major Sherman, of the 12th Illinois Cavalry; the other was low in stature, coarse in appearance, with a mean, vile expression of countenance, and a grizzly beard, which, it was evident, had not made the acquaintance of water or a comb for weeks at least. His small, restless eyes glanced here and there, with an expression of incessant watchfulness and suspicion. All his features were repulsive in the extreme, denoting a mixture of cowardice, ferocity, and cunning. In a word, his mien was unmistakably that of a finished villain, who was capable of perpetrating any act, however atrocious, when stimulated by the promise of a reward in money.

This man was a good type of his order: he was one of Secretary Stanton's minions—a detective belonging to, and employed and paid by, that honourable branch of Mr. Lincoln's Government, the Secret Service Department.

I had not been in the room more than a few moments when Major McEnnis turned to me and said —

"Miss Boyd, Major Sherman has come to arrest you."

"Impossible! For what?" I cried.

Major Sherman here interposed, and, speaking in a very kind manner, assured me that, although the duty he had to perform was painful to his feelings, he was, nevertheless, forced to execute the orders of the Secretary of War, Mr. Stanton; and, as he finished speaking, the detective produced from his pocket the document, which I transcribe as nearly as I can recollect: —

"War Department.

"SIR, - YOU will proceed immediately to Front Royal, Virginia, and arrest, if found there, Miss Belle Boyd, and bring her at once to Washington.

"I am, respectfully,
"Your obedient Servant,
"E. M. STANTON."

Such was the curt order that made me a prisoner; and, as remonstrance would have been idle and resistance vain, nothing was left for me but quiet, unconditional obedience.

The detective then informed me that it was his duty to examine all my luggage.

To this I could not do otherwise than assent, and only begged that a few minutes might be granted, to enable my servant to prepare my room, which was in great confusion, and that I might also be permitted to retire. I made this request to the detective, for it had not escaped my notice that Major Sherman was acting a subordinate part, and was virtually at the disposal and under the orders of the former.

As no answer was returned to my question, I took it for granted I had tacit permission to withdraw; but my disgust was great when, turning round upon the stairs, I saw my persecutor silently following at my heels.

I stopped short, and said —

"Sir, will not you wait until I see if my room is in a suitable condition for you to enter?"

The reply was characteristic, though not urbane.

"No, yer don't: I'm agoin' with yer. Yer got some papers yer want to get rid on;" and, with these words, he pushed violently past me, and hastily entered my room.

My clothes were first seized, and searched with the utmost scrutiny. My dresses were examined closely, and, after being turned inside out, and distorted into all sorts of fantastic shapes, were flung in a pile upon the floor, much to the horror and amazement of my maid, who had employed a great part of the previous night in packing them safely and neatly, and who was at a loss to understand the meaning of such treatment, which appeared to her, naturally enough, so strange and unseemly.

My under-clothing next underwent an ordeal precisely similar to that which my upper garments had passed through; and, finally, my desk and portfolio were discovered; but here very fortunately my devoted servant came to the rescue with the promptitude and courage of a heroine.

She well knew the value I attached to the contents of my portfolio, and made a shrewd guess as to how far they would compromise me with my captor and his employers. Acting upon a sudden impulse, she made a swoop upon the repository of the greatest part of the evidence that could be adduced against me; and, rushing at headlong speed down-stairs, she gained the kitchen in time to burn all the papers it contained. But some important papers were, unfortunately, in my writing-desk, and these fell into the possession of the detective who also, much to my regret, made prize of a handsome pistol, with belt and equipments complete, which had been presented to me on the 4th July, by a Federal officer on the staff, as a token, he was pleased to say, of his admiration of the spirit I had shown in defence of my mother and my home.

It had always been my hope to have some day an opportunity of begging General Stonewall Jackson's acceptance of a present made to me, under very trying circumstances, by a gallant and generous enemy; but this could not be done. The pistol now occupies a conspicuous place in the War Department at Washington, and is entered in the catalogue of spoils in the following words: —

"A trophy captured from the celebrated rebel Belle Boyd."

Not contented with the seizure of my own papers, the emissary of Mr. Stanton proceeded to break open the private *escritoire* of my uncle, who was a lawyer, and who had left it in my room for safekeeping during his absence from Front Royal.

The detective, bundling up the law-papers with mine, bade me, in the roughest manner, and in the most offensive language, be prepared to start within half an hour.

I asked permission to be indulged with the attendance of my maid; but this request was refused, with imprecations, and she was only allowed to pack one trunk with apparel absolutely necessary to comfort, if not to decency. Brief time was granted for the packing; and, before many minutes, my solitary trunk was strapped to the back of the carriage.

I then nerved myself, and, walking into the drawing-room, announced, in firm, unbroken accents, that I was ready to start.

I preserved my composure unshaken; although it was a hard trial to me to see my grandmother and cousin weeping piteously, and beseeching Major Sherman, in the most moving terms, to spare me. Their supplications were vain; and the detective, stepping up close to my side, ordered me to get into the carriage forthwith.

Then came the final parting, bitter enough, God knows; for I was being dragged from those to whom I was endeared by the associations of my happy youth, no less than by the ties of nature, and consigned to the safe-keeping of a man whose countenance alone would have immediately convicted him of any crime of which he might anywhere have been accused.

Belle Boyd, *Belle Boyd, In Camp and Prison,*
2 vols. (London: Saunders, Otley, and Co., 1865),
1: 157–170.

Women's Pennsylvania Branch of the United States Sanitary Commission's Call for Contributions (March 1863)

Established on June 18, 1861, the United States Sanitary Commission (USSC) organized the efforts of thousands of female volunteers. Members worked as nurses, raised money, ran hospital ships, donated clothing, sewed clothing and blankets, and ran sanitary fairs on behalf of the Union army. An institution of the federal government, the USSC provided an umbrella organization for hundreds of local ladies' aid societies. In the following newspaper excerpt, the Pennsylvania Branch of the USSC called on patriotic women in the area to join in the cause and to donate items that were needed immediately.

WOMEN'S PENNSYLVANIA BRANCH OF THE U. S. SANITARY COMMISSION.

The women of the Pennsylvania Branch of the United States Sanitary Commission, appeal to the women of Pennsylvania, and of the neighboring counties of adjoining States, for assistance in their new enterprise—not as to those who have been unmindful of our sick and wounded soldiers—but fully cognizant of the great amount of supplies which their industry has prepared and sent for distribution to various Aid Societies.

Our appeal is based upon the knowledge that this Commission has greater facilities for doing this work than any State or Local Agency—that out of the thousands of boxes distributed by them, but one has been lost—that their Agents are notified of the time of an army's advance, and permitted to transfer their stores to as near the front as possible—and that they are the only organization authorized by Government to pass within the lines, and administer their supplies on the field of battle for the saving of life and the relief of suffering, knowing no difference between men from any section who are nobly fighting for the preservation of the Union.

This work must be left undone if THE WOMEN of the land do not keep the Sanitary Commission supplied with the means of doing it. For this purpose, some of the women of Philadelphia have organized under the name of the "Women's Pennsylvania Branch of the United States Sanitary Commission," and we invite every loyal woman in the city and State and surrounding counties of other States, to co-operate with us.—A small amount of self-denial, or of exertion on the part of each, would insure to the Commission and exhaustless supply of those needed stores. There is no time to be lost. Let every county, every town organize and put themselves in communication with us without delay. We know not how many lives depend upon our exertions—how much suffering rests with us to relieve. Let us assume these duties solemnly, with the determination that while the war lasts, we will devote our energies to this sacred cause.

LIST OF ARTICLES NEEDED
Flannel Shirts, ordinary size and make
Flannel Drawers, " "
Calico Wrappers
Blankets and Quilts for single beds.
Cotton Shirts and Drawers.
Bed Sacks, 7 feet by 3 feet; slit in the middle, with strings.
Carpet Slippers, with stiff soles.
Woolen Sacks, Towels.
Handkerchiefs, made of old chintz or lawn dresses.

Wines, Syrups and Jellies should be packed in separate boxes. Jellies should be covered with cloth, pasted over the mouth of the jar. Bottles should have the cork tied or sealed over. They should be packed in saw-dust, as firmly as possible. Every bottle should be labeled.

On the top of the contents of each box, under the cover, a list of what it contains, with the name and address of the donor, should be placed; a duplicate of this list should be sent by mail.

Each box should be marked on the outside with the name of the Society, Town and State from which it is sent. Boxes should be directed:

WOMEN'S PENN. BRANCH, U. S. SAN. COM.
1307 Chestnut Street Philadelphia.

Women's Pennsylvania Branch of the U. S. Sanitary Commission, *The Saturday Evening Post* (March 28, 1863): 2.

Mrs. Moore, Corresponding Secretary of the Women's Pennsylvania Branch of the U.S. Sanitary Commission, Calls for More Soldiers Aid Societies to be Formed (April 1863)

The United States Sanitary Commission relied on communities of local women to organize themselves on behalf of the national organization. Donations of food, uniforms, money, and other needed items were usually raised locally. In the following newspaper article from the Saturday Evening Post, *the USSC provided a how-to guide to urge women to form local aid societies.*

SANITARY COMMISSION DEPARTMENT
Our Sick and Wounded Soldiers

We last week published in this paper the circular of the Women's Pennsylvania Branch of the U.S. Sanitary Commission, and the list of supplies most needed; to which we invite the attention of existing Aid Societies, soliciting them to unite with this Association, under the assurance that their stores will be sent where they are *the most needed;* and distributed with the least possible waste and delay. All applications made to Independent Aid Societies and referred by them to the Sanitary Committee, will be attended to with far greater despatch than any other Association can command; and if the existing Aid Societies co-operate with this Commission, they will enable the latter to meet all the urgent demands made upon them.

After the delivery of an address in behalf of the Sanitary Commission at Rochester recently, an aged man arose, and with tears rolling down his cheeks, thus gave in his testimony,

"After the battle of Fredericksburg, hearing that my boy was wounded, I went on to look after him; but I found the Sanitary Commission had been *looking after him* from the time he fell, and after sixteen other Rochester boys; and I say, God bless everyone connected with the Sanitary Commission!"

He sat down in a silence so profound that one could have heard a pin drop.

A well known lady of this city who has returned within the last week from Falmouth, where she has been ministering in the Hospitals, gives the most powerful testimony to the efficiency of the work which the Sanitary Commission are doing. She says, "Hearing of great distress at a Hospital some miles distant, we went there in all haste, but found that the Sanitary Commission had been twelve hours before us." On her way home quite a number of sick soldiers were put under her care. Not knowing the provision made for them at Washington, by the Sanitary Commission, she was at a loss what to do; but all her anxiety was relieved, when upon the boat touching the wharf, she found the Agent of the Commission ready to convey these men to the comfortable beds awaiting them at "The Home," which the Commission have provided.

Is it any wonder that those who know the workings of this humane Association call upon God to bless all connected with it?

The only wonder is that the various societies whose supplies are not distributed under their supervision, do not make the Commission almoner of their bounties; and that societies do not spring up wherever there is a mother who has a boy exposed to the dangers of camp or battle, and pour in an exhaustless supply of stores!

In the towns and villages where no such organization exists, a few simple directions may be necessary for starting them. When once organized, we hope to keep up their enthusiasm by the interesting matter which we proposed to publish in these columns, by frequent correspondence, and in other ways. Acknowledgments will be made to all those who forward parcels; and a final report to the Secretary of War will be published, recording the names of all contributors. Circulars, with the names of the officers for 1863, can be procured at 1307 Chestnut street.

DIRECTIONS FOR FORMING SOCIETIES

Let the first woman whose heart is stirred with a desire to do something in her own town, go to two or three of her neighbors and take counsel.

Let them agree on some convenient day and hour for a meeting of ladies, in the lecture-room of some place of worship, or in the town-house, or school-house.

Let notices of this be written, and carried to the pastors of all the churches in town, with a request that they be read, with comments by the pastor, in each society, at the close of service.

Let the ladies meet—select a President and Secretary, and form themselves into a Soldiers' Relief Circle, to meet once a week from 1 to 4 P. M.—the time to be spent in sewing or knitting for the soldier.

Let them, in addition to the President and Secretary already elected, choose a Treasurer and two committees—one on supplies and work, of three ladies, and one on correspondence, forwarding, and all other business, such as storing, engaging rooms, &c., of the same number.

The duty of the officers should be as follows:

I.—The President—to call and preside at all meetings, and have a general charge of the interests of the Circle.

II.—The Secretary—to enroll the names of the members (each lady simply pledging herself to give three hours per week, either in the meeting or at home, to the service of the soldier)—to keep a record of the meetings—the amount of work done weekly—the number present, and their names—and to make a monthly report, to be read at the first meeting in each month.

III.—The Treasurer—to keep all donations of money, collections in churches, or funds raised by other means, and disburse them at the order of the President, on vote of the Circle, and to make a monthly report of receipts and expenditures.

IV.—The Committee on Supplies—to solicit donations in kind from stores, farmers, and citizens in general, in yarn, wool, cotton cloth, and other articles, to be made up by the industry of the Circle; also, to determine the kind of work to be engaged in by the Circle, and to distribute it properly; to put out work to those willing to receive it at home, but unable to attend, and to see to its collection; to form, with the President's advice, plans of work, and endeavor to get the largest possible stock of goods against the monthly reckoning. This Committee, on the first meeting in each month, shall report a plan of work for that month, and report in full the results of the work of the last month.

V.—The Committee on Correspondence, forwarding, storage—shall have for their duties, first, the custody, care, and storage; then, the packing and forwarding of the goods; and, finally, all the correspondence with the "Women's Penn. Branch," either for instructions, counsel, sympathy, or business. They shall send a monthly letter, and if possible a monthly package, directed to U.S. Sanitary Commission, 1307 Chestnut street, Philadelphia.

With these hints, and in view of the pressing need of our army, it is difficult to see how any patriotic village will be without its "Soldier's Aid," and we hope soon to hear from many who have been newly incited to this work, as well as from those whose labors commenced with the war. For further information address

Mrs. Moore,
Cor. Secretary W. P. B.
1307 Chestnut street, Philadelphia.

Sanitary Commission Department, Mrs. Moore, Cor. Secretary, *The Saturday Evening Post* (April 4, 1863): 8.

Frustrated Women in Richmond Participate in Bread Riot (1863)

In the spring of 1863, hundreds of women across the South took to the streets to protest the price of bread and other necessities. These rioters were primarily poor white women who were frustrated that they were making sacrifices for the Confederacy while their government ignored their immediate needs. Rather than expressions of disloyalty or Unionism, the riots were in fact public statements that called on the Confederate government for assistance and an end to policies that magnified their economic troubles. In the following excerpt, the New York Herald *details the upheaval in Richmond, the largest of the bread riots. Similar uprisings took place in North Carolina, Georgia, Alabama, and elsewhere across the South.*

A refugee from Richmond, who left that city on Tuesday, gives an interesting account of the riot of the 2d inst [April 2].

Considerable excitement had prevailed for some time in consequence of the exorbitant prices, and rumors of a popular movement had been in circulation for several days. Females had begged in the streets and at the stores until begging did no good, and many had been driven to robbery to sustain life. On the morning of the 2d inst a large meeting, composed principally of the wives and daughters of the working classes, was held in the African church, and a committee appointed to wait upon the Governor to request that articles of food should be sold at government rates. After the passage of sundry resolutions the meeting adjourned, and the committee proceeded to wait upon Governor Letcher. The functionary declined to take any steps in the matter, and upon urging the case the ladies were peremptorily ordered to withdraw. The result of the interview was soon made public, when a body of females, numbering about three hundred, collected together and commenced helping themselves to bread, flour, meat, articles of clothing, &c. The entire city was at once thrown into consternation.

Stores were closed, the windows barred, doors bolted, and every precaution taken against forcible entries; but hatchets and axes in the hands of women rendered desperate by hunger made quick work, and building after building was rapidly broken open. The destruction commenced on Carey street, above Fifteenth street, and was becoming general in that section of the city, when the City Guard, with fixed bayonets, arrived at the scene of operations. A few individuals attempted to resist the women, but without success. One man who struck a female was wounded in the shoulder by a shot from a revolver, and the threatening attitude of those armed with hatchets, &c. intimidated others from attempting force. The Mayor soon appeared, and, mounting a stool on the sidewalk, proceeded to read the Riot Act. During the reading of that document a portion of the crowd suspended operations; but no sooner had the Mayor concluded than the seizure of provisions commence again more vigorously than before. At this juncture an attempt was made to arrest the more violent; but the party immediately scattered, and, entering Main street, resumed operations.

Gov. Letcher then appeared, and, mounting a vehicle in the centre of the street, addressed the throng, characterizing the demonstration as a disgrace and a stigma upon the city, and announcing that but five minutes would be given them in which to disperse. If in that time the order was not complied with, the troops would be called upon to act. Again the crowd broke up, and in a few moments burst into the stores of Franklin street, But little damage was done here, however, and the riot finally subsided; but not until after the arrest of about forty of the women, and the promise of the Governor to relieve the wants of the destitute. A large amount of bread and bacon was carried off, and all engaged in the riot succeeded in getting a good supply of provisions. Steps have been taken to provide for the immediate wants of some of the families; but great suffering still prevails and is daily increasing. Another uprising is feared, and precautionary measures for its suppression have been instituted; but great uneasiness is felt throughout the city, and merchants are adding to the strength of doors and shutters in every possible manner. The effect of this riot upon the troops about Richmond was very demoralizing. The authorities are much exercised over it, and the greatest vigilance is enjoined upon the police force. The leading men of the city attempted to circulate the report that the women were *"Irish and Yankee hags,"* endeavoring to mislead the public concerning the amount of loyal sentiment in the city, miserably failed. The fact of their destitution and respectability was too palpable, and the authorities are forced to admit the conclusion that starvation alone incited the movement.

Troops are being hurried up from Richmond to Fredericksburg. There is still a large force in the vicinity of Richmond; but these, it is believed, are about to leave for the Rappahannock. Fortifications are being thrown up on the Rapidan river, and the force in that section is being augmented. No work is going on upon the defenses about Richmond. Two gunboats (iron clads) are afloat in James river. The Virginia Vessel has been trying to get below the obstructions, and now lies near Drury Bluff. The third is unfinished, but is rapidly approaching completion. The iron works are worked to their utmost in the manufacture of munitions of war; but the iron is of miserable quality, and many of their projectiles contain pieces of stone.

The railroads have almost entirely given out, and no material is to be had for their repair. Great despondency prevails, and the events of the next three months are awaited with most absorbing anxiety.

New York Herald (April 2, 1863).

Farmers' Wives Overtaxed (1863)

During the Civil War, the number of voices increased that were demanding equality or a greater public voice for women. Much of the discussion revolved around suffrage, which would be granted, through the Fifteenth Amendment, to African American men but not to white or black women. The struggle for equality meant more than political or economic equality; it also meant recognizing the essential functions of women in American society. In the following 1863 article, the author proclaims that proper recognition is rarely given to the wives of common farmers. Instead, women are treated without the respect or deference that should accompany their importance to the household.

There is scarcely any lot in life, in this country, which promises so much quiet enjoyment, such uniform health and uninterrupted prosperity, as that of a gentleman's farmer's wife; of a man who has a well-improved, well-stocked plantation, all paid for, with no indebtedness, and a sufficient surplus of money always at command, to meet emergencies, and to take advantage of those circumstances of times, and seasons, and changing conditions which are constantly presenting themselves. Such a woman is incomparably more certain of living in quiet comfort to a good old age than the wife of a merchant prince, or one of the money-kings of Wall Street; who, although they may clear thousands in a day, do, nevertheless, in multitudes of cases, die in poverty, leaving their wives and daughters to the sad heritage of being slighted and forgotten by those who once were made happy by their smiles; and to pine away in tears and destitution. On the other hand, it is often a sad lot indeed to be the wife of a farmer who begins married life by renting a piece of land or buying a "place" on credit, with the moth of "interest" feeding on the sweat of his face every moment of his existence.

The affectionate and steady interests, the laudable pride, and the self-denying devotion which wives have for the comfort, prosperity, and respectability of their husbands and children, is a proverb and a wonder in all civilized lands. There is an abnegation of self in this direction, as constant as the flow of time; so loving, so uncomplaining, so heroic, that if angels make not of mortal things, they may well look down in smiling admiration. But it is a melancholy and undeniable fact, that in millions of cases, that which challenges angelic admiration fails to be recognized or appreciated by the very men who are the incessant objects of these high, heroic virtues. In plain language, in the civilization of the latter half of the nineteenth century, a farmer's wife, as a too general rule, is a slave and a drudge; not of necessity, by design, but for want of that consideration, the very absence of which, in reference to the wife of a man's youth, is a crime. It is perhaps safe to say, that, on three farms out of four, the wife works harder, endures more, than any other on the place; more than the husband, more than the "farm-hand," more than the "hired help" of the kitchen. Many a farmer speaks to his wife, habitually, in terms so imperious, so impatient, so petulant, that if repeated to the scullion of the kitchen, would be met with an indignant and speedy departure, of if to the man-help, would be answered with a stroke from the shoulder, which would send the churl reeling a rod away!

In another way a farmer inadvertently increases the hardships of his wife; that is, by speaking of her or treating her disrespectfully in the presence of the servants of children. The man is naturally the ruling spirit of the household, and if he fails to show his wife, on all occasions, that tenderness, affection and respect which is her just due, it is instantly noted on the part of menials, and children too, and they very easily glide into the same vice and interpret it as an encouragement to slight her authority, to undervalue her judgment and to lower that high standard of respect which of right belongs to her. . . .

The indisputable truth is, that there is no other item of superior, or perhaps equal importance, in the happy and profitable management of any farm, great or small, than that every person on it should be made to understand that deference, and respect, and prompt and faithful obedience, should be paid, under all circumstances, to the wife, the mother, and the mistress. . . .

"Farmers' Wives Overtaxed," *New England Farmer* 15, no. 5 (May 1863), 141–142.

Louisa May Alcott, *Hospital Sketches* (1863)

New Englander and abolitionist author Louisa May Alcott spent six weeks as a nurse in a Georgetown, Virginia hospital tending to wounded Union soldiers. She had to leave nursing after contracting typhoid fever. She used her experiences at the Union Hotel Hospital as the basis for Hospital Sketches, *which was first published in serial form. She later gained fame for* Little Women (1868). *In the following excerpt from* Hospital Sketches, *Alcott details daily life in the hospital and the situations faced by nurses.*

In most Hospitals I hope there are [services by hospital death beds]; in ours, the men died, and were carried away, with as little ceremony as on a battle-field. The first event of this kind which I witnessed was so very brief, and bare of anything like reverence, sorrow, or pious consolation, that I heartily agreed with the bluntly expressed opinion of a Maine man lying next his comrade, who died with no visible help near him, but a compassionate woman and a tender-hearted Irishman, who dropped upon his knees, and told his beads, with Catholic fervor, for the good of his Protestant brother's parting soul. . . .

To me, the saddest sight I saw in that sad place, was the spectacle of a grey-haired father, sitting hour after hour by his son, dying from the poison of his wound. The old father, hale and hearty; the young son, past all help, though one could scarcely believe it; for the subtle fever, burning his strength away, flushed his cheeks with color, filled his eyes with lustre, and lent a mournful mockery of health to face and figure, making the poor lad comelier in death than in life. His bed was not in my ward; but I was often in and out, and for a day or two, the pair were much together, saying little, but looking much. The old man tried to busy himself with book or pen, that his presence might not be a burden; and once when he sat writing, to the anxious mother at home, doubtless, I saw the son's eyes fix upon his face, with a look of mingled resignation and regret, as if endeavoring to teach himself to say cheerfully the long good bye. And again, when the son slept, the father watched him as he had himself been watched; and though no feature of his grave countenance changed, the rough hand, smoothing the lock of hair upon the pillow, the bowed attitude of the grey head, were more pathetic than the loudest lamentations. The son died; and the father took home the pale relic of the life he gave, offering a little money to the nurse, as the only visible return it was in his power to make her; for though very grateful, he was poor. Of course, she did not take it, but found a richer compensation in the old man's earnest declaration:

"My boy couldn't have been better cared for if he'd been at home; and God will reward you for it, though I can't."

My own experiences of this sort began when my first man died. He had scarcely been removed, when his wife came in. Her eye went straight to the well-known bed; it was empty; and feeling, yet not believing the hard truth, she cried out, with a look I never shall forget:

"Why, where's Emanuel?"

I had never seen her before, did not know her relationship to the man whom I had only nursed for a day, and was about to tell her he was gone, when McGee, the tender-hearted Irishman before mentioned, brushed by me with a cheerful—"It's shifted to a better bed he is, Mrs. Connel. Come out, dear, till I show ye;" and, taking her gently by the arm, he led her to the matron, who broke the heavy tidings to the wife, and comforted the widow.

Another day, running up to my room for a breath of fresh air and a five minutes rest after a disagreeable task, I found a stout young woman sitting on my bed, wearing the miserable look which I had learned to know by that time. Seeing her, reminded me that I had heard of some one's dying in the night, and his sister's arriving in the morning. This must be she, I thought. I pitied her with all my heart. What could I say or do? Words always seem impertinent at such times; I did not know the man; the woman was neither interesting in herself nor graceful in her grief; yet, having known a sister's sorrow myself, I could have not leave her alone with her trouble in that strange place, without a word. So, feeling heart-sick, home-sick, and not knowing what else to do, I just put my arms about her, and began to cry in a very helpless but hearty way; for, as

I seldom indulge in this moist luxury, I like to enjoy it with all my might, when I do.

It so happened I could not have done a better thing; for, though not a word was spoken, each felt the other's sympathy; and, in the silence, our handkerchiefs were more eloquent than words. She soon sobbed herself quiet; and leaving her on my bed, I went back to work, feeling much refreshed by the shower, though I'd forgotten to rest, and had washed my face instead of my hands. I mention this successful experience as a receipt proved and approved, for the use of any nurse who may find herself called upon to minister to these wounds of the heart. They will find it more efficacious than cups of tea, smelling-bottles, psalms, or sermons; for a friendly touch and a companionable cry, unite the consolations of all the rest for womankind; and, if genuine, will be found a sovereign cure for the first sharp pang so many suffer in these heavy times.

I am gratified to find that my little Sergeant has found favor in several quarters, and gladly respond to sundry calls for news of him, though my personal knowledge ended five months ago. Next to my good John—I hope the grass is green above him, far away there in Virginia!—I placed the Sergeant on my list of worthy boys; and many jovial chat have I enjoyed with the merry-hearted lad, who had a fancy for fun, when his poor arm was dressed. While Dr. P. poked and strapped, I brushed the remains of the Sergeant's brown mane—shorn sorely against his will—and gossiped with all my might, the boy making odd faces, exclamations, and appeals, when nerves got the better of nonsense, as they sometimes did:

"I'd rather laugh than cry, when I must sing out anyhow, so just say that bit from Dickens again, please, and I'll stand it like a man." He did; for "Mrs. Cluppins," "Chadband," and "Sam Weller," always helped him through; thereby causing me to lay another offering of love and admiration on the shrine of the god of my idolatry, though he does wear too much jewelry and talk slang.

The Sergeant also originated, I believe, the fashion of calling his neighbors by their afflictions instead of their names; and I was rather taken aback by hearing them bandy remarks of this sort, with perfect good humor and much enjoyment of the new game.

"Hallo, old Fits is off again!" "How are you, Rheumatiz?" "Will you trade apples, Ribs?" "I say, Miss P. may I give Typus a drink of this?" "Look here, No Toes, lend us a stamp, there's a good feller," etc. He himself was christened "Baby B.," because he tended his arm on a little pillow, and called it his infant.

Louisa May Alcott, *Hospital Sketches* (Boston: James Redpath, 1863), 86–94.

Document: A Letter from the Mother of a Black Union Soldier to President Abraham Lincoln (1863)

In 1863, after President Abraham Lincoln issued the Emancipation Proclamation, the United States Army began organizing an African American regiment. Led by Colonel Robert Gould Shaw, the Fifty-fourth Massachusetts Infantry Regiment became the nation's first colored unit. Members of the Fifty-fourth soon faced problems specific to their race. First, although the Federal government promised recruits the same pay as white soldiers, this was not initially the case. In addition, the Confederate government vowed to treat any captured black soldiers as runaway slaves and send them back to slavery. Members of the regiment proved their capabilities as soldiers in the attack on South Carolina's Battery Wagner in July 1863. In the following letter, a mother asks the president to protect her son in the Fifty-fourth from Southern retaliation.

Buffalo [N.Y.] July 31 1863

Excellent Sir My good friend says I must write to you and she will send it. My son went in the 54th regiment. I am a colored woman and my son was strong and able as any to fight for his country and the colored people have as much to fight for as any. My father was a Slave and escaped from Louisiana before I was born morn forty years agone I have but poor edication but I never went to schol, but I know just as well as any what is right between man and man. Now I know it is right that a colored man

should go and fight for his country, and so ought to a white man. I know that a colored man ought to run no greater risques than a white, his pay is no greater his obligation to fight is the same. So why should not our enemies be compelled to treat him the same, Made to do it.

My son fought at Fort Wagoner but thank God he was not taken prisoner, as many were I thought of this thing before I let my boy go but then they said Mr. Lincoln will never let them sell our colored soldiers for slaves, if they do he will get them back quck he will rettallyate and stop it. Now Mr Lincoln dont you think you oght to stop this thing and make them do the same by the colored men they have lived in idleness all their lives on stolen labor and made savages of the colored people, but they now are so furious because they are proving themselves to be men, such as have come away and got some edication. It must not be so. You must put the rebels to work in State prisons to making shoes and things, if they sell our colored soldiers, till they let them all go. And give their wounded the same treatment. it would seem cruel, but their no other way, and a just man must do hard things sometimes, that shew him to be a great man. They tell me some do [sic] you will take back the Proclamation, don't do it. When you are dead and in Heaven, in a thousand years that action of yours will make the Angels sing your praises I know it. Ought one man to own another, law for or not, who made the law, surely the poor slave did not. so it is wicked, and a horrible Outrage, there is no sense in it, because a man has lived by robbing all his life and his father before him, should he complain because the stolen things found on him are taken. Robbing the colored people of their labor is but a small part of the robbery their souls are almost taken, they are made bruits of often. You know all about this

Will you see that the colored men fighting now, are fairly treated. You ought to do this, and do it at once, Not let the thing run along meet it quickly and manfully, and stop this, mean cowardly cruelty. We poor oppressed ones, appeal to you, and ask fair play. Yours for Christs sake

Hannah Johnson.

Hannah Johnson to Hon. Mr. Lincoln, July 31, 1863, J-17 l863, Letters Received, ser. 360, Colored Troops Division, Adjutant General's Office, Record Group 94 (Washington, D.C.: National Archives).

A Noble Enterprise: The Loyal Women's Petition to Get a Federal Amendment Passed to End Slavery (1863)

In 1863, Elizabeth Cady Stanton and Susan B. Anthony called for a constitutional amendment to end slavery in the United States. The amendment would extend the recent Emancipation Proclamation to include slaves living within the Union as well as preclude future slavery in the United States. The National Women's Loyal League organized the petition drive and called on local affiliates to gather a million signatures and support for the cause. The group disbanded with the passage of the Thirteenth Amendment. The following article from The Liberator *explains the rationale and importance of the movement and petition.*

A NOBLE ENTERPRISE

We have been remiss in not earlier calling the attention of our readers to the great work undertaken by the Women's Loyal League of New York, at their meeting last May. They then formed an organization, of which Mrs. E. C. Stanton is President, and Miss Susan B. Anthony Secretary, for the purpose, first, of procuring a *million signatures* to a petition to Congress, for the emancipation by law of all the slaves in the country. This petition, drawn up by Hon. Robert Dale Owen, and already signed by thousands of men and women in all parts of the land, is printed to-day at the head of our columns, and will remain there until the meeting of Congress, for the convenience of our readers who may wish to sign or circulate it. It is a petition that few of the loyal people of the North can refuse to sign; for if it be objected that Congress has no power to pass such an act, and if this objection be well founded (which we deny,) then of course "the earliest practicable day" will be after such changes have been made in the Constitution as will allow such a law to be passed.

Certainly, there can be few *loyal* men in the North, who do not earnestly pray for the emancipa-

tion of the slaves at the "earliest practicable day," since Reverdy Johnson, the Maryland lawyer, has just declared that to be his prayer. This petition, then, if Congress decide the matter to be out of its jurisdiction, will serve as an indication of the popular wish for such action in other ways as shall bring about the same result. Therefore all who honestly prefer Freedom to Slavery can and ought to sign it.

Miss Anthony, the efficient Secretary of the League, which is extending itself over the whole North and West, is now in Boston, making arrangements for the circulation of the petition throughout New England, where, as yet, few signatures have been procured. We commend her and her enterprise to the assistance of our readers, and of all friends of the Union and of Freedom. It will be seen by the following pledge, adopted by the League last May, how broad is the basis of principles on which it is proposed to operate:—

We, the Undersigned, Women of the United States, agree to become members of the Women's Loyal National League; hereby pledging our most earnest influence in support of the Government, in its prosecution of the War for Freedom, and for the restoration of the National Unity.

God speed these patriotic women in their labor of love!—*Commonwealth*

THE LOYAL WOMEN'S PETITION

Subscription papers were sometime since sent to several ladies in this city, with the request that they would interest themselves in procuring signatures. We do not know what has been done in the matter, but presume not much, as we have heard of no plan of systematic action being adopted; and without some systematic method, such a work cannot be properly accomplished.

Mr. Willits, of Mercer County, has lately undertaken to set the ball in motion in this and adjoining counties, and is devoting himself to the cause. In some places, he calls public meetings, at which the people are stirred up to the importance of the subject, and committees appointed to canvass towns and neighborhoods for the signatures of all women who wish to hasten the day of universal emancipation for our slavery-cursed country—and there are few women who do not. In other places, he finds individuals who volunteer to go out independently, and canvass for signatures.

There is another petition, similar to the foregoing, for subscription by men. They will generally be circulated together, and it is hoped the men will not fall behind the women in the number of their signatures, but that a full million at least of them will be sent into Congress, to plead for the regeneration of our country.

This is the most important petition that was ever circulated for signatures, and we hope the means will be adopted to insure its presentation to every woman in the North. We have no doubt but a million of names, and more, will be obtained if proper exertions are made; and we have very little doubt but Congress will pass the act thus petitioned for before its adjournment next summer. We hope Mr. Willits will find ready co-operators here, and wherever he goes in the good work of making arrangements for the circulation of the petition.—*Galesburg Free Democrat*

"A Noble Enterprise," *The Liberator* 33, no. 42 (October 16, 1863): 167.

Augusta Jane Evans, *Macaria; Or, Altars of Sacrifice* (1864)

Southern author Augusta Jane Evans wrote Macaria; Or, Altars of Sacrifice *while nursing Confederate soldiers at a makeshift hospital. The novel praised Southern soldiers and the Southern cause, and Evans dedicated it to Confederate soldiers' sacrifices. In addition, the novel offered female readers, barred from the battlefield by virtue of their sex, ways to support their nation. Macaria's heroine, Irene Huntingdon, sacrifices her luxurious antebellum lifestyle to aid the Confederacy in any way possible. In the following excerpt, she explains the importance of women's sacrifice to the success of the Confederacy.*

TO THE
ARMY OF THE SOUTHERN CONFEDERACY,
WHO HAVE DELIVERED THE SOUTH FROM
    DESPOTISM, AND WHO HAVE WON FOR

GENERATIONS YET UNBORN THE PRECIOUS
    GUERDON OF
CONSTITUTIONAL REPUBLICAN LIBERTY:

TO THIS VAST LEGION OF HONOR,
WHETHER LIMPING ON CRUTCHES THROUGH
THE LAND THEY HAVE SAVED AND IMMORTALIZED,
OR SURVIVING UNINJURED TO SHARE THE
    BLESSINGS THEIR
UNEXAMPLED HEROISM BOUGHT, OR SLEEPING
    DREAMLESSLY IN NAMELESS
MARTYR-GRAVES ON HALLOWED BATTLE-FIELDS
    WHOSE
HISTORIC MEMORY SHALL PERISH ONLY WITH
THE REMNANTS OF OUR LANGUAGE,
THESE PAGES ARE
GRATEFULLY AND REVERENTLY DEDICATED
BY ONE WHO, ALTHOUGH DEBARRED FROM THE
DANGERS AND DEATHLESS GLORY OF THE
    "TENTED FIELD,"
WOULD FAIN OFFER A WOMAN'S INADEQUATE
    TRIBUTE TO THE NOBLE
PATRIOTISM AND SUBLIME SELF-ABNEGATION OF HER
DEAR AND DEVOTED COUNTRYMEN.

. . .

Electra had finished the bandages and was walking slowly before the windows, and, without looking up from the lint, which she was tying into small packages, Irene answered:

"The safeguards will be found in the mothers, wives, and sisters of our land."

"Ah! but their hands are tied; and they walk but a short, narrow path, from hearthstone to threshold, and back again. They have, I know, every inclination to exert a restraining influence, but no power to utilize it. Sometimes I almost fear that the fabled Norse *Ragnarök* is darkening over this continent. The monsters, Midgard Serpent, Fenris, and all, have certainly been unloosed at the North."

"Electra, though we are very properly debarred from the 'tented field,' I have entire confidence that the cause of our country may be advanced, and its good promoted, through the agency of its daughters; for, out of the dim historic past come words of encouragement. Have you forgotten that, when

Sparta forsook the stern and sublime simplicity of her ancient manners, King Agis found himself unable to accomplish his scheme of redeeming his degenerate country from avarice and corruption, until the ladies of Sparta gave their consent and support to the plan of reform? Southern women have no desire to usurp legislative reins; their appropriate work consists in moulding the manners and morals of the nation; in checking the wild excesses of fashionable life, and the dangerous spirit of extravagance; of reckless expenditure in dress, furniture, and equipage, which threatened ruinous results before the declaration of hostilities. Noble wives, who properly appreciate the responsibility of their position, should sternly rebuke and frown down the disgraceful idea, which seems to be gaining ground and favor in our cities, that married women may, with impunity, seek attentions and admiration abroad. Married belles and married beaux are not harmless, nor should they be tolerated in really good society. Women who so far forget their duties to their homes and husbands, and the respect due to public opinion, as to habitually seek for happiness in the mad whirl of so-called fashionable life, ignoring household obligations, should be driven from well-bred, refined circles, to hide their degradation at the firesides they have disgraced. That wives should constantly endeavor to cultivate social graces and render themselves as fascinating as possible, I hold their sacred duty; but beauty should be preserved, and accomplishments perfected, to bind their husband's hearts more closely, to make their homes attractive, instead of being constantly paraded before the world for the unholy purpose of securing the attentions and adulation of other gentlemen. I do not desire to see married women recluses; on the contrary, I believe that society has imperative claims upon them, which should be promptly met and faithfully and gracefully discharged. But those degraded wives, who are never seen with their husbands when they can avoid it—who are never happy unless riding or walking with strangers, or receiving their attentions at theatres, concerts, or parties—are a disgrace to the nation which they are gradually demoralizing and corrupting. From the influence of these few deluded weak libels on our sex may God preserve our age and country! They are utterly unworthy the noble work which calls loudly to every true Southern woman. Statesmen are trained up around the mother's armchair, and she can imbue the boy with lofty sentiments, and inspire him with aims which, years hence, shall lead him in congressional halls to adhere to principles, to advance the Truth—though, thereby, votes for the next election fall away, like stricken leaves in autumn. What time has the married belle for this holy hearthstone mission? The conscientious, devoted, and patriotic Christian women of a nation are the safeguards of its liberties and purity."

Augusta Jane Evans, *Macaria; Or, Altars of Sacrifice* (Richmond, VA: West & Johnson, 1864), 163.

Special Field Orders, Number 67 for the Evacuation of Atlanta, Georgia (1864)

Before his famous March to the Sea, Union General William Tecumseh Sherman laid siege to and then occupied Atlanta, Georgia. Upon taking control of the city, Sherman ordered the evacuation of Atlanta's civilians—men, women, and children. He also confiscated, on behalf of the Union army, the valuable raw materials that were stored there. These decisions turned hundreds of families into refugees and set the stage for the hard war policies that Sherman used on his march through Georgia and the Carolinas. Issued on September 8, 1864, Special Field Orders, Number 67 detailed Sherman's decision as a wartime necessity. Sherman and his men set fire to buildings in Atlanta before they left the city in November 1864.

SPECIAL FIELD ORDERS, NO. 67
HDQRS. MIL. DIV. OF THE MISSISSIPPI,

In the Field, Atlanta, Ga.
September 8, 1864.

I. The City of Atlanta, being exclusively required for warlike purposes, will at once be vacated by all except the armies of the United States and such civilian employees as may be retained by the proper departments of government.

II. The chief quartermaster, Colonel Easton, will at once take possession of buildings of all kinds, and of all staple articles, such as cotton, tobacco, &c.,

and will make such disposition of them as is required by existing regulations, or such orders as he may receive from time to time from the proper authorities.

III. The chief engineer will promptly reconnoiter the city and suburbs, and indicate the sites needed for the permanent defense of the place, together with any houses, sheds, or shanties that stand in his way, that they may be set apart for destruction. Colonel Easton will then, on consultation with the proper officers of the ordnance, quartermaster, commissary, medical, and railroad departments, set aside such buildings and lots of ground as will be needed for them, and have them suitably marked and set apart. He will then, on consultation with Generals Thomas and Slocum, set apart such as may be necessary to the proper administration of the military duties of the Department of the Cumberland and of the post of Atlanta, and all buildings and materials not thus embraced will be held subject to the use of the Government as may hereafter arise, according to the just rules of the quartermaster's department.

IV. No general, staff, or other officers, or any soldier will on any pretense occupy any house or shanty, unless it be embraced in the limits assigned as the camp of the troops to which such general or staff belongs, but the chief quartermaster may allow the troops to use boards, shingles, or materials of buildings, barns, sheds, warehouses, and shanties, not needed by the proper departments of government, to be used in the reconstruction of such shanties and bivouacs as the troops and officers serving with them require, and he will also provide as early as practicable the proper allowance of tents for the use of the officers and men in their encampments.

V. In proper time just arrangements will be made for the supply to the troops of all articles they may need over and above the clothing, provisions, &c., furnished by Government, and on no pretense whatever will traders, manufacturers, or sutlers be allowed to settle in the limits of fortified places, and if these manage to come in spite of this notice, the quartermaster will seize their stores and appreciate them to the use of the troops, and deliver the par-

ties or other unauthorized citizens who thus place their individual interests above that of the United States, in the hands of some provost-marshal, to be put to labor on the forts or conscripted into one of the regiments or batteries already in service.

VI. The same general principles will apply to all military posts south of Chattanooga.

By order of Major General W. T. Sherman:
L. M. DAYTON,

Special Field Orders No. 67, *The War of the Rebellion: A Compilation of the Official Records of the Union and Confederate Armies*, Series 1, Vol. 38, Part 5 (Washington, DC: U.S. Government Printing Office, 1880–1901), 837–838.

Charlotte Forten, "Life on the Sea Islands" (1864)

Charlotte Forten became the first African American to teach the freed slaves in the South Carolina Sea Islands. Born free in Philadelphia, Pennsylvania, Forten began her teaching career in Salem, Massachusetts. Her family's long abolitionist roots inspired her to do something to aid the Union cause during the Civil War. Beginning in 1862, she spent two years on St. Helena teaching the freed slaves, in what became known as the Port Royal Experiment. Forten's essays about her experiences there offered Northern readers insight into the Port Royal Experiment. They were published in The Atlantic Monthly *in 1864.*

The first day at school was rather trying. Most of my children were very small, and consequently restless. Some were too young to learn the alphabet. These little ones were brought to school because the older children—in whose care their parents leave them while at work—could not come without them. We were therefore willing to have them come, although they seemed to have discovered the secret of perpetual motion, and tried one's patience sadly. But after some days of positive, though not severe treatment, order was brought out of chaos, and I found but little difficulty in managing and quieting the tiniest and most restless spirits. I never before saw children so eager to learn, although I had had several years' experience in New England schools. Coming to school is a constant delight and recreation to them. They come here as other children go to play. The older ones, during the summer, work in the fields from early morning until eleven or twelve o'clock, and then come into school, after their hard toil in the hot sun, as bright and as anxious to learn as ever.

Of course there are some stupid ones, but these are the minority. The majority learn with wonderful rapidity. Many of the grown people are desirous of learning to read. It is wonderful how a people who have been so long crushed to the earth, so imbruted as these have been,—and they are said to be among the most degraded negroes of the South,—can have so great a desire for knowledge, and such a capability for attaining it. One cannot believe that the haughty Anglo Saxon race, after centuries of such an experience as these people have had, would be very much superior to them. And one's indignation increases against those who, North as well as South, taunt the colored race with inferiority while they themselves use every means in their power to crush and degrade them, denying them every right and privilege, closing against them every avenue of elevation and improvement. Were they, under such circumstances, intellectual and refined, they would certainly be vastly superior to any other race that ever existed.

After the lessons, we used to talk freely to the children, often giving them slight sketches of some of the great and good men. Before teaching them the "John Brown" song, which they learned to sing with great spirit, Miss T. told them the story of the brave old man who had died for them. I told them about Toussaint, thinking it well they should know what one of their own color had done for his race. They listened attentively, and seemed to understand. We found it rather hard to keep their attention in school. It is not strange, as they have been so entirely unused to intellectual concentration. It is necessary to interest them every moment, in order to keep their thoughts from wandering. Teaching here is consequently far more fatiguing than at the North. In the church, we had of course but one room in which to hear all the children; and to make

one's self heard, when there were often as many as a hundred and forty reciting at once, it was necessary to tax the lungs very severely.

My walk to school, of about a mile, was part of the way through a road lined with trees,—on one side stately pines, on the other noble live-oaks, hung with moss and canopied with vines. The ground was carpeted with brown, fragrant pine-leaves; and as I passed through in the morning, the woods were enlivened by the delicious songs of mocking-birds, which abound here, making one realize the truthful felicity of the description in "Evangeline,"—

"The mocking-bird, wildest of singers, Shook from his little throat such floods of delirious music

That the whole air and the woods and the waves seemed silent to listen."

The hedges were all aglow with the brilliant scarlet berries of the cassena, and on some of the oaks we observed the mistletoe, laden with its pure white, pearl-like berries. Out of the woods the roads are generally bad, and we found it hard work plodding through the deep sand.

Charlotte Forten, "Life on the Sea Islands," *The Atlantic Monthly* 13 (May 1864): 587–596.

The Capture and Rescue of Union Spy Pauline Cushman (1864)

An actress by trade, Pauline Cushman served as a Union spy during the Civil War. She posed as a Confederate sympathizer and went behind enemy lines in Louisville, Kentucky, to determine troop movements and how Southerners were smuggling medical supplies. Cushman was caught in 1863 and sentenced in a court-martial to hang. Before the Confederates could mete out their punishment, Cushman escaped. The following article from the New York Times *detailed some of Cushman's exploits and helped her reputation for bravery grow in the postwar years.*

Among the women of America who have made themselves famous since the opening of the rebellion, few have suffered more or rendered more service to the Federal cause than Miss Maj. PAULINE CUSHMAN, the female scout and spy.

At the commencement of hostilities she resided in Cleveland, Ohio, and was quite well known as a clever actress.

From Cleveland she went to Louisville, where she had an engagement in Wood's Theatre. Here, by her intimacy with certain rebel officers, she incurred the suspicion of being a rebel, and was arrested by Federal authorities. She indignantly denied that she was a rebel, although born at the South, and having a brother in a rebel Mississippi regiment.

In order to test the love for the old flag, she was asked if she would enter the secret service of the Government. She readily consented, and was at once employed to carry letters between Louisville and Nashville. She was subsequently employed by Gen. ROSECRANS, and was for many months with the Army of the Cumberland. She visited the rebel lines time after time, and was thoroughly acquainted with all the country and roads in Tennessee, Northern Georgia, Alabama and Mississippi, in which sections she rendered our armies invaluable service. She was twice suspected of being a spy, and taken prisoner, but managed to escape.

At last, however, she was not so fortunate. After our forces had captured Nashville, Maj. CUSHMAN made a scout towards Shelbyville to obtain information on the strength and position of the enemy, and while returning to Nashville, was captured on the Hardin pike, eleven miles from the latter city. She was placed on a horse, and in charge of two scouts, was being taken to Spring Hill, the headquarters of FORREST.

While on the way to this place, she feigned sickness, and said she could not travel any further without falling from her horse. Her captors stopped at a house on the roadside, when it was ascertained that a Federal scouting party had passed the place an hour before. Knowing that her guards had important papers for Gen. BRAGG, the quick-witted spy seized the fact and schemed to use it to her advantage.

Seeing an old negro, who appeared to commiserate her unfortunate plight, she watched her opportunity and placed $10 in Tennessee money in his hand, saying: "run up the road, Uncle, and come back in a few minutes, telling us that four hundred Federals are coming down the street." The faithful negro obeyed the order literally, and soon came back in the greatest excitement, telling the story. The two "rebs" told him he lied. The old colored man got down on his knees, saying: "Massa, dey's cumin, sure nuff; de Lord help us, dey is cumin."

The scouts at this believed his story, mounted their horses, and "skedaddled" for the woods. Miss CUSHMAN, seizing a pistol belonging to a wounded solider in the house, also mounted her horse and fled towards Franklin. She travelled through the rain, and, after nightfall, lost her way. Soon came the challenge of a picket, "Who comes there?" Thinking she had reached the rebel line, she said: "A friend of JEFF. DAVIS." "All right," was the reply, "advance and give the countersign."

She presented the countersign in the shape of a canteen of whisky. She passed five pickets in this way, but the sixth and last was obdurate. She pleaded that she was going to see a sick uncle in Franklin, but the sentry couldn't see it. Sick and disheartened, she turned back. Seeing a light at a farmhouse, she sought shelter. An old man received her kindly, showed her to a room, and said he would awake her at an early hour in the morning, and show her the road to Franklin.

A loud knock awoke her in the morning from her Lethean slumbers, and upon arousing she found her horse saddled and the two guards from whom she had escaped the previous afternoon. She was taken to the headquarters of FORREST and he sent her, after a critical examination, to Gen. BRAGG. Nothing could be found against her until a secesh woman stole her garters, under the inner sole of which were found important documents which clearly proved her to be a spy.

She was tried and condemned to be executed as a spy, but being sick, her execution was postponed. She finally, after lying in prison three months, sent for Gen. BRAGG, and asked him if he had no mercy. She received from him the comforting assurance that he should make an example of her, and that he should hang her as soon as she got well enough to be hung decently.

While in this state of suspense, the grand army of ROSECRANS commenced its forward movement, and one fine day the rebel town where she wos [sic] imprisoned was surprised and captured, and the heroine of this tale was, to her great joy, released. She is now in this city visiting friends, having arrived at the Biddle House one day last week. — *Detroit Tribune, Tuesday.*

New York Times (May 28, 1864): 9.

Letter to the Editor from "Many Wives and Mothers of Charleston" (1865)

As Union General William Tecumseh Sherman waged hard war on the civilians of Georgia, many residents of Charleston, South Carolina discussed evacuating women and children from the city. Sherman's men foraged their way across the lower South, destroying crops, homes, livestock, and railroad lines. The Confederate army seemed powerless to stop the march, and many rightfully feared that Sherman would target Charleston for destruction. In the following letter to the editor of the Charleston Mercury, "Many Wives and Mothers of Charleston" rejected this as an appropriate course of action and continued to declare their Confederate patriotism.

Many Wives and Mothers of Charleston to the Editor of the *Charleston Mercury*

We beg through your columns to address the General Commanding South Carolina, and the Governor of the State. We, women of Charleston, not enthusiastic girls, but women whose hair has whitened through the anguish of this awful war, whose husbands, sons, brothers, have died for South Carolina and Charleston, entreat to be heard. We would say that we have listened with grief and horror inexpressible to the hints of abandoning to our foes, without a struggle, the city of our love. We urge by all our titles to regard; we implore, as the greatest boon, fight for Charleston! At every point, fight for every inch, and if our men must die, let them die amid the blazing ruins of our homes; their souls rising upwards on the flames which save our city from the pollution of our enemy.

Send out the women and children yet in the city. Thousands of Charleston women scattered through the land will share with them their all. They shall not starve. But let there be no excuse for deserting the sacred homes of us and our ancestors. What! the four years of proud defence to be rendered nugatory? The battle flag of Sumter to veil its proud defiance without a cannon shot? The churches where we heard the burial services of our dead who died around our walls, to ring with the triumphant Te Deums of the invaders? Oh, men! it is impossible! By the rain of blood and tears which has fallen upon our hearts, never quenching, but brightening the flame of patriotism there, do not utterly crush those true hearts by this blow.

We *know*, each of us, *our* husbands, *our* brothers, *our* sons, are not shrinking now. They are chafing at this fatal policy of retreat. They who have won their fame from the Savannah River to Charleston Harbor, they ask but leave to fight as they have fought. Do you but lead them on, not keep them back. We call upon the Commanding General to stand by us, to fight with us, heart and soul. We call upon our Governor, sworn to defend Carolina and her honor, to defend it here. Let the mantle of the Dictator fall upon him, and if Charleston, defended to the hour, must then fall, let the Governor and her homes—to sound of the guns of our forts, as they send out their last defiance to the baffled foe.

Charleston Mercury (January 24, 1865).

Reverend Hatfield Reminds Women of their Christian Duty (1865)

The enlistment of millions of men in the Union and Confederate armies created a moral crisis for many religious leaders. American men were forced to live without the civilizing influences of women, and the weighty responsibilities of the homefront were placed in the hands of women. In the following sermon, Reverend Edwin F. Hatfield of New York calls on his Christian sisters to ensure that the church will continue its moral and religious functions during the war.

Abundant, as are always the opportunities for being of service in the cause of her Redeemer, woman is called upon, with far more earnestness, and much more constantly, to work for her Saviour in time of war; especially, such a war as is now raging over the breadth of this great land. The necessities of the country demand that the time, attention, and services of nearly a million of the most active, enterprising and laborious of her sons should be diverted from the peaceful pursuits and occupations in which they are ordinarily employed, and devoted, almost or quite exclusively to the work of suppressing this gigantic rebellion. This vast number of men must, then, be separated for one, two, or three years, as the case may be, from their homes, the social circles in which they are accustomed to move, and the Christian congregations to which they have been attached. Old associations, in consequence, are broken up; new combinations, commercially and socially, are demanded; other than the ordinary agencies, for the promotion of many of the educations and reformatory schemes of the age are called for; and any of our dearest and most cherished institutions of benevolence are put into serious jeopardy. The exigencies of the occasion require, to some extent, a re-adjustment of our plans and calculations in almost all the departments of business, and of social, home and religious life.

Two evils of great magnitude are to result from this social revolution, and are to be met with energy, and, if possible, to be overcome. The one necessarily results from the segregation of large bodies of men by themselves, afar from the mollifying refining, restraining, and sanctifying influences of the home, the family, and the church. Universal experience has conclusively demonstrated the wisdom of that providential arrangement, by which the sexes are do distributed in society, as to exert a constant influence over each other, stimulating, restraining, and all-pervading. Break up this arrangement, and separate the sexes entirely from each other, and the invariable tendency is to a greater laxity in manners and morals, to deterioration and demoralization . . .

The other evil to which I would refer, resulting from this great revolution, is the withdrawal of such an immense number of the most vigorous, active and enterprising men from posts of usefulness, from positions of great importance, and from associations of the most sacred character at home. The husband disappears from the quiet abode, where the fond wife was wont to meet and greet him, on his daily return from labor and business, and where she looked to him for counsel and support. The father is taken from his children, and separated from them for months and years, at a period, when most they need his instructions and his paternal care. A sad and wearisome change comes over the loved home, where the son and brother gave such a charm to the domestic sanctuary. What shall fill the void—who make good the terrible privation? . . .

It devolves on you, my Christian sisters, to make good, to the extent of your abilities, the deficiencies occasioned by the absence of your brothers, and their devotion to the cause of their suffering country. Our churches must not be suffered to languish for want of appropriate laborers. Women labored with Paul in the gospel, as they have with others of Christ's ministers in every age. None have labored so much as they. But for them, their prayers, their endeavors, their self-denying and unwearied services in the cause of Christ, the kingdom of God would have advanced but slowly on the earth. They are now the most reliable and the most efficient helpers in many of our Churches. But for them what would become of our mission and Sunday-schools, our prayer meetings and our tract visitations? . . . All honor to the sex! Let it be known what the church owes to woman. . . .

Here is something that you, my Christian sisters, can do for your Saviour. You are wanted at the prayer meeting. Your presence there cannot be dispensed with. Your brothers are away, and you must take their place. You cannot have their attendance as formerly, but you can come alone. . . .

So, too, you can do much for your Saviour, by your prompt and faithful attendance on the services of the sanctuary every Sabbath-day. Never were you more needed there. Never could you absent yourselves with so little reason. . . .

You could be of service, also, in the Sunday-school and mission-school . . .

Our churches, it is evident, while sending so many of their sons to the Army and Navy, so many to whom they have been wont to look for the prosecution of their work of evangelization at home and abroad, and from whom they have received their main support, must now, more than ever, depend on the reserve force of their sisters and daughters; and, we trust, will not depend in vain. You, my sister, must not be deaf to the call, not backward to follow where God leads. . . .

Edwin F. Hatfield. "Woman's Work in Time of War," *The National Preacher and Village Pulpit* 39, no. 3 (March 1865): 70-76.

"The Unconquered Class" in Georgia (1865)

When the military struggle ended, many Southerners were less than eager to return to the Union or accept the changes imposed on their lives. Many white Southerners resisted Reconstruction policies, the presence of Union soldiers, and efforts by African Americans to define what their freedom would mean. Women participated as part of this resistance, often in attempts to prevent freedwomen from enjoying their new liberties. The Ku Klux Klan and other militant groups formed to "redeem" the south and prevent significant changes in their society. As the following newspaper article, "The Unconquered Class," from The Liberator *demonstrates, many white women tried to prevent African American women from enjoying even the most basic freedoms.*

General Carl Schurz, who, at the request of President Johnson, is making an extended tour of observation at the South, has send to the Boston *Daily Advertiser* a series of interesting letters, from the last of which, dated Savannah, July 31, we make the following extract.

"But there is another class of people here, mostly younger men, who are still in the swearing mood. You can overhear their conversations as you pass them on the streets, or even sitting near them on the stoop of the hotel. They are not conquered, but only 'overpowered.' They are only smothered for a time. They want to fight the war over again, and they are sure in five years we are going to have a war bigger than any we have seen yet. They are impatient to get rid of 'this d—d military despotism.' They will show us what stuff Southern men are made of. They will send their own men to Con-

gress, and show us that we cannot violate the Constitution with impunity. They have a rope ready for this or that Union man, when the Yankee bayonets are gone. They will show the Yankee interlopers, who have settled down here to live upon their subsistence, the way home. They will deal largely in tar and feathers. . . . Now, there may be much of the old Southern braggadocio in this, and I do not believe that such men will again resort to open insurrection. But they will practice private vengeance whenever they can do it with impunity, and I have heard sober-minded Union men express their apprehension of it. This spirit is certainly no evidence of true loyalty. . . ."

Unfortunately, this spirit receives much encouragement from the fair sex. We have heard so much of the bitter resentment of the Southern ladies that the tale becomes stale by frequent repetition. But when inquiring into the feelings of the people, this element must not be omitted. There are certainly a good many sensible women in the South who have arrived at a just appreciation of the circumstances with which they are surrounded. But there is a large number of Southern women who are vindictive and defiant as ever, and whose temper does not permit them to lay their tongue under any restraint. You can see them in every hotel, and they will treat you to the most ridiculous exhibitions whenever an occasion offers. A day or two ago, a Union officer, yielding to an impulse of politeness, handed a dish of pickles to a Southern lady at the dinner-table of a hotel in this city. A look of unspeakable scorn and indignation met him. "So you think," said the lady, "a Southern lady will take a dish of pickles from a hand that is dripping with the blood of her countrymen!" It is remarkable upon what trifling materials this female wrath is feeding and growing fat. In a certain district in South Carolina, the ladies were some time ago, and perhaps are now, dreadfully exercised about the veil question. You may ask me what the veil question is. Formerly—under the old order of things—negro women were not permitted to wear veils. This is an outrage which must not be permitted to. The white ladies of that neighborhood agree in being indignant beyond measure.

Some of them declare that whenever they meet a colored woman wearing a veil, they will tear the veil from her face. Others, mindful of the consequences which such an act of violence might draw after it under this same new order of things, declare their resolve never to wear veils themselves as long as colored women wear them. That is the veil question, and this is the way it stands at present.

Such things may seem trifling and ridiculous. But it is a well-known fact that a silly woman is sometimes able to exercise a powerful influence over a man not half as silly; and the class of "unconquered" above described is undoubtedly in a great measure composed of individuals that are apt to be influenced by silly women. It has frequently been said that, had it not been for the spirit of Southern women, the rebellion would have broken down long ago, and there is, no doubt, a grain of truth in it. The same spirit of the female part of the community, although undoubtedly at present much less powerful in a quantitative sense, is now contributing to keep those bitter feelings alive, which, as long as kept under a sufficient control, may be harmless, and gradually die away; but which, if prematurely relieved of that control, may lead to serious conflicts.

The Liberator 35, no. 36 (September 8, 1865): 144.

Clara Barton Becomes a Wartime Nurse

Clara Barton provided medical assistance at some of the bloodiest battles of the Civil War. She tended to the wounded at the Second Bull Run, Antietam, Fredericksburg, the Wilderness, Spotsylvania, Petersburg, and elsewhere. Although she did not arrive at the battlefield as an official nurse or as a member of an organization, she and other female nurses transformed the nature of nursing in the United States. Before the war, nursing was widely considered menial labor, and it was exclusively performed by men. When the war ended, nursing was considered an honorable profession in which women were widely accepted. Barton later founded and became the first president of the American Red Cross. In the following description, Barton explains her original decision to dedicate herself to wounded soldiers.

I was strong and thought I might go to the rescue of the men who fell. The first regiment of troops, the old 6th Mass. that fought its way through Baltimore, brought my playmates and neighbors, the partakers of my childhood; the brigades of New Jersey brought scores of my brave boys, the same solid phalanx; and the strongest legions from old Herkimer brought the associates of my seminary days. They formed and crowded around me. What could I do but go with them, or work for them and my country? The patriot blood of my father was warm in my veins. The country which he had fought for, I might at least work for, and I had offered my service to the government in the capacity of a double clerkship at twice $1400 a year, upon discharge of two disloyal clerks from its employ,—the salary never to be given to me, but to be turned back into the U.S. Treasury then poor to beggary, with no currency, no credit. But there was no law for this, and it could not be done and I would not draw salary from our government in such peril, so I resigned and went into direct service of the sick and wounded troops wherever found.

But I struggled long and hard with my sense of propriety with the appalling fact that I was only a woman whispering in one ear, and thundering in the other the groans of suffering men dying like dogs—unfed and unsheltered, for the life of every institution which had protected and educated me!

I said that I struggled with my sense of propriety and I say it with humiliation and shame. I am ashamed that I thought of such a thing.

Percy H. Epler, *The Life of Clara Barton* (New York: Macmillan, 1915), 31-32.

Susie King Taylor Recalls Her Time as a Camp Follower

Many women joined their husbands when they left their homes to serve in the Union and Confederate armies. Susie King Taylor was an African American camp follower whose husband served in the Thirty-third Colored Regiment. She and her husband had escaped from slavery earlier in the war by taking refuge among Union soldiers. When her husband enlisted, Taylor became a laundress for the company. She performed many tasks, including tending to the wounded, cleaning guns, cooking food, and cleaning clothes. In the following reminiscence, she details her life in the Union army.

FORT WAGNER being only a mile from our camp, I went there two or three times a week, and would go up on the ramparts to watch the gunners send their shells into Charleston (which they did every fifteen minutes), and had a full view of the city from that point. Outside of the fort were many skulls lying about; I have often moved them one side out of the path. The comrades and I would have quite a debate as to which side the men fought on. Some thought they were the skulls of our boys; others thought they were the enemy's; but as there was no definite way to know, it was never decided which could lay claim to them. They were a gruesome sight, those fleshless heads and grinning jaws, but by this time I had become accustomed to worse things and did not feel as I might have earlier in my camp life.

It seems strange how our aversion to seeing suffering is overcome in war,— how we are able to see the most sickening sights, such as men with their limbs blown off and mangled by the deadly shells, without a shudder; and instead of turning away, how we hurry to assist in alleviating their pain, bind up their wounds, and press the cool water to their parched lips, with feelings only of sympathy and pity.

About the first of June, 1864, the regiment was ordered to Folly Island, staying there until the latter part of the month, when it was ordered to Morris Island. We landed on Morris Island between June and July, 1864. This island was a narrow strip of sandy soil, nothing growing on it but a few bushes and shrubs. The camp was one mile from the boat landing, called Pawnell Landing, and the landing one mile from Fort Wagner.

Colonel Higginson had left us in May of this year, on account of wounds received at Edisto. All the men were sorry to lose him. They did not want him to go, they loved him so. He was kind and devoted to his men, thoughtful for their comfort, and we missed his genial presence from the camp.

The regiment under Colonel Trowbridge did garrison duty, but they had troublesome times from Fort Gregg, on James Island, for the rebels would throw a shell over on our island every now and then.

Finally orders were received for the boys to prepare to take Fort Gregg, each man to take 150 rounds of cartridges, canteens of water, hard-tack, and salt beef. This order was sent three days prior to starting, to allow them to be in readiness. I helped as many as I could to pack haversacks and cartridge boxes.

The fourth day, about five o'clock in the afternoon, the call was sounded, and I heard the first sergeant say, "Fall in, boys, fall in," and they were not long obeying the command. Each company marched out of its street, in front of their colonel's headquarters, where they rested for half an hour, as it was not dark enough, and they did not want the enemy to have a chance to spy their movements. At the end of this time the line was formed with the 103d New York (white) in the rear, and off they started, eager to get to work. It was quite dark by the time they reached Pawnell Landing. I have never forgotten the good-bys of that day, as they left camp. Colonel Trowbridge said to me as he left, "Good-by, Mrs. King, take care of yourself if you don't see us again." I went with them as far as the landing, and watched them until they got out of sight, and then I returned to the camp. There was no one at camp but those left on picket and a few disabled soldiers, and one woman, a friend of mine, Mary Shaw, and it was lonesome and sad, now that the boys were gone, some never to return.

Mary Shaw shared my tent that night, and we went to bed, but not to sleep, for the fleas nearly ate us alive. We caught a few, but it did seem, now that the men were gone, that every flea in camp had located my tent, and caused us to vacate. Sleep being out of the question, we sat up the remainder of the night.

About four o'clock, July 2, the charge was made. The firing could be plainly heard in camp. I hastened down to the landing and remained there until eight o'clock that morning. When the wounded arrived, or rather began to arrive, the first one brought in was Samuel Anderson of our company. He was badly wounded. Then others of our boys, some with their legs off, arm gone, foot off, and wounds of all kinds imaginable. They had to wade through creeks and marshes, as they were discovered by the enemy and shelled very badly. A number of the men were lost, some got fastened in the mud and had to cut off the legs of their pants, to free themselves. The 103d New York suffered the most, as their men were very badly wounded.

My work now began. I gave my assistance to try to alleviate their sufferings. I asked the doctor at the hospital what I could get for them to eat. They wanted soup, but that I could not get; but I had a few cans of condensed milk and some turtle eggs, so I thought I would try to make some custard. I had doubts as to my success, for cooking with turtle eggs was something new to me, but the adage has it, "Nothing ventured, nothing done," so I made a venture and the result was a very delicious custard. This I carried to the men, who enjoyed it very much. My services were given at all times for the comfort of these men. I was on hand to assist whenever needed. I was enrolled as company laundress, but I did very little of it, because I was always busy doing other things through camp, and was employed all the time doing something for the officers and comrades.

Susie King Taylor, *Reminiscences of My Life in Camp with the 33rd United States Colored Troops* (Boston: Self-published, 1902), 31–35.

Mary Livermore Remembers the Sanitary Commission

Mary Livermore served as an associate manager of the Northwestern Branch of the United States Sanitary Commission. She raised money for the organization, oversaw its charity work, gave countless public speeches, and recruited volunteers to serve as nurses. She also helped plan two charitable fairs in Chicago, which raised more than $1 million for relief efforts. In the following excerpt, Livermore explains the importance of the commission, the reasons for its formation, and her personal path to becoming a public official.

It was months after the war opened before the Sanitary Commission was organized and in the field, and it was yet longer, before relief work for the soldiers was generally carried forward under its admirable system. But women did not wait for that.

They refused to release their hold upon the men of their households, although the government had taken them out of the home and organized them into an army. Whether sick or well, the women were determined that they should receive home care, such as had never before been known to soldiers, and that was the prevalent feeling of the country. No failure of their plans of relief abated the ardor of the women, and no discouragements stayed the stream of their beneficence. Relief societies were organized everywhere, working independently, and in accordance with their best judgment. There was very little co-operation of societies in the beginning, and not unfrequently there was clashing.

Some of them proposed to follow the volunteers of their neighborhoods with their benefactions, or, as they phrased it, "to provide them with home comforts when well, and with hospital supplies and nurses when wounded and sick. If such a plan could have been carried out, it would have been admirable, but the difficulties in the way, and the failure of their attempts, soon brought that method into disrepute. The constant movement of troops rendered it impossible for express agents to forward boxes to special regiments, and, as much of the freight sent to the soldiers by these Relief Societies was perishable, baggage cars were flooded with decaying fruit and vegetables, pastry and cake, and badly canned meats and soups, which became spoiled and were thrown away en route. For a time there was great waste of the lavish outpouring of women. It did not, however, check their liberality, but it compelled better methods, and out of this chaos of individual benevolence and abounding patriotism, the Sanitary Commission finally emerged with its marvelous system.

I was reluctant to enter upon the work of the Commission in an official capacity, for I saw that it would take me from home, break up my habits of study and literary work, and take me altogether too much from my husband and children. But the need of relief work for the sick and wounded men of the army became more and more imperative,—the necessity of a better organization and wiser methods were more keenly felt,—and the government was preparing for a more vigorous prosecution of the war than it had yet ventured upon,—and I felt compelled to withdraw all objections and obey the call of my country. My husband was very desirous that I should enroll myself regularly in the work of the Commission, and aided me in finding a suitable housekeeper, and governess for the children, so that home interests should not suffer because of my absences. And when Dr. Bellows, president of the United States Sanitary Commission, proposed that my friend, Mrs. Jane C. Hoge, and myself should become associate members of the Commission, with headquarters at Chicago, we consented, and remained at our posts until the October after the war closed.

The Relief Societies, all through the Northwest, very quickly affiliated themselves in some way with the Northwestern branch of the Sanitary Commission at Chicago. And, as new societies were formed, they also wheeled into line, and adopted our methods of work, until we had, not only through the Northwest, but through the entire North, a compact organization of aid societies, auxiliary to the Commission.

The work of the next three or four years was severe in the extreme. Many women broke down under the incessant strain, and some of them died. I resigned all positions save that on my husband's paper, and subordinated all demands on my time to those of the Commission. I organized Soldiers' Aid Societies, delivered public addresses, to stimulate supplies and donations of money in the principal cities and towns of the Northwest; wrote letters by the thousand, personally and by amanuenses; answered all that I received, wrote the circulars, bulletins, and monthly reports of the Commission; made trips to the front with sanitary stores, to the distribution of which I gave personal attention; brought back large numbers of invalid soldiers, who were discharged that they might die at home, and accompanied them in person, or by proxy, to their several destinations; assisted to plan, organize, and conduct colossal sanitary fairs, the histories of which I wrote at their close; detailed women nurses for the hospitals by order of Secretary Stanton, and accompanied them to their posts; in short, the story

of women's work during the war has never been fully told, and can never be understood save by those connected with it. Whatever of mine was published during this period, or whatever related to my work during those stormy times, was carefully preserved by my husband.

> Mary Ashton Rice Livermore, *The story of my life; or, The sunshine and shadow of seventy years / by Mary A. Livermore . . . with hitherto unrecorded incidents and recollections of three years' experience as an army nurse in the great Civil War, and reminiscences of twenty-five years' experiences on the lecture platform . . . to which is added six of her most popular lectures . . . with portraits and one hundred and twenty engravings from designs by eminent artists* (Hartford, CT: A. D. Worthington and Company, 1897), 469–472.

Former Slave Hannah Austin Recalls Slavery and the War (April 8, 1937)

As one of many New Deal projects designed to create jobs for unemployed Americans, the Works Progress Administration (WPA), as part of its Federal Writers Project, hired writers to interview former slaves about their experiences. Formed in 1935, the WPA assembled hundreds of interviews of elderly African Americans. Despite their shortcomings, these sources provide some of the most vivid firsthand accounts of the slave experience before, during, and after the Civil War. In the following interview, Hannah Austin recalls some of her wartime experiences as well as her life as a slave.

When the writer was presented to Mrs. Hannah Austin she was immediately impressed with her alert youthful appearance. Mrs. Austin is well preserved for her age and speaks clearly and with much intelligence. The interview was a brief but interesting one. This was due partly to the fact that Mrs. Austin was a small child when The Civil War ended and too because her family was classed as "town slaves" so classed because of their superior intelligence.

Mrs. Austin was a child of ten or twelve years when the war ended. She doesn't know her exact age but estimated it to be between seventy and seventy five years. She was born the oldest child of Liza and George Hall. Their master Mr. Frank Hall was very kind to them and considerate in his treatment of them.

Briefly Mrs. Austin gave the following account of slavery as she knew it. "My family lived in a two room well built house which had many windows and a nice large porch. Our master, Mr. Hall was a merchant and operated a clothing store. Because Mr. Hall lived in town he did not need but a few slaves. My family which included my mother, father, sister, and myself were his only servants. Originally Mr. Hall did not own any slaves, however after marrying Mrs. Hall we were given to her by her father as a part of her inheritance.

My mother nursed Mrs. Hall from a baby, consequently the Hall family was very fond of her and often made the statement that they would not part with her for anything in the world, besides working as the cook for the Hall family my mother was also a fine seamstress and made clothing for the master's family and for our family. We were allowed an ample amount of good clothing which Mr. Hall selected from the stock in his store. My father worked as a porter in the store and did other jobs around the house. I did not have to work and spent most of my time playing with the Hall children. We were considered the better class of slaves and did not know the meaning of a hard time.

Other slave owners whipped their slaves severely and often, but I have never known our master to whip any one of my family. If any one in the family became ill the family doctor was called in as often as he was needed.

We did not have churches of our own but were allowed to attend the white churches in the afternoon. The white families attended in the forenoon. We seldom heard a true religious sermon; but were constantly preached the doctrine of obedience to our masters and mistresses. We were required to attend church every Sunday.

Marriages were conducted in much the same manner as they are today. After the usual courtship a minister was called in by the master and the marriage ceremony would then take place. In my opinion people of today are more lax in their attitude toward marriage than they were in those days. Following the marriage of a slave couple a celebration would take place often the master and his family would take part in the celebration.

I remember hearing my mother and father discuss the war; but was too young to know just the effect the war would have on the slave. One day I remember Mr. Hall coming to my mother telling her we were free. His exact words were quote—'Liza you don't belong to me any longer you belong to yourself. If you are hired now I will have to pay you. I do not want you to leave as you have a home here as long as you live.' I watched my mother to see the effect his words would have on her and I saw her eyes fill with tears. Mr. Hall's eyes filled with tears also.

Soon after this incident a Yankee Army appeared in our village one day. They practically destroyed Mr. Hall's store by throwing all clothes and other merchandise into the streets. Seeing my sister and I they turned to us saying, 'Little Negroes you are free there are no more masters and mistresses, here help yourselves to these clothes take them home with you.' Not knowing any better we carried stockings, socks, dresses, underwear and many other pieces home. After this they opened the smoke house door and told us to go in and take all of the meat we wanted.

On another occasion the mistress called me asking that I come in the yard to play with the children." Here Mrs. Austin began to laugh and remarked, "I did not go but politely told her I was free and didn't belong to any one but my mama and papa. As I spoke these words my mistress began to cry.

My mother and father continued to live with the Halls even after freedom and until their deaths. Although not impoverished most of the Halls' fortune was wiped out with the war."

Mrs. Austin married at the age of 16 years; and was the mother of four children, all of whom are dead. She was very ambitious and was determined to get an education if such was possible. After the war Northern white people came south and set up schools for the education of Negroes. She remembers the organization of the old Storrs School from which one of the present Negroes Colleges originated.

Mrs. Austin proudly spoke of her old blue back speller, which she still possesses; and of the days when she attended Storrs School.

As the writer made ready to depart Mrs. Austin smilingly informed her that she had told her all that she knew about slavery; and every word spoken was the truth.

Hannah Austin, Works Progress Administration Interview, Library of Congress (April 8, 1937).

Bibliography

Aaron, Daniel. 1987. *The Unwritten War: American Writers and the Civil War.* Madison: University of Wisconsin Press.

Abel, E. Lawrence. 2000. *Singing the New Nation: How Music Shaped the Confederacy, 1861–1865.* Mechanicsburg, PA: Stackpole Books.

Abel, Emily K. 2000. *Hearts of Wisdom: American Women Caring for Kin, 1850–1940.* Cambridge, MA: Harvard University Press.

Ahlstrom, Sydney. 1972. *A Religious History of the American People.* New Haven, CT: Yale University Press.

Albers, Henry, ed. 2001. *Maria Mitchell: A Life in Journals and Letters.* Clinton Corners, NY: College Avenue Press.

Alcott, Louisa May. 1960. *Hospital Sketches,* edited by Bessie Z. Jones. Cambridge, MA: Harvard University Press. (Reprint of Boston: James Redpath, 1863.)

Aleman, Jesse, ed. 2003. *The Woman in Battle: The Civil War Narrative of Loreta Velazquez, Cuban Woman and Confederate Soldier,* with introduction by Jesse Aleman. Madison: University of Wisconsin Press.

Alleman, Tillie Pierce. 1994. *At Gettysburg or What a Girl Saw and Heard of Battle.* Baltimore, MD: Butternut & Blue.

An Act for Enrolling and Calling Out the National Forces, and for Other Purposes. 1863. HR 125, 37th Congress, 3rd Session. *Statutes at Large of the United States.* Vol. 12. Boston: Little, Brown and Company.

Anderson, John Q., ed. 1955. *Brokenburn: The Journal of Kate Stone, 1861–1868.* Baton Rouge: Louisiana State University Press. (Reprinted 1995 with Introduction by Drew Gilpin Faust.)

Andrews, Eliza Frances. 1908. *The War-Time Journal of a Georgia Girl, 1864–1865.* New York: D. Appleton & Co.

Andrews, Eliza Frances. 2002. *Journal of a Georgia Woman 1870–1872,* edited with an introduction by S. Kittrell Rushing. Knoxville: University of Tennessee Press.

Andrews, Melodie. 1990. "'What the Girls Can Do': The Debate over the Employment of Women in the Early American Telegraph Industry." *Essays in Economic and Business History* 8: 109–120.

Andrews, William L., and William S. McFeely. 1997. *Narrative of the Life of Frederick Douglass, an American Slave, Written by Himself: Authoritative Text, Context, Criticism.* New York: W. W. Norton & Company.

Ash, Stephen V. 1988. *Middle Tennessee Society Transformed, 1860–1870: War and Peace in the Upper South.* Baton Rouge: Louisiana State University Press.

Ash, Stephen V. 1990. "White Virginians under Federal Occupation, 1861–1865." *Virginia Magazine of History and Biography* 98: 169–192.

Ash, Stephen V. 1995. *When the Yankees Came: Conflict and Chaos in the Occupied South, 1861–1865.* Chapel Hill: University of North Carolina Press.

Ashdown, Paul. 2002. *The Mosby Myth: A Confederate Hero in Life and Legend.* Wilmington, DE: Scholarly Resources.

Ashendel, Anita. 1997. "Fabricating Independence: Industrial Labor in Antebellum Indiana." *Michigan Historical Review* 23 (2): 1–24.

Atkinson, Maxine P., and Jacqueline Boles. 1985. "The Shaky Pedestal: Southern Ladies Yesterday and Today." *Southern Studies* 24: 398–406.

Attie, Jeanie. 1998. *Patriotic Toil: Northern Women and the American Civil War.* Ithaca, NY: Cornell University Press.

Austin, Anne. 1971. *The Woolsey Sisters of New York: A Family's Involvement in the Civil War and a New*

Profession (1860–1900). Philadelphia, PA: American Philosophical Society.

Bacon, Margaret Hope. 1896. *Mothers of Feminism: The Story of Quaker Women in America.* New York: Harper & Row.

Bacon, Margaret Hope. 1980. *Valiant Friend: The Life of Lucretia Mott.* New York: Walker & Company.

Bacon, Margaret Hope. 2000. *Abby Hopper Gibbons: Prison Reformer and Social Activist.* Albany: State University of New York Press.

Baer, Elizabeth R., ed. 1997. *Shadows on My Heart: The Civil War Diary of Lucy Rebecca Buck of Virginia.* Athens: University of Georgia Press.

Bailey, Anne J. 2000. *The Chessboard of War: Sherman and Hood in the Autumn Campaigns of 1864.* Lincoln: University of Nebraska Press.

Baird, Nancy Chappelear, ed. 1984. *Journals of Amanda Virginia Edmonds: Lass of the Mosby Confederacy, 1857–1867.* Stephens City, VA: Commercial Press.

Bakeless, John. 1970. *Spies of the Confederacy.* Philadelphia, PA: J. B. Lippincott Co.

Baker, Jean. 1983. *Affairs of Party: The Political Culture of Northern Democrats in Mid-Nineteenth-Century America.* Ithaca, NY: Cornell University Press.

Baker, Jean H. 1987. *Mary Todd Lincoln: A Biography.* New York: W. W. Norton.

Baker, Nina Brown. 1952. *Cyclone in Calico: The Story of Mary Ann Bickerdyke.* Boston: Little, Brown and Company.

Baker, Paula. 1984. "The Domestication of Politics: Women and American Political Society, 1780–1900." *American Historical Review* 89 (June): 620–647.

Bakker, Jan. 1987. "Overlooked Progenitors: Independent Women and Southern Renaissance in Augusta Jane Evans Wilson's *Macaria; or, Altars of Sacrifice.*" *The Southern Quarterly* 25: 131–141.

Banner, Lois W. 1980. *Elizabeth Cady Stanton: A Radical for Woman's Rights.* Boston: Little, Brown and Company.

Barber, E. Susan. 2000. "Cartridge Makers and Myrmidon Viragos: White Working-Class Women in Confederate Richmond." In *Negotiating the Boundaries of Southern Womanhood: Dealing with the Powers That Be,* edited by Janet Coryell, 199–214. Columbia: University of Missouri Press.

Barber, E. Susan. 2002. "'Depraved and Abandoned Women': Prostitution in Richmond, Virginia, across the Civil War." In *Neither Lady Nor Slave: Working Women of the Old South,* edited by Susanna Delfino and Michele Gillespie, 155–173. Chapel Hill: University of North Carolina Press.

Bardaglio, Peter. 1995. *Reconstructing the Household: Families, Sex, and the Law in the Nineteenth-*

Century South. Chapel Hill: University of North Carolina Press.

Barney, William. 1974. *The Secessionist Impulse: Alabama and Mississippi in 1860.* Princeton, NJ: Princeton University Press.

Barry, Kathleen. 1988. *Susan B. Anthony: A Biography of a Singular Feminist.* New York: New York University Press.

Barton, George. 1898. *Angels of the Battlefield: A History of the Labors of the Catholic Sisterhoods in the Late Civil War.* Philadelphia, PA: Catholic Art Publishing Company.

Baym, Nina. 2000. "Introduction." In *Three Spiritualist Novels,* by Elizabeth Stuart Phelps, vii–xxiii. Urbana: University of Illinois Press.

Bearden, Jim, and Linda Jean Butler. 1977. *Shadd: The Life and Times of Mary Shadd Cary.* Toronto: N. C. Press.

Beecher, Catharine. 1850. *Miss Beecher's Domestic Receipt-Book: Designed as a Supplement to Her Treatise on Domestic Economy.* New York: Harper.

Bennett, Paula Bernat. 2003. *Poets in the Public Sphere: The Emancipatory Project of American Women's Poetry, 1800–1900.* Princeton, NJ: Princeton University Press.

Bercaw, Nancy. 2003. *Gendered Freedoms: Race, Rights, and the Politics of Household in the Delta, 1861–1875.* Gainesville: University Press of Florida.

Berlin, Ira. 1974. *Slaves without Masters: The Free Negro in the American South.* New York: New Press.

Berlin, Ira. 2003. *Generations of Captivity: A History of African-American Slaves.* Cambridge, MA: Harvard University Press.

Berlin, Ira, Steven F. Miller, Joseph P. Reidy, and Leslie S. Rowland, eds. 1982–present. *Freedom: A Documentary History of Emancipation, 1861–1867.* New York: Cambridge University Press.

Berlin, Ira, Barbara J. Fields, Steven F. Miller, Joseph P. Reidy, and Leslie S. Rowland. 1992. *Slaves No More: Three Essays on Emancipation and the Civil War.* Cambridge, UK, and New York: Cambridge University Press.

Berlin, Ira, and Leslie Rowland, eds. 1997. *Families and Freedom: A Documentary History of African-American Kinship in the Civil War Era.* New York: New Press.

Berlin, Jean V., ed. 1994. *A Confederate Nurse: The Diary of Ada W. Bacot, 1860–1863.* Columbia: University of South Carolina Press.

Berlin, Jean V. 2001. "Did Confederate Women Lose the War? Deprivation, Destruction, and Despair on the Homefront." In *The Collapse of the Confederacy,* edited by Mark Grimsley and Brooks D. Simpson, 168–193. Lincoln: University of Nebraska Press.

Bernard, Jacqueline, with Introduction by Nell Irvin Painter. [1967] 1990. *Journey toward Freedom: The Story of Sojourner Truth.* New York: Feminist Press at The City University of New York.

Berry III, Stephen W. 2003. *All That Makes a Man: Love and Ambition in the Civil War South.* New York: Oxford University Press.

Berwanger, Eugene. 1975. "Reconstruction on the Frontier: The Equal Rights Struggle in Colorado, 1865–1867." *Pacific Historical Review* 44 (3): 313–329.

Birney, Catherine H. [1885] 1969. *The Grimké Sisters: Sarah and Angelina Grimké: The First American Women Advocates of Abolition and Women's Rights.* Westport, CT: Greenwood Press.

Black, Linda. 1994. "A Wife's Devotion: The Story of James and Fanny Ricketts." *Blue and Gray Magazine* 11: 22–28.

Black, Linda. 1994. "Three Heroines of Gettysburg." *Gettysburg Magazine* 11:119–125.

Blackwell, Elizabeth. 1895. *Pioneer Work in Opening the Medical Profession to Women.* London and New York: Longmans, Green & Company.

Blainey, Ann. 2001. *Fanny and Adelaide.* Chicago: Ivan R. Dee.

Blair, William A. 1998. *Virginia's Private War: Feeding Body and Soul in the Confederacy, 1861–1865.* New York: Oxford University Press.

Blair, William. 2004. *Cities of the Dead: Contesting the Memory of the Civil War in the South, 1865–1914.* Chapel Hill: University of North Carolina Press.

Blakey, Arch Fredric, Ann Smith Lainhart, and Winston Bryan Stephens Jr., eds. 1998. *Rose Cottage Chronicles: Civil War Letters of the Bryant-Stephens Families of North Florida.* Gainesville: University Press of Florida.

Blanton, DeAnne, and Laura M. Cook. 2002. *They Fought Like Demons: Women Soldiers in the American Civil War.* Baton Rouge: Louisiana State University Press.

Bleser, Carol, ed. 1991. *In Joy and in Sorrow: Women, Family, and Marriage in the Victorian South.* New York: Oxford University Press.

Bleser, Carol K., and Lesley J. Gordon, eds. 2001. *Intimate Strategies of the Civil War: Military Commanders and Their Wives.* New York: Oxford University Press.

Blight, David. 2001. *Race and Reunion: The Civil War in American Memory.* Cambridge, MA: Harvard University Press.

Blom, Ida. 1991. "The History of Widowhood: A Bibliographic Overview." *Journal of Family History* 16 (2): 191–210.

Blumenthal, Walter Hart. 1974. *Women Camp Followers of the American Revolution.* New York: Arno Press.

Blumhofer, Edith L. 2005. *Her Heart Can See: The Life and Hymns of Fanny J. Crosby.* Grand Rapids, MI: William B. Eerdmans Publishing Company.

Bollet, Alfred J. 2002. *Civil War Medicine: Challenges and Triumphs.* Tucson, AZ: Galen Press.

Bonner, Robert E. 2002. *Colors and Blood: Flag Passions of the Confederate South.* Princeton, NJ: Princeton University Press.

Boritt, Gabor S., ed. 1999. *The Gettysburg Nobody Knows.* New York: Oxford University Press.

Botume, Elizabeth Hyde. 1968. *First Days Amongst the Contrabands.* New York: Arno Press and the New York Times.

Boyd, Belle. 1998. *Belle Boyd in Camp and Prison,* with Foreword by Drew Gilpin Faust and Introduction by Sharon Kennedy-Nolle. Baton Rouge: Louisiana State University Press.

Boyd, Melba Joyce. 1994. *Discarded Legacy: Politics and Poetics in the Life of Frances E.W. Harper, 1825–1911.* Detroit, MI: Wayne State University Press.

Bradford, Sarah H. 1869. *Scenes in the Life of Harriet Tubman.* Auburn, NY: W. J. Moses.

Bradford, Sarah H. 1886. *Harriet, The Moses of Her People.* New York: Geo. R. Lockwood & Son.

Bradley, Mark L. 2000. *This Astounding Close: The Road to Bennett Place.* Chapel Hill: University of North Carolina Press.

Breckenridge, Lucy. 1979. *Lucy Breckinridge of Grove Hill: The Diary of a Virginia Girl, 1862–1864,* edited by Mary D. Robertson. Kent, OH: Kent State University Press.

Bremner, Robert Hamlett. 1890. *The Public Good: Philanthropy and Welfare in the Civil War Era.* New York: Alfred A. Knopf.

Brevard, Keziah Goodwyn Hopkins. 1993. *A Plantation Mistress on the Eve of the Civil War: The Diary of Keziah Goodwyn Hopkins Brevard, 1860–1861,* edited by John Hammond Moore. Columbia: University of South Carolina Press.

Broadwater, Robert P. 1993. *Daughters of the Cause: Women in the "Civil War."* Santa Clarita, CA: Daisy Publishing Company.

Brockett, L. P., and Mary C. Vaughn. 1867. *Women's Work in the Civil War: A Record of Heroism, Patriotism and Patience.* Philadelphia, PA: Zeigler, McCurdy & Co./Boston: R. H. Curran.

Brown, Alexis Girardin. 2000. "The Women Left Behind: The Transformation of the Southern Belle, 1840–1880." *The Historian* 62: 759–778.

Brown, Elizabeth Potts, and Susan Mosher Stuard, eds. 1989. *Witnesses for Change: Quaker Women over Three Centuries.* Piscataway, NJ: Rutgers University Press.

Brown, Thomas. 1998. *Dorothea Dix: New England Reformer.* Cambridge, MA: Harvard University Press.

Browne, Stephen Howard. 1999. *Angelina Grimké: Rhetoric, Identity, and the Radical Imagination.* East Lansing: Michigan State University Press.

Brumgardt, John R., ed. 1980. *Civil War Nurse: The Diary and Letters of Hannah Ropes.* Knoxville: University of Tennessee Press.

Bruyn, Kathleen. 1970. *"Aunt Clara Brown:" Story of a Black Pioneer.* Boulder, CO: Pruett Publishing Company.

Bucklin, Sophronia E. 1869. *In Hospital and Camp: A Woman's Record of Thrilling Incidents among the Wounded in the Late War.* Philadelphia, PA: John E. Potter and Co.

Bulloch, Joseph Gaston Baillie. 1901. *A history and genealogy of the Habersham family: in connection with the history, genealogy, and mention of the families of Clay, Stiles, Cumming, King, Elliott, Milledge, Maxwell, Adams, Houstoun, Screvens, Owens, Demere, Footman, Ellis, Washington, Newell, deTreville, Davis, Barrington, Lewis, Warner, Cobb, Flournoy, Pratt, Nephew, Bolton, Bowers, Cuthbert, and many many other names.* Columbia, SC: R.L. Bryan Company.

Bunch, Jack A. 2000. *Military Justice in the Confederate States Armies.* Shippensburg, PA: White Mane Publishing Co.

Burgess, Lauren Cook, ed. 1994. *An Uncommon Soldier: The Civil War Letters of Sarah Rosetta Wakeman, alias Pvt. Lyons Wakeman, 153rd Regiment, New York State Volunteers, 1862–1864.* New York: Oxford University Press.

Burlingame, Michael. 1994. *The Inner World of Abraham Lincoln.* Urbana: University of Illinois Press.

Burnham, John C. 1971. "Medical Inspection of Prostitutes in America in the Nineteenth Century: The St. Louis Experiment and Its Sequel." *Bulletin of the History of Medicine* 45: 203–218.

Burton, David H. 1995. *Clara Barton: In the Service of Humanity.* Westport, CT: Greenwood Press.

Burton, David L. 1982. "Richmond's Great Homefront Disaster: Friday the 13th." *Civil War Times Illustrated* 21 (6): 36–41.

Burton, Georganne B., and Orville Vernon Burton, eds. 2002. *The Free Flag of Cuba, The Lost Novel of Lucy Holcombe Pickens.* Baton Rouge: Louisiana State University Press.

Burton, Orville Vernon. 1985. *In My Father's House Are Many Mansions: Family and Community in Edgefield, South Carolina.* Chapel Hill: University of North Carolina Press.

Butchart, Ronald E. 1980. *Northern Schools, Southern Blacks, and Reconstruction: Freedmen's Education, 1862–1875.* Westport, CT: Greenwood Press.

Butler, Anne M. 1985. *Daughters of Joy, Sisters of Misery: Prostitutes in the American West, 1865–90.* Chicago: University of Chicago Press.

Butler, Benjamin F. 1892. *Autobiography and Personal Reminiscences of Major-General Benjamin F. Butler.* Boston: A. M. Thayer & Co.

Bynum, Hartwell T. 1970. "Sherman's Expulsion of the Roswell Women in 1864." *Georgia Historical Quarterly* 54: 169–182.

Bynum, Victoria E. 1992. *Unruly Women: The Politics of Social and Sexual Control in the Old South.* Chapel Hill: University of North Carolina Press.

Bynum, Victoria. 2001. *The Free State of Jones: Mississippi's Longest Civil War.* Chapel Hill: University of North Carolina Press.

Campbell, Edward D. C. Jr., and Kym S. Rice, eds. 1996. *A Woman's War: Southern Women, Civil War, and the Confederate Legacy.* Richmond, VA: Museum of the Confederacy/Charlottesville: University Press of Virginia.

Campbell, Jacqueline Glass. 2003. *When Sherman Marched North from the Sea: Resistance on the Confederate Home Front.* Chapel Hill: University of North Carolina Press.

Campbell, James. 1998. *Songs of Zion: The African Methodist Episcopal Church in the United States and South Africa.* New York: Oxford University Press.

Cannon, Devereux D. 1994. *Flags of the Confederacy: An Illustrated History.* Gretna, LA: Pelican Publishing Company.

Cannon, Devereux D. 1994. *Flags of the Union: An Illustrated History.* Gretna, LA: Pelican Publishing Company.

Capers, Gerald M. Jr. 1964. "Confederates and Yankees in Occupied New Orleans, 1862–1865." *Journal of Southern History* 30: 405–426.

Capers, Gerald M. 1965. *Occupied City: New Orleans under the Federals, 1862–1865.* Lexington: University of Kentucky Press.

Carmichael, Peter S. 2001. "'All Say They Are under Petticoat Government': Lizinka Brown and Richard Ewell." In *Intimate Strategies: Military Marriages of the Civil War,* edited by Carol Bleser and Lesley Gordon, 87–103. New York: Oxford University Press.

Carroll, Anna Ella. 1861. *Reply to the Speech of Hon. J. C. Breckinridge.* Washington, DC: Henry Polkinhorn.

Carroll, Anna Ella. 1861. *The War Powers of the General Government.* Washington, DC: Henry Polkinhorn.

Carter, Christine Jacobson, ed. 1997. *The Diary of Dolly Lunt Burge, 1848–1879.* Athens: University of Georgia Press.

Carter III, Samuel. 1973. *The Siege of Atlanta, 1864.* New York: St. Martin's Press.

Cashin, Joan E. 1990. "The Structure of Antebellum Families: 'The Ties That Bound Us Was Strong.'" *Journal of Southern History* 56: 55–70.

Cashin, Joan E. 1992 "'Since the War Broke Out': The Marriage of Kate and William McLure." In *Divided Houses: Gender and the Civil War,* edited by Catherine Clinton and Nina Silber, 200–212. New York: Oxford University Press.

Cashin, Joan E. 1996. *Our Common Affairs.* Baltimore, MD: Johns Hopkins University Press.

Cashin, Joan E. 2002. "Deserters, Civilians, and Draft Resistance in the North." In *The War Was You and Me: Civilians in the American Civil War,* edited by Joan E. Cashin, 262–285. Princeton, NJ: Princeton University Press.

Cashin, Joan E., ed. 2002. *The War Was You and Me: Civilians in the American Civil War.* Princeton, NJ: Princeton University Press.

Caskie, Jacquelin Ambler. 1928. *The Life and Letters of Matthew Fontaine Maury.* Richmond, VA: Richmond Press, Inc.

Cassedy, James H. 1992. "Numbering the North's Medical Events: Humanitarianism and Science in Civil War Statistics." *Bulletin of the History of Medicine* 66 (2): 210–233.

Castel, Albert. 1992. *Decision in the West: The Atlanta Campaign of 1864.* Lawrence: University Press of Kansas.

Castel, Albert. 1999. *William Clarke Quantrill: His Life and Times.* Norman: University of Oklahoma Press.

Catton, Bruce, and James McPherson, eds. 1996. *The American Heritage New History of the Civil War.* New York: MetroBooks.

Cazalet, Sylvain. 1866. *History of the New York Medical College and Hospital for Women.* New York: University of the State of New York.

Censer, Jane Turner, ed. 1986. *The Papers of Frederick Law Olmsted,* vol. IV: *Defending the Union.* Baltimore, MD: Johns Hopkins University Press.

Censer, Jane Turner. 1987. *North Carolina Planters and Their Children, 1800–1860.* Baton Rouge: Louisiana State University Press.

Censer, Jane Turner. 2003. *The Reconstruction of White Southern Womanhood, 1865–1895.* Baton Rouge: Louisiana State University Press.

Ceplair, Larry, ed. 1989. *The Public Years of Sarah and Angelina Grimké, Selected Writings, 1835–1839.* New York: Columbia University Press.

Channing, Steven. 1970. *A Crisis of Fear: Secession in South Carolina.* New York: Simon & Schuster.

Chartrand, René. 1996. *Napoleonic Wars, Napoleon's Army.* Washington, DC: Brassey's.

Chesson, Michael B. 1984. "Harlots or Heroines? A New Look at the Richmond Bread Riot." *Virginia Magazine of History and Biography* 92: 131–175.

Cimbala, Paul A. 1997. *Under the Guardianship of the Nation: The Freedmen's Bureau and the Reconstruction of Georgia, 1865–1870.* Athens: University of Georgia Press.

Cimbala, Paul A., and Randall M. Miller, eds. 1999. *The Freedmen's Bureau and Reconstruction: Reconsiderations.* New York: Fordham University Press.

Cimbala, Paul A., and Randall M. Miller, eds. 2002. *Union Soldiers and the Northern Home Front: Wartime Experiences, Postwar Adjustments.* New York: Fordham University Press.

Cimbala, Paul, and Randall Miller, eds. 2002. *An Uncommon Time: The Civil War and the Northern Home Front.* New York: Fordham University Press.

Cimprich, John. 1985. *Slavery's End in Tennessee, 1861–1865.* Tuscaloosa: University of Alabama Press.

Clayton, Sara "Sallie" Conley. 1999. *Requiem for a Lost City: A Memoir of Civil War Atlanta and the Old South,* edited by Robert Scott Davis Jr. Macon, GA: Mercer University Press.

Cliff, Michelle. 1993. *Free Enterprise: A Novel of Mary Ellen Pleasant.* New York: Dutton.

Clifford, Deborah Pickman. 1978. *Mine Eyes Have Seen the Glory: A Biography of Julia Ward Howe.* Boston: Little, Brown and Company.

Clifford, Deborah Pickman. 1992. *Crusader for Freedom: A Life of Lydia Maria Child.* Boston: Beacon Press.

Clinton, Catherine. 1982. *The Plantation Mistress: Woman's World in the Old South.* New York: Pantheon Books.

Clinton, Catherine. 1984. *The Other Civil War: American Women in the Nineteenth Century.* New York: Hill and Wang.

Clinton, Catherine. 1991. "'Southern Dishonor': Flesh, Blood, Race, and Bondage." In *In Joy and in Sorrow: Women, Family, and Marriage in the Victorian South,* edited by Carol Bleser, 52–68. New York: Oxford University Press.

Clinton, Catherine. 1995. *Tara Revisited: Women, War, and the Plantation Legend.* New York: Abbeville Press.

Clinton, Catherine. 1998. *Civil War Stories.* Athens: University of Georgia Press.

Clinton, Catherine. 2000. *Fanny Kemble's Civil Wars.* New York: Simon & Schuster.

Clinton, Catherine, ed. 2000. *Southern Families at War: Loyalty and Conflict in the Civil War South.* New York: Oxford University Press.

Clinton, Catherine, and Nina Silber, eds. 1992. *Divided Houses: Gender and the Civil War,* with Introduction by James M. McPherson. Oxford: Oxford University Press.

Cochran, Hamilton. 1973. *Blockade Runners of the Confederacy.* Westport, CT: Greenwood Press.

Coleman, Penny. 1992. *Spies! Women in the Civil War.* White Hall, VA: Shoe Tree Press.

Connelly, Thomas. 1971. *Autumn of Glory: The Army of Tennessee, 1862–1865.* Baton Rouge: Louisiana State University Press.

Connelly, Thomas L. 1977. *The Marble Man: Robert E. Lee and His Image in American Society.* New York: Alfred A. Knopf.

Cook, Cita. 2003. "Winnie Davis: The Challenges of Daughterhood." In *Mississippi Women: Their History, Their Lives,* edited by Martha Swift et al., 21–38. Athens: University of Georgia Press.

Coontz, Stephanie. 1999. "Working-Class Families, 1870–1890." In *American Families: A Multicultural Reader,* edited by Stephanie Coontz, Maya Parson, and Gabrielle Raley, 94–127. New York: Routledge.

Cooper, Edward S. 2004. *Vinnie Ream: An American Sculptor.* Chicago: Academy Chicago Publishers.

Cooper, William J. 2000. *Jefferson Davis, American.* New York: Alfred A. Knopf.

Corbin, D. T. 1866. *Digest of Opinions of the Judge Advocate General of the Army.* Washington, DC: U.S. Government Printing Office.

Coryell, Janet L. 1990. *Neither Heroine Nor Fool: Anna Ella Carroll of Maryland.* Kent, OH: Kent State University Press.

Coski, John M. 1996. *Capital Navy: The Men, Ships, and Operations of the James River Squadron.* Campbell, CA: Savas Woodbury.

Cott, Nancy F., ed. 1993. *History of Women in the United States. Historical Articles on Women's Lives and Activities,* vol. 12: *Education.* Munich: K. G. Saur Publishing.

Cottom, Robert I., and Mary Ellen Hayward. 1994. *Maryland and the Civil War: A House Divided.* Baltimore: Maryland Historical Society.

Coulling, Mary P. 1987. *The Lee Girls.* Winston-Salem, MA: John F. Blair.

Coulter, E. Merton. 1948. *Travels in the Confederate States: A Bibliography.* Norman: University of Oklahoma Press.

Coultrap-McQuin, Susan. 1990. *Doing Literary Business: American Women Writers in the Nineteenth Century.* Chapel Hill: University of North Carolina Press.

Coultrap-McQuin, Susan, ed. 1992. *Gail Hamilton: Selected Writings.* Piscataway, NJ: Rutgers University Press.

Cox, Karen L. 2003. *Dixie's Daughters: The United Daughters of the Confederacy and the Preservation of Confederate Culture.* Gainesville: University Press of Florida.

Cox, LaWanda. 1985. *Lincoln and Black Freedom: A Study in Presidential Leadership.* Urbana: University of Illinois Press.

Cozzens, Peter. 1992. *This Terrible Sound: The Battle of Chickamauga.* Urbana: University of Illinois Press.

Crabtree, Beth G., and James W. Patton, eds. 1979. *Journal of a Secesh Lady: The Diary of Catherine Ann Devereux Edmondston, 1860–1866.* Raleigh: North Carolina Division of Archives and History.

Crawford, Richard. 1977. *The Civil War Songbook.* New York: Dover Publications.

Creighton, Margaret S. 2005. *The Colors of Courage: Gettysburg's Forgotten History: Immigrants, Women, and African Americans in the Civil War's Defining Battle.* New York: Basic Books.

Crenshaw, Ollinger. 1945. *The Slave States in the Presidential Election of 1860.* Baltimore, MD: Johns Hopkins University Press.

Crofts, Daniel. 1989. *Reluctant Confederates: Upper South Unionists in the Secession Crisis.* Chapel Hill: University of North Carolina Press.

Cromwell, Otelia. 1958. *Lucretia Mott.* Cambridge, MA: Harvard University Press.

Cullen, Jim. 1995. *The Civil War in Popular Culture: A Reusable Past.* Washington, DC: Smithsonian Institution Press.

Culpepper, Marilyn Mayer. 1991. *Trials and Triumphs: The Women of the American Civil War.* East Lansing: Michigan State University Press.

Culpepper, Marilyn Mayer. 2002. *All Things Altered: Women in the Wake of Civil War and Reconstruction.* Jefferson, NC: McFarland.

Cushman, Stephen. 1999. *Bloody Promenade: Reflections on a Civil War Battle.* Charlottesville: University of Virginia Press.

Cutter, Barbara. 2003. *Domestic Devils, Battlefield Angels: The Radicalization of American Womanhood, 1830–1865.* DeKalb: Northern Illinois University Press.

Dale, Edward Everett, and Gaston Litton. 1939. *Cherokee Cavaliers.* Norman: University of Oklahoma Press.

Dall, Caroline, ed. 1860. *A Practical Illustration of "Woman's Right to Labor;" or, A Letter from Marie E. Zakrzewska.* Boston: Walker, Wise & Co.

Daly, Maria Lydig. 1962. *Diary of a Union Lady 1861–1865,* edited by Harold Earl Hammond. New York: Funk & Wagnalls.

Daniel, Larry J. 1997. *Shiloh: The Battle That Changed the Civil War.* New York: Simon & Schuster.

Daniel, Larry J. 2004. *Days of Glory: The Army of the Cumberland, 1861–1865.* Baton Rouge: Louisiana State University Press.

Dannett, Sylvia G. L. 1959. *Noble Women of the North.* New York: Thomas Yoseloff.

Dannett, Sylvia G. L. 1960. *She Rode with the Generals: The True and Incredible Story of Sarah Emma Seelye, Alias Franklin Thompson.* New York: Thomas Nelson & Sons.

Dargan, Elizabeth Paisley, ed. 1994. *The Civil War Diary of Martha Abernathy: Wife of Dr. Charles C. Abernathy of Pulaski, Tennessee.* Beltsville, MD: Professional Printing.

Davis, Jefferson. 1881. *Rise and Fall of the Confederate Government.* 2 vols. New York: D. Appleton & Co.

Davis, Jefferson. 1971–present. *The Papers of Jefferson Davis.* 11 vols. to date. Baton Rouge: Louisiana State University Press.

Davis, Varina Howell. 1890. *Jefferson Davis, A Memoir.* 2 vols. New York: Belford.

Davis, William C. 1991. *Jefferson Davis: The Man and His Hour.* New York: HarperCollins.

Davis, William C. 1999. *Lincoln's Men: How President Lincoln Became Father to an Army and a Nation.* New York: Free Press.

Decker, William Merrill. 1998. *Epistolary Practices: Letter Writing in America before Telecommunications.* Chapel Hill: University of North Carolina Press.

DeForest, John William. 1969. *Miss Ravenel's Conversion from Secession to Loyalty.* Columbus, OH: Charles E. Merrill Publishing Company. (Reprint of 1867 edition. New York: Harper & Brothers.)

Degler, Carl N. 1974. *The Other South: Southern Dissenters in the Nineteenth Century.* New York: Harper & Row.

Degler, Carl. 1980. *At Odds: Women and the Family from the Revolution to the Present.* New York: Oxford University Press.

Dehart, William C. 1869. *Observations on Military Law and the Constitution and Practice of Courts Martial.* New York: D. Appleton & Co.

Delauter Jr., Roger U. 1992. *Winchester in the Civil War.* Lynchburg, VA: H. E. Howard.

Delfino, Susanna, and Michelle Gillespie, eds. 2002 *Neither Lady Nor Slave: Working Women of the Old South.* Chapel Hill: University of North Carolina Press.

Denney, Robert E. 1994. *Civil War Medicine: Care and Comfort of the Wounded.* New York: Sterling Publishing Co.

Denton, Lawrence M. 1995. *A Southern Star for Maryland: Maryland and the Secession Crisis, 1860–1861.* Baltimore, MD: Publishing Concepts.

De Pauw, Linda Grant. 1998. *Battle Cries and Lullabies: Women in War from Prehistory to the Present.* Norman: University of Oklahoma Press.

Detzer, David. 2001. *Allegiance: Fort Sumter, Charleston, and the Beginnings of the Civil War.* New York: Harcourt Brace.

Detzer, David. 2004. *Donnybrook: The Battle of Bull Run, 1861.* Orlando: Harcourt.

Dickinson, Anna Elizabeth. [1868] 2003. *What Answer?* New York: Humanity Books.

Diedrich, Maria. 1999. *Love Across Color Lines: Ottilie Assing and Frederick Douglass.* New York: Hill and Wang.

Diffley, Kathleen. 2002. *To Live and Die.* Durham, NC: Duke University Press.

Diner, Hasia R. 1983. *Erin's Daughters in America: Irish Immigrant Women in the Nineteenth Century.* Baltimore, MD: Johns Hopkins University Press.

Dix, Dorothea L. 1975. *On Behalf of the Insane Poor: Selected Reports 1842–1862.* North Stratford, NH: Ayer Company.

Dobson, Joanne. 1986. "The Hidden Hand: Subversion of Cultural Ideology in Three Mid-nineteenth-century American Women's Novels." *American Quarterly* 38 (2): 223–242.

Dolensky, Suzanne T. 1985. "Varina Howell Davis, 1889 to 1906." *Journal of Mississippi History* 47 (May): 90–109.

Donald, David Herbert. 1995. *Lincoln.* New York: Simon & Schuster.

Dorr, Rheta Childe. 1970. *Susan B. Anthony: The Woman Who Changed the Mind of a Nation.* New York: AMS Press. Reprint.

Dorsey, Bruce. 2002. *Reforming Men and Women: Gender in the Antebellum City.* Ithaca, NY: Cornell University Press.

Douglas, Ann. 1974. "Heaven Our Home: Consolation Literature in the Northern United States, 1830–1880." *American Quarterly* 26 (5): 496–515.

Douglas, Ann. 1998. *The Feminization of American Culture.* New York: Farrar, Straus and Giroux. (Orig. pub. 1977.)

Douglass, Frederick. 1962. *Life and Times of Frederick Douglass: His Early Life as a Slave, His Escape From*

Bondage, and His Complete History Written by Himself. New York: Collier Books.

Douglass, Frederick. 1976. *Frederick Douglass on Women's Rights,* edited by Philip S. Foner. Westport, CT: Greenwood Press.

Dowdy, Clifford. 1964. *The Seven Days: The Emergence of Lee.* Boston: Little, Brown.

DuBois, Ellen Carol. 1978. *Feminism and Suffrage: The Emergence of an Independent Women's Movement in America 1848–1869.* Ithaca, NY: Cornell University Press.

Dulles, Foster Rhea. 1950. *The American Red Cross, a History.* New York: Harper & Row.

Durrill, Wayne K. 1990. *War of Another Kind: A Southern Community in the Great Rebellion.* New York: Oxford University Press.

Dyer, Thomas G. 1992. "Vermont Yankees in King Cotton's Court: The Case of Cyrena and Amherst Stone." *Vermont History* 60: 205–229.

Dyer, Thomas G. 1995. "Atlanta's Other Civil War Novel: Fictional Unionists in a Confederate City." *Georgia Historical Quarterly* 79: 147–168.

Dyer, Thomas G. 1999. *Secret Yankees: The Union Circle in Confederate Atlanta.* Baltimore, MD: Johns Hopkins University Press.

East, Charles, ed. 1991. *Sarah Morgan: The Civil War Diary of a Southern Woman.* New York: Simon & Schuster.

Edmonds, S. Emma. 1864. *Unsexed; or, The Female Soldier: The Thrilling Adventures, Experiences and Escapes of a Woman, as Nurse, Spy and Scout, in Hospitals, Camp and Battlefields.* Philadelphia, PA: Philadelphia Publishing.

Edmonds, S. Emma E. 1865. *Nurse and Spy in the Union Army.* Hartford, CT: W. S. Williams and Company.

Edmonds, Sarah Emma. 1999. *Memoirs of a Soldier, Nurse and Spy: A Woman's Adventures in the Union Army.* DeKalb: Northern Illinois University Press.

Edward, Laura F. 1997. *Gendered Strife and Confusion: The Political Culture of Reconstruction.* Urbana: University of Illinois Press.

Edwards, Laura F. 1999. "Law, Domestic Violence, and the Limits of Patriarchal Authority in the Antebellum South." *Journal of Southern History* 65: 733–770.

Edwards, Laura F. 2000. *Scarlett Doesn't Live Here Anymore: Southern Women in the Civil War Era.* Urbana: University of Illinois Press.

Edwards, Stewart C. 2001. "'To Do the Manufacturing for the South.'" *Georgia Historical Quarterly* 85 (4): 538–554.

Eggleston, G. K. 1929. "The Work of Relief Societies during the Civil War." *Journal of Negro History* 14 (3): 272–299.

Eggleston, Larry G. 2003. *Women in the Civil War: Extraordinary Stories of Soldiers, Spies, Nurses, Doctors, Crusaders, and Others.* Jefferson, NC: McFarland.

Eiselein, Gregory, and Anne K. Phillips, eds. 2001. *The Louisa May Alcott Encyclopedia.* Westport, CT: Greenwood Press.

Elder, Donald C. III, ed. 2003. *Love amid the Turmoil: The Civil War Letters of William and Mary Vermillion.* Iowa City: University of Iowa Press.

Ellefson, Cheryl. 1996. "Servants of God and Man: The Sisters of Charity." In *Valor and Lace: The Roles of Confederate Women, 1861–1865,* edited by Mauriel Phillips Joslyn, 175–184. Murfreesboro, TN: Southern Heritage Press.

Elmore, Grace Brown. 1997. *A Heritage of Woe: The Civil War Diary of Grace Brown Elmore, 1861–1868,* edited by Marli F. Weiner. Athens: University of Georgia Press.

Emerson, Sarah Hopper, ed. 1986. *The Life of Abby Hopper Gibbons, Told Chiefly through Her Correspondence.* New York: G.P. Putnam's Sons.

Englizian, H. Crosby. 1968. *Brimstone Corner: Park Street Church, Boston.* Chicago: Moody Press.

Eppes, Susan Bradford. [1926] 1968. *Through Some Eventful Years.* Gainesville: University Press of Florida.

Escott, Paul D. 1977. "'The Cry of the Sufferers': The Problem of Welfare in the Confederacy." *Civil War History* 23: 228–240.

Escott, Paul D. 1978. *After Secession: Jefferson Davis and the Failure of Confederate Nationalism.* Baton Rouge: Louisiana State University Press.

Evans, Augusta Jane. 1992. *Macaria; or, Altars of Sacrifice,* with Introduction by Drew Gilpin Faust. Baton Rouge: Louisiana State University Press. (Reprint of 1864 edition. Richmond: West & Johnston.)

Evans, Clark. 1994. "*Maum Guinea:* Beadle's Unusual Jewel." *Dime Novel Roundup* 63 (4): 77–80.

Evans, David. 1996. *Sherman's Horsemen: Union Cavalry Operations in the Atlanta Campaign.* Bloomington: Indiana University Press.

Evans, Sara M. 1997. *Born for Liberty: A History of Women in America.* New York: Free Press.

Everett, Robinson O. 1956. *Military Justice in the Armed Forces of the United States.* Harrisburg, PA: Military Service Publishing Company.

Fahs, Alice. 1999. "The Feminized Civil War: Gender, Northern Popular Literature and the Memory of the Civil War, 1861–1900." *Journal of American History* 85: 1461–1494.

Fahs, Alice. 2001. *The Imagined Civil War: Popular Literature of the North and South, 1861–1865.* Chapel Hill: University of North Carolina Press.

Farnham, Christie Anne. 1994. *The Education of the Southern Belle: Higher Education and Student Socialization in the Antebellum South.* New York: New York University Press.

Farnham, Thomas J., and Francis P. King. 1996. "'The March of the Destroyer': The New Bern Yellow Fever Epidemic of 1864." *North Carolina Historical Review* 73: 435–483.

Farrell, James J. 1980. *Inventing the American Way of Death, 1830–1920.* Philadelphia, PA: Temple University Press.

Faulkner, Carol. 2003. *Women's Radical Reconstruction: The Freedmen's Aid Movement.* Philadelphia: University of Pennsylvania Press.

Faust, Drew Gilpin. 1988. *The Creation of Confederate Nationalism: Ideology and Identity in the Civil War South.* Baton Rouge: Louisiana State University Press.

Faust, Drew Gilpin. 1989. "Race, Gender, and Confederate Nationalism: William D. Washington's *Burial of Latane.*" *Southern Review* 25: 297–307.

Faust, Drew Gilpin. 1990. "Altars of Sacrifice: Confederate Women and the Narratives of War." *Journal of American History* 76 (4): 1200–1228.

Faust, Drew Gilpin. 1992. "Introduction: *Macaria,* A War Story for Confederate Women." In *Macaria; or, Altars of Sacrifice,* by Augusta Jane Evans, xiii–xxvi. Baton Rouge: Louisiana State University Press.

Faust, Drew Gilpin. 1992. *Southern Stories: Slaveholders in Peace and War.* Columbia: University of Missouri Press.

Faust, Drew Gilpin. 1992. "'Trying to Do a Man's Business': Gender, Violence, and Slave Management in Civil War Texas." *Gender and History* 4: 197–214.

Faust, Drew Gilpin. 1996. *Mothers of Invention: Women of the Slaveholding South in the Civil War.* Chapel Hill: University of North Carolina Press.

Faust, Drew Gilpin. 1998. "'Ours as Well as That of the Men': Women and Gender in the Civil War." In *Writing the Civil War: The Quest to Understand,* edited by James M. McPherson and William J. Cooper Jr., 228–240. Columbia: University of South Carolina Press.

Faust, Drew Gilpin. 2000. "A Moment of Truth: A Woman of the Master Class in the Confederate South." In *Slavery, Secession and Southern History,* edited by Robert Louis Paquette and Louis A. Ferleger, 126–139. Charlottesville: University Press of Virginia.

Faust, Drew Gilpin. 2005. "'The Dread Void of Uncertainty': Naming the Dead in the American Civil War." *Southern Cultures* 11 (2): 7–32, 113.

Fellman, Michael. 1989. *Inside War: The Guerrilla Conflict in Missouri During the American Civil War.* New York: Oxford University Press.

Fellman, Michael. 1994. "Women and Guerrilla Warfare." In *Divided Houses,* edited by Catherine Clinton and Nina Silber, 147–165. New York: Oxford University Press.

Fellman, Michael. 1995. *Citizen Sherman: A Life of William Tecumseh Sherman.* New York: Random House.

Fellman, Michael. 2000. *The Making of Robert E. Lee.* New York: Random House.

Felton, Rebecca Latimer. 1911. *Memoirs of Georgia Politics.* Atlanta, GA: Index Publishing Co.

Felton, Rebecca Latimer. 1919. *Country Life in Georgia in the Days of My Youth.* Atlanta, GA: Index Publishing Co.

Fidler, William Perry. 1951. *Augusta Evans Wilson, 1835–1909.* Tuscaloosa: University of Alabama Press.

Fields, Catherine Keene, and Lisa C. Kightlinger, eds. 1993. *To Ornament Their Minds: Sarah Pierce's Litchfield Female Academy, 1792–1833.* Litchfield, CT: Litchfield Historical Society.

Finley, Randy. 1996. *From Slavery to Uncertain Freedom: The Freedmen's Bureau in Arkansas, 1865–1869.* Fayetteville: University of Arkansas Press.

Fishel, Edwin C. 1996. *The Secret War for the Union: The Untold Story of Military Intelligence in the Civil War.* Boston: Houghton-Mifflin.

Fisher, Clyde Olin. 1971. "The Relief of Soldiers' Families in North Carolina during the Civil War." *Southern Atlantic Quarterly* 16: 60–72.

Fladeland, Betty. 1972. *Men and Brothers: Anglo-American Antislavery Cooperation.* Urbana: University of Illinois Press.

Fleischner, Jennifer. 2003. *Mrs. Lincoln and Mrs. Keckly.* New York: Broadway Books.

Foner, Eric. 1970. *Free Soil, Free Labor, Free Men: The Ideology of the Republican Party before the Civil War.* New York: Oxford University Press.

Foner, Eric. 1988. *Reconstruction: America's Unfinished Revolution, 1863–1877.* New York: Harper & Row.

Foner, Philip Sheldon. 1979. *Women and the American Labor Movement: From Colonial Times to the Eve of World War I.* New York: Free Press.

Forbes, Ella. 1998. *African American Women during the Civil War.* New York: Garland Publishing.

Foster, Frances Smith. 2005. "Frances Ellen Watkins Harper." In *Black Women in America,* edited by Darlene Clark Hine, 2: 532-537. New York: Oxford University Press.

Foster, Gaines M. 1987. *Ghosts of the Confederacy: Defeat, the Lost Cause, and the Emergence of the New South.* New York: Oxford University Press.

Fought, Leigh. 2003. *Southern Womanhood and Slavery: A Biography of Louisa S. McCord, 1810–1879.* Columbia: University of Missouri Press.

Fox, Arthur B. 2002. *Pittsburgh during the American Civil War, 1860–1865.* Chicora, PA: Mechling Books.

Fox-Genovese, Elizabeth. 1988. *Within the Plantation Household: Black and White Women of the Old South.* Chapel Hill: University of North Carolina Press.

Frank, Joseph Allan. 1998. *With Ballot and Bayonet: The Political Socialization of American Civil War Soldiers.* Athens: University of Georgia Press.

Frank, Lisa Tendrich. 2001. "To 'Cure Her of Her Pride and Boasting': The Gendered Implications of Sherman's March." Ph.D. diss. University of Florida.

Frank, Lisa Tendrich. 2005. "War Comes Home: Confederate Women and Union Soldiers." In *Virginia's Civil War,* edited by Peter Wallenstein and Bertram Wyatt-Brown, 123-136. Charlottesville: University of Virginia Press.

Franklin, John Hope. 1963. *The Emancipation Proclamation.* Garden City, NY: Doubleday.

Frederickson, George M. 1965. *The Inner Civil War: Northern Intellectuals and the Crisis of the Union.* Urbana: University of Illinois Press.

Freehling, William W. 2001. *The South vs. the South: How Anti-Confederate Southerners Shaped the Course of the Civil War.* New York: Oxford University Press.

Freeman, Douglas Southall. 1942–1944. *Lee's Lieutenants: A Study in Command.* 3 vols. New York: Scribner's.

Freemon, Frank R. 2001. *Gangrene and Glory: Medical Care During the American Civil War.* Urbana: University of Illinois Press.

French, Stanley. 1974. "The Cemetery as Cultural Institution: The Establishment of Mount Auburn and the 'Rural Cemetery' Movement." *American Quarterly* 26 (1): 37–59.

Friedman, Jean E. 1985. *The Enclosed Garden: Women and Community in the Evangelical South, 1830–1900.* Chapel Hill: University of North Carolina Press.

Furgurson, Ernest B. 2004. *Freedom Rising: Washington in the Civil War.* New York: Alfred A. Knopf.

Furnas, J. C. 1982. *Fanny Kemble: Leading Lady of the Nineteenth-Century Stage.* New York: Dial Press.

Gabaccia, Donna. 1994. *From the Other Side: Immigrant Life in the U.S., 1820–1990.* Bloomington: Indiana University Press.

Gaines, W. Craig. 1989. *The Confederate Cherokees: John Drew's Regiment of Mounted Rifles.* Baton Rouge: Louisiana State University Press.

Galbraith, William, and Loretta Galbraith, eds. 1990. *A Lost Heroine of the Confederacy: The Diaries and Letters of Belle Edmondson.* Jackson: University Press of Mississippi.

Gallagher, Gary. 1986. "A Widow and Her Soldier: LaSalle Corbell Pickett as Author of the George E. Pickett Letters." *The Virginia Magazine of History and Biography* 94: 329–344.

Gallagher, Gary, ed. 1989. *Fighting for the Confederacy: The Personal Recollections of General Edward Porter Alexander.* Chapel Hill: University of North Carolina Press.

Gallagher, Gary, ed. 1996. *Chancellorsville: The Battle and Its Aftermath.* Chapel Hill: University of North Carolina Press.

Gallagher, Gary W. 1997. *The Confederate War: How Popular Will, Nationalism, and Military Strategy Could Not Stave Off Defeat.* Cambridge, MA: Harvard University Press.

Gallagher, Gary W., ed. 1997. *The Wilderness Campaign.* Chapel Hill: University of North Carolina Press.

Gallagher, Gary W., ed. 1999. *The Antietam Campaign.* Chapel Hill: University of North Carolina Press.

Gallagher, Gary W., ed. 2006. *The Shenandoah Valley Campaign of 1864.* Chapel Hill: University of North Carolina Press.

Gallman, J. Matthew. 1994. *The North Fights the Civil War: The Home Front.* Chicago: Ivan R. Dee.

Gallman, J. Matthew. 2006. *America's Joan of Arc: The Life of Anna Elizabeth Dickinson.* New York: Oxford University Press.

Gardner, Sarah E. 2001. "'A Sweet Solace to My Lonely Heart': 'Stonewall' and Mary Anna Jackson and the Civil War." In *Intimate Strategies of the Civil War: Military Commanders and their Wives,* edited by Carol K. Bleser and Lesley J. Gordon, 49–68. New York: Oxford University Press.

Gardner, Sarah E. 2004. *Blood and Irony: Southern White Women's Narratives of the Civil War, 1861–1937.* Chapel Hill: University of North Carolina Press.

Garfield, Deborah, and Rafia Zafar, eds. 1996. *Harriet Jacobs and 'Incidents in the Life of a Slave Girl': New Critical Essays.* New York: Cambridge University Press.

Garrison, Nancy S. 1999. *With Courage and Delicacy: Civil War on the Peninsula: Women and the U.S. Sanitary Commission.* Mason City, IA: Savas Publishing Company.

Garrison, Webb. 1995. *Atlanta and the War.* Nashville, TN: Rutledge Hill Press.

Gay, Mary A. H. [1892] 2001. *Life in Dixie during the War*. Edited by J. H. Segars. Macon, GA: Mercer University Press.

Geer, Emily Apt. 1984. *The First Lady, The Life of Lucy Webb Hayes*. Kent, OH: Kent State University Press.

Geisberg, Judith Ann. 2000. *Civil War Sisterhood: The U.S. Sanitary Commission and Women's Politics in Transition*. Boston: Northeastern University Press.

Genovese, Elizabeth Fox. 1988. *Within the Plantation Household: Black and White Women of the Old South*. Chapel Hill: University of North Carolina Press.

Genovese, Eugene D. 1991. "Toward a Kinder and Gentler America: The Southern Lady in the Greening of the Politics of the Old South." In *In Joy and in Sorrow: Women, Family, and Marriage in the Victorian South*, edited by Carol K. Bleser, 125–134. New York: Oxford University Press.

Gienapp, William. 1987. *The Origins of the Republican Party, 1852–1856*. New York: Oxford University Press.

Giesberg, Judith Ann. 1995. "In Service to the Fifth Wheel: Katharine Prescott Wormeley and Her Experiences in the United States Sanitary Commission." *Nursing History Review* 3: 43–53.

Giesberg, Judith Ann. 2000. *Civil War Sisterhood: The U.S. Sanitary Commission and Women's Politics in Transition*. Boston: Northeastern University Press.

Gilbert, Olive. [1878] 1968. *Narrative of Sojourner Truth: A Bondswoman of Olden Time*. New York: Arno Press.

Gilbo, Patrick F. 1981. *The American Red Cross: The First Century*. New York: Harper & Row.

Gilmore, Donald L. 2006. *Civil War on the Missouri-Kansas Border*. Gretna, LA: Pelican Publishing Company.

Ginzberg, Lori D. 1990. *Women and the Work of Benevolence: Morality, Politics, and Class in the Nineteenth-Century United States*. New Haven, CT: Yale University Press.

Glatthaar, Joseph T. [1985] 1995. *The March to the Sea and Beyond: Sherman's Troops in the Savannah and Carolinas Campaigns*. Baton Rouge: Louisiana State University Press.

Goen, C. C. 1985. *Broken Churches, Broken Nation: Denominational Schisms and the Coming of the American Civil War*. Macon, GA: Mercer University Press.

Goldin, Claudia D., and Frank D. Lewis. 1975. "The Economic Cost of the American Civil War: Estimates and Implications." *Journal of Economic History* 35 (2): 299–326.

Goodrich, Thomas. 1995. *Black Flag: Guerilla Warfare on the Western Border, 1861–1865*. Bloomington: Indiana University Press.

Gordon, Beverly. 1998. *Bazaars and Fair Ladies: The History of the American Fundraising Fair*. Knoxville: University of Tennessee Press.

Gordon, Lesley J. 1998. *General George E. Pickett in Life and Legend*. Chapel Hill: University of North Carolina Press.

Gordon, Lesley J. 2001. "'Cupid Does Not Readily Give Way to Mars': The Marriage of LaSalle Corbell and George E. Pickett." In *Intimate Strategies of the Civil War: Military Commanders and Their Wives*, edited by Carol K. Bleser and Lesley J. Gordon, 69–86. New York: Oxford University Press.

Gorman, Kathleen. 1999. "Confederate Pensions as Southern Social Welfare." In *Before the New Deal: Social Welfare in the South, 1830–1930*, edited by Elna C. Green, 24–39. Athens: University of Georgia Press.

Gould, Virginia Meacham. 1998. *Chained to the Rock of Adversity: To Be Free, Black, and Female in the Old South*. Athens: University of Georgia Press.

Graf, Mercedes. 2001. *A Woman of Honor: Dr. Mary E. Walker and the Civil War*. Gettysburg, PA: Thomas Publications.

Grant, Mary H. 1994. *Private Woman, Public Person: An Account of the Life of Julia Ward Howe from 1819 to 1868*. Brooklyn, NY: Carlson Publishing..

Greeley, Horace, and John Cleveland. 1860. *A Political Text-Book for 1860*. New York: Tribune Association.

Green, Carol C. 2004. *Chimborazo: The Confederacy's Largest Hospital*. Knoxville: University of Tennessee Press.

Greene, Dana, ed. 1980. *Lucretia Mott, Her Complete Speeches and Sermons*. Lewiston, NY: Edwin Mellen Press.

Greene, Elna C., ed. 1999. *Before the New Deal: Social Welfare in the South, 1830–1930*. Athens: University of Georgia Press.

Greenhow, Rose O'Neal. 1863. *My Imprisonment and the First Year of Abolition Rule in Washington*. London: Richard Bentley.

Greer, Jack. 1975. *Leaves from a Family Album*. Waco: Texian Press.

Griffin, Farah Jasmine, ed. 1999. *Beloved Sisters and Loving Friends: Letters from Rebecca Primus of Royal Oak, Maryland, and Addie Brown of Hartford, Connecticut, 1854–1868*. New York: Alfred A. Knopf.

Griffith, Elisabeth. 1984. *In Her Own Right: The Life of Elizabeth Cady Stanton*. New York: Oxford University Press.

Griffith, Helen. 1966. *Dauntless in Mississippi: The Life of Sarah A. Dickey.* South Hadley, MA: Dinosaur Press.

Griffith, Lucille. 1953. "Mrs. Juliet Opie Hopkins and Alabama Military Hospitals." *Alabama Review* 6: 99–120.

Grimsley, Mark. 1995. *The Hard Hand of War: Union Military Policy toward Southern Civilians, 1861–1865.* New York: Cambridge University Press.

Grimsley, Mark, and Brooks D. Simpson, eds. 2001. *The Collapse of the Confederacy.* Lincoln: University of Nebraska Press.

Grivetti, Louis E., Jan L. Corlett, and Cassius T. Lockett. 2002. "Food in American History. Part 5: Pork: A Nation Divided: The American Civil War Era (1861–1865)." *Nutrition Today* 37 (3): 110–118.

Groce, W. Todd. 1999. *Mountain Rebels: East Tennessee Confederates and the Civil War, 1860–1870.* Knoxville: University of Tennessee Press.

Gross, Jennifer Lynn. 2001. *"Good Angels": Confederate Widowhood and the Reassurance of Patriarchy in the Postbellum South.* Ph.D. diss., University of Georgia.

Guelzo, Allen C. 2004. *The Emancipation Proclamation: The End of Slavery in America.* New York: Simon & Schuster.

Guerin, Elsa Jane. 1968. *Mountain Charley, or the Adventures of Mrs. E. J. Guerin, Who Was Thirteen Years in Male Attire: An Autobiography Comprising a Period of Thirteen Years Life in the States, California, and Pike's Peak,* with Introduction by Fred W. Mazzulla and William Kostka. Norman: University of Oklahoma Press.

Guilfoyle, Timothy. 1992. *City of Eros: New York City Prostitution and the Commercialization of Sex, 1790–1920.* New York: W. W. Norton.

Guterman, Benjamin. 2000. "Doing 'Good Brave Work'. Harriet Tubman's Testimony at Beaufort, South Carolina." *Prologue* 42: 155–165

Gutman, Herbert G. 1977. *The Black Family in Slavery and Freedom, 1750–1925.* New York: Vintage.

Hague, Parthenia Antoinette. [1888] 1991. *A Blockaded Family: Life in Southern Alabama During the Civil War.* Lincoln: University of Nebraska Press.

Hall, Richard. 1993. *Patriots in Disguise: Women Warriors of the Civil War.* New York: Paragon House.

Halttunen, Karen. 1982. *Confidence Men and Painted Women: A Study of Middle-Class Culture in America, 1830–1870.* New Haven, CT: Yale University Press.

Hanna, William F. 1990. "The Boston Draft Riot." *Civil War History* 36: 262–273.

Hansen, Debra Gold. 1993. *Strained Sisterhood: Gender and Class in the Boston Female Anti-Slavery Society.* Amherst: University of Massachusetts Press.

Hansen, Karen. 1995. "'No Kisses Is Like Youres': An Erotic Friendship between Two African American Women during the Mid-Nineteenth Century." *Gender and History* 7 (2): 151–182.

Harker, Jaime. 2001. "'Pious Cant' and Blasphemy: Fanny Fern's Radicalized Sentiment." *Legacy* 18 (1): 52–64.

Harper, Ida Husted. 1898. *The Life and Work of Susan B. Anthony.* Vol. 1. Indianapolis, IN: Hollenbeck Press.

Harrington, Fred Harvey. 1948. *Fighting Politician: Major General N. P. Banks.* Philadelphia: University of Pennsylvania Press.

Harris, Sharon M. 1991. *Rebecca Harding Davis and American Realism.* Philadelphia: University of Pennsylvania Press.

Harrison, Kimberly. 2003. "Rhetorical Rehearsals: The Construction of Ethos in Confederate Women's Civil War Diaries." *Rhetoric Review* 22 (3): 243–263.

Harrison, Lowell H. 1975. *The Civil War in Kentucky.* Lexington: University Press of Kentucky.

Hart, John S. 1852. *The Female Prose Writers of America, with Portraits, Biographical Notices, and Specimens of their Writing.* Philadelphia, PA: E. H. Butler & Co.

Harwell, Richard Barsdale. 1950. *Confederate Music.* Chapel Hill: University of North Carolina Press.

Harwell, Richard Barsdale, ed. [1959] 1998. *Kate: The Journal of a Confederate Nurse.* Baton Rouge: Louisiana State University Press.

Hauptman, Laurence. 1993. *The Iroquois in the Civil War: From Battlefield to Reservation.* Syracuse, NY: Syracuse University Press.

Haviland, Laura Smith. 1881. *A Woman's Life Work: Labors and Experiences of Laura S. Haviland.* Cincinnati, OH: Walden and Stowe.

Headley, John W. 1906. *Confederate Operations in Canada and New York.* New York: Neale Publishing Company.

Heaps, Willard A., and Porter W. Heaps. 1960. *The Singing Sixties: The Spirit of Civil War Days Drawn from the Music of the Times.* Norman: University of Oklahoma Press.

Hearn, Chester. 1997. *When the Devil Came Down to Dixie: Ben Butler in New Orleans.* Baton Rouge: Louisiana State University Press.

Hennessy, John J. 1993. *Return to Bull Run: The Campaign and Battle of Second Manassas.* New York: Simon & Schuster.

Hennessy, John. 2005. "For All Anguish, For Some Freedom: Fredericksburg in the War." *Blue and Gray Magazine* 22: 6–53.

Hennig, Helen Kohn, ed. 1936. *Columbia, Capital City of South Carolina, 1786–1936.* Columbia, SC: Columbia Sesquicentennial Commission, R. L. Bryan Co.

Henshaw, Sarah Edwards. 1868. *Our Branch and Its Tributaries.* Chicago: Alfred L. Sewell & Co.

Henwood, Dawn. 1999. "Slaveries 'In the Borders': Rebecca Harding Davis's 'Life in the Iron Mills' in its Southern Context." *Mississippi Quarterly* 52 (4): 567–596.

Herr, Pamela. 1988. *Jessie Benton Frémont: A Biography.* Norman: University of Oklahoma Press.

Herr, Pamela, and Mary Lee Spence, eds. 1993. *The Letters of Jessie Benton Frémont.* Urbana: University of Illinois Press.

Herran, Kathy Neill. 1997. *They Married Confederate Officers: The Intimate Story of Anna Morrison, Wife of Stonewall Jackson and Her Five Sisters.* Davidson, NC: Warren Publishing.

Hess, Earl J. 1997. *The Union Soldier in Battle: Enduring the Ordeal of Combat.* Lawrence: University Press of Kansas.

Higginbotham, Evelyn Brooks. 1994. *Righteous Discontent: The Women's Movement in the Black Baptist Church, 1880–1920.* Cambridge, MA: Harvard University Press.

Higonnet, Margaret R. 1989. "Civil War and Sexual Territories." In *Arms and the Woman: War, Gender, and Literary Representation,* edited by Helen M. Cooper, Adrienne Auslander Munich, and Susan Merrill Squier, 80–96. Chapel Hill: University of North Carolina Press.

Hill, Marilyn Wood. 1993. *Their Sisters' Keepers: Prostitution in New York City, 1830–1870.* Berkeley: University of California Press.

Hodgson, Godfrey. 2005. "Storm over Mexico." *History Today* 55: 34–39.

Hoff, Joan. 1991. *Law, Gender, and Injustice: A Legal History of U.S. Women.* New York: New York University Press.

Hoffert, Sylvia D. 2004. *Jane Grey Swisshelm: An Unconventional Life, 1815–1884.* Chapel Hill: University of North Carolina Press.

Hoffman, Nancy, ed. 1981. *Woman's "True" Profession: Voices from the History of Teaching.* Old Westbury, NY: Feminist Press/New York: McGraw-Hill.

Hoffman, Nicole Tonkovich. 1990. "Legacy Profile: Sarah Josepha Hale." *Legacy* 7 (2): 47–55.

Hoge, Jane (Mrs. A. H.). 1867. *The Boys in Blue, or Heroes of the "Rank and File."* New York: E. B. Treat and Company.

Hoisington, Daniel John, ed. 2001. *My Heart toward Home: Letters of a Family during the Civil War.* Roseville, MN: Edinborough Press.

Holdredge, Helen. 1953. *Mammy Pleasant.* New York: G.P. Putnam's Sons.

Holland, Mary Gardner, with Introduction by Daniel John Hoisington. 1998. *Our Army Nurses: Stories from Women in the Civil War.* Roseville, MN: Edinborough Press.

Holland, Rupert Sargent, ed. 1969. *Letters and Diary of Laura M. Towne: Written from the Sea Islands of South Carolina, 1862–1884.* New York: Negro University Press.

Hollandsworth, James G. 1998. *Pretense of Glory: The Life of Nathaniel P. Banks.* Baton Rouge: Louisiana State University Press.

Holman, Harriet R. 1965. *The Verse of Floride Clemson.* Columbia: University of South Carolina Press.

Holmes, Amy. 1990. "'Such Is the Price We Pay': American Widows and the Civil War Pension System." In *Toward a Social History of the American Civil War: Exploratory Essays,* edited by Maris Vinovskis, 171–195. Cambridge University Press.

Holt, Thad, Jr., ed. 1964. *Miss Waring's Journal, 1863 and 1865: Being the Diary of Miss Mary Waring of Mobile, during the final days of the War Between the States.* Chicago: The Wyvern Press of S. F. E.

Holtzman, Robert S. 1959. "Sally Tompkins, Captain, Confederate Army." *American Mercury* 127–130.

Hoogenboom, Ari. 1995. *Rutherford B. Hayes.* Lawrence: University Press of Kansas.

Hopley, Catherine Cooper. 1863. *"Stonewall" Jackson, Late General of the Confederate States Army. A Biographical Sketch, and an Outline of His Virginia Campaigns.* London: Chapman and Hall.

Hopley, Catherine Cooper. 1971. *Life in the South from the Commencement of the War by a Blockaded British Subject. Being a Social History of Those Who Took Part in the Battles, from a Personal Acquaintance with Them in Their Own Homes.* 2 vols. New York: Augustus M. Kelley Publishers. (Reprint of 1863 edition.)

Horn, John. 1993. *The Petersburg Campaign: June 1864–April 1865.* Conshohocken, PA: Combined Books.

Horn, Pamela. 1985. *The Victorian Country Child.* Wolfeboro Falls, NH: Alan Sutton.

Horn, Stanley. 1952. *The Army of Tennessee.* Norman: University of Oklahoma Press.

Horton, James Oliver, and Lots E. Horton. 1979. *Black Bostonians: Family Life and Community Struggle in the Antebellum North.* New York: Holmes and Meier Publishers.

Hoy, Claire. 2004. *Canadians in the Civil War.* Toronto: McArthur & Company.

Hudson, Linda S. 2001. *Mistress of Manifest Destiny; A Biography of Jane McManus Storm Cazneau, 1807–1878.* Austin: Texas State Historical Association.

Hudson, Lynn M. 2003. *The Making of "Mammy" Pleasant: A Black Entrepreneur in Nineteenth-Century San Francisco.* Urbana: University of Illinois Press.

Humez, Jean M. 2003. *Harriet Tubman: The Life and the Life Stories.* Madison: University of Wisconsin Press.

Humphreys, Margaret. 1992. *Yellow Fever and the South.* Piscataway, NJ: Rutgers University Press.

Hunter, Tera W. 1997. *To 'Joy My Freedom: Southern Black Women's Lives and Labors After the Civil War.* Cambridge, MA: Harvard University Press.

Hurn, Ethel Alice. 1911. *Wisconsin Women in the War between the States.* Madison: Wisconsin History Commission.

Hutchinson, John F. 1996. *Champions of Charity: War and the Rise of the Red Cross.* Boulder, CO: Westview Press.

Hutton, Paul Andrew. 1985. *Phil Sheridan and His Army.* Lincoln: University of Nebraska Press.

Hyman, Harold M. 1954. *Era of the Oath: Northern Loyalty Tests during the Civil War and Reconstruction.* Philadelphia: University of Pennsylvania Press.

Hyman, Harold M. 1973. *"A More Perfect Union": The Impact of the Civil War and Reconstruction on the Constitution.* New York: Alfred A. Knopf.

Inscoe, John. 1992. "Coping in Confederate Appalachia: A Portrait of a Mountain Woman and Her Community at War." *North Carolina Historical Review* 69: 388–413.

Inscoe, John. 1996. "The Civil War's Empowerment of an Appalachian Woman: The 1864 Slave Purchases of Mary Bell." In *Discovering the Women in Slavery: Emancipating Perspectives of the American Past,* edited by Patricia Morton, 61–81. Athens: University of Georgia Press.

Inscoe, John C., and Robert C. Kenzer, eds. 2001. *Enemies of the Country: New Perspectives on Unionists in the Civil War South.* Athens: University of Georgia Press.

Jackson, Mary Anna. 1892. *Life and Letters of General Thomas J. Jackson.* New York: Harper and Brothers.

Jackson, Roswell F., and Rosalyn M. Patterson. 1989. "A Brief History of Selected Black Churches in Atlanta, Georgia." *Journal of Negro History* 74 (Winter): 31–59.

Jackson-Coppin, Fanny. [1913] 1995. *Reminiscences of School Life and Hints on Teaching.* Introduction by Shelley P. Haley. Boston: G. K. Hall & Co.

Jacob, Katherine Allamong. 2000. "Vinnie Ream: The 'Prairie Cinderella' Who Sculpted Lincoln and Farragut—And Set Tongues Wagging." *Smithsonian* 31 (5): 104–115.

Jacobs, Harriet A. [1861] 1987. *Incidents in the Life of a Slave Girl,* edited by Jean Fagan Yellin. Cambridge, MA: Harvard University Press.

Jacobs, Joanna. 1988. "Eugenia Levy Phillips vs. The United States of America." *Alabama Heritage* 50: 22–29.

Jaquette, Henrietta Stratton, ed. 1937. *South after Gettysburg: Letters of Cornelia Hancock, 1863–1865.* New York: Thomas Y. Crowell & Company.

Jeffrey, Julie Roy. 1998. *The Great Silent Army of Abolitionism: Ordinary Women in the Antislavery Movement.* Chapel Hill: University of North Carolina Press.

Jenkins, Wilbert L. 2002. *Climbing up to Glory: A Short History of African Americans during the Civil War and Reconstruction.* Wilmington, DE: Scholarly Resources.

Jepsen, Thomas. 2000. *My Sisters Telegraphic: Women in the Telegraph Office, 1846–1850.* Athens: Ohio University Press.

Johannsen, Albert. 1950. *The House of Beadle and Adams.* Norman: University of Oklahoma Press.

Johnson, Carolyn Ross. 2003. *Cherokee Women in Crisis: Trail of Tears, Civil War, and Allotment.* Tuscaloosa: University of Alabama Press.

Johnson, Michael P., ed. 2001. *Abraham Lincoln, Slavery, and the Civil War: Selected Writings and Speeches.* Boston: Bedford/St. Martin's.

Johnston, Mary Tabb, with Elizabeth Johnston Lipscomb. 1978. *Amelia Gayle Gorgas: A Biography.* Tuscaloosa: University of Alabama Press.

Jolly, Ellen Ryan. 1927. *Nuns of the Battlefield.* Providence, RI: Providence Visitor Press.

Jones, Ann Goodwyn. 1981. *Tomorrow Is Another Day: The Woman Writer in the South, 1859–1936.* Baton Rouge: Louisiana State University Press.

Jones, Jacqueline. 1980. *Soldiers of Light and Love: Northern Teachers and Georgia Blacks, 1865–1873.* Chapel Hill: University of North Carolina Press.

Jones, Jacqueline. 1985. *Labor of Love, Labor of Sorrow: Black Women, Work and the Family from Slavery to the Present.* New York: Vintage.

Jones, James Boyd. 1985. "A Tale of Two Cities: The Hidden Battle against Venereal Disease in Civil War Nashville and Memphis." *Civil War History* 31 (3): 270–276.

Jones, Katharine M., ed. 1962. *Ladies of Richmond, Confederate Capital.* Indianapolis, IN: Bobbs-Merrill.

Jones, Katherine M., ed. 1964. *When Sherman Came: Southern Women and the "Great March."* Indianapolis, IN: Bobbs-Merrill.

Jones, Mary Sharpe, and Mary Jones Mallard. 1959. *Yankees a'Coming: One Month's Experience during the Invasion of Liberty County, Georgia, 1864–1865,* edited by Haskell Monroe. Tuscaloosa, AL: Confederate Publishing Company.

Jones, Paul Christian. 2001. "'This Dainty Woman's Hand . . . Red with Blood': E. D. E. N. Southworth's *The Hidden Hand* as Abolitionist Narrative." *American Transcendental Quarterly* 15 (1): 59–80.

Jordan, Waymouth T. Jr. 1979. *North Carolina Troops 1861–1865: A Roster.* Raleigh, NC: Division of Archives and History.

Josephy, Alvin M. Jr. 1992. *The Civil War in the American West.* New York: Alfred A. Knopf.

Joslyn, Mauriel Phillips, ed. 2004. *Confederate Women.* Gretna, LA: Pelican Publishing Company.

Kadzis, Peter, ed. 2000. *Blood: Stories of Life and Death from the Civil War.* New York: Thunder's Mouth Press.

Kaestle, Carl. 1983. *Pillars of the Republic: Common Schools and American Society, 1780–1860.* New York: Hill and Wang.

Kampmeier, Rudolph H. 1982. "Venereal Disease in the United States Army, 1775–1900." *Sexually Transmitted Diseases* 9 (2): 100–108.

Kane, Harnett T. 1954. *Spies for the Blue and Gray.* New York: Hanover House.

Karcher, Carolyn L. 1994. *The First Woman in the Republic: A Cultural Biography of Lydia Maria Child.* Durham, NC: Duke University Press.

Karcher, Carolyn L., ed. 1996. *An Appeal in Favor of That Class of Americans Called Africans.* Amherst: University of Massachusetts Press.

Katcher, Phillip, and Richard Scollins (illus.). 2000. *Flags of the Civil War.* Oxford: Osprey Publishing.

Kaufmann, Janet E. 1984. "Under the Petticoat Flag: Women Soldiers in the Confederate Army." *Southern Studies* 23: 363–375.

Kaufman, Janet E. 1986. "Working Women of the South: 'Treasury Girls.'" *Civil War Times Illustrated* 25: 32–38.

Keckley, Elizabeth. [1868] 1988. *Behind the Scenes, or Thirty Years a Slave and Four Years in the White House.* New York: Oxford University Press.

Kelley, Mary. 1984. *Private Woman, Public Stage: Literary Domesticity in Nineteenth-Century America.* New York: Oxford University Press.

Kelly, Bruce C., and Mark A. Snell, eds. 2004. *Bugle Resounding: Music and Musicians of the Civil War Era.* Columbia: University of Missouri Press.

Kelly, Lori Duin. 1983. *The Life and Works of Elizabeth Stuart Phelps, Victorian Feminist Writer.* Albany, NY: Whitston Publishing Company.

Kemble, Frances Anne. 1961. *Journal of a Residence on a Georgian Plantation: 1838–1839,* with Introduction by John A. Scott. Athens: University of Georgia Press. (Reprint of 1863 edition.)

Kennett, Lee. 1995. *Marching through Georgia: The Story of Soldiers and Civilians during Sherman's Campaign.* New York: HarperPerennial.

Kenzer, Robert C. 1987. *Kinship and Neighborhood in a Southern Community: Orange County, North Carolina, 1849–1881.* Knoxville: University of Tennessee Press.

Kerr, Andrea Moore. 1992. *Lucy Stone: Speaking out for Equality.* Piscataway, NJ: Rutgers University Press.

Kerr, Andrea Moore. 1995. "White Women's Rights, Black Men's Wrongs, Free Love, Blackmail, and the Formation of the American Woman Suffrage Association." In *One Woman, One Vote: Rediscovering the Woman Suffrage Movement,* edited by Marjorie Spruill Wheeler, 61-80. Troutdale, OR: NewSage Press.

Kessler, Carol Farley. 1982. *Elizabeth Stuart Phelps.* New York: Twayne Publishers.

Kessler-Harris, Alice. 1982. *Out to Work: A History of Wage-Earning Women in the United States.* Oxford: Oxford University Press.

Kete, Mary Louise. 2000. *Sentimental Collaborations: Mourning and Middle-Class Identity in Nineteenth-Century America.* Durham, NC: Duke University Press.

Kinchen, Oscar A. 1972. *Women Who Spied for the Blue and the Gray.* Philadelphia, PA: Dorrance & Company.

King, Spencer Bidwell, Jr., ed. 1958. *Ebb Tide: As Seen through the Diary of Josephine Clay Habersham, 1863.* Athens: University of Georgia Press.

King, Wendy A. 1992. *Clad in Uniform: Women Soldiers of the Civil War.* Collingswood, NJ: C. W. Historicals.

King, Wilma, ed. 1993. *A Northern Woman in the Plantation South: Letters of Tryphena Blanche Holder Fox, 1856–1876.* Columbia: University of South Carolina Press.

Klein, Maury. 1997. *Days of Defiance: Sumter, Secession, and the Coming of the Civil War.* New York: Alfred A. Knopf.

Klement, Frank L. 1999. *Lincoln's Critics: The Copperheads of the North,* edited by Steven K. Rogstad. Shippensburg, PA: White Mane Publishing Co.

Kohlstedt, Sally Gregory. 1978. "Maria Mitchell and the Advancement of Women in Science." *New England Quarterly* 51: 39–63.

Kolchin, Peter. 2003. *American Slavery: 1619–1877.* New York: Hill and Wang.

Korn, Bertram W. 1961. *American Jewry and the Civil War,* with Introduction by Allan Nevins. Cleveland, OH, New York, and Philadelphia, PA: Meridian Books and Jewish Publication Society.

Kraditor, Aileen S. 1969. *Means and Ends in American Abolitionism: Garrison and His Critics on Strategy and Tactics, 1864–1850.* New York: Random House.

Kurant, Wendy. 2002. "The Education of a Domestic Woman in Mary Boykin Chesnut's *Two Years.*" *The Southern Literary Journal* 34 (2): 14–29.

Laas, Virginia Jeans, ed. 1991. *Wartime Washington: The Civil War Letters of Elizabeth Blair Lee.* Urbana: University of Illinois Press.

Laas, Virginia Jeans. 2001. "'A Good Wife, the Best Friend in the World': The Marriage of Elizabeth Blair and S. Phillips Lee." In *Intimate Strategies of the Civil War: Military Commanders and Their Wives,* edited by Carol K. Bleser and Lesley J. Gordon, 225–242. New York: Oxford University Press.

Ladies' Christian Commission. 1864. *Ladies' Christian Commissions: Auxiliary to the U.S. Christian Commission.* Philadelphia: C. Sherman.

Lancaster, Jane. 2001. "'I Would Have Made Out Very Poorly Had It Not Been for Her': The Life and Work of Christiana Bannister, Hair Doctress and Philanthropist." *Rhode Island History* 59 (4): 103–122.

Lane, Mills, ed. 1990. *"Dear Mother: Don't grieve about me. If I get killed, I'll only be dead": Letters from Georgia Soldiers in the Civil War.* Savannah, GA: Beehive Press. (Reprint of 1977 edition.)

Larsen, Arthur J., ed. 1934. *Crusader and Feminist: Letters of Jane Grey Swisshelm 1858–1865.* Saint Paul: Minnesota Historical Society Press.

Larsen, Lawrence H. 1961. "Draft Riot in Wisconsin, 1862." *Civil War History* 7: 421–427.

Larson, C. Kay. 1992. "Bonny Yank and Ginny Reb Revisited." *Minerva, Quarterly Report on Women and the Military* 10 (2): 33–48.

Larson, Kate Clifford. 2004. *Bound for the Promised Land: Harriet Tubman, Portrait of an American Hero.* New York: Ballantine Books.

Larson, Rebecca D. 1996. *Blue and Grey Roses of Intrigue.* Gettysburg, PA: Thomas Publications.

Lassen, Coralou Peel, ed. 1999. *"Dear Sarah:" Letters Home from a Soldier of the Iron Brigade.* Bloomington: Indiana University Press.

Lawson, Melinda. 2002. *Patriot Fires: Forging a New American Nationalism in the Civil War North.* Lawrence: University Press of Kansas.

Lease, Benjamin. 1990. *Emily Dickinson's Readings of Men and Books: Sacred Soundings.* New York: St. Martin's Press.

Lebsock, Suzanne. 1984. *The Free Women of Petersburg: Status and Culture in a Southern Town, 1784–1860.* New York: W. W. Norton & Company.

Leckie, Shirley A. 1993. *Elizabeth Bacon Custer and the Making of a Myth.* Norman: University of Oklahoma Press.

Leckie, Shirley A. 2001. "The Civil War Partnership of Elizabeth and George A. Custer." In *Intimate Strategies of the Civil War: Civil War Commanders and their Wives,* edited by Carol K. Bleser and Lesley J. Gordon, 178–198. New York: Oxford University Press.

LeConte, Emma. 1987. *When the World Ended: The Diary of Emma LeConte,* edited by Earl Schenck Meirs, with Foreword by Anne Firor Scott. Lincoln: University of Nebraska Press.

Leonard, Ann. 1991. "Red Rover, The Civil War, and the Nuns." *Lincoln Herald* 93 (4): 136–140.

Leonard, Ann. 2000. "Catholic Sisters and Nursing in the Civil War." *Lincoln Herald* 102 (2): 65–81.

Leonard, Elizabeth D. 1994. *Yankee Women: Gender Battles in the Civil War.* New York: W. W. Norton.

Leonard, Elizabeth D. 1995. "Civil War Nurse, Civil War Nursing: Rebecca Usher of Maine." *Civil War History* 41 (3): 190–208.

Leonard, Elizabeth D. 1999. *All the Daring of a Soldier: Women of the Civil War Armies.* New York: W. W. Norton & Company.

Leonard, Elizabeth D. 2004. *Lincoln's Avengers: Justice, Revenge, and Reunion after the Civil War.* New York: W. W. Norton & Company.

Lerner, Gerda. 1998. *The Grimké Sisters from South Carolina: Pioneers for Women's Rights and Abolition.* New York: Oxford University Press.

Leslie, Edward E. 1998. *The Devil Knows How to Ride: The True Story of William Clarke Quantrill and His Confederate Raiders.* New York: Da Capo Press.

Lewis, Charles Lee. 1927. *Matthew Fontaine Maury: The Pathfinder of the Seas.* Annapolis, MD: U.S. Naval Institute.

Lewis, Elizabeth Wittenmyer. 2002. *Queen of the Confederacy, the Innocent Deceits of Lucy Holcombe Pickens.* Denton: University of North Texas Press.

Lightener, David L., ed. 1999. *Asylum, Prison, and Poorhouse: The Writings and Reform Work of Dorothea Dix in Illinois.* Carbondale: Southern Illinois University Press.

Linderman, Gerald E. 1987. *Embattled Courage: The Experience of Combat in the American Civil War.* New York: Free Press.

Link, William. 2003. *Roots of Secession: Slavery and Politics in Antebellum Virginia.* Chapel Hill: University of North Carolina Press.

Lively, Robert A. 1957. *Fiction Fights the Civil War: An Unfinished Chapter in the Literary History of the American People.* Chapel Hill: University of North Carolina Press.

Livermore, Mary Ashton Rice. 1890. *My Story of the War: A Woman's Narrative of Four Years Personal Experience as a Nurse in the Union Army.* Hartford, CT: A. D. Worthington and Company. (Reprinted 1974 in Women in America, from Colonial Times to the Twentieth Century series. New York: Arno Press.)

Logan, Kate Virginia Cox. 1932. *My Confederate Girlhood: The Memoirs of Kate Virginia Cox Logan,* edited by Lily Logan Morrill. Richmond, VA: Garrett and Massie.

Long, David. 1994. *Jewel of Liberty: Abraham Lincoln's Reelection and the End of Slavery.* Mechanicsburg, PA: Stackpole Books.

Long, Ellen Call. [1882] 1962. *Florida Breezes; or, Florida, New and Old.* Gainesville: University Press of Florida.

Lonn, Ella. 1928. *Desertion during the Civil War.* New York: American Historical Association.

Lonn, Ella. 2002. *Foreigners in the Confederacy.* Chapel Hill: University of North Carolina Press.

Loughridge, Patricia R., and Edward D. C. Campbell Jr. 1985. *Women and Mourning.* Richmond, VA: Museum of the Confederacy.

Lowry, Thomas P. 1994. *The Story the Soldiers Wouldn't Tell: Sex in the Civil War.* Mechanicsburg, PA: Stackpole Books.

Luebke, Frederick C. 1971. *Ethnic Voters and the Election of Lincoln.* Lincoln: University of Nebraska Press.

Lutz, Alama. 1940. *Created Equal: A Biography of Elizabeth Cady Stanton, 1815–1902.* New York: John Day Company.

Lutz, Alma. 1959. *Susan B. Anthony: Rebel, Crusader, Humanitarian.* Boston: Beacon Press.

Lystra, Karen. 1989. *Searching the Heart: Women, Men, and Romantic Love in Nineteenth-Century America.* New York: Oxford University Press.

Mabee, Carleton, with Susan Mabee Newhouse. 1993. *Sojourner Truth: Slave, Prophet, Legend.* New York: New York University Press.

Macaulay, John Allen. 2001. *Unitarianism in the Antebellum South: The Other Invisible Institution.* Tuscaloosa: University of Alabama Press.

MacDonald, Joanna M. 1999. *"We Shall Meet Again": The First Battle of Manassas (Bull Run), July 18–21, 1861.* Shippensburg, PA: White Mane Publishing Co.

MacDonald, Rose. 1939. *Mrs. Robert E. Lee.* Boston: Ginn & Company.

MacKethan, Lucinda H., ed. 1998. *Recollections of a Southern Daughter: A Memoir by Cornelia Jones Pond of Liberty County.* Athens: University of Georgia Press.

Mackey, Robert R. 2004. *The Uncivil War: Irregular Warfare in the Upper South, 1861–1865.* Norman: University of Oklahoma Press.

Maher, Sister Mary Denis. 1989. *To Bind up the Wounds: Catholic Sister Nurses in the U.S. Civil War.* Westport, CT: Greenwood Press.

Mahin, Dean B. 2002. *The Blessed Place of Freedom: Europeans in Civil War America.* Washington, DC: Brassey's.

Marchalonis, Shirley. 1988. "Lucy Larcom." *Legacy: A Journal of American Women Writers* 5 (1): 45–52.

Marchalonis, Shirley. 1989. *Worlds of Lucy Larcom, 1842–1893.* Athens: University of Georgia Press.

Markle, Donald E. 2000. *Spies and Spymasters of the Civil War.* New York: Hippocrene Books. (Revised edition in 2004.)

Marsh, Thomas O., and Marlene Templin. 1988. "The Ballad of Lottie Moon." *Civil War: The Magazine of the Civil War Society* 21: 40–45.

Marshall, H. E. 1937. *Dorothea Dix, Forgotten Samaritan.* Chapel Hill: University of North Carolina Press.

Marshall, Megan. 2005. *The Peabody Sisters: Three Women Who Ignited American Romanticism.* Boston: Houghton Mifflin Company.

Marszalek, John F. 1993. *Sherman: A Soldier's Passion for Order.* New York: Free Press.

Marszalek. John F., ed. 1994. *The Diary of Miss Emma Holmes, 1861–1866.* Baton Rouge: Louisiana State University Press. (Reprint of 1979 edition.)

Marszalek, John F. 2001. "General and Mrs. William T. Sherman, A Contentious Union." In *Intimate Strategies of the Civil War, Military Commanders and Their Wives,* edited by Carol K. Bleser and Lesley J. Gordon, 138-156. New York: Oxford University Press.

Marszalek, John F. 2005. *Sherman's March to the Sea.* Civil War Campaigns and Commanders Series. Abilene, TX: McWhiney Foundation Press.

Marten, James. 1990. *Texas Divided: Loyalty and Dissent in the Lone Star State.* Lexington: University of Kentucky Press.

Marten, James. 1998. *The Children's Civil War.* Chapel Hill: University of North Carolina Press.

Marvel, William. 1991. *Burnside.* Chapel Hill: University of North Carolina Press.

Marvel, William. 2000. *A Place Called Appomattox.* Chapel Hill: University of North Carolina Press.

Massey, Mary Elizabeth. 1949. "The Food and Drink Shortage on the Confederate Homefront." *North Carolina Historical Review* 26: 306–334.

Massey, Mary Elizabeth. 1952. *Ersatz in the Confederacy: Shortages and Substitutes on the Southern Homefront.* Columbia: University of South Carolina Press.

Massey, Mary Elizabeth. 1964. *Refugee Life in the Confederacy.* Baton Rouge: Louisiana State University Press.

Massey, Mary Elizabeth. 1973. "The Making of a Feminist." *Journal of Southern History* 39 (1): 3–22.

Massey, Mary Elizabeth. 1994. *Women in the Civil War.* Lincoln: University of Nebraska Press. (Reprint of *Bonnet Brigades.* New York: Alfred A. Knopf, 1966.)

Matthews, Glenna. 1992. *The Rise of Public Woman: Woman's Power and Place in the United States, 1630–1970.* New York: Oxford University Press.

Matthews, Glenna. 1997. *"Just a Housewife": The Rise and Fall of Domesticity in America.* New York: Oxford University Press.

Maxwell, William Quentin. 1956. *Lincoln's Fifth Wheel: The Political History of the United States Sanitary Commission.* New York: Longmans, Green & Company.

Mayer, Henry. 1998. *All on Fire: William Lloyd Garrison and the Abolition of Slavery.* New York: St. Martin's Griffin.

McAllister, Anna. 1936. *Ellen Sherman, Wife of General Sherman.* New York: Benziger Brothers.

McClintock, Megan J. 1996. "Civil War Pensions and the Reconstruction of Union Families." *Journal of American History* 83: 456–479.

McCrumb, Sharyn. 2003. *Ghost Riders.* New York: Dutton.

McCurry, Stephanie. 1992. "The Politics of Yeoman Households in South Carolina." In *Divided Houses: Gender and the Civil War,* edited by Catherine Clinton and Nina Silber, 22–38. New York: Oxford University Press.

McCurry, Stephanie. 1992. "The Two Faces of Republicanism: Gender and Proslavery Politics in Antebellum South Carolina." *Journal of American History* 78: 1245–1264.

McCurry, Stephanie. 1995. *Masters of Small Worlds: Yeoman Households, Gender Relations and the Political Culture of the Antebellum South Carolina Low Country.* New York: Oxford University Press.

McDevitt, Theresa R. 2004. "'A Melody before Unknown': The Civil War Experiences of Mary and Amanda Shelton." *Annals of Iowa* 63 (2): 105–136.

McDonald, Cornelia Peake. 1992. *A Woman's Civil War: A Diary with Reminiscences of the War from March 1862,* edited by Minrose C. Gwin. Madison: University of Wisconsin Press.

McElligott, Mary Ellen, ed. 1977. "'A Monotony Full of Sadness': The Diary of Nadine Turchin, May, 1863–April 1864." *Journal of the Illinois State Historical Society* 70: 27–89.

McGee, Charles M. Jr., and Ernest M. Landers Jr., eds. 1989. *A Rebel Came Home: The Diary and Letters of Floride Clemson, 1863–1866.* Columbia: University of South Carolina Press.

McGuire, Judith W. 1995. *Diary of a Southern Refugee during the War, by a Lady of Virginia,* with Introduction by Jean V. Berlin. Lincoln: University of Nebraska Press.

McKay, Charlotte E. 1876. *Stories of Hospital and Camp.* Philadelphia, PA: Claxton, Remsen & Haffelfinger.

McKnight, Brian D. 2006. *Contested Borderland: The Civil War in Appalachian Kentucky and Virginia.* Lexington: University Press of Kentucky.

McMurry, Richard M. 2000. *Atlanta 1864: Last Chance for the Confederacy.* Lincoln: University of Nebraska Press.

McMurry, Sally. 1995. *Transforming Rural Life: Dairying Families and Agricultural Change, 1820–1885.* Baltimore, MD: Johns Hopkins University Press.

McPherson, James M. 1964. *The Struggle for Equality.* Princeton, NJ: Princeton University Press.

McPherson, James M. 1965. *The Negro's Civil War: How American Blacks Felt and Acted during the War for the Union.* New York: Ballantine Books.

McPherson, James M. 1982. *Ordeal by Fire: The Civil War and Reconstruction.* New York: Alfred A. Knopf.

McPherson, James M. 1996. *Drawn with the Sword: Reflections on the American Civil War.* New York: Oxford University Press.

McPherson, James M. 1997. *For Cause and Comrades: Why Men Fought in the Civil War.* New York: Oxford University Press.

McPherson, James M. 2002. *Crossroads of Freedom: Antietam.* New York: Oxford University Press.

McPherson, James M. 2003. *Battle Cry of Freedom: The Civil War Era.* New York: Oxford University Press. (Reprint of 1988 edition. New York: Ballantine Books.)

McPherson, James M., and William J. Cooper Jr., eds. 1998. *Writing the Civil War: The Quest to Understand.* Columbia: University of South Carolina Press.

Melder, Keith E. 1963–1965. "Angel of Mercy in Washington: Josephine Griffing and the Freedmen, 1864–1872." *Records of the Columbia Historical Society of Washington, DC.*

Menendez, Albert J. 1986. *Civil War Novels: An Annotated Bibliography 1986.* New York: Garland Publishing.

Merington, Marguerite, ed. 1950. *The Custer Story: The Life and Intimate Letters of General George Armstrong Custer and His Wife Elizabeth.* New York: Devon-Adair.

Meriwether, Elizabeth Avery. 1880. *The Master of Red Leaf.* New York: E. J. Hale & Son.

Meriwether, Elizabeth Avery. 1958. *Recollections of 92 Years.* Nashville: Tennessee Historical Commission.

Miller, Edward A. 1997. *Lincoln's Abolitionist General: The Biography of David Hunter.* Columbia: University of South Carolina Press.

Miller, Randall M., Harry S. Stout, and Charles Reagan Wilson, eds. 1998. *Religion and the American Civil War.* New York: Oxford University Press.

Mills, Cynthia, and Pamela H. Simpson, eds. 2003. *Monuments to the Lost Cause: Women, Art, and the Landscapes of Southern Memory.* Knoxville: University of Tennessee Press.

Mitchell, Reid. 1988. *Civil War Soldiers.* New York: Viking.

Mitchell, Reid. 1993. *The Vacant Chair: The Northern Soldier Leaves Home.* New York: Oxford University Press.

Mohr, Clarence L. 1986. *On the Threshold of Freedom: Masters and Slaves in Civil War Georgia.* Athens: University of Georgia Press.

Moon, Virginia B. No date. "Experiences of Virginia B. Moon, during the War between the States." Moon Collection. Oxford, OH: Smith Library of Regional History.

Moore, Frank. 1997. *Women of the War: Their Heroism and Self-Sacrifice.* Alexander, NC: Blue/Gray Books. (Reprint of 1866 edition. Hartford, CT: S. S. Scranton & Co.)

Moore, John Hammond. 1993. *Columbia and Richland County: A South Carolina Community, 1740–1990.* Columbia: University of South Carolina Press.

Morgan, David T. 1984. "Eugenia Levy Phillips: The Civil War Experiences of a Southern Jewish Woman." In *Jews of the South: Selected Essays from the Jewish Historical Society,* edited by Samuel Proctor and Louis Schmier with Malcolm Stern, 95–106. Macon, GA: Mercer University Press.

Morris, Roy. 1992. *Sheridan: The Life and Wars of General Phil Sheridan.* New York: Crown.

Morrow, Sara S. 1980. *The Legacy of Fannie Battle.* Nashville, TN: Fannie Battle Social Workers.

Morton, Patricia, ed. 1996. *Discovering the Women in Slavery: Emancipating Perspectives of the American Past.* Athens: University of Georgia Press.

Moss, Elizabeth. 1992. *Domestic Novelists in the Old South: Defenders of Southern Culture.* Baton Rouge: Louisiana State University Press.

Moss, Lemuel. 1868. *Annals of the United States Christian Commission.* Philadelphia, PA: J. B. Lippincott Co.

Moulton, Louise Chandler. 1909. *The Poems and Sonnets of Louise Chandler Moulton.* Boston: Little, Brown and Company.

"Mrs. Edmund Kirby Smith." 1907. *Confederate Veteran* 15: 563.

Muhlenfeld, Elisabeth. 1981. *Mary Boykin Chesnut: A Biography.* Baton Rouge: Louisiana State University Press.

Muhlenfeld, Elisabeth. 1985. "The Civil War and Authorship." In *The History of Southern Literature,* edited by Louis Rubin, 178–187. Baton Rouge: Louisiana State University Press.

Muhlenfeld, Elisabeth, ed. 2002. *Two Novels by Mary Chesnut,* with an introduction by Elizabeth Hanson. Charlottesville: University Press of Virginia.

Murdock, Eugene C. 1971. *One Million Men: The Civil War Draft in the North.* Madison: State Historical Society of Wisconsin.

Murrell, Amy E. 2000. "'Of Necessity and Public Benefit: Southern Families and Their Appeals for Protection." In *Southern Families at War: Loyalty and Conflict in the Civil War South,* edited by Catherine Clinton, 77–100. New York: Oxford University Press.

Neff, John R. 2005. *Honoring the Civil War Dead: Commemoration and the Problem of Reconciliation.* Lawrence: University Press of Kansas.

Nelson, Claudia, and Lynne Vallone, eds. 1994. *The Girl's Own: Cultural Histories of the Anglo-American Girl, 1830–1915.* Athens: University of Georgia Press.

Nelson, Michael C. 1997. "Writing during Wartime: Gender and Literacy in the American Civil War." *Journal of American Studies* 31 (1): 43–68.

Nevins, Allan. 1950. *The Emergence of Lincoln.* 2 vols. New York: Scribner's.

Newman, Richard S. 2002. *The Transformation of American Abolitionism: Fighting Slavery in the Early Republic.* Chapel Hill: University of North Carolina Press.

Noble, Jeanne L. 1956. *The Negro Woman's College Education.* New York: Teachers College, Columbia University, Bureau of Publications.

Oakes, Sister Mary Paullina, ed. 1998. *Angels of Mercy: An Eyewitness Account of the Civil War and Yellow Fever; A Primary Resource by Sister Ignatius Sumner.* Baltimore, MD: Cathedral Foundation.

Oates, Stephen B. 1977. *With Malice toward None: A Life of Abraham Lincoln.* New York: Harper & Row.

Oates, Stephen B. 1994. *A Woman of Valor: Clara Barton and the Civil War.* New York: Free Press.

O'Brien, Sean Michael. 1999. *Mountain Partisans: Guerrilla Warfare in the Southern Appalachians, 1861–1865.* Westport, CT: Praeger.

O'Connor, Thomas H. 1997. *Civil War Boston: Home Front and Battlefield.* Boston: Northeastern University Press.

Odendahl, Laura. 2003. "A History of Captivity and a History of Freedom." In *Searching for Their Places: Women in the South across Four Centuries,* edited by Thomas H. Appleton Jr. and Angela Boswell, 122–143. Columbia: University of Missouri Press.

O'Donnell-Rosales, John. 1997. *Hispanic Confederates.* Baltimore, MD: Clearfield Co.

Okker, Patricia. 1995. *Our Sister Editors: Sarah J. Hale and the Tradition of Nineteenth-Century American Women Editors.* Athens: University of Georgia Press.

Olsen, Christopher. 2000. *Political Culture and Secession in Mississippi: Masculinity, Honor, and the Antiparty Tradition, 1830–1860.* New York: Oxford University Press.

Olson, Kenneth E. 1981. *Music and Musket: Bands and Bandsmen of the American Civil War.* Westport, CT: Greenwood Press.

O'Reilly, Francis Augustin. 2002. *The Fredericksburg Campaign: Winter War along the Rappahannock.* Baton Rouge: Louisiana State University Press.

O'Sullivan, John, and Alan M. Meckler, eds. 1974. *The Draft and Its Enemies: A Documentary History.* Urbana: University of Illinois Press.

Oubre, Claude F. 1978. *Forty Acres and a Mule: The Freedman's Bureau and Black Landownership.* Baton Rouge: Louisiana State University Press.

Owsley, Frank Lawrence. 1926. "Defeatism in the Confederacy." *North Carolina Historical Review* 3: 446–456.

Owsley, Frank Lawrence. 1949. *Plain Folk of the Old South.* Baton Rouge: Louisiana State University Press.

Padilla, Genaro M. 1993. *My History, Not Yours: The Formation of Mexican American Autobiography.* Madison: University of Wisconsin Press.

Painter, Nell Irvin. 1990. "The Journal of Gertrude Clanton Thomas: An Educated White Woman in the Eras of Slavery, War, and Reconstruction." Introduction to *The Secret Eye: The Journal of Gertrude Clanton Thomas, 1848–1889,* edited by Virginia Ingraham Burr, 1–67. Chapel Hill: University of North Carolina Press.

Painter, Nell Irvin. 1996. *Sojourner Truth: A Life, A Symbol.* New York: W. W. Norton & Company.

Painter, Nell Irvin. 2002. *Southern History across the Color Line.* Chapel Hill: University of North Carolina Press.

Paludan, Phillip Shaw. 1975. *A Covenant with Death: The Constitution, Law and Equality in the Civil War Era.* Urbana: University of Illinois Press.

Paludan, Phillip Shaw. 1988. *"A People's Contest": The Union and Civil War, 1861–1865.* New York: Harper & Row.

Paludan, Phillip Shaw. 1994. *The Presidency of Abraham Lincoln.* Lawrence: University Press of Kansas.

Paludan, Phillip Shaw. 1998. *War and Home: The Civil War Encounter.* Milwaukee, WI: Marquette University Press.

Parks, Joseph H. 1982. *General Edmund Kirby Smith C.S.A.* Baton Rouge: Louisiana State University Press. (Reprint of 1954 edition.)

Parrish, T. Michael. 1992. *Richard Taylor: Soldier Prince of Dixie.* Chapel Hill: University of North Carolina Press.

Parsons, Theophilus. 1880. *Memoir of Emily Elizabeth Parsons.* Boston: Little, Brown and Company.

Pease, Jane H., and William H. Pease. 1999. *A Family of Women: The Carolina Petigrus in Peace and War.* Chapel Hill: University of North Carolina Press.

Peavy, Linda, and Ursula Smith. 1994. *Women in Waiting in the Westward Movement.* Norman: University of Oklahoma Press.

Pember, Phoebe Yates Levy. [1879] 2002. *A Southern Woman's Story,* with Introduction by George C. Rable. Columbia: University of South Carolina Press.

Penningroth, Dylan. 1997. "Slavery, Freedom, and Social Claims to Property among African Americans in Liberty Country, Georgia, 1850–1880." *Journal of American History* 84: 405–436.

Penny, Virginia. 1870. *How Women Can Make Money.* Springfield, MA: Fisk.

Perdue, Theda. 1999. *Cherokee Women: Gender and Culture Change, 1700–1835.* Lincoln: University of Nebraska Press.

Perry, Carolyn, and Mary Louise Weeks, eds. 2002. *The History of Southern Women's Literature.* Baton Rouge: Louisiana State University Press.

Perry, John. *The Lady of Arlington: The Life of Mrs. Robert E. Lee.* 2001. Sisters, OR: Multnomah Publishers.

Perry, Mark. 2001. *Lift Up Thy Voice: The Grimké Family's Journey from Slaveholders to Civil Rights Activists.* New York: Viking Penguin.

Peterson, Carla L. 1995. *"Doers of the Word": African-American Women Speakers and Writers in the North (1830–1880).* Piscataway, NJ: Rutgers University Press.

Pfaelzer, Jean, ed. 1995. *A Rebecca Harding Davis Reader: "Life in the Iron Mills," Selected Fiction, and Essays,* with a Critical Introduction, by Jean Pfaelzer. Pittsburgh, PA: University of Pittsburgh Press.

Pfaelzer, Jean. 1996. *Parlor Radical: Rebecca Harding Davis and the Origins of American Social Realism.* Pittsburgh, PA: University of Pittsburgh Press.

Pfanz, Donald C. 1998. *Richard S. Ewell: A Soldier's Life.* Chapel Hill: University of North Carolina Press.

Phipps, Sheila R. 2004. *Genteel Rebel: The Life of Mary Greenhow Lee.* Baton Rouge: Louisiana State University Press.

Piehler, G. Kurt. 1995. *Remembering War the American Way.* Washington DC: Smithsonian Institution.

Pike, Martha V., and Janice Gray Armstrong. 1980. *A Time to Mourn: Expressions of Grief in Nineteenth Century America.* Stony Brook, NY: Museums at Stony Brook.

Pinkerton, Allan. 1883. *The Spy of the Rebellion; Being a True History of the Spy System of the United States Army during the Late Rebellion.* New York: G.W. Carleton.

Pleck, Elizabeth. 1999. "The Making of the Domestic Occasion: The History of Thanksgiving in the United States." *Journal of Social History* 32 (4): 773–790.

Plum, William R. 1882. *The Military Telegraph during the Civil War in the United States.* 2 vols. Chicago: Jansen, McClurg & Company.

Pollak, Vivian R., ed. 2004. *A Historical Guide to Emily Dickinson.* New York: Oxford University Press.

Porter, Dorothy B. 1935. "Sarah Parker Remond, Abolitionist and Physician." *Journal of Negro History* 20 (3): 287–293.

Potter, David. 1976. *The Impending Crisis 1848–1861.* New York: Harper & Row.

Power, J. Tracy. 1998. *Lee's Miserables: Life in the Army of Northern Virginia from the Wilderness to Appomattox.* Chapel Hill: University of North Carolina Press.

Poynter, Lida. 1946. "Dr. Mary Walker, M.D. Pioneer Woman Physician." *Medical Woman's Journal* 53 (10): 43–51.

Prushankin, Jeffery S. 2005. *A Crisis in Confederate Command: General Edmund Kirby Smith, Richard Taylor, and the Army of the Trans-Mississippi.* Baton Rouge: Louisiana State University Press.

Pryor, Elizabeth Brown. 1987. *Clara Barton: Professional Angel.* Philadelphia: University of Pennsylvania Press.

Pryor, Sara Rice (Mrs. Roger A.). 1905. *Reminiscences of Peace and War.* New York: Grosset & Dunlap.

Putnam, Sallie Brock. 1996. *Richmond during the War: Four Years of Personal Observation*, with Introduction by Virginia Scharff. Lincoln: University of Nebraska Press.

Quarles, Benjamin. 1953. *The Negro in the Civil War.* Boston: Little, Brown and Company. (Reprinted 1989. New York: DeCapo Press.)

Rable, George C. 1989. *Civil Wars: Women and the Crisis of Southern Nationalism.* Urbana: University of Illinois Press.

Rable, George C. 1992. "'Missing in Action': Women of the Confederacy." In *Divided Houses: Gender and the Civil War*, edited by Catherine Clinton and Nina Silber, 134–146. New York: Oxford University Press.

Rable, George C. 1994. *The Confederate Republic: A Revolution against Politics.* Chapel Hill: University of North Carolina Press.

Rable, George C. 2002. *Fredericksburg! Fredericksburg!* Chapel Hill: University of North Carolina Press.

Raboteau, Albert J. 2004. *Slave Religion: The "Invisible Institution" in the Antebellum South.* New York: Oxford University Press.

Rafuse, Ethan S. 2002. *A Single Grand Victory: The First Campaign and Battle of Manassas.* Wilmington, DE: Scholarly Resources Books.

Ramage, James A. 1999. *Gray Ghost: The Life of Col. John Singleton Mosby.* Lexington: University Press of Kentucky.

Ramsdell, Charles W. 1943. *Behind the Lines in the Confederacy.* Baton Rouge: Louisiana State University Press.

Randall, Ruth Painter. 1962. *I, Varina.* Boston: Little, Brown and Company.

Ream, Debbie Williams. 1993. "Mine Eyes Have Seen the Glory." *American History Illustrated* 27: 60–64.

Regosin, Elizabeth. 2002. *Freedom's Promise: Ex-Slave Families and Citizenship in the Age of Emancipation.* Charlottesville: University Press of Virginia.

Reilly, Tom. 1981. "Jane McManus Storms, Letters from the Mexican War, 1846–1848." *Southwestern Historical Quarterly* 85: 21–44.

Reilly, Wayne E., ed. 2001. *Sarah Jane Foster: Teacher of the Freedman, The Diary and Letters of a Maine Woman in the South after the Civil War.* Rockland, ME: Picton Press.

Remond, Sarah P. 1942. "The Negroes in the United States of America." *Journal of Negro History* 27 (2): 216–218.

Reveley, Bryce. 1993. "The Black Trade in New Orleans: 1840–1880." *Southern Quarterly* 31 (2): 119–122.

Revels, Tracey J. 2004. *Grander in Her Daughters: Florida's Women during the Civil War.* Columbia: University of South Carolina Press.

Reverby, Susan M. 1987. *Ordered to Care: The Dilemma of American Nursing, 1850–1945.* New York: Cambridge University Press.

Reynold, Arlene. 1994. *The Civil War Memories of Elizabeth Bacon Custer.* Austin: University of Texas Press.

R.G. 153. No date. Records of the U.S. Army, Office of the Adjutant General. Washington, DC: National Archives and Records Service.

Rhea, Gordon C. 2004. *The Battle of the Wilderness May 5–6, 1864.* Baton Rouge: Louisiana State University Press.

Rhodes, Jane. 1998. *Mary Ann Shadd Cary: The Black Press and Protest in the Nineteenth Century.* Bloomington: Indiana University Press.

Richard, Patricia L. 2003. *Busy Hands: Images of the Family in the Northern Civil War Effort.* New York: Fordham University Press.

Richardson, Marilyn. 1995. "Edmonia Lewis's 'The Death of Cleopatra.'" *The International Review of African American Art* 12 (2): 36–52.

Richter, William L. 1991. *Overreached on All Sides: The Freedmen's Bureau Administration in Texas, 1865–1868.* College Station: Texas A&M University Press.

Rikard, Marlene Hunt, and Elizabeth Wells. 1997. "'From It Begins a New Era': Women and the Civil War." *Baptist History and Heritage* 32 (3): 59–73.

Riley, Glenda. 1981. *Frontierswomen: The Iowa Experience.* Ames: Iowa State University Press

Roark, James L. 1977. *Masters without Slaves: Southern Planters in the Civil War and Reconstruction.* New York: W. W. Norton.

Roark, James L. 1998. "Behind the Lines: Confederate Economy and Society." In *Writing the Civil War: The Quest to Understand,* edited by James M. McPherson and William J. Cooper Jr., 201–227. Columbia: University of South Carolina Press.

Roberts, Giselle. 2003. *The Confederate Belle.* Columbia, OH: University of Missouri Press.

Robertson, Mary D., ed. 1992. *A Confederate Lady Comes of Age: The Journal of Pauline DeCaradeuc Heyward.* Columbia: University of South Carolina Press.

Rodgers, Mark E. 1999. *Tracing the Civil War Veteran Pensions System in the State of Virginia: Entitlement or Privilege.* Lewiston, NY: Edwin Mellen Press.

Rogers, Sherbrooke. 1985. *Sarah Josepha Hale: A New England Pioneer 1788–1879.* Grantham, NH: Thompson and Rutter.

Romero, Laura. 1997. *Home Fronts: Domesticity and Its Critics in the Antebellum United States.* Durham, NC: Duke University Press.

Ronda, Bruce, ed. 1984. *Letters of Elizabeth Palmer Peabody, American Renaissance Woman.* Middletown, CT: Wesleyan University Press.

Ronda, Bruce. 1999. *Elizabeth Palmer Peabody: A Reformer on Her Own Terms.* Cambridge, MA: Harvard University Press.

Rose, Anne C. 1992. *Victorian America and the Civil War.* New York: Cambridge University Press.

Rose, Willie Lee. 1999. *Rehearsal for Reconstruction. The Port Royal Experiment.* Athens: University of Georgia Press. (Reprint of 1964 edition. Indianapolis, IN: Bobbs-Merrill Company.)

Ross, Ishbel. 1949. *Child of Destiny.* London: Gollancz.

Ross, Ishbel. 1954. *Rebel Rose: Life of Rose O'Neal Greenhow, Confederate Spy.* New York: Harper & Brothers, Publishers. (Reprinted 1989. New York: Ballantine Books.)

Ross, Ishbel. 1959. *The General's Wife: The Life of Mrs. Ulysses S. Grant.* New York: Dodd, Mead and Company.

Ross, Ishbel. 1973. *First Lady of the South.* Westport, CT: Greenwood Press. (Reprint of 1958 edition. New York: Harper & Brothers, Publishers.)

Ross, Kristie. 1992. "Arranging a Doll's House: Refined Women as Union Nurses." In *Divided Houses: Gender and the Civil War,* edited by Catherine Clinton and Nina Silber, 97–113. New York: Oxford University Press.

Royster, Charles. 1991. *The Destructive War: William Tecumseh Sherman, Stonewall Jackson, and the Americans.* New York: Vintage.

Rubin, Anne Sarah. 2005. *Shattered Nation: The Rise and Fall of the Confederacy.* Chapel Hill: University of North Carolina Press.

Rubin, Louis D. 1958. "The Image of an Army: Southern Novelists and the Civil War." *Texas Quarterly* 1: 17–34.

Rubin, Louis D. Jr., ed. 1985. *The History of Southern Literature.* Baton Rouge: Louisiana State University Press.

Ruiz De Burton, Maria Amparo. 1995. *Who Would Have Thought It?* Houston, TX: Arte Público Press.

Russell, James M. 1988. *Atlanta, 1847–1890: Citybuilding in the Old South and the New.* Baton Rouge: Louisiana State University Press.

Ryan, David D. 1996. *A Yankee Spy in Richmond: The Civil War Diary of "Crazy Bet" Van Lew.* Mechanicsburg, PA: Stackpole Books.

Ryan, Mary P. 1981. *Cradle of the Middle Class: The Family in Oneida County, New York, 1790–1865.* New York: Cambridge University Press.

Ryan, Mary P. 1982. *The Empire of the Mother: American Writing about Domesticity, 1830–1860.* New York: Institute for Research in History and Haworth Press.

Ryan, Mary. 1990. *Women in Public: Between Banners and Ballots, 1825–1880.* Baltimore, MD: Johns Hopkins University Press.

Rybczynski, Witold. 1999. *A Clearing in the Distance: Frederick Law Olmsted and America in the Nineteenth Century.* New York: Scribner's.

Saint-Amand, Mary Scott. 1941. *A Balcony in Charleston.* Richmond, VA: Garrett & Massie.

Sally Louisa Tompkins Papers. Eleanor S. Brockenbrough Library, Museum of the Confederacy, Richmond, VA.

Samuelson, Nancy. 1989. "Employment of Female Spies in the American Civil War." *Minerva* 7: 57–66.

Sanchez, Regina Morantz. [1985] 2000. *Sympathy and Science: Women Physicians in American Medicine.* Chapel Hill: University of North Carolina Press. Reprint with new preface.

Sarmiento, Ferdinand L. 1865. *Life of Pauline Cushman, The Celebrated Union Spy and Scout.* Philadelphia, PA: John E. Potter.

Saville, Julie. 1994. *The Work of Reconstruction: From Slave to Wage Laborer in South Carolina, 1860–1870.* New York: Cambridge University Press.

Saxon, Elizabeth Lyle. 1905. *A Southern Woman's War Time Reminiscences, by Elizabeth Lyle Saxon, for the Benefit of the Shiloh Monument Fund.* Memphis, TN: Press of the Pilcher Printing Co.

Scadron, Arlene, ed. 1988. *On Their Own: Widows and Widowhood in the American Southwest, 1848–1939.* Urbana: University of Illinois Press.

Scarborough, Ruth. 1983. *Belle Boyd: Siren of the South.* Macon, GA: Mercer University Press.

Schultz, Duane. 1996. *Quantrill's War: The Life and Times of William Clarke Quantrill.* New York: St. Martin's Press.

Schultz, Jane E. 1989. "Mute Fury: Southern Women's Diaries of Sherman's March to the Sea." In *Arms and the Woman: War, Gender, and Literary Representation,* edited by Helen M. Cooper, Adrienne Auslander Munich, and Susan Merrill Squier, 59–79. Chapel Hill: University of North Carolina Press.

Schultz, Jane E. 1992. "The Inhospitable Hospital: Gender and Professionalism in Civil War Medicine." *Signs* 17 (2): 363–392.

Schultz, Jane E. 1994. "Race, Gender and Bureaucracy: Civil War Army Nurses and the Pension Bureau." *Journal of Women's History* 6: 45–69.

Schultz, Jane E. 2004. *Women at the Front: Hospital Workers in Civil War America.* Chapel Hill: University of North Carolina Press.

Schulz, Karen. 1966. "Descendant of Woman Captain Remembers Heroine of Civil War." *Richmond News Leader,* July 21.

Schwalm, Leslie A. 1997. *A Hard Fight for We: Women's Transition from Slavery to Freedom in South Carolina.* Urbana: University of Illinois Press.

Schwartz, Gerald, ed. 1984. *A Woman Doctor's Civil War: Ester Hill Hawks' Diary.* Columbia: University of South Carolina Press.

Scott, Anne Firor. 1970. *The Southern Lady: From Pedestal to Politics, 1830–1930.* Charlottesville: University of Virginia Press.

Sears, Stephen W. 1983. *Landscape Turned Red: The Battle of Antietam.* New Haven, CT: Ticknor and Fields.

Sears, Stephen W. 1988. *George B. McClellan: The Young Napoleon.* New York: Ticknor & Fields.

Sears, Stephen W. 1992. *To The Gates of Richmond: The Peninsular Campaign.* New York: Ticknor & Fields.

Sears, Stephen W. 1996. *Chancellorsville.* Boston: Houghton-Mifflin.

Sears, Stephen W. 2003. *Gettysburg.* Boston: Houghton Mifflin Company.

Selby, John G. 2002. *Virginians at War: The Civil War Experiences of Seven Young Confederates.* Wilmington, DE: Scholarly Resources.

Selleck, Linda B. 1995. *Gentle Invaders: Quaker Women Educators and Racial Issues during the Civil War and Reconstruction.* Richmond, IN: Friends United Press.

Shaffer, Donald R. 2004. *After the Glory: The Struggles of Black Civil War Veterans.* Lawrence: University Press of Kansas.

Shammas, Carole, Marylynn Salmon, and Michel Dahlin. 1987. *Inheritance in America from Colonial Times to the Present.* Piscataway, NJ: Rutgers University Press.

Shankman, Arnold. 1980. *The Pennsylvania Antiwar Movement, 1861–1865.* Madison, NJ: Fairleigh Dickinson University Press.

Shattuck, Gardiner. 1987. *A Shield and Hiding Place: The Religious Life of the Civil War Armies.* Macon, GA: Mercer University Press.

Sherman, William T. 1875. *Memoirs of General William T. Sherman.* 2 vols. New York: D. Appleton & Co.

Siguad, Louis. 1944. *Belle Boyd: Confederate Spy.* Petersburg, VA: Dietz Press.

Silber, Nina. 1993. *The Romance of Reunion: Northerners and the South, 1865–1900.* Chapel Hill: University of North Carolina Press.

Silber, Nina. 2002. "A Compound of Wonderful Potency: Women Teachers of the North in the Civil War South." In *The War Was You and Me: Civilians in the American Civil War,* edited by Joan E. Cashin, 35–59. Princeton, NJ: Princeton University Press,.

Silber, Nina. 2005. *Daughters of the Union: Northern Women Fight the Civil War.* Cambridge, MA: Harvard University Press.

Silbey, Joel. 1977. *A Respectable Minority: The Democratic Party in the Civil-War Era.* New York: W. W. Norton & Company.

Simkins, Francis Butler, and James Welch Patton. 1936. *The Women of the Confederacy.* Richmond, VA: Garrett & Massie.

Simmons, James C. 2000. *Star Spangled Eden.* New York: Carroll and Graf Publishers.

Simmons, Michael K. 1976. "Maum Guinea: or, A Dime Novelist Looks at Abolition." *Journal of Popular Culture* 10 (1): 81-87.

Simon, John Y., ed. 1975. *The Personal Memoirs of Julia Dent Grant.* New York: G.P. Putnam's Sons.

Simon, John Y. 2001. "A Marriage Tested by War: Ulysses and Julia Grant." In *Intimate Strategies of the Civil War: Military Commanders and their Wives,* edited by Carol K. Bleser and Lesley J. Gordon, 123–137. New York: Oxford University Press.

Simonhoff, Harry. 1963. *Jewish Participants in the Civil War.* New York: Arco Publishing.

Sinha, Manisha. 2000. *The Counterrevolution of Slavery: Politics and Ideology in Antebellum South Carolina.* Chapel Hill: University of North Carolina Press.

Sizer, Lyde Cullen. 1992. "Acting Her Part: Narratives of Union Women Spies." In *Divided Houses: Gender and the Civil War,* edited by Catherine Clinton and Nina Silber, 114–133. New York: Oxford University Press.

Sizer, Lyde Cullen. 2000. *Political Work of Northern Women Writers and the Civil War, 1850–1872.* Chapel Hill: University of North Carolina Press.

Skaggs, Merrill Maguire. 1972. *The Folk of Southern Fiction.* Athens: University of Georgia Press.

Sklar, Katherine Kish. 1973. *Catharine Beecher: A Study in American Domesticity.* New Haven, CT: Yale University Press.

Skocpol, Theda. 1992. *Protecting Soldiers and Mothers: The Political Origins of Social Policy in the United States.* Cambridge, MA: Harvard University Press.

Slaughter, Linda Warfel, ed. 1869. *The Freedmen of the South.* Cincinnati, OH: Elm St. Printing Co.

Smith, Andrew F. 2005. "The Civil War and American Food, or How Nationalized, Industrialized American Cookery Got Its Start." *The Food Journal* 5 (Winter): 4–5.

Smith, Anna Habersham Wright, ed. 1999. *A Savannah Family, 1830–1901: Papers from the Clermont Huger Lee Collection.* Milledgeville, GA: Boyd Publishing Company.

Smith, Diane Monroe. 1999. *Fanny and Joshua: The Enigmatic Lives of Francis Caroline Adams and Joshua Lawrence Chamberlain.* Gettysburg, PA: Thomas Publications.

Smith, Jennifer Lund. "The Reconstruction of 'Home': The Civil War and the Marriage of Lawrence and Fannie Chamberlain." In *Intimate Strategies of the Civil War: Military Commanders and their Wives,* edited by Carol K. Bleser and Lesley J. Gordon, 157–177. New York: Oxford University Press.

Smith, Orphia. 1962. *Oxford Spy: Wed at Pistol Point.* Oxford, OH: Cullen Printing Co.

Smith, Timothy B. 2004. *This Great Battlefield of Shiloh: History, Memory, and the Establishment of a Civil War National Military Park.* Knoxville: University of Tennessee Press.

Snyder, Charles McCool. 1974. *Dr. Mary Walker: The Little Lady in Pants.* New York: Arno Press.

Solomon, Barbara Miller. 1985. *In the Company of Educated Women: A History of Women and Higher Education in American.* New Haven, CT: Yale University Press.

Solomon, Clara. 1995. *The Civil War Diary of Clara Solomon: Growing Up in New Orleans 1861–1862,* edited, with introduction, by Elliott Ashkenazi. Baton Rouge: Louisiana State University Press.

Sommerville, Diane M. 2004. *Rape and Race in the Nineteenth-Century South.* Chapel Hill: University of North Carolina Press.

Southworth, Emma Dorothy Eliza Nevitte. 1997. *The Hidden Hand,* with Introduction by Nina Baym. New York: Oxford University Press.

Speer, Lonnie R. 1997. *Portals to Hell: Military Prisons of the Civil War.* Mechanicsburg, PA: Stackpole Books.

Spiegel, Marcus. 1985. *Your True Marcus: The Civil War Letters of a Jewish Colonel,* edited by Frank L. Byrne and Jean Powers Soman. Kent, OH: Kent State University Press.

Stackpole, Edward J. 1959. *From Cedar Mountain to Antietam: August–September, 1862.* Harrisburg, PA: Stackpole Books.

Stansell, Christine. 1986. *City of Women: Sex and Class in New York, 1789–1860.* New York: Alfred A. Knopf.

Stanton, Elizabeth, Susan B. Anthony, and Matilda Joslyn Gage. 1970. *History of Woman Suffrage.* Vol. 2. New York: Source Book Press.

Stanton, Elizabeth, Susan B. Anthony, and Matilda Joslyn Gage. 1970. *History of Woman Suffrage.* Vol. 2. New York: Source Book Press.

Starobin, Robert S. 1970. *Industrial Slavery in the Old South.* New York: Oxford University Press.

Staudenraus, P. J. 1961. *The African Colonization Movement, 1816–1865.* New York: Columbia University Press.

Stearns, Amanda Akin. 1909. *Lady Nurse of Ward E.* New York: Baker & Taylor Company.

Steers, Edward. 2001. *Blood on the Moon: The Assassination of Abraham Lincoln.* Lexington: University Press of Kentucky.

Sterkx, H. E. 1970. *Partners in Rebellion: Alabama Women in the Civil War.* Madison, NJ: Fairleigh Dickinson University Press.

Sterling, Dorothy, ed. 1984. *We Are Your Sisters: Black Women in the Nineteenth Century.* New York and London: W. W. Norton.

Sterling, Dorothy. 1991 *Ahead of Her Time: Abby Kelley and the Politics of Antislavery.* New York: W. W. Norton & Company.

Stern, Philip Van Doren. 1959. *Secret Missions of the Civil War.* Chicago: Rand McNally.

Stevens, Bryna. 1992. *Frank Thompson: Her Civil War Story.* Toronto: Maxwell MacMillian Canada.

Stevens, Peter F. 2000. *Rebels in Blue: The Story of Keith and Malinda Blalock.* Dallas, TX: Taylor Publishing Company.

Stevenson, Brenda E., ed. 1988. *The Journals of Charlotte Forten Grimké.* New York: Oxford University Press.

Stevenson, Brenda E. 1996. *Life in Black and White: Family and Community in the Slave South.* New York: Oxford University Press.

Stevenson, Louise L. 1991. *The Victorian Homefront: American Thought and Culture, 1860–1880.* New York: Twayne Publishers.

Stewart, James Brewer. 1997. *Holy Warriors: The Abolitionists and American Slavery.* New York: Hill and Wang.

Still, William N. Jr. 1971. *Iron Afloat: The Story of the Confederate Armorclads.* Nashville, TN: Vanderbilt University Press.

Still, William. [1872] 1970. *The Underground Railroad: a record of facts, authentic narratives, letters, &c., narrating the hardships, hair-breadth escapes, and death struggles of the slaves in their efforts for freedom, as related by themselves and others or witnessed by the author: together with sketches of some of the largest stockholders and most liberal aiders and advisers of the road.* Chicago, IL: Johnson Publishing.

Stock, Mary Wright, ed. 1975. *Shinplasters and Homespun: The Diary of Laura Nisbet Boykin.* Rockville, MD: Printex.

Storey, Margaret M. 2004. *Loyalty and Loss: Alabama's Unionists in the Civil War and Reconstruction.* Baton Rouge: Louisiana State University Press.

Stowe, Harriet Beecher. [1852] 2001. *Uncle Tom's Cabin, or Life among the Lowly,* with Introduction by Jane Smiley. New York: Modern Library.

Stowell, Daniel. 1998. *Rebuilding Zion: The Religious Reconstruction of the South, 1863–1877.* New York: Oxford University Press.

Streeby, Shelley. 2002. *American Sensations: Class, Empire, and the Production of Popular Culture.* Berkeley: University of California Press.

Sullivan, Regina Diane. 2002. "Woman with a Mission: Remembering Lottie Moon and the Woman's Missionary Union." Ph.D. diss. University of North Carolina, Chapel Hill.

Sullivan, Walter. 1953. "Southern Novelists and the Civil War." In *Southern Renascence: The Literature of the Modern South,* edited by Louis D. Rubin Jr. and Robert D. Jacobs, 123–125. Baltimore, MD: Johns Hopkins University Press.

Sutherland, Daniel. 1995. *Seasons of War: The Ordeal of a Confederate Community, 1861–1865.* New York: Free Press.

Sutherland, Daniel E., ed. 1996. *A Very Violent Rebel: The Civil War Diary of Ellen Renshaw House.* Knoxville: University of Tennessee Press.

Swint, Henry L., ed. 1966. *Dear Ones at Home: Letters from Contraband Camps.* Nashville, TN: Vanderbilt University Press.

Swint, Henry L. 1967. *The Northern Teacher in the South, 1862–1870.* New York: Octagon Books.

Swisshelm, Jane Grey Cannon. [1880] 1970. *Half a Century.* New York: Source Book Press.

Tackach, James. 2002. *Lincoln's Moral Vision: The Second Inaugural Address.* Jackson: University Press of Mississippi.

Talmadge, John Erwin. 1960. *Rebecca Latimer Felton: Nine Stormy Decades.* Athens: University of Georgia Press.

Taylor, Amy Murrell. 2005. *The Divided Family in Civil War America.* Chapel Hill: University of North Carolina Press.

Taylor, Lou. 1983. *Mourning Dress: A Costume and Social History.* London: George Allen & Unwin.

Taylor, Susie King. 1988. *A Black Woman's Civil War Memoirs,* edited by Patricia W. Romero and Willie Lee Rose. Princeton, NJ: Markus Weiner Publisher. (Orig. pub.1902 as *Reminiscences of My Life in Camp: With the 33rd United States Colored Troops, late 1st S.C. Volunteers.*)

Taylor-Colbert, Alice. 1997. "Cherokee Women and Cultural Change." In *Women of the American South,* edited by Christie Anne Farnham, 43–55. New York: New York University Press.

Thomas, Ella Gertrude Clanton. 1990. *The Secret Eye: The Journal of Ella Gertrude Clanton Thomas, 1848–1889,* edited by Virginia Ingraham Burr. Chapel Hill: University of North Carolina Press.

Thomas, Emory M. 1979. *The Confederate Nation, 1861–1865.* New York: Harper & Row.

Thomas, Emory M. 1991. *The Confederacy as a Revolutionary Experience.* Columbia: University of South Carolina Press. (Reprint of 1971 edition. Englewood Cliffs, NJ: Prentice-Hall.)

Thomas, Emory M. 1995. *Robert E. Lee.* New York: Random House.

Thompson, E. P. 1971. "The Moral Economy of the Crowd in the Eighteenth Century." *Past and Present* 50: 76–136.

Thompson, Jerry D. 2000. *Vaqueros in Blue and Gray.* Austin, TX: State House Press.

Tidwell, William A., with James O. Hall and David Winfred Gaddy. 1988. *Come Retribution: The Confederate Secret Service and the Assassination of Lincoln.* Jackson: University Press of Mississippi.

Tinling, Marion. 1986. *Women Remembered: A Guide to Landmarks of Women's History in the United States.* Westport, CT: Greenwood Press.

Todras, Ellen. *Angelina Grimké: Voice of Abolition.* 1999. North Haven, CT: Linnet Books.

Tonkovich, Nicole. 1997. *Domesticity with a Difference: The Nonfiction of Catharine Beecher, Sarah J. Hale, Fanny Fern, and Margaret Fuller.* Jackson: University Press of Mississippi.

Trindal, Elizabeth Steger. 1996. *Mary Surratt: An American Tragedy.* Gretna, LA: Pelican Publishing Company.

Trowbridge, John Townsend. 1956. *The Desolate South, 1865–1866; A Picture of the Battlefields and of the Devastated Confederacy,* edited by Gordon Carroll. New York: Duell, Sloan and Pearce.

Trudeau, Noah Andre. 1989. *Bloody Roads South: The Wilderness to Cold Harbor May–June 1864.* Boston: Little, Brown and Company.

Trudeau, Noah Andre. 1995. *National Parks Civil War Series: The Siege of Petersburg.* Fort Washington, PA: Eastern National Park and Monument Association.

Trudeau, Noah Andre. 2002. *Gettysburg: A Testing of Courage.* New York: HarperCollins.

Trulock, Alice Rains. 1992. *In the Hands of Providence: Joshua L. Chamberlain and the American Civil War.* Chapel Hill: University of North Carolina Press.

Truth, Sojourner. 1997. *Narrative of Sojourner Truth.* New York: Dover Publications.

Tucker, St. George, ed. 1803. *Blackstone's Commentaries.* New York: Augustus M. Kelley Publishers. (Reprinted 1969. South Hackensack, NJ: Rothman Reprints.)

Turner, Justin G., and Linda Levitt Turner, eds. 1987. *Mary Todd Lincoln: Her Life and Letters.* New York: Fromm International Publishing Corporation.

United States Sanitary Commission. 1972. *The Sanitary Commission of the United States Army: A Succinct Narrative of Its Works and Purposes.* New York: Arno Press and New York Times. (Reprint of 1864 edition.)

U.S. War Department. 1880–1902. *The War of the Rebellion: A Compilation of the Official Records of the Union and Confederate Armies.* 130 vols. Records and Pension Office. Washington, DC: U.S. Government Printing Office.

Van der Heuvel, Gerry. 1988. *Crowns of Thorns and Glory: Mary Todd Lincoln and Varina Howell Davis.* New York: Dutton.

Varon, Elizabeth R. 2003. *Southern Lady, Yankee Spy: The True Story of Elizabeth Van Lew, A Union Agent in the Heart of the Confederacy.* New York: Oxford University Press.

Velazquez, Loreta Janeta. 1876. *The Woman in Battle: A Narrative of the Exploits, Adventures, and Travels of Madame Loreta Janeta Velazquez, Otherwise Known as Lieutenant Harry T. Buford, Confederate States Army,* edited by C. J. Worthington. Richmond, VA: Dustin, Gilman & Co.

Venet, Wendy Hamand. 1991. *Neither Ballots Nor Bullets: Women Abolitionists and the Civil War.* Charlottesville: University Press of Virginia.

Vietor, Agnes C., ed. [1924] 1972. *A Woman's Quest: The Life of Marie E. Zakrzewska, M.D.* New York: Arno Press.

Vinovskis, Maris A. 1990. *Toward a Social History of the American Civil War.* New York: Cambridge University Press.

Vorenberg, Michael. 2001. *Final Freedom: The Civil War, the Abolition of Slavery, and the Thirteenth Amendment.* New York: Cambridge University Press.

Walker, Nancy A. 1993. *Fanny Fern.* New York: Twayne Publishers.

Walkowitz, Judith R. 1980. *Prostitution in Victorian Society: Women, Class, and the State.* New York: Cambridge University Press.

Wall, Barbra Mann. 1998. "Called to a Mission of Charity: The Sisters of St. Joseph in the Civil War." *Nursing History Review* 80 (1): 36–57.

Warren, Edward. 1885. *A Doctor's Experiences in Three Continents.* Baltimore, MD: Cushings and Bailey.

Warren, Joyce W. 1992. *Fanny Fern: An Independent Woman.* Piscataway, NJ: Rutgers University Press.

Waugh, Charles, and Martin Greenburg, eds. 1999. *The Women's War in the South: Recollections and Reflections of the American Civil War.* Nashville, TN: Cumberland House.

Waugh, Joan. 1997. *Unsentimental Reformer: The Life of Josephine Shaw Lowell.* Cambridge, MA: Harvard University Press.

Weatherford, Doris. 1986. *Foreign and Female: Immigrant Women in America, 1840–1930.* New York: Schocken Books.

Weathers, Willie T. 1974. "Judith W. McGuire: A Lady of Virginia." *Virginia Magazine of History and Biography* 82 (1): 100–113.

Weiner, Marli F. 1997. *A Heritage of Woe: The Civil War Diary of Grace Brown Elmore, 1861–1868.* Athens: University of Georgia Press.

Weiner, Marli F. 1998. *Mistresses and Slaves: Plantation Women in South Carolina, 1830–80.* Urbana: University of Illinois Press.

Weitz, Mark A. 2000. *A Higher Duty: Desertion among Georgia Troops during the Civil War.* Lincoln: University of Nebraska Press.

Welter, Barbara. 1966. "The Cult of True Womanhood: 1820–1860." *American Quarterly* 18 (Summer): 151–174.

Wert, Jeffry D. 1990. *Mosby's Rangers.* New York: Simon & Schuster.

Wertheimer, Barbara M. 1977. *We Were There: The Story of Working Women in America.* New York: Pantheon.

Wheeler, Richard. 1986. *Sword Over Richmond: An Eyewitness History of McClellan's Peninsular Campaign.* New York: Harper.

White, Barbara A. 2003. *The Beecher Sisters.* New Haven, CT: Yale University Press.

White, Deborah Gray. 1985. *Ar'n't I a Woman? Female Slaves in the Plantation South.* New York: W. W. Norton.

Whites, LeeAnn. 1992. "The Civil War as a Crisis in Gender." In *Divided Houses: Gender and the Civil War,* edited by Catherine Clinton and Nina Silber, 3–21. New York: Oxford University Press.

Whites, LeeAnn. 1995. *The Civil War as a Crisis in Gender, Augusta, Georgia, 1860–1890.* Athens: University of Georgia Press.

Whites, LeeAnn. 2005. *Gender Matters: Civil War, Reconstruction, and the Making of the New South.* New York: Palgrave Macmillan.

Whiting, Lilian. 1910. *Louise Chandler Moulton: Poet and Friend.* Boston: Little, Brown and Company.

Whitney, Louisa M. 1903. *Goldie's Inheritance: A Story of the Siege of Atlanta.* Burlington, VT: Free Press Association.

Wiggins, Sarah Woolfolk. 1998. "Amelia Gayle Gorgas and the Civil War." *Alabama Review* 51 (2): 83–95.

Wiggins, Sarah Woolfolk. 2001. "The Marriage of Amelia Gayle and Josiah Gorgas." In *Intimate Strategies of the Civil War: Military Commanders and their Wives,* 104–119. New York: Oxford University Press, 2001.

Wiggins, William H., Jr. 1987. *O Freedom!: Afro-American Emancipation Celebrations.* Knoxville: University of Tennessee Press.

Wiley, Bell Irvin. 1943. *The Life of Johnny Reb: The Common Soldier of the Confederacy.* Indianapolis, IN: Bobbs-Merrill Company.

Wiley, Bell Irvin. 1952. *The Life of Billy Yank: The Common Soldier of the Union.* Indianapolis, IN: Bobbs-Merrill Company.

Wiley, Bell Irvin. 1970. *Confederate Women.* Westport, CT: Greenwood Press.

Williams, David. 2005. *A People's History of the Civil War: Struggles for the Meaning of Freedom.* New York: New Press.

Williams, Gary. 1999. *Hungry Heart: The Literary Emergence of Julia Ward Howe.* Amherst: University of Massachusetts Press.

Williams, Julieanna. 1996. "The Homefront: 'For Our Boys—The Ladies' Aid Societies.'" In *Valor and Lace: The Roles of Confederate Women 1861–1865,* edited by Mauriel Phillips Joslyn, 16–33. Murfreesboro, TN: Southern Heritage Press.

Williams, Kenneth P. 1950. "The Tennessee River Campaign and Anna Ella Carroll." *Indiana Magazine of History* 46: 221–248.

Williams, Teresa Cusp, and David Williams. 2002. "'The Women Rising:' Cotton, Class, and Confederate Georgia's Rioting Women." *Georgia Historical Quarterly* 86 (1): 49–83.

Willingham, Robert M., Jr. 1976. *No Jubilee: The Story of Confederate Wilkes.* Washington, GA: Wilkes Publishing.

Wilson, Charles Reagan. 1980. *Baptized in Blood: The Religion of the Lost Cause 1865–1920.* Athens: University of Georgia Press.

Wilson, Dorothy C. 1975. *Stranger and Traveler.* Boston: Little, Brown and Company.

Wilson, Edmund. 1984. *Patriotic Gore: Studies in the Literature of the American Civil War,* with a foreword by C. Vann Woodward. Boston: Northeastern University Press. (Also published: New York: Farrar, Straus and Giroux, 1962 and New York: W. W. Norton, 1972.)

Wilson, Mark R. 2001. "The Extensive Side of Nineteenth-Century Military Economy: The Tent Industry in the Northern United States during the Civil War." *Enterprise and Society: The International Journal of Business History* 2: 297–337.

Wise, Stephen. 1988. *Lifeline of the Confederacy: Blockade Running during the Civil War.* Columbia: University of South Carolina Press.

Wittenmyer, Annie Turner. 1895. *Under the Guns: A Woman's Reminiscences of the Civil War.* Boston: E. B. Stillings & Co.

Wolf, Simon. 1972. *The American Jew as Patriot, Soldier and Citizen,* with new Introduction and Preface by George Athan Billias. Boston: Gregg Press.

Wolff, Cynthia Griffin. 1987. *Emily Dickinson.* New York: Alfred A. Knopf.

Woloch, Nancy. 2000. *Women and the American Experience.* 3rd ed. New York: McGraw-Hill.

Wood, Ann Douglas. 1972. "The War Within a War: Women Nurses in the Union Army." *Civil War History* 18: 197–212.

Wood, Kirsten E. 2004. *Masterful Women: Slaveholding Widows from the American Revolution through the Civil War*. Chapel Hill: University of North Carolina Press.

Woodward, C. Vann, and Elisabeth Muhlenfeld, ed. 1981. *Mary Chesnut's Civil War*. New Haven, CT: Yale University Press.

Woodward, C. Vann, and Elisabeth Muhlenfeld, ed. 1984. *The Private Mary Chesnut: The Unpublished Civil War Diaries*. New York: Oxford University Press.

Woodworth, Steven E. 2001. *While God Is Marching On: The Religious World of Civil War Soldiers*. Lawrence: University Press of Kansas.

Woody, Thomas. 1929. *A History of Women's Education in the United States*. 2 vols. New York: Science Press.

Woolsey, Jane Stuart. 2001. *Hospital Days: Reminiscence of a Civil War Nurse*. Roseville, MN: Edinborough Press.

Wooster, Ralph. 1962. *The Secession Conventions of the South*. Princeton, NJ: Princeton University Press.

Wormeley, Katharine P. 1889. *The Other Side of War: With the Army of the Potomac*. Boston: Ticknor.

Wright, Helen. 1949. *Sweeper in the Sky: The Life of Maria Mitchell, First Woman Astronomer in America*. New York: Macmillan.

Wudarczyk, James. 1999. *Pittsburgh's Forgotten Allegheny Arsenal*. Apollo, PA: Closson Press.

Wyatt-Brown, Bertram. 1982. *Southern Honor: Ethics and Behavior in the Old South*. New York: Oxford University Press.

Wyatt-Brown, Bertram. 2001. *The Shaping of Southern Culture: Honor, Grace and War, 1760s–1880s*. Chapel Hill: University of North Carolina Press.

Yellin, Jean Fagan. 2004. *Harriet Jacobs: A Life*. New York: Basic Civitas Books.

Young, Agatha. 1959. *The Women and the Crisis: Women of the North in the Civil War*. New York: McDowell, Obolensky.

Young, Elizabeth. 1999. *Disarming the Nation: Women's Writing and the American Civil War*. Chicago: University of Chicago Press.

Young, James R. 1982. "Confederate Pensions in Georgia." *Georgia Historical Quarterly* 62: 47–52.

Young, Mel. 1991. *Where They Lie: The Story of the Jewish Soldiers of the North and South Whose Deaths—Killed, Morally Wounded or Died of Disease or Other Causes—Occurred During the Civil War, 1861–1865*. Lanham, MD: University Press of America.

About the Editor

Lisa Tendrich Frank is an Independent Scholar who received her Ph.D. from the University of Florida. She has taught courses in the American Civil War and Women's History at various universities, including the University of North Florida, University of California, Los Angeles, and Occidental College. She is the author of numerous articles and is currently writing a book on the experiences of Confederate women and Sherman's March. She lives in Tallahassee, Florida.